Scott and Amundsen

Roland Huntford

Scott and Amundsen

Atheneum *New York* 1984

Library of Congress Cataloging in Publication Data

Huntford, Roland, ———
    Scott and Amundsen.

    Bibliography: p.
    Includes index.
    1. Scott, Robert Falcon, 1868-1912. 2. Amundsen,
Roald, 1872-1928. 3. Explorers—Great Britain—
Biography. 4. Explorers—Norway—Biography. 5. South
Pole. I. Title.
G875.S35H86 1984   919. 8′9′0922   83-6393
ISBN 0-689-70656-1

To my wife

It is more important to provide material for a true
verdict than to gloss over disturbing facts so that
individual reputations may be preserved.

Sir Basil Liddell Hart in the preface to *History of the First World War*

Contents

ACKNOWLEDGMENTS   9
AUTHOR'S NOTE   12
LIST OF ILLUSTRATIONS   13
LIST OF MAPS   14

PART ONE

1   Rivals for the Pole   17
2   The Forerunners   18
3   'The Last of the Vikings'   25
4   The Nansen Spirit   31
5   A Sailor on Skis   46
6   Into the Antarctic Night   60
7   Amundsen's First Command   76
8   Arctic Apprenticeship   94
9   Robert Falcon Scott, R.N.   118
10   Divided Aims   132
11   An Antarctic Winter   148
12   Scott's Furthest South   166
13   Return of the *Discovery*   176
14   'You shall have *Fram*'   191
15   Facing Due South   204
16   Territorial Waters   215
17   An Edwardian Marriage   225

PART TWO

18   Volte-Face   241
19   On the *Terra Nova*   254
20   The Secret Disclosed   272
21   Scott Sails On   299

22 The Base at Framheim   315
23 Sledging with 'the Owner'   337
24 The Pole-Seeker Prepares   350
25 Wintering at Cape Evans   367
26 False Start   376
27 Scott's Caravan   389
28 The Devil's Ballroom   399
29 Man-Hauling Begins   429
30 The Race Won   446
31 The Race Lost   475
32 Back to the *Fram*   491
33 The Ultimate Defeat   498
34 Birth of a Legend   510
35 The Last Adventure   525

NOTE ON DIET   545
BIBLIOGRAPHY   546
INDEX   549

Acknowledgments

MANY PEOPLE, IN England, Norway, and elsewhere helped in the preparation of this book. With great injustice, there is no space here to thank each individually. I cannot, however, be sufficiently grateful to all my unnamed helpers, who gave so generously of their time, and never failed to answer calls for help. I hope they will accept this as an expression of my heartfelt thanks.

Mr. Oddvar Vasstveit, of the Department of Manuscripts at the University Library in Oslo, is one of the few for whom anonymity must be drawn aside. Mr. Vasstveit piloted me through the unfamiliar waters of Norwegian primary sources. Without his unstinting help, this book would have been immeasurably harder to write. To him, my very warmest thanks are due.

The author and publisher are grateful to the following for permission to use copyright material:

Mrs. Alda Bittemor Amundsen, for the diaries and papers of Roald Amundsen; Mr. M. L. Bernacchi, for the diaries of L. C. Bernacchi; Mr. Olav Bjåland for the Antarctic diaries of Olav Bjaaland; Mr. Marcus Clements, for the diaries and papers of Sir Clements Markham; Miss Barbara Debenham, for the diaries of Frank Debenham; the family of Mr. O. Ditlev-Simonsen, for *En Sjøgutt Ser Tilbake*; Miss E. Ellison-Macartney, Mr. Jack Ellison-Macartney, for the Scott family papers in their possession; Mrs. Minna Eyre, for the diaries of Vice Admiral C. R. Royds; Mrs. Evelyn Forbes, for the diaries of H. T. Ferrar; Major Tryggve Gran, for *En Hjelt, Fra Tjuagutt til Sydpolfarer, Hvor Sydlyset Flammer, Kampen om Sydpolen, Slik var Det*; Mrs. Marion Gregory, for the correspondence of Prof. J. W. Gregory; Mr. Tim Greve, for the papers and printed work of Fridtjof Nansen and Liv Nansen Højer; Sir Geoffrey Harmsworth, for a letter from Lord Northcliffe; Mr. E. Helland-Hansen, for the correspondence of Prof. Bjørn Helland-Hansen; Houghton Library, Harvard University, for the correspondence between Roald Amundsen and F. Herman Gade; Mrs. Margaret Hubert, for the diaries and papers of Sir Raymond Priestley; Mrs. D. Irving-Bell, for permission to quote from her diary; Miss Margit Johansen, for the letters and diaries of Hjalmar Johansen; Mr. Dag Juul-Møller, for the correspondence between J. Daugaard-Jensen and Roald Amundsen; Miss Sue Limb, for *Soldier*; her then unpublished biography of Captain L. E. G. Oates; Mr. Angus McMillan, for the letters and diaries of Lieutenant H. R. Bowers; Mrs. Angela Mathias, for the Antarctic diaries of A. Cherry-Garrard, and *The Worst Journey in the World*; The Trustees of the National Maritime Museum, Greenwich, for the diaries of Admiral Sir Barry Domville, *The Life of a Sailor*, by Admiral of the Fleet Sir Henry May, and the diaries of Admiral Sir Herbert Richmond; Norsk Sjøfartsmuseum, for the diaries of Sverre Hassel and Captain Thv. Nilsen; The Norwegian Ministry of Foreign Affairs, for despatches concerning Don Pedro Christophersen; Lieutenant Colonel E. B. G. Oates, for the papers of Captain L. E. G. Oates; Rigsarkivet, Copenhagen, for J. Daugaard-Jensen's despatches to Greenland, and Admiral Godfred Hansen's naval papers; The Royal Geographical Society, for correspondence and papers of Major Leonard Darwin, Sir Clements Markham and John Scott Keltie; The Royal Society, for the letter from Admiral Mostyn Field to Sir Archibald Geikie; Sir Peter Scott, for the diaries and papers of his father and mother; Scott Polar Research Institute, for material in their archives; Lord Shackleton, for the papers of Sir Ernest Shackleton; Dr. Oliver Simpson, for the diaries of Sir George Simpson; Commander W. F. Skelton, R.N., for the diaries and papers of Engineer Admiral R. W. Skelton, R.N.; Mr. Jakob Vaage, for *Roald Amundsens første skiturer til Fjells*, published in *Snø og Ski*, 1954; Miss Janet Vetter, for the unpublished memoirs of Dr. F. A. Cook; Mr. E. P. Wilson, for the diaries and correspondence of Dr. E. A. Wilson.

It goes without saying that acknowledgment of help is not angling for endorsement of the views expressed in this book. They remain my responsibility alone. Likewise, any errors must be laid at my door. Nonetheless, in the original edition, circumstances required the printing of the following passage:

Sir Peter Scott, son of the late Captain Scott, has requested me to make clear to all readers that the thanks I have expressed to him in the list of acknowlegdments for material which he made available to me must under no circumstances be interpreted as approval of anything in the book, from which he totally dissociates himself and which he did not moreover see before printing. His view is that in order to make a comparative study of Amundsen and Scott it was not necessary to denigrate Scott, let alone his wife. I do not accept that this is what I have done but I greatly regret any distress that my treatment of the subject has caused to Sir Peter or others.

All other copyright holders allowed me to use the material under their control without any caveat whatsoever, before or after publication.

Finally, I want to thank my wife, to whom this book is dedicated, for her patience during its writing and her support in moments of despair. I owe her more than I can ever repay.

Author's Note

OSLO, THE CAPITAL city of Norway, was called Christiania (sometimes Kristiania) until 1925. The older form is used when the period demands it.

For similar reasons, the Ross Ice Shelf in the Antarctic is called by its old names of Ross Barrier or Great Ice Barrier.

Following the original logs and journals, the mile used in this book for ocean voyages and Polar land travel is the nautical or geographical mile. In other cases it is the statute mile. The nautical mile is one sixtieth of a degree, or one minute of latitude. It is fixed at 6,080 feet, equivalent to 1⅓ statute miles, or 1.85 kilometres.

A nunatak is a rock peak protruding through the ice.

Sastrugi are irregularities formed by the wind on the surface of the snow. They may be anything from a few inches to a few feet high, and all shapes from regular ripples to abstract oculpated forms.

The Norwegian letter a is pronounced like u in run; aa or å like aw in law; j like y in yell; ø like i in first, and u like oo in loose. Askeladden (Chapter 4) is pronounced with four distinct syllables, the accent on the first.

The rate of exchange of the Norwegian krone from 1900 to 1910 varied between 18.40 and 18.60 to the £ sterling; 3.78 and 3.82 respectively to the U.S. $.

Illustrations

Mt. Don Pedro Christophersen, the edge of the Polar plateau (David J. Drewry).
Amundsen aged three years (Universitetsbiblioteket, Oslo).
The first ski tour – Amundsen poses in studio (Jakob Vaage).
Nansen on skis (Kunnskapsforlaget, Oslo).
Magdalena (Norsk Sjøfartsmuseum, Oslo).
Scott in 1895 (Miss E. Ellison-Macartney).
Cook and Amundsen in Eskimo garments, winter 1898 (Miss Janet Vetter).
In Eagle City, Alaska (Tom Scott, Eagle, Alaska).
Amundsen on *Gjøa* at Framnesbryggen, Oslo (Norsk Folkemuseum, Oslo).
Scott aboard *Discovery* (Miss E. Ellison-Macartney).
Discovery's crew (Miss E. Ellison-Macartney).
Shackleton, Scott and Wilson (The Royal Society).
Discovery with the relief ships (The Royal Society).
'Cock o' the walk' (Norsk Folkemuseum, Oslo).
Fram's first crew (Norsk Polarinstitutt, Oslo).
Before the last expedition (Miss E. Ellison-Macartney).
Kathleen Scott.
Fram under full sail (Norsk Folkemuseum, Oslo).
Oates with the ponies aboard *Terra Nova* (Herbert Ponting and Scott Polar Research Institute Picture Collection).
Midwinter 1910, the Norwegian party (*Aftenposten* and Olav Bjåland).
Scott's birthday dinner (Scott Polar Research Institute Picture Collection).
The Devil's Glacier (Kunnskapsforlaget, Oslo).
Entry from Amundsen's diary (Universitetsbiblioteket, Oslo).
Norwegians at the Pole (Mrs. Alda Amundsen).
Scott's diary (The British Library).
The British at Polheim (Scott Polar Research Institute Picture Collection).
Amundsen, Shackleton and Peary in New York (Scott Polar Research Institute Picture Collection).
The last photograph (Norsk Polarinstitutt, Oslo).

Maps

Early Antarctic Exploration   19
Amundsen's Ski Journeys in Norway   47
The Drift of the *Belgica*   66
Arctic Regions   78–9
The North-West Passage   98
The *Discovery* Expedition   155
The Antarctic   316–17
McMurdo Sound   347
Framheim and the Bay of Whales   347
Amundsen's Crossing of the Transantarctic Mountains   413
Amundsen's Route to the South Pole   449
Scott's Route to the South Pole   477
The South Pole   483

Part One

Rivals for the Pole

ON THE MORNING of November 1st, 1911, a little cavalcade left Cape Evans in the Antarctic, straggled over the sea ice and faded into the lonely wastes ahead. Their leader was Captain Robert Falcon Scott.

'The future is in the lap of the gods,' he had written in his diary the night before. 'I can think of nothing left undone to deserve success.'

Two hundred miles ahead, on the same white southward road, another man was already well on his way. He was the Norwegian, Roald Amundsen. He had uncharacteristically blundered into a fog-bound labyrinth of chasms and led his companions through the shadow of death that day. They all, Amundsen wrote in his diary, 'were determined to get through – cost what it may'.

Thus began the race for the South Pole. For the privilege of being the first to tread this useless yet so desirable spot, both men were prepared to drag themselves 1,500 miles across a frozen wilderness, and face any extremity of suffering and danger. The poles of the earth had become an obsession of Western man. It could be argued against, but not argued away. Since the obsession was there, it had to be exorcised, and the sooner the better.

The Forerunners

IT WAS THE last act of an ancient tale.

Out of the cloud of myth and tradition rises the misty figure of the earliest known Antarctic voyager, a Polynesian chief called Ui-te-Rangiora who, about A.D. 650, reached the frozen sea. But the first polar explorer in recorded history was Pytheas, a Greek. He came from the Greek colony of Massilia, the present Marseilles. He was born in the fourth century, B.C., during the full flowering of the restless, inquisitive Greek spirit of the age of Aristotle. In about 320 B.C., Pytheas sailed on one of the great pathfinding voyages. He circumnavigated the British Isles, reached the Arctic pack ice, and became the first civilized man known to have crossed the Arctic Circle and seen the midnight sun. He brought the Polar regions into the consciousness of Western man.

After the lapse of a thousand years the Norwegian Vikings took up Pytheas' work in the north. During the Middle Ages they roamed the Arctic waters. They sailed to the White Sea and possibly Spitsbergen. They landed in America and reached Labrador. They colonized Greenland and travelled up the west coast almost to the 76th parallel, a respectable 'Furthest North' that stood for over 250 years.

With the end of the Norse medieval empire, Arctic exploration once more lapsed. When it recommenced in the sixteenth century, the English made the running. Spain and Portugal had appropriated South America and the sea route to the east round the Cape of Good Hope. England, the rising Naval power, turned her attention to less crowded waters. Ferdinand Magellan's circumnavigation had confirmed the ancient belief that the world was round. For the first time, the oceans and the globe seemed one. The notion was still fresh and intoxicating, and the English sought an easy path to the riches of the glorious East through two short seaways across the top of the globe; the North-East Passage along the Siberian coast, and the North-West Passage along the upper reaches of the North American continent. They were grand illusions both, driving men back to the ice and cold, in the face of setback and disaster, in search of a mythical open Polar sea; but in the process the Arctic was explored.

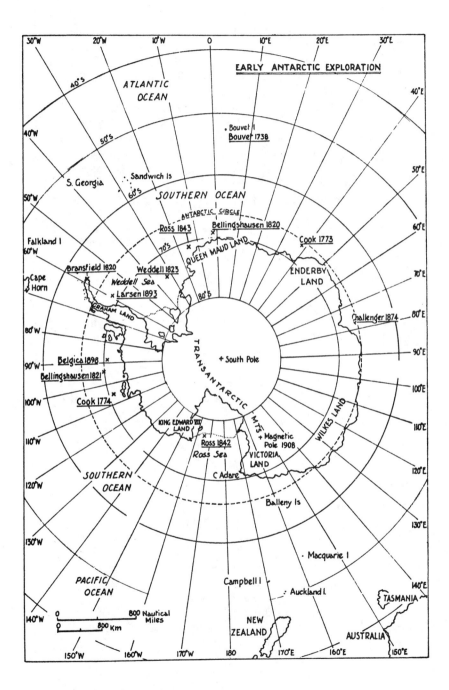

EARLY ANTARCTIC EXPLORATION

ATLANTIC OCEAN

· Bouvet I
Bouvet 1738

· Sandwich Is

S. Georgia

SOUTHERN OCEAN

ANTARCTIC CIRCLE

Falkland I

Ross 1843 ×   Bellingshausen 1820 ×

Cook 1773 ×

QUEEN MAUD LAND

Cape Horn

Bransfield 1820 ×   Weddell 1823 ×

ENDERBY LAND

Weddell Sea
× Larsen 1893

Challenger 1874

GRAHAM LAND

+ South Pole

Belgica 1898 ×

Bellingshausen 1821 ×

TRANSANTARCTIC MTS

WILKES LAND

Cook 1774 ×

KING EDWARD VII LAND

+ Magnetic Pole 1908

× Ross 1842
Ross Sea

VICTORIA LAND

SOUTHERN OCEAN

C Adare

Balleny Is

· Macquarie I

PACIFIC OCEAN

Campbell I

· Auckland I

TASMANIA

0   800 Nautical Miles
0   800 Km

NEW ZEALAND

AUSTRALIA

30°W 20°W 10°W 0 10°E 20°E 30°E
40°W 40°S 40°E
50°W 50°S 50°E
60°W 60°S 60°E
70°S 70°E
80°S 80°E
80°W 90°E
90°W 100°E
100°W 110°E
110°W 120°E
120°W 130°E
130°W 140°E
140°W 150°E
150°W 160°W 170°W 180 170°E 160°E 150°E

Men were looking hopefully south as well. There, the illusion that enticed mariners from Sir Francis Drake, and perhaps before, was a great fertile Southern continent, an Eldorado round the Pole. It was a Frenchman, suitably enough a contemporary of Voltaire, who first glimpsed the baleful truth.

In 1738, Captain Jean-François-Charles Bouvet de Lozier sailed out with two ships, the *Aigle* and *Marie*, to annex the *Terra Australis* – the South Land. On New Year's Day, 1739, he sighted a dismal, fogbound, ice-covered foreland, part of what today is called Bouvet Island.

It was hardly the promised land, but it was a foretaste of what lay ahead. Bouvet brought back the first fairly complete description of the Antarctic scene, with its tabular icebergs

2 or 300 feet high ... up to 10 miles long [with] all sorts of shapes; islands, fortresses, battlements ... like floating reefs [and] penguins, amphibious animals like huge ducks, but with flippers instead of wings.

The English too, were turning their eyes to the South. In 1769, there was to be a transit of the planet Venus across the disc of the sun, a rare event which astronomers wanted to observe. The newly discovered island of Tahiti was judged the perfect site. The Royal Society in London asked the Royal Navy to organize the expedition. The Navy obliged. This was to have profound and unlooked-for consequences. It led to the virtual monopolization by naval officers of British Polar exploration until the first decade of this century.

The voyage inspired by the transit of Venus was commanded by a man of quiet genius, James Cook, one of the greatest of discoverers.

The motives for Cook's voyage were mixed. Astronomy was only one part, and politics lurked just beneath the surface. In the days of Anglo-French rivalry, the French could not be left to roam the south unchallenged. When, in August 1768, Cook left England in *Endeavour*, he carried secret instructions to search for the mysterious southern continent, and find it before the French.

Three years later, after circumnavigating the globe, Cook returned home with the news that altered the mental horizons of his time and changed the politics of an age. There was no land flowing with milk and honey down there in the south. If a southern continent existed, it lay in the bleak expanses beyond the 40th parallel. There was to be no great power struggle for the possession of such unattractive property. Cook, however, suggested another circumnavigation at a higher latitude merely to 'settle the question' of what lay beyond. The Admiralty, to their everlasting credit, agreed.

So in 1772 Cook, newly promoted Commander, once more left England, this time with two ships, *Resolution* and *Adventure*. It was the first Antarctic expedition in the modern sense, for it had no motive beyond the fulfilment of personal ambition: exploration was an end in itself and discovery its own reward.

On Sunday, January 17th, 1773, Cook sailed over the Antarctic Circle, 'undoubtedly the first', as he put it, 'that ever crossed that line'. Next day, solid pack ice forced him back. The following year, after wintering in New Zealand, he went south again. On January 30th, 1774 he reached 71° 10′, 300 miles beyond the Antarctic Circle, before being stopped once more by ice. No one came this far south again for almost fifty years, and, to this day, it remains the furthest south anyone has ever sailed at that particular longitude, 106° W.

On both occasions, Cook turned back scarcely a day's sailing from the coast of the hidden continent. He never saw it, shrouded as it was in a fog of inaccessibility. Nonetheless, he firmly believed in its existence.

The death of Cook in 1779, at the hands of natives in Hawaii, was the end of an era. For a generation, Polar exploration virtually lapsed while the French Revolution and Napoleonic Wars took their course. When the Battle of Waterloo was fought, the Antarctic Continent still had not been sighted.

In 1819, an English merchant ship, *Williams*, was blown off her course sailing round Cape Horn and discovered the South Shetland Islands. When *Williams* reached Valparaiso, Captain Shireff, a Royal Naval officer commanding H.M.S. *Andromache*, stationed there at the time, thought the discovery ought to be investigated. As a private venture, he chartered *Williams*, put Edward Bransfield his master (i.e. navigator) in command, and sent her south.

Bransfield sailed beyond the South Shetlands. On January 30th, 1820, he sighted the north tip of Graham Land and briefly went ashore. Such was the discovery of Antarctica.

Three days earlier, some 1,500 miles to the east, Captain Thaddeus Bellingshausen, a Russian naval officer sent out by the Tsar Alexander I in a burst of expansionistic fervour, recorded what may be interpreted as a sighting of the Antarctic ice cap where it meets the sea. Bellingshausen did not, however, recognize what he saw as land. Bransfield very definitely did, seeing in his landfall, moreover, 'the long sought southern continent'.

The next Antarctic discoverers were American sealing captains like Nathaniel Palmer, who explored the coast of Graham Land, and British ones like James Weddell, who discovered the Weddell Sea in 1823.

In 1827, a Royal Naval officer, Captain William Edward Parry, led an expedition to Spitsbergen with the express purpose of reaching the North Pole. He reached 82° 45′, over the Polar pack ice; the furthest north for half a century. This was the first recorded occasion on which an explorer had gone out with a pole of the earth as his sole and ultimate aim.

The Pole, north or south, has been a symbol of the ultimate. Ever since the earth was known to be a sphere, men have wished to see the point about which it turns. Parry was the first to translate this into action. He was the original Pole seeker, and his expedition was the start of the race for the Poles.

Two years after Parry, Lieutenant James Clark Ross, another Royal Naval officer, set out to reach the North Magnetic Pole. This he achieved on May 31st, 1831. Eight years later Ross, promoted to Captain, was sent out by the Navy to make a magnetic survey of the southern hemisphere, with the aim of reaching the South Magnetic Pole as well. In August 1840, when he reached Hobart, Tasmania, with his two ships, *Erebus* and *Terror*, he was met with the news that a French and an American expedition had each gone south to forestall him.

Faced with what he considered an ill-mannered intrusion, Ross acted characteristically and changed the course of Antarctic history.

> Impressed with the feeling that England had *ever* led the way of discovery [he wrote in his diary], I considered it would have been inconsistent with the pre-eminence she has maintained, if we were to follow in the footsteps of the expedition of any other nation. I therefore resolved at once to avoid all interference with their discoveries, and selected a much more easterly meridian (170° E) on which to endeavour to penetrate to the southward.

Nobody had followed this course before. Ross left Hobart in November and in January he met the pack ice. He plunged in and, after four days, ran out into clear water stretching to the horizon. He had discovered the open sea that now bears his name.

Ross then headed south-west for the Magnetic Pole, in the belief that it was plain sailing. But an unknown range of lofty, snow-covered mountains barred the way. This new coast Ross called South Victoria Land in honour of the young Queen.

Then followed a cruise quite extraordinary in the annals of Polar exploration. In the course of the following six weeks, Ross discovered and charted five hundred miles of coastline. Mountain after mountain, glacier after glacier, fjord upon icy fjord opened, it seemed endlessly, to the south.

On January 27th, Ross sighted an island with a smoking volcano, which he called Mount Erebus in honour of his ship. An extinct crater nearby he named Mount Terror. They were to become household names to generations of explorers.

As we approached the land under all studding sails, [Ross wrote in his journal] we perceived a low white line extending ... as far as the eye could discern eastward. It presented an extraordinary appearance, gradually increasing in height as we got nearer to it, and proving at length to be a perpendicular cliff of ice, between one hundred and fifty and two hundred feet above the level of the sea.

Such is the record of the discovery of an entirely new natural phenomenon: the Antarctic ice shelf or, as Ross called it 'The Great Icy Barrier' for, in his words, 'we might with equal chance of success try to sail through the Cliffs of Dover, as penetrate such a mass'. From this it got its original name of the Great Ice Barrier.

Ross followed the cliffs of the 'icy barrier' as far east as the icebergs and gathering pack ice allowed. At a point where the cliffs descended below the mast heads, he first saw the surface of the 'barrier', and glimpsed its true nature. 'It appeared to be quite smooth,' he wrote, 'and conveyed to the mind the idea of an immense plain of frosted silver.'

Ross then turned back and wintered in the Pacific. The next Southern summer, he returned to the Ross Sea and reached 78° 10′, the furthest south for over half a century. Towards the eastern end of the 'icy barrier' he discovered a bay which turned out to be of enduring importance. He returned to England in September 1843, a famous and applauded man. He discovered more of the Antarctic than anyone else. His were the last Antarctic discoveries until the end of the century.

Ross's two ships, the *Erebus* and the *Terror*, were refitted on their return to England and two years later, under the command of Captain Sir John Franklin, sailed out in an expedition to find the North-West Passage. This had long been abandoned as a commercial quest for a sea route to the east; now it had been revived as a blend of romantic harkback and a hard-headed desire to push back the northernmost frontier of Empire along the Arctic coast of Canada.

Franklin's was the expedition that finally found a North-West Passage, for in fact there are several. He did not actually navigate it from end to end, but his companions traced the frozen channels linking earlier advances, thus showing that there was a seaway from the Atlantic to the Pacific, and bringing to a victorious conclusion two and three-quarter centuries of martyrdom and struggle.

Unfortunately, neither Franklin nor any of his 128 men survived to tell the tale. They all perished of starvation, exposure and disease. It was the supreme and, it may be, the characteristic disaster of the country and the age. While Franklin and his men were dying of hunger, Eskimos around them were living off the land in comparative plenty. But Franklin was hampered by grotesquely unsuitable methods, the product of rigid thought and incapacity to adapt to circumstances.

This was the state of Polar exploration when Roald Amundsen and Robert Falcon Scott were born. The coast of Antarctica was known along a fraction of its length. Whether it was a continent or an archipelago was still unsettled. Nobody had yet wintered there. In the Arctic, the North-West Passage had not yet been navigated. Neither the South nor the North Pole had yet been attained. The last frontiers were waiting to be breached.

3

'The Last of the Vikings'

SCOTT AND AMUNDSEN were ideal antagonists: on almost every point they stood opposed. Scott came from a rich and mighty empire, albeit in decline; Amundsen from a small, poor country, with a sparse and scattered population, not even independent when he was born.

Someone who, as a child, met Amundsen, remembers his mother saying in awe: 'He is the last of the Vikings.' Over six feet tall, fair, with piercing blue eyes, he looked the part. An enormous aquiline nose gave just the touch of mastery and suggestion of the bird of prey that expresses one side of the Viking spirit.

Roald Engebreth Gravning Amundsen, to give him his full name, was born on July 16th, 1872, into a family of seamen and shipowners. Engebreth and Gravning commemorated particularly respected ancestors, for this was a clannish society, almost an informal aristocracy.

The Amundsens came from Hvaler, a cluster of islands at the mouth of the Christiania Fjord. It is a typical Norwegian archipelago; granite polished by wind and weather; shapes oddly truncated, like mountains drowned by the sea. It is a harsh country, storm-beaten, and ice-ground. Through the ages it has been the home of fishermen and sailors. A race of individualists, with their own standards of behaviour, they were marked by their surroundings, men apart.

The Amundsen surname first appeared in the eighteenth century, as the patronymic of the explorer's great-grandfather Amund Olsen Utgård. This was a common device to distinguish branches of a large family. It usually occurred when someone of sufficient pride, success or force of character felt he ought to impress his identity on those who came after.

By the time Amund's son (and Roald's grandfather) Ole Amundsen grew up, the family were established as seagoing masters and shipowners of considerable wealth for the islands. Ole Amundsen had twelve children, five of whom were boys. All five sons went to sea, and all became ship's captains, shipowners, and men of property. The fourth son, and ninth child, was Jens Engebreth Amundsen, the explorer's father.

The early nineteenth century had been a time of poverty and want.

Norway was then almost devoid of industry, self-supporting in almost nothing, her only significant resources being timber and fish. Obtaining the necessities of life, depended on the ability of her shipowners to export timber and uphold foreign trade, so she had suffered calamitously from the British blockade during the Napoleonic Wars. By the time Jens Engebreth had become a captain in 1853, Britain had repealed the Navigation Act which favoured British ships for carrying British goods. That, and the removal of similar barriers elsewhere, changed Norwegian fortunes. Her shipowners took on work that others despised, becoming, as it were, shipping scavengers to the world. They set a splendid example of percipience and initiative, achieving a position out of all relation to their numbers and the size of their country.

Jens Engebreth was a good specimen of his kind. In 1854, together with a partner, he bought the wreck of a burnt-out sealer for her scrap value. The partner owned a small shipyard. There, like Phoenix, the hulk was restored to life from the ashes and as *Phoenix* rebaptized.

The Crimean War then broke out. Jens Engebreth, now captain as well as part owner of *Phoenix*, had heard of fabulous money to be made from the British and French fighting the Russians in the Black Sea, so to the Black Sea he sailed. Upon arrival, *Phoenix* was snapped up as officers' winter billets for the British Army before Sebastopol. Thereafter, for the rest of the war, she carried forage and straw under charter to the Allies. With the profits, the wartime profits of a neutral, Jens Engebreth laid the foundations of his fortunes.

Jens Engebreth married late. He was forty-two when he met Hanna Henrikke Gustava Sahlquist, the daughter of a country tax-collector. As a result of his voyages, Jens Engebreth, captain and shipowner, was distinguished by a foreign manner. In Norway at the time there was a reverence for things foreign as the evidence of culture. Miss Sahlquist was impressed. Besides, Jens Engebreth was tall and presentable. He was also, when they met in 1862, a man of means. In the following year they were married.

They made their home not on Hvaler, but on the mainland, on a property called Hvidsten bought by the Amundsen brothers a few years before. It lay near Sarpsborg, one of the chief seafaring towns of Norway.

By now, Jens Engebreth, together with his brothers, had established their own shipping company. It was the largest in that part of the country. But moneyed as he was, Jens Engebreth, in the distinctive Norwegian custom of the day, still went to sea and Gustava sometimes sailed with him. Indeed, she gave birth to her eldest son, Jens Ole Antonio (called Tonni) in China. But the remaining children, all boys, were born at

Tomta, Jens Engebreth's house at Hvidsten. The second son, Gustav Sahlquist, arrived in June 1858 and the third in September 1870, christened Leon Henry Benham.

At the end of July 1872, Amanda, a niece of Jens Engebreth, wrote to her father that: '*Long John* has gone to London ... on the 16th Aunt Gustava was delivered of another son. The lady is hale and hearty as usual, and on the sixth day was already out for a walk.'

Amanda's lighthearted announcement of Roald's birth concealed tensions in the Amundsen household. To be absent when his children came into the world was doubtless a seaman's lot. But, after nine years of marriage, Gustava felt she was not cut out for a seaman's wife. She had never been at ease among the salty merchant skippers who were Sarpsborg society. As the daughter of a Government official, she considered greater refinement to be her due. Three months after Roald was born the Amundsens, with Jens Engebreth's unenthusiastic acquiescence, moved to Christiania, as Oslo, the capital, then was called, having been named after the reigning Danish king, Christian IV, following rebuilding in the seventeenth century. It had become a standing reminder that Norway was no longer independent but under foreign rule. The old name was once more assumed in the twentieth century as a symbol of sovereignty regained.

Amundsen was born into an inspiring environment. Though now subject to Sweden after four hundred years under Denmark, Norway in the nineteenth century was no stagnant backwater. It was seized by the nationalism of the age. It was there that the European nationalist movement came earliest to fruition. Norway was the first of the subject nations of the post-Napoleonic settlement to attain independence. And within less than a century, she had transformed herself from a poor, backward country into a modern industrialized state.

But the factory was kept in its place. Norway is a country where Nature reigns supreme. Through the ages, man's foothold has been precarious. Three-quarters of the country is mountain. Where the sea has drowned the deepest valleys lie the celebrated fjords. It is an overwhelming landscape, with violent contrasts, set in a harsh climate. It is a country where men, even in the towns, have never lost their awareness of the powers of Nature. All this has put its stamp on the national character.

When the Amundsens came to Christiania, they lived within a stone's throw of the centre, but theirs was the last house before the wilds began. It lay in its own grounds, not a garden in the English sense, but a forest clearing, fenced off and imperfectly tamed. A two-storeyed villa, it was a typical 'good residence' of the Norwegian bourgeoisie at the time. It lay on the crest of a knoll and was called Little Uranienborg.*

An old shipwright called Erik (his surname has not survived), who for years had sailed under Jens Engebreth, followed him to Little Uranienborg as general factotum. The domestic staff was completed by a cook-housemaid and nursemaid, a typical upper class Christiania establishment. Erik was a kind of reserve father. The move had not reduced Jens Engebreth's activity, and he was still frequently away with his ships.

Both by sons and shipmates Jens Engebreth seems to have been liked. But he was unmistakably a disciplinarian. Jens Engebreth was bred and born a sailing-ship skipper; his fortune was built on exploiting the cheapness of sail against steam where speed did not matter. His milieu was therefore distinctive. A sailing skipper is not like the captain of any other ship. Because the swift handling of intricate rigging may be a matter of life and death, he expects instant execution of orders. But if he is a good skipper, he will not offend a sense of natural justice. He cannot be an unreasoning despot. Once he has made up his mind, however, his word is law. Jens Engebreth seems to have been a good skipper and ran his home like one of his ships: this is very important for an understanding of Roald Amundsen's character. There is also something else. Jens Engebreth was a respected member of the society in which he lived. He was a success. His sons looked up to him. This is important for the comparison with Scott.

Roald had the rumbustious outdoor childhood of the average Norwegian boy. He was the youngest of a gang that played in the forest around Uranienborgveien. By an improbable coincidence, one of them, Carsten Borchgrevink, also became a Polar explorer.

The Amundsen brothers loved to fight. Their father's advice on the subject, no doubt remembering his own pugnacious boyhood, was ambivalent: 'I don't want you to get into any fights. But if you must, get in the first blow – and see that it's enough.'

Roald was remembered for airing his opinions and rising to a bait. Both, together with his being the youngest among a lot of older boys, led naturally to bullying and teasing. One day according to Borchgrevink, he ran to a woodshed and, like a Viking berserk, emerged brandishing an axe, yelling horrible threats. 'After which,' so Borchgrevink says, 'he was left alone.'

It was the time when team games and formalized sports were making their way into Norway. Gymnastics was becoming popular; the

---

* Literally. 'The little castle of Uranus'.

Amundsen brothers rigged up bars in a tree on their grounds and became notably adept. But skiing was the native sport, and at that time was what distinguished a Norwegian childhood from any other. As soon as he could walk, Roald was put on skis. His first pair were made by Erik; primitive contrivances, little more than barrel staves with an osier toe loop for a binding. They were difficult to master. Proper children's skis with modern bindings were on the market but Roald's father, although well able to afford them, had no desire to spoil his sons.

The Amundsen children learned, or rather taught themselves, to ski on their doorstep. It was the Norwegian's all-round concept of cross-country, jumping and downhill. For their nursery slope, they used the road outside their garden gate.

By and large, the Amundsen household was a happy one. Father and sons were intensely loyal to each other. The verdict of one of the servants was that 'They were people who knew how to stick together and raise themselves above the crowd'.

But what of Gustava's rôle? Subdued at Hvidsten by the proximity of her husband's numerous brothers and sisters (especially his maiden sisters), she now in Little Uranienborg relaxed and developed in a way impossible before. For the first time in her married life, Gustava was able to create a home of her own.

She mitigated Jens Engebreth's discipline; she tried to enter into the spirit of her children's play (at least the quieter kind), becoming almost an elder sister instead of a mother with a tendency perhaps to mollycoddle. For all that she remains a shadowy figure and clearly an unhappy one, with few contacts outside her own home. Certainly Roald looked elsewhere for affection; to his Aunt Olava and, above all, to Betty, his nursemaid.

Few Norwegians have been entirely naturalized city-dwellers. Little Uranienborg to an outsider might have appeared distinctly rural, to Jens Engebreth it was uncomfortably urban. His roots were in the country, by the water. For the summer and Christmas school holidays, the Amundsens regularly went back to Hvidsten – although often without Gustava, who preferred the company of her own family scattered over Southern Norway. Jens Engebreth had sold his house at Hvidsten, but a nephew was the buyer. Hvidsten remained an Amundsen family colony, and there was always room, somewhere, for the Christiania cousins. Hvidsten was part of Roald's school.

Maritime and rural, Hvidsten lay on the navigable lower reaches of the River Glomma. Playing hide and seek among the ships at anchor, learning how to manage small boats in shoals and rushing water, the

Amundsen boys acquired the first glimmerings of seamanship. Across the river lay Jens Engebreth's shipyard; the Amundsens prudently kept repairs and building in the family as far as they were able.

In the shipyard, Roald learned the feel of wooden hulls. The foreman, an old shipwright wise in the ways of ships and children, gave him his first lessons in Naval architecture. The boy was remembered for incessant questioning, seriousness, and a taste for laying down the law about rigging.

It was in the winter that Hvidsten, like most of the Norwegian landscape, really came into its own. The river froze up. Through a window framed in frost crystals, to the nostalgic accompaniment of logs crackling in a wood stove, Roald could look out on the masts and rigging of laid-up ships starkly standing out like lattice-work against the snow. The countryside would be silent; rolling, white, sparsely dotted with houses, broken here and there by forest patches, the only movement an occasional human figure drifting across the scene.

When the cold was deep enough, the Amundsen boys would skate out miles over the sea ice towards the inner islands of the Hvaler archipelago. It was a typical Scandinavian winter waterway, broken by the dark silhouettes of rounded skerries; ice underfoot, a hard white expanse to the horizon, a border country where land and sea, ice and water flow together, almost into an element of its own.

Roald mirrored this in himself. He was absorbing the elements of skiing and seafaring; growing up a man of sea and rock, water, ice, forest and snow; someone of the coast; half mariner, half *montagnard*. It is a rare combination, but one that is authentically Norwegian. It is halfway to the Polar environment.

4

The Nansen Spirit

THE NORWEGIANS ARE a coastal people, and the sea permeates their lives. On the long, deeply indented coastline are concentrated their cities. The mountains cut off communications overland, so that the sea has historically been the escape from isolation, the window on the world, the road to survival.

Those connected with the sea have, therefore, possessed distinction and respect. But, unlike other maritime societies, it was not in the Navy that honour lay, but the mercantile marine. This is understandable in a small country without a modern independent military tradition, where war meant not foreign adventure but domestic calamity. The merchant service, on the other hand, has always been the very embodiment of national wealth and prestige. Success at sea meant respect ashore. A merchant skipper was looked up to; the title 'Captain' meant much. A shipowner took precedence over other businessmen. To be a shipowner *and* a captain was to be high in the social scale indeed.

Norwegian society in the nineteenth century was, by and large, a meritocracy. It was related to the old hunting communities, with the best hunters and their families at the top. Class broadly followed function. Family meant much, but not all. Each generation was expected to prove itself.

In contrast to England, trade was never a taint. Seamen of all degrees possessed a higher social standing than their English counterparts. And so Roald Amundsen had all the advantages of being born into the upper reaches of society.

His father, however, lacked the cachet of ultimate respectability. This was the so-called 'students cap', a grey peaked quasi-military affair with a tassel dangling from the top. It was the mark of those who had passed the *examen artium*, or matriculation examination. It was a social distinction as much as an academic attainment. It was almost a kind of secular confirmation into the middle classes. To have children so distinguished was, apart from any advantage to the children themselves, to acquire merit and fortify one's own social standing.

Going to sea young, Jens Engebreth had had only elementary schooling. This had not prevented his learning how to navigate or rising to the top. But, like many self-made men, he felt acutely his imperfect formal education. He saw to it that his sons did not suffer the same disadvantage. They were sent to a private school, with the tasselled student's cap their goal.

Jens Engebreth, so fated to be away from home on days of importance, was in France when Gustav got his cap in 1886. He fell ill on the way back to Norway and died at sea. Roald, was fourteen; instinctively he turned to the Hvidsten cousins, and to Karen Anna Amundsen, his favourite among them, he now wrote:

> Sad times have come to me since I last was home. I have never known what sorrow is, but now I have formed an idea. It is hard to lose a father like ours, as you may imagine, but it was God's will, and that must be done, above all. We have much to be grateful to God for. He brought our father home to us, even if not alive, but dead, when he so easily could have been thrown overboard, and how much worse it would have been for us then, but now we have the consolation that we can go and see him in the chapel. He is unchanged, he is exactly as he was when he walked among us. He is so lovely, as he lies, in his long white shroud, strewn with flowers. Last night at 8 o'clock we were there for the last time to see him and say farewell. It was with heavy hearts that we left him, but it had to be. Today we will presumably go to the chapel and screw down his coffin. For none of us want to take the lid off and look at him, after we had got such a good impression of him, since it is impossible to know if he has not changed a little between yesterday and today. I have felt so relieved every time I was able to cry a little next to his coffin. Today we were on board the *Rollo* – where father drew his last breath – to give the 2nd class steward some recompense for being so kind to father. He sat next to father night and day until father's time had come. The whole Saturday he was out of his mind, but not in the sense that he was delirious, since he was quite calm the whole time, but he spoke in such a way that the steward could not understand him. The last half hour that he lived he recognized all who cared for him, and when his time had come he died without pain and without a change of expression on his face. I hope you come to the funeral. Greetings to all! Love from all here, but most love from your
> Roald!

In this lies much of conventional Norwegian attitudes, but the appeal to God is sincere and personal. It is something that never left Amundsen. Whether he was a Lutheran of the Norwegian established Church in which he was brought up, or even whether he was a Christian in the accepted sense of the word, may be open to doubt. But that he was a Theist is certain. It is almost a form of natural, as opposed to revealed, religion, ignoring cult and form; a kind of primitive Monotheism not uncommon among Norwegians. In moments of profound emotion, it emerges half reluctantly, as if wrung from the depths. Amundsen was one of those who knew the religious emotions.

The letter to Karen Anna was his farewell to innocence.

Soon after Jens Engebreth had died the three older boys left home to make their own way in the world. They had not entirely fulfilled their parents' expectations. Only Gustav, the second son, had achieved his student's cap, and he almost immediately went to sea. Roald, alone, the youngest, remained at home to bear Gustava's ambition of academic study for her sons. Her heart was set on a medical career for him. Roald did not share her ambitions.

It was now, so he maintained in after years, that Amundsen came to the turning point of his life. At the age of fifteen he stumbled on the works of Sir John Franklin, and decided to become a Polar explorer.

> Oddly enough it was the sufferings that Sir John and his men had to go through which attracted me most in his narrative. A strange urge made me wish that I too one day would go through the same thing. Perhaps it was the idealism of youth, which often takes the form of martyrdom, that got me to see myself as a kind of crusader in Arctic exploration.

This refers, not to Franklin's last calamitous voyage but to his overland expeditions in the Canadian Arctic in 1819 and 1825, which he survived with lurid tales of suffering, murder and cannibalism. Amundsen was looking back with detachment on a stage through which he had passed. He had left behind romantic longings for martyrdom with adolescence.

The young Amundsen's sensibilities would have gone beyond the melodramatic appeal to the adolescent mind. He would have understood the conditions against which Franklin had struggled; they were different only in degree from the ski tours he was now beginning to make. He was even then in a position to appreciate the heroism of men fighting a cold climate. But it was an ironic comment on the age that inspiration had to come from a man who, looked at in the cold light of history, is one of the great bunglers of Polar exploration. And it may also seem odd that a Norwegian boy had to depend on an English hero. But Norwegian exploration did not yet exist; it was even then being born.

One of the myth figures, perhaps *the* myth figure of Norway is Askeladden. He is a kind of male Cinderella: the underdog with hidden powers who eventually uses them and comes out on top. Most significant, he is a favourite of Fortune. A revealing Norwegian comment on this myth is that is symbolizes

The Norwegian people's life [which is] the saga of powers held back. It shows us the long damming of powers which so suddenly has a violent release. Nature herself provides the elements in this saga, where contradictions pile up steeply against each other and history has swung in time with Nature's tremendous swings of the pendulum ... In the long winter the country sleeps under its covering of snow, then comes a late and reluctant spring, and then the water-falls suddenly burst forth, the avalanches fall, and the birches break their flags.

This is not a bad characterization of the spirit of the age in which Amundsen grew up. Askeladden is one of those myths in which whole nations see themselves. He made a crucial intrusion into Amundsen's life in 1887.

In that year, the same in which by his own account Amundsen was inspired by Franklin, there appeared in a Norwegian children's annual an article called 'Across Greenland?'

You all surely know the story about the Princess who sat on top of the mountain made of glass, holding three apples in her lap [it began]. And Knights came from far and near to ride up to her and take the apples. For the king had promised her hand in marriage and half his kingdom as the prize. And all the gallant knights rode and rode, but they never got further than the beginning. The harder they rode, the harder they fell, for the glass moun-tain was hard and smooth as flint, and they could make no headway at all. But then one fine day, along came Askeladden. He rode up the mountain, took the apples, and so he gained both the princess and half the kingdom – That, more or less is how the story goes. But what has all this got to do with Greenland? Well, Greenland is just like a huge glass mountain, and many are they who have tried to conquer it, but Askeladden has not yet arrived ... Askeladden who will go right in, across Greenland from one side to the other, has not yet come.

    You have perhaps heard that I want to try a crossing right through the country, but if I can do so, if I will come home with the princess – well, on that we must put a big question mark.

The writer who invoked such myth, indeed myth at all, to describe an expedition, was no ordinary man. He was Fridtjof Nansen, who became one of the great Polar explorers. His life was to be curiously intertwined with Amundsen's. The expedition of which he wrote was no ordinary one. It was the expedition that thrust Norway into Polar exploration: the first crossing of Greenland.

Many, as Nansen said, had vainly attacked the Greenland Ice Cap. Among them had been Edward Whymper, Robert Peary, and A. E. Nordenskiöld. Whymper was a famous English mountaineer, the con-queror of the Matterhorn; Peary an officer in the United States Navy.

Nordenskiöld, who at the end of the previous decade had become the first man in history to navigate the North-East Passage, was, besides a celebrated explorer, a baron, a Swede, and therefore one of the Norwegians' overlords.

In the summer of 1888, Nansen, together with five companions (including two Norwegian Lapps) crossed the Greenland Ice Cap from Umivik to Godthaab. The prize, after all, had been snatched by the unknown citizen of a small country. When Nansen had chosen Askeladden to address his audience, he had chosen well.

It was the introduction of modern technique to Polar exploration. Its achievements form a monotonous catalogue of 'firsts'. By Amundsen's own account, it inspired him quite as much as Franklin's tale of disaster.

Nansen had moreover introduced a startling new concept into Polar exploration. He had deliberately cut off his lines of retreat. His route was from the desolate east coast to the inhabited west. This was not bravado, but calculated exploitation of the instinct of self-preservation. It drove him on; there was no incentive to look back.

In the technique of Polar travel, Nansen broke new ground. For the heavy, narrow-runnered sledge traditionally used, he had substitued a new, lighter, flexible one running on skis. It was adapted from a traditional Norwegian pattern. It was the prototype of the modern expedition sledge. Nansen also demonstrated the necessity of designing special clothing, tents and cooking equipment. He also devised a saucepan, 'the Nansen cooker' to conserve heat and fuel. He was the first Polar explorer to work out rations scientifically on fundamental principles - and proved by bitter experience the need to have fat in the Polar diet.

It was the launching of the Norwegian school of Polar exploration; the school that for a short, intense, fertile period was to supplant the British and dominate the field. The heart of that school, and Nansen's most conspicuous achievement, was the application of skis to Polar travel. It took place at the same time as modern skiing was developing in Norway. Norwegian Polar exploration went hand in hand with the rise of skiing, and they shared some of the same pioneers.

Every skier knows how capricious and variegated snow is. It is best to take nothing for granted. Although skis were proven in the sub-Arctic conditions of the Scandinavian peninsula, it was not certain that they would function at the altitude and under the conditions of the Greenland Ice Cap. Nansen spectacularly showed that they did. This was the first major Polar journey carried out on skis; it also brought skiing to the attention of the world and launched it as a mountain sport.

The first crossing of Greenland was also the first identifiable goal attained in high latitudes since the discovery of the North-West Passage forty years before. Nansen returned to a hero's welcome. On May 30th, 1889, he sailed up the Christiania Fjord, escorted by an armada of boats with flags flying, flower bedecked, and bands playing. Ashore, he and his companions drove through streets black with cheering crowds. It was the return of Askeladden triumphant.

It was more than a personal triumph; it was a national demonstration of the very deepest significance. Like Ibsen's plays from *A Doll's House* onwards, it brought Norway out of the obscurity of Northern mists and gave her a reputation abroad. It was a stride in the search for national identity. Bjørnstjerne Bjørnson, the national poet and a fiery patriot, wrote to Nansen that

> Every deed like yours is a tremendous contribution. It strengthens the nation's courage and sense of honour, and it awakens foreign sympathy ...

Among the welcoming crowds stood Amundsen, an impressionable seventeen-year-old schoolboy. It was, he wrote years afterwards,

> A red letter day in many a Norwegian youngster's life. It was at any rate in mine. It was the day that Fridtjof Nansen came home from his Greenland expedition. The young Norwegian skier sailed up the Christiania fjord on that calm and sunny day, his tall form glowing with the admiration of a whole world for the deed he had accomplished: 'A madman's work'; the impossible! ... With beating heart I walked that day among the banners and cheers and all the dreams of my boyhood woke to storming life. And for the first time I heard, in my secret thoughts, the whisper clear and insistent: If *you* could do the North-West Passage!

The last sentence is Amundsen's own. The remainder is cliché. It is a cliché that appears in many reminiscences of the time, and catches the essence of Nansen's achievement. For unlike most other Polar explorers who had gone out to grapple with an alien environment, Nansen had stayed within his own world. He had kept, as it were, within an extension of his own familiar environment. At home, he was one of the pioneers of mountain skiing. In 1884, he had made one of the first winter crossings from Bergen to Christiania. The crossing of Greenland was different only in degree. To the world, it was a staggering, heroic, almost incomprehensible achievement. To his own countrymen it was an achievement too, but not strange; a glorification of what they themselves could quite well do; a ski tour writ large. The outside world looked up to Nansen; the Norwegians identified with him. He had discovered for his countrymen a field to which they were by nature suited.

Nansen's exploits inspired a front-page article in a Christiania news-paper:

> Norway lies closer to the Polar Regions than any other country, and because of their occupation many of our compatriots have penetrated far into Northern waters.
>
> The Arctic sealing skippers from Tromsø and Hammerfest annually navigate north of a latitude which does not exist on other seamen's charts....
>
> If a Norwegian North Pole expedition were to be organised, we could provide an elite corps of experienced and tough men, used to travel in ice and snow, on ski or snowshoes. In that field we ought to have the advantage of the Englishmen, Dutchmen, Austrians and other nationalities which have been engaged in the task.
>
> We have thus long had the people specially fitted to participate in such an expedition, but what we have lacked until very recently is the man with the qualifications to be the leader.
>
> Now, however, I believe that we have such a man: he who has had his Arctic baptism with an enterprise which has aroused attention all over the civilised world.

The author was a Christiania chemist called Ludvig Schmelck, a friend of Nansen, who had helped with the preparations for the crossing of Greenland. The lesson of Nansen's success, continued Schmelck, was that it had been

> carried out by a 'new method', one might call it the sportsman's method which, used in an expedition to the North Pole, possibly could attain the goal.
>
> Previous foreign expeditions have gathered a large number of hetero-geneous elements as participants and in general worked with a clumsy and expensive organisation.
>
> The principle of the new method consists in limiting the number of par-ticipants, and selecting a small party able to achieve the greatest possible degree of physical stamina: a small, trained group, in which all keep pace with each other in the coming trials.

This is a good definition of the Norwegian school of Polar explora-tion and a prophetic explanation of it successes.

The first crossing of Greenland also inspired Amundsen and three of his schoolmates in January 1889 to go on their first long ski tour. This took place in the hinterland of Christiania, a tract of pine forest, low mountain and lake as big as an English county, rolling down to the edge of the city. It has survived to become the playground of modern Oslo. The main part to the north is called Nordmarka, a name that looms large in the folklore of Norwegian skiing. Amundsen on this occasion chose the terrain to the west known as Krogskogen.

His jaunt was a little expedition, lasting twenty hours without sleep, across fifty miles of country, still untamed and the preserve of skiing pioneers. Equipment in many ways was still more a handicap than a help. Skis were heavy, made of solid wood, with circumscribed capacity to slide. Waxing, the process of preparing skis to slide forwards but not slip backwards, was embryonic,* and defeated by most of the many splendoured forms of snow. Bindings were cumbrous affairs of cane and osier. Skiing technique was uncertain. The ancient single stick was used in place of the later pair. Clothing was stiff, heavy and awkward. Amundsen's was distinguished by a violet waistcoat.

Their goal was a particularly ferocious slope called Krokkleiva, to reach which they skied hours on end for the privilege of running down – once. Even today it is a slope that demands respect. Amundsen's companions dealt with it by squatting and braking with their stick between their legs.† Amundsen tried to run straight, unbraked and upright. It was too much for the technique and equipment of the times. He paid for it by a terrible fall, from which, however, he emerged unscathed. They skied on far into the night. In the small hours they found themselves on a frozen lake under a fine display of the Aurora Borealis.

That boyhood journey had a profound effect on Amundsen. Thenceforth, he regularly went on long ski tours, mainly across Nordmarka. How much it was to prepare himself for a career in Polar exploration, and how much sheer enjoyment, it is difficult to say. The one did not of course exclude the other.

At school Amundsen seems to have been remembered, not so much for his strong enthusiasm, as for obstinacy and an implacable sense of rectitude. On one occasion, he is supposed to have defended a classmate against a teacher who had cast aspersions on his origins; on another, to have stood up to a teacher because of a supposed injustice to himself until the headmaster intervened in his favour.

Amundsen did consistently badly at school, so badly that his head-

---

* The traditional method was to apply pine pitch by melting it on to the soles of the skis over a naked flame. Tallow and candlewax were used in an attempt to cope with the most intractable of snow; fresh flakes at around freezing point that cling in sheaves to the skis. At the annual Holmenkollen ski-jumping competitions in Nordmarka, a large fatty cheese was provided as a wax for wet conditions.

† At that time the usual way of dealing with steep slopes. The 'Christiania' turn had not yet come into common use. A military ski race in 1767 offered '6 prizes ... for those, who without riding or resting on their ski stick best can ski down the steepest slope without falling'. The problem was not new.

master refused to allow him to sit for matriculation for fear of being disgraced by so monumentally unpromising a pupil. Amundsen did not particularly want his matriculation certificate; even less did he want to be told he could not have it. In sheer obstinacy, he sat the examination as a private candidate so that the school was not involved. In July 1890 he passed; only just, but he had passed. He had made his point – and so, one feels, had his headmaster.

The term after obtaining the prized student's cap, Amundsen, now eighteen, entered the medical faculty of Christiania University.* It was against his own inclinations, but it was what his mother wanted. Since she held the purse strings, it was the only reasonable course.

By law, the brothers were eventually to inherit equally their father's estate. But first it passed in its entirety to Gustava, who found herself in the possession of a reasonable income. Roald clearly understood that he would have to respect her wishes, at least if he was to enjoy a comfortable allowance and avoid gratuitous inconvenience. Whatever his reluctance – or inability – to pursue academic studies, he had no objection, for a while, to the life of a student.

Soon after he entered University, he moved to a comfortable flat on his own, taking Betty, his old nurse, as housekeeper. Gustava sold Little Uranienborg and went to live in a pension. She never remarried. Outside her immediate family, she does not appear to have had any emotional engagements.

Amundsen's attitude to her was of pity more than anything else. It was also contractual. In return for independence and financial support, he would study as Gustava prescribed. When he reached the age of majority, he would feel morally released from those obligations.

Of one thing – being reasonably free of self-delusion – he was certain. He was constitutionally unsuited to formal academic study, and conventional examinations. Of that he was to have ample proof in another field, even when he had the strongest conceivable motivation. It is hard to discern how far his aversion to medicine was rooted in dislike for the subject and how far in a belief that, however hard he tried, he would not be able to pass the examinations. He had to find himself, a condition to which the only reasonable answer – sometimes – is to do nothing in particular.

Norway was now approaching nationhood, and politics, industry, art – all the aspects of civilization – were rapidly maturing. It was a country making up for a late start. Besides Nansen and Ibsen there was Grieg,

*At the time, the only university in Norway.

bringing folk music to the concert platform, and Edvard Munch, one of the exponents of Expressionist painting and a prophetic interpreter of the neurotic in art. These are the household names that have burst out of their environment. Behind them were others of formidable accomplishment like the novelist Knut Hamsun, the precursor of existentialism. But for all its talent it could be claustrophobic. Christiania was unmistakably the small capital of a small country on the periphery of Europe. The whole population of Norway in 1880 was 1,800,000 when that of Great Britain was 20,000,000. In many ways, said one Norwegian writer,

> It was hard to be a citizen in a small country. He who is gifted does not get so far as in a big one. A big man in a little country is like the fully fledged chicken in the egg. Either he breaks it to pieces, or he himself is suffocated.

It was indeed a time and place not without strain. The individualism of the age found fruitful soil in Norway. The country, as one of its historians has said, was almost too small to contain all the different warring, cantankerous, opinionated, determinedly independent characters who sprang up.

The cult of the individual was taken to inspiring lengths. Ibsen articulated it in *Brand*, his dramatic poem about a country priest who sacrifices all to the consummation of his own individuality. Brand, the hero of the poem, is made to say,

> Room within the world's wide span,
> Self completely to fulfil.
> That's a valid right of Man,
> And no more than that I will!

It is a telling point that Nansen, the most Norwegian of them all, made Brand his ideal.

Individualism, says Gerhard Gran, a Norwegian scholar and contemporary of Amundsen,

> the violent drive to self-assertion, is characteristically Norwegian, I believe. Our history can scarcely be termed one of discipline; we have never suffered any brutal, exaggerated harmony. The drive to self-assertion is one of the strongest traits in our national character. There is undoubtedly something in every Norwegian's soul that strongly and quite definitely answers Yes to Brand's words: 'compromise is Satan's work!'

Such was the spirit and such the atmosphere in which Amundsen spent his formative years. Conceivably he may have been attracted to exploration in the first place because he saw in it a way of moving beyond the confines of Norway into wider fields.

However, Amundsen gave no hint of sharing the political and intellectual ferment of his University. He was quiet, and preferred the company of a few trusted friends. He was courtly towards women and appears to have been a good dancer, but reserved. There is no hint of any love affair from his University days. His contemporaries all remark on his reticence about sex. They were struck by a rigid purity about his attitudes. This did not, of course, exclude sexual adventures; indeed, it might argue in favour of them. But if he was sowing his wild oats, his discretion was impenetrable. The women in his life were his Hvidsten cousin Karen Anna (with whom perhaps he was secretly a little in love) and Betty; buxom, motherly, so obviously his mother-substitute.

Betty Gustavson was Swedish. In 1865, at the age of eighteen, she had gone aboard *Constantin*, one of Jens Engebreth's ships at Gothenburg, as mother's help to Gustava, who was then expecting Tonni and sailing to China with her husband. Betty never returned to Sweden, staying with the Amundsens for the rest of her life.

When she moved with Roald to his flat, she had been with the family almost twenty-five years. She was one of the few women for whom Roald ever admitted affection. In the Antarctic, he named a mountain after her; he did not similarly commemorate his mother.

Not many students could boast a housekeeper. Even among the richer ones, Amundsen was distinguished by his style of living. Not many could afford, or were allowed by their families, to keep independent establishments. His flat was large and, in a gloomy way, of some elegance. It lay round the corner from Little Uranienborg in Parkveien, behind the Royal Palace. It was a very good address.

Such was the way Amundsen spent his creative pause. His chief interest was outdoor life: skiing in winter, long forest walks in summer. He neglected his work. He ought to have sat for his first University examination in 1891, but he waited another two years before doing so. On February 25th, 1893, still at University, he went to hear Eivind Astrup lecture at the Students' Union.

Astrup was another Askeladden figure. He was of an age with Amundsen; also one of the school of long-distance Nordmarka cross-country skiers, like Amundsen, profoundly moved by Nansen's first crossing of Greenland; just another Christiania boy. At the age of nineteen, he went to America to complete his education, but instead, by chance and cheek, found himself with Peary on his second Greenland expedition in 1891–92, and turned into a celebrated explorer. He had been Peary's sole companion on his journey from McCormick Bay to Independence Bay and back; a tale of 1,300 miles of difficulties, privation and triumph. It was the first crossing of the Greenland Ice Cap so far north.

It was about this classic Polar journey that Astrup lectured to the Christiania students.

He described how he proved the superiority of Norwegian ski over the North American snowshoe. But what he really had to talk about was Peary's pioneering work. His theme was the journey on which Peary showed that Eskimo dogs could be successfully used by Europeans for Polar travel. Astrup concentrated on how Peary made friends with the Polar Eskimos to learn how to build igloos; how to make clothes adapted to the environment; how, in short, to live under Polar conditions. The lesson was that primitive people had something to teach, and civilized men did not enjoy a monopoly of knowledge. It was a lesson brought back by Nansen from Greenland a few years before, after spending a year with the Godthaab Eskimos.

Astrup spoke with originality and charm. To finish off, he conveyed an appealing vision of the life of the Eskimo, a noble Polar savage. It appealed profoundly to the romantic nature worship which then was taking hold of the Norwegians. The effect on Amundsen was immediate.

He commandeered an old school friend who had been with him on the ski tour four years earlier, and persuaded him then and there to repeat the performance. They collected their skis and went straight from Astrup's lecture into Nordmarka skiing in the dark. The night was far advanced when they reached their destination. Amundsen appeared to have gathered strength, as if, paradoxically, through physical exhaustion he had achieved a state of spiritual exaltation.

In the snow, resting on his ski stick under the clear, cold glistening starlit sky of a Northern winter night, Amundsen harangued his companion on the splendours of the Polar regions and the attraction which they held for him. It was a rare outburst. Besides Astrup's lecture there was something else to cause tension, ambition, excitement, dissatisfaction.

For over a year Norway had been full of Nansen's plans for a new expedition. This was no less than letting a ship freeze into the Arctic pack ice, and using ocean currents for a drift across the Polar basin. It was an original concept, and therefore foredoomed to failure by most experts, especially the old British Naval officers who later advised Scott. Nansen, utterly self-confident, ignored them. He could afford to. He was not only a proven explorer but an accepted scientist. He was a marine biologist with research to his credit and a doctor's degree,* and he was helping to develop modern oceanography.

* He had handed in his thesis before leaving for Greenland in 1888. The first greeting he received on coming down from his historic crossing of the ice cap was congratulation on getting his doctorate.

Nansen had ordered a revolutionary type of ship, with round bilges, to lift when squeezed in order to withstand the pressure of the sea ice. Her designer and builder was Colin Archer, a Norwegian of Scottish origins. He was a naval architect with a touch of genius; who had devised a new, almost unsinkable lifeboat.

Nansen's reputation was now such that he could command Government support and he had Government money to spend. It is a sidelight on Norwegian life at the time, that Archer, even although a solid citizen with a well-known shipyard, suffered acutely from a shortage of capital.

We have had so many outgoings for the ship this week [runs a typical letter of his to Nansen], that there will not be enough left over for the wages on Saturday, and I am therefore once more compelled to ask for a transfer before then.

The progress of the ship – although not such domestic detail – was well reported. Nansen's new expedition was a national affair consciously exploited in the drive to independence. The launching on October 26th, 1892, was an emotional, patriotic event. Thousands of spectators gathered at Archer's yard at Larvik in Southern Norway. Nansen knew how to squeeze drama from the occasion. He surrounded the name with mystery; Eva, his wife, christened the ship, not with some predictable chauvinistic name, but *Fram* ('Forwards').

The building of *Fram* fired Amundsen's Polar ambitions, and Astrup's lecture fanned the flames. On Midsummer's Day, 1893, filled with longing and enthusiasm, he went to see Nansen sail from Christiania in triumph, the water thick with an escorting fleet of little boats.

Earlier in June, Amundsen had failed his University examinations. He must have expected it since (as his companions had noticed) he had neglected his work. But it was failure and it rankled. He did not like to admit this failure to anyone and kept it a secret as long as he lived. He did not even tell his mother, pretending that nothing had happened. In September she died, and Amundsen then left the University, free at last to follow his own desires.

Amundsen's Polar interests had so far been little more than day-dreaming; arguably a retreat from uncongenial outer circumstances. He now had spurs enough to action. Within a few months, he had failed his examinations, his mother had died, and Nansen had departed. It is at this time that Amundsen crossed the frontier of reality and made his first attempt to join a Polar expedition.

He had heard of a Norwegian Arctic traveller, Martin Eckroll, who was then at Tromsø, in Northern Norway, preparing an expedition to

Spitsbergen. On October 23rd, Amundsen wrote to Eckroll, asking to accompany him. The letter is revealing:

> I have long been possessed of a great desire to join one of these interesting Arctic expeditions, but various circumstances have prevented me. First and foremost, my parents wanted me to study. Secondly, there was my age. Now, however, circumstances have changed. My father died several years ago, and my mother – the last tie that bound me to my home – died a month ago of inflammation of the lungs. My brothers – I have 3, and they are all older than myself – are spread all over the world as businessmen. I thus remain alone, and my desire for this great enterprise is correspondingly greater. I matriculated three years ago, and in the intervening time have studied medicine. My experience in this subject is therefore not great, but can always be of use. I intend to spend the coming winter in the study of meteorology, mapmaking, surveying, and other subjects which possibly could be of use on such an expedition. I am 21 to 22 years old. I am a little short sighted, but not seriously. Thus I have never worn spectacles. I am always ready to provide certificates for anything required. A medical certificate goes without saying, and I therefore enclose one. My conditions for accompanying you are not great. I want no salary, and am prepared to submit to anything whatsoever. Should you require a personal interview with me, I am prepared to come whenever you want. Many candidates have presumably applied already, possibly with better qualifications than mine, so my chances are small. I conclude my appeal to you, however, with profound hopes for a favourable reply.

Without waiting for an answer, Amundsen was already trying elsewhere. In the middle of November, he wrote to the Swedish-Norwegian Consulate in London, and *The Times* (signing himself 'medical student') and asked about the Jackson–Harmsworth expedition. This was going to Franz Josef Land under the leadership of Frederick Jackson, an English traveller and big game hunter, financed by Alfred Harmsworth, later Lord Northcliffe, the celebrated newspaper magnate, but then merely a magazine proprietor.

Neither the Consulate nor *The Times* could help. Eckroll's reply, when it came, was also discouraging, but instructive. The subjects mentioned by Amundsen

> would undoubtedly be an advantage.... Familiarity with the care and training of dogs will likewise be of use on any Arctic expedition.... I will not demand more of the participants than any normal outdoor person can manage, and prefer doggedness and stamina to forced sporting enthusiasm.

Eckroll went on to say that he would only take people that he knew. He was sufficently interested to suggest a meeting if he visited Christiania.

That you only want to take companions whom you have already learned to know, I consider to be thoroughly reasonable [was Amundsen's reply], since on an expedition of this nature one is exclusively confined to one's immediate surroundings. . . .

I had considered an Arctic voyage in a sealer in the spring, in order to accustom myself both to the climate and to the difficulties to which one would be exposed . . . Concerning the care and training of dogs, I must unfortunately confess my complete ignorance. If I knew some way of learning these things, I would immediately set to . . .

Nothing came of it, at least as far as Amundsen was concerned, but several interesting things are revealed by the exchange. One of them is Amundsen's combination of forthrightness and secretiveness. He gives the gist of his family situation – vital in a society where the family meant much and a man was the sum of his ancestors and relatives – and candidly explains how the removal of ties and the age of majority allow him to follow his own bent. On the other hand, he covers up his University failure with some adroitness. He misleads without the lie direct. But most interesting of all, is the grasp of the principles of Polar exploration. There is the recognition of the necessity of prior training; of acclimatization; of understanding dogs.

Amundsen was perfectly aware of his own deficiencies. Even before Eckroll's reply arrived, he had set about the process of acquiring the necessary qualifications. Dog-driving was difficult, because the dog as a draught animal hardly existed in Norway; it was only later imported from Greenland and Alaska. Amundsen therefore began with what lay closest; the art of mountain skiing. That, together with dog-driving, seemed to him the fundamental qualifications of a Polar explorer. It was not universally self-evident. At almost exactly the same time, Sir Clements Markham, the father of modern British Antarctic exploration was laying down the rule of Polar travel as 'No ski. No dogs'.

5

A Sailor on Skis

To LIVE IN Norway in the last decade of the nineteenth century was to live with quasi-Polar exploration on the doorstep. In winter, the great upland ranges were virtually *terra incognita*. Between November and March few ventured into their high valleys and plateaux.

It was the middle-class men from the towns, inspired by a romantic upsurge of Nature-worship, who were pushing back the frontier and opening up the mountains in winter. Amundsen wanted to learn from these pioneers, but they were an exclusive little coterie, not easily approached. He turned for help to Gustav, his elder brother.

Gustav had married a relative of one of those early mountain skiers, a journalist called Laurentius Urdahl, and Roald wanted an introduction.

So far, Roald had kept his plans very much to himself. He did not like revealing what was in his mind until he had accomplishments to show. Now, somewhat reluctantly, he disclosed his aims, because Gustav wanted to know what lay behind the request.

Gustav was beginning to be worried about his younger brother's future. Polar exploration hardly seemed a dependable profession; however for the moment he decided that the best course was to humour Roald so he asked Urdahl to take him under his wing. Gustav was by now a shipowner and established citizen; he was therefore not a relative to be ignored. Urdahl agreed to take Roald skiing in the Western Mountains over the New Year.

Although, as the saying goes, born with skis on his feet, Amundsen had so far skied only on the protected lowland snowfields of Nordmarka. This trip to the Western Mountains was to be his first taste of mountain skiing. It was a considerable transition. The Norwegian mountains are not high, but they are wild. The Western ranges are exposed to the ocean, bearing the brunt of the North Atlantic storms. Their weather is capricious. Except for the occasional hut, there is no trace of civilization for mile upon mile. With blizzard, burning cold, and the hiss of drift – fine grains of loose snow seized by the wind and swept over the surface from one place to the other, like sand blown across the desert – with snow in all its forms from feather-like powder to steel-hard crust, and

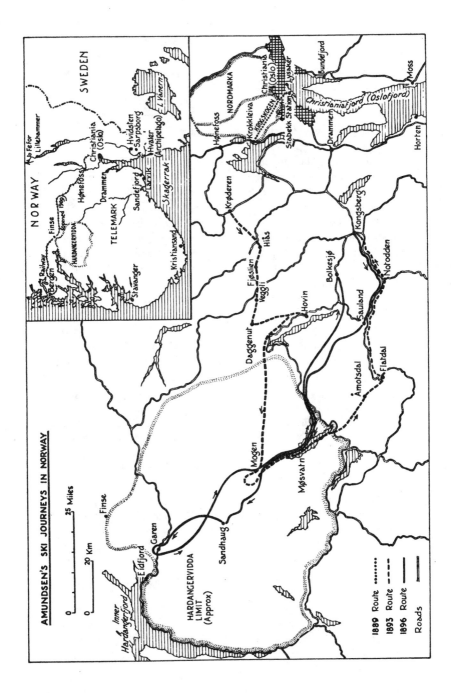

AMUNDSEN'S SKI JOURNEYS IN NORWAY

0   25 Miles

0   20 Km

Finse

Eidfjord

Garen

Inner Hardangerfjord

HARDANGERVIDDA
LIMIT
(Approx)

Sandhaug

Mogen

Møsvatn

Dæggenut

Hovin

Åmotsdal

Flatdal

Sauland

Notodden

Bolkesjø

Vågsli

Fjøslien

Hitås

Kongsberg

Krøderen

Hønefoss

NORDMARKA

Krokkleiva

KRISTVOGEN

Christiania (Oslo)

Stabekk Station

Lysaker

Sundefjord

Bundefjord

Drammen

Moss

Horten

Christianiafjord (Oslofjord)

1889 Route
1893 Route
1896 Route
Roads

NORWAY

SWEDEN

To Fefor
Lillehammer

Bergen

Finse
(opened 1909)

Railway

HARDANGERVIDDA

Hønefoss

Drammen

Christiania
(Oslo)

Hvidsten
Sarpsborg

Sandefjord

Larvik

Hvaler
(Archipelago)

Skagerrak

Kristiansand

Stavanger

TELEMARK

the wind-carved furrows, ridges and waves that are called sastrugi, this
landscape is a convincing approximation of the Polar regions.

Urdahl proposed taking Amundsen on a crossing of Hardangervidda.
He had chosen something rather special in the way of terrain. Hardangervidda is a mountain plateau which (for the initiate) holds an austere
nostalgic charm. Nansen compared it with the Arctic, 'where it was so
high under the heavens, the air was clean and life was simple ... back
to solitude–silence–greatness ...'

In some ways, Hardangervidda is as formidable as Antarctica. It is,
at any rate, untamed, exposed, and not to be trifled with; and open,
treeless, windswept, hummocked land. In winter, it is a rolling desert
of snow.

In 1893, Hardangervidda in winter had hardly been explored. The
first recorded crossing had been made in 1884 by a Norwegian Army
officer, Captain H. A. Angell. A few years later, Urdahl had attempted
to cross from Mogen to Eidfjord, on the Hardangerfjord, a route not
yet done from east to west. He was beaten back by blizzards, and now
proposed to try again. Amundsen was promised a piece of mountain
pioneering.

Anticipation was very much part of the pleasure of this enterprise.
Urdahl and Amundsen met frequently in the autumn of 1893, mostly
in Amundsen's impressive bachelor flat. At the time, as Urdahl put it,
Amundsen was for him

> the younger companion, comparatively unfamiliar with skiing, who had come
> to me to be initiated into the mysteries of the high mountains in midwinter.
> But we were both drenched with interest in Polar expeditions and other ad-
> ventures. Therefore we got on very well, and we could build castles in the
> air so well together.
>
> The only difference is that all mine have crumbled into the dust, while
> Roald's steadily grew in pomp and splendour.

Urdahl's contemporary accounts of their experiences were not quite
so respectful. They left Christiania on Christmas Day, 1893 by train.
From Krøderen, the railhead, they then had to ski over forty miles of
foothills before reaching Hardangervidda and starting on their journey
proper.

> We were [wrote Urdahl of the first day on skis] sluggish and completely out
> of the habit of taking exercise. The tallest in the company, 'The Arctic Ex-
> plorer', had nothing to do for half a year, and was therefore well nourished
> and untrained. 'The Doctor' had had far too much to do, and for that reason
> was worn out and thin, and I myself felt – as I thought at the time – the
> effects of age and the result of a sedentary life.

'The Arctic Explorer', needless to say, was Amundsen. Urdahl also called him 'Goliath', for even in a company of tall people Amundsen was of a noticeable height. 'The Doctor' was a relative of Urdahl's, a medical student called Vilhelm Holst, invited along to make up the party. As soon as they started, climbing from the valley, their difficulties began.

The snow was ... loose and soft to the bottom.

Oddly enough, the little bookworm of a 'Doctor' was the fittest and best. While we others lay far down the slopes and flailed about with cramp in our legs, so that we were in danger of drowning in the sea of snow, he would already have reached the top, and would be inspecting us through his gold-framed spectacles. But good eyesight was necessary to discover us, since often our noses alone stuck out of the snow.

'The Explorer', who had done nothing for a whole month but equip himself for the tour, was worst off – since none of his equipment was usable.

Now and then I heard from the depths of the nearest snowdrift a more forceful than elegant outburst concerning ski makers and sports shops who could not deliver proper wares   and shortly afterwards a tall, completely snow-covered form with long, iced-up moustaches, emerged into the open and struggled a few feet upwards – whereupon the owner sank helplessly once more into the deep, deep snow.

This hid in fact considerable preparation. Sleeping bags had been specially sewn of reindeer fur similar to those used by Nansen on the first crossing of Greenland. Their wind jackets were also copied from Nansen; a model with hood attached, which he had adapted from the Eskimo anorak. Both were warm, functional; (if heavy) a reasonable success. The same could not be said of the skis, or at least the bindings, for equipment was still rudimentary.

Bindings were primitive, various, and a fruitful source of dispute (as they remain among skiers even today). Amundsen was ill served by the pattern he had chosen. They did not fit his boots, so that the skis could not be steered properly at speed. On their first downhill run, he turned a spectacular somersault into the loose snow at the end, on the banks of a frozen lake.

'These skis are quite impossible,' he said. 'Each one insisted on going its own way; the one to the right, and the other to the left ...'

'Ah well,' said 'the Doctor' drily, 'you have always been a man of the Centre ... you don't happen to have broken any of your arms or legs, or perhaps a cervical vertebra?' He added teasingly, 'You know I have bandages enough.' 'Goliath' simply growled, and set off over the ice-covered lake at a hundred miles an hour.

Amost every misery known to the mountains was visited on them.

There was a *föhn*, an unseasonal thaw, snow that stuck to the skis and stopped them from sliding. There was that abomination of abominations, a warm blizzard. They were now so delayed that, because of his work, Urdahl could not continue. At a mountain called Daggrønut, having ignominiously taken a week for thirty miles and not yet reached Hardangervidda proper, they turned and skied down to a village called Hovin. Thence, Urdahl went back to Christiania, while Amundsen and Holst returned to the attack. Near Mogen, a mountain farm and the last habitation before the actual crossing of Hardangervidda began, they were forced to spend a night out in the open at a temperature of $-40°$ (C.). The snow was too hard to dig themselves in, so they had to lie on top, as a result of which, in spite of their reindeer furs, they froze horribly. A few miles further on they were overtaken by a blizzard, and they, too, had to turn back with unaccomplished errand. Hardangervidda had won again.

Six weeks later, Amundsen was on his way to the Arctic. As he had written to Eckroll, he wanted to accustom himself 'both to the climate and to the difficulties to which one would be exposed' on a real expedition. After mountain skiing, Polar navigation was logically the next stage in his instruction.

There was, however, more to it than that. Amundsen had abandoned a medical career. This, his family agreed, was not necessarily a disgrace but they suggested that without formal qualifications he would find obstacles in his way. He really ought to take up another profession. What more natural for someone of his background and tastes than that of ship's officer? When he was qualified, his family would be prepared to help him on his chosen path. A master's certificate ought to be his aim, and he could start putting in his sea time as soon as he liked. He accepted their advice; after all, to be a captain would mean he could have the command at sea and on land; the undisputed leader of his expeditions. At the beginning of March, 1894, nursing his Polar interests, he shipped before the mast on the sealer *Magdalena* for a season in the ice. It was a harsh but privileged initiation into the life of a sailor.

Sealing, together with whaling, held a high place in the Norwegian imagination. It was a respected occupation, 'a manly exercise', to quote a Norwegian historian, 'comparable with Nansen's great deeds of exploration in the Polar regions'.

For a first-time sailor, *Magdalena* was a hard school. A small, weather-beaten, wooden sailing ship, barque rigged, with inadequate auxiliary engine, she pitched, tossed and heaved before the wind in notably violent and moody waters. In August, when Roald returned from the Arctic on *Magdalena*, he wrote to his brother Gustav, at Gustav's request, giving an account of the voyage. Although writing for the information (and presumably entertainment) of another, Amundsen seems to be concerned with his own instruction. Few words are wasted on his state of mind. Everything is to the point. He shows a capacity, indeed a determination, to learn from what he sees and hears. From the beginning, his letter reads like a student's notebook:

... first a description [of a sealer] First and foremost, what distinguishes a sealer, is its stout construction. Iron and steel will not do, since they would be crushed to pieces by the ice. A strong kind of wood is required, and they are therefore all built of oak. The latter is not quite correct, since the hull itself is built of a lighter kind of wood, which outside is clad by the so-called ice sheath. The ice sheath is a layer of oak several feet thick surrounding the inner structure, and which thereby serves to resist the pressure of the ice which sometimes can be monstrous. *Magdalena* was said to be 12 feet thick at the bows; a pretty thickness, as you can see. On the mainmast, a little below the top, the sealer has its most characteristic feature; to wit, the crow's nest. This is a large, capacious barrel fixed to that point on the mainmast where the royal yard is placed on other ships. The captain and first mate take their places there alternately either to look for seal or to navigate the ship through thick and heavy ice ...

Aft [lies the] Captain's cabin [and] a cabin with four bunks for both mates, chief engineer and steward ... Right up forrard lies the mess deck ... [with] space for 50 men ... each bunk holds two men. Before each bunk stands a little chest in which each man keeps his food, and all the little things for which space can be found ...

This is a good description of the way a wooden ship was built for the Polar seas. Amundsen then turns to the essentials of sealing and his first lesson in the behaviour of Arctic ice.

Now comes the most difficult part of sealing. That is finding the pups. All seal are protected until April 3rd. 14 days before, the seal go in huge herds on to the ice to give birth to their young, *throw*, as it is called ... At these latitudes, the ice forms a large bay, and the seal like to throw their young at the end of this bay. It is only necessary, therefore, to find the bay.

On March 28th, they found a herd of about 5,000 seal, but four ships waiting. *Magdalena* approached one of them, *Morgenen* of Sandefjord.

'I think there are too few for 5,' our skipper sings out as we glide alongside ... 'What about you and me sneaking West; that's where the main herds are; you can bet your boots.'
You have got to use cunning and craft everywhere in order to get on.

This is illuminating; not only for Amundsen but for the whole milieu out of which he came. So too is the next passage:

Our skipper is well aware that with our inadequate engine we cannot work further [through the ice] with any success. He therefore wants *Morgenen* to sail ahead in order to follow in her wake. *Morgenen*'s skipper, who has less experience in the Arctic, immediately submits to the other's greater insight.

On March 30th, the main herd was found. There were about 50,000 seal, and eight ships lying in wait. That meant, at a reasonable estimate, three or four thousand for each ship; a good catch, and reasonable shares for each man. Sealers were paid by results. Amundsen continues his story:

Sunday, the first of April, we had unusually fine weather; dead calm with sunshine and air that was crystal clear. All the captains had once and for all agreed that in weather like this they would let their fires go out; while lying among the seal, that is to say. For in such weather, if the fires are lit, the smoke rises straight up into the air, and can be seen miles away. Those ships which had not found the seal, and lay so far off that they could not see our ships, would then be able to see the smoke. Attracted by it, they would then come in towards us. Today we therefore had to be on our best behaviour. But what happens? The skipper of *Haardraade* who, without doubt, must have been afraid of freezing in – the temperature was – 15° – and finding it difficult to manoeuvre among the seal on the 3rd, lights his fires to break a channel in the ice.

Smoke pours in huge masses up from the funnel. 'That bloody fool of a skipper on the *Haardraade* had gone stark raving mad,' yells our skipper. The whole crew was furious.

Results were not wanting. In the afternoon we caught sight of 4 ships working their way towards us. That was a blow. There we lost 1,000 seal for a certainty   and all because of a little smoke ...

His one trace of emotion, Amundsen reserves for the start of the sealing itself. He was an oarsman in one of the ship's boats from which the work was done. He had never seen animals hunted before.

Seven o'clock struck.

'Prepare to launch the boats,' the skipper orders from aloft. In a flash, everybody is in their respective boats, with the exception of 2 men from each boat standing ready by the ropes which let them down into the water.

'Let go,' comes the order from the crow's nest. A whirring and screeching comes from the tackle and immediately afterwards all the boats are lying in the water at the ship's sides. Those who have lowered the boats now shin down the ropes, which are still attached to the boats. As soon as they are aboard, the ropes are flung out of the boats, and each man takes his place. A course is set for where seal have been observed.

'Steady as she goes,' the rifleman commands; and 1, 2, 3, shots ring out. I cannot let be – I must turn my head a little. 3 large carcasses tell me that the shots are well placed. The mothers have been shot as they suckled their

young. Still the little ones try to feed at their mothers' nipples. Now all the
boats surge towards the floe.

'Every man out and flense,' rings out the command. The coxwain has in
the meanwhile grabbed one of the small picks lying in the boat and drives
it hard to the ice. In this way the boat is kept next to the floe. The oarsmen
have let go the oars, grabbed each his pick, and in an instant are out on the
floe ... they spread out ... each with a pick in his hand. The little pups have
now caught sight of us, and with the most appealing eyes they seem to beg
for their lives. But there is no mercy. The pick is lifted and with well-placed
blow of the blunt end the creature's skull is crushed ... and immediately after
we turn to flensing ... To flense is no easy affair, and requires great practice.
A slaughtered animal is turned over with its underside topmost. With a slash
the skin is cut from the mouth right down to the hind flippers. After that, skin
and blubber are cut away from the rest of the carcass. The blubber lies just
under the skin, and comes away together in the flensing. The remainder of
the carcass is left lying in the ice.

The letter ends there. Only by oblique references in later years is the
depth of underlying emotion revealed. Amundsen is counterpoint both
to his mentor, Nansen and his future rival, Scott; in them, feeling produced eloquence; in him, a bland and easily misinterpreted understatement verging on the inarticulate.

Amundsen was shaken by his introduction to the wholesale slaughter
of wild animals. He was not particularly squeamish, but he was appalled
by the cruelty he saw and the effect on his shipmates.

This was one of the experiences that moulded Amundsen. He hunted
when he had to, but he questioned the necessity for such prodigal and
inhumane slaughter. He turned his back on blood-sports. He could never
understand those who killed a fellow creature for pleasure.

After paying off from *Magdalena*, Amundsen signed on *Valborg*, one
of the family ships, for his next voyage. His heart, however, was not
really in ordinary sailing nor, yet, in mate's or master's rank. He had
been introduced to the navigation of Polar ice and to working in Polar
conditions. From his abortive attempt on Hardangervidda he had
glimpsed the technique of Polar travel and now, at the age of twenty-two,
felt confident enough to make his first definite plans for exploration.

In November 1894, he was considering a voyage to Spitsbergen.
Spitsbergen's status was unclear, and he wanted to organize an expedition
to take possession for Norway. Two months later, he had turned his
attention to the Antarctic.

This was a rather more serious project. His eldest brother, Tonni,
was also involved. Tonni, after two years working in Algiers, had re-

turned to Christiania. He was a very good skier, the best of the brothers, in fact (Roald was not, by Norwegian standards, exceptionally brilliant on skis). There was a perfectly good reason for the direction their thoughts had taken.

The previous August, Captain C. A. Larsen, in the sealer *Jason* of Sandefjord, had returned from an Antarctic voyage, on which he had discovered Oscar II Land, on the Weddell Sea coast of Graham Land. Exploration had not been his aim. He had been sent to look for new sealing and whaling grounds, one of the pioneering ventures of the Norwegian Antarctic whale fishery. He had, nevertheless, contrived to come home with the first major Antarctic discovery since Sir James Clark Ross, fifty years before.

Larsen was a prince among whaling skippers. He was a leader of men. By sheer force of character he had quelled a drunken mutiny on *Jason* in the Straits of Magellan. He had all the instincts of an explorer. From a hasty landing on Seymour Island, off Graham Land, he had brought back the first fossils from Antarctica. A popular hero he was not, but he kindled a flutter of interest. He kindled rather more in Roald and Tonni Amundsen. They drafted a letter to Christen Christensen of Sandefjord, *Jason*'s owner, asking

> if a ski expedition would not be the best method of exploring unknown lands in the South, i.e., if snow and ice conditions resemble those on the Greenland Ice Cap ...
>
> if Graham Land would be suitable ... or if you know some other relatively unknown land better suited for an expedition such as ours ...
>
> if there is good opportunity for hunting seal ... for food, and if we could get enough to feed a number of dogs to pull sledges ... for an estimate for a sealer to land us and fetch us.

The plan behind these questions is eminently sane. The essence of Antarctic exploration has already been grasped – before a single person has landed to explore the interior. There are no doubts over the use of skis and dogs on the yet unknown continent; decades later, English explorers were still debating the point.

It is hard to know how far the Amundsens' plan was the product of an enthusiastic moment; how far, serious intention. With the least encouragement, Roald would probably have rushed into some enterprise. But some sobering hand, probably that of Gustav, restrained him. He went neither to Spitsbergen nor to Graham Land, but continued humdrum sailing in temperate seas on family ships to make up qualifying sea time. A cabin mate from this period recalled him as hard working, serious, and determined to learn. 'We knew that he had something at the back of his mind, but he didn't say what it was.' This was a common impression.

On May 1st, 1895, Amundsen obtained his mate's certificate, to his disappointment, only with a second class. He was not made for examinations, but he had passed. All he needed was a few months more at sea to qualify as a mate. But first he had to do his military service.

He very much wanted, as he said, to do his 'duty as a citizen'. This was not sententious bombast; nor, at that particular time was it an unusual feeling. In the summer of 1895, one of the periodical crises between Norway and Sweden over Norwegian sovereignty reached the brink of war. At the last moment Norway, unarmed and unready, had to back down. The national mood was now one of chagrin and defiance. The Norwegians, so notably unwarlike, reluctantly were forced to recognize that they might one day have to fight for independence. As best they could, they began to arm, and patriotic feeling ran high.

But in Amundsen's case, there was something beyond patriotism. He was morbidly afraid of rejection on account of his short sight. He felt it, not as a simple disability, but as a shameful stigma to be hidden from the world. His admission to Eckroll had been a momentary lapse; he revealed it to no one else, not even his family. Clandestinely, he had spectacles prescribed but, to the end of his life, shunned them in public as a badge of dishonour. Much of his ludicrous misadventure on Hardangervidda had been due to this. Only in middle age, as a famous man, was he prepared to admit his defect. It is connected with something obsessive in his cultivation of the physical virtues.

Since the age of fifteen, he had religiously done physical exercises to make himself fit and as he said, prepare himself for the life of exploration inspired by the heroic difficulties of Sir John Franklin. Doubtless there is something in this. But at the time the cult of sport and physical fitness was taking root among Norwegians. In the competitive sports then current in Norway – ski racing, ski jumping and association football – Amundsen did not shine. To turn to some non-competitive recreation instead is a not unknown reaction. Amundsen was devoted to physical perfection as an end in itself besides training for a purpose. Beneath it all, there lurks the hint of some dark anxiety.

The story of his Army medical examination is best told in his own words, written thirty years later:

> The doctor was elderly and, to my great pleasure and surprise, a keen student of the human body. Naturally I was entirely without clothes during the examination. The old doctor inspected me with minute care, and suddenly burst out into rhapsodic praise over my appearance. Apparently eight years'

uninterrupted training had not been without effect. He said: 'Young man, what on earth have you been doing to acquire such muscles?'

I explained that I was fond of physical exercise, which I practised assiduously. The old gentleman was so enthused by his discovery, which he regarded as something quite unusual, that he called some officers from the next room to look at the wonder. I need not say that I was terribly embarrassed by this public viewing, so that I wanted the ground to open and swallow me.

But this episode had a profitable consequence. In his enthusiasm over my physical condition, the old doctor forgot to examine my eyes. Consequently I got through the examination as easily as I could have wished, and was able to do my military service.

His service lasted the statutory seven months and five days. It consisted of parade ground drill at the Gardemoen barracks outside Christiania. Amundsen did not feel it was enough. He continued extra training on his own. One of the stories told about this period is that he obtained permission for himself and a companion to do a long private cross-country run. The companion acted pacemaker, lightly clad. Amundsen carried full field equipment, with rifle and rucksack, wearing heavy, cumbersome regulation knee-length boots.

Their own writers have frequently remarked that the Norwegians are people of extremes. In a famous passage quoted with particular relish by generations of his countrymen, Ibsen says:

> Whatever you are, be out and out.
> Not divided or in doubt.

It is at any rate Amundsen to the life. The man possessed by a single goal, to the exclusion of all else, begins to take shape.

At the end of January, 1896, the headline MISSING SKIERS appeared on the front pages of the Christiania press. It was Amundsen's debut in the news.

Early in the New Year, Amundsen and his brother, Leon, had left Christiania to ski over Hardangervidda to Western Norway. They should have taken a week; nothing had been heard from them for over a fortnight. Hardangervidda in midwinter had a quality of mystic foreboding; and a disaster in the snow was then very much in men's minds. Eivind Astrup had disappeared on a ski tour in the Rondane Mountains in Eastern Norway, and was later found dead. From Nansen, hidden in the Arctic, there had been no news for over two years, and gloomy speculation had begun. From this, the Amundsens had duly benefited. The alarm was raised, a search begun. After three weeks, given up for lost, they reappeared under their own steam – just.

This was part of Amundsen's Polar training. After military service, he decided next on another bout of mountain skiing. He chose, characteristically, the midwinter crossing of Hardangervidda which had defeated him two years before. Urdahl being unable to go with him again, Leon was persuaded to take his place.

It was to be no slavish repetition, but an exercise in applying lessons learned. Skis were lighter; bindings gave more control. Food, clothing and equipment had been changed. Now imbued with a seaman's awareness of weather and navigation, Amundsen took a pocket barometer (missing on the previous occasion) and *three* compasses to check against each other.

For the provincial newspaper of which Urdahl was now editor, Amundsen immediately afterwards wrote an account of the tour. It was his first published work. It was a piece of genre writing. In the pioneering days of Norwegian mountain skiing, articles about notable routes were a regular feature of the Press.

Amundsen was reluctant to burst into print. He had got into a scrape, and, being *au fond* a perfectionist, only wanted to write about perfection. Urdahl, however, persuaded him that the readers preferred scrapes. Amundsen had no literary pretensions and, at Urdahl's suggestion, wrote in the form of a long letter to him. It was published, in several instalments, under the title of 'The Amundsen Brothers' Adventurous Journey over Hardangervidda'.*

It differs from others of its kind only in being more than usually unvarnished and underplayed. The adventure, Amundsen was careful to explain, ensued when things went wrong. His plan was to follow Urdahl's proposed route from Mogen to Eidfjord, starting, however from Kongsberg instead of Krøderen, as on the previous occasion. This meant skiing 170 kilometres, (100 statute miles) but the critical part was the last sixty kilometres (forty miles) from Mogen, over the deserted heights of Hardangervidda to Garen, the first habitation on the western side. All went reasonably well until the last thirty kilometres after leaving an uninhabited hut called Sandhaug. Then everything went wrong.

> Although the weather was fine – clear and cold – minus 25° (C.)   the ski glided badly. The dry, grainy drift snow was the cause. At about midday ... thick, grey-black masses of fog rolled up, and scarcely half an hour later we had a N.W. storm upon us ... the only correct thing would undoubtedly have been to turn round. But our ski tracks were already drifted over and

---

* It is an illuminating point that the Norwegian word for adventurous, *eventyrlig*, can also mean risky, or like a fairy tale.

drift and thick weather surrounded us on all sides, so there was no question of finding the hut again ...

The brothers were now treated to a selection of the teasing little foibles of the snows. They were battered by a relentless wind that erased the landscape in a cauldron of boiling drift. They were disoriented by white-out, when sky and ground melt into one, there is no horizon, and up and down are confused. Despite the three compasses, they lost their bearings. For days, they wandered in circles, sleeping in the snow, unable to cook warm food because their spirit stoves were useless out of doors. The sand-like drift snow penetrated everything; it melted and ran in rivulets down the insides of their sleeping bags. On the second night out, their food bag, rashly dumped in the snow, mysteriously disappeared, taken perhaps by the wind or a wolverine. It is all stirring stuff. Amundsen, however, presented it, not as noble adventure, but as a somewhat reprehensible cautionary tale. The climax came on the fourth successive night, sleeping out:

> We spent it on a steep mountain slope. As there was a lot of snow, we took the opportunity to dig ourselves well down, in order to get some protection against wind and drift. I slept unusually well that night. When I woke, I discovered that I was snowed in. I thought that by pressing my shoulders up against the covering of snow above me, I would break it. But I was mistaken. The snow had clearly been wet when it fell, and had since frozen into a compact mass around me. My brother had, however, been more alert. Several times, he told me afterwards, he had been up during the night and brushed the snow off me. I, on the other hand, had slept through it all. When the first daylight appeared, he had looked out to see the weather. Then he discovered that I was snowed in. My feet were all that were visible, and showed where I lay. After frantic digging for an hour or more, he was able to set me free. We agreed that after so much misfortune, something better had to come, and trustfully we started off.

Within a few hours, they found themselves on the way down from Hardangervidda. They passed the tree line, came upon ski tracks, and returned to civilization – at the same Mogen from which they had started ten days before. They had not eaten for the past two and a half days. Meanwhile, at Garen during the blizzard, mysterious ski tracks had appeared from the east which could only have been theirs. Without knowing it at the time, they had been within a few yards of their goal.

Amundsen had been in deeper trouble than his narrative suggested. He had nearly suffocated the last night buried in the snow. He was threatened with the amputation of several frostbitten fingers. It was his hardest journey. He would break records and breach frontiers, but

Hardangervidda he never overcame. It taught him, however, a variety of lessons. It was his Polar nursery, and allowed him to make his beginner's mistakes in time.

Next, needing sea time before being allowed to serve as mate, Amundsen sailed on a second Arctic voyage – on *Jason*, no less, which had returned to Northern sealing after her foray in the South.

The story now turns elsewhere.

6

Into the Antarctic Night

AMUNDSEN'S OLD PLAYMATE Carsten Borchgrevink had inveigled himself as supercargo on *Antarctic*, a Norwegian whaler sent out to investigate Sir James Clark Ross's reports of commercially profitable whales. This was the first voyage to the Ross Sea since its discovery in 1841. The right whales were not found, but at Cape Adare, Leonard Kristensen, *Antarctic*'s captain, lowered a boat and went ashore. Borchgrevink was with him. They were the first men to set foot on South Victoria Land. The date was January 24th, 1895. It was the first step on the road to the Pole.

The Sixth International Geographical Congress was meeting in London that July, and Borchgrevink hurried halfway round the world at his own expense to burst in on it and bring the news. He immediately offered himself as leader of an expedition to go out to Cape Adare and become the first to winter on the Antarctic continent. The Congress passed a resolution that

> the exploration of the Antarctic regions is the greatest piece of geographical exploration still to be undertaken ... this work should be undertaken before the close of the century.

After decades of neglect, interest in the Antarctic had revived.

The talk first bore fruit in Belgium, where a Naval officer, Lieutenant Adrien de Gerlache, was preparing to mount an expedition. This smacked of the improbable for, as de Gerlache himself put it, Belgium was 'a country without a seafaring background, if not without seafarers [where] the taste for far-flung enterprises is little developed'. But the spirit of the age descends where it lists.

Four years before, Baron Adolf Erik Nordenskiöld, the illustrious conqueror of the North-East Passage, Nansen's precursor on the first crossing of Greenland, had tried to organize an Antarctic expedition. De Gerlache wrote volunteering, or rather begging, to go. He got no reply; nor did the expedition materialize. But he had been fired by an idea. If he could not join someone else's expedition, if indeed there was no expedition for him to join, he would organize one of his own. It was a profound act of faith. Belgium was then absorbed by the heady business of colonizing the Congo. King Leopold of the Belgians frowned on anything which distracted from that enterprise. He did not approve of de Gerlache. Getting money for Antarctic exploration was going to be more than usually difficult.

However, de Gerlache had the sublime determination before which difficulties wilt and brick walls open. Somehow he found money and bought his expedition ship. In the best traditions of Polar exploration, she was an old sealer, a Norwegian one, none other than the *Patria* which Amundsen had encountered on his first Arctic voyage a year or two before. Renamed *Belgica*, she entered Sandefjord on July 4th, 1896 to refit.

To the same harbour came *Jason* from the Arctic with Amundsen on board. Here was the kind of chance for which he had been waiting. On July 29th, he wrote volunteering to join de Gerlache.

Amundsen was unknown; only one of many offering to sail on *Belgica* to the mysterious South. De Gerlache showed his letter to Johan Bryde, a Sandefjord shipowner, the honorary Belgian consul, and *Belgica*'s agent. Bryde's comment, written in the margin was: 'Take him, my friend!'

Bryde was an old Arctic skipper, used to judging seamen. He, at any rate, was the adviser on whom de Gerlache leaned. De Gerlache accepted Amundsen. Amundsen offered to serve without pay, which undoubtedly told in his favour. On the other hand, de Gerlache was prepared to take qualified Polar travellers where he could find them and, as he said, he saw before him a 'sailor and skier'. He was also influenced by the fact that Amundsen was a compatriot of Nansen. Nansen fever had just broken out.

On August 13th, Nansen had landed at Vardø, in Northern Norway. It was the first sign of him since he had vanished into the Arctic ice three years before. He came ashore like a man returning from the dead.

With a single companion, Hjalmar Johansen, he had left *Fram* with sledges, dogs and skis, for a dash to the Pole. They did not reach it; but they reached 86° 14′, the furthest north that human feet had ever trod, 170 miles further than anyone before; closer than anyone yet to either Pole of the earth. This in itself was enough to make them heroes for a day; but what caught the imagination of the public was what then happened. Their retreat over the drifting pack ice became one of the classic journeys of Polar exploration. It was 500 miles of difficulty but never, somehow, despair. It ended with a Robinson Crusoe winter alone in a makeshift hut on an Arctic desert island among the forlorn archipelagos of Franz Josef Land and a miraculous encounter with the

Jackson–Harmsworth expedition. *Windward*, the expedition's relief ship, brought Nansen and Johansen back to civilization. Exactly one week after they landed, *Fram* returned to Norway. She had drifted across the Polar basin as Nansen had foreseen. She had come through her ordeal in the ice with hardly a crack to her timbers. Unlike almost every other Arctic expedition, not a man had been lost. Best of all, Nansen had routed all the experts, the pontificators, the Arctic authorities who had prophesied disaster. Some of them, of course, never forgave him. But it was the way to the public heart.

Norway erupted in an orgy of patriotic fervour. Nansen had emerged from the ice to give his countrymen self-confidence and national pride when they needed both in their fight for independence. With no politicians of his personal stature, he did duty for a national leader. 'Until now, nobody thought that little Norway could be concerned in something so big,' said Bjørnstjerne Bjørnson, the national poet, in his welcoming oration to Nansen in Christiania before a crowd of 30,000. 'And the Great Deed is like a confirmation for the whole nation.'

Tall, blond, with the aura of invincibility, Nansen was made into a demi-god by his countrymen. A well-known artist, Erik Werenskiold, used him as a model in illustrations for a popular edition of the Sagas, so that Nansen entered thousands of Norwegian homes in the likeness of a medieval Norse hero, King Olav Yrygvason. Thus, in Norway, the Polar explorer became the national ideal; there have been worse.

Abroad, Nansen made an impact far exceeding that attained after his first crossing of Greenland. It was not only because the deed was bigger, but because the medium of presentation was different. Then, it had been a book written by Nansen himself; now it was the popular Press. His personality appealed to journalists because it lent itself to simplification and easy comprehensibility, bringing life to the puppet show of people in the news. He had the correct touch of vanity: appearing in a black matador has and a distinctive jacket buttoned up to the neck that became known as the Nansen jacket. Thus framed, his long Nordic visage, with its intense melancholy, bordering on the fierce, became a familiar tableau in newspaper photographs all over the world. He was the stuff of headlines and the instant public personality. In that sense, he was a creation of the Press: the first of the popular modern Polar heroes.

The yet youthful art of popular journalism needed a supply of heroes as an outlet for patriotic fervour and as figures with whom to identify in an escape from the creeping uniformity of industrial civilization. The explorer was a good hero; the Polar explorer, with his easily dramatized surroundings, even better. Thus entered Nansen, the man of the frozen outlands, playing to demotic audiences in search of vicarious adventure. He opened what has imprecisely been called the heroic age of Polar exploration. It was understandable that Amundsen should profit by his reflected glory.

Amundsen had now served his sea time, and was appointed as second mate to *Belgica*. But, since taking his certificate eighteen months before, he had been in near waters where one sailed 'by guess and by God'. It was a condition of his appointment that he brush up his navigation. He also had to learn some French and Flemish to be able to give orders to the Belgian sailors. He combined both by going to a navigation tutor in Antwerp early in 1897.

De Gerlache, meanwhile, spent the winter in Norway to learn skiing and the Norwegian language. On *Belgica*, languages were going to be desirable. Officers and crew would be part Belgian, part Norwegian. The scientific staff would be built round a Polish geologist, Henryk Arctowski, and a Romanian zoologist, Emile-G. Racovitza. They were the only suitable volunteers to turn up. De Gerlache was perhaps making a virtue of a necessity when in his polyglot company he saw a grand experiment in advancing the comity of nations. During the apotheosis of the age of nationalism, it was at any rate an unusual ideal.

Belgica was almost a year at Sandefjord fitting out. On June 26th, 1897, she sailed for Antwerp with a skeleton crew. Amundsen returned to join her. Nansen came down from Christiania to say farewell.

De Gerlache, like Borchgrevink (from whom he probably got the idea) intended to land at Cape Adare and become the first man to winter in the Antarctic. En route, he proposed to explore Graham Land and the intervening waters, a little matter of half the circumnavigation of a yet virtually unknown continent.

It was more than enough for three expeditions; and when *Belgica* left Sandefjord, there was not even money for one. De Gerlache still needed 80,000 Belgian francs* before he could start for the south. First, he was going to Antwerp where that detail would be settled. He was certain that by sailing day the money somehow would materialize. Somehow it did; even, at the eleventh hour, a Government grant. De Gerlache had brought to a glorious conclusion three years of humiliating mendicancy. From start to finish he had collected no more than £12,000 and, on this grotesquely inadequate sum, he set out on the first modern expedition to the Antarctic continent.

* £3,150 or $15,000; £54,000 or $108,000 in present terms.

Various hitches delayed sailing. At the last moment the doctor resigned. But among the original motley deluge of unsuccessful volunteers had been a certain Dr. Frederick A. Cook from Brooklyn, N.Y., who had been with Peary on his expedition to North Greenland in 1892. De Gerlache now cabled to offer him the post. Cook instantly accepted, and was told to join *Belgica* at Rio de Janeiro.

At Ostend, five days before departure, a young man presented himself on board unannounced with a change of clothes, a little linen, a great deal of energy and a request to join the expedition. He was a Pole called Antoine Dobrowolski. He appeared to have a solid scientific training. He was engaged on the spot as assistant meteorologist. He refused all offers of money to fit himself out, his only regret being that he was not rich enough to help financially.

On August 23rd, *Belgica* sailed for the south, arriving on October 22nd at Rio de Janeiro. There, Dr. Cook came aboard. As an accomplished Polar explorer he was the subject of Amundsen's particular attention from the start, especially as he had with him two Peary sledges to add to the three brought from Norway.

Christmas found *Belgica* at Lapataïa, in the Beagle Channel, near Cape Horn. As Christmas presents for the officers and scientists, De Gerlache gave novels, carefully selected according to the tastes of each. For Amundsen, there was Pierre Loti's *Pêcheur d'Islande*.

In Big Yann, the hero of Loti's novel, Amundsen saw a little of himself. Big Yann is a Breton fisherman, completely absorbed in his calling, not for what he earns, but for sheer pleasure in the harvest of the sea and the battle with the elements.

> What a man was this Yann, with his disdain for women, his disdain for money, his disdain for everything ...

When taxed with his single state and self-sufficiency he answers:

> 'One of these days, I will indeed celebrate my wedding ... but with none of the girls of the country; no, it will be with the sea.'

In the proverbially stormy seas off Cape Horn, *Belgica* had the luck to find good weather. On January 19th, the first iceberg, gleaming, flat-topped, was sighted and, next day, the South Shetland Islands. *Belgica* now had several narrow escapes. She hit a reef and, somehow, came off again unscathed. With sketch charts, and navigation a wild surmise, De Gerlache pressed on, full speed ahead.

Blindly sailing on, *Belgica* passed through a strait between Snow Island and Smith's Island, the first ship ever to do so. She had arrived at the fringes of the unknown. Almost immediately, in a storm, Wiencke, one of the Norwegian sailors, was washed overboard and drowned.

Never were taut, imagination on edge. One death already. What omen was this? How many victims would yet fall? Would anyone see their homes again? Whose turn next?

Of this Amundsen gives no hint. In his diary, he reproaches himself as the officer of the watch, and therefore responsible. He reproaches himself doubly because, being the only Norwegian officer he felt a particular responsibility for his countrymen on board. Grimly he considers that with greater attention he could have prevented the calamity. That Wiencke was careless, and he at the time engrossed in steering the ship clear of an iceberg, he considers no excuse. To Amundsen there were no excuses.

Belgica ran into clear weather, and appeared before the coast of Antarctica with flags at half mast. The motley crew, depressed at the death of a shipmate, were awed by the first sight of a strange new world; land, desolate, uninhabited, with dark pinnacles of rock piercing endless snowfields sweeping down to the shores of a bitter sea.

Belgica was off the west coast of Graham Land, unvisited for more than 60 years. They now found the entrance to an uncharted channel. De Gerlache hoped it led to the Weddell Sea. He was hoping, in his innocence, for solid land to open up. What he found was a strait between the mainland and the coastal archipelago. He called the strait after the ship, but today it bears his name. It was the great discovery of the voyage.

De Gerlache and Lieutenant Georges Lecointe, the second in command, feeling perhaps that the season was closing in, wanted to hurry now as much as they could.

When I came on deck at midnight [Amundsen wrote on January 29th, the day after entering the strait], a minor storm was blowing, with heavy wet snow and thick fog. We simply lay and drove before the wind. This kind of navigation is dangerous but enticing. Land on all sides, without knowing where. The officer I relieved informed me that in his opinion we were well clear of land now. This did not however prevent my taking very good care to carry out my duty properly. It is ahead and to leewards that my gaze is riveted. At half past twelve, I see on the lee bow a dark stripe, which seems to stay in the same place. There is not much time to decide. Engine ahead, and tiller to leewards. We turn away and leave the dark stripe astern. It now clears enough for me to convince myself of what I have seen. It was big, high land, and far away it was not, of that I am certain. It was during a brief interval that I caught sight of that black stripe. A little before or after, it would have been impossible to see anything in the impenetrable snowdrift and thick fog. Precisely the same thing has been repeated several times. That it is Thou, God, who are steering and watching over everything, I do not doubt for a moment.

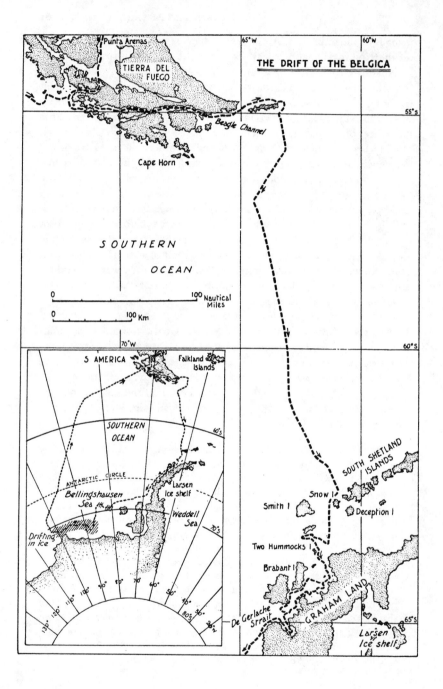

THE DRIFT OF THE BELGICA

Punta Arenas
TIERRA DEL FUEGO
Beagle Channel
Cape Horn

SOUTHERN OCEAN

0   100 Nautical Miles
0   100 Km

65°W
60°W
55°S
60°S

S AMERICA
Falkland Islands
SOUTHERN OCEAN
60°S
ANTARCTIC CIRCLE
Bellingshausen Sea
Larsen Ice shelf
Weddell Sea
70°S
Drifting in ice
70°W
60°
50°
40°
30°
80°
90°
100°
110°
120°
130°

SOUTH SHETLAND ISLANDS
Snow I
Smith I
Deception I
Two Hummocks I
Brabant I
De Gerlache Strait
GRAHAM LAND
Larsen Ice shelf
65°S

Looking back, Amundsen felt he had been saved from shipwreck by divine protection. He had that quality of good fortune indispensable for great generals and explorers.

The expedition spent three weeks in the Straits and made a score of landings, Like some wild Wagnerian scene, the air rang with the clink of the geologist's hammer and the massed cries of agitated penguins. It was the first invasion of the Antarctic by men of science.

On January 26th, Amundsen landed on an island called Two Hummocks to try his skis. He was probably the first man to ski on Antarctic terra firma. He could, if he liked, reason that he had staked a claim to the South Pole.

January 31st, was another memorable day. It was the day on which the first Antarctic sledging journey began. The participants were de Gerlache, Amundsen, Cook, Arctowski and Emile Danco, a Belgian army officer, who had paid to join the expedition. With two sledges and supplies for a week, they landed on the just-discovered Brabant Island to survey the de Gerlache Strait from the heights. It was a cameo of Antarctic exploration to come.

They began by manhandling the sledges up to the ice sheet that covered the island. They had to struggle and strain over a steep ice slope round evil crevasses. Those few hours burned their way into Amundsen's consciousness; man-hauling was vividly shown to be neither glorious nor heroic, but unpleasant, sweaty, toilsome and stupid.

At the top of the climb on that January 31st, 1898, the first camp in Antarctic exploration was made. This is Amundsen's diary entry of the historic event:

> The snow was very loose, and we were therefore compelled to dig out a place for the tent. 3 make this ready, 2 proceed to prepare the evening meal in the lee of the sledge. The first occasion takes the longest time, but it is not long before our little tent raises its ridge against snow and wind. Our necessities for the night, sleeping bags and dry stockings, are put into the tent; the rest is left on the sledge, well protected by covers. With the boiling pea soup between us, snow and wind are forgotten, and one could not be happier in a royal palace ...

They reached their goal on the heights and were able to see almost the whole length of the Strait. Amundsen, however, was more interested in learning the technique of Polar travel. On February 4th, leaving the others to their theodolite and plane table, he went with Cook on an excursion to an ice fall that had defeated them.

This was Amundsen's initiation into ice work.

It was a long tour and a hard day. We passed huge uncounted crevasses. We were forced to cut our way along a perpendicular ice wall ... The Doctor, the experienced Polar explorer, goes ahead, I follow ... It is interesting to see the practical and calm manner in which this man works ...

After eight hours' incessant battling with the ice, constantly in danger, they finally returned to their camp. 'These excursions are wonderful,' was Amundsen's comment, 'and I hope to have frequent opportunities for more.'

On February 6th, he returned to the ship. The same evening, he summarized his experience before first impressions faded. He ignores the historic significance of what he has helped to do. He does not expatiate on the glories of discovery, there are no rhapsodies on the sensation of treading where human feet have never trod before. He is wholly and soberly occupied with the lessons he has learned. He notes that the tent, of the traditional ridge pattern, is unsatisfactory because it

presents too great a surface to the wind. It is made of oiled silk ... not practical ... heavier than untreated material ... the most practical form ... is undoubtedly the conical. It is easier to pitch and doesn't offer so much wind resistance ... The Doctor had [Eskimo] sealskin clothes, which proved very practical. They dry easily ... Be lightly clothed. Wool everywhere. Waterproof tin for matches. Snow goggles absolutely necessary. The country here is ... just one single glacier ... to go alone in it is pure madness. Two roped together absolutely necessary.

Amundsen was learning from the start, and Cook was his teacher, the disciple of Peary, one of the masters of Polar travel. That to Amundsen was the real privilege of having sailed on *Belgica*.

Keeping the coast of Graham Land at a respectful distance, *Belgica* crossed the Antarctic Circle and found the pack ice. Like a glistening crust, it stretched to the horizon, floe rafting lazily on floe, with the noise likened by a French explorer to 'the distant murmur of a great city at the bottom of a valley'.

Belgica sheered off to follow the edge of the pack away from land. It was now late in February, with winter on its way. It was the time of year when most captains would think of turning home. But de Gerlache was loath to leave the ice. His original plan was in shreds; it was obvious now that he could not survey the Weddell Sea, and then sail on to go ashore on South Victoria Land. He could not get anywhere near South Victoria Land. But he was unwilling to renounce his ambition of being the first man to winter in the Antarctic. He sailed on with the new idea of emulating Nansen, deliberately letting *Belgica* freeze in, and attaining a Furthest South by drifting with the pack.

De Gerlache would not openly admit this, because he knew that most of his followers would disapprove. Suspicions were nonetheless aroused by his attempts to probe the outskirts of the pack. On February 23rd, after one of these forays, Amundsen wrote that

> the scientists unfortunately display clear signs of fear. They are reluctant to go further into the ice. Why, may I ask, have we come here? Is it not to explore the unknown regions? That can't be done by lying still outside the ice.

On February 28th, a storm blew up from the north-east. The ice opened before *Belgica*. To de Gerlache it seemed a heaven-sent alibi. For who could argue with the wind? He approached Lecointe, who had the watch, and found him of the same mind. With a solemn handshake, they turned the ship southwards into the heaving, crashing floes. She drove before the storm and, on March 2nd, when it had blown itself out she was surrounded by ice, and almost certainly beset for the winter.

Belgica had crossed the 71st parallel, and was still being carried south by the pack. But de Gerlache could not yet trust his shipmates with the truth. He falsified his observations to suggest a northerly movement and held out fictitious hopes of imminent release. Amundsen and Lecointe alone were party to the secret.

When the ice slackened, de Gerlache made a show of getting out. Predictably he failed, but, being seen to have made the effort, he made his shipmates resigned to what was in store. They nonetheless accused him of not honestly trying. To this, Lecointe somewhat disingenuously commented that

> it is *certain* that we *honestly* tried to return northwards, but it is also certain that de Gerlache and myself were happy at the failure of our attempt.

De Gerlache originally had intended landing with a few companions at Cape Adare, sending *Belgica* away to winter in Australia. The men about to make history by being the first to winter in the Antarctic were mostly tricked into it against their will.

In that ill-assorted and fortuitously assembled ship's company, few were mentally or physically suited to the demands of Polar exploration. Fewer still were able to cope with their own special predicament. The normal stresses of an expedition would be trying enough. There is the sense of isolation; the being cooped up with a few companions, seeing the same old faces day after day, month after month; the threat of a hostile environment; the wind, the cold and, above all, the darkness of the Polar winter, when the sun never rises for months at a time. The darkness alone can be an ordeal. The men on *Belgica* were the first to go through all this in the south; it was no consolation to say that it was already known from the north. Besides, they were lost in an uncharted sea; alone off an unknown coast. They could not know if they could ever escape from the ice. They were plagued by uncertainty and fear. And to add to it all, because of the way they had been forced into it, they were prey to frustration, cold panic and resentment. Two sailors lost their reason. At one time or another they all trod the borderlands of sanity. 'Mentally,' Cook afterwards wrote, 'the outlook was that of a madhouse.'

Belgica was ill prepared for a winter in the ice. On board there were cold weather clothes for exactly four men, and food for a year at the most. Scurvy descended like a plague.

Scurvy is caused by an acute lack of Vitamin C. This is a substance essential for life, although its specific function is not yet fully understood. Man shares with guinea pigs and monkeys the inability to synthesize it, and must get it from what he eats. Vitamin C, however, is unstable, destroyed by traditional methods of preserving, and found only in fresh food.

Scurvy was the historic plague of communities cut off from fresh provisions and forced to live on preserved victuals for any length of time. It haunted ships at sea. In bygone days, it killed more than the sword. It was the scourge of voyages of exploration. In the graphic (and clinically accurate) words of Camoens, the sixteenth-century Portuguese poet of the age of discovery, it was

> The loathsom'st, the most fell Disease ...
> In such dire manner would the gums be swelled
> In our mens Mouths; that the black flesh thereby
> At once did grow, at once did putrifie.

> With such a horrid stench it putrified,
> That it the neighb'ring Air infected round.

Untreated, scurvy is alway fatal. When *Belgica* went South, vitamins had not yet been discovered, and the cause of the disease was therefore still unknown. Fresh food, however, was a proven cure, although orthodox medicine clouded the issue with elaborate and irrelevant theories. Dr. Cook, after his Arctic experience, ignored the theories, and put his trust in fresh, underdone seal meat. He was far ahead of the medical profession of his day and he was right. The ice around the *Belgica* teemed with seals and penguins. A stock was laid in, the skins to be used for clothes, the blubber to eke out fuel. Cook wanted the meat as a staple food to keep scurvy at bay. De Gerlache regarded this as criticism of his choice of food and took offence; as a compromise he allowed seal and penguin to be served occasionally for those who wanted it, most did not and the expedition continued to live on tinned food. Scurvy, with its swollen limbs, bleeding gums, loosening teeth, its depression and mental aberrations, was the inevitable result.

Scurvy killed Danco. He died on June 5th, having been unfit when he sailed. He had an irrational aversion to seal and penguin, saying that he would rather die than eat either. He was buried without ceremony in a hole in the ice. His shipmates were haunted by the thought of their late companion floating just beneath their feet, the eerie groaning of the ice preying on their minds.

On June 20th, Midwinter's Eve, the sun gone a month, with disease, darkness, depression and insanity around him, Amundsen writes:

The sun finishes its wandering northwards tomorrow, and begins its return. I will naturally be glad to see it again; but I have ... not missed it for *one moment*. On the contrary, it is this that I have waited for so long. It was not a childish impulse that persuaded me to come. It was a mature thought. I regret nothing and hope I have the health and strength to continue the work I have now begun.

Amundsen looked on his surroundings as a school for Polar exploration to teach him lessons for the future. While those around him were going through their little private hells, he was dispassionately recording what he learned. At the worst moments, even when *Belgica* is threatened with destruction by the ice, they are preparing to abandon ship and prospects are exceptionally bleak, he is learning, always learning.

Like a doctor in search of clinical objectivity, he deliberately keeps his shipmates at arm's length looking on them as case studies, in the pursuit of his professional training. Early in July, in the middle of the winter night, with everybody more or less scurvy-ridden, de Gerlache and Lecointe particularly bad, even Cook gloomy and discouraged, perhaps the darkest moment of the whole expedition, Amundsen is principally concerned with the defects of his wolfskin clothing. He has the quite phenomenal insight to see that the mental aberrations which he observes within himself are the consequences of scurvy.

Lecointe was convinced he was going to die. De Gerlache had become morose and shunned company. The sailors were growing apathetic. It was Cook who now saved the expedition. He could inspire faith in him-self, and was able to make his patients take penguin meat as medicine where they refused it as food. De Gerlache took longest to convince. Obstinately he would hear of no antiscurbutic but lime juice because it was what the British Navy used and 'What is good enough for the British Navy,' he said, 'is good enough for me.' But in the end, he too submitted, and rapidly improved. By now, scurvy was in retreat, with everybody on the mend – physically. The mental price, no one ever knew.

The atmosphere, however, was not one of wholly unrelieved gloom. There were intervals of humour. Lecointe produced a mildly ribald magazine called *The Ladysless South*; touching incidentally on a tabu. Sexual deprivation is an obvious consequence of Polar exploration, and Lecointe made one of the very few explicit references on record. In the process, he showed some insight. Amundsen, for example, is made to say in an imaginary comment on *The Ladysless South*, "Yes, sir, I love it', while the others were expressing frustration in various ways. Lecointe had detected the vein of asceticism and misogyny, perhaps of monasticism, that was part of Amundsen's make-up.

On July 23rd, the sun returned. What it showed were pallid com-plexions, unkempt hair, drawn features, and faces that had aged years in a few months. Amundsen's hair had turned grey. Personalities had changed. The first Antarctic night experienced by man had taken its toll.

In some ways, Cook and Amundsen had weathered the ordeal best of all. They had a common interest that kept their minds off disaster. Both were fascinated by Polar equipment, and all winter they worked hard at improving what they had. This drew them together, set them apart from the others, and probably helped to keep them reasonably balanced.

Their *chef d'oeuvre* was an igenious new tent of Cook's design, with an aerodynamic shape to reduce wind resistance, far in advance of its time. Testing the new outfit gave Cook and Amundsen, accompanied by Lecointe, the pretext to sledge at the end of July to an iceberg on the horizon. It was, as Amundsen proudly headed his diary, 'The first sledge journey on the Antarctic pack ice.'

Amundsen afterwards wrote for his own benefit an exhaustive analysis of what he had learned. Food, sleeping bags, tent, sledge, clothing, all come in for critical examination. Of one thing alone is he satisfied: on the pack ice, skis are the best form of transport. He travelled on them, and tried them against Cook on snow shoes. Cook was constantly in difficulties, while he was not. Skis were faster and, spreading the weight, were able to cross thin ice without breaking through.

Amundsen's judgment of his companions is penetrating. It explains much about his attitude to people and how later he chose his followers:

It is a pleasure to make excursions with the company that I had. Lecointe; small, cheerful, witty; never losing hope. Cook, the calm and imperturbable never losing his temper; and in addition, there are the many small things one can learn in the society of such a thoroughly practical Polar explorer like Cook. In his contact with the North Greenland Eskimos, and in his profound study of everything concerning Polar life, he has, without doubt, greater insight in these matters than most men in the field ... He has advice on everything. He gives it in a likable and tactful manner; not with fuss and noise ...

As the sun rose higher, and hopes revived, De Gerlache held long formal committee meetings to discuss plans for the approaching summer. At one of these, in November, Amundsen discovered for the first time that by a confidential agreement de Gerlache had promised the Belgian Geographical Society that, whatever their rank, Belgian officers were to take precedence in the succession of command. This meant that Melaerts, the third mate, in spite of being subordinate to Amundsen, would take over command before him.

De Gerlache said that he had been forced into this by political and financial pressures. Amundsen took it as insulting discrimination. They quarrelled and exchanged acrimonious missives.

I followed you without pay [wrote Amundsen]. It was not a question of money, but honour. That honour you have insulted by denying me my right.

Amundsen then resigned.

A Belgian Antarctic Expedition no longer exists for me [he told de Gerlache]. I see in *Belgica*, an ordinary vessel, beset in the ice. My duty is to help the handful of men gathered here on board. For that reason, Captain, I continue my work as if nothing had happened, trying to do my duty as a *human being* ...

They had now been imprisoned in the pack for nine months, drifting helplessly over the Bellingshausen Sea at about 70° south. The ice still held *Belgica* firmly in its grip, showing no signs of letting her go free. Another winter beset in the Antarctic was too horrible to contemplate. Tempers were naturally frayed. Three sailors were insane. Cook felt that the mental state of de Gerlache and Arctowski was giving cause for concern. Christmas and New Year were gloomy. Apathy and resignation descended.

For a second time, Cook saved the expedition. About a mile from the ship was a lead that had remained open all through the winter. Cook proposed cutting a canal towards it, so that the ship could get into the lead and, when the pack next worked, try to escape. This was the spark that roused his companions and broke their lethargy; it gave them something to do instead of passively waiting for their fate.

On January 11th, 1899, they started sawing and blasting the ice. It was not easy; they had their fill of setbacks and disappointments. At one stage, they despaired of ever getting out, preparing to abandon ship and sledge over the ice to land.

And then, at two o'clock in the morning of February 15th, 1899, the canal, having been shut by the pressure of the ice, unbelievably opened. *Belgica* once more reverberated to the music of her engines. After a year as a hulk beset, she had been reborn. A living ship once more, she worked her way into the lead. But for another month she remained imprisoned within tantalizing sight of the open sea. On March 14th, she began heaving to the swell. But, to the last, the ice played cat and mouse. Within sight of safety, *Belgica* was thrown against an iceberg. Thus Amundsen recorded the scene:

> If we cannot go ahead, we are irretrievably lost ... the engineer comes on deck to say he cannot keep up steam any longer. He sees the gravity of the situation for himself. It is unnecessary to ask him to keep steam up. In the winking of an eye he is below again, and the engine is working as it has never worked before, and never will work again. We fight our way ahead, inch by inch, foot by foot, metre by metre. We are saved. At the critical moment, the ice slackened ... Now we are sailing northwards quickly. The ice slackens more and more and we work our way ahead without difficulty. At midday we are out in a huge lead. At 2 in the afternoon we have the pack behind us. Thus ended the first wintering by men in the Antarctic.

On March 27th, *Belgica*, long since given up for lost, sailed into Punta Arenas. While she had been away, the Spanish American and Boer Wars had broken out; *Turbinia*, the first turbine ship had broken the forty knot barrier; air had been liquefied, Marconi had made his first wireless transmissions. It was the first expedition to be confronted with the modern pace of change.

At Punta Arenas, the expedition came to an end. There was neither the money nor the will for the second season so optimistically discussed in the prison of the pack.

De Gerlache and Lecointe took *Belgica* home. Amundsen, still brooding on his quarrel with de Gerlache, preferred not to sail with them. He returned to Norway by mailboat, escorting Tollefsen, one of the Norwegian seamen, who had lost his reason, a victim of the first Antarctic night.

Fifty years on, Dobrowolski, the enthusiast who had appeared on board at Ostend, summed up what de Gerlache had done. He had not only been the first to winter in the Antarctic, he discovered so many miles of the continental archipelago. His expedition had brought back

the first complete year's meteorological record ... the first foundation of an Antarctic climatology; the first proof of a ring of low pressure surrounding the anticyclone of the Antarctic continent; and also the first collection of [Antarctic] oceanic organisms spanning a whole year ... And finally, our voyage was the first school of that extraordinary explorer, the Napoleon of the Polar regions; Amundsen.

7

Amundsen's First Command

IT TOOK POSTERITY to appreciate what *Belgica* had done. She was no passport to contemporary fame. When Amundsen returned to Norway towards the end of May 1899, he came quietly and without remark.

De Gerlache, Cook and Lecointe all wrote books about the *Belgica*. It is characteristic of Amundsen that he wrote not a word for publication. He did not need money, which sometimes is a sufficient reason for not getting into print. Besides, to him his first Antarctic Night was a private experience, one stage in his professional training. He wanted to get on to the next as quickly as he could. His first step was to write to Fridtjof Nansen:

> Just returned home from the Belgian Antarctic Expedition, I take the liberty of asking if the Herr Professor would be interested in hearing something of the voyage. Should that be the case, I would with pleasure be at the professor's disposal.

Nansen was by then the undisputed oracle on Polar matters. At home, he exercised the kind of autocratic domination only found in small countries. To acquire public credibility, his blessing was essential. That was what Amundsen now was seeking. It was the first step towards an expedition of his own.

Since the first crossing of Greenland, Nansen had been convinced that the South Pole was waiting to be conquered by Norwegian skiers. He was nursing the idea of leading an expedition himself. Anyone back from the Antarctic was bound to be welcome. Amundsen's approach therefore fell on fertile ground. 'I permit myself once more to thank you for the friendliness you showed me on my return from the ... Antarctic,' he wrote to Nansen in September.

Amundsen had attained his purpose of securing Nansen's goodwill in general. But before he could profit in particular, there were duties to be done.

First there was military service. He had hurried home from Punta Arenas for an obligatory refresher course. He had obtained a postponement to go with de Gerlache and, although only a humble corporal or perhaps on that account, made it a point of honour not to be late. Immediately after military service, Amundsen went to sea again to complete as quickly as he could the qualifying time afloat for his Master's Certificate. He was to do so on *Oscar*, the family barque on which he had sailed before. *Oscar* lay at Carthagena in Spain. For the sake of the exercise he decided to cycle most of the way. Cycling over such distances was still distinctly uncommon but with his brother Leon, who was working for a firm of wine shippers at Cognac, near Bordeaux, he left Christiania on September 9th, to pedal across the Continent.

Oscar was bound for Pensacola, the Florida timber port. The voyage took two months entirely under sail. The chief event, as far as Amundsen was concerned, was eating raw dolphin to prove that it was edible; a useful piece of knowledge for shipwreck and survival.

In Pensacola, Amundsen bought a load of hickory. A hard, tough, elastic wood, it had been used in Norway for skis since the 1880s. Amundsen thought it might some day be useful for making sledges and skis for an expedition. He had it shipped to Gustav in Christiania.

The voyage both outwards and home, Amundsen spent seriously studying Polar literature. He filled the two exercise books with notes on Frederick Jackson's recently published *A Thousand Days in the Arctic*, an account of the Jackson–Harmsworth expedition to Franz Josef Land in 1894–97. I was the latest Polar work available.

In April 1900, he returned to Norway having now completed his sea time and finished his mariner's training. He felt ready – almost – for the first expedition of his own.

It was the ambition of his boyhood, the North-West Passage. Since its discovery by Franklin half a century before, no one had yet sailed through from end to end on one and the same keel. Amundsen intended to be the first and therefore the man to attain one of the historic goals of exploration.

Although Amundsen was setting out to realize a schoolboy ambition, he had by now divested himself of schoolboy attitudes. He was unburdened by the desire to be a martyr or a hero. Any thoughts in that direction, *Belgica* effectively had quashed. Heroism in the corrupt sense of the age almost by definition, meant wanton self-sacrifice and bungling. For neither had he any taste. He wanted rational attainment; victory but not at any price. No point upon the globe was worth the cost of a single life. Preparation would be meticulous, he would learn from the past. He would avoid the disasters of his predecessors. His mistakes would be his own.

One of the unfulfilled objects of the *Belgica* expedition had been the

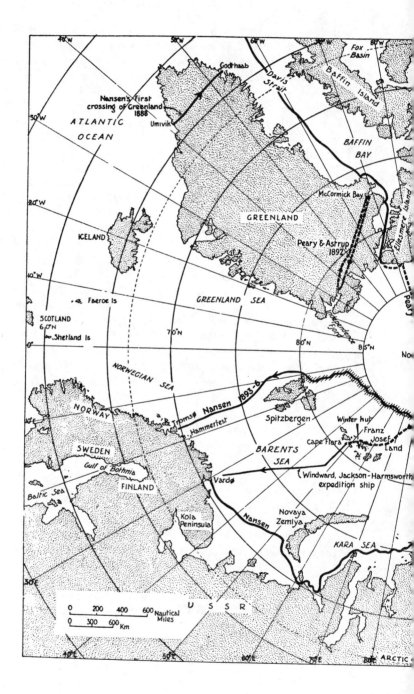

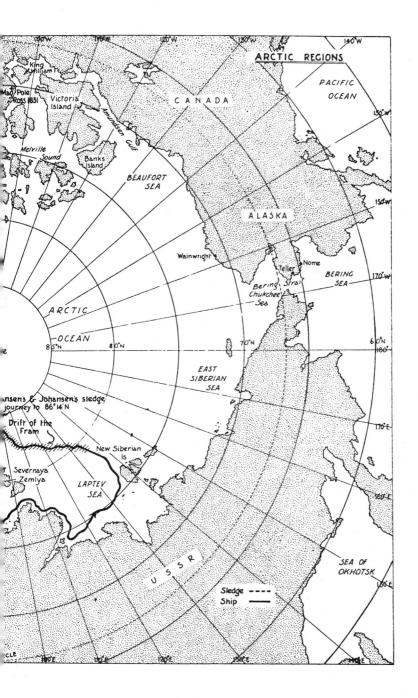

ARCTIC REGIONS

PACIFIC OCEAN

CANADA

ALASKA

King William I.

Mag. Pole Ross 1831

Victoria Island

Amundsen Gulf

Melville Sound

Banks Island

BEAUFORT SEA

Wainwright

Teller   Nome

Bering Strait

Chukchee Sea

BERING SEA

ARCTIC

OCEAN

85°N   80°N   70°N   60°N   180°

EAST SIBERIAN SEA

nsen's & Johansen's sledge journey to 86°14′N

Drift of the Fram

Severnaya Zemlya

New Siberian Is

LAPTEV SEA

U S S R

SEA OF OKHOTSK

Sledge ----
Ship ——

150°W

150°W

170°W

170°E

160°E

160°E

100°E   110°E   120°E   130°E   140°E

CLE

fixing of the South Magnetic Pole. On board there was much talk about terrestrial magnetism in general, and the North Magnetic Pole in particular. It alone of the poles of the earth had yet been reached once before by Sir James Clark Ross in 1831. Some of the *Belgica* scientists maintained that it still was in the the same place; others that it was not. This introduced Amundsen to the learned controversy over the magnetic poles; were they movable or fixed? There was only one way of settling the point; to visit the North Magnetic Pole and compare the position with that obtained by Ross. Thus it was, to quote his words to the Norwegian Geographical Society, that 'at 72 degrees South latitude, the idea of reaching the North Magnetic Pole and exploring the surroundings first occurred to me'.

To be the man who showed whether the magnetic poles were movable or fixed would doubtless be an achievement. But it was not Amundsen's meat; he was an explorer, not a scientist. He wanted to be first, to show the way, not follow in someone else's wake.

One thing however he had learned from de Gerlache; even more from Nansen; exploration now had to be dressed in scientific clothes. For the North-West Passage alone, Amundsen knew he could not get a serious hearing. For respectability he needed a scientific pretext. The North Magnetic Pole might do. It lay somewhere along the channels of the North-West Passage. The attainment of both could be combined.

Amundsen went methodically to work. On his return from *Belgica* he collected all possible literature. He persisted until he found Sir James Clark Ross' account of his attainment of the North Magnetic Pole, a rare work. Amundsen later maintained that this first gave him some feeling for the project of the Magnetic Pole. It is not at all implausible; Ross was a transparently honest man, and his writing – to a receptive mind – quietly inspiring.

Having read up the subject historically Amundsen then sought modern opinion. He began with Dr. Axel Steen, the deputy director of the Meteorological Institute in Christiania.

Sensing perhaps that to a scientist the North-West Passage might be frivolity, Amundsen concentrated on the Magnetic Pole. Steen approved enthusiastically. He explained, however, that training was needed for the necessary observations. This, said Steen, could best be done at the Deutsche Seewarte in Hamburg, the Director of which, Professor Georg Neumayer, was an authority on terrestrial magnetism. Apart from anything else, this would give Amundsen a foreign qualification. In Norway, there was prestige in foreign qualifications.

So, late in 1900, Amundsen went to Neumayer, unannounced, with a letter of introduction from Steen.

I found myself before an elderly gentleman with long white hair ... On my asking whether it would be of great interest to have the position of the North Magnetic Pole more closely investigated, he answered: 'A precise determination of the North Magnetic Pole would be of immense value to science.' If I had previously had any doubts about the realisation of my contemplated enterprise, they were instantly dispelled by this answer, coming as it did from what is probably the greatest authority of our day on terrestrial magnetism.

Neumayer took Amundsen under his wing, making sure that he was given a thorough grounding in taking magnetic observations and doing the computations needed in the field. Amundsen noted just before he left that he had worked '250 hours in 40 days, a daily average of 6.3 hours'.

Amundsen now felt he had an acceptable technical foundation. But all plans were vain imaginings until granted Nansen's approval. Amundsen obtained an interview to explain his intentions. Nansen was a man of awesome dignity and reserve. He shared a sleeping bag with Hjalmar Johansen on Franz Josef Land, yet maintaining the formal mode of address. After six months he consented to the more familiar *du*, second person singular. Surnames were still insisted on. Nobody dared call Nansen 'Fridtjof'.

Between Nansen and Amundsen there was never warmth or ease. They respected each other, but their feelings stopped at respect. They were cast in incompatible moulds. It is no wonder that Amundsen felt so uncertain before that particular encounter, upon which his whole future seemed to turn.

He need not have worried. Nansen was intrigued by the idea of an expedition to the North Magnetic Pole. He gave his approval. From that moment, Amundsen once said, he reckoned that his expedition came into being.

For all his conscientious preparation Amundsen still felt unready. He told Nansen that before starting on his enterprise, he wanted more experience in navigating small ships in Arctic ice. From that fateful interview he went immediately to Tromsø.

Beyond the Arctic Circle, on the edge of the Polar Sea, Tromsø was the old whaling and sealing port of Northern Norway. It was more than that. With its wooden houses huddled on a rocky island amongst craggy fjords, in a windswept archipelago, forested with stumpy masts of stocky wooden ships, redolent of fish and blubber, swung between the violent contrasts of the Polar seasons, it had character and ambience. There gathered the sealers of Northern Norway, a special breed of men, independent, weathered, inured to hardship; wonderful in ship-handling and icecraft; hunters of the sea. It was *the* Polar milieu; it was to this school of Arctic lore that Amundsen now turned and, with his usual singleness of purpose, set to work.

North Norwegians are notably clannish. For their own countrymen from below the Arctic Circle, they reserve a portion of mistrust. The man from the south is *a priori* an alien. In those days, when the mountains cut off communications overland, when the sea was the only connection with the outside, when a letter from Tromsø to Christiania took a week or more, and the 700 miles between them were a barrier in space and time, the isolation of the North Norwegians was great, and their clannishness formidable. Amundsen now proceeded to break into this society. That he had been one of the first men to go through an Antarctic winter did not impress men professionally disinclined to be impressed, and ever on the lookout for airs and affectation. Of this Amundsen was not guilty. He made it clear that he had come to learn, showing respect for experience and age. He quickly became acquainted with most of the Arctic skippers in Tromsø. 'Any other acquaintances,' he told Gustav, 'I have neither the time nor the opportunity to make.'

Amundsen originally had intended sailing as a passenger on a sealing vessel to the east coast of Greenland, where ice conditions are particularly difficult, and therefore particularly instructive. But berths were few and expensive. 'Seeing that I must have a vessel next year anyway,' he wrote to Gustava on January 14th, 1901, soon after arriving in Tromsø, 'I consider it most sensible to try and buy one now. I am therefore in the process of negotiation.'

Amundsen was quite simply preparing to spend his patrimony on a ship. His money was tied up in shares and property, administered by Gustav. He asked for his assets to be realized quickly so that the purchase could go ahead as soon as he had made up his mind.

Gustav doubted the wisdom of the transaction, but he had ceased trying to make Roald see reason. Gustav, then practising as an accountant, was headed for financial difficulties, but towards his brother he acted with scrupulous rectitude. He let Roald have the 10,000 kroner* he required, and Roald bought his ship.

She was called *Gjøa*, an old Norsewoman's name from Western Norway, after the wife of a former owner. Amundsen kept the name, and *Gjøa* she remained. Twenty-nine years old, she was exactly as old as he. She was a sloop, a sturdy, square-sterned, seaworthy wooden vessel of a type much used in the rough waters along the coast. She had been

* £540 or $2,600; £9,000 or $18,000 in present terms.

in the herring fishery – and showed it. She was a derisory forty-seven tons, far too small, they said, to try conclusions with the real Polar pack. But Amundsen had read his history and put his trust in smallness. He faced narrow waters and treacherous shoals; safety lay in a nimble ship with shallow draft. Others had come to grief trying to crush their way through the ice; he would push his way between the floes. 'What has not been accomplished with large vessels and main force,' he said, 'I will attempt with a small vessel and patience.'

Amundsen had grasped that in the Arctic there was danger in numbers. If Franklin had had eight instead of 128 companions, they would probably all have survived. At those latitudes, the land could not support many people, and Amundsen proposed living off the land. He intended living like the Eskimos, sleeping where necessary in igloos. In a lecture to the Norwegian Geographical Society, Amundsen pointed out that although 'going native' was unusual, he would not be the first to do so in those regions,

> since one of the Hudson's Bay Company's travellers, Dr. Rae, spent a whole winter with his people there on the North Coast of America and found [living in an igloo] an excellent way of wintering.

Dr. John Rae was an Orkneyman who worked in the Canadian Arctic between 1834 and 1854. He pioneered the small expedition, living like the natives. 'Extent of Land, Coast Line and River added to chart, 1,135 statute miles,' he wrote, summarizing his achievements, 'at the expense of about £2.15s per mile.' He lost very few men. His success with small means was a standing reproach to the elaborate, costly and disastrous Naval expeditions that dominated British Polar exploration until the First World War. Because his methods differed from 'official' ones he was derided and neglected at home. Foreigners learned from him. It says something for Amundsen's sense of history that he went beyond immediate prophets of the small expedition to the source of their idea. He too would take a small expedition and adopt the best of Eskimo lore.

Such then was the vessel, and such the plan for sailing the North-West Passage and triumphing after centuries of calamity and setback. But first, Amundsen insisted on a training cruise with the very best available tuition. He took along as mate *Gjøa*' s previous owner, Hans Christian Johannesen, an old sealing skipper, one of the finest Arctic seamen of his day. Amundsen was very proud of having sailed with Johannesen – as pupil. The crew were sealers, for they were going after seal in order to cover the costs of the voyage.

Amundsen also took Peder Ristvedt, his sergeant during military service. He was considering Ristvedt for the main voyage; his first candidate for any of his expeditions.

On April 15th, 1901, *Gjøa* left Tromsø for the Barents Sea, between Spitsbergen, Franz Josef Land and Novaya Zemlya. Amundsen had his wish for training thoroughly gratified. The Arctic, as it were, pulled out all the stops for him. The sealing was bad, the weather worse, the ice worst of all, and Amundsen received all the lessons he wanted in handling *Gjøa* under difficult conditions.

He was learning much in various departments. The crew were all from the Tromsø region, engaged for specialized experience, not forgetting the cook.

Early this morning [Amundsen wrote on May 10th] we were served with fresh seal steak, which tasted magnificent – exactly like tender beefsteak. For dinner we had fried guillemot and for supper seal ragout, that was simply magnificent. It was a genuine Arctic day, as far as food went. It is a pleasure to see how everybody here in Northern Norway   Tromsø – appreciates the wonderful fresh seal meat. A mass of different dishes are made out of it.

Amundsen had grasped that in northern waters seal ought to be a staple food, and its preparation needed special skill. On *Belgica* he had learned the misery bad cooking caused, and hence that the most important single member of a Polar expedition was probably the cook.

On September 4th, after a cruise in the ice of almost five months, *Gjøa* returned to Tromsø. When she paid off, Amundsen recorded a catch of 1,200 seal, two walruses, two polar bears and one narwhale, total value 4,800 kroner, plus a barrel of blubber, 21.50 kroner. For those days and that particular season it was a respectable result. By ancient custom the thirteen men aboard shared the sum equally; as captain, Amundsen's only privilege was an extra share 'for the boat'. He had cleared the costs of his training cruise, but not much more. He had been prevented from carrying out all the observations he had promised Nansen. He telegraphed a promise to finish them the following year. Nansen considered this an unjustifiable delay to the more important enterprise, and dissuaded Amundsen from doing so. He found it hard going. Amundsen had a deep-rooted repugnance for not doing what he had set out to do.

Meanwhile *Gjøa* had shown serious deficiencies. She moved by sail alone and displayed weakness in the ice. Soon after returning from the Arctic, Amundsen ordered a complete refit and a new ice sheathing for the hull. He also installed a 'hot bulb' paraffin motor, making *Gjøa* one of the early motor-driven ships. The patronage of Nansen, discreetly bruited, helped to secure the necessary credit.

For money there was none. Amundsen needed at least another 70,000 kroner before he could set off. That was beyond his means. To those who asked him how he was going to raise it – and Nansen was among them – he had the same reply: 'I will have to depend on my credit and good fortune.'

He now made the timely acquaintance of a man called Fritz Zapffe, a pharmacist who also was a part-time correspondent in Tromsø for *Morgenbladet*, a Christiania newspaper. Zapffe has left a description of Amundsen at this time:

> Every day for a few weeks I had seen a young stranger pass the pharmacy where I was working. I could not avoid noticing his peculiar gait. When he thrust his legs forwards, he bent his knees gently   approximately as one does when skiing ...

Zapffe, smelling a 'story', proceeded to investigate. His contacts could tell him very little. Nobody seemed to know what *Gjøa* was intended for. Amundsen 'did not reply when he was asked'. So Zapffe bearded him in his lodgings.

At first he was met by a barrage of evasion. The answer, when it came, was a trifle naive:

> 'I don't want to say anything before I have accomplished something,' said Amundsen. 'I wish to leave with the least possible attention. I want to have done something before letting anything appear in the press.'

Zapffe now wormed his financial predicament out of him, then artfully suggested how publicity might persuade right-minded philanthropists to support him.

The thought had clearly never occurred to Amundsen. Zapffe pressed home his advantage. Times were bad in Norway; money was tight. Amundsen agreed to talk.

It was a front-page story. It helped Gustav, who had gone begging on his brother's behalf, to get 15,000 kroner* from two moneyed shipowners. Amundsen had learned the uses of publicity; he did not need to be shown twice.

With Zapffe there sprang up an intimacy beyond the symbiosis of journalist and news fodder. He became one of the few friends that Amundsen kept. He was rather more than either a pharmacist or a journalist. He was a skier and a climber. He had the local contacts that Amundsen needed. He shared Amundsen's passion for equipment. Amundsen now settled down in Tromsø to fit out his expedition, and

---

* £800 or $3,900; £14,000 or $28,000 in present terms.

Zapffe became his enthusiastic helper. It was Zapffe who, through friends among the Lapps of the hinterland, got good reindeer furs, and had sleeping bags, clothes, *finnesko* (soft reindeer-fur boots) sewn with a craftsmanship usually denied expeditions that depended on ordinary agents.

In the days before synthetic materials and industrialized equipment, Polar travellers had to depend on natural substances and (if they were sensible) native lore. Zapffe was a good example of the Norwegian who learned from the Lapps.

Northern Norway is a sub-Arctic territory shared by the Norwegians and the Lapps, the aboriginal inhabitants of the Scandinavian peninsula. The Lapps, who live by the reindeer, a highly adapted Arctic animal, are themselves highly adapted to a cold climate. In prehistoric times, they brought skis to Norway, and the North Norwegians learned from them how to cope properly with the Arctic environment.

This profitable interaction with a primitive culture predisposed Norwegians to learn from native peoples, at least in Polar exploration. Nansen, for example, took two Lapps with him on the first crossing of Greenland to benefit from their skills if he could. Amundsen was following a long tradition.

One of the Lapp materials acquired by Zapffe was sennegrass, a North Norwegian grass that absorbed moisture and was a good insulator. It was used to line the *finnesko* to keep the feet dry and warm. It could be dried and used again, but eventually had to be replaced. A large supply was required, and it needed patience and contacts to get the best quality. It was gathered on the remote heathlands, and the Lapps liked to keep the best for themselves.

At the end of May, 1902, Amundsen had finished his work in Tromsø, and sailed *Gjøa* down to Christiania. There, he turned his attention to pemmican, the time-honoured Polar sledging ration. Originating among the Chree Indians of North America, it consists of lean ground dried meat mixed with melted fat. Until the advent of dehyrated food, it was the most concentrated nourishment available.

Again, Amundsen mistrusted the commercial product. He set Ristvedt to work in a disused bakery, making the pemmican he required. Professor Sophus Torup, a friend of Nansen, who held the chair of physiology at Christiania University, supervised the preparation.

In the meantime, Amundsen contrived to work at magnetic observations. In the summer of 1902 he accompanied Axel Steen on a magnetic survey in Northern Norway, and later in the year returned to the Deutsche Seewarte, going on to the magnetic observatory in Potsdam for training by the scientists who were designing his instruments. In October he was granted his Master's Certificate, entitling him to command a foreign vessel under the Norwegian flag. Hitherto he had only been allowed to command a ship in home waters; now he could take *Gjøa* overseas.

Soon after *Gjøa* arrived in Christiania, Otto Sverdrup returned to Norway in *Fram* after four years in the Canadian Arctic. Sverdrup had been with Nansen, both on the first crossing of Greenland, and then on the drift of the *Fram*. On that voyage he had been master. Not long after landing in Norway, he was given the command of *Fram* for another expedition during which he had discovered and charted about 300,000 square kilometres of new land, approaching the total of all expeditions of the preceding sixty years put together – at a fraction of the cost.

Sverdrup's great achievement had been to improve the technique of Polar travel. He had developed the methods pioneered by Nansen, finding out how to run dogs with men moving on skis and brought out the creative interplay between the two.

Sverdrup and his men had no adventures; they sought no heroics. With ease, although not without effort, they covered the same country that had meant horror and disaster to others before them. It was an interesting lesson for those who wanted to learn. Amundsen was one. Sverdrup settled much. He proved that skis could be used on most kinds of snow and sea ice. Above all, he showed how skis could be used to keep up with dogs, instead of riding on the sledges, so that more useful loads could be carried. He showed that Europeans could learn to drive dogs as well as Eskimos. All his experience on the first voyage of the *Fram* proved that the Eskimo dogs from Greenland were better than the Siberian breed. He also had something to teach about dog psychology. The relation between dog and driver had to be that between equals: a dog was not a horse, he was a partner, not a beast of burden. And the Eskimo dog was a comfort in the Polar wastes. He was a companion, amusing, touching, exasperating, but always diverting.

'Ah, the dogs,' Sverdrup said. 'It is they who give a Polar journey its character; without them travel would indeed be grim.'

It was fortunate for Amundsen that Sverdrup returned when he did. For he was able to tell Amundsen all he knew about dogs. Amundsen realized that dog-driving would be his best way to reach the Magnetic Pole but he had no experience of this method of travel. It could not be practised in Norway, and there had been no dogs on *Belgica*. In dog-driving, Amundsen had to start as an absolute beginner.

From Sverdrup, at any rate, he got all that vicarious experience could convey. He got more. Sverdrup gave him his own dog team and from Sverdrup, Amundsen secured for *Gjøa* Adolf Henrik Lindstrøm, *Fram*'s cook and handyman.

But Amundsen also suffered from what Sverdrup had done. After two voyages of the *Fram* in nine years, the Norwegians felt that national honour was satisfied, and another Polar expedition unnecessary. Also, times were bad. It became virtually impossible to raise more money.

Amundsen nonetheless serenely continued his preparations, convinced that, somehow, he would be able to sail in the middle of 1903. Late in 1902, he proposed visiting England to talk to people who knew the region for which he was bound. As a useful acquaintance he was introduced by Nansen in the autumn to Sir Clements Markham, President of the Royal Geographical Society.

Sir Clements was in Norway to take his annual cure at Larvik, a spa on the south coast, where he had been coming since 1894 for his gout. Amundsen explained his plans and took him for an afternoon cruise in *Gjøa* down the Christiania Fjord. 'I gave him every encouragement,' Sir Clements said. 'Nansen has a high opinion of young Amundsen.'

To Scott Keltie, the Secretary of the R.G.S., Sir Clements wrote: 'There is at least no want of pluck and enterprise in the scheme. I wish Englishmen would do these things.'

With introductions from Sir Clements, Amundsen went to London in November, visiting Dundee on the way to arrange with some whaling captains for the shipping of supplies for him to Dalrymple Rock, off North-West Greenland. *Gjøa* was too small to carry her whole cargo safely across the hazardous waters of Melville Bay.

There is a story that the captains began by asking whether he was the man who was going to sail through the North-West Passage.

'No,' the answer is supposed to have been. 'It is I who will attempt it on the experience of others.' If the story is not true, it ought to be; it illuminates one side of Amundsen's character. In London, however, he committed the gaffe of calling on Sir Clements Markham, but not on Scott Keltie; courting the President, but ignoring the Secretary of the Royal Geographical Society. Nansen subsequently felt obliged to apologize on Amundsen's behalf.

> It is simply because he is an exceedingly modest young man in spite of his appearance and self reliance, when it is wanted.

Amundsen had come to London partly to visit two Arctic veterans. One was Admiral Sir Leopold McClintock, the man who had discovered Franklin's fate almost half a century before. When Amundsen called in the middle of the morning, Sir Leopold had not yet got out of bed. 'But that can be forgiven,' Amundsen wrote to Gustav, 'as he is 85 years old and deaf.'

At least Amundsen had paid his respects. McClintock was one of the Arctic pioneers. Nansen freely acknowledged the debt he owed to him.

Next Amundsen lunched with Sir Allen Young. Sir Allen, an old merchant captain, had in 1876 taken his yacht *Pandora* far down the Franklin Strait, between Prince of Wales Land and Boothia Felix; the most likely approach to a successful North-West Passage. He was, as Amundsen told Gustav, 'also very old – but nevertheless in full possession of his faculties. He was able to tell me much that was useful.'

From Sir Allen, Amundsen went to the Admiralty, with an introduction from Sir Clements to ask about charts.

> I was [he wrote] most cordially received, and will be sent all the charts ... I want, as a gift, together with 'The Arctic Pilot', the printing of which will be hurried to reach me in time.

Amundsen then hurried to Potsdam for more instruction in terrestrial magnetism. He was met on returning to Christiania in late December by financial disarray. He had gone on piling up debts in the vague and innocent belief that credit would be limitless because his plans were big and his intentions honourable. But the whiff of insolvency had reached the sensitive nostrils of his creditors. They wanted cash, quickly.

Nansen now came to his rescue, perhaps the only man in Norway who could do so. Nansen appealed for help to Oscar II, the reigning King of Sweden-Norway in Stockholm. Amundsen, he wrote,

> inspires confidence ... he has particularly good qualifications both as the organiser and leader of an Arctic expedition. He has made his preparations ... with care, thought, and self-control that I have never seen bettered ... Should Your Majesty be pleased to support the enterprise with a donation, I believe Amundsen would be doubly helped, for besides the support itself ... Your Majesty's example ... would help by making it comparatively easy to raise money from our wealthy men.

It says much for Oscar's magnanimity (or political sense) that he immediately responded with a gift of 10,000 kroner.* He was, after all, a Swedish king, the campaign for Norwegian independence from Sweden was approaching its culmination, and Nansen was one of its leaders.

It was that campaign which in part dictated Nansen's tenacious support of Amundsen. Through his Arctic exploits, Nansen had acquired

---

* £540 or $2,600; £9,000 or $18,000 in present terms.

a standing that went far beyond the confines of Norway and Polar exploration. He was the one living Norwegian of international stature. He stood head and shoulders above his fellow Scandinavians. He became the spokesman of the Norwegian case abroad: he was a weapon that the Swedes could not hope to match. He threw his whole reputation into the work of creating international goodwill for Norway. He was a pioneer in the exploitation of what is broadly termed 'culture' to political ends. He foresaw that if Amundsen snatched the honour of the North-West Passage, it would enhance national prestige which, in a time of crisis, would be a valuable commodity. It was not only the respect it would win abroad, but the self-confidence it would encourage at home; and self-confidence discouraged rash adventures. Nansen disliked rash adventures, especially in politics. He wanted independence, but without the war which the militant Swedes and radical Norwegians seemed heading for.

Compared to political troubles, the actual preparations for the expedition were painless and straightforward. Equipment – paid for or not – was being designed and delivered. The crew were being gathered.

Whatever his financial complications, Amundsen had made certain, with his brother Leon's help, that he was in a position to pay the wages of his men throughout the four years that the expedition was expected to last. He wanted the best and he paid well.

With Ristvedt as first engineer and Lindstrøm as cook, Amundsen had a good nucleus. Through Zapffe he got two experienced Arctic navigators from Northern Norway: Anton Lund, who knew the pack ice as sealing skipper and harpooner, and Helmer Hanssen, who for almost two decades was to be his faithful companion.

Helmer Hanssen came from the Vesterålen Islands, on the edge of the Arctic. He belonged to a breed of farmers and fishermen who in summer tended smallholdings on the islands and in winter fished for cod in small boats. Theirs was a hard life; their folklore is full of violent storms, evil sea spirits and tragic sagas. From the age of twelve, Helmer Hanssen followed his family in the tossing little clinkered fishing craft, with lines so very like the Viking boats, and learned the feel of the Arctic waves. When he grew up, he went sealing and whaling, the islanders' traditional way of getting out. He took his mate's certificate; and sailed to Novaya Zemlya on a private expedition run by Henry Pearson, a well-to-do Englishman. Afterwards he settled down, married, and made his home in Tromsø.

Hanssen first met Amundsen at Sandefjord in 1897, where his ship put in just before *Belgica* sailed. In his words, despite a large notice saying 'Entry forbidden', Hanssen just had to see this vessel which was going on an adventure to the Antarctic; it was almost the end of the world. [I was sent to the mate and] met a tall, stately young man.

'Are you the mate?' I asked.

'Yes,' he said, 'so I'm told.' [And] he showed me round everywhere. From the first moment, I had a lot of time for this tall, handsome man with the kindly face ... and so I parted from Roald Amundsen on that occasion. He went South, and I North.

Hanssen was sailing with a North Norwegian line of coastal steamers when Zapffe told him about the vacancy on *Gjøa*. Nonetheless he instantly applied for the vacancy, and left a wife and small son for no one knew quite how many years in the Arctic.

Amundsen's one difficulty was finding a second in command. He wanted a Naval officer, chiefly because of the theoretical training, which meant a competent scientific leader. But no Norwegian volunteered, and the only candidate was a Danish Naval lieutenant, Godfred Hansen. As a Dane and a brother Scandinavian, speaking (roughly) the same language, Hansen was the next best thing to a Norwegian. He had sailed in Icelandic waters; besides, he had a thoroughgoing Copenhagener's sense of humour. Amundsen decided to take him.

Hansen prudently asked Nansen to endorse his request for Naval leave of absence. 'It is a well laid plan,' Nansen wrote. 'The expedition is as thoroughly and splendidly provisioned and equipped as any earlier one.'

Hansen was released for four years and he duly became Amundsen's second in command.

The company was made up with a second engineer; Gustav Juel Wiik, a gunner in the Norwegian Navy.

These six men were all. By any standards it was a small expedition.

In February, Amundsen found time for a final visit to Potsdam to make absolutely sure of understanding the instruments on which the fixing of the Magnetic Pole depended. The last 20,000 kroner remained obstinately elusive, but he took it for granted, that with the patronage of Nansen and the King, his creditors would trust him until the expedition was completed. He was going to earn money by newspaper articles; already Nansen had started the negotiations on his behalf for international syndication. The North-West Passage was worth a headline or two, and there would be money for the bills – in time. He assumed that in the meanwhile he could concentrate on essentials and complete his preparations with the thoroughness demanded by his perfectionist soul.

On his return to Christiania, he was swiftly disabused of his naive illusions. The creditors were yet more strident, insisting on settlement before sailing. The most importunate now threatened to have *Gjøa* impounded unless their bills were paid.

For three months, Amundsen struggled to raise the money. But even with Nansen's help, until the eleventh hour the issue was in doubt. At this moment of despair Amundsen's family rallied round.

A second cousin, Olav Ditlev-Simonsen, a rising shipowner (later one of the biggest in Norway), felt the ties of kinship and lent the last few thousand kroner.

On June 16th, matters were finally arranged, and Amundsen could sail at last. In an act of deliberate symbolism, he cast off at midnight. The city was veiled in cloudy gloom; rain was pelting down. Nobody was on the obscure, dilapidated jetty to say goodbye. Quietly, almost furtively, *Gjøa* slipped away down the fjord towards the open sea.

Thus began Amundsen's first command. It says something about his capacity for leadership that in his travail, with nothing but personal qualities to support him, his men instinctively identified themselves with him; even Godfred Hansen, who clearly saw his business failings. None of them felt quite at ease until they had left territorial waters. When the Norwegian coast was finally lost to sight, Amundsen appeared with a bottle of rum, and poured out drinks all round. 'Well, boys, we're clear of the creditors,' he said. 'All that matters now is that every man does his duty. That's easy. Skål and bon voyage.'

A man is known (amongst other things) by those whom he admires. Of all the explorers of the North-West Passage, Amundsen had chosen for his model one of the most neglected; Richard Collinson.

Collinson was a Royal Navy captain who commanded one of the many expeditions that went in search of Franklin. On H.M.S. *Enterprise*, he spent between 1850 and 1854 in the Arctic. He found no sign of Franklin, but he discovered hundreds of miles of new coastline, never lost a man, and got back safely with his ship. Captain Robert Le Mesurier McClure, who sailed on H.M.S. *Investigator* under Collinson's command, lost his ship, some of his crew and had to be rescued by an expensive relief expedition. He was a notable bungler. But he had all the lurid adventures. He was the first man to complete the North-West Passage, albeit as a shipwrecked mariner, ingloriously trudging to safety over the ice. He got all the glory. Collinson, not having had proper adventures, was deprived of his rightful due.

It took an Amundsen to understand a Collinson. Collinson's diary, published after his death, was one of Amundsen's favourite texts. On the title page was a couplet, from Addison's *Cato*, which he took as his motto:

'Tis not in mortals to command success,
But we'll do more, Sempronius, we'll
deserve it.

8

Arctic Apprenticeship

AMUNDSEN NOW RECORDED the pleasing discovery that he could 'run a happy ship' as the seamen say. It is an indefinable gift, an extension of the personality. It can neither be acquired, nor is it invariably associated with command. Amundsen was blessed with it. In his own revealing words:

> We have established a little republic on board *Gjøa* ... After my own experience, I decided as far as possible to use a system of freedom on board let everybody have the feeling of being independent within his own sphere. In that way, there arises   amongst sensible people · a spontaneous and voluntary discipline, which is worth far more than compulsion. Every man thereby has the consciousness of being a human being; he is treated as a rational being, not as a machine ... The will to do work is many times greater   and thereby the work itself. We were all working towards a common goal and gladly shared all work.

Respect was given not to rank, but the man; the concept of the superior personality was accepted.

One pilot said that Amundsen's ship was the most astonishing he had ever seen. 'No orders were given, but everyone seemed to know exactly what to do.'

Helmer Hanssen wrote that he 'did not come to a strict captain, not to a boss, but it was as if I had been met by a kind of father'.

Not everybody who encountered Amundsen felt that way; but he tried to select those who did. He did not, on the other hand, allow sentiment to cloud judgment. There is a story that he told an aspirant for *Gjøa* to stow dried fish (for dog food) in the after hold. 'It can't be done,' was the answer. 'There's no space.'

'There's no space for you either on board this ship,' said Amundsen, biting his lip. 'Get your traps and go.'

Amundsen wanted no hacks; he required extraordinary initiative. One of the great lessons of *Belgica* had been that under stress, passivity dissolved into apathy. He devised little tests, like the stowing of the dried fish, to eliminate the weaklings before it was too late.

Although this was (in part) a scientific enterprise, there were deliberately no scientists. Amundsen mistrusted academics on an expedition. He believed that, consciously or otherwise, they showed off their superior knowledge, thus undermining the authority of the leader. He was convinced he could do without them. The necessary observations were repetitive and routine. Any intelligent layman could be trained to do them. Wiik, the second engineer, was sent to Potsdam for instruction in magnetism; likewise, Ristvedt was taught the meteorology required. Amundsen thus avoided the strain of hostile cliques that followed from having scientists as a separate class on board. That at least was the way he interpreted his observations on *Belgica*. *Belgica* had been a profoundly formative experience.

There was also – deliberately – no doctor. Amundsen had a curious predjudice against one on an expedition. He believed that a doctor created sickness and, because of his priest-like rôle, meant divided command. He would have liked a pharmacist if he could have got one. He asked Zapffe to come, but Zapffe had family commitments. Amundsen made do with common sense, medical encyclopaedias, first-aid training, and the mystique of having been a medical student.

This then was the minuscule company that was setting out in the path of Franklin and his tragic entourage.

On July 25th, *Gjøa* entered Godhavn in North-Western Greenland. There she took on board ten more Eskimo dogs, complete with harnesses; also sledges and kayaks, ordered through the Danish authorities in Copenhagen, and Amundsen found time to take his first steps in dog driving behind a sledge on bare, stony ground. Then for twelve days *Gjøa* slowly sailed across Melville Bay, through floes and the raw Arctic ice-fog. On the thirteenth day, Amundsen recorded in his diary, she

shot out of the bank of fog. Behind us, it lay dark and black, but before us appeared a magnificent picture. Cape York with the surrounding York Mountains straight ahead ... As if at God's command ... the ice opened, and without hindrance we advanced swiftly towards land ... Without the least obstacle Melville Bay that dreaded bight had been overcome. Heartfelt thanks to Thou, O God, who led us through.

What Amundsen considered the worst of the North-West Passage, at least for so small a ship, was over. *Gjøa* now made for Dalrymple Rock to fetch the supplies sent with Milne and Adams, the Scottish whaling captains. As she closed land, the silence was riven by the rat-tat-tat of a fusillade. From behing an iceberg darted a flotilla of Eskimo kayaks; one flying the Danish flag, the other, the Norwegian; a welcoming committee, no less. Two of the kayak rowers turned out to be Danish;

Knud Rasmussen and Mylius-Erichsen. They belonged to the Danish Greenland Literary Expedition, which was recording the culture of the Polar Eskimos before it was submerged by the advancing tide of civilization. The encounter was not as improbable as it might seem. Dalrymple Rock is an Arctic crossroad. A natural point of departure for the crossing of the top of Baffin Bay, it is also on the Eskimo migration routes along the coast of Greenland.

The two Danes never forgot that meeting with Amundsen. They had lost their books, and faced a winter without anything to read. Amundsen gave them a spare set of Goethe's works that he had on board. The pleasure of that unexpected gift in the Polar darkness was a delighted memory for the rest of their lives.

With the willing help of Rasmussen, Mylius-Erichsen, and their Eskimo companions, Amundsen quickly re-stowed *Gjøa* and took the new supplies on board. As a parting gift, Mylius-Erichsen presented Amundsen with four of his best dogs.

Gjøa now resembled a waterlogged pantechnicon. A hundred and five packing cases crammed the deck almost to the main spar; atop the mound were perched seventeen raucous Eskimo dogs straining for a fight; and underneath the gunwhale was at the waterline. This was no state in which to face the swells and storms and meandering icebergs of Baffin Bay.

But, in a notoriously capricious sea, an almost unrelieved calm was vouchsafed Amundsen for his passage. Where others had so often suffered, he slipped across unhindered and untroubled.

Through Lancaster Sound, *Gjøa* sailed and on August 22nd made her first landing in the New World; at Erebus Bay on Beechey Island. This was the last of Franklin's winter stations definitely known. To Amundsen it was holy ground. Far into the night, he stayed alone on deck, sitting on an anchor chain and meditating on Franklin, his unfortunate precursor. As he sat and peered into the gloom, he could see the faint outlines of burial crosses, like the ghosts of the doomed expedition. In a characteristic tribute, he wrote:

> Franklin and all his men gave their lives in the struggle for the North-West Passage. Let us raise them a memorial, more lasting than any monument of stone; *the recognition that it was they who were the first discoverers of the North-West Passage.*

After all those years, with the way ahead clear and unequivocal, Amundsen at Beechey Island saw his paths divide.

Several North-West Passages had already been discovered, but none proved wholly navigable. *Gjøa* could now head either west through

Barrow Strait or south-west through Peel Sound and Franklin Strait. Nothing in Amundsen's knowledge or experience gave him rational guidance, but intuition said south-west. It was now that this man of action, not normally prey to doubt or indecision, deliberately renounced the exercise of free will. He took the auguries; he let the magnetic needle decide.

In the regions round the Magnetic Pole, the directional force of the earth's magnetic field is so weak that the ordinary compass is useless. A special instrument called a declination needle is required. On August 23rd, Amundsen and his assistant, Wiik, ceremonially erected one ashore in the shade of Franklin. They set the needle free. The whole of the little expedition crouched round to watch the languid oscillations that would decide their lot.

The instrument, when it gave its answer, said south-west.

It was with profound satisfaction that Amundsen saw the impersonal needle pointing the way his instincts told him to go. He had needed a sign, and now he could sail on with unimpaired self-confidence.

Soon after leaving Beechey Island, *Gjøa* passed the De La Roquette Islands, the furthest point yet reached by any vessel on her own keel. Half incredulous, Amundsen observed that where everyone before had been beset, the ice obediently opened for his entry into virgin waters.

For the next ten days, however, he suffered a succession of near calamities. Instead of ice, he was faced with fog and storms. In the midst of a bad blow, there was an engine-room fire, luckily extinguished before damage was done. Twice in four days *Gjøa* ran aground. The second time it was touch and go. After two days and a night gripped by a reef, in a wild and wind-lashed sea, Amundsen prepared to abandon ship. But, urged by Anton Lund, the first mate, he made a final effort to save her. The deck cargo was jettisoned. Thus lightened, and with a wind that obligingly veered at the right moment to dead astern, *Gjøa* was sailed off to float once more. It was a near thing. Splinters from the false keel boiled up in the waves. Had the wind shifted or *Gjøa* drawn two feet more, her crew would not have lived to tell the tale.

Amundsen expressed gratitude for deliverance by immediately studying the lessons for the future. The reef was large, and, from a modest height, quite obvious. Had the crow's nest been manned, *Gjøa* would never have struck. But the crow's nest was associated with ice alone, and, the waters being clear, had been ignored. Henceforth, Amundsen firmly noted, *Gjøa* would not move a foot through uncharted waters without one man in the crow's nest and another in the chains.

Now she sailed through untroubled waters. On September 9th, at the

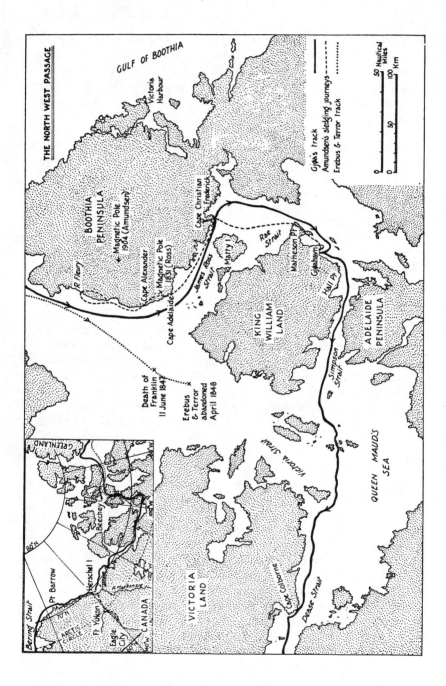

THE NORTH WEST PASSAGE

GULF OF BOOTHIA

Victoria
Harbour

BOOTHIA
PENINSULA

◆ Magnetic Pole
1904 (Amundsen)

Cape Alexander
× Magnetic Pole
1831 (Ross)

Cape Christian
Frederick

Cape Adelaide

James Ross Strait

Rae Strait

Matty I.

Death of
Franklin
11 June 1847 ×

Erebus
& Terror
abandoned
April 1848 ×

KING
WILLIAM
LAND

Matheson Pt.

Gjøahavn

Hall Pt.

ADELAIDE
PENINSULA

Simpson Strait

Victoria Strait

QUEEN MAUD'S
SEA

VICTORIA
LAND

Cape Colborne

Dease Strait

GREENLAND

Pt Barrow

Bering Strait

Herschel I.

Beechey

ARCTIC CIRCLE

Ft. Yukon

Eagle City

R. Mackenzie

CANADA

70°N

Gjøa's track _____
Amundsen's sledging journeys --------
Erebus & Terror track ....

Nautical
Miles 50
0

Km 100
0   50

entrance to Simpson Strait, on the southern coast of King William Land, a landlocked cove was sighted. A narrow, curving entrance was as if made for keeping heavy ice at bay. A ring of hills made a shield against the prevailing northerly winds. There was plenty of fresh water in the vicinity. *Gjøa* could anchor in comfort a yard or two from the shore. 'If one had sat at home and thought out a winter harbour,' Amundsen remarked, 'it would have been impossible to conceive a better one.'

Ahead, Simpson Strait rolled on, ice free, and underfoot the rhythmic surge of an unseen swell told of open seas to the west. But westwards was away from the Magnetic Pole, which lay somewhere on the peninsula of Boothia Felix. In the conflict between open waters and so opportune a haven, the haven won. He put *Gjøa* into the haven. Gjøahavn – Gjøa Haven – he called it. On October 1st, ice began to form and, by the 3rd, *Gjøa* was frozen in. She was not to sail out again for almost two years.

Now the first caribou (American reindeer) appeared so Amundsen told his men to drop everything for the hunt. After his ordeal on *Belgica*, he took the danger of scurvy very seriously indeed. Moreover his reading had taught him that it was the worst danger in the Arctic, killing more than blizzard, hunger or cold.

No significant progress had been made since *Belgica* had sailed in finding out its causes. One medical theory, following the fashion of seeing all disease in terms of bacterial infection, held that eating 'untainted' food in tins was enough to prevent scurvy. Another theory just coming into vogue when *Gjøa* left, explained scurvy as acid intoxication of the blood, but was hazy over what this actually meant in practice. Amundsen was unimpressed by medical theories. He stuck to his own experience on *Belgica*, Dr. Frederick Cook's unconventional observations of Eskimo diet, the traditional lore of Norwegian sealers and put his trust in fresh meat as a preventive. He also took with him the Arctic cloudberry (*Rubus Chameomorus L.*) already known to the Vikings as an effective antiscorbutic.

Gjøahavn lay on the caribou migration routes. Herd after herd swept across the landscape, but hunting was not easy, for the caribou is shy, and the dreary tundra of King William Land devoid of cover. But Amundsen's men, being passionate hunters, enjoyed themselves hugely. Amundsen contented himself with transporting the carcasses to the ship. His short-sightedness (for which he still refused to wear glasses) made him a bad shot. He did not enjoy hunting: 'I cannot,' he once said, 'imagine shooting an animal for pleasure.' And, in any case as the first snow had fallen, he wanted to start dog driving. Back and forth he shuttled with his sledge, suffering the indignities of everybody's first efforts with the unruly, exasperating but lovable Eskimo dogs. The pile of caribou carcasses mounted on *Gjøa*'s deck. Within a few weeks, there was more than enough meat, deep frozen in the Arctic autumn frosts, to last the winter.

On Thursday, October 29th, Amundsen came on deck as usual at eight-thirty a.m.

> Up on the hillside to the north, I saw a herd of what I first assumed to be reindeer, but which on more careful examination turned out to be human beings. Our first Eskimos. I got ready with all possible speed and ordered Lund and Hansen to follow me with rifles. When we finally left the ship – myself in the lead, the two others about 10 paces after with rifles over their shoulders – the Eskimos had already reached the sea ice and we quickly approached each other. The Eskimos were 5 in number, and advanced directly to us in a line. Without a trace of fear they came closer, and about 100 metres from the vessel we met.

The military precautions turned out to be superfluous – or outstandingly effective?

> Our meeting was as if between old friends. They gave their greeting of friendship by rubbing us on the chest and shouting in chorus: '*Minaktumi.*' We did the same, and our friendship was sealed.

Amundsen had hoped for an encounter such as this. The strange men with brown skins, Mongoloid eyes, black hair matted and hanging down to their shoulders, clad, almost like furry animals themselves, in compact, bristling, mottled caribou furs, were Netsiliks, the least known of the Canadian Eskimos, and the most isolated. Some of their ancestors had seen the explorers of the previous century. But these standing before *Gjøa* had never seen white men before. It was an ethnographer's paradise.

With the arrival of the Eskimos there springs into Amundsen's diaries a breath of life otherwise so strangely lacking. Too often his followers and even he himself seem paper figures; it is the Eskimos who live. It is almost as if he were capable of finding human contact among primitive people alone.

He had brought with him Eskimo glossaries, and with these proceeded to open communication with the newcomers. They slept the night on board *Gjøa* – in the hold – returning the following day whence they came. The visits were soon repeated and, on the third occasion, Amundsen went back with the Eskimos to their camp.

After six or seven hours they reached a cluster of igloos, drifted up like molehills in the snow, on the banks of a frozen lake in a valley among low hills. The inhabitants came tumbling out to greet the *kabluna* – the white man.

> It was a strange scene [wrote Amundsen], which I will never forget. Out in the desolate snow landscape I was surrounded by a crowd of wild people who cried and shrieked ... stared me in the face, pinched my clothes, stroked and felt me. The gleam of light from the igloos filtered out in a dark green glow against the fading day in the west.

Amundsen had come alone and unarmed. Although his raucous hosts, in the manner of nomads, proved spontaneously hospitable, it was nonetheless an act of courage. Amundsen had demonstratively put himself in their power as the only way of winning their trust.

He spent the night in an igloo as the guest of the two families inhabiting it. Next day, he returned to *Gjøa* escorted by three Eskimo men. The Eskimos trotted without snowshoes of any kind; Amundsen had 'the greatest difficulty in keeping up with them on skis with 2 sticks and good snow.'

Such was Amundsen's introduction to the life of the Eskimo. It was enough to confirm, what he had long accepted, that living like the Eskimos was the best way of coping with the Arctic. He now had experienced the comfort and advantages of an igloo as compared to a tent at low temperatures.

The visit secured the friendship sought by Amundsen. *Gjøa* now had a stream of visitors. Trade was their spur and in Amundsen they found an enthusiastic partner.

His motives at the start were wholly utilitarian. Under the influence of Nansen, Astrup and Dr. Frederick Cook, Amundsen had set out to learn about living under Polar conditions from the indigenous people. With his mentors, he believed that civilization held no monopoly of wisdom, and that primitive people might well have something to teach civilized man.

The Netsiliks were still living in the Stone Age. Their weapons were bows and arrows; their cooking utensils of soapstone; their only means of striking a light was by rubbing two pieces of wood together. But they had much to teach. They belonged to the circumpolar Eskimo tribes, the most highly adapted of mankind to a Polar environment. Uncontaminated by civilization, their sophisticated technology was still intact. This, Amundsen discerned. These would be his masters in the art of living in deep cold. After a decade of preparation, he was still acutely aware of the defects in his technique.

He found himself recording the whole material culture of the Eskimos whom he met. This was a task to which he was entirely suited. He was observant and perceptive. Where the primitive mind was concerned, he had the rare gift of empathy. Without professional training as an ethnographer, he yet had a professional touch; his notebooks and collections are models of their kind. He was the first to record the Netsilik culture and make a collection of their artefacts. It has taken a later generation to appreciate his worth.

On Christmas Day, one of the Netsiliks, a man of about fifty called Teraiu, appeared on *Gjøa* with a piteous tale of desertion by unfeeling fellow tribesmen. Unless helped over the dead season between the disappearance of the caribou in October and the arrival of the first seal in February or March, he, his wife and child would simply starve to death.

Here, Amundsen realized, was an opportunity to practise the Eskimo language and study Eskimo life in comfort and at leisure. Teraiu was told to move in with his family and make his winter home next to *Gjøa*. He was provided with food and fuel. Together with Kaiogolo, his wife, he took over many of *Gjøa*'s domestic chores.

But it was neither as domestic servant nor language teacher nor ethnographical guinea pig that Teraiu proved his greatest worth. He turned out to be a past-master in building igloos. He became Amundsen's first instructor in that basic art of survival: how to build with the materials of the country.

After the Christmas and New Year holidays Amundsen, with Lieutenant Hansen, Ristvedt and Helmer Hanssen presented themselves before Teraiu's igloo every morning after breakfast for their building lesson.

The Norwegians began by watching Teraiu work. Then, after several demonstrations, they started to help, advancing finally to building on their own under Teraiu's more or less taunting supervision. They used only the Eskimo tools; a special implement to probe the consistency of the snow, and a villainous-looking knife to cut the blocks.

> In the forenoon we built igloos, [runs a typical entry in Amundsen's diary]. We built in two parties, two to each. In 3 hours we had erected 2 magnificent igloos. We lack practice, which we will get later. The building itself is not difficult.

Three weeks before, he had begun to dress completely as an Eskimo. Amundsen had been assiduously trading. Besides acquiring samples for his ethnographical collection, he had amassed a stock of Netsilik fur clothing for his own use. He noted the results of his first attempt at wearing them:

Both inner and outer anorak hang loosely outside the trousers and the air has free access all the way up the body. Inner and outer trousers are held up round the waist with a cord and hang free over the *kamikks* (boots), so that the air can circulate freely. I find it excellent, and the only way to wear fur clothes, if one is to avoid sweating. Now I can move as I want to. Am always warm, without sweating.

This was quite extraordinary. There are very few civilized men – even today – who can immerse themselves in a primitive culture without trying to improve on it. Amundsen had set out with the perception and humility to learn from anyone who had something to teach. Eskimos might be dirty, pick their noses, and have peculiar habits; but in the matter of Polar living, they displayed a sophistication which civilization so patently lacked. He realized that millenia of evolution and specialized adaptation had taught the Netsiliks how to survive in the cold, and he was only too happy to learn all he could from them. Amundsen had firmly committed himself to an 'anthropological' approach.

He rapidly learnt the principles of cold-weather clothing. Man is better adapted to extremes of cold than heat, for the human body is a furnace requiring only insulation to maintain a proper temperature; cooling is more difficult. Insulation quite simply works on layers of trapped air, a poor conductor of heat. To this end, garments had to fit loosely, so as to form insulating pockets of air. They also had to allow air to circulate, so as to prevent sweating; a dangerous enemy, for it dissipates heat, and makes protective clothing freeze, thus destroying its insulation.

These principles were understood by all the Polar Eskimos. Their basic garment was the anorak or parka, a large jacket with attached hood, ingeniously designed to protect the face against wind and cold. Furs of Arctic animals were the traditional material.

It so happened that the Netsilik culture particularly suited Amundsen's methods. The Netsiliks used reindeer fur, supple and light. Their clothes were designed for travelling fast. Their particular development matched the needs of men on skis.

The most efficient of Nature's insulators is the reindeer or caribou fur. The individual hairs are hollow, so that the pelt is a honeycomb of air chambers, extraordinarily light in weight. It is a material which has required the technology of space travel to surpass, and in certain respects still has no synthetic peer. The Netsiliks wore caribou fur underwear, specially worked for suppleness, over which they put anoraks with a long tail behind to protect the vital organs from the wind, and improve the general insulation and air circulation. By adopting these garments,

Amundsen had taken himself to the forefront of Polar technique – by learning from a Stone Age tribe.

The winter was devoted to preparing for the journey to the North Magnetic Pole, and Gjøahavn became a school for Polar travel. Everyone now, willy nilly, wore Eskimo clothes. Igloo-building was systematically practised; so too was dog-driving, for that, above all, was what the Eskimos had to teach.

There lives around the Arctic a large, wolf-like dog, inured to cold and adapted to Polar conditions, possibly the closest existing relative of the first domesticated dogs. The Eskimo dog is the variety found in the Western Hemisphere, spread over three thousand miles from Greenland to Alaska; the domain of the Eskimo, in fact. Hardy, strong, and compactly built, the Eskimo dog is mentally and physically made for pulling. He has thick coarse fur of various colours, usually mottled brown, grey, white, yellow or black, and is found in several breeds.

The dog is the one animal that has followed man into civilization, but the Eskimo dog is distinguished by having kept one foot firmly in the wild. This explains his captivating personality. Watchdog, hunter, draught animal, he works under conditions in which no other beast of burden could survive. Without him, life in a cold and hostile environment would have been infinitely more difficult. Loyal, intelligent, brave, persevering; possessed also of quasi-human peccadillos like thieving, bullying and malingering, the Eskimo dog is part of the legend and literature of the North. Like most Polar sledge dogs, he is a compulsive fighter and a social animal, accepting a hierarchy and an uninhibited struggle for supremacy within the pack (or sledge team). As among men, a good leader is beyond price. His relation to his master is not that of servile beast, but of contractual dependant, performing certain duties in return for food and protection. Understanding the subtleties of the contract is the secret of managing the Eskimo dog.

This, then, was the dog that Helmer Hanssen was learning to drive before a sledge. He had a trained team, the example of the Eskimos before him; all possible advantages. Nonetheless, his progress was astonishing. He had turned out to be a born dog-driver, with the intuition necessary for contact between man and animal.

Wiik and Godfred Hansen were occupied with magnetic observations; Ristvedt forged iron arrow heads and knives for trading with the Eskimos. It was all hard work, learning and training. But at long last, Amundsen felt ready for his journey to the Pole, and on March 1st, 1904, he set off, together with Lieutenant Godfred Hansen, Ristvedt, and Helmer Hanssen.

The Magnetic Pole was only about ninety miles away, but they had set off too early in the season. The second night out the thermometer fell to − 61.7° (C.). At that temperature mercury freezes (a spirit thermometer is required), petrol will not burn, and even an Eskimo dog cannot work for long. A working dog breathes through its mouth, panting hard and, if the air inhaled is too cold, his lungs cannot cope. The limit of his endurance is about − 50° (C.). There were too few dogs, so Amundsen, Ristvedt and Godfred Hansen were harnessed to a sledge and man-hauled on their own. In such extreme cold the snow stuck like glue to the skis and the sledge runners; moving a heavy load was backbreaking torture. Altogether man and beast were thoroughly miserable.

The third day out Amundsen decided to cut his losses and turn back to wait for milder weather. He dumped the loads, abandoned what he called the 'futile toil' of man-hauling, and returned to *Gjøa*. In four hours he covered the distance that had taken two and a half days, all of six miles. Such was the first sledging journey under Amundsen's command; an inglorious fiasco. 'Yet,' he noted in his diary, 'we harvested experience.' An exhaustive analysis follows, written while impressions were still fresh.

Two great lessons stood out for the future. Starting too early in the season was risky. Manhauling was inefficient, and therefore stupid.

Henceforth Amundsen would use only dogs. This meant that instead of adapting transport to his men, he would go the other way about. The Magnetic Pole party had to be reduced to the number the dogs could bear. That meant two, and no more.

Amundsen learned quickly. On March 16th, ten days after the great fiasco, he was on his way again. He was accompanied now by Helmer Hanssen alone; he had waited until the temperature had risen. Even so, with new-found caution, he declined to risk too much too soon.

The Polar journey itself would now have to wait until the cold was broken and spring manifestly on the way. Instead, he would take a preliminary canter to advance the loads dumped on the first abortive start.

We had one sledge ... with about 300 kilos, and all 10 dogs [Amundsen wrote in his diary]. At 3 in the afternoon we reached the depot after 3½ hours at the double. It was only by the utmost exertion that we were able to keep up.

Picking up their depot, they had double the load; still the dogs went on with their tireless gait between a trot and a scamper, paws padding on the wind crust; tails raised like pennants in the wind. After two days, they reached Matty Island in James Ross Strait. Out on the sea ice they met a crowd of Netsiliks – no less than thirty-four. Amundsen was delighted to note that it was almost at the same spot that McClintock had found Eskimos in 1859, and that they were of the same tribe.

Amundsen, ever keen to learn and ever more interested in Eskimos than magnetism, turned aside to visit their camp. From one of them he obtained a set of new caribou fur underwear. Etiquette demanded that he put it on immediately, still warm from the donor. He complied, with a silent prayer that there were no lice; most Eskimos he met had lice.

It was a risk he was prepared to take. He had (rightly) concluded that it was a mistake to mix Eskimo and European clothing. Woollen underwear rapidly became sweaty and dirty, losing its warmth; fur kept dry, clean and warm. It was essential to be dressed in fur throughout, and only the Eskimos could cure and sew the pelts so that they could be worn next to the skin in comfort. Amundsen was building up a stock of undergarments for present and future travel.

He remained with the Netsiliks long enough to see the start of their spring migration to the sealing grounds. He was probably the first European to do so. Most urgently he wanted to see how the Netsiliks ran their dogs.

When the caravan of dogs and sledges had straggled over the horizon, Amundsen returned to *Gjøa*, arriving on March 25th. On April 6th, he set out for the third time. Spring was finally on the way; this was the real start for the Pole. As his companion, he now took Ristvedt instead of Helmer Hanssen. Hanssen was the better dog driver, but magnetic observations were the purpose of the journey, and Ristvedt could help where Hanssen could not. 'Such changes of mind,' Amundsen remarked, 'easily cause discontent, and are therefore tiresome. But now there was no way out.'

As a school for travel, the Polar journey was undeniably instructive. In that short distance, it supplied a comprehensive sample of hardships and obstacles. There was wet snow; clinging snow; sea ice rafted and twisted into ridges that barred the way and tried the patience of man and dog. There was fog. There was wind that seared and sun that burned in the way it only can at high latitudes, where snow and ice focus its rays at a low malicious angle.

At the start, Amundsen and Ristvedt had the company of their old friend, Teraiu. The second day out, Teraiu turned off to rejoin his tribe in their summer hunting grounds. The two Norwegians were left to carry on alone. 'It was,' Amundsen noted, 'extraordinarily heavy going now that we had no one in front of us.'

He now grasped the full force of something he had observed on the Netsilik migration. Someone had been sent ahead of the dogs to encourage them. This was evidently because even a trained dog disliked advancing into a void – sensible creature, one might say. He preferred some fellow creature to draw him on. On the previous journey this had been obscured by good going and Helmer Hanssen's talent. Amundsen quickly acted on what he had perceived. He went ahead as forerunner; his own dogs followed at his heels, Ristvedt's coming on behind. 'It has been extremely exhausting,' Amundsen recorded at the end of the day, not forgetting to reproach himself for doing only ten miles. His perfectionist severity conceals accomplishment.

After picking up the main depot at Matheson Point on the east coast of King William Land, the dogs had pulled 500 kilos: fifty-five kilos each. This is something over their own weight; under any circumstances a respectable performance. That day, the going was notably discouraging. The snow was loose, so the dogs (and men) sank in, the sledge runners stuck and the loads dragged. Still, the animals pulled not only well but willingly. Amundsen had learned how to run dogs under varying conditions with drivers of different capacity.

Eskimos have always disliked hurrying to orders; Europeans usually interpreted this as cowardice and sloth. Amundsen saw otherwise. The Eskimo did not hurry, firstly because he wanted to avoid sweating, the enemy of warmth. But also his whole being rebelled at overtaxing his strength. There is a proper pace of working, and it must be respected. To an outsider it may appear as an incomprehensible inertia but to those who understand the climate it is common sense.

Amundsen thus learned a cardinal rule of Polar travel: not to exceed what the body and spirit of man or dog could comfortably bear. It is not an obvious lesson, and one which civilized man frequently ignores. Conservation of energy also leaves resources which can be drawn upon in an emergency. At Cape Christian Frederick on the coast of Boothia Felix, he broke the glass of a pocket chronometer. Ristvedt returned to *Gjøa* for a new one. Travelling light, with one sledge and all the dogs, he was able to cover the distance, fifty-four geographical miles, in twenty-four hours at a stretch, and the same coming back. On the evening of April 20th, he reappeared, having rested on board for a day.

They now continued their journey. The dogs were pulling well; travel was a pleasure. Fanning out from the sledges, like a pack of hounds in full cry, the animals hauled away in their tireless scamper. The sledges, packed high, swung along, pitching and tossing slightly to follow the terrain, like ships riding to the waves. Men and dogs seemed to understand each other.

On April 26th, they reached the position of the North Magnetic Pole found by James Clark Ross on Boothia Felix near Cape Adelaide, to discover that it had moved somewhere to the north. Thus Amundsen became the first man to prove that the Magnetic Pole indeed migrated. He was profoundly unimpressed with himself, as if attainment were anticlimax and, by definition, sterile. He was more concerned with the storm that blew up and with the fact that Ristvedt had to shoot Nakdio, a dog obtained from the local Eskimos, because it absolutely refused to pull. Nakdio was served, as an experiment, to his comrades who, Amundsen noted, dispassionately 'partook of it with relish. We ourselves tried some substantial steaks and found the meat excellent.' Amundsen had verified that the Eskimo dog was both a cannibal and edible for men. On the sea ice off Matty Island, he met some Eskimos hunting seal. He obtained from them fresh seal meat and blubber, allowing his dogs to gorge on both. The effect was remarkable. They had been feeding on pemmican and were losing condition; with the fresh meat they rapidly acquired new vigour, and pulled as well as before. That, too, was a valuable lesson.

From Ross' Pole, Amundsen struck out northwards to find the new one.

For three weeks, Amundsen and Ristvedt travelled to and fro near the coast of Boothia Felix hunting for the Pole. It was rather a monotonous business, enlivened chiefly by Eskimo and polar-bear spoors crisscrossing on the ice, and finally an encounter with a bear itself, which cost the lives of two of their dogs. By May 11th, they were back at Ross' Pole on the way to Victoria Harbour, Ross' winter harbour on the east coast of Boothia Felix in 1831–32. This was partly an historical pilgrimage; partly to 'ring' the Pole and fix its new position accurately.

Amundsen was now reminded, and philosophically accepted, that in the snows, the plans of men often go awry. At Ross' Pole, he was immobilized by an injured left ankle – probably a strained tendon – and had to rest for a week. There was little to do except hunt rock ptarmigan and observe the dogs who, in Amundsen's words, were

> now turning their noses up at pemmican. They consider old pieces of fur a delicacy. 'The menu of the Polar dog is comprehensive,' said Ristvedt. 'I think I can manage many dishes, but I don't think I could have managed your old underpants.' The dogs smacked their lips over them like a bear with honey.

Continuing their journey, they found their depot at Cape Christian Frederick plundered by Eskimos, which left them with just enough food to get home, and forced them to give up the visit to Victoria Harbour. On May 27th, they arrived back at *Gjøa*, after an absence of seven weeks.

Our journey was not a brilliant success, [ran Amundsen's summing-up] but considering the many unfavourable circumstances ... we had to be satisfied with the results ...

Final calculations showed that he had missed the new Magnetic Pole by thirty miles. At the time, he suspected that he had not reached the mathematical point. The reason is obscure but, whatever it was, Amundsen had failed to attain one of his goals. To the end of his days it was a source of the deepest mortification.

The journey, however, short as it was, had taught him much. The three attempts together amounted to less than 500 miles, but from them Amundsen had learned how to travel over pack ice and snow-covered land; how to manage a party on the move. He had suffered setbacks under conditions in which they were instructive rather than dangerous. He had shown the ability to learn quickly from his mistakes; and, what is much more difficult and rare, from his success. Above all, he had learned the management of dogs. He had done between ten and twenty-four miles a day in all conditions, a respectable performance by most standards. He had, as it were, graduated as a Polar traveller. That, and not the failure to reach a particular point on the surface of the globe, was the true outcome of the journey to the North Magnetic Pole.

Ten days after returning to *Gjøa*, Amundsen was out again making magnetic observations in the field. He had planned a second winter in the vicinity of the Pole, and wished to make the most of his time.

Amundsen was following conscientiously the instructions of Neumayer and the scientists at Potsdam. But he did not enjoy the tedious and repetitive attendance upon scientific instruments. He never pretended that science for him was anything more than a necessary evil which others saw as a justification for Polar travel. For him the act of travel was justification in itself. His heart was in perfecting his technique.

Although he had learned, he felt he still had not learned enough, especially about dogs and skis. The adaptability of skis was not yet fully proven. Summer skiing with its ever changing thaws and re-freezing, was an excellent laboratory, but he was glad of the opportunity to spend another winter mastering travel in extreme cold.

Winter was early that year. At the end of September, when the ice was firm, some Netsiliks moved to the vicinity of *Gjøa*, and Amundsen proceeded to collect their artefacts and study their behaviour. His observations, incidentally, say as much about himself as about those whom he is observing.

Amundsen's relationship with the Netsiliks went beyond that of ethnographer and specimen. He made friends among them; two in particular, Ugpik, whom he called 'The Owl', and Talurnakto. The Owl was a natural aristocrat. Talurnakto, on the other hand,

> was considered by his fellow tribesmen to be a kind of idiot, but in reality was the cleverest of them all. He laughed and clowned incessantly, had no family and hadn't a care in the world [but] he was a good worker. If his honesty was not as marked as 'The Owl's', he was nonetheless reliable.

During the winter, Amundsen made what he called 'the horrifying discovery' that one of the Netsilik children was suffering from congenital syphilis. He lectured his men on the danger this implied, for he did not want them to sleep with the Eskimo women, and on this point there is evidence that discipline broke down. Amundsen had an obsessive horror of venereal disease which, in some way, appears to have been connected with a fear of the sexual act. In any case, he decided that good morale on an expedition could only be achieved by pretending that the female sex did not exist. The table talk on *Gjøa* was rigidly sexless, at least in his presence.

Earlier in February, Amundsen went with Talurnakto (as teacher) on a journey with sledge and dogs. The temperature was about $-45°$ (C.).

One piece of Eskimo technique Amundsen was anxious to acquire. Eskimos were able to travel at any temperature, because they could make their sledges slide on any kind of snow. They did this by coating the runners with ice. It is a skilled operation: the ice has to be applied in thin layers so that it is elastic and does not flake off. There are various methods. Talurnakto's was this. A mixture of moss and water was applied to the runners, freezing solid as an undercoating. Then, water warmed in the mouth was spat on to a bearskin mitten, and applied with a few deft strokes, forming the layers of ice. This surface would slide effortlessly on the worst of the crystalline, drift snow that clung like the sands of the desert to all civilized contrivances.

Amundsen got Talurnakto to prepare one of the Norwegian sledges, to see whether the method would work on its broad ski-like runners as well as the narrow ones of the Eskimo models. It worked. After preliminary trials around *Gjøa* before setting off, Amundsen could record that 'if the temperature is lower than $-30°$ (C.) I find that the iced

runners glide far better than any other kind,' and on the journey with
Talurnakto under proper travelling conditions, he observed that 'they
glide just as easily on the arid drift snow as ash wood on wind crust.'
Thus did Amundsen learn to overcome the worst vagaries of snow and
approach mastery of the Polar environment.

In the New Year Amundsen found a fault in a magnetic instrument.
This might have explained his failure the previous summer, and he
decided to make another attempt to reach the Pole. But various ailments
had ravaged the dogs, and when spring came, there were only enough
for one party. Lieutenant Godfred Hansen had planned a journey to
Victoria Land. Amundsen felt it would be unfair – and bad leadership
– to assert his privilege and commandeer the dogs; his failings did not
include jealousy. He gave up his own season's travelling to let Hansen
carry out his. He himself stayed behind at Gjøahavn to take another series
of magnetic observations and repair what damage he could.

Hansen, accompanied by Ristvedt, left on April 2nd, returning on
June 25th. In that time, they covered 800 miles, and charted 150 miles
of Victoria Land; one of the last stretches of unexplored coastline on the
North American Continent.

The work was now done. Later in the summer the ice melted; the
waters to the west opened up. At three in the morning of August 13th,
1905, Amundsen sailed out of Gjøahavn, into Simpson Strait, and bore
up to Hall Point where two of Franklin's men were buried.

With our flag hoisted in honour of the dead [Amundsen wrote], we glided past
the grave in ceremonial silence ... Our little ... *Gjøa* saluted her unhappy
predecessors.

No vessel had yet sailed through Simpson Strait. It was a labyrinth of
shoals and narrows; drifting ice and treacherous currents, uncharted
and unknown. Only a boat journey by Lieutenant Hansen the summer
before had shown a way through. Only *Gjøa*'s petrol motor enabled her
to twist and turn through the maze and save her from disaster. With
lead going all the time, helm constantly put about, men standing watch
and watch, she inched her way along. After four days she reached Cape
Colborne, at the entrance to Victoria Strait, Collinson's furthest east on
his voyage from the Pacific fifty years before. *Gjøa* had survived the last
stretch of the North-West Passage yet untamed by the keel of a ship –
at the cost of no more than a broken gaff.

Still there were the foul and sketchily charted channels of Dease Strait and Coronation Gulf. At last, on August 21st, *Gjøa* ran out into Dolphin and Union Straits. 'My relief over thus having cleared the last awkward stretch of the North-West Passage,' Amundsen wrote, 'was indescribable.'

To his men he had seemed an icy pool of imperturbability. But the fortnight since leaving Gjøahavn, he had been living on his nerves, haunted by the near disaster off Matty Island two years before. For him there was no glorious failure: no prize for trying. Victory was all he could look forward to.

At eight in the morning of August 26th, Amundsen came off watch and went below to his bunk.

> After I had been asleep for some time, I was woken by a tremendous running back and forth on deck. There was clearly something afoot, and I merely was annoyed that they should make such a fuss for the sake of a bear or seal. For something of that kind it must be. But then Lt. Hansen burst into the cabin and shouted the unforgettable words, '*Vessel in sight!*'
>
> The *North-West Passage* was done. My boyhood dream – at that moment it was accomplished. A strange feeling welled up in my throat; I was somewhat overstrained and worn – it was weakness in me – but I felt tears in my eyes. '*Vessel in sight*' . . . *Vessel in sight.*

After weeks of fog and miserable weather, the sky was burning clear; against a backdrop of distant snow peaks, glittering (like a stage set) in the Arctic sun, a schooner bore down, out of the west, all sail set. It was an obligingly fitting *mise en scène* for Askeladden triumphant; *Gjøa*, that Cinderella of a ship victorious, where all the armadas and captains and expensive legions of seamen had failed.

The ship bearing down on *Gjøa* flew the Stars and Stripes. She was the whaler *Charles Hansson* of San Francisco; her captain was James McKenna. 'Are you Captain Amundsen?' were his first words when they met. Amundsen had not expected to be recognized in this remote corner of the world. 'How surprised was I not,' he wrote in his diary, 'when Captain McKenna wrapped his fist round mine and congratulated me on a brilliant success.'

The North-West Passage was accomplished. Three centuries of human endeavour and a whole martyrology were at an end.

Until the news got through, the North-West Passage was only half done. *Gjøa* sailed urgently on towards the cable stations of the Pacific. But a thousand miles short of the Bering Strait, at King Point on the Yukon Coast of Canada, she was stopped by ice, and frozen in for a third winter.

At Herschel Island, a little to the west a fleet of American whalers was wintering. One of them had the 'pleasant surprise' of post for Amundsen. His brother Leon, who had done so much to help before *Gjøa* had left Norway, had got the expedition publicized through the Norwegian consul in San Francisco, Henry Lund. Leon had done this with the aid of a letter from Nansen. Nansen's name had pursuaded the American Government and the whaling companies to send out orders for all possible assistance to be given *Gjøa*.

I do not know [Amundsen wrote when he received his mail], how I can ever show Prof. Nansen . . . how much I respect and honour him for the invaluable services he has given the *Gjøa* expedition.

Civilization was now within reach. Amundsen had to be the first with his story. On October 24th, two Eskimos left Herschel Island overland with post from the whaling fleet. They were joined by William Mogg, captain of the *Bonanza*, a whaler wrecked near *Gjøa* off King Point. With them went Amundsen, bound for the nearest telegraph station at Eagle City in Alaska.

This journey by itself was a minor accomplishment. It was 500 miles to Eagle City, dog-driving all the way, over a route rarely attempted so early in the season. In the short, bleak days of autumn, on snow not properly settled, along the Herschel river leaking through imperfect ice, they crossed a windswept pass 3,000 feet high over the Brooks range of coastal mountains. For week after week they followed frozen water-courses, the caravan routes of the north.

Amundsen skied; the Eskimos walked on foot or snow shoes; Mogg alone rode on a sledge. It was his first sledging journey. Short and squat, an old salt of about sixty, his place was on the bridge, not tramping the snows. He was making for San Francisco overland to find another ship for the next season. For a man of his age, it was a sporting effort. He was financing the expedition. Amundsen, the conqueror of the North-West Passage, had not a penny to his name and Mogg took him as his guest.

Amundsen began by noting the superiority of the cold weather technique he had learned from the Netsiliks.

I was the only one to avoid getting my fur clothing wet with sweat. The reason is that I carry my clothes loose & allow the air to circulate between them. The others have their fur garments tightly fastened.

But when they crossed the mountains, reached the tree line, and entered the deep, loose powder snow of the North American forests, he found more to learn. There he discovered the first (and only) conditions which defeated skis, and where the snowshoe was superior. The snow also defeated sledges, whose runners, designed for the hard crust of open country, sank in to the hilt as if fallen into quicksands, and tangled with the tree roots. The sledges were changed for Indian toboggans, flat-bottomed sledges like shallow barges that floated on the snow. That was one lesson for the future. Another was the Alaskan way of running dogs, which Amundsen now had ample opportunity to observe. The dogs were harnessed in a straight line, pair by pair, to a central trace; a contrast to the usual Eskimo system of letting them fan out with individual traces attached to a single point. The Alaskan harness too was different, a padded ring like a horse's halter, with the traces at the side, instead of the single strap over the neck, with a trace running under the dog's belly. Each system had its drawbacks. All this Amundsen carefully noted in his diary.

At midday on December 5th, they reached Eagle City, a gold mining town of rough wooden buildings huddled on the banks of the Yukon. The temperature was − 52° (C.). Amundsen hurried into Fort Egbert, the United States military outpost, and the terminal of the telegraph line to the United States. There he sent Fridtjof Nansen the telegram for which he had striven so hard: the announcement that, first of all men, he had navigated the North-West Passage – 'In the tracks of Collinson', as he remembered to report – paying his historical debts even at seventy-five cents a word.

Immediately afterwards, the line was broken by the cold. When it was repaired, a few days later, Amundsen was a famous man. But it was not fame with which he was first called upon to deal.

For two years, Amundsen had lived in Eden. When he skied out of the wilderness into Fort Egbert, he returned to the world of money and its worries; and money he had absolutely none. He had travelled from Herschel Island on Captain Mogg's charity. He was an explorer in distress. He was in no position to pay for his telegram to Nansen: 1,000 words and a matter of $755.28.* He sent it, perforce, collect.

But collect facilities had not been arranged beforehand. Amundsen was taken on trust at Fort Egbert; not so further down the line. His telegram was stopped en route at Valdez, and a resumé transmitted to the head of the U.S. Signals Corps Telegraph system in Alaska, Major W. A. Glassford, at Seattle.

Major Glassford immediately disclosed the contents to the local Press, whence it made its way across the world. Unfortunately, the telegram

* £155; £2,600 or $5,200 in present terms.

contained the news which Nansen had placed exclusively with *The Times* of London, and other newspapers.

The major argued plausibly that the cable fees had to be guaranteed before the message could be transmitted, and using the Press was the quickest way of letting Nansen know. In the background there was probably a deal with some enterprising newspaper willing to pay for a scoop. It would not be the only example of its kind.

When Brigadier General Adolphus Greely, head of the U.S. Signals Corps was told of the affair, he ordered Glassford *not* to divulge anything to anyone. Greely then approached the Norwegian Legation in Washington, who guaranteed the fees. The telegram was sent on to Nansen three days later and practically worthless as marketable news. The newspapers, with whom he had made agreements, declined to pay since the story was no longer exclusive. Nansen refused to pay for the cable because of Major Glassford's 'violation of trust'.

It is a piquant detail that Greely, a well-known Arctic explorer in his own right, was an enemy of Nansen's. He disliked the whole idea of the drift of the *Fram*, and he condemned Nansen's dash to the Furthest North as desertion of his men and ship.

This then greeted Amundsen when the lines to Eagle City were re-opened. Major Glassford had acted behind his back. The financial loss was considerable but Amundsen did not whine. He took it as an expensive, elementary and unpalatable lesson in the handling of news. At least he had learned the penalties of naiveté.

Ruefully, Amundsen admitted his mistake. 'In future,' as he wrote to Nansen's brother Alexander, the expedition's business manager, 'I will try to be more careful.'

The affair of the stolen cable was one of the first contentious issues to face the newborn Norwegian Diplomatic Service in the United States. While Amundsen had been in the wilderness, Norway had become independent. He learned this for the first time in Eagle City. It had happened on June 7th, 1905, a bare six months before. He had left owing allegiance to Oscar II, the Swedish King; now it was to a Norwegian monarch, the Danish Prince Carl, who had taken the name of Haakon VII. Amundsen was hugely pleased; this was news indeed to take back to King Point.

Amundsen had asked Nansen to tell the families of his men that letters sent immediately would arrive in time for him to take back to *Gjøa*. This was a little surprise that he had arranged. He settled down for two months to wait for the replies.

On February 3rd, 1906, with the post from Norway, Amundsen once more got on to his skis behind a dog sledge, and headed north away from Eagle City on the way back to *Gjøa*. The snow was better, there was no passenger and the journey was easier than the outward one. On March 12th, he arrived back at *Gjøa*, having been away five months and skied over 1,000 miles.

The heartfelt welcome [he wrote], was more than a reward for the long and exhausting journey. From vessel and huts the Norwegian flag waved ... How glad I was to be able to bring these splendid lads news from their dear ones. They were all pleased and excited.

The following day they declared

a holiday. Again all flags are flying. It is our first opportunity to honour our new king. God save him.

While Amundsen had been away, Helmer Hanssen had travelled hundreds of miles on hunting trips into the Mackenzie Delta. There, among the twisted frozen channels in sparse, difficult snow, he became the complete dog driver; it had taken him three seasons from scratch.

Hanssen had great feeling for his animals as he revealed in an anecdote about his leader dog, a bitch called Gjøa after the ship. She had a phenomenal sense of smell. One day, returning to King Point after a hunting trip, she declined to go where she was told. Usually, said Hanssen,

she obeyed commands [but now] she went off in the way she had decided. I will confine myself to saying that I lashed her, but nothing helped. So I gave up the struggle and let Gjøa take command ... finally ... she stopped ... and started digging in the snow ... to my great surprise I saw that it was my mittens, which I had lost on the outward journey [a week before]. Now I regretted bitterly having whipped her ... I decided it was my duty to make amends which I did by immediately serving a half hare to everyone in the team ... After that journey I never touched Gjøa with the lash.

Four four months, Amundsen was still imprisoned by the ice. Amongst other things, he took the opportunity to learn how the whalers at Herschel Island hunted the Bowhead whale. He was shocked to discover that they took only the whalebone – long, narrow, bony plates growing from the jaw. 'Everything else,' as he put it, 'is fed to the fishes.'

I asked what ... the ... valuable whalebone ... was used for, and received the answer that it was mostly used in the manufacture of corsets!
A woman's figure is a precious thing!
But I think that after my experience as a polar explorer, I would vote for a fashion reform.

On July 10th, *Gjøa* left King Point and crawled through the ice and between the shoals along the top of the North American Continent. She rounded Point Barrow on August 30th, passed through the Bering Strait, and left the Arctic, hounded by a storm.

> I had thought of celebrating our passage through the Bering Strait [said Amundsen], but we could just manage a little glass of whisky on deck in a hurry – there was no question of flying a flag. It was with happiness we emptied our glasses, for whatever happens now, we have brought the Norwegian flag through the North-West Passage on *one* ship.

What remained now was the public acclaim. *Gjøa* reached San Francisco on October 19th, and one month later Amundsen and his men returned to Norway. He received his accolade, as it were, in London on February 11th, 1907, when he lectured on the expedition to the Royal Geographical Society. Nansen, now the first ambassador in London of an independent Norway, was present. After the lecture, he spoke:

> As Captain Amundsen has already pointed out himself, the fact that it has been possible for him to accomplish that great deed is due entirely to the work of British seamen ... But a Norwegian has been the lucky man to finish this quest for the North-West Passage ... I think we may say we belong to the same race, and ... of these ... gallant achievements we may say with Tennyson

> 'One equal temper of heroic hearts,
> Made weak by time and fate, but
> strong in will
> To strive, to seek, to find, and
> not to yield'.

9

Robert Falcon Scott, R.N.

NANSEN HAD, ONCE more, invoked the Askeladden–Cinderella myth. In the nicest possible way he celebrated the triumph of little Norway over a great, albeit a friendly power. He also made a point of which some of his audience were uncomfortably aware. Britain, having been ahead so long, had faltered and lost the prize. The issue went beyond Polar exploration. Kipling had expressed the feeling in the *Recessional*, written for Queen Victoria's Diamond Jubilee, ten years before:

> Far-called, our navies melt away;
> On dune and headland sinks the fire:
> Lo, all our pomp of yesterday,
> Is one with Nineveh and Tyre!
> Judge of the Nations, spare us yet,
> Lest we forget – we forget!

These intimations of decline seem curiously personified in Robert Falcon Scott. He was born on June 6th, 1868, at a watershed in English life.

In 1870 Dickens died. Darwin's last great work, *The Descent of Man* appeared in 1871. Livingstone died in 1873; Wheatstone, the English inventor of the telegraph in 1875. The race of giants which had adorned the early years of Queen Victoria's reign was passing away.

In 1870, too, erupted the Franco-Prussian War, the prelude to Armageddon which, transferring to Germany the ascendancy in Europe and inaugurating the modern era of mass, technological warfare, exposed Britain's relative impotence to influence events on the Continent and heralded her decay abroad.

In a manner familiar in history, an age of greatness was starting to fade. Within the edifice of Imperial grandeur, the structure was beginning to rot. In almost every field the story was the same. During the years of very occasionally interrupted peace since Waterloo, the armed services (despite colonial sallies) had forgotten how to fight. They laboured under a rigid and uncreative discipline that stifled thought and rendered them unfit for modern war. Industry was beginning to wilt because of related sins. Exports were falling, notably in favour of Germany and the United States. Most inventions of importance were coming from abroad. After the generations as 'the workshop of the world', Britain was forgetting how to think, how to compete and how to adapt.

1870, or thereabouts, may be taken as the manifest start of the collapse of British power. If Scott's birth had been chosen as a symbol, it could scarcely have been better timed.

Robert Falcon Scott was born, of Devonshire stock, near Plymouth. He grew up with parents, four sisters, a younger brother, a maiden aunt, and a staff of servants in a house standing in its own grounds, but a little dilapidated and too small for its inhabitants.

The Scott property, 'Outlands', lay in Devonport, where lies also the Plymouth Naval dockyard. This was wholly appropriate. It was from the Navy that the Scotts derived their money and their standing. Scott's mother Hannah neé Cuming was the sister of a Naval captain, and the niece of a vice admiral. His father, John Edward Scott, was the son of a Naval purser. It was from his father that the money came.

John Edward's father Robert, together with a brother, also a Naval purser, made their fortunes, partly in prize money from the Napoleonic Wars, but mostly from the perquisites of their branch of the Navy. They retired to buy 'Outlands' and a small brewery in Plymouth. After various quarrels, Robert eventually found himself in sole possession.

What then happened was a moral tale for the times. Robert's three older sons joined the Indian Army. John Edward Scott, the son left at home to carry on the business, was the youngest, weakest and least qualified to do so. Eventually he inherited both 'Outlands' and the brewery. He ran the brewery with a cavalier insouciance which, incidentally, gives credence to the romantic claim that his forebears were fugitive Scots from the 1745 Rebellion. John Edward Scott had the authentic touch of a supporter of lost causes. He sold his inheritance, lived off the proceeds, he and all seventeen members of his household, and occupied himself with gardening.

Behind the paterfamilias immersed in the characteristic English middle-class pastime of playing the country gentleman was a quiet, morose, anxious man, plagued by a sense of inadequacy, prone to violent outbursts of temper. Mrs. Scott had a struggle to run her extensive household and keep up appearances. She was, in any case, beside being socially superior the stronger of the two; a matriarch thinly disguised as a dutiful wife, the real ruler of the family. She had the Victorian solicitude for the spiritual welfare of others which has destroyed faith more effectively than the most militant atheism. She possessed the special English brand of middle-class matronly charm that concealed a debilitating despotism. From that Scott never entirely escaped.

'Con', as his family always called him (after his middle name Falcon, the surname of his godparents), had a sheltered upbringing. The Victorian nursery, with its nursemaids, its romps, its idealization of childhood, was a protected haven, and the most Scott had to put up with was gentle bullying by two older sisters. He suffered from the mysterious, possibly psychosomatic sickliness of so many Victorian childhoods that commonly presaged robust maturity. He was taught at home by a governess until he was eight, then sent to a day school. He was an ordinary, affable little boy, with a touch of temper and a hint of idleness to whom no legends clung.

John Edward Scott chose service in the armed forces as the profession for his sons. It was a family tradition, it was socially acceptable and it avoided the taint of trade. He decided to send Con, the eldest son, into the Royal Navy, and Archibald, the next son, into the Army. Each uncomplainingly did as he was told.

To make certain that Con passed the entrance examinations, he was taken away from school and sent to a cramming establishment which specialized in teaching to the educational standards required by the service. In 1881, at the age of thirteen, he passed as a cadet into the training ship *Britannia* at Dartmouth.

The Royal Navy of the last two decades of the nineteenth century, although numerically imposing, was backward, drowsy and inefficient. One of its own admirals called it 'a menagerie of unruly and curiously assorted ships'.

Yet Britannia really did rule the waves. The victory under Nelson at Trafalgar had turned the Royal Navy into a legend. This inevitably led to smugness, closed minds, resistance to technical progress and living in the past. In the mid 1880s, when younger fleets had converted to breechloaders, British battleships were still armed with obsolete muzzle-loading guns, not much more efficient than those of Nelson's day. Tastefully decked out with black sides, yellow funnels and pink boot-topping, with gilding here and there, Her Majesty's ships resembled yachts more than men o'war. As the autobiographies of nineteenth-century admirals illustrate so well, the Royal Navy was more like an exclusive yacht club than a warlike institution. Spit and polish were more important than preparation for war.

This was one side of the Navy that Scott had joined. Another was the system of blind obedience and rigid centralization that maintained the hierarchy of rank rather than efficiency of function. Trivialities were minutely regulated from above. Officers, even captains of Her Majesty's ships, became automata, acquiring life only through orders from a superior. The least threat of independent thought was treated as subversion.

Naval education began at Dartmouth which, in Scott's day, was modelled on the minor Victorian public school. It has been well described by Vice Admiral K. G. B. Dewar, an unusually critical officer, and one of the little band of Naval reformers early in this century. In his words,

> the repressive atmosphere ... checked initiative and self-confidence ... the greater part ot the syllabus was allotted to navigation, mathematics and seamanship. Navigation was taught by Naval instructors who had no practical experience of navigating a ship ... The ... syllabus ... omitted the study and use of the English language. This was particularly unfortunate, for the efficiency of Naval administration often depends on the powers of clear expression ...
>
> Although the instruction methods were not calculated to stir up the interest or enthusiasm of the cadets, the majority worked hard because their future seniority depended on the result of the passing-out examination. According to their position on the list, cadets might be rated midshipmen at once or have to wait anything from one to twelve months.
>
> Thus it was not intelligence, character, aptitude for command nor professional zeal that started a young officer on his upward career, but mastery of such subjects as algebra, the binomial theorem or trigonometrical equations.

This almost exactly sums up Scott's Dartmouth years. In July 1883, he passed out seventh in a class of twenty-six, and on August 14th, was rated midshipman. His career then followed the usual pattern. After four years at sea, he obtained automatic promotion to sub-lieutenant, and spent a year at the Royal Naval College, Greenwich, for more theoretical instruction to qualify for lieutenant. He obtained four out of a maximum of five first class certificates, coming out near the top of his class.

He then was appointed to H.M.S. *Amphion*, a cruiser posted to Esquimalt, the Canadian Naval base at Victoria, B.C. on the Pacific Station. She sailed from Devonport round Cape Horn on January 20th, 1889. On April 14th, at Octavia Bay in Colombia, Scott was lent to H.M.S. *Caroline*, a corvette, which was short of officers. He left her on August 1st, at Callao in Peru. A fortnight later he received automatic promotion to lieutenant. After that, he disappears from Naval records for some time.

In fact, after leaving *Caroline*, he appeared in Guatemala City. There, he made the acquaintance of Addison Mizner, the son of the United States Ambassador, Lansing Bond Mizner, 'the original Benjamin

Harrison man'; a wealthy politico from Benicia, near San Francisco. To Addison, a raffish seventeen-year-old, Scott (just turned twenty-one) 'was the nicest, most thoughtful fellow I think I have ever known'. They sailed on the same ship to San Francisco, where Addison had been sent back to school.

Scott was introduced to Addison's sister Mary Ysabel, or Minnie, a somewhat flamboyant character. She was married to Horace Blanchard Chase, a wealthy Chicago businessman settled in San Francisco.

Scott's relations with Minnie became warm enough to detain him in San Francisco and inspire her to write these verses in his address book:

> The night has a thousand eyes,
>   And the day but one;
> Yet the light of the bright world dies,
>   With the dying sun.
>
> The mind has a thousand eyes,
>   And the heart but one;
> Yet the light of a whole life dies,
>   When love is done.

But what happened at this time is obscure. Admiralty records are incomplete; they have almost certainly been pruned. There is the hint of an irregular trip home, the protection of a superior officer, and a cover-up. None of it is particularly remarkable. For the reputation of the Service, young officers were periodically got out of scrapes. The two indisputable facts in this case are that Minnie's verses, with their heavy intimation of the end of the affair, are dated March 20th, 1890, and on March 24th the log book of *Amphion* records Scott's return on board at Esquimalt, having apparently been adrift for the past eight months. It is an unexplained gap in his career. He was at any rate in a state of considerable emotional turmoil, as this suggests:

After many more or less futile attempts I again decide on starting a diary ... The greatest of men have deplored the want of power of expression. Lytton in a preface to a novel has uttered the restraint of this limitation very eloquently (tho' in making up for understanding what he cannot write, the eminent novelist often writes what he does not understand) ... How much have I often felt the restriction ... It is in face of such difficulties that I commence to control my pen ... even as an ordinary gentleman should ... there seems too a growing fear of my own thoughts; at times too they almost frighten me ... It is only given to us cold, slowly-wrought natures to feel this dreary, deadly tightening at the heart ... How can I bear it? I write of the future, of the hopes of being more worthy, but shall I ever be? ... No one will ever see these words, therefore I may freely write, 'What does it all mean?'

There is little outside testimony to what lay behind this; few eye-witness accounts survive of Scott up to the age of thirty and beyond. Scott was ignored by his service contemporaries. Many of his shipmates became senior officers; some wrote their memoirs. He figures in few even after he became famous; often he was pointedly passed over. He seems enveloped in a conspiracy of silence. This is significant because Naval officers, on the whole, have a keen eye for character. Their memoirs are gossipy, shot with vivid pen portraits. Scott clearly did not make an impression on his brother officers, or perhaps he was under a cloud, or both.

At Esquimalt Scott passed the normal tour of duty at a colonial station, in drills, routine, showing the flag, and being received into the homes of local dignitaries. One of these was Judge Peter O'Reilly, at Victoria.

Scott pursued a decorous flirtation with the judge's daughter, Kathleen. It never became much more. For seventeen years they maintained a sporadic correspondence in which he kept her at arm's length; she probably imagined that he was more interested in her than he really was. Scott, in the words of his sister Grace, 'had a capacity for appearing wholly absorbed in the person he was talking to while all the time he was really quite detached'. In any case, like the other young lieutenants received by the O'Reillys, he was probably more interested in the parents, who entertained the senior Naval officers and thus were a path to useful introductions. Scott felt the need of introductions more than most, for he was now worried about his future and feared he would not rise.

Specialization seemed the remedy. Gunnery was the premier branch, but it attracted the best officers, and Scott sensed his chances there were slim. He chose torpedoes instead.

The torpedo was a new weapon, just coming into service. Specialists were still relatively few. Joining their ranks would enhance prospects of promotion, so Scott applied for a training course. Late in 1890, he left Esquimalt in *Amphion* for the Mediterranean via Hong Kong. Finally, the following June, after some hesitation at the Admiralty, he was told by telegram at Malta that he had been accepted for a course at H.M.S. *Vernon*, the torpedo training school at Portsmouth, starting in October.

The torpedo branch then dealt not only with torpedoes, but with all the electrical installations and the mechanical equipment of a warship except propulsion. This seemed to suit Scott and, at *Vernon*, he showed definite technical leanings. In August 1893, he qualified for torpedo lieutenant with a first-class certificate. Just before, he had been given temporary command of a torpedo boat for manoeuvres and promptly ran her aground in Falmouth harbour. In the measured phrases of

Admiralty reprimand (or praise), 'Due care does not appear to have been exercised ... [Lt. Scott] cautioned to be more attentive in future.'

It was an odd incident in a first command. There is the suggestive image of excellence in theory and deficiencies in practice following hard upon each other. There is the glimpse of an unlucky officer. Scott left *Vernon* with a tiny question mark hanging over him.

At this point, his family suffered upheaval. Mr. Scott had run through his money and, after some trouble, found work as a brewery manager near Bath. 'Outlands' was let. The two older daughters profited by the opportunity to get away on their own, Ettie going on the stage, Rose nursing in Nigeria.

For Scott himself, the change did not affect his career. In the Navy, a private income was not required, at least up to the rank of captain. It was one of the features that made the Navy a resort of impecunious middle-class sons. Living on one's pay was socially acceptable, and that is what Scott had been doing for some time.

Archibald, his younger brother, was a subaltern in the Royal Artillery, and therefore differently circumstanced. In the Army, at least in a fashionable regiment or a distinguished corps, officers were expected to have private means. Mr. Scott had made Archibald an allowance; this now ceased. Archibald also promptly went out to Nigeria, where pay was higher, and joined the Lagos Constabulary. It is not clear whether it was solely the money that sent him to West Africa, or whether, like his two sisters, he seized the opportunity to get away from their mother.

In 1898, Archibald died of typhoid when home on leave. The year before, their father had died. Monsie (Grace), and Kitty, the two daughters still remaining at home, now had to earn their living and went into dressmaking. They all moved to London, together with their mother, and set up house in Royal Hospital Road, Chelsea. At least, as Scott put it, the series of calamities had jerked them out of the 'sleepy hollow' of Plymouth life. The one bright spot on the horizon was that Ettie had married well. Her husband was William Ellison-Macartney, Unionist M.P. for South Antrim, and Parliamentary Secretary to the Admiralty.

Scott was now torpedo lieutenant of H.M.S. *Majestic*, flagship of the Channel Squadron; the same appointment he had held on a succession of cruisers and battleships since leaving *Vernon* five years before. His prospects were not bad. Europe's 'Vigil under Arms', after the Franco-Prussian War, was approaching its violent culmination. The Royal Navy was starting to expand. Officers of Scott's rank and seniority would be in demand. As long as he avoided the grosser forms of incompetence, he could expect a reasonable career. But he was typed as a torpedo specialist. The summit of his profession, the captain on the bridge of a battleship, the admiral commanding a fleet, seemed beyond his reach. The old fear which had driven him to specialize, welled up again. In his own revealing words at the time: 'They may not think me sufficiently good as a general service officer.'

Behind a conventional mask of self-effacement, Scott smouldered with ambition. It was not, however, the kind directed to a particular goal. Although he was by now thirty years old, Scott still seemed somehow uncertain and immature. He possessed an inchoate passion to get on without any definite aim.

Scott had not impressed the captains under whom he had served. In the background lurked mistrust of his capacity to deal with men and ships. Nor could he exploit the discreet nepotism and intrigue which were recognized ways to the top. He was not well born or well connected. He did not (until Ettie married) have Admiralty influence. He lacked the talent that could overcome obstacles of money and birth. In a service rich in characters, not to say eccentrics, he did not stand out. He made little impression on shipmates and superiors. He was unlikely to rise by sheer force of personality. Scott looked for another way to the top.

A nineteenth-century British Naval officer could hardly fail to notice that serving on a Polar expedition frequently meant promotion over the heads of one's contemporaries. The Navy List from the Board of Admiralty downwards bore eloquent testimony to *that*.

After the Napoleonic Wars, there was not much demand on the Royal Navy as a fighting force, and Polar expeditions were taken as a means of usefully employing officers and men. The precedent set by Captain James Cook had turned into tradition, and British Polar exploration was made into what was virtually a Naval preserve. Those who took part were all volunteers. The sought escape from peacetime monotony. They were also in search of promotion, for during the middle years of the Pax Britannica, Polar exploration became a surrogate for active service.

Thus arose a distinctively British type, of whom Scott became the most famous example; the Naval officer who took to Polar exploration as part of his ordinary career.

The most pertinacious advocate of this service was the President of the Royal Geographical Society, Sir Clements Markham. He has already appeared fleetingly in Amundsen's story. He was the *deus ex machina* in Scott's life.

*

Solemn bishop's face staring out of a frame of whiskers like a figure in early daguerreotype, Sir Clements Markham was the image of one of the formidable Victorians. The ruling passion of his later years was a long, lone crusade for the revival of British Antarctic exploration, lapsed since Sir James Clark Ross went south in 1839.

Because Nelson, when a young midshipman, had been on an Arctic expedition Sir Clements, in his own words, saw Polar exploration

as a nursery for our seamen, as a school for our future Nelsons, and as affording the best opportunities for distinction to young naval officers in times of peace.

He determined therefore that the Antarctic expedition for which he was working should be a Naval one.

Sir Clements had himself a Naval background. In 1844, at the age of fourteen, he entered the Royal Navy as a cadet, leaving prematurely seven years later, in hazy circumstances. His last Naval service was in the Arctic, on the second Franklin search expedition under Captain Horatio Austin in 1850–51. From this experience, he derived his lifelong passion for Polar exploration and the welfare of the Navy or, more precisely, young Naval officers.

Through Naval friends and relations he was able in the liberal custom of the day to go cruising as their guest on Her Majesty's ships. He was frequently at the Royal Naval College, Greenwich. He cultivated young lieutenants and midshipmen. He received favoured ones at 21, Eccleston Square in Pimlico, his London home. He went by family and appearances. He liked good looks, fresh complexions, nice manners. He was suffused by an ill-disguised feeling of romantic attachment.

Though married, with a daughter, Markham was a homosexual. He sometimes went south to indulge his proclivities safe from criminal prosecution. He liked earthy Sicilian boys. At home, he kept his affairs decorous, or at least discreet.

At the age of thirty he had successfully led an expedition to South America to collect the cinchona plant, the source of quinine, the only known anti-malarial drug, and transplanted it to India. He knew half a dozen languages, was a garrulous conversationalist and a prolific writer on the history of exploration. He had a gift for orotund rhetoric. At the meetings of the R.G.S., in the words of one of its officials

he seemed the embodiment of the romance of Geography; his bosom swelled, and his shirt front billowed out like the topsail of a frigate, and as his voice rose in praise of 'our glorious associates', he often roused a rapturous response.

Sir Clements had the true Victorian evangelizing fervour; a missionary (or a moralizing politician) manqué. 'What new worlds are opened,' a young Naval officer wrote after hearing him speak for the first time. 'How small [everything] seems by the side of great endeavours and heroic sacrifice like Ross, Parry and Franklin.'

It was indeed the glorification of suffering as an ideal that moved Sir Clements to his highest flights of oratory. He saw Polar exploration as an exercise in heroism for heroism's sake. He answered to the spirit of the age.

Self-sacrifice as such was praised as the highest human quality, especially by the Anglican Church. Thus Francis Paget, Dean of Christ Church, Oxford:

> Surely war, like every other form of suffering and misery, has its redeeming element in the beauty and splendour of character men, by God's grace show in it ... men rise themselves and raise others by sacrifice of self, and in war the greatness of self-sacrifice is set before us.

In Polar exploration, this had its exact parallel:

> How nobly those gallant seamen toiled ... sent to travel upon snow and ice, each with 200 pounds to drag ... No man flinched from his work; some of the gallant fellows really died at the drag rope ... but not a murmur arose ... as the weak fell out ... there were always more than enough of volunteers to take their places.

This comes from Captain McClure's search for Franklin in H.M.S. *Investigator* in 1850–54. It was to this era that Sir Clements harked back. He proposed to revive the earlier Naval expeditions of the century; cumbrous, ill-equipped, burdened with numbers, doing their work at an awful cost in suffering.

Such deeds, however, cost the Navy too much money for comfort and, after McClure, in his turn, had to be rescued, official British Polar exploration lapsed. It recommenced in 1873, with the cruise of H.M.S. *Challenger*, a Naval survey vessel, which was allowed to enter Antarctic waters, the first powered vessel to do so. In 1875–76, *Challenger*'s commander, Captain Sir George Nares, R.N., led a Naval expedition which attempted to reach the North Pole via Smith Sound, the channel between America and Greenland, and reached a new 'Furthest North' of 83°20'. But the expedition was an expensive débâcle. Its methods were outmoded. Men went down like ninepins from scurvy. On his return, Nares had to face what amounted to a court martial. Official interest in Polar exploration once more lapsed.

By the time Clements Markham was elected President of the R.G.S. in 1893 with power at last to achieve his aims, he had been overtaken by events. The same international tension that enhanced Scott's prospects of advancement, hampered Sir Clements' crusade. With conflict in the air, the Admiralty scorned side-shows round the Poles. Not even the patriotic fervour of Queen Victoria's Diamond Jubilee in 1897 dented official obduracy. But, whether the Navy wished or no, Sir Clements was determined to arrange a supply of heroes. Since his ambition for a grand Naval expedition was to be denied him, he settled in the end for the next best thing; a private expedition with a Naval crew.

Sir Clements now set about raising money. He persuaded the Royal Society to join forces with the R.G.S., hoping that their 'great name' as the august doyen of national academies and official scientific advisers to the Government would appeal to the public. But even with the Royal Society behind him, by the end of 1898, he had only collected £12,000 of the £50,000 wanted: and of that, £5,000 had been subscribed by the R.G.S. This was humiliating. Single-handed, Alfred Harmsworth, the future Lord Northcliffe, had wholly financed the Arctic expedition to Franz Josef Land organized by Major Frederick Jackson,* at a cost of £20,000.

But most galling to Markham was the success of Amundsen's childhood friend, Carsten Borchgrevinck.

Unable to find the backing in Norway for his project of becoming the first man to winter on the Antarctic Continent, Borchgrevink tried his luck in London. In October 1897, Sir George Newnes, another early newspaper baron, gave him £35,000. He had got the money needed before Sir Clements had managed to set in motion his own cumbrous machinery. Borchgrevink, a private citizen, an outsider, an intruder, an adventurer, and a foreigner to boot, had succeeded where all Sir Clements' position and authority had failed. Sir Clements found it hard to forgive Borchgrevink.

Why had Newnes backed this man who walked in from the street, while ignoring Sir Clements' soapy blandishments? Partly it was due to the personality of Sir Clements. He was widely mistrusted, partly from suspicion of his homosexuality, partly because of a deal in bogus Angolan railway shares. Also, he was thought to be after a peerage; too obviously, that is. But ultimately the explanation lay in the nature of the R.G.S. itself.

It was a self-perpetuating clique. Its Polar experts were old 'Arctic' admirals, who had not seen the ice for twenty years or more. The really able men were excluded from the clique, and carefully avoided the R.G.S.

*The Jackson–Harmsworth expedition encountered by Nansen and Johansen after their winter in the hut.

In other words, the R.G.S. was a typical moribund stronghold of institutionalized mediocrity. It was not an enterprise in which the sagacious investor sank his money. Borchgrevink *inspired* altogether more confidence. He might be brash and a bit of a bounder, but at least he had drive and he had recently been to the Antarctic.

Newnes' only stipulation was that the expedition sailed under the British flag. Borchgrevink bought a Norwegian sealer, *Pollux*, renamed her *Southern Cross*, and registered her in London. In all but name, it was a Norwegian expedition. Officers and crew were mostly sealers and whalers from Norway. The technique, based on skis, dogs, smallness and mobility, followed the now familiar Norwegian pattern established by Nansen.

As a concession to Sir George, Borchgrevink took three British subjects: William Colbeck, a merchant officer, Hugh Blackwell Evans, a naturalist, and Louis Bernacchi, an Australian physicist.

Markham refused to have anything to do with what he called 'this disgraceful business'. Like many ageing radicals, he had developed mild *folie de grandeur*. He believed he had a prescriptive right to control Antarctic exploration. He henceforth tried to stop all British expeditions which competed with his own. He bludgeoned their leaders, quarrelled with their benefactors and intrigued as best he could. When he found he could not stop Borchgrevink, he saw to it that the R.G.S. ostentatiously snubbed him.

The historic fact is that Borchgrevink sailed from the Port of London on August 22nd, 1898, while the 'official' expedition was still only a committee and a hope.

On February 17th, Borchgrevink sighted once again the shores of the Antarctic Continent where, as he put it, 'No human being had lived before. Here we would live or die under conditions which were an unopened book for the world.' He landed at Cape Adare, put up a hut and, with nine companions prepared for the first winter ever spent by men on the Antarctic Continent. All the while Sir Clements floundered on, vainly questing for money.

On March 15th, 1899, when Sir Clements' prospects distinctly seemed on the wane, and, as it happened the same day that *Southern Cross* sighted New Zealand on her return from Cape Adare, an offer of assistance providentially appeared. It came from Llewellyn Longstaff, a wealthy London businessman, who, through the Press, had been moved to sympathy. After a meeting with Sir Clements, Mr. Longstaff promised £25,000

At the end of March, Sir Clements triumphantly announced this 'munificient gift'. He now had about £40,000. It was the turn of the tide. On April 10th, Queen Victoria wished the expedition success. The Prince of Wales agreed to be Patron and the Duke of York, Vice Patron. Two months later, A. J. Balfour, First Lord of the Treasury, overturned the official policy of the past twenty years and promised a Parliamentary grant.

It was not private munificence, Sir Clements' pertinacity or even Royal patronage that spurred Mr. Balfour, so much as foreign rivalry. The Reichstag in Berlin had been asked to vote £50,000 for a German Antarctic expedition. In every field – Naval expansion, trade diplomacy, military power – Germany was the looming and aggressive threat. She could not be left unchallenged in Polar exploration. Politics, which for so long had hindered Sir Clements, now helped him.

The Government gave £45,000, with the entirely typical caveat that it must be matched by equal contributions 'from other sources'. Sir Clements persuaded the R.G.S. to vote £5,000 in order to meet the stipulation. At last he was in business.

It is part of the Scott legend that, years before, when he was still a midshipman, Sir Clements had already chosen him to command the future expedition. Sir Clements told the tale himself. He, however, was looking back to put a gloss upon the past.

Autocrat as he was, Sir Clements from the outset had always planned not only to launch the expedition, but to run it according to his own ideas. He had always known it would be years before it sailed, so he had undoubtedly been looking among junior Naval officers for a commander well in advance. He was keenly interested in family background, for he believed in heredity, and thought that Polar explorers were bred.

In 1887 Sir Clements, then Secretary of the R.G.S., and as yet unknighted, went cruising in the West Indies on H.M.S. *Active*, with the Training Squadron. He was the guest of the cousin, Captain (later Vice Admiral Sir) Albert Markham, the Squadron's Commodore, who had been on the Nares Expedition eleven years before and commanded the sledge party that reached the Furthest North – the last time Britain was to hold the record, as it turned out.

In the Training Squadron at the same time as Clements Markham, aboard H.M.S. *Rover*, happened to be Scott, then an eighteen-year-old midshipman. On March 1st, off the island of St Kitts, Markham recorded in his diary that there was

a 'service race' for cutters ... The *Rover*'s boat won (mid-Scott) but the *Calypso*'s (Hyde Parker) held the lead for a long time.

Two days later, at Barbados, Markham attended a dinner at which the guests included 'young Scott from the *Rover*, who won the race at St. Kitts, a charming boy'.

Markham, however, knew many a 'charming boy'. In his exhaustive diaries, he meticulously kept notes of the hundreds of Naval officers he met.

In any case, the predestined post of Antarctic leader had been reserved for Tom Smyth, a midshipman on *Active*. Smyth, not Scott, was the star of Markham's diaries. At one point, forty-two close-written pages were devoted to an encomiastic survey of his career. Indeed, Midshipman Thomas C. Smyth, son of General Smyth, great-grandson of the Duchess of Grafton, and a Walpole to boot, had the character, family and pedigree for which Markham was looking.

Scott's and Markham's paths, however, crossed again. They next met, by chance, on October 18th, 1891, at the London Zoo. Within the next six months there were two further encounters at the Royal Naval College, Greenwich, as brief and fortuitous as the first. They did not meet again until February, 1897. Markham, now Sir Clements Markham, K.C.B., knighted the previous year for services to geography, and President of the R.G.S., was cruising with the Channel Squadron in H.M.S. *Royal Sovereign*. Invited to dine on H.M.S *Empress of India*, he found Scott on board as torpedo lieutenant, a not unlikely coincidence, since Sir Clements, immersed in the tight little world of Naval officers, was always running into 'old friends and acquaintances' as he put it. Their next meeting was two years later, on June 5th, 1899, soon after the announcement of the Antarctic Expedition.

That afternoon, Scott unexpectedly appeared at the Markhams' home in Eccleston Square. Over tea, he volunteered to command the expedition. A week later he was back, Sir Clements recorded blandly, again 'wanting to command the Antarctic Expedition'.

Divided Aims

ON THE FACE of it, nothing could be more improbable. Until now, Scott had shown no interest in snow and ice. He himself said that he had no 'predilection' for Polar exploration. But, as he wrote at the time, he had 'neither rest nor peace to pursue anything but promotion'.

Scott had now been a lieutenant for ten years. He was facing the awesome jump to Commander, the crisis through which every Naval officer had to go.* Automatic promotion by seniority was behind him. Further advance was now by merit alone, or at least special recommendation. Scott was haunted by the lieutenant's nightmare of being left on the shelf.

His first visit to Eccleston Square was on the eve of his thirty-first birthday. He had the anguished sense of time flowing past, and no accomplishment to show. It was not because he was one of the rebels and reformers who dragged the Royal Navy out of its Victorian torpor, antagonizing superiors with unpopular opinions, for Robert Falcon Scott was an orthodox officer; nobody had anything to fear from his ideas. His anxiety was rooted much more in a sense of personal inadequacy and a feeling that even on his own unexceptionable terms as a conformist trying hard to please, he was not well thought of in the Service. Each month the Navy List rubbed in the point with its tale of contemporaries getting on and leaving him behind. The path ahead seemed blocked.

On their fleeting encounters Sir Clements, expatiating on his favourite theme of Polar service as a 'training squadron with double pay and promotion', had planted a seed in Scott's mind. The thought was refreshed by two recent examples at close quarters. Vice Admiral Sir Henry Stephenson, Commander of the Channel Squadron until the beginning of the year, and Captain George LeClerc Egerton, about to take over H.M.S. *Majestic* from Captain Prince Louis of Battenberg, had both been to the Arctic in the Nares expedition. When the Antarctic Expedition was announced, Scott saw in it the much sought passport to promotion.

In retrospect, Scott maintained – against the evidence of Sir

---

* The rank of Lieutenant-commander was introduced into the Navy in 1914. After that, the crisis came between Lieutenant-commander and Commander.

Clements Markham's diary – that he had met Sir Clements by chance in the street and that it was then, in his own words, that he 'learned for the first time that there was such a thing as a prospective Antarctic expedition'. This may be no more than paying lip service to the amateur ideal. The 'prospective Antarctic expedition' was attended by considerable publicity, and Scott is unlikely to have been as ignorant of its existence as he wished to pretend.

For the past few months, since the expedition had become a practical possibility, Sir Clements had been seriously considering the choice of a commander. He had got his money, but he was not sure of getting his officers, at least the kind he wanted. Germany had started building her battle fleet; the Boer War was about to break out; the Pax Britannica was coming to an end; real instead of substitute action was in the offing. First-class officers would not now want to bury themselves in the Polar regions for two or three years; the Navy would be unwilling to let its best men go.

Of all this, Scott was well aware, and it was there he saw his chance. When he entered the high, narrow hallway at Eccleston Square that day in June, 1899, he found Sir Clements – as perhaps he had foreseen – in a vulnerable mood. The right officers were out of reach. Tommy Smyth had disgraced himself (mainly by drink) and dropped out of the running. The post of expedition commander was waiting to be filled.

Sir Clements, rising seventy, believed in youth; being a romantic, he worshipped it. It was a point at which emotion overcame judgment. Like many men of his age, Sir Clements was looking for a protégé through whom he could live vicariously.

Scott was hardly an obvious candidate. Sir Clements demanded the highest social and professional standing in his favourites. An obscure, rather dull torpedo lieutenant with mediocre prospects, the son of a provincial brewer, under the plebeian necessity of living on his pay to boot, was not the kind of officer whom Sir Clements normally sought out. Moreover Sir Clements, who went by appearances, usually preferred blander, epicene good looks to Scott's sensual features. Sir Clements was taken aback by Scott's unsolicited approach.

Scott, however, of whom a companion once said that there was nobody 'man or woman who could be so attractive when he chose', knew how to play up to the susceptibilities of older men, and soon found favour in Sir Clements' eyes. It was a situation in which each saw that he could make use of the other. Scott appeared when there was no other volunteer for command, and secured Sir Clements' fanatical espousal of his claims.

Strictly speaking, it was all unnecessary. The day after his original appearance at Eccleston Square, Scott, without Sir Clements' help, received his first recommendation for promotion and, as he put it, joined 'the ranks of the advancers'. Within three or four years, barring some unspeakable catastrophe, he would be a commander. He had got through the eye of the needle. But Scott wanted more, much more. He was not satisfied with having caught up with his contemporaries, he wanted to leave them behind. He looked beyond the first modest step to Commander, to the four stripes of a Captain and, more distantly, to an admiral's broader acreage of gold. He wanted immediate promotion.

'You must have patience,' Sir Clements admonished him, discerning a fateful propensity to hurry at the wrong time. 'If you are promoted this time [next] year, it will do very well. You will make a great mistake if you do anything at the Admiralty before you get the signal.' Scott was 'to do nothing until October beyond making interest with the Naval officers on the Joint Committee'.

The R.G.S. had now entered into a coalition with the Royal Society, not only to collect money but to run the expedition. The Joint Committee managed its affairs, 'a very ponderous machine', as Sir Clements put it, of twenty-eight members, drawn equally from both Societies. Among them were eleven Naval officers, mostly old 'Arctic' Admirals. A sub-committee of ten Naval officers would choose the commander of the expedition, hence Sir Clements' advice to Scott about 'making interest'.

After four decades in the ruling circles of the R.G.S., Sir Clements had a working knowledge of jobbery and gerrymandering. He knew that his finger must not be seen in this particular pie. He advised Scott to proceed as if acting entirely on his own. Scott had to 'square' Vice Admiral A. H. Markham, Sir Clements' cousin; he was to get Admiral Sir Leopold McClintock on his side. 'Your sister Mrs. Macartney knows him', and so on.

At this point, in fact, there was no certainty of getting any Naval officers at all. A few months later the Boer War broke out; the international horizon was more then usually clouded, and every available man, as the Admiralty explained, was needed at his post. More to the point, the Government did not want to get involved; if they stopped at money, they could, if need be, wash their hands of the affair; with men, they would be saddled with responsibility. While Scott was 'making interest', therefore, Sir Clements nagged persistently at the Government. In April, 1900, George (later Viscount) Goschen, the First Lord of the Admiralty, finally capitulated to the extent of promising two officers, doubtless seeing this as a cheap way of ridding himself of Sir Clements' attentions.

In the meanwhile, Sir Clements, through tactful intermediaries, had nobbled Lord Walter Kerr, the First Sea Lord, and Admiral Douglas, Second Sea Lord, who would actually name the officers. Amongst others, Sir Clements used Scott's brother-in-law, William Ellison-Macartney.

Macartney took advantage of his position as Parliamentary Secretary to the Admiralty and saw both Douglas and Lord Walter. He wrote to reassure Scott that it was 'quite settled that you should go ... Mr. Goschen has agreed to a Commander and Lieutenant, and you are to be the former, so I take it your promotion is all right'.

Lord Walter had been persuaded to appoint Scott to command the expedition, with Lieutenant Charles Rawson Royds, also chosen by Sir Clements, as his assistant.

Royds had been one of the first to volunteer, approaching Sir Clements two months before Scott. Royds was genuinely interested in Polar exploration. This, together with the right kind of good looks, and the fact that he was the nephew of Wyatt Rawson, who had been on the Nares expedition, was enough to make Sir Clements decide that 'he should be one of the Antarctic heroes'.

The Naval officers on the Joint Committee assumed that they had been appointed to select a commander. They now discovered that they had been co-opted merely to rubber-stamp Sir Clements' nominees, for his hand was not entirely indiscernible. 'Clements meddles re Scott', as Vice Admiral Markham had succinctly noted in the margin of a letter from his cousin.

There welled up a compact, sometimes virulent, opposition, which went beyond the usual chagrin at finding that someone else's favourite was getting in. The Victorian Navy was the home of violent characters and monumental nepotism; but this kind of delicate machination, with its hint of political influence, transgressed the acceptable limits of gentlemanly jobbery. Worse; it was being dragooned by an outsider. And Scott's manifest deficiencies also played a part;

> All experience must be purchased [wrote Captain Mostyn Field, with unconscious prophecy], and if an officer inexperienced in these matters be appointed, the price will be paid in time and material, neither of which can be afforded on an Antarctic Expedition ... the Commanding officer should have every trick of the trade at his fingers ends, and must not attain this knowledge at the expense of the work he has in hand.

Captain Field expressed the feelings of many Naval officers on the Joint Committee. There was among them considerable hostility to

Scott. He seemed to have a black mark against his name. Rear Admiral Sir William Wharton, the Hydrographer (chief surveyor) of the Navy, clearly mistrusted him. Sir William had been one of the few English authorities to support Nansen's plans for the drift of the *Fram* against the pooh-poohings of the old 'Arctic' admirals, and he had some understanding of Polar exploration.

But the admirals and captains, not to mention the scientists of the Royal Society, were no match for Sir Clements on the warpath. By a combination of quick footwork and sheer effrontery he got his way. On Friday, May 25th, 1900, the full Joint Committee as he put it, 'most fully confirmed a foregone conclusion', and Scott was appointed Commander of the National Antarctic Expedition.

Captain George LeClerc Egerton, Scott's commanding officer on H.M.S. *Majestic*, who had known him on H.M.S. *Vernon* some years before, was strangely tepid when asked for a recommendation. 'No officer having previous knowledge of Arctic or Antarctic work being forthcoming,' he wrote, 'I am at a loss to name any officer who is likely to be more suitable.' Of Royds, by contrast, one of his captains had written that he was 'one in a thousand and if I had to select a man from the whole navy to follow me into action or to spend an arctic winter with, I should certainly choose Royds'.

On June 30th, Scott was promoted Commander. Sooner than he otherwise might have expected, he had achieved the coveted third stripe of gold braid on his arm: Polar exploration was, after all, a path to 'double pay and promotion'.

A year after volunteering for command Scott was still astonishingly ignorant of Polar exploration. He had done very little reading on the subject. He was entirely in the hands of Sir Clements Markham.

Sir Clements was clinging to methods long outmoded. He contemptuously dismissed Amundsen's model, Dr. John Rae. He ignored contemporary British Polar travellers like Sir Martin Conway, who made the first crossing of Spitsbergen. Sir Martin was an accomplished exponent of the small private expedition, besides being a good mountaineer and experienced on ice. He had the quality of leadership, and would have been an ornament to the national enterprise. He was not even asked to join.

Sir Clements had amassed £90,000*, the largest sum yet collected for Polar exploration. It was seven times the cost of the whole *Belgica* expedition. It was enough to have a ship specially built.

*£1,500,000 or $3,000,000 in present terms.

A wooden ship was needed; but in Britain the art of building large wooden ships was dying. The capacity to build them for the ice lingered among a few Scottish yards specializing in Arctic whalers. Instead of trusting to such expertise, Sir Clements prepared an uneasy compromise. He ordered his ship from a Dundee yard, but got an Admiralty Naval architect, W. E. Smith, to design her. Smith had no experience of Polar vessels. Crass technical defects were built into the ship, a curious parallel with British Naval construction at the time.

Although official British exploration had lapsed since the Nares Arctic expedition of 1875–76, Sir Clements Markham, with ossified insularity, disparaged progress abroad, preferring homely obsolescence to foreign efficiency. It was almost inevitable that he should display a violent and irrational aversion to dogs as draught animals. Sir Clements had never driven dogs; except for one brief sledge trip on the Franklin search expedition which ended his Naval service, almost fifty years before, he had no practical Polar experience at all. His opinions were the product of theory and emotion. Dogs, he said in a telling passage, were 'useful to Greenland Eskimos and Siberians', the implication being that they were somehow degrading to Englishmen. He advocated instead the grotesquely outmoded system of man-hauling.

In August 1899, two months after Scott volunteered to command the expedition, Sir Clements sent him a paper he was to read at the Seventh International Geographical Congress in Berlin in September. It contained this passage:

In recent times much reliance has been placed upon dogs for Arctic travelling. Yet nothing has been done with them to be compared with what men have achieved without dogs. Indeed, only one journey of considerable length has ever been performed, in the Arctic regions, with dogs   that by Mr. Peary across the inland ice of Greenland. But he would have perished without the resources of the country, and all his dogs, but one, died, owing to overwork, or were killed to feed the others. It is a very cruel system.

At the Congress, Nansen got up and answered:

I have tried with and without dogs; in Greenland I had no dogs; then in the Arctic I used dogs, and I find that with dogs it is easier ... I agree it is cruel to take dogs; but it is also cruel to overload a human being with work. Likewise, it is cruel to kill dogs. But at home, we kill animals as well ...

This did not appeal to Sir Clements: 'The discussion after my paper,' as he put it, 'was of no value.' Sir Clements had been misled by the achievement of man-hauling on the Franklin searches, half a century before. He was fond of extolling the then Lieutenant Leopold McClintock 'who, without the aid of dogs, was away in a tent for one hundred and five days and travelled over 1328 miles'. The issue was further obscured by the failure of dogs on the Nares expedition; mainly because the British officers did not understand them.

Sir Clements, however, ignored the experience of an earlier generation of British explorers. In the 1820s, Sir Edward Parry in the Canadian Arctic had successfully learned from the Eskimos the use of dogs and shown the way ahead. Parry was indeed the father of modern sledge travelling. But it was abroad that his lessons were mostly learned. Nansen, for example, freely acknowledged what he owed to him. At home, in official exploration, the all too familiar sequel was stagnation and retrogression.

When Nansen said that 'to do everything with human beings causes much work and much suffering' he was denouncing culpable stupidity; but to Sir Clements the squandering of human effort was the expression of an ideal. One aspect of the English romantic movement was to equate suffering with achievement. There was a virtue in doing things the hard way. Contemporary drawings show British bluejackets straining in serried ranks before grotesquely overladen sledges, like soldiers marching into battle; humbly heroic figures overcoming the power of Nature by brute force and sheer grit. Dogs interfered with this vision; they made things seem too easy. That really was their crime.

This feeling also played a part in Sir Clements' bias against skis. Nothing, he declared, could compare with the British bluejacket plodding through the snow on his own two feet. Sir Clements had never seen skis in use.

It is a paradox that Englishmen, who pioneered skiing in the Alps, should have neglected it in the Polar regions. Of course English skiing was downhill and a sport; in its original form as transport across country it was neglected and misunderstood. Sir Clements' adviser on the subject was D. M. Crichton-Somerville, an Englishman living in Norway. To Crichton-Somerville, skis were 'over-rated' as a means of transport. In the Antarctic,

> They would be useful for ... light work over soft snow ... I have been accustomed to ski since 1877 ... but should never think of using them if I had to drag anything after me – that would be well nigh an impossibility – or of wearing them on firm snow, for which they are not suited.

This flew in the face of all experience. But it was what Sir Clements chose to believe. It was the origin of another fatal misconception.

*

Scott assumed his duties with the expedition in September, 1900. Sir Clements was then in Norway, taking his annual cure for gout at Larvig Spa. He wrote to Scott, insisting that he join him in a visit to Nansen at Christiania.

In the words of Knud Rasmussen, the great Danish Polar explorer, Nansen had become 'like a John the Baptist. [His] blessing on an expedition was like a baptism, an inauguration, an accolade of knighthood .' A visit to him was obligatory for aspiring Polar explorers. In practical terms, Nansen had made Christiana into a centre for the manufacture and supply of sledges, skis, sleeping bags, and all the impedimenta of Polar travel. These were virtually unobtainable in England.*

So, on October 8th, Scott duly arrived as bidden in Christiania. Nansen, as he wrote to his mother, he found 'quite a great man'. Nansen, however, did not quite know what to make of Scott, with his tensed figure, his permanent shadow of a frown, and his strange combination of uncertainty and self-satisfaction.

Few of those who approached Nansen had been so ignorant or ill advised. Out of charity, he devoted some time to lecturing Scott on the elements of snow travel. Scott, hardly having seen snow, had to grapple with the problem theoretically. Nansen did his best to overcome Scott's received and outdated opinions, and succeeded to the extent of persuading him to take some dogs and skis.

Unfortunately, although skiers were now going over to the modern system of two sticks, Nansen obstinately clung to the obsolescent style of the single stick, and it was this prejudice which he explained to Scott. Since Scott had never seen anyone on skis, he had to imagine how they were used as best he might, and accept what Nansen said.

Talking to experts, Scott proposed to learn by theory in a week or two what Amundsen had taken a decade of practice to acquire. He kept a notebook of what he was told. Nansen, for example, advised him to obtain foreign oceanographical thermometers suggesting that 'the want of exactitude & progress in English instrument makers is directly due to the lack of those qualities in English public offices'. But, wrote Scott,

What was principally brought to my notice & serious consideration is That the crew is ridiculously large in the eyes of all foreigners. *The crew must be largely reduced.*

In the same notebook, Scott revealed a curious limitation. There was in Christiania at the time the Duke of Savoy, fresh from leading an

---

*It is a telling point that the most important advance in expedition equipment for a decade, the Primus stove (the first device efficiently to burn paraffin) was a Swedish invention.

Italian expedition which happened to have attained a new Furthest North of 86°31′, beating by seventeen miles Nansen's six-year-old record, the closest anyone had yet come to either Pole of the earth and, incidentally, validating once more the use of dogs. Scott, however, remarking that the Duke had 'nice manners', decided that there was 'not much to be learned here'. Away from the influence of Nansen's overwhelming personality, Scott seemed to close his mind to the experience of Polar explorers; perhaps from a streak of obstinacy, but sometimes it was almost as if he were jealous.

Thus, Scott's sole recorded comment on Borchgrevink was that Nansen called him a 'fraud'. The two Norwegians had quarrelled and Borchgrevink had been rather rude. Nonetheless, he had opened Antarctic land exploration. He had returned to civilization in March, having become the first man to winter on the Antarctic continent, and the first to land on the Ross Ice Barrier, at the inlet to the east discovered by James Clark Ross sixty years before. There, Borchgrevink set up a record for the Furthest South, 78°50′, and opened the race for the South Pole. More, he had shown the way ahead. He had set his record with dogs and skis, and proved that both could be used in the south as they had been in the north. His historic accomplishment was to show that the Barrier was not a barrier but a highway to the South. As a pioneer effort it was not bad, but Scott was unimpressed.

He was equally unimpressed by Colin Archer, *Fram*'s designer, and possibly the greatest living authority on Polar vessels. 'Rather wasted time', was his verdict on a visit, arranged by Nansen. The trouble here seems to have been that Scott was unable to penetrate Archer's unassuming manner to see the qualities lying underneath.

Behind his interviewing and note-taking, Scott gives the impression of not really wanting to learn, as if he were guided by the unofficial Royal Naval motto that 'There is nothing the Navy cannot do'. Like most of his brother officers at the time, he really scorned careful preparation, at heart believing only in common sense and improvisation when the time came.

Scott had to find time for various social functions, at one of which he confessed himself 'much interested' in Mrs. Reusch, the wife of the President of the Norwegian Geographical Society, because she was an artist. Nansen introduced him to '"Grieg" (composer)' as he put it in his notebook. As a Royal Naval officer Scott was made much of, a handicap, perhaps, for a beginner who had come to learn.

After ten days in Christiania Scott – again at Sir Clements Markham's bidding – went to Copenhagen to interview Beauvais, Nansen's pemmican supplier. Thence he continued to Berlin, in order to investigate the

German Antarctic expedition which, under Erich von Drygalski, one of the Professors of Geography at Berlin University, was to leave at about the same time as the British. Drygalski was going to the regions facing the Indian Ocean, while Scott was bound for the Ross Sea, in another quarter of the continent.

On the train, Scott read *Through the First Antarctic Night*, Dr. Frederick A. Cook's account of the *Belgica* expedition, just published. 'They must be a poor lot,' was his sole comment.

In Berlin, Scott was disabused of further complacency. The Germans were ahead and better organized. Thoroughly alarmed, he returned to London, going straight from Liverpool Street Station to the Royal Geographical Society's rooms at 1, Savile Row, where he saw Sir Clements Markham, and 'fully impressed him with our backwardness'.

Not only the Germans were in the field. The Swedes were preparing an expedition to Graham Land under Otto Nordenskjöld. As things stood, both were likely to leave before the British.

An edifice of sub-committees was partly – but not wholly – responsible for the backwardness of British preparations. In Berlin, what impressed Scott was that Drygalski 'has emancipated himself from all control. He has refused to be subject to any order.' If a Prussian professor could do this, why not a Commander in the Royal Navy? It was the example of Drygalski that now inspired Scott to take command of the whole expedition instead of remaining its paid servant. To push forward the work he now demanded, and got, what amounted to full, independent, executive powers, with only Sir Clements above him.

Since Scott had been forced on the expedition, the Royal Geographical Society, or rather Sir Clements Markham, and the Royal Society had been at loggerheads. The Royal Society had assumed that Scott would merely be the captain of the ship, the technical consultant, as it were, to get the expedition to the Antarctic and back again. Since this was a scientific enterprise, the Royal Society assumed a scientist would be in charge. Professor J. W. Gregory was appointed to the post. He would lead the landing party.

Gregory, then thirty-six years old, was a Londoner, recently appointed to the Chair of Geology at Melbourne University. He was, in that order, a mountaineer, an explorer and a distinguished geologist. He had done the classic Alpine climbs; he was practised on ice slopes and glacier work. He had been with Sir Martin Conway on the first crossing of Spitsbergen. He had grasped the principles of Polar travel. Dogs, he wrote in his plan for the expedition, were essential, because

every extra pound of food that we can carry will enable us to go four miles further South. Secondly, one cannot expect men who are harnessed to heavy sledges to keep sufficiently alert mentally to ... solve the new problems that will be presented to them.

This was prophetic. Gregory had forebodings about Scott. He thought Scott 'a bad organizer, and that he was trying to get all the glory of the show ... that Scott's slack methods would land us in some holes.' Gregory did not want a Naval captain. He wanted a whaling skipper with Newfoundland and Norwegian sailors for their familiarity with pack ice. He wanted a landing party 'as small as possible', with Swiss mountain guides for glacier and climbing. He aimed to travel fast, with plenty of dogs. The landing party were to practise ice work and skiing in Switzerland before departure. Compared with what was otherwise being proposed, it was a model of percipience and sanity. It was in fact the only plan worthy of the name in a torrent of verbose generalities. It could have got the British first to the South Pole. It was not so very different from the methods of the eventual victor. But it had to remain a tantalizing might-have-been.

Sir Clements could not stomach the idea of anyone but a Naval officer being in command, anywhere. He manoeuvred Gregory into resigning, thus depriving the expedition of its only first-class talent.

The consequences were to go far beyond this particular enterprise. Sir Clements Markham had changed the course of British Polar exploration. Had Gregory got his way, scientists and civilians would have taken over, and a breath of fresh air would have entered. Sir Clements upheld Naval domination and ensured, at a critical time, the rule of regimented mediocrity.

Sir Clements, however, did not go quite unchallenged. Alfred Harmsworth (later Lord Northcliffe) had given the expedition £5,000, on condition that two of his nominees were appointed; a safeguard for his investment, as it were. He selected Albert Armitage and Dr. Reginald Koettlitz, who had spent three years in the Arctic with the Jackson–Harmsworth expedition. They were definitely outside the R.G.S. clique, and when Sir Clements objected, Harmsworth answered that Koettlitz's

best testimonial is the fact that the men all came back in better health than that in which they started ... Nobody except myself knows what [Armitage] went through ... His sense of duty ... developed to a degree I never hitherto encountered ...

Armitage was a merchant officer with the P. & O. line. Besides his Arctic experience, he was a good navigator and ship handler. He was made second in command.

In spite of their experience, Scott wanted neither Koettlitz nor Armitage. He also tried to get rid of Charles Royds. He resented having men imposed on him, and felt entitled to choose his own since he was, after all, supposed to be in command. The organizers, however, still saw him as their paid servant, and were in a position to call the tune. Scott was now obliged to accept a young merchant officer from the Union Castle Line called Ernest Shackleton.

An Irishman from Co. Kildare, Shackleton, like Scott, had no particular bent for Polar exploration but, like him, wanted to get on. Each, in his way, was an adventurer. Chance showed Shackleton the Antarctic as a path to fame. He met Mr. Longstaff's son on a troopship going out to South Africa at the beginning of the Boer War, and got an introduction to his father. Mr. Longstaff, impressed by Shackleton's buccaneering eloquence, recommended him for the expedition: as the chief benefactor he could not be denied.

With so many appointments thrust upon him, Scott got his own way where he could. He used a medical technicality to remove Dr. (later Sir) George Simpson, a rising meteorologist to whom he had taken a personal dislike. On the other hand, when a Royal Society nominee, Dr. Edward Wilson, was declared unfit because of tuberculotic scars on one lung, Scott quashed the medical report to take him.

There was chance over Wilson's as over Shackleton's appointment. One of the organizers choosing the scientific staff, Dr. Philip Sclater, President of the Zoological Society, saw Wilson at the London Zoo, painting birds for an illustrated magazine. Sclater was looking for an assistant doctor to double as zoologist under Koettlitz and, seeing in Wilson a competent scientific illustrator, asked him to apply for the post.

The son of a Cheltenham doctor, Wilson had just taken his medical degree at Gonville and Caius College, Cambridge. He had been delayed by pulmonary tuberculosis, which sent him to sanatoriums in Norway and the Swiss Alps. He had no particular interest in Polar exploration; he seemed uninterested in practising medicine, either. Dr. Sclater relieved him of the necessity of choice, appealing to a passive, fatalistic, perhaps drifting streak in his nature.

But Wilson took no initiative. It was his uncle, Major-General Charles Wilson, on the Council of the R.G.S., who approached Sir Clements Markham and arranged an interview. Scott recognized something congenial in Wilson and insisted on taking him whatever the doctors said.

Another fresh Cambridge graduate, Hartley Ferrar, went as geologist; Thomas Vere Hodgson, curator of the Plymouth Museum, was taken as marine biologist. Dr. Simpson's successor, also proving uncongenial to Scott, was removed on another medical technicality. Sir Clements now took a hand, and appointed as physicist Louis Bernacchi, who had been with Borchgrevink. (Sir Clements' vendetta against Borchgrevink did not extend to his men).

Scott's preoccupation now was getting Naval officers and crew, having, as he put it, 'grave doubts as to my own ability to deal with any other class of men'. The Admiralty, justifiably afraid of involvement in an enterprise over which they had no control, originally limited the Naval contingent to Scott and Royds. Sir Clements, however, had extracted further concessions. Scott was able to take Lieutenant Michael Barne, and Engineer Lieutenant Reginald Skelton, old shipmates from H.M.S. *Majestic*. He was also allowed about twenty petty officers and ratings, selected by officers he knew. It was not quite enough, and Scott had to man his ship with a mixed crew of Naval and merchant seamen. Given the antagonism between the two Services at the time, and their wholly different outlooks, it was a risky compromise.

Besides the Germans and the Swedes two other nations were now also on their way to the Antarctic. William Spiers Bruce, an Edinburgh naturalist, was organizing a rival Scottish National expedition to the Weddell Sea. In France, Dr. Jean Charcot, who thought that his country ought also to be represented in the Antarctic rush, was preparing to go to the West Coast of Graham Land. With five expeditions making for the south, Scott had competition enough.

Bruce had spent seven years in the Arctic and Antarctic fitting himself for his task. Charcot went to Jan Mayen Island in the Barents Sea on a training cruise. During the winter of 1900–01, Scott, too, ought to have been acquiring the elements of snow craft and learning how to ski in Norway or the Alps. Instead, he stayed in London to supervise the paperwork.

The expedition had a full-time secretary, Cyril Longhurst, the son of a doctor, an ex-public schoolboy, and a future distinguished civil servant.* Scott, however, did not quite trust Longhurst, because he was not only another of Sir Clements' nominees, but one of Sir Clements' homosexual attachments into the bargain. Scott felt justified in staying close to the expedition offices in Burlington Gardens. When there was trouble during the building of the ship, however, the yard manager acidly remarked that it 'might have been avoided, had Captain Scott [sic] devoted one half hour to me when I had expressly come up for that purpose'.

Scott, enjoying what he called the 'greater dignity' of a Commander's

*Assistant Secretary to the Committee of Imperial Defence.

rank, was in fact spending some time on the social round. He was also keeping watch on the seats of power. For the latter he had good reason. He still faced mistrust of his abilities, and had to fight off attempts to remove him. He was burdened by committees and intrigues. Nansen was one of the few whom Scott trusted to relieve his feelings:

> Whilst I have been trying to carry out the equipment ... on the precepts you taught me in Norway, a committee of 32 scientific men have been quarrelling as to where the Expedition is to go! & what it is to do! 'too many cooks spoil the broth' and too many men on a committee are 'the devil'!!

Scott was involved in another of the running fights between Sir Clements and the Royal Society.

Sir Clements (and Scott) wanted the ship to winter in the ice for no other reason than that it was the heroic thing to do, and had usually been the case in the rather different conditions of the north. The Royal Society and the Admiralty were very sensibly against it. It seemed a gross waste of money to immobilize a ship equipped for oceanographical work. It would also introduce uncertainty. *Belgica* had been a warning of the risks. 'Did any misfortune occur,' Captain Tizard wrote to Sir Clements, 'you would hardly be able to forgive yourself.' Borchgrevink had, once and for all, set the pattern: the ship ought to land the wintering party, return to civilization for the winter and come back the next season. That it was Borchgrevink who had done so, was enough to condemn it in Sir Clements' eyes.

Sir Clements was now thoroughly suspect, and influential members of his own R.G.S. approached the Royal Society for a 'stop Markham' campaign. Sir William Huggins, President of the Royal Society, wanted to stop the Government grant to prevent the ship wintering. Sir Clements overcame them all.

Because of muddles and delays, preparations had to be rushed and obtaining dogs had been left until late. It was Armitage who saved the day. On the Jackson–Harmsworth expedition, he had met a Scots Polar enthusiast, D. W. Wilton, who lived in Russia, knew Siberia, and was a practised skier and dog driver. He now asked Wilton to find some dogs. Wilton knew that Trontheim, the Russian of Norwegian descent who had got Nansen's dogs, was collecting some hundred or so in Siberia for an American expedition. He persuaded Trontheim to add his modest order of twenty-five, bring the whole pack to Archangel, and let him have first choice. Wilton offered to join Scott as dog driver, but was refused. Thus Scott bought dogs, but went south without anybody who knew how to work them.

The dogs were sent out separately to join Scott in Australia. They were trans-shipped in London and quartered in the London Zoo for the first ten days of July. Scott did not make the time to go and see them. There was another curious incident. Although Scott was told that he could obtain all the butter he needed in Australia or New Zealand, he insisted on buying it in Denmark, and carrying it all through the tropics, because, it seems, Nansen had taken Danish butter to the Arctic.

On March 21st, the expedition ship was launched by Sir Clements Markham's wife. Sir Clements, after careful consideration, chose the name *Discovery*, sixth in a line going back to the sixteenth century. Early in August, she went to the Isle of Wight for her send off.

It was Cowes Week; a very public, indeed, a Royal occasion; one of the first of the new reign. Queen Victoria had died in January, and Edward VII was now on the throne. It was the opening summer of the short Edwardian age, the glorious spree before Armageddon, with what John Buchan called 'a vulgar display of wealth, and a rastaquouere [a foreign adventurer's] craze for luxury'. It was at any rate luxurious. *Discovery*, black, squat and workaday, anchored among a glittering fleet of sleek, white, gilt and mahogany yachts. Admirals and people in society came to see Scott off; a novel experience he quietly enjoyed. His mother and sisters were also there to say goodbye: 'a sad time indeed,' he remarked, 'but the womenfolk are always brave'. The King came on board to inspect the ship and presented Scott with the insignia of the M.V.O.

Naval officers and ratings were in full uniform. Armitage and Shackleton appeared as R.N.R. lieutenants. The civilians were pressed into a Naval semblance by monkey jackets and yachting caps. Sir Clements Markham surveyed the scene with justifiable pride. It was, after all, nearly the Naval expedition on which he had set his heart. Thus had three decades of effort been crowned with achievement. The only blemish was the ensign at the stern; blue and second best. Scott had been made a member of the Harwich Yacht Club. This entitled him to fly the Blue Ensign, instead of the humble Red Ensign, the merchant flag, and allowed *Discovery* to be registered as a yacht, exempting her from the tiresome regulations of the Board of Trade. Sir Clements had wanted the White Ensign, the Royal Naval flag. But the Admiralty, very reasonably maintaining that *Discovery* was no man o'war, categorically refused. An exception could have been made, but this was a heaven-sent opportunity to spite Sir Clements for all his intrigues and importunities.

At a little before noon on August 6th, *Discovery* sailed from Cowes down the Solent and into the Channel.

You are now opening a new period in Antarctic Exploration [Nansen wrote in a farewell letter to Scott]. That you will make great discoveries on land, I feel certain but I hope also that you will manage to get time and opportunity to make great discoveries in the southern seas, for every sounding and ... water sample ... is new land conquered for science ... And now ... I can give you no better wish than the Eskimo do: 'May you always sail in open water'!

Scott stood on the deck of *Discovery*, not like Amundsen, an insolvent buccaneer, but a Naval officer at the helm of a national enterprise, glistening in new gold braid. He owed it all to Sir Clements Markham: 'Sad to see the last of the Grand old man,' he wrote in his diary as the shores of England slipped astern.

Ten days later, after leaving Madeira, Scott ordered the photograph of Sir Clements in the wardroom to be taken down.

The wide Atlantic had given Scott his first feelings of achievement. He no longer wished to be reminded of his benefactor.

An Antarctic Winter

'THE VOYAGE OUT TO NEW ZEALAND,' wrote Frank Wild, one of *Discovery*'s seamen, in a letter home, 'was neither eventful nor happy.' Discontent was a pervasive theme on board. Command is a brutal touchstone. Not until he has borne its indivisible responsibility does a sea officer know the truth about himself.

In his ten years as a lieutenant, Scott had been sidetracked, as a technical specialist, from the mainstream of executive responsibility. There seemed to be doubts over his capacity for command. Now, he soon showed the evidence of strain. His subordinates observed that he was impatient and easily flustered. He enjoyed no confidence in his person, as distinct from obeisance to his rank.

Scott was lucky, however, in his officers. Armitage had the knack of getting on with the men. Royds was a loyal and capable first lieutenant who saved his captain from some of his worst mistakes. Koettlitz was an accomplished expedition doctor who, amongst other things, while on the Jackson–Harmsworth expedition had made a notable advance in Polar equipment by inventing the pyramid tent* and, the year before sailing on *Discovery*, had gone up the Amazon on a zoological expedition.

Scott, however, went by appearances and, because of an unfortunate manner, dismissed Koettlitz as a 'good-natured duffer'. He repaid Royds with snubs and petty persecution because, as he told Armitage, Royds was 'out to make all he could of the business for his promotion'. Behind this lay jealousy of well-connected brother officers. One of Royds' uncles happened to be Vice Admiral Sir Harry Rawson, who had given Scott his first recommendation for promotion to Commander. After quarrelling with Scott, George Murray, the scientific director, left the expedition at the Cape.

To make matters worse, *Discovery* turned out to be a sluggish sailer. She had been taken off to the other end of the world without trials, and her engines proved to be inefficient, burning too much coal. She made only six knots. Somewhere in the middle of the Atlantic, it

---

*The advantages being ease in pitching and lower wind resistance.

dawned on Scott that this would mean an extra three weeks on the voyage to New Zealand and a corresponding delay in reaching the ice. At Royds' suggestion, Scott decided to omit a planned stop at Melbourne and go straight to Lyttelton, New Zealand, from Cape Town. This involved tons of equipment and supplies being sent on, and the diversion of the dogs, who were travelling out separately. All of which, in turn, meant a flurry of cables from the Cape.

But all this was minor irritation by the side of *Discovery*'s leak. Most wooden ships make water, especially when new; but this was something else. After leaving Madeira Scott was alarmed to find the holds awash. 'To tell the truth,' Royds wrote, 'I am pleased, as ever since the ship got to London, I have spoken about the leak, and have been laughed at for my reports.' When the ship was dry-docked at Lyttelton, the workmanship below the waterline proved to be conscienceless. Seams were loose. The leak came from holes bored too big for some through-bolts in the keel. Instead of being plugged, the fault was hidden by washers, which let the water stream through. Ironwork was criminally poor; spars had carried away in light winds when the parrels broke. *Discovery*'s designer explained that none of this was extraordinary. Shipyard workers could not be trusted, for it was 'impossible to get each individual workman to take a proper view of the responsibility of his work', words that have a familiar ring.

After three weeks at Lyttelton being repaired and restowed, *Discovery* sailed on December 21st now, in Hodgson's words,

> bunged up. From the wardroom skylight aft she is paved with coal bags, 25 dogs amidships and 50 sheep astern; it is a splendid steeplechase from one end of the ship to the other ...

As the ship left harbour, a sailor fell to his death climbing the mainmast when he was drunk.

In a farewell letter to Nansen, Scott wrote:

> The Expedition has a Crew with little knowledge and no experience except such as pertains to the sea and its moods.
> It seems that if success is to attend us it will be like the successes of our army, due to the rank and file.
> Moreover I am distinctly conscious of want of plan · I have a few nebulous ideas centreing round the main object, to push from the known to the unknown, but I am quite prepared to find that such imaginings of inexperience are impracticable and that hasty and possibly ill conceived plans must be made on the spot.
> Thoughts such as these cannot but show me how very much I am removed from the illustrious men who have led successful polar ventures hitherto.

Not that I feel despondent, but face to face with the work I cannot but feel a lively sense of my own shortcomings ...

I send you a last assurance that I do not pin my faith or fortune to Geographical Discovery – but fully appreciate the great Scientific discoveries that await the explorer in paths that have already been trodden.

Scott first saw Antarctica on January 8th, 1902. Through the limpid air of high latitudes, the ice-clad summits of Mount Sabine and the Admiralty Range glittered in the midnight sun like a cluster of rock crystal, almost a hundred miles away. But it was not until January 29th, after touching at Cape Adare, and following in the tracks of Borchgrevink as far as the inlet where he landed on the Ross Ice Barrier, that *Discovery* entered virgin waters. On January 30th, her logbook tells the tale:

4.30 p.m. Stood into a bay. Hills plainly seen inland. 5.50. Observed land over ice cap. 6.45 Observed bare rock projecting through snow capped hills.

This was the discovery of King Edward VII Land (King Edward VII Peninsula today). It established the eastern end of the Barrier. It was the first Antarctic discovery of the twentieth century. 'A unique sort of feeling,' Shackleton remarked, 'to look on land that has never been seen by human eyes before.' It was the last quarter of the world where this experience was easily to be had. Antarctica was a blank on the map, broken by sporadic landfalls. The interior was totally unknown.

Mildly intoxicated by the sensations of discovery, Scott pushed eastwards to add miles to the map. He was rashly plunging into one of the most dangerous parts of the whole Ross Sea, with treacherous, swirling pack ice.

Early on February 1st, Royds came on deck to find Shackleton 'explaining to the Captain that we were going round in a circle'. They were embayed in sea ice with a hint of rafting floes encircled by a ring of virtually indistinguishable icebergs. It was not the first time that Scott, in his ignorance of ice, had got the ship into a trap. With some difficulty Royds managed to convince Scott, who seemed to be in a state bordering on panic, that Shackleton was right, and extricated *Discovery* from danger. Scott now precipitately retreated, making for the west again.

The same day, A. B. Thomas Williamson observed that

this monotonous idea of scrubbing the decks every morning in the Antarctic, with the temperature far below freezing point, is something terrible; it seems as though they cannot forget the Navy idea or commandment (thou shalt not miss scrubbing decks no matter under what circumstances,) ... as soon as you turn the water on it is frozen and they have to come along with shovels to pick the ice up which the water has made.

The sailors were not only depressed by unnecessary routine, they felt uninformed and nervous. No one had bothered to tell them where they were going, nor for how long. Only now for the first time did Scott tell the officers his intentions. They were elaborate and diffuse; but the nub was that *Discovery* would winter in the Antarctic, and head westwards in search of harbour.

On the way Scott landed on the Barrier in a bay near Borchgrevink's inlet, and sent up a captive balloon, to make the first flight in the Antarctic. It was, in Wilson's words,

a great function ... some 20 or 30 hydrogen cylinders were laid near, the fixings attached and the balloon filled. The Captain, knowing nothing whatever about the business, insisted on going up first and through no fault of his own came back safely ... The whole ballooning business seems ... an exceedingly dangerous amusement. There is one man who is supposed to know all about it, who has had a week's instruction ... He was not the one to go up.

From the air, the Barrier swept uninterruptedly to the horizon, in long, endless waves. It was, as Borchgrevink had said, the highway to the south. The surface was hard, wind-packed snow with patches of drift. Skelton wrote:

I have an idea that a motor car, driven by petroleum, could be constructed to do very good work on [the Barrier] ... of course the design would have to be greatly different from ordinary cars especially in the matter of wheels, and the body would have to be a van to use as a hut   precautions would have to be taken in case of breakdown to take sledges, and the car could drag a large supply of oil and with depots laid out at intervals, I believe 5 or 600 miles each way could be covered   that is of course over the surface we saw   in all probability it does not extend that distance   if it did the pole could be reached.

This is one of the first recorded suggestions of motor transport in the Antarctic. It was half a century before its time; not until 1958 did Dr. Vivian Fuchs and Edmund Hillary reach the South Pole by Sno-cat; another generation of technology was needed to overcome Polar conditions. But Skelton had seen; and he planted a seed in Scott's mind.

Like schoolboys on a holiday, officers and men spread over the surroundings; for many, it was their first contact with snow. Williamson followed Ferrar to look for land, and was 'away 4 hours, covering about 10 miles altogether, not so bad for my first experience on Skis. All's well.' Later the same day (February 3rd) Williamson joined Armitage, Bernacchi and three seamen in an overnight excursion to the south. The dogs remained tethered on the ship, while the men hauled their own sledge. They slept crammed into a tent made for three, going without warm food, because nobody had learned to use the Primus stove. However, they returned safely, having covered thirty miles, in Williamson's words,

therefore beating Borchgrevink's record [for the Furthest South] and gaining the honour of holding the record for this year, and which we hope to knock spots off next season, but by that time, I expect we shall see many changes, with dark and stormy nights to contaminate (sic) with.

On February 4th, after twenty-four hours, they left what Williamson called 'Discovery Nook' but what later was officially named Balloon Bight, and continued westwards towards winter quarters.

Sir Clements Markham had ordained Robertson Bay on the coast of South Victoria Land as winter quarters. But Scott had also consulted Hugh Robert Mill.

Mill, a well-known geographer and former R.G.S. Librarian, cordially disliked Sir Clements Markham. He was unconnected officially with the expedition. That, partly, may have been why Scott asked his advice. Scott wanted to know the best point from which to penetrate the interior of the Antarctic continent. Considering the scanty evidence, it was a formidable brief. Mill advised

landing ... at the head of McMurdo Bay on the ground that, where the South-running mountains of Victoria Land met the coast running east from Mount Erebus, there was sure to be an important valley to serve as access to the interior.

Scott ditched Sir Clements, listened to Mill, and headed for McMurdo Bay. On February 8th, *Discovery* rounded a headland, entered the bay which so far had only been seen at a distance and, in Royds' words,

We made the great discovery that Mts. Erebus and Terror form an island ... and that as far as eye could see the way was open to the South on good ice.

McMurdo was no bay; it was McMurdo Sound.

At the head of the Sound, where the open water lapped at the foot of the ice, under Erebus, towering high with its frozen cataracts and smoking plume, Scott found his winter haven. It was a shallow cove sheltered in most directions from ice pressure. It was near the Barrier where it debouched through an archipelago of nunataks into the sea.

'So here we are,' as Williamson put it, 'doomed for at least 12 months and probably more.' The first notable event at winter quarters was that Brett, the cook, was put in irons, not for incompetence, but insubordination. A civilian shipped from New Zealand, he did not understand Naval discipline. Where discipline was concerned, Scott had no sense of humour. The offender twice escaped and was finally chained on deck to the windlass where, says Scott, 'Eight hours brought him to his senses and a condition of whining humility'.

Next, the hut was erected. It had been supplied on the assumption that a landing party would be left while the ship returned to civilization for the winter. It would now be used as a storeroom and emergency shelter. It had been ordered in Australia; a bungalow, with a sun verandah, supported by many posts sunk deep into the soil. It was admirably adapted to Australia. It was less suitable for Antarctica, where the ground is perennially frozen hard as rock – the so called permafrost. Such, in little things, was the collective ignorance of the expedition.

It is entirely characteristic, both of the expedition and the Royal Navy at the time, that much money had been spent on equipment, and nothing done about learning how to use it. To Scott, brought up with a belief in the virtues of improvisation, this was perfectly acceptable. He now proposed to turn out Polar travellers in a week or two of uninstructed experiment. While *Discovery* was waiting to be frozen in, he made his first serious attempts on skis. Ford, the officers' steward, acquired a kind of immortality by becoming the first man to break a leg skiing in the Antarctic.

After a few days on skis, Scott was dogmatically asserting that they were 'certainly of great assistance to travelling on the level and for a slight incline ... but they will be of little use [for] dragging and some sort of slight snow shoe must be devised in the winter'. He seems to have forgotten all that Nansen had told him and had apparently not read Nansen's *First Crossing of Greenland*, then (as now) one of the classics both of skiing and Polar exploration. It had been in circulation in English for a decade.

> For those who understand how to use them [Nansen wrote], ski are ...
> superior, even to haul with ... For 19 days on end we moved on our ski
> from early morning to late at night ... [covering] 350 miles.

A message with *Discovery*'s position now had to be taken to a prearranged rendezvous at Cape Crozier. Without it, a relief ship would be unlikely to find her, for no one yet knew where she was. This viatal task was given to Royds.

Cape Crozier was at the eastern end of Ross Island, as it had been named, a mere forty miles away. But to Scott it was a major undertaking. After a month ashore, he still had made no attempt to organize systematic training. Royds was casually given some dogs, and told to learn how to run them on the way. He was also given Barne, Koettlitz, Skelton and eight sailors, with more or less the same instructions. Except for Koettlitz, they were all absolute beginners.

The dogs refused to work; the men had to pull the sledges themselves. Each man had been left to teach himself to ski then allowed to choose whether to take skis on the journey or not. A debate of rising acrimony was waged as the party stumbled knee-deep through the snow, like lost souls in Dante's *Inferno*. The anti-skiing faction was in the majority; only Royds, Koettlitz and Skelton were on skis. In the words of a seaman,

> they could get along much better on them than on foot ... It was very much regretted that we had not all brought 'ski' ... We could only pull a few hundred yards at a time and as soon as the leaders cried out 'spell ho!' we at once stretched ourselves on the snow – panting and hot, although the temperature was below zero.

In the end Royds, considering Barne (anti-ski), dogs and ratings equally useless sent them all back to the ship, while he led the pro-skiing party on. First, however, they had to discover whether a man could, in fact, haul a sledge on skis. So they camped for a day to experiment. Skelton, as he put it,

> was awfully surprised at the ease with which we dragged the sledge as I always considered it impractical to pull any load with skis – but it appears they are first-rate hauling gear.

As a setting for a ski school the southern slopes of Mount Terror, towering ten thousand feet in cold majesty above their heads, growling with avalanches, never seen by human eyes before, was undeniably impressive. 'We got on famously with our ski,' Skelton recorded, 'and went along steadily up hill and down dale.' Royds a little later was not quite so rhapsodic:

> We have had to stop so many times on account of ski's clogging and upsetting one. Awful going, real bullock's work [man-hauling].

Still, both belong to early efforts on skis, and they covered their distances. But in the end, they were defeated. The Barrier, flowing northwards to the sea, pressed up against Cape Crozier in splintered waves like breakers frozen in a storm. Ignorance of simple ice craft stopped Royds at this elementary obstacle. Inexperienced and untaught, he was forced to turn back in sight of the beach.

The same shortcoming on Barne's return party killed a seaman called

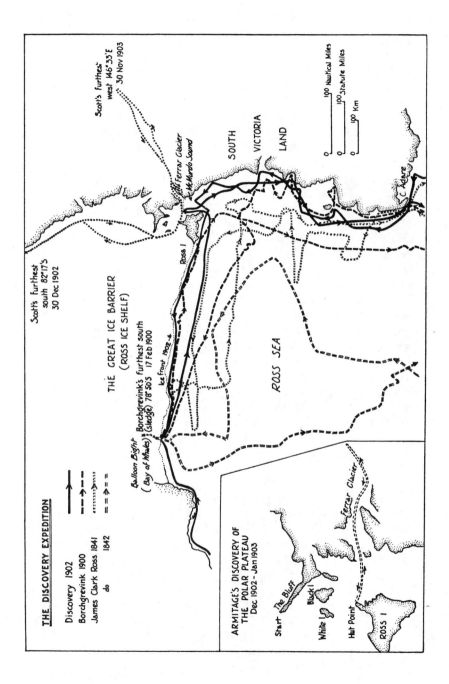

THE DISCOVERY EXPEDITION

Discovery 1902
Borchgrevink 1900
James Clark Ross 1841
  do   1842

Scott's furthest west 146°33'E 30 Nov 1903

Scott's furthest south 82°17'S 30 Dec 1902

SOUTH VICTORIA LAND

C. Adare

Mt Ferrar Glacier
McMurdo Sound

Ross I

THE GREAT ICE BARRIER
(ROSS ICE SHELF)

Ice Front 1902

ROSS SEA

Balloon Bight
(Bay of Whales)

Borchgrevink's furthest south (sledge) 78°50'S 17 Feb 1900

100 Nautical Miles
100 Statute Miles
100 Km

ARMITAGE'S DISCOVERY OF THE POLAR PLATEAU
Dec 1902 - Jan 1903

Start
The Bluff
Black I
White I
Ferrar Glacier
Hut Point
ROSS I

Vince, who fell over an ice cliff in a blizzard. 'All hands despondent,' as one of the seamen put it. 'Captain Scott showing deep feeling.' Scott was glum for several days as he counted the cost of the Cape Crozier expedition. Besides the death of Vince, half a dozen others had been incapacitated by frostbite, and a dog had been lost. 'The responsibility,' Scott wrote in his diary, 'must rest with the officer in charge. [Barne].' Scott did not consider how he might have prevented the disaster by proper training; his instincts were to evade responsibility and shift the blame.

Since landing in Antarctica, Scott himself had kept close to the ship, while sending his subordinates out to make the first experiments in sledge travel. After Royds returned from Cape Crozier, he finally made his own first attempt. This was a journey on to the Barrier to lay a depot for the next season's work. Scott left Royds, Koettlitz and Skelton behind, however, although they were by now his most experienced Antarctic travellers, and proceeded to repeat their mistakes. He went, without skis, hauling side by side with the dogs. It was Cape Crozier *da capo*. The dogs refused to pull; the men floundered in the snow. For good measure, the thermometer descended to the lower depths of the forties and fifties below zero. Shivering in his sleeping bag, Scott had a foretaste of the Barrier late in March. After three days' struggle for less than ten miles, he saw that the game was up. He dumped his loads and turned tail, arriving back to the ship on April 3rd, to close the season with a pathetic little saga of failure. Such was the outcome of Scott's optimistic hope of making Polar travellers in a week or two.

By the end of March, *Discovery* had frozen in. On April 23rd, the sun disappeared for over a hundred days. Scott prepared to face the third Antarctic winter experienced by man. At 78° South latitude, he was about 500 miles nearer the Pole than Borchgrevink's or de Gerlache's winter station. He was even further south than either of the expeditions with whom he was sharing Antarctica: the Germans under Drygalski beset in *Gauss* off Kaiser Wilhelm II Land, which they had just discovered, and the Swedes under Nordenskjöld on Snow Hill Island in the Weddell Sea. Scott faced the longest Antarctic winter night of all; and his test as an expedition leader.

Although *Discovery* was technically a merchant vessel, Scott, by what he called 'a pleasing fiction', ran her under Naval discipline with rigid segregation of officers and men. This is a far cry from Amundsen's 'little republic' on *Gjøa*, his 'spontaneous discipline' and absence of formal hierarchy and rank. But, besides the fact that Amundsen was leading a small expedition and Scott a large one, each was the product of his society. Given the militarized discipline of the Victorian Navy, and the great divide between wardroom and messdeck, it was logical to maintain it in the snows.

Still there are good and bad exponents of any system. Other British officers had also brought Naval routine to the wilds. But, whatever their failings as explorers, they were often good leaders of men. Sir James Clark Ross could cock a snook at the Admiralty; Parry, the original Pole seeker, kept his companions happy; Franklin, though a tragic bungler, was liked by officers and men. By the standards of his own kind, Scott was found wanting. Because of his personal failings, this was one of the unhappier Polar expeditions.

As Williamson with feeling recorded:

> Fancy all hands being drove on deck on a day like this just because the skipper wants to inspect the mess deck, it's a bit thick you know. Why, one of our men had most of his toes frostbitten whilst waiting for the above mentioned individual to go his cursed rounds as they call it. This and a few more petty items is causing a lot of discontent on the mess deck. (Navy routine again.)

In the words of a steward, life on board was 'very monotonous ... many are short tempered and low spirited'. There was open fighting on the messdeck, partly due to drink.

Among the officers, Royds caught the atmosphere in his diary:

> Wilson said it was going a bit far when [bridge] leads to swearing and quick temper ... the conversation was really against the Captain's behaviour last night. He came into breakfast, and told all hands that he had heard every word of the conversation, and so the barometer is decidedly low.

Skelton recorded in his diary that when an experimental wind generator broke down, Scott went 'raging about in a panic; going for everybody about it'.

The picture that emerges is one of an insecure, unhappy, emotional disciplinarian. It existed side by side with a considerate man who insisted on doing his own washing so as not to overburden his personal servant. There seemed no connection between the two, and it was a rash person who presumed to judge the one Scott by the behaviour of the other. He was a kind of Dr. Jekyll and Mr. Hyde, and he had a heavy vein of irrationality in his make-up.

In any leader, these are uncomfortable defects. In one called upon to deal with the strains of a small isolated community, where gloom, quarrelling, paranoiac resentment and brooding on trifles loom large, they are dangerous flaws.

In Polar expeditions, as in most tight-knit groups, there is usually a process of selecting a natural or psychological leader. It is a conflict akin to the fight for domination within a wolf pack or dog team; a more or less overt challenge to the established, formal leadership. How he deals with this threat to his authority is one of the tests through which most commanders have to go, and upon the outcome depends the cohesion of the group. Amundsen, by his moral strength and sheer force of personality, held the psychological as well as the formal leadership on *Gjøa*. On *Discovery*, Scott was found wanting and Shackleton became the psychological leader.

Forceful, outward going, with a personality that could be felt, Shackleton overshadowed Scott, and, although equally inexperienced in Polar matters, established a moral ascendancy in wardroom and messdeck. To begin with even Scott (to Skelton's amazement) seemed to bow to Shackleton. But it was a dangerous situation, with tension underneath the surface. Scott lacked the strength of character to resolve the conflict. He had not, said Armitage, 'that magnetic quality which could have made me follow him in all things'. It is revealing that Scott needed the rigid Naval hierarchy to assert his authority.

But perhaps Scott's saddest flaw was his isolation. He seemed to be incapable of sensing the psychological undercurrents which rule human behaviour, the understanding and exploitation of which is the heart of leadership. He found it especially difficult to understand men not of his own background. One seaman, for example, whom Scott dismissed as 'simple, ignorant and discontented', Barne, an officer of a different stamp, called 'the most amusing tent mate I have come across ... keeps me in convulsions ... with his dry remarks'.

Scott was so lacking in insight that he could say there was 'not one individual who is not on excellent terms with his messmates', when Ferrar recorded 'a feeling of "Everyone for himself"'; when Wilson was sniping at Koettlitz; 'nothing so nasty in science as some of the people working in it'; Skelton at Shackleton, and he himself had taken a very obvious dislike to Ferrar, once driving him to tears with taunts of cowardice.

Royds was the unsung hero of *Discovery*; in Wilson's words, 'a marvel of patience, [taking] any amount of snubbing from superiors'. He grasped that Scott's isolation was the root of the trouble, and tried to counteract it. Where Scott never spoke to the seamen except at formal inspections, Royds would regularly 'have a yarn' with them. He bridged the gap between wardroom and lower deck. As Wilson put it, he made 'a great difference to the Mess'.

Royds, young as he was, understood how to support, with tact, a weak and unpopular captain, and supply some of the missing fibre of command. It was largely due to him that the morale of *Discovery* was as high as it was. He did more for Scott than he was ever given credit for.

The technical defects of the expedition were mirrored in the ship. No attempt had been made to apply recent lessons in preparing her for the conditions it was known she would meet. In *Fram*, the first modern vessel specifically designed for a Polar winter, the hitherto intractable problems of insulation and ventilation in deep cold had been solved. When *Discovery* was on the drawing board, *Fram*'s first drift had been over for three years, and literature about her freely available. *Discovery*'s designer, however, chose to ignore it all because it was foreign. As Scott put it, he used 'good and well-tried English lines', and contrived to make her notably uncomfortable. Ventilation was bad, with nothing between draught and stuffiness. The stoves smoked. All that separated the living quarters from the unheated space below, was a flimsy deck of single planking. Water froze in the cabins. Bedding was soaked with condensation. 'At the back of the drawers under my bunk,' wrote Wilson, 'are icicles and stalagmites of ice.'

The long winter wore on with scarcely any attempt to remedy the failings which had been so ingloriously revealed by the autumn sledging. At the eleventh hour Scott considered plans for the journeys before him, but stayed in the realms of theory, omitting practical preparations. Skiing and dog-driving were neglected, although much of the time wind and cold were moderate, and there was light enough from moon, stars or the dim glow on the horizon at noon for both to have been practised. Time that might profitably have been spent on learning the elements of Polar travel in which they were so patently defective, was frittered away on moonlight football, academic discussions and amateur theatricals.* An entry in Royds' diary summed it up: 'Had a debate on "The best means of travelling in the Antarctic" ... but having to leave in the middle for a meeting concerning the Nigger Troupe, I missed one or two speakers.'

Time went, too, on another hallowed custom; a magazine. *Discovery*'s was called *The South Polar Times*. Scott wrote for it, one of his contributions being an imaginary newspaper interview after *Discovery*'s return to England. Like most fiction, it contains revealing glimpses of the author.

---

* *Discovery*'s cargo included a full set of stage make-up.

As I approached maturer years, the action of my heart caused my parents some anxiety; on ... examining me ... the doctor observed ... that it seemed to be beating in rhythm with two short words ... South Pole! South Pole! From this moment it became obvious that the words were written there.

This was only half in jest. Scott, in the months of blizzard and cold, under the shimmering streamers of the Aurora Australis, had become a Pole-seeker. He decided that the main enterprise of the summer would be a journey to set a southern record. He would lead it himself. He had vague, optimistic hopes of reaching the Pole itself.

Scott long concealed this; during the winter he became secretive and withdrawn. On June 12th, he called Wilson into his cabin, revealed his plan and asked him to go with him.

Wilson was surprised, as well he might have been. With a shipload of Naval men at his disposal, besides three more or less experienced Polar travellers, Scott had turned to a civilian and a novice. He needed a prop and Wilson filled the bill.

Wilson was born to live in the shadow of other men. That he was outside the Navy, was to Scott his greatest asset. Scott was suspicious of brother officers. Wilson was no threat professionally. He could be trusted not to gossip. Scott already accepted him sufficiently to bow to his advice. Usually Scott treated advice as bordering on mutiny.

Bernacchi, for example, observing the ship's boats put out on to the sea ice for the winter, warned Scott that from what he had seen under Borchgrevink they would probably be frozen in. The result, in his words, 'was an experience I did not care to repeat, for I was told, in no uncertain terms, to attend to my own speciality' and the boats were duly encased in tumuli of ice.

Wilson was a complement to Scott. Scott was an agnostic; Wilson profoundly religious. Scott was pursued by nameless anxieties. In Wilson who, under the Anglican umbrella, was devoted to St. Francis of Assisi, there lurked the thirst for suffering and something close to a death wish that was a Victorian perversion of the Franciscan ideal.

'It is no sin to long to die,' Wilson had once written, adding the rider that 'the sin is in the failure to submit our wills to God to keep us here as long as He wishes.'

Where Scott was short-tempered, Wilson was bitter, and controlled. Wilson provided the calm, patience, detachment, perhaps even the contact with reality that Scott so sorely lacked. In the end, Scott seemed as incomplete without Wilson as Don Quixote without Sancho Panza.

The plan that Scott revealed to Wilson threw Sir Clements Markham overboard. The first whiff of reality had suggested that the heroic charms of man-hauling might well exist chiefly in retrospect. It was to Nansen that Scott now turned. With all the dogs, he proposed getting as far south as he could.

His original intention was to take one companion; Wilson successfully argued for two. Scott then selected Shackleton, because he knew he was Wilson's particular friend. This was another example of sentimentality and defective judgment; it was rash to take a potential rival.

Wilson had become the associate of both Shackleton and Scott. He recognized in the one the psychological as in the other the formal leader of the expedition. Like some doctors and priests, Wilson enjoyed the sense of power over patient and penitent. He gravitated towards the leadership of his little community.

Towards Scott, Wilson was on his guard. With Shackleton he had no reserve. Shackleton (or 'Shackle') is mentioned more in Wilson's diary than anyone else. Wilson loved talking to Shackleton. More openly ambitious than Scott, lively with poetic instincts and a curiosity about men and morals, Shackleton appealed to Wilson, acting as counterpoint to his essentially negative virtues.

Shackleton was 'overjoyed' to hear he was going south. He instantly wanted to turn his restless energy to the project, but Scott told him not to talk about the southern journey with the others, since all plans were still 'private'; not to be divulged for another month.

Most of the winter having been wasted in irrelevant diversions, there was now a rush to be ready in time. The responsibility was by no means Scott's alone. His companions shared his invincible faith in gentlemanly improvisation. The Navy, in the words of Admiral Sir Herbert Richmond, was 'breeding amateur Naval officers'. The study of strategy and tactics was considered almost bad form, chiefly because Nelson was erroneously believed to have triumphed at Trafalgar without a plan of battle. Most officers believed that the old hereditary idea of gallantry and dash would see them through. *Discovery* was offering a scenario familiar in British history.

At the eleventh hour, Scott had to read up Polar literature of which, three years since offering himself for command of *Discovery*, he was, in his own words, still 'woefully ignorant'. For over a year, whilst preparing for the expedition, he had worked in the next street to the Royal Geographical Society, whose incomparable library contained in English all the latest books of Peary, Nansen and the other founders of modern Polar exploration. But Scott, somehow, had not found the time to read these useful works. On board, he did not have much to choose from. Those who selected *Discovery*'s library had made certain he would not be troubled by the latest experience. The medieval charlatan Sir John Mandeville was included, and the records of British Naval expeditions of fifty years before, but not Nansen's *Farthest North* and other modern works.

Scott slaved away at writing out last-minute instructions. There were to be a dozen different journeys besides his own. Instead of allowing each leader independence within general directions, he drafted, Naval fashion, copious and detailed orders leaving little to individual initiative. These orders, as he abundantly made plain, had to be absolutely unquestioningly and literally obeyed. It was an attitude that would eventually cost him dear.

Dog-driving was first seriously considered in August. Fights and other mishaps had reduced the original twenty-five dogs to nineteen. Most of the winter they had languished in their kennels like neglected pets, ill fed and ill cared for. Scott now put Shackleton in charge, and told him to learn how to drive them. Scott believed – seconded enthusiastically by Shackleton – that there was nothing that a British sailor cannot do and that a few weeks of hurried improvisation would produce the necessary skill.

Normally, dog-driving takes at least a year or two of hard practice to learn. Experienced drivers never let a beginner loose in a good team, for he would be almost certain to ruin it. And these beginners were singularly handicapped.

Scott, Wilson and Shackleton all failed to understand dogs; nor, in their heart of hearts, did they believe in them. Scott could not tell whether they wanted 'whip or encouragement, it is doubtful when to use which and what to make of the beasts at all'. Scott often called the dogs 'beasts', almost exclusively referring to them with pity or contempt, a telling pointer to his fundamental estrangement from the animal world.

Scott was horrified at the sledge dog's love of fighting. When he noticed that the breed was capable of friendship, he made the revealing comment that it was 'rather surprising to find even this amount of honour amongst such unscrupulous creatures'. Scott expected dogs to act like human beings instead of trying to understand them as animals. He forced observed facts to fit preconceived ideas, which argues a reluctance to face reality and difficulty in learning from experience.

Amundsen, Peary and all successful exponents of dog-driving learned their technique from contact with Polar peoples, on the principle that centuries of evolution and manifestly successful adaptation must have something to teach. But learning from native cultures (as distinct from observing from above), requires a particular cast of mind which was alien to Scott. He came from a tradition which assumed that civilized man always knew best.

Thus, although he had never been to the Arctic or seen dogs in action, he believed he could improve on the Siberian harnesses with which he had been supplied. Instead of trying to discover how they worked, he spent much of the winter designing from theory a new dog harness; a contrivance of stiff canvas and steel wire like a piece of dockyard tackle, 'guaranteed', in Bernacchi's words, 'to twist up the dogs and chap their hair off in a surprisingly short space of time'. It was characteristically his sole attempt to improve his equipment. When he tried the harness on the dogs, it was a ludicrous fiasco and the original outfit was soon put on again.

After the sun returned on August 22nd, Scott sent out various parties for a hurried bout of training before the summer's exploration began. He himself departed on a last-minute foray to experiment with dog-driving. It was not a success. Impatient and insensitive to the animal mind, he found it hard to get the dogs to work. His main object was to test a theory that dogs ought to be divided into small teams among many sledges, only to make the instructive discovery that this multiplied the opportunity for fighting, since each team behaved like a pack, making war on the next. He could have learned this from Astrup's *With Peary Near the Pole*, and other books he had neglected to read in London.

But it was men, not dogs, who caused the real surprise. After a week or two, scurvy broke out among the sledging parties. 'History,' as Wilson despondently put it, 'is evidently going to repeat itself in the south.' He was referring to the disastrous record of British Naval expeditions in the Arctic; especially that of Nares a quarter of a century before.*

In the prevention of scurvy, Scott on *Discovery* had as little help from established nutritional science as Amundsen on *Gjøa*. It was to be another decade before vitamins were discovered, and more than a quarter of a century before Vitamin C, and hence a specific cure for scurvy, was isolated. The attitude of each man to the scourge lying in wait says a great deal about them. Scott took it much less seriously than Amundsen, although he had the plainest warning from history.

In the Polar regions, scurvy was preeminently the disease of the Royal Navy; a strange postscript to an enlightened era. During the eighteenth century, a Scottish Naval surgeon, James Lind, carried out a remarkable

* See p. 127.

clinical experiment which virtually identified scurvy as a deficiency disease. Captain James Cook applied the results to his voyages of discovery, and pioneered the use of fresh food as a preventative, with citrus fruit as the proven antiscorbutic. He achieved the unheard of result of not losing a single man from scurvy. By the beginning of the nineteenth century, scurvy had been practically eliminated from the Navy, and the drinking of lemon juice made compulsory.

For economy and convenience, the Admiralty then changed over to tinned and preserved foods, leading to a shipboard diet deficient in Vitamin C, the only certain source of which was now the daily dose of lemon juice. This, however, instead of being issued fresh, as Lind and Cook had insisted, was bottled under conditions which rapidly destroyed the vitamin. Also for economy, the Navy changed from European lemons to West Indian limes, with half the Vitamin C content. The outcome was the return of scurvy and the lessons of the previous century were obscured. The true concept of a deficiency disease was buried for a spell, and orthodox medicine went off on a wild goose-chase to fit the observed facts into the fashionable theory of sepsis and asepsis, leaving a later age to honour Lind and Cook as prophets before their time.

Scott accepted official medical theory, wide of the mark as it was. He was in good company. Amundsen was exceptional in his acceptance of useful folk medicine (such as the antiscorbutic property of the cloudberry), and his critical capacity to reject medical fashion. History, however, could have helped Scott, as it helped Amundsen. Scurvy was practically unknown among the private expeditions   both British and foreign – living off the land. There, the proven antiscorbutic was fresh meat. A considerable body of evidence was in print. Scott, in fact, had with him a practical authority on the subject.

Koettlitz had kept the Jackson Harmsworth expedition healthy on fresh meat, and wanted to do the same for Scott. With seal meat strewn in battalions over the ice, Koettlitz proposed to slaughter enough for everyone to have fresh meat daily throughout the winter. Scott forbade him to do so, partly because he disliked Koettlitz, and found it difficult to separate persons from ideas. He gave the somewhat illogical reason that killing many seals, for food, as distinct from a few, for scientific specimens, was 'cruel'. The truth of the matter was, Scott was squeamish and could not stand the sight of blood. As his companions were beginning to understand, he allowed emotion to sway his judgment.

Even though Koettlitz was demonstrably on the right track with his insistence on fresh meat, Scott preferred conventional wisdom. Koettlitz persisted, but he was not born to persuade. After some argument, Scott reluctantly allowed some seals to be slaughtered, but not enough – a typical official compromise. He fell back on the familiar Naval diet of tinned food that had proved so disastrous in the past. The precaution against scurvy was to examine each tin for 'tainted' contents, an essentially irrelevant proceeding.

The upshot was that by midwinter Vitamin C deficiency was rife, one sailor developing plain scurvy. It did not take long on sledging rations – pemmican and patent foods devoid of Vitamin C – to generate scurvy *en masse.*

Scott had to pay doubly for allowing emotion to cloud judgment. With fresh meat for the taking, the dogs had to make do with inadequate biscuits resulting amongst other things in a Vitamin B deficiency. This made them nervous and difficult to control.

Armitage, returning from a trip with scurvy-ridden men, found Scott away. As second in command he took the law into his own hands. He stopped all tinned meat, had plenty of seal slaughtered, ordered it to be served daily – and had the moral authority to enforce the new diet. Under his regime, Brett, the same cook who all winter had been cursed for his ineptitude, suddenly produced palatable food.

Scott, when he came back, was astonished by the improvement. Armitage 'must have tackled … this wretched creature … in just the right way'. Ferrar suggested that the change was accomplished 'chiefly by treating the cook as a cook and not a beast'.

At any rate, Scott had had the point about scurvy and fresh meat proved. For the moment, he now accepted the Koettlitz Armitage diet, and October was devoted to convalescence and feeding up.

The southern journey began on the morning of Sunday, November 2nd. There was a demonstrative send off. Scott, Wilson and Shackleton were photographed with their sledging flags; personal ensigns designed by Sir Clements Markham like the pennants of medieval chivalry.

At ten o'clock, Scott gave the order to depart and, to a chorus of cheers, set off on what one of the seamen called 'the long trail, the lone trail, the outward trail, the darkward trail'.

Scott's Furthest South

As Scott set out, on the other side of the continent the first major sledge journey in the history of Antarctic exploration was coming to an end. This was the traverse of the Larsen Ice Shelf by the leader of the Swedish expedition, Otto Nordenskjöld. Scott, on the other hand, was making the first thrust into the interior.

In this historic journey, Scott revealed many personal failings. Going where none has trod before, especially in the subtle Polar world, needs originality, perception, adaptability, perhaps a touch of art, none of which Scott possessed. He was vacillatory and obtuse. His Naval training had taught him form, routine, discipline, obedience, but stifled independent thought. He lacked the capacity to learn from experience. He revealed an alarming lack of judgment, an interesting example being a point which, with or without Polar experience, he could have grasped: feeding his men.

Although the apprentice of a backward school, Scott accepted modern ideas to the extent of taking dogs and skis. He had neither the foresight nor resolution, however, to prepare himself by acquiring a mastery of either. Having reached the Antarctic uninstructed, he dabbled desultorily in both, but neglected systematic and patient experiment to work out proper techniques for himself. This was not impossible. A seaman on *Discovery* called Dell, also a product of the same rigid Naval discipline, caught young and cast in a mould, equally ignorant of sledge dogs, contrived of his own accord to practise intelligently and make himself into a passable driver with a team running smoothly on the sea ice.

Scott marched off into the unknown, singularly ill prepared. Beyond a hazy hope of reaching the Pole, he had no plan of campaign. With a lordly disregard for his technical insufficiency, he believed that British guts would see him through. He thought that snow and ice could be overcome by brute force. He did not understand the world he had chosen to invade. It was do or die. Scott was setting off for the south in the spirit of Balaclava.

All nineteen dogs were harnessed to a single trace before a cumbrous train of five awkwardly-loaded sledges, the product of Scott's theories, ensuring minimum traction and maximum friction. Floundering through loose snow and slithering over hard, Scott, Shackleton and Wilson laboured to keep up on foot, while their skis were carried on a sledge. They looked like an historical charade, dressed in an outdated Naval style. Instead of the Eskimo anorak or parka adopted by foreign contemporaries, they wore awkward canvas blouses, tight in the wrong places, impeding circulation and giving ineffective defence against the cold, with separate hats and helmets, guaranteed to let in the wind through the joins.

After a few hours, they overtook Barne, who had started three days earlier, man-hauling, to advance supplies for them. Barne and the twelve men with him were all on foot, trudging ankle deep in the snow. On catching up, Scott ordered them on to the skis which, at the last minute, he had decided to bring out on his sledges. Although they had now been in the Antarctic for a whole year, and Royds, Skelton and Koettlitz had shown the way, none had hauled on skis before. Yoked to their laden sledge on skis for the first time, their legs flailed ludicrously, like the wheels of an overloaded locomotive starting, as their skis slipped uselessly backwards. They soon jettisoned the despised implements and, with every sign of equanimity, continued to flounder along on foot, pulling 200 pounds a man, at the rate of a mile an hour.

Finally Scott followed the advice he had given Barne, and tried to ski for himself. But he was setting off to unravel the mysteries of the Antarctic virtually as a beginner and found it hard going. His ignorance of snowcraft meant that the varied forms of snow took him by surprise. He was, for example, astonished by the friction of cold drift snow, 'much different' as he put it in his diary, 'from any met with by travellers in the north'. However, in *The First Crossing of Greenland*, Nansen had clearly described 'drift snow, upon which as is well known, ski as well as sledges glide sluggishly ... it was, as we put it, rough as sand'.

Scott was also handicapped by his equipment. Although skiing was then going through rapid technical development, he kept to the old-fashioned single stick, bindings little more than toestraps, and *finnesko*, soft, slipper-like reindeer fur Lapp boots advocated by Nansen, that made control of the skis difficult and demanded good technique. Scott had early embraced the misconception that skis worked only on a certain kind of soft snow and, when faced with any other, he took them off to flounder along on foot. He was often in trouble from his skis slipping backwards as he tried to push forwards and kick off on the flat. 'Some other footgear wants to be invented,' he announced, calling also for 'some slip preventing arrangement'. In fact, as every skier knew, such already existed, in the shape of fur attached to the soles of the skis, a device known to prehistoric tribesmen, and mentioned by Nansen in *The First Crossing of Greenland*.* Scott, however, had never seen experts ski; he was working from hearsay and theory. Incapable of the specialized interplay of arms, torso and legs that has always been the heart of cross-country skiing, he struggled awkwardly to the south, squandering energy with every step. The interior of the Ross Ice Barrier, never yet beheld by human eye, was hardly the place for a nursery slope.

Scott fared little better with his dogs. He noticed that, with Barne ahead, they raced willingly along, but could not understand why, after Barne had turned back on November 15th, they refused to pull. He plaintively recorded that 'we can't imagine how to get them on better'. He seemed unable to make the connection between Barne being ahead and the dogs' need for a goal in sterile and featureless snowfields. It did not occur to Scott to send someone ahead to reproduce the conditions because he was the prisoner of a preconceived notion that a beast of burden was exclusively driven from behind. A month before, Otto Nordenskjöld, faced with the identical situation under the considerably more trying circumstances of the Larsen Ice Shelf, and as inexperienced with dogs as Scott, did not find it hard to draw the obvious conclusion. 'I went ahead as fast as I could,' he wrote, 'and the dogs had no difficulty following.'

Scott was incapable of understanding the mentality of the dog. Wilson and Shackleton were not much better. They were all poor drivers relying, in the last resort, on brute force. But the dog cannot be driven like a horse or a bullock. He will only serve a master he respects. He will not work for a bully, and he cannot suffer fools gladly. All three men were brought up with the English sentimentality towards the dog as a pet, but they calmly allowed those animals to work while horribly chafed by badly fitted harnesses without doing anything about it. 'Nigger', the leader dog, decided these masters were not worth working for, and early declined to pull his weight.

The animals started off undernourished and in poor condition. All winter they had been fed on a biscuit allowance more suitable for a pet than a working dog. Scott's ignorance of the whole species was such that he did not know that a working dog needs a different diet from a household pet, and that to get him into proper trim it is necessary to feed him up. To cap it all, when the journey started, the dogs were

---

* The forerunner of the modern sealskins used for climbing on skis in alpine terrain. In the Royal Navy there was an apocryphal rubber stamp to reject innovations: N.I.H., 'Not Invented Here'.

suddenly given stockfish instead of biscuits, which meant an abrupt change of diet. At no time did they receive the fat essential for a sledge dog working hard. Moreover, the stockfish had lain in *Discovery's* hold unexamined since delivery from Norway eighteen months before. Having gone through the tropics and suffered heat, damp and bad storage, it was loaded in the original bundles on the sledges. Not surprisingly it was found to have rotted. The dogs consequentially weakened with violent gastro-enteritis.

To add to their woes, Scott tried to force them into a working pattern which suited his own dour, self-punishing temperament. But dogs work in bursts, needing frequent rest. They cannot keep up a steady grind hour after hour. The sum of it all was that the dogs were hungry, tired, unwilling and overloaded. Wrongly handled, they had to be lashed on, yard by yard. It was not long before the men had to get into harness themselves and help.

The journey became a dirge of struggle and setback. For thirty days they relayed; i.e. taking half the loads on for a spell, and returning for the other half. It was enough, said Scott, 'to last a lifetime'. In that time, they made a farcical 109 miles southing, and to do this they had to cover 327 miles, struggling nine or ten hours a day.

The querulous, self-pitying tone in Scott's diary rises to a crescendo, as the sledges stick, and the dogs refuse to pull. Nature, it seems, would never arrange herself to his convenience. The snow was either too hard or too soft; the sun too weak or too strong. Yet Scott was phenomenally lucky with the weather; no blizzards, little wind, moderate temperatures, and the terrain he describes – 'a broad white plain' – is patently made for skis, sledges and dogs. It would be hard to deduce from his diary that he was a discoverer at every step. Just occasionally a hint escapes as, on November 25th, when he wrote that, 'We have at last crossed the 80th parallel and entered that blank space shown on the popular charts.'

On December 10th, Snatcher, the first dog, died from exhaustion and maltreatment, confronting Scott with the possibility of losing all the animals. His requiem for Snatcher was that it 'put a stop to all hope of a high latitude [leaving] us to do the best with what we have got'. It was not entirely the dogs' fault. The unknown mountains appearing on their right, trended south-east across their bows; to cross them almost certainly meant climbing a range higher than the Alps.

Scott was ill-suited to bear the strains of Polar travel, let alone the burden of disappointed hopes. His nerves were soon on edge from the stress of isolation and of an environment to which he was not attuned.

The little irritations of travel from the miseries of snow-blindness to the exasperation of driving dogs, tried him from the start. He was in no state to deal with the tensions of conflicting personality.

Soon after starting, Shackleton accidentally burned a hole in the tent floor while cooking. This made Scott erupt with wrath. The two men were wholly incompatible; the strains of the journey made feelings boil over and any triviality was enough to detonate an explosion.

Taking Shackleton on that journey showed a high degree of obtuseness. He and Scott ought not to have been on the same expedition let alone sharing the same tent. Their suppressed conflict was coming to a head.

One morning, when Wilson and Shackleton were packing the sledges, Scott suddenly shouted to them, 'Come here, you bloody fools.'

They went up to him, and Wilson said quietly, 'Were you speaking to me?'

'No,' said Scott.

'Then it must have been me,' said Shackleton.

He received no answer.

'Right,' said Shackleton. 'You're the worst bloody fool of the lot, and every time you dare to speak to me like that, you'll get it back.'

This was the almost inevitable moment of mutiny. Had it been left to Scott (or Shackleton) the journey would have been broken off then and there. It was Wilson who, by common consent, took over the moral leadership, forced them to patch up their differences, and persuaded them to carry on. It was not because he himself any longer wanted to; in his diary he soon deplored 'this tedious plod to the south simply to beat a southern record'. After his original enthusiasm, that entry says something of his somersault of feeling. But he felt that to turn so soon for such a reason would be a disgrace from which the whole expedition would suffer.

Survival in extreme conditions depends on judgment and intuition. Conflict, suppressed or not, disturbs both. It is an invitation to disaster. Before the tensions within the party, and the defects of Scott's personality, the dangers of the Polar regions paled. Men, as Amundsen liked to say, are the unknown factor in the Antarctic.

Exceptionally fine weather and sunshine favoured Scott. He took these to be the rule, almost his right. In the confused and shifting plans he improvised from day to day, he assumed the best conceivable conditions would continue and left no margin of safety. Thus was revealed the recklessness and collapse of judgment under stress that his superior officers had already discerned. Scott was now blind to everything except a southern record. The lives of all three – Scott, Shackleton and Wilson – depended on Wilson's ability to make him turn back before it was too late; which meant controlling an obstinate man in an irrational state of mind. This was Wilson's burden, besides keeping the peace between Scott and Shackleton, from 80 deg. South.

When Snatcher died, he was experimentally fed to his companions and, having seen (as had Nansen) that dog does indeed eat dog, Scott decided to depot some of his load and

> make a dash south with a month's provisions & without food for the dogs, leaving them to feed on one another ... I have some hope that dieted on themselves they will do better ...

Scott had come far since his first sledge journey seven months before when, as Ferrar ironically observed, 'dogs had to be treated kindly'.

Relaying now ceased. Killing dogs, more or less according to plan, Scott trudged his way south at the rate of seven miles a day. It was not much, but at least the same ground no longer had to be covered three times.

Scott had originally intended to be away for ten weeks. To get another week of southing, he increased this to twelve, reducing rations to eke out his food. Unfortunately, he had planned badly and behaved reck-lessly:

> The somewhat careless way in which we started with our provisions & oil and our savings for an extra week have reduced our present allowance con-siderably & we are really hard pressed.

They were now literally starving; plagued with dreams of food. They were eating less than any Polar explorers since Sir Edward Parry's first Arctic expedition in 1820, a fact of which Scott was perversely proud.

On Christmas Eve, Wilson found that Shackleton and Scott had scurvy. Both displayed the classic symptoms of swollen and inflamed gums. Their diet had contained no fresh food for two months, just pemmican, bacon and patent concentrated foods totally lacking in Vitamin C.

Wilson had seen that things were being run too close. They ought to have turned long before, but Scott had been almost impossible to convince. Disease came as an unanswerable argument. Wilson pressed for an immediate turnabout and race for home. Scott, however, was in an emotional state now, seeing only a southern record at all costs. He was impervious to reason. After some argument, in his words, they came to something like the following conclusion. To push on till the 28th when we should be well over the 82nd parallel, then to turn to the shore & investigate if possible the high & interesting cliff & rock formation that are now abreast of us ...

It was a compromise that Wilson was reluctantly forced to accept. On December 28th, they passed the 82nd parallel, and pitched their southernmost camp the following day at 82°15′ South. A monstrous bergschrund where the Barrier piled up against the land, effectually quashed all thoughts of geologizing.

Scott and Wilson skied on southwards for a mile or two, reaching 82°17′. Shackleton was left behind to look after the dogs. He was not invited to share the distinction of the Furthest South. It was a slight he never forgot.

On December 31st, Scott at last, and none too soon, gave the order to turn for home.

The best of good luck to all of us [wrote Wilson], we don't know anything about the snow surface of the Barrier during the summer. It may be quite different to what it was on the way south. One *must* leave a margin for heavy surfaces, bad travelling, and weather.

The *must* is telling. For one of Wilson's restraint, it implies severe disapproval. Scott had risked his companions' lives for his own ambition. He had even been prepared to take greater risks than he admitted. A very private entry in his navigation notebook indicates that he had been planning to be another fortnight on the march, returning to the first depot from the ship on February 14th; food calculated to last until that same evening and no longer.

He was taken completely by surprise when the weather changed after he turned; and the going became difficult. The mutability of snow, fast one day, sticky the next, caught him off guard, although it had been demonstrated amply for a year. It was all part of his curious lack of foresight and adaptability.

In his diary, Scott revealed how he swung from recklessness to remorse. The day they turned, it was

impossible not to feel some anxiety for the future   it is impossible not to appreciate that we have a shortage of provisions.

And two days later:

It is ludicrous to think of the ease with which we expected to make our return journey in comparison with the struggle which it has become.

Their lives depended on finding their depot, a hundred miles away, with the food to reach home. Like everything else, that too had been left with no margin of safety. The depot was poorly marked by a single flag; a pinpoint in a trackless desert. Scott had fixed it inadequately by bad cross bearings on the uncharted land to the west. He assumed that because he had the best conceivable visibility when taking the observations, it would be the same when he came back. He was naively surprised and vaguely resentful to find that it was not, that it was foggy instead. It does seem amazing that after twenty years in the Navy, having seen wind and weather in all their caprice, he could still lament over the elementary phenomenon of fog.

At a critical moment, the fog lifted, and the depot appeared, a dot, far off, in an unexpected quarter. Had the weather been a little worse, things would have gone ill. A blizzard would almost certainly have killed them. They had no reserves; their food was almost gone.

By now, all three men were suffering from obvious scurvy, with swollen limbs and aching joints. They were hauling the sledge themselves now; in Scott's words, 'Slow, monotonous & tiring, but ... infinitely preferable to driving a team of tired & hungry dogs.' The few surviving dogs, having long since lost all respect for their masters, refused to work, and were allowed to walk by the side of the sledge, in the hope of a pull later on.

But after two days' pulling dog food himself, Scott saw the futility. He ordered Wilson (who usually acted butcher; a brutal business without a gun) to kill Nigger and Jim, the last survivors.

From the depot, the retreat turned into a headlong flight from disaster. Scott, Wilson and Shackleton were all weakening from scurvy and starvation. One blizzard would have finished them. Scott had brought it all on himself by his haphazard and incompetent planning. It is hard to feel sympathy for him, but one can feel sorry for his companions, as for any victims of bad leadership.

To save weight, Scott jettisoned his skis, which he now blamed for his woes, although the real explanation was that he was still unable to use them properly. 'One grows accustomed to steady plodding, even in soft snow,' he reasoned in his diary on January 5th, 'and much of the relief we used to feel on getting on skis at such times is now unnecessary.'

On January 18th, about 100 miles from the ship, Shackleton collapsed with pains in the chest. He had been the weakest and sickest of the three since the scurvy began. With giddiness, breathlessness and coughing up blood, scurvy may not have been his only ailment. He had a mitral murmur: a weakness of the heart usually caused by rheumatic fever in childhood. Normally it may give no trouble, but may do so under stress. On another Polar journey Shackleton had a heart attack.

His collapse was partly due to overwork. He had strained every muscle and fibre, hauling at the sledge. He never spared himself. He had the kind of ardent, demoniac energy which pulled for two. Also, he had a fierce desire to show Scott what he was good for. He felt his predicament keenly.

Long afterwards Shackleton told a story of overhearing Wilson tell Scott outside the tent that he would not last the march, and that he then said to them that he would outlive them both.

'Ten years later,' Shackleton used to say, 'within a mile of the same spot, Wilson and Scott were both dead, and I was still alive.' Whatever the literal truth of this tale, it reflects something that had its roots in that caricature of a Polar journey. By sheer willpower, Shackleton forced himself to carry on, sometimes helping to pull; more often not; but nearly always under his own steam. Such were his passions, and such the tensions within the party, that he construed Scott's orders to avoid strain and overwork, not as well-meant kindness, but as a deliberate attempt to humiliate him.

As dislike or vaguely hostile pity, the conflict persisted. Once too often Scott lost his temper with Shackleton and Wilson had to impose a truce. They could hardly afford the luxury of quarrelling. Scott had led them into manifest danger. He had overrun his supplies. There was every possibility of food running out again before the next depot. Fog and a few warning gales cut down their marches, so that doubts about getting through loomed large. In this crisis, Scott once more was taken unawares by the snow; this time by breakable crust. 'We regret,' wrote Wilson drily after hours breaking through and jarring sore, inflamed, scurvy-ridden joints at every step. 'We regret that we threw away our ski.' But at least he had persuaded Scott not to jettison one pair in case anyone fell ill.

Shackleton owed his life to those skis. Putting them on at the breakable crust, he was supported on the surface instead of sinking through, and thus saved exhaustion he was too ill to bear.

By a neat little irony, it was Shackleton who sighted the next depot. Poor visibility and bad marking had again put them in danger of missing the depot altogether. Their food was all but exhausted. A few hours after arrival, their first real blizzard descended. In Scott's words, 'If all this had happened a day or two ago, the circumstances would have been very different.' They had got through just in time. It was a dress rehearsal for disaster.

At the depot, Shackleton had his worst attack, and again Wilson hardly expected him to survive but again he rallied and, when they reached the ship on February 3rd, he was moving under his own power; the embodiment of his family motto – *Fortitudine Vincimus* – 'By endurance we conquer'.

13

Return of the Discovery

IT WAS THE historical hiatus between the invention of the submarine cable and the advent of wireless. Western man was acquiring the habit of instant global contact. Away from the cablehead, however, he was as of old, adrift in a sea of silence, but with a new and poignant appetite for voices from the outside that he could not as yet assuage.

When Scott returned to *Discovery* it was not only to reach safety by a short head, but to find isolation breached. A relief ship had arrived.

The relief ship was none other than *Morgenen*, the sealer Amundsen had met on his first Arctic voyage ten years before. Sir Clements Markham had gone to Norway for a ship. Renamed *Morning*, *Morgenen* was refitted in London, and in command Sir Clements put William Colbeck. This showed how, once away from the field of his obsessions, Sir Clements was a shrewd old fox.

Colbeck, who had been with Borchgrevink on the *Southern Cross*, was one of the very few people who knew the Ross Sea. A merchant officer from Yorkshire, he was a very fine seaman into the bargain. Seven weeks after leaving New Zealand, he ran *Discovery* to earth, at the end of a meagre trail of messages over five hundred miles of imperfectly charted coastline.

Scott expected to find *Discovery* floating free; instead he found her still firmly beset with five miles of solid ice between her and *Morning*, riding gently to the swell in open waters.

Ten days after his return, it dawned on him that he might not get out that year. He was not overly distressed. It provided a legitimate pretext for disregarding the official orders to return, brought by *Morning*, and following Sir Clements' secret instructions to remain. Scott wanted time to redeem himself.

82° 17′ was not particularly impressive. There was a feeling that the southern journey had been mishandled. The outcome, in Hodgson's words, was rated 'fairly satisfactory ... They seem to have had a far rougher time than they admitted at first.' At home, when comparisons were made with Nansen, the result would seem even less impressive, and out of all proportion to the cost.

'We don't seem to have done much in any one direction,' Scott himself wrote to Scott Keltie. This however was not quite fair. While Scott was in the south, Armitage had led a party to the Western Mountains, and become the first man to reach the Antarctic Ice Cap. He may be called its discoverer. It was a more significant achievement than Scott's, and it was immediately recognized as such. Bernacchi catalogued Armitage's accomplishments in his diary:

A typical [Antartic] glacier followed to its source ... A distance of about 240 miles ... sledged over in a mountainous, glacial region at ... 78 deg. South [reaching] an altitude of ... about 14,500 feet ... accomplished by ... men [with] little or no previous experience of glacial travelling.

Armitage's performance was more impressive than it seems, and he showed himself a better and more balanced leader than Scott. He took no chances. He successfully coped with crevasses and altitude sickness. Koettlitz, a better clinical diagnostician than Wilson, was able to give a warning of incipient scurvy, and Armitage turned while he still had food, energy and health in reserve, although the plateau rolled seductively on to the horizon. He did not get as far as he would have liked, but he brought his men back without misery or accident. His return to *Discovery* was far removed from Scott's theatrical shambles. Unfortunately, it did not make such a good story. 'Adventure,' as the American explorer Vilhjalmur Stefansson liked to say, 'is a sign of incompetence.'

In the middle of February, Scott began preparing for a second winter. He decided to send most of the merchant seamen home because, as he wrote to Admiral Markham, 'it was a mistake to try and mix the merchant service & Naval element ... they have never pulled well together'.

The anathematized cook was, understandably, among the contingent to return and undoubtedly there were some misfits. But it was for Shackleton that Scott reserved the full flood of his bitterness.

Scott, looking for excuses, blamed his mediocre southern latitude on Shackleton's collapse, forgetting that it happened *after* he had turned. Scott had a strange contempt for invalids. He invalided Shackleton home. Shackleton, who took this as a reflection on his manliness, was profoundly distressed. He seemed to have recovered more quickly than Wilson, yet it was Wilson who was staying on. Shackleton turned to Armitage, as second in command, for help.

Having had Shackleton's recovery – at least from scurvy – confirmed by Koettlitz, Armitage tackled Scott who, after some temporizing, said,

'If he does not go back sick, he will go back in disgrace.' Scott apparently had not told Shackleton this to his face. But he had not forgotten Shackleton's mutinous behaviour on the southern journey; nor could he any longer face the challenge posed by the strength and personality radiating from Shackleton. Shackleton was a little naive in believing that Scott could forgive or forget. No leader can tolerate a rival; he must be contained or removed. There was no place for Shackleton and Scott on *Discovery*, and Shackleton had to go.

As Shackleton left *Discovery* for *Morning* on the first stage of his reluctant journey home, he was spontaneously cheered by the crew. It was almost subversion, and interpreted by the officers as such. Shackleton could handle Naval and merchant seamen alike; to Scott, who self-confessedly could only deal with Naval ratings, it was more fuel for the dislike born of a sense of inadequacy.

On March 2nd, *Morning* sailed, seen off by Scott and a few companions. One of her officers was Sub-Lieutenant E. R. G. R. Evans, R.N., the future Admiral Lord Mountevans, who has left a description of the scene, as *Morning* drew away, escorted by whales blowing and curvetting and skuas swooping overhead:

> We ... gazed astern at the little group of men, huddled in pathetic loneliness on the edge of the frozen sea ... We watched till Scott's men vanished out of sight, when poor Shackleton ... broke down altogether and wept ...

When Scott, planning a western journey for the next season, asked Skelton, who had been with Armitage, to come along as guide, Skelton's reaction was that he would 'go there as soon as anywhere else; – not that I particularly want to go anywhere – but of course one must go somewhere'.

In some ways, however, life was better than before. There was less wind. There was no fighting on the messdeck. Scurvy had overcome Scott's scruples about taking seal, so that there was now plenty of fresh meat with better health all round.

But without Shackleton the wardroom was a gloomier place. Lieutenant George Mulock, a Naval officer on *Morning*, who had replaced him, could not fill the gap.

Reading an account of Sverdrup's expedition brought out by *Morning*, Wilson was 'struck at the amount of sledging they did ... his record shows the great value of having plenty of dogs to do the hauling'. To Scott, on the other hand, the failure of the dogs on the southern journey did not suggest shortcomings in himself, but damned the dog for Polar travel. He developed an almost neurotic hatred of the breed for having, as it were, let him down. It reached a pitch that, when puppies were born to some bitches who had not gone south, he ordered a wholesale slaughter because 'it was getting a positive nuisance to see so many of these wretched undersized little beasts for ever gorging themselves on the midden heap'.

With Shackleton gone, conflict centred on Scott and Armitage instead. Scott had hinted to Armitage that, for domestic reasons, he ought to go home on *Morning*. It is a comment on the atmosphere on *Discovery* that, although Scott actually was justified by confidential news about Armitage's wife, Armitage construed it not as kindness but as a devious attempt to get rid of him. He believed that jealousy was the real reason – Scott fearing that he would steal some of the kudos if he stayed. Armitage, in Scott's words, 'didn't rise', and insisted on remaining. Armitage believed that he had antagonized Scott by thwarting designs to turn the expedition into a grand Naval one. All but two of the merchant seamen had been sent home, and he was the sole remaining merchant officer.

Armitage could not be ordered home like the rest because he had guarded against it in his contract. He declined to go because he rightly realized that he would be stigmatized for leaving before the end of the expedition. As it was, he laboured under a sense of grievance, because Scott refused to allow him to make a southern journey the next summer for fear, so he believed, of seeing his own record beaten.

Armitage brooded much that winter. Years later he wrote that he

> found much that was lovable in [Scott's] character, but was quite aware that he would allow nothing to stand in his way, and that he was of a most suspicious nature ... Scott would, apparently, make a great friend of a man, use him and throw him to one side.

He went on to remark that Shackleton, by contrast, 'never forgot a friend'.

By then, Armitage knew that Scott had been loath to give him credit for covering the Antarctic Ice Cap. Scott had played down his achievement in the Press despatch sent home with *Morning* and patronizingly wrote to his mother that Armitage was 'an excellent chap but *entre nous* a little old for the work. [He] was the man who got the stockfish for the dogs.'

This was another step in shifting the blame for the failure of the dogs and the unsatisfactory result of the Southern Journey. In fact, Armitage had got good quality fish in Ålesund, in Norway, with the help of Nansen. He could hardly be blamed for what subsequently happened, since it had been taken out of his hands. But Scott had by now consistently revealed an instinct for evading responsibility for his mistakes.

The second spring came round, and with it another season of sledge travel. The main enterprise was that of Scott, in the steps of Armitage. Armitage, dourly resentful, stayed by order on the ship while Scott proceeded to break a record for the Furthest West.

This journey – like the others – was man-hauling. Scott gloried in it, displaying an appetite for sheer physical exertion, almost as an end in itself. It seemed like a manic reaction to the winter indolence; a love of punishment, a ferocious need perhaps to prove himself.

From the start, the journey bore a familiar stamp. There was a false start caused by sledges breaking down from poor maintenance and inefficient loading. Setting off finally on October 26th, Scott discovered that he had lost the *only* set of navigational tables possessed by the party, and took the chance of pushing on without any.

Following the route pioneered by Armitage up the Ferrar Glacier, Scott climbed to the plateau. Without the restraining presence of Wilson (who had gone to Cape Crozier to visit the Emperor Penguin rookery discovered by Royds; the first of its kind) Scott revealed himself uncurtained to his companions. One of them was Skelton, a blunt and uninhibited diary writer.

Breaking the canons of mountaineering, Scott started off at a rush, as if trying to eclipse Armitage by sheer speed. He was stopped only by gales that kept him tentbound. 'The skipper,' wrote Skelton in a passage, the theme of which was to be all too familiar to Scott's followers, 'gets very impatient under these delays.' Scott drove himself and his men to the limit; dragging 240 pounds each upwards, nine and ten inhuman hours a day.

On November 20th, about 9,000 feet above sea level, Handsley, one of the seamen, collapsed from altitude sickness. It can be quite distressing, but, knowing Scott's intolerance of invalids, Handsley was afraid to own up. Skelton had to tell Scott, going on to say that

> we couldn't go on at that sort of hauling ... that the boatswain [Thomas Feather] was [also] ill only hadn't the moral courage to say so & that we were being overworked, he made a fuss [complaining] of want of candour, but he is not the sort of person to encourage it.

For two days more, Skelton was obliged to continue what he called 'the back-breaking work' of keeping up with Scott. They were now on the plateau, and, having shown Scott the way up he was ordered back with Handsley and Feather. Skelton resignedly told Scott 'it was hard lines to come up here a 2nd time and not get Furthest West – to which he answered that it was hard lines'. And he turned, and got his men safely back to the ship.

With the two apparently fittest seamen, Petty Officer Edgar Evans and Leading Stoker William Lashly, Scott continued to the west. It was a bizarre repetition of the old blunders. Once more, Scott and his companions froze and starved because food and clothing were inadequate. Once more Scott assumed the best possible conditions, to be surprised when they turned for the worse. Once more he was reckless where caution was needed, and overran his supplies. When he turned, on December 1st, it was once again a race for life, with food and fuel running out, and nothing but luck to save him. Once more, his luck held, and all three returned to the ship on Christmas Eve. They had travelled 600 miles in two months, at the cost of hideous toil, dragging the sledge for up to twelve hours at a stretch. Scott, alone, had the double trophy of Furthest South and Furthest West.

> The circumstances were hard [he wrote to Hugh Robert Mill], I cannot find anything in polar history to equal them ... I am rather proud of my journey although as long as I live I never want to revisit the summit of Victoria Land. The conditions were so hard that three of my people couldn't stick it and were sent back.

This was boastful language, specially when so much had depended on luck.

Scott afterwards considered this the best of his journeys. It was at any rate the happiest. It was the only one he made exclusively with long service Naval men, cast in the same mould as himself. He was safe in a familiar hierarchy, supported by the unquestioning respect for his rank upon which he depended for authority.

With everyone reunited at McMurdo Sound, there remained only the tedious wait for the ice to go out.

Before that happened, as A. B. Williamson recorded on January 5th, 1904, '2 ships sighted. Oh, what joy, we all started jumping round like wild men.'

Scott was not quite so pleased. The relief ships – for it was they; *Morning*, and a Dundee whaler called *Terra Nova* – brought peremptory orders from the Admiralty that

> If the 'Discovery' cannot be got out of the ice, you will abandon her and bring your people back ... in the relief ships ... as ... My Lords cannot under existing circumstances consent to the further employment of officers and men of the Royal Navy in the Antarctic Regions.

When Scott had digested the news from home and grasped the reason for two relief ships instead of the one he had only half expected, he was even more depressed.

By letting *Discovery* be frozen in two seasons in a row, he had caused an impressive rumpus. In apocalyptic terms, Sir Clements Markham had appealed for a second relief expedition. He was helped by trouble hanging over Nordenskjöld, whose ship, *Antarctic*, had been crushed in the ice. A search was being hastily organized. Antarctic disaster hung in the air. The organizers of the *Discovery* expedition were accused of extravagance and mismanagement, and Sir Clements' enemies – of whom there were many – saw their opportunity and turned on him. The Royal Society dissociated themselves from the whole affair; the R.G.S. passed a resolution condemning Sir Clements. Major Leonard Darwin, the R.G.S Honorary Secretary (and son of Charles Darwin), intrigued against him.

The upshot of it all was that the Government, after twice refusing help, and accusing the Royal Society and R.G.S. of bad faith, agreed to undertake the relief of *Discovery*. They insisted on full control and the Admiralty demanded that *Morning* be turned over to them. Sir Clements was outraged. He refused to hand over *Morning*, claiming that as he bought her in his name, he had the final say. The R.G.S. had to threaten legal action to force him to comply.

Since Naval officers and men were involved, the Admiralty could not afford to fail. They insisted on two ships, buying and refitting *Terra Nova* in a hurry, no expense spared. Shackleton, by then home again and medically fit, was asked to go as Chief Officer. It would have been a neat revenge on Scott but, wisely for himself, perhaps, he refused.

The Admiralty were not amused by the affair, and blamed Scott for allowing *Discovery* to be frozen in. To add to their displeasure, *Terra Nova* had to be towed by relays of Royal Naval cruisers as far as the Arabian Gulf to reach her rendezvous with *Morning* at Hobart, Tasmania, in time, thus considerably increasing the expense.

Scott settled down to wait until the last possible moment, in the hope of the ice breaking up. Meanwhile, Hodgson had an apoplectic fit, and Whitfield, one of *Discovery*'s stokers, became mildly insane. The atmosphere was sombre.

On February 14th, with hope swiftly waning, the ice for no apparent reason suddenly began to break up. Like an armada leaving port, the floes sailed one after the other out to sea. On the 16th, *Discovery* was free at last, floating again after two years of immobility. As if the

Antarctic were reluctant to unhand her, a storm sprang up at the last moment, driving her on to a reef, but she got off again more or less undamaged. Before finally sailing away, she collided with an ice floe, broke her rudder, her leak reappeared, and her pumps clogged. Scott, in the words of the long-suffering Royds, was 'continually in a panic, just the same as ever, everything expected to be done at once, & rows if nothing is done'.

Out of McMurdo Sound, into the Ross Sea, *Discovery* at last sailed on February 19th and, with her two escorts, shaped a course for New Zealand. On March 5th, she crossed the Antarctic Circle. 'I have hopes,' wrote Royds, 'that I will never cross it again.'

On April 1st, Scott reached Lyttelton, New Zealand, and there received a frigid cable: 'Admiralty congratulates you on safe return.' Allowing *Discovery* to be frozen in was evidently a *very* black mark. It gave Scott doubts about promotion and soured existence. Achievement was not to him its own reward. Unless he could exploit the Antarctic in terms of gold braid, the past two years would go for nought. At least where the Navy was concerned, he was a realist, and he knew that much was against him. Promotion over the heads of his contemporaries, especially of the kind secured through *Discovery*, was not popular in the Service. He had enemies at the Admiralty, particularly Captain Mostyn Field, who had opposed his appointment in the first place. The old doubts about his professional ability would be intensified when the stories of his conduct on *Discovery* filtered through.

But Scott had friends working for him. Sir Clements Markham had his official report sent to the King, with a hint that a cable of appreciation would be acceptable. The King obliged: 'I congratulate you and your gallant crew on your splendid achievements, and I hope to see you all on your return to England.'

When, as Sir Clements had intended, this was published in the Press, he gleefully said that Scott's enemies 'would not dare to spite him ... He stands too high now'. Edward VII was the last monarch under whom Royal patronage counted for something. And a letter from his mother told Scott that his brother-in-law, Sir William Ellison-Macartney, now knighted and Deputy Master of the Mint, was again, under her prompting, using his influence.

But when Scott sailed in *Discovery* on June 8th to go home round Cape Horn, he was still a commander, and worried about it. His place on the captains' list would determine when – or whether – he would get his flag; and what kind: would he end as Rear Admiral, retired; or rise to full Admiral and – who knew – perhaps even First Sea Lord? Another 'Polar' officer, Sir William May, with far less claim to distinction, had done so. The ambition burned through the bland exterior.

I persuade myself that even if I was promoted it is not likely anyone would have thought of sending a wire – I contain my soul in patience, but it is a nuisance having to wait another 2 months for news ...

Promotion did come but only, as Scott feared, when he returned to England. It was pointedly dated September 10th, the day that *Discovery* berthed at Portsmouth; a hint, perhaps, for all to read, that it was due to the Antarctic and not merit as a Naval officer.

Promotion came to Scott just in time. A few months later, Lord Walter Kerr was replaced as First Sea Lord by Admiral Sir John Fisher, who could not have been less sympathetic to Scott or the patrons on whose influence he depended.

It was the opening of the tempestuous reign of the great, hated, lovable 'Jackie' Fisher, who swept down like a tornado and, in six years, dragged the Royal Navy out of its peacetime torpor to turn it into a fighting service. The old ways were swept into the sea. Especially did Sir John scorn Polar service as a school for fighting officers. 'What on earth good accrues from going to the North and South Poles,' he once said, 'I never could understand – no one is going there when they can go to Monte Carlo!'

The *Discovery* expedition especially aroused his antagonism because, as he later said, the money it cost might have been better spent on 'the purchase of a new battleship'. 'It is worse than a crime, it is a blunder', about summed up Sir John's opinion. In spite of promotion, Scott was under a cloud.

Scott was not what Sir John called 'a doer of imperishable deeds'. By his record for the Furthest South, Scott had provided the patriotic accomplishment for which the British were hungering in the twilight of Empire and the bitter aftertaste of the Boer War. But 82° 17′ South latitude was not by itself sensation. It was only the raw material of success. It needed the touch of a Stanley – the impresario of Darkest Africa – or a Nansen to make the transmutation. Lecturing on *Discovery*, Scott found he could not touch his listeners. He did not have presence.

Soon after *Discovery* returned to civilization, *The Times* reviewed *New Land*, the English translation of *Nyt Land*, Otto Sverdrup's book about the second *Fram* expedition.* Comparison was invited between

* See p. 87.

Sverdrup, who had discovered 100,000 square miles of new land with obvious efficiency, and Scott who, with six times as many men, at an eightfold cost, and far more trouble, had not done as much. The expeditions sharing the Antarctic with Scott offered more fruit for comparison. Bruce had discovered Coats Land and added more to the continental coastline than *Discovery*. Charcot's charting of land in the Bellingshausen Sea exceeded both in quantity and quality the slipshod surveying under Scott. Nordenskjöld was a model scientific leader; so was Drygalski.

Sir Clements Markham was driven to complain,

> People do not understand the greatness of [Scott's] achievement. The sledge journeys *without dogs* are quite unequalled. It is a very much easier matter when Peary or Nansen or Sverdrup make dogs drag their things, while they stroll along.

This is a classic statement of the English device – still by no means dead – of explaining away material inferiority by inventing some factitious ideal. It was part of the moralistic approach that bedevilled English public life. But in Polar exploration, at least, the country was interested only in results. Scott had to justify himself.

As the leader of the expedition, he was privileged, indeed, expected, to write a book about it, and requested Naval leave to do so. The Admiralty were only too happy to comply. In Scott, they had a problem on their hands.

He had been away from the Fleet for four years, a long time for any officer, especially at a time of rapid technical development, and, in effect, had been hoisted straight from Lieutenant (Torpedo) to Post Captain. He was of a rank to command a battleship, but by the Navy's own standards, lacked either the experience or the personal qualities to do so. Enjoying Royal patronage, however (a visit to Balmoral emphasized that), he could not be dropped into oblivion. If he went off to write his book, My Lords of the Admiralty could postpone any decision about his future.

Sir Clements Markham lent Scott a room in his house where he could write, away from the attentions of his mother and sisters in their Chelsea home. The outcome was *The Voyage of the 'Discovery'*, published in 1905.

The Voyage of the 'Discovery' was a minor masterpiece of the literature of apologetics. It sowed the seeds of a legend. As *The Seven Pillars of Wisdom* (to which it bears a considerable resemblance) created Lawrence of Arabia, so out of *The Voyage of the 'Discovery'* came Scott of the Antarctic. Scott's salvation was his literary talent.

Exculpation was Scott's theme. He used the device of turning a fault into a virtue. He flaunted his inexperience to be praised for his frankness. He turned his saga of obstinacy, bungling and near-disaster into a stirring tale of heroism against overwhelming odds.

The Voyage of the 'Discovery' is based on what purport to be untouched extracts from the author's diaries. This method attains a degree of immediacy and authenticity difficult to achieve in other literary forms.

The kernel of the book is the great Southern Journey. One of the celebrated passages is that describing the last day's march before reaching the Furthest South. In *The Voyage of the 'Discovery'* the account runs thus:

> *December 27* . . there stood revealed one of the most glorious mountain scenes we have yet witnessed . . . Pelion was heaped on Ossa, and it can be imagined that we pressed the pace to see what would happen next, till the end came in a gloriously sharp double peak crowned with a few flecks of cirrus cloud . . . We have decided that at last we have found something which is fitting to bear the name of him whom we must always the most delight to honour, and 'Mount Markham' it shall be called in memory of the father of the expedition.

The diary actually reads:

> We have had a most interesting day from the spectacular point of view – . . . there appeared . . . a magnificent mountain peak with other noticeable peaks about it. With so much new land and so much new matter for discussion we begin to think that our trip will really find a corner in polar history – If so our hard work and short commons will be repaid.

This kind of elaboration is perfectly legitimate, so long as it does not pretend to be a literal quotation of the original document. But as it stands, it is falsification, the effect of which is deliberately to self-ennoble Scott.

Again, to describe an incident which played a leading rôle in shaping his image, Scott in the book apparently quotes his diary:

> The dogs have done little but they have all walked, except Stripes, who broke down and had to be carried on the sledge; he was quite limp when I picked him up, and his thick coat poorly hides the fact that he is nothing but skin and bone . . .

This led an American critic to write that:

> these heavily burdened men . . . not sure of fighting their way back to the ship . . . loaded the weak animals upon sledges, hoping to save them. Such humanity is unprecedented, I think, in the annals of Polar exploration.

It certainly would have been. The diary itself says:

The dogs on the whole were brighter today with the exception of Stripes, who gave out in the afternoon and had to be carried on the sledge. I fear he must be the next victim — Brownie lasts over tomorrow or three days and others I hope will last longer as the number to be fed diminishes.

The vital entry on December 10th, 'we shall make a dash south ... with a month's provisions and without food for the dogs, leaving them to feed on one another ...' was suppressed altogether from the book. The effect was to pretend that Stripes was being carried out of spontaneous humanity where in reality it was premeditated cannibalism as supper for his friends.

In tampering with the record, Scott was playing to the gallery. Modesty, even if false, was required. Kindness to animals was expected.

There is an unconscious two-edged bite to Scott's remark in *The Voyage of the 'Discovery'* that in sledging 'the fraud must be quickly exposed'. The book is a sustained reworking of reality. Perhaps the subtlest and, in its consequences, the most fateful example of the process is the treatment of Shackleton on the Southern Journey. The book, still pretending to quote the diary, says:

> January 21 [1903] ... we have had a brisk southerly breeze and, setting our sail, got along at a fine rate. For a time Shackleton was carried on the sledges ...

The diary itself, however, runs:

> Shackleton started in his harness but after an hour we put him on the sledge to break the speed when it tended to overrun ...

which is rather different. And a later entry recording that Shackleton went 'on ahead on ski with the compass [to navigate]', was omitted altogether from the book. So were all the references proving that Shackleton fought through to the end. *The Voyage of the 'Discovery'* was written so as to suggest that he broke down completely, becoming a passenger and a drag on the return.

Whether the Scott of the diaries is the real Scott, it would be difficult to say. He is at any rate different from the one who appears in the book. The Scott of the diaries is rash, then rueful; timid and dangerously reckless by turns; palpably lacking in judgment; uncertain, indecisive, confused by emergencies, incapable of learning from experience; totally lacking in foresight, and trusting to luck. The Scott of the book, on the other hand, is the gentlemanly and slightly conceited amateur, making a virtue of inexperience by implying that efficiency and the avoidance of unnecessary danger are somehow unmanly. Both versions have this in common. Their judgment is consistently clouded by emotion; and they inhabit the borderland between illusion and reality.

The two glaring failures of the expedition had been skis and dogs. Discussing skis in *The Voyage of the 'Discovery'*, he suppressed the favourable evidence in his diary to dimiss them with the characteristically phrased opinion, with echoes of Sir Clements Markham, 'that in the Antarctic Regions there is nothing to equal the honest and customary use of one's own legs'.

And about the dogs, this was his conclusion:

> To say that they do not greatly increase the radius of action is absurd; to pretend that they can be worked to this end without pain, suffering and death is equally futile. The question is whether the latter can be justified by the gain, and I think that logically it may be; but the introduction of such sordid necessity must and does rob sledge-travelling of much of its glory. In my mind no journey ever made with dogs can approach the height of that fine conception which is realised when a party of men go forth to face hardships, dangers, and difficulties with their own unaided efforts, and by days and weeks of hard physical labour succeed in solving some problem of the great unknown. Surely in this case the conquest is more nobly and splendidly won.

This is Scott's profession of the heroic delusion; the ultimate justification of man-hauling. It is a paean to adversity and setback as morally desirable; yet another embodiment of the ideal of personal gallantry as an end in itself. The book, for all its flourishes, is a curiously barren one. Much of it is nonsense. All the same, it is literate nonsense. It has unity, style, atmosphere, conviction. *The Voyage of the 'Discovery'* was a considerable literary achievement. With it, Scott had vindicated himself. He had written himself into a rôle; out of his setbacks he had spun the web of an heroic legend.

The Voyage of the 'Discovery' was a success. Almost without exception, the reviews were favourable. And yet, underneath the chorus of praise, there lurks a suspicion of reserve, as if the book somehow left a little nagging doubt.

Away in the Arctic, Amundsen had gone through the North-West Passage and was skiing down the Yukon with the news. He, too, had a book to write but, with another year before him in the wilds, it was not published until 1907, two years later than Scott's. As *The North-West Passage*, the English translation appeared in 1908.

The Times called it 'a worthy record of a memorable achievement'. To *The Anthenaeum*, then the organ of the English literary establishment, Amundsen had 'written with sailorlike simplicity and ... an attractive enthusiasm'. All this is very true, yet as a literary work, *The North-*

West Passage will not stand comparison with *The Voyage of the 'Discovery'*. It is a rough record; a captain's log.

Amundsen was no writer. When he quotes his diaries, he does so faithfully. He is selective – the stolen telegram from Eagle City; a quarrel with Wiik are two examples of omission. But, in what he tells, there is no tampering with the record. A compelling naiveté shines through to disarm the critics. 'Simplicity' and 'sincerity' recur in reviews of the book; words scarcely applied to *The Voyage of the 'Discovery'*.

Amundsen was an individualist, a buccaneer; though a patriot, he was not, like Scott, a public servant, imbued with the team spirit. Yet *The North-West Passage* is the less self-centred book. Partly this is because Amundsen followed the time-honoured practice of letting his men tell their own tales when they had tales of their own to tell. He lets Godfred Hansen tell his own story of the sledge journey to Victoria Land and Hansen gets his due recognition in the reviews. Also, in his own text, Amundsen allows his men to play their proper part, rather than paying lip-service to their deeds. To all this *The Voyage of the 'Discovery'* makes a poor contrast. Scott paints, as Lawrence of Arabia frankly called the *Seven Pillars of Wisdom*, 'a self-regardent picture'. Scott does not allow his followers to tell their own tales; he tells them himself, and does so in such a way as subtly to disparage their achievements in order to enhance his own.

One of the expedition's discoveries was that by Colbeck of two small islands on the first voyage of the *Morning*. This included a landing and survey which, on the rough coasts and turbulent waters of the Antarctic, was a feat of seamanship. Scott dealt with it in a single sentence:

> On December 25th he [Colbeck] crossed the Antarctic Circle and a short way to the south, to his great surprise, discovered some small islands which he has since done me the great honour of naming the Scott Islands.

Colbeck in fact called them after Sir Clements Markham. It is unclear who made the change. It is a tiny but significant incident; Scott was trying to build up an image of himself as a leader engaging the spontaneous respect and affection of all within his orbit.

Armitage was not given the credit he deserved for his discovery of the Antarctic Ice Cap; nor Royds for a rather important piece of exploration.

In the second season, Royds led a party south-east over the Barrier. 'It was a short journey,' Scott casually remarks, 'as it only occupied thirty days.' During those thirty days, Royds happened to reach a point 157 miles from the ship, a good half of what Scott had attained on his Southern Journey, in one-third the time and with rather less misery, man-hauling though they were. It was also a happier effort. Royds had the capacity to inspire and lead: he did not have to drive his men. Finally, it was the pioneer enterprise that showed the Ross Ice Barrier to be a single, extensive and unbroken ice sheet. Scott buried it in four patronizing paragraphs, concealing its true significance. He buried it so well, that later workers in the field, to whom it would have been important, remained unaware of it for at least sixty years.

In *The Voyage of the 'Discovery'*, he obscured the scurvy outbreak. He suppressed Koettlitz's belief in fresh meat as a preventative, confusing if not misrepresenting the incident, in order to evade any suspicion of responsibility.

Scott wished to present himself as a hero battling against the Fates; Amundsen as commanding them. *The Voyage of the 'Discovery'* is romantic, histrionic and, in the last resort, an illusion. *The North-West Passage* is earth-bound to the point of baldness, although it does have humour, which Scott's book so conspicuously lacks. Scott presents a heroic vision, Amundsen keeps a sense of proportion and a firm contact with reality. He, after all, had mastered the Polar environment; Scott, despite his undoubted achievements, had been defeated by it. That was how each emerged from the first expedition that he led.

14

'You shall have Fram'

IN OCTOBER 1906, when Amundsen first saw the Golden Gate and reached San Francisco after the attainment of the North-West Passage, Norway had been independent for little more than a year. Amundsen was the first Norwegian to have achieved anything spectacular since his country separated from Sweden and became a sovereign state.

He was for that reason hurrying home. Nansen, now Norwegian Minister in London, was a pioneer in the use of non-political celebrities for political propaganda. He saw in the conqueror of the North-West Passage a useful diplomatic weapon. Norway's continued existence as an independent country turned on the indulgence of the Great Powers. Amundsen could be used to generate goodwill among their rulers, and hence help Norwegian leaders in their work. Nansen therefore wanted Amundsen back in Europe as soon as possible for the greatest possible effect. Amundsen was accordingly rushing home, although his inclinations were all the other way. He wanted to start immediately on an American lecture tour to strike while the iron was hot. But he was enough of a patriot to obey Nansen's call. Nansen had told the Norwegian authorities that 'they ought to help Amundsen, and see that he is brought home in proper style, for he will be in financial difficulties when he arrives.'

On November 18th, Amundsen and his men returned by mailboat to Norway, landing at Kristiansand, on the south coast. Willy-nilly they were transferred, by Government order, to a warship to sail in state up the fjord to Christiania. There they were met by the same massed bands, cheering crowds, and cannons thundering a royal salute, that had greeted Nansen. Snow was falling as Amundsen and his men stepped ashore on the red carpet laid out on the ceremonial quay, and got into horse-drawn carriages for their triumphant procession through the streets.

After the procession, Amundsen and his men were taken to the balcony of the Grand Hotel – the customary place for celebrities – to acknowledge the plaudits of the multitude.

It was all very different from the gloomy summer's night three years before when Amundsen had slunk away down the fjord like a fugitive. Now he was selected to deliver the oration then traditionally given by the 'man of the hour' before the medieval Akershus Castle in Christiania on May 17th, the Norwegian national day.

May 17th usually brings the breath of spring. On that occasion it was cold, overcast, and, in the words of the French Ambassador, who was present with the diplomatic corps,

> snow began to fall while the explorer of the Polar regions was speaking ... a fact widely remarked at the time ... sometimes he achieved ... a lyric tone, but only for a little while; his emotions [were] expressed with a reserve which, perhaps, increased their power.

Amundsen's address was mostly conventional, faithfully reproducing Norwegian patriotic feeling, with its vein of Nature worship and love of the native soil. But he had something personal to say:

> There is no man or woman so humble that he or she cannot work for the good of the fatherland. In that, we are all equal. The goal is the same, if the means must vary according to talent, destiny, and a view of life.

In the midst of the acclaim, Amundsen found that he was being threatened in America with legal proceedings for unpaid bills, because the organizers of a reception had defaulted, and he, as the guest of honour, was considered the most promising person to sue. It was a ludicrous reminder that he had returned, as he had sailed, in debt. He now had to set about paying what he owed, a matter of some 60,000 kroner.* However he had friends, who, all unbidden, were working to help him. One of them was Axel Heiberg, rich, philanthropic and a patron of science and exploration, who was to be one of his most loyal supporters. Before Amundsen returned home, Heiberg sent out an appeal for help:

> By his brilliant attainment of the North-West Passage, Amundsen has finally completed a task which has been the goal for a long succession of expeditions over 400 years ... His voyage in the little *Gjøa* is a worthy parallel to the old Norsemen's bold voyages in their small ships to Greenland and Vinland, and a visible proof to the world that the determination which led a Leif Erikson on the first crossing of the Atlantic in history, still lives in the Norwegians of our day ... It will be unworthy of us, his countrymen, not to do all in our power to help cover costs, and thus show him some proof of our gratitude for what he has done for the honour of Norway.

Patriotism, alas, while it elicited cheers, did not touch pockets. Heiberg's appeal fell flat, and Amundsen pinned his hopes on lecture tours.

* £3,250 or $15,800; £52,500 or $103,000 in present terms.

En route for the Pole – the sheer face of Mt. Don Pedro Christophersen, named after Amundsen's lifelong patron, on the edge of the Polar Plateau.

The earliest photograph of Roald Amundsen, aged about three.

1893 – the year of
Amundsen's first ski tour.
A sleeping bag strapped
to his back, he poses in a
studio between his friends
Laurentius Urdahl
(leading) and Vilhelm
Holst.

Amundsen's "prophet",
Nansen, in
characteristically
autocratic pose.

Amundsen's first voyage and his first journey to the Arctic were on the wooden sealing vessel *Magdalena*.

Scott off duty in 1895.

Dr. Frederick A. Cook
(left) and Amundsen clad
in Eskimo fur garments
from Greenland in the
winter of 1898.

Amundsen sledged 600 miles
to Fort Egbert, Eagle City,
Alaska, to cable the news of
his completion of the North-
West Passage.

Gjøa in June 1903 at the ramshackle jetty on the western outskirts of Oslo from which she set sail.

Commander Scott, R.N.,
aboard *Discovery*.

Discovery's crew, 1904: seated
(*l-r*) Royds, Sir Clements
Markham, Scott, Armitage,
Skelton and Wilson. Lashly
standing behind and to the right
of Royds. Seated on deck in
front of Scott (*l-r*) Wild and
Evans.

Shackleton, Scott and Wilson just before the start of the southern journey, November 2nd, 1902.

Discovery's relief ships in 1904 – *Morning* to her left and *Terra Nova* to her right.

Cock o' the walk: Amundsen on his borrowed ship, *Fram*, moored on Oslo waterfront, hugs the secret of his proposed southern destination to himself.

Among *Fram*'s first crew on the 1893-96 voyage were two of Amundsen's mentors, Sverdrup (seated third from left) and the vessel's owner, Nansen. Hjalmar Johansen (standing extreme right) was also on board.

He declined one in England because, as he wrote to Nansen, it would probably

> be poorly attended, [and] have a damaging effect on my proposed lecture tour in America afterwards. On the other hand ... the invitations from the various geographical societies ought to be accepted, as publicity for my American journey.

This utilitarian view of honours was characteristic. He embarked on a European tour which turned into a triumphal progress. He was showered with most of the major geographical medals and awards.

Amundsen bore it all very well. Restless, driven, man of action as he was, he nonetheless had seized the opportunity to enjoy success. He was now thirty-four, a good age for doing so, and he seemed to sense that the moment might not return. Before it was too late, Amundsen had understood the words of Ecclesiastes, 'To every thing there is a season, and a time to every purpose under the heaven.'

There are two impressions of Amundsen about this time. The French Ambassador to Norway, after meeting him at dinner, wrote that

> this man, whose energy and modesty I had often the occasion to admire, had never given me such an impression of power ... that he had authority and charm, nobody denies, who has approached him ... Without chasing people, he does not flee them. [He possesses] simplicity ... and a charm of conversation enlivened by sharp remarks, but without malice. Far from seizing the occasion to shine, as he could easily do, he listens more than he speaks, quite happily keeping in the background, smiling a little vaguely, and always he avoids speaking of himself.

Hugh Robert Mill, who knew most of the explorers of the day, found Amundsen

> of a reserved and very sensitive nature. Although brave, daring and self-reliant above most men, he shrank from criticism, and withered under any suspicion of ridicule. He was, I think, the most successful and most unhappy of all the Polar explorers whom I have met.

Amundsen enjoyed a joke, except when it was against himself. On *Belgica*, when this happened, he would retire in dudgeon to his cabin, convinced of a malicious attempt to humiliate him although, when he could be persuaded that there was in fact no malice, he would emerge in good humour again.

Amundsen was undoubtedly shy but, at the same time, he had a touch of vanity. He would unconsciously steal glances at himself whenever he was near a mirror. He looked equally at home in Eskimo furs or white tie and tails. Clothes were to him an extension of the personality, not a façade behind which to hide. He liked giving away signed photographs of himself. Perhaps there was within him a streak of narcissism. But he was modest withal.

Despite a thick accent and a high-pitched voice incongruous in his giant frame, he had presence. Lurking in his public manner was a hint of scorn for his audience – all audiences. Yet, in spite of this, perhaps because of it, his lecture in London on February 11th, 1907 at the R.G.S. was a notable triumph. Amundsen had a personality that was able to communicate across the barrier of language to sympathetic listeners – particularly those who had experienced exploration and discovery. He impressed the old 'Arctic' admirals of the R.G.S. In the discussion after Amundsen's lecture, Admiral Sir Vesey Hamilton said,

I do not think an Arctic expedition ever did so much with such small means ... I have had the experience of three Arctic winters and five Arctic summers, and I can say that nothing I have heard of surpasses the work of Captain Amundsen.

Since Vesey Hamilton had been one of Sir Clements Markham's henchmen in appointing Scott, and knew the inner history of the *Discovery* expedition, this was praise enough. Amundsen's European tour had been a national triumph. He had generated the goodwill Nansen wanted. He had struck a shrewd blow for his country by charming the Kaiser, for Germany was a supporter of Sweden, and would have liked to see Norway back under Swedish rule. In England, the principal friend of Norway among the Great Powers, Amundsen had stoked the fires of goodwill.

Belgica and the First Antarctic Night; *Gjøa* and the North-West Passage were not enough. Amundsen wanted something more. In London, meeting Nansen for the first time since returning from the North-West Passage, he asked if he could have *Fram*.

Amundsen wanted the yet unattained North Geographical Pole itself. Robert Edwin Peary had returned from yet another rebuff in the long march across the pack ice from the shores of the frozen sea. To Amundsen, this seemed a profitless route, and he decided on another. His idea was to repeat Nansen's drift on the *Fram* but, by entering the pack further to the east, use wind and currents to reach a higher latitude; perhaps passing over the Pole itself but at least coming within range of a short dash with ski, sledge and dogs.

But Nansen could not give an answer. He was still Norwegian Ambassador in London. It was a decade since he had returned from the drift of the *Fram*. Politics, science, writing, diplomacy, the conflict of wife and mistress, absorbed him. But he was haunted by the passage of time. He hankered after action. He clung to the idea of one more expedition, for which he would need his old ship. His desire – perhaps his delusion; what Ibsen calls the 'life lie' – was to crown his career by the conquest of the South Pole.

He had toyed with the thought ever since returning from the first crossing of Greenland in 1889. That expedition convinced him that for trained skiers a Polar Ice Cap was no hurdle but a highway made to order. Two decades before the proof, he decided that the South Pole lay on an ice cap, and therefore was waiting for swift and elegant conquest by a small party of Norwegian skiers.

This was not vanity but sober judgment. To Nansen, reaching the South Pole would be merely a ski tour – a long one, a dangerous one, requiring careful organization – but still essentially a ski tour, no different in kind from one over the familiar mountains of his homeland, as the crossing of Greenland had hinted. Nothing in the intervening years altered that opinion; certainly not the grotesque travesties of snow travel portrayed by Scott in *The Voyage of the 'Discovery'*. If anything, Scott suggested that the field was waiting for professionals to replace the incompetent, albeit heroic, amateurs.

But the years passed; plans lay fallow. Norwegian independence arrived, sucking Nansen into politics and the embassy in London. And over all lay the sense that the drift of the *Fram* had killed something in him. 'None of us,' he wrote to Eva, his wife, 'goes unpunished through three such years.' Yet still the thought refused to die, and when Amundsen asked about *Fram* that day in London, Nansen answered with his own Antarctic plans. But Amundsen discerned the self-delusion that lay behind it all. Within three months, he was writing to Nansen:

> Have you made any decision with respect to the journey we talked about when I was in London in February? I should prefer to be able to follow you and possibly be of some use; but should it be that this journey does not materialize, then I should very much like to have my plan – or to use a more correct expression, your original plan – of going through the Bering Strait and over the pole ready by the autumn.

There was also a sound practical reason for this strangely self-confident letter. Nansen had been badgering the Norwegian Government to clear Amundsen's debts, and his efforts had just then borne fruit. On April 20th, the Storting (the Norwegian Parliament) granted Amundsen 40,000 kroner.*

* £2,200 or $11,000; £35,500 or $71,000 in present terms.

The grant was conditional on the ethnographical collections of the Netsilik Eskimos made on *Gjøa* being handed over to the Norwegian State. It was a good bargain, but unnecessary, since Amundsen already had offered to make the gift. But if the explorer was hurt at the mean spirit that this implied, he did not show it. The grant had relieved his financial troubles. His forthcoming lecture tour in America would not now be the depressing prospect of simply clearing old debts, but the start of a new enterprise.

Nansen had promised a decision about *Fram* when he returned to Norway, and one day early in September, 1907, Amundsen went to learn his fate.

Amundsen was eleven years younger than the man he was going to meet. He was the claimant to the throne, going to ask the old king to hand over the sceptre. It was a prospect to daunt the boldest for, even among his countrymen, Nansen was a distant and intimidating figure.

A friend of Nansen described how once they were discussing the meaning of life:

> Nansen said: 'Life has no meaning. There is nothing called meaning in nature. Meaning is a purely human concept which we put into existence.'
> It was like a chill blast from another mental world.

Polhøgda was the name of Nansen's home, The Polar Heights, a symbol and extension of his own personality. He had designed the place himself. It was a tall forbidding mansion, like some castle in a Nordic folk tale, rising on a knoll above the forest. High up in a tower in one corner lay a study from which, in splendid isolation, Nansen could look down on a sea of sombre treetops and the glinting waters of the fjord.

Amundsen knocked on the heavy door; was shown into the high, forbidding hall with its gallery and the centrepiece, the staircase, at the head of which Nansen would appear. Thus Nansen received visitors; a stage-set consciously arranged.

Within Polhøgda's walls another drama, intertwined with Amundsen's, was being played out. Nansen's marriage was at a crisis. Eva had not followed him to England. They had grown apart; had other affairs, yet still loved each other. Eva said little, but could not bear the thought of her husband's absence on another expedition. Their daughter, Liv, has left an account of what happened.

> As time passed [Father] grew more indecisive. In the end he could stand it no longer and revealed all his doubts to Eva. Without regard to herself, she entered into his thoughts with an understanding that overwhelmed him.

Nonetheless he could not make up his mind and when the day came and Amundsen stood downstairs in the hall and waited, Eva was unable to hide her distress either. She stood in the bedroom and heard Fridtjof's slow footsteps above her on the attic floor. With raised eyebrows she looked at him as he entered. 'I know what it's going to be,' was all she said. Without a word Fridtjof went out again and continued down the stairs to the hall. There he met another pair of tensed eyes. 'You shall have *Fram*,' said father.

Nansen's promise of *Fram* was not a gift, but the cession of a claim. *Fram* was State property, and now Amundsen had first call on her. She was laid up in the Naval Yard at Horten, on the Oslo Fjord. She needed an extensive refit but Amundsen at least had a ship waiting for him. Now all he needed was to pay off the remaining debts on *Gjøa* and find money for the third voyage on the *Fram*. (Nansen's and Sverdrup's had been the first two.) In the autumn of 1907 he embarked on an American lecture tour, that Eldorado of the times, hoping to raise a fortune by talking about the North-West Passage.

He started off in New York, as he put it in a letter to Alexander Nansen, with 'a cold douche at my opening lecture. 2 to 300 people were all that were present in Carnegie Hall, which can hold as many thousands.'

His concern was not for himself but because it would be

impossible to help Ristvedt, as I had promised ... This hurts me so much, I don't know what I can turn to in order to help him. If matters change for the better here, I shall inform you; if not, I must beg you to do everything in human power to find him a job.

Ristvedt, his companion in the journey to the North Magnetic Pole, and the first volunteer for *Gjøa*, was someone to whom Amundsen felt much in debt. Amundsen was fanatically loyal to those who served him loyally, and he had a deep, paternalistic sense of responsibility towards those who depended on him.

The lectures were going well; in Amundsen's words, 'Full houses everywhere' and three weeks after starting, he sent Gade with no little pride $1,000 'to be looked after', as he put it, 'in the best way'. Gade was acting as his American financial manager.

But, after the New Year, reaction came. 'I simply cannot travel into the depths of North Dakota again and give a demonstration in the attics,' he told Gade early in April. 'I retch when I think of it.'

As Amundsen later put it, he was 'merely a part of a lecture machine set in motion between New York through intermediate stops to San Francisco ... a lecture tour is not the same as a holiday excursion, but a journey full of work and strain and the profits hard earned'.

It was now that Amundsen, at the age of thirty-five, had his first recorded sexual adventures. The central figure is a mysterious lady called 'Carrey', evidently a procuress, and well known to Gade. Amundsen wrote to Gade from Butte, Montana, in April, towards the end of his tour,

> I should very much like to dash out to Lake Forest on Sunday to look in on you and your family. But what shall I do with Saturday night? My old friend Carrey possibly has a solution? Ask her if the little French one, *the nice and tidy one* is free, and get her to arrange a meeting in her house at 9 o'clock on Saturday evening.

In a farewell letter from the boat, just before sailing for Norway, Amundsen wrote to Gade: 'A thousand thanks for your great kindness on all occasions.' 'Kindness', 'Friendliness', are two concepts that seem to haunt Amundsen. He thirsted for them; and could not find enough.

In May 1907, Amundsen returned home, disillusioned. The lecture tour, though profitable, had not been the financial sensation he had hoped. *The North-West Passage* had disarmed the critics, but not, alas, fulfilled the secret wistful faith of every author that *this* will be a best seller. He had cleared *Gjøa*'s debts but not much more. Of money for the next expedition there was none in sight, and poor *Fram* still languished, gathering barnacles in a backwater.

For a while, Amundsen put all this out of his mind, and made himself a home; for a home, the conqueror of the North-West Passage had none. He was alone, with no prospect of marriage, but he bought himself a house. It was large, two storeyed, built of wood like a Swiss chalet; lying about ten miles outside Christiania in a dark pine forest called Svartskog, – 'The Black Forest' – on Bundefjord, an inner arm of the Christiania Fjord. He installed Betty, his old nursemaid, as housekeeper, and with the same meticulous attention to detail that marked his exploration, set up house.

The house was being furnished like a ship's saloon; solid, comfortable, the decor slightly dark. On a glass door between the entrance hall and living room there was mounted, as a large transparency, a photograph of Amundsen's old friend Ugpik, 'The Owl', from Gjøahavn, aiming a bow and arrow. Other transparencies depicting scenes from the North-West Passage were mounted on various fanlights and, as an ironic trophy perhaps, there was hung in the living room a print of Sir John Millais' painting called *The North-West Passage*, with its legend, 'It can be done and England shall do it'.

Among the amenities being installed was a tap on the dining room floor for a miniature fountain that Amundsen liked as a table decoration. Also, his bedroom and dressing room were being fitted up to look like cabins, so that he could feel as if he were on a ship.

However, Amundsen was soon, at Nansen's suggestion, on his way to Bergen for an oceanographical course. Oceanography was to be part of the work on *Fram* and opportunities for instruction were rare. Professor Bjørn Helland-Hansen, a leading oceanographer, gave the course. 'I think it best to mention that I possess no prior knowledge,' Amundsen wrote to him, to make it clear that the conqueror of the North-West Passage was not afraid to learn, 'and I beg you to consider me as someone going to school for the first time.'

In Helland-Hansen, Amundsen found a loyal and understanding friend.

The wonderful two months I spent in Bergen with you went all too quickly, [Amundsen wrote after the course]. It was wonderful how we combined business with pleasure an art, you see, that very few people really understand.

The expedition was still no more than a private notion shared by a few. After finishing the oceanographical course, Amundsen unveiled his plans on November 10th at a grand soirée of the Geographical Society in Christiania. In his words to Gade, 'Naturally, not a fifth of the audience understood what I was talking about, but the enthusiasm was great, just the same.'

An occasion it most certainly was. Or, as *Aftenposten*, the leading Norwegian exponent of the new popular journalism put it:

The sense of great events surged over the distinguished gathering ...

The King was present, the Diplomatic Corps was copiously represented. This Day will certainly be long remembered by the Geographical Society; the day when Roald Amundsen presented the plans for his Polar Voyage over an unknown part of the World!

Amundsen was pre-eminently a Pole-seeker. He did not like boasting beforehand. As he had half-concealed his designs on the North-West Passage under the cloak of the North Magnetic Pole, so he now veiled his plans for the North Pole in a passage of apologia:

Many people believe that a Polar Expedition is merely an unnecessary waste of money and life. With the concept of Polar Expedition they generally associate the thought of a record; to reach the Pole or Furthest North. And in that case, I must declare myself in agreement. But I want to make it absolutely clear that this – the assault on the Pole, will not be the aim of the expedition. The main object is a scientific study of the Polar Sea itself.

He then outlined his plan:

> With *Fram* fitted out for 7 years, and with a good crew, I propose to leave
> Norway at the beginning of 1910. My course will run round Cape Horn to San
> Francisco, where we will coal and provision. Thence, our course will be set
> for Point Barrow, America's Northernmost promontory. The last news will
> be sent home from there, before the voyage itself starts. On departing from
> Point Barrow, it is my intention to continue with the smallest possible crew.
> A course will be set in a North-North-West direction, where we will seek the
> most favourable point from which to force a way further to the North. When
> that has been found, we will try and get on as far as possible, and prepare for
> a drift of 4 to 5 years over the Polar Sea ... from the moment the vessel has
> been frozen into the ice, the observations begin with which I hope to solve
> some of the hitherto unsolved mysteries.

A long ovation greeted Amundsen's address which, as *Aftenposten*'s
reporter put it, 'clearly showed the trust placed in the bold Seaman and
Scientist, who had just presented his daring Plans'.

Nansen afterwards took the floor, to give Amundsen his benediction
as it were; and seal the plan with his approval. In his combination of
understatement and hyperbole, he is characteristically Norwegian. He
succinctly expresses the Norwegian attitude to Polar exploration and
he makes a profession of faith which will stand for the Polar explorer
in any age and any country in the West. What drove men to the Polar
regions was

> the power of the unknown over the human spirit. As ideas have cleared with
> the ages, so has this power extended its might, and driven Man willy-nilly
> onwards along the path of progress.
> It drives us in to Nature's hidden powers and secrets, down to the immeasur-
> ably little world of the microscopic, and out into the unprobed expanses of the
> Universe.
> ... it gives us no peace until we know this planet on which we live, from
> the greatest depth of the ocean to the highest layers of the atmosphere.
> This Power runs like a strand through the whole history of polar explora-
> tion. In spite of all declarations of possible profit in one way or another, it was
> that which, in our hearts, has always driven us back there again, despite all
> setbacks and suffering.

The next day, King Haakon and Queen Maud opened the subscription list for what came to be known as the third *Fram* expedition
with 20,000 kroner. Amundsen told Gade that 'People are simply
touching in the way they are showing their enthusiasm for "the great
national undertaking".'

But this was defensive optimism. When a letter arrived from Gade offering to raise money in America, he answered:

> My dear friend, if you with your contacts can manage anything in that direction you will do me a greater service than I can possibly explain. Attitudes here are miserably mean and parochial, and disproportionately hard work is needed to drum up the necessary means.

This is one of the first explicit hints of a bitterness that had started to appear within Amundsen since he returned, somehow a changed man, from the North-West Passage. He was beginning to fret under the claustrophobic strain of a small country. He was too big for his surroundings; America, with all its failings, was more to his taste. 'If you meet Armour,' he told Gade, 'tell him that the chances of sending his products to the Pole are now better than ever.'

Armour was one of the celebrated Chicago meat-packing magnates. Amundsen hoped he could be induced to present all the pemmican and tinned meat in return for free publicity.

Amundsen was one of the first of the Polar explorers to grasp fully the potentialities of commercial promotion. But, somehow, he could not turn things properly to account.

By the beginning of 1909, contributions had dried up. Hardly a quarter of the necessary sum was in sight. This expedition was too big for the Amundsen family to rescue, as they had rescued *Gjøa*. Amundsen turned to the State.

Fram had not yet been secured; he now formally asked the Storting for her loan and, crucial addendum, 75,000 kroner* to refit her. The outcome was by no means certain.

Repugnant as the concept was to a man of his independent soul, Amundsen had to ask for a committee to give him a semblance of formal standing. A small one was formed, with Nansen as chairman and Axel Heiberg as one of the members.

In January 1909, they issued an appeal to the public, probably drafted by Heiberg. Amundsen's expedition, it said, would be

> of such great value for ... Norway, that no efforts must be spared to carry it out. It is clear that especially for a small nation it is important to unite in the solution of cultural tasks as often as the opportunity arises, and preferably in those fields to which it is especially adapted. Here the small nations stand on an equal footing with the big ones. By making the ... greatest possible efforts in the fields of exploration, art or science, they demonstrate their right to exist as an independent nation and show their significance for world culture. Every

* £8,660 or $42,200; £140,000 or $280,000 in present terms.

such effort, big or small, helps to give the people backbone and self-confidence at home and recognition abroad.

This was aimed at the public pocket, but above all Storting votes. The Storting debate was expected soon. To improve his chances, Admundsen wrote to Scott Keltie, the R.G.S. Secretary, in London.

I shall feel most obliged to receive from the Royal Geographical Society its opinion & views concerning the plan of my next expedition to the arctic according to the lecture which I have already sent you.

My demand to the Norwegian Parliament to obtain the *Fram* will be discussed in the first days of January and it will be of great importance and interest to have a word from you before that time.

This is a breathtakingly forthright letter. It expresses – and exploits – something common to many small countries: a respect, not to say veneration, for what comes out of bigger ones.

Before replying, Scott Keltie consulted Albert Markham and Sir Lewis Beaumont, two of the old 'Arctic' admirals. Both disapproved.

Now Keltie was not only the Secretary of the R.G.S., but also he wrote for *The Times* on exploration. He had no desire to kill a good story. His reply to Amundsen was a model of encouragement discreetly given, and responsibility avoided.

Your scheme ... has been submitted to several Arctic experts here, and after consideration of their views ... I am directed by the President to say that the Council of the Society consider it most desirable that in the interests of ... science there should be a thorough investigation of the Arctic ...

If you are able to carry out your proposed expedition with anything like the thoroughness indicated in the paper which you have sent us, there is no doubt that it will go a very long way to solve all the problems which still remain to be solved.

To which Amundsen replied:

Please accept my very best thanks for your letter ... which will have great interest when my demand of the *Fram* will be discussed in the Norwegian Parliament.

On January 25th, 1909, Amundsen visited London to present his plans to an R.G.S. meeting.

I welcome the resolution of my friend Amundsen to follow in the footsteps of Nansen [said Sir Clements Markham in the discussion that ensued]. That it will be a very perilous undertaking cannot be disguised. But the guidance of a really capable man very largely reduces the danger. Like the enterprise of Nansen, it is a grand conception, worthy of the first navigator of the North-West Passage.

Before this authoritative endorsement, criticism wilted. Sir Lewis Beaumont did, however, suggest taking wireless; which by now was in regular use from ship to shore over oceanic distances. Amundsen's reply was characteristic:

> I have decided not to carry a wireless, and the reason is this. Imagine that we have spent two years in the drifting-pack, and still have three more years to spend - imagine that we suddenly get a despatch stating that some of our dear ones are seriously ill ... What would be the result? Nobody can tell, but the worst might happen.

From the R.G.S. Amundsen went to an audience with King Edward VII at Windsor. It 'went very well', he wrote to Scott Keltie. 'The King was much interested and asked a good many questions.'

With this sort of approval in England, Amundsen returned to face the verdict of his own country's legislature.

The smaller the country, on the whole, the more passionate its politics. On February 6th, when the Storting debated whether to let Amundsen have *Fram* and whether to grant him 75,000 kroner to refit her, there was more than a soupçon of dramatization. Bitter and repetitive, the debate dragged on for three hours.

In the end, by eighty-seven votes to thirty-four, Amundsen got *Fram* and the 75,000 kroner. Doubtless the prestige of the R.G.S. had helped to carry the day. Amundsen wrote off to Scott Keltie with the news. 'I have not yet got all the money I want,' he was compelled to add, 'but I must go on nevertheless.'

15

Facing Due South

AMUNDSEN BELIEVED THAT, since he was doing so much for his country, he was entitled to his country's aid. Since returning from the North-West Passage, his sense of prerogative had grown, and he assumed that money would eventually appear in the natural order of things. In the meantime, the new expedition began like the old. Amundsen used Nansen's name -- besides his own reputation - to raise credit, and cheerfully went ahead with his preparations.

After all his experience, Amundsen was still in search of perfection. At the very least, he could avoid the repetition of old mistakes. On the North-West Passage, for example, he had been troubled by unsuitable reindeer furs from inferior animals slaughtered at the wrong time of year. Sleeping bags in which they were used became stiff, wet and cold. The pelts he wanted were one year calves of a certain kind slaughtered in the autumn. For this, he turned to his friend Zapffe in Tromsø, who had helped him with equipment for the *Gjøa*.

Amundsen was also meticulous with the preparation of *Fram*; he had her rerigged as a topsail schooner because the fore and aft sails on which it is based are easier to handle than square ones, and this particular rig saved crew. The mainsails could be set from the deck. Going aloft, that romantic feature of old windjammer tales, was cut to the bone. Six men could handle *Fram* thus rigged.

Amundsen, moreover, had *Fram* converted from steam to diesel propulsion, because of its advantages in ice navigation. This demands the ability to seize opportunity; to exploit each arbitrary slackening of the floes, every providentially opening lead, and the diesel motor, unlike a steam engine, would give instant power without wasting fuel while at rest. Also, a diesel motor would give greater range under power, besides saving space and crew.

The marine diesel, however, was still new and unproven. When *Fram* started her refit, motor vessels could be counted on the fingers of one hand. The reversible engine, on which marine propulsion depended, had only been invented about five years earlier, in 1904, by Jonas Hesselman, a Swedish engineer. It was first put into production by the Diesels Motorer Co. of Stockholm in 1907. *Fram*'s engine was the fourth to go into service. She was the first Polar ship to be diesel powered, a notable pioneering enterprise.

Unlike Scott, Amundsen did not organize from a desk. For that he could thank his family. Leon, his brother, installed himself in a small Christiania office as expedition secretary, and dealt with all the paperwork. Roald was able to keep away from the office, and devote himself to the proper business of preparation.

There was plenty to do. All the numberless items of Polar equipment had to be tested, considered and, usually, redesigned. Constantly, Amundsen went down the fjord to the Naval yard at Horten, where *Fram* was refitting, to oversee the work. It was a busy but exciting time. Organizing an expedition can be the keenest of pleasures; it is anticipation and hope unjaded.

At the age of thirty-seven, Amundsen now fell in love, probably for the first time in his life. He had chosen a married woman: Sigrid Castberg, the wife of a lawyer belonging to a well-known family. In the tight little society of a small city (the population of Christiania was then 240,000) it was hard to keep such affairs entirely secret, and Amundsen had a horror of scandal. He wanted Sigrid to get a divorce and marry him immediately. She naturally hesitated.

But in the months before he sailed, she gave him a touch of human warmth. His family generally believed that Amundsen was not interested in women. That may have been due to the absence of an understanding woman. Sigrid at any rate seems to have found the key. She was pretty, amusing, and altogether womanly; exactly what Amundsen needed. A postcard written by both at midnight from the Grand Hotel – the Ritz, as it were, of Christiania – hints at high jinks. That release, too, he probably needed. This was among the few contented times Amundsen knew in civilization.

Hidden in the Arctic, meanwhile, Peary was trying yet again to reach the North Pole.

For *Gjøa*, Amundsen had been obliged to seek out his crew; now he was inundated with volunteers. As second in command he chose a Norwegian Naval officer, Commander Ole Engelstad. At the end of July 1909, Engelstad was killed by a lightning discharge while testing one of the man-lifting kites to be taken on *Fram* for observation in the ice.

Amundsen now cabled another Naval officer, Lieutenant Thorvald Nilsen, who had unsuccessfully applied to join the expedition, asking if he still was interested. 'To that', Nilsen laconically recorded in his diary, 'I answered Yes, and thereupon received the appointment as the expedition's second in command.'

On his way to London at the end of January, 1909, to lecture on his forthcoming expedition to the R.G.S., Amundsen had to change trains at Lübeck, in Northern Germany. There he chanced to meet a Norwegian ski team travelling to Chamonix, in French Savoy for a demonstration. In the historic Nordic disciplines of ski-jumping and cross-country, the Norwegians were still the undisputed masters.

Between trains Amundsen entertained his countrymen at the station restaurant. The conversation, not unnaturally, turned to his expeditions, past and future.

'Do you know,' said one of the team, a lithe, dark-haired, moustachioed figure, with a glint in his eye. 'Do you know, it would be fun to be with you at the North Pole.' He happened to be one of the finest living skiers, a man called Olav Bjaaland.

'Indeed?' was Amundsen's reply. 'Well, if you really mean it, I think it could be arranged. Just look me up in Christiania when you get home from Chamonix. But – think it over carefully. It won't only be fun.'

This is how Bjaaland told the story afterwards. His motives for asking Amundsen were mixed. Of course, being a Norwegian, he had the customary desire to emulate Nansen. But also, here was a way of seeing the world and being paid for it. At the age of nearly thirty-six, he was now making his first visit abroad. Chamonix and the North Pole were both part of the great outside. To him, both seemed merely variations on the same theme; ski races both, with the North Pole perhaps a little bit more fun.

Before the chance encounter at Lübeck station, the two had never met, although each knew of the other through the headlines.

Bjaaland was more than just a ski champion. He came from Morgedal, in Telemark, the cradle of modern skiing. It was the men of Morgedal who turned skiing, which had existed as transport in Scandinavia since the Stone Age, into the sport we know. Bjaaland was of the pioneer generation that brought skiing out into the world. He was a farmer and a Montagnard. He was a skilled carpenter; a violin and ski maker; and he worked in wrought iron too. He was a bit of an artist, a bit of a poet, a bit of a child, a bit of a jester. And he had in the very highest degree the natural dignity and ceremoniousness traditionally associated with his native Telemark. He was a natural aristocrat. Amundsen discerned these qualities. When Bjaaland returned to Morgedal from Chamonix in February, he had joined the expedition.

Preparations, one way and another, were progressing reasonably. Money was still the great obstacle. But Amundsen, with unquenchable faith in himself, believed that this would somehow disappear. He still believed that he could leave, as he had originally intended, in January 1910. On September 1st, 1909, he opened his afternoon newspaper to read:

THE NORTH POLE REACHED
... Dr. Cook reached the North Pole on the 21st April 1908, arrived in May 1909 from Cape York at Upernavik [Greenland].

It was his old friend from the *Belgica*. Immediately he had to give interviews to the Press. He did so with becoming poise, although with a touch perhaps of disingenuousness. What did he think of the man?

Cook has made thorough studies in connection with Polar exploration. But he is first and foremost a sportsman, a pot hunter, and his main goal has been to reach the North Pole.

Did he believe the news? (To this, polite evasion.) Would it have any effect on his own plans? To this, the answer was an unequivocal 'Absolutely not'.

Cook was on his way to Copenhagen from Greenland on *Hans Egede*, a Danish ship. 'Warmest congratulations with splendid deed,' Amundsen cabled him. 'Regret I cannot be with you in Copenhagen. Hope to see you in the States.'

That was on Friday, September 3rd. The following Tuesday, Amundsen's newspaper had more headlines: 'Peary: Has he also planted the Stars and Stripes on the North Pole?'

The *New York Times* had no doubts:

Peary Discovers the North Pole after Eight Trials in 23 Years ... I have the D.O.P. Peary cables Wife. That Means the Damned Old Pole, Happy Wife of the Explorer Declares.

Peary claimed to have reached the Pole on April 6th, 1909, a year after Cook.

Again Amundsen was asked for his opinion. In an interview with the *New York Times* he suggested that

It would be useless to make speculations as to the points arrived at by the two explorers. It is not important if the exact mathematical pole was reached or not, but it is important that the geographical conditions of the spot were observed. Probably something will be left to be done. What is left will be sufficient for all of us.

This was undoubtedly true, but it rang somewhat hollow, especially to Amundsen himself. In any case, Peary's news sent Amundsen by the first train to Copenhagen, where he arrived early on Wednesday morning. He found himself plunged into what a Danish journalist called the 'jumble of demonstrations, ceremonies, misunderstandings and idiocies, which may be characterized as "The Cook days".' Cook had been spontaneously welcomed as the conqueror of the North Pole, and swiftly given an honorary doctorate by Copenhagen University. But there was a school of thought that, from the start, considered it all a hoax, and controversy waxed fierce.

Amundsen went straight from the station to the Hotel Phoenix, where Cook was staying. According to Cook this is what happened:

> Amundsen told me ... that he was about ready to take the *Fram* ... for another try at the Pole. He asked me about the currents, the weather, and what I thought of the prospects. I advised against the execution of the enterprise because at best I believed he could only duplicate the voyage of Nansen and Sverdrup. Furthermore, I said the North Pole is now out of the picture. Why not try for the South Pole.

This was written with hindsight a quarter of a century after the event. The idea, Cook goes on to say,

> almost took Amundsen's breath. He sat in meditation for a while as was his custom when new ideas were suddenly flashed. Then said Amundsen 'The *Fram* is not a good sea boat for the heavy South Seas. But this is the thing to do. Let me think it over.'

Amundsen's own published version of events is somewhat different. When the news arrived from Peary, he wrote,

> I clearly understood that the original plan of the third *Fram* expedition — the investigation of the North Polar basin   was in jeopardy. If the expedition was to be saved, I had to act quickly and without hesitation. I decided on a change of front — to turn about and point my bows South ... the North Pole, the penultimate question of popular interest in Polar exploration, had been settled. If I was to succeed in rousing interest in my enterprise, nothing else remained for me to do than try to solve the last great question - the South Pole.

Or, as he also put it, 'I decided to postpone my original plan by a year or two in order to raise the funds still lacking.' In other words, to raise money for his drift across the Arctic, a stunt was needed, and it would have to be the South Pole.

But this is a shade too glib. 'I do not deny,' he wrote afterwards, 'that I should have liked to be the first man at the [North] Pole.' Perhaps he came closest to the truth in his memoirs, when he said that 'If I were to maintain my reputation as an explorer, I had to win a sensational victory one way or another. I decided on a coup.' Somehow, the heart had gone out of his Arctic expedition. As he said in later years, he could not understand why anyone should 'want to go to a place where somebody else had been ... or go there for the sake of doing it a different way'. Despite his gibe at Cook for being only interested in the Pole, Amundsen was himself in every fibre a Pole seeker. The North Pole had gone; he had the sweep of imagination to take the simple but vast step of turning to the South Pole instead.

Whether Cook or Peary had been first at the Pole was soon the battle of the headlines. In the end, Cook's claims were officially rejected and Peary's confirmed. But to this day, the polemics smoulder still. Did Cook reach the Pole? Did Peary? Did either? Did both? To Amundsen, the verdict was irrelevant from the start. He understood that it was the claim that counted. Once made, it destroyed all chance of uncontested primacy and by leaving the issue for ever wreathed in doubt, killed the goal. That a man with Amundsen's inner sense of greatness should be bitterly disappointed and perplexed, is quite understandable. That he at once looked for new worlds to conquer in place of the old one snatched away, is entirely in keeping with his character.

Amundsen wanted to be the first man at the South Pole. He had no illusions as to its intrinsic worth, but he wanted to be first. And, incidentally, he thought he could raise money for his Arctic drift as well. He had the Napoleonic audacity to swing from one Pole to the other. The audacity was so great that the public, and certainly his backers, would be unlikely to understand it. After all, he was going south with money given him to go north. From the outset, Amundsen decided that if he were to succeed, he would have to act in secret. He pretended that his sudden Danish journey was for a reunion with Dr. Cook, his old companion from the ordeal on *Belgica*, and to get information for his northern drift. But that was a blind to defeat potential enemies and ill-wishers. In reality, it was to begin his Antarctic preparations. In an Englishman of another age, it would have been called the Drake Touch.

The road to the South Pole quite naturally started in Copenhagen. It was there that the sledge dogs had to be ordered. Dogs were to Amundsen without question the kernel of success The best came from Greenland, a Danish colony, all trade with which went by law through a State monopoly in the Danish capital.

It so happened that Jens Daugaard-Jensen, the Inspector (i.e. chief administrative officer) for North Greenland had sailed on the same ship as Cook, and was now in Copenhagen. Amundsen wanted the Polar dogs from North Greenland – the hardiest breed, best adapted to Antarctic conditions. To get what he wanted, Daugaard-Jensen's help was crucial. It was to see Daugaard-Jensen rather than Cook that Amundsen had gone to Copenhagen.

Soon after arriving, Amundsen met Daugaard-Jensen, and in a letter dated September 9th, wrote thanking him for his

> kind willingness to obtain sledge dogs, Eskimo equipment etc., from the Danish colonies in Greenland. I now take the liberty of specifying in greater detail what I require
> 50 dogs.
> 14 complete Eskimo suits of sealskin.
> 20 prepared sealskins to repair the suits ...
> 20 dog whips ... sealskin straps ...
> As far as the dogs are concerned, it is absolutely essential that I obtain the very best it is conceivable to obtain. Naturally I am fully aware that as a result the price must be higher than that normally paid, but I am absolutely willing to adapt myself accordingly.

On several counts, this is an interesting document. It illustrates Amundsen's method of working; his thoroughness; his caution; his pain-staking refusal to leave preparation and equipment to chance. It is the first proof positive of his change of plan. His original intention had been to get his dogs in Alaska, on his way to the Bering Strait for his northern drift. This is the proof that he had now turned to the Antarctic. It dates his change of plan not later than Friday, September 9th, 1909. *It is written on Cook's notepaper.*

This has some bearing on Cook's version of events. That he should have told Amundsen to go south is in character and quite likely, and that Amundsen should have been taken aback, equally so. To have his secret surprised, even by a chance shot, was wholly disconcerting. Read-ing between the lines of what Cook wrote, it is evident that Amundsen tried to head him off. Amundsen was a loyal friend of Cook's; but he would not trust him with a secret; he would trust very few people with one. He did not even trust Daugaard-Jensen, who was under the im-pression that Amundsen was still going north.

At any rate, Amundsen's turbulent state of mind is graphically suggested by that use of Cook's notepaper for the fateful letter of his life. One can picture the scene: Amundsen has been to see Daugaard-Jensen; he can get what he wants. He goes back to his hotel; the same one as Cook's. In suppressed excitement, he talks to his old friend;

borrows some notepaper, and hurries out to his own room to write the letter that changed history.

One question remains obscure: why did Amundsen wait for Peary before going to Copenhagen and taking the first step on the road to the south? Perhaps the answer is suggested by Cook's cheeky cable to the *New York Times* that 'Two records are better than one'.

Cook had gone North quietly, without revealing his intentions. His news, therefore, came as a shock to Amundsen, because it was so grotesquely unexpected. It took Peary to jolt him into action.

After Cook had left Copenhagen, on September 10th, Daugaard-Jensen, for whom the 'Cook days' had been particularly hectic, immediately devoted himself to Amundsen's business. He went far beyond the arid confines of official duty. Daugaard-Jensen was devoted to Greenland and its people; a dedicated paternalist with a sense of mission. He helped Amundsen as a personal favour, to the utmost of his ability: Amundsen had the gift of arousing in others a spontaneous urge to help him; one of the attributes of leadership that Scott conspicuously lacked. It says something for Amundsen's stature that a senior public servant pushed official business aside to look after his affairs. It was just as well: Daugaard-Jensen held the key to the whole enterprise. By the quality of the dogs, Amundsen would stand or fall. He had secured his most vital ally, Nansen not excepted. The visit to Copenhagen had paid off.

Amundsen sailed with Cook across the Skagerrak as far as Kristiansand, where Cook caught the ship for America. That was on Sunday, September 11th, the day the *New York Times* printed on its front page a cable from Peary, at Battle Harbour, Labrador saying that Cook had 'not been at the Pole on April 21st, 1908, or at any other time. He has simply handed the public a gold brick.'

It was Peary's first denunciation of his rival and the start of their celebrated brawl. Naturally Amundsen was again interviewed. Did he believe in Dr. Cook?

'Unreservedly,' he replied. 'How can you explain this affair with Peary?' 'Well,' answered Amundsen, 'Peary has got it into his head that he is entitled to a monopoly of everything up there in the North.'

Whether Amundsen believed in Cook as much as he made out, was open to question: privately he told Daugaard-Jensen that he found Cook 'unfathomable'. Cook had aroused considerable scepticism by failing to produce original navigational records; even more perhaps by his explanation that they had been left behind in Greenland. But Cook was an old friend; more, Amundsen believed that on *Belgica* he had saved all their lives. Amundsen's code made him stand by an old friend in public, whatever the rights and wrongs of the case.

But, when all was said and done, it was to strike at Peary as much as to defend Cook that Amundsen took his stance. Amundsen blamed Peary for having helped to drive Eivind Astrup to suicide, as his death in 1896 while skiing was widely interpreted to be.* Astrup meant a great deal to Amundsen; almost as much as Nansen, in fact. Nansen, as he told a journalist about this time, 'was the master, but he has always been an awesome, distant figure ... Astrup was much closer; from him I got my inspiration.'

Amundsen had never forgotten what he owed Astrup for the timely encouragement of his lecture to the Christiania students fifteen years before on the crossing of the Greenland Ice Cap with Peary. On *Belgica*, he had named an Antarctic cape in Astrup's memory. He never forgot, and he found it hard to forgive.

Amundsen was also scandalized by Peary's assumption of a prescriptive right to any territory he had chosen to explore. Imbued as he was with the mariner's — and the buccaneer's — belief in the freedom of the seas, Amundsen considered that the waves and the wilds belonged to no one and everyone. He recognized no exclusive claims and believed that, in the Polar regions, he — or anyone else — had the right to go where he chose, whenever he liked.

The day after Cook left for New York, Amundsen cabled Daugaard-Jensen, asking for a hundred instead of fifty dogs. Probably talking to Cook, and reflection over his own experience on *Gjøa*, had induced second thoughts about margins of safety.

Next day, Tuesday, September 13th, *The Times* of London announced that 'Captain Scott informs us that another expedition ought to be arranged for at once ... [It] will, it is hoped start in August next.'

This was the announcement of Scott's next expedition. It was Amundsen's first intimation of a rival in the field. His expedition had been turned into a race. If his mind worked that way, he might well have asked — who is the interloper now?

The day after Scott's announcement, Amundsen revealed that his own departure had been delayed six months, to July 1st, 1910. The reason he gave was a general strike in Sweden that would delay the delivery of the diesel motor for *Fram*. This was merely a pretext. Amundsen had to find a convincing way to gain time for the extra work his change

---

* See p. 56.

of plan involved, besides starting at the right moment for the southern summer, without arousing suspicions.

Scott's appearance on the scene made secrecy yet more urgent. Amundsen knew very well by now that the Ross Sea, from which at the outset he had decided to attack the Pole, was by the British – at least in the persons of Sir Clements Markham and Scott – loudly claimed to be their fief. As his acidulous remark on Peary showed, this did not impress him. Amundsen seems to have taken a dislike to Scott, partly perhaps because of his claims of prescriptive right; partly from the tone of *The Voyage of the 'Discovery'*; whose particular combination of smugness and ignorance can be antagonizing. If he could steal a march on a rich and mighty Empire so much the better; it would show that God was not always on the side of the big battalions.

There were more cogent reasons for secrecy. At that time, the Norwegian Government was bent, at all costs, on cultivating British goodwill; for upon the support of Britain, Norway depended for the maintenance of her independence and neutrality. Amundsen believed that the Norwegian Government, had they had the slightest inkling of his plans, would have stopped him and sacrificed his expedition to the Minotaur of the national interest.

Prudence was indeed necessary. About the same time, Wilhelm Filchner, a lieutenant in the German Army, was also preparing an Antarctic expedition. The British, said Filchner,

> accused me of unfair competition. It was unfair, so one read [in the Press] that I was preparing an expedition to the Antarctic at the same moment that Captain Scott was about to start on a long planned expedition ... Priority of enterprise belonged to the British expedition and no nonsense ... The correct solution seemed to me ... to take the bull by the horns. I went to London. Captain Scott received me in his office. We had a frank conversation and arrived at full understanding.
>
> As Scott wanted to push into the interior from the Ross Sea, and I, on the other hand, from the Weddell Sea, our fields of work were generously separated by Nature ... on this basis we agreed to a 'co-operation of the British and German Antarctic Expeditions in doing exploring work!' We sealed our pact with a handshake, and Scott immediately made certain that the British Press told their readers in favourable terms about the complete Scott–Filchner understanding.

If the subject of a great Power, doubtless on official prompting, saw fit to conduct himself so carefully, it is easy to see how the citizen of a small country would have been persuaded to act with the very greatest circumspection.

Nearer home, there were also grounds for secrecy. Amundsen was afraid of Nansen. The circumstances holding Nansen back in 1907 had now changed. He was no longer Ambassador in London. Eva, his wife, was dead. He made no effort to start another expedition. He gave no hint of wanting to go back on his cession of *Fram*. A terrible world-weariness had overcome him. But Amundsen feared that his reactions would be unpredictable; that he might stop the enterprise. He therefore had to be deceived, along with everybody else. Knowing what Nansen claimed to have given up for him Amundsen felt a sense of guilt, even if he suspected an element of self-deception in what Nansen had said.

Amundsen – justifiably – was also convinced that the Storting and private subscribers would have stopped him for one reason or another. And there was one other tactical reason.

An avowed rival would have been God-given to Scott. The threat of foreign competition would have opened British purses. Scott could have got all the money and equipment he wanted. Without the threat, complacency would do its work.

Three weeks after the British expedition was announced, Amundsen wrote to Daugaard-Jensen, saying, 'If you receive other orders for dogs I hope you will remember that I was first.' This was clearly aimed at forestalling Scott. It was unnecessary. The Danish Ministry of the Interior gave instructions that 'in obtaining the ... dogs, the necessary consideration is taken to the preservation of the stock of dogs in Greenland', so that in any case, no one else would have been allowed to obtain any more. Amundsen wanted to be certain of every conceivable advantage, and to deprive your opponent of the best dogs was to beat him in the first round.

Amundsen had no scruples over his deception, at least as far as Scott was concerned. Scott's plans, as he later wrote, were

completely different from mine ... The English expedition was based entirely on scientific research. The Pole was only a subsidiary matter, while my extended plans made the Pole the first objective.

Scott's aims were what he set forth in his original announcement, and thereafter consistently maintained. He may not have been entirely honest, but Amundsen could scarcely be blamed for taking him at his word. Besides, Amundsen could quite reasonably say that the British had had their chance. It was his – or anyone else's turn now.

16

Territorial Waters

WHEN ERNEST SHACKLETON returned from the Antarctic in 1903, he seemed to have left the quarrels on *Discovery* behind. He was too warm and volatile to nurse a grudge and coldly plan his moves. The publication of *The Voyage of the 'Discovery'* in October, 1905, changed all that. It rekindled all Shackleton's resentment and thirst for revenge. From that moment, he started trying to organize another expedition. His object was the South Pole itself.

Shackleton could see the fraud within Scott's book. He was angered and humiliated at being portrayed as a weakling who had failed. He resented being made the scapegoat, along with the dogs, for the failure of the Southern Journey. He protested. Scott published rectification of a kind that still left the stigma of collapse. It did nothing to resolve the misrepresentation of the facts. In public Shackleton abandoned further pursuit of restitution. But in the secret recesses of his heart, he burned with the fire of the wronged. *The Voyage of the 'Discovery'* gave Shackleton a bitter dislike of his old leader, and caused a lifelong breach between the two.

Even without *The Voyage of the 'Discovery'*, Shackleton might eventually have gone south again. But the book decided the spirit and the timing, goading Shackleton to show himself a better man than Scott and exact retribution for the disgrace of having been invalided home. It was as an avenging angel that he acted.

Shackleton had left the sea to try his luck ashore. After various schemes, he went to work in Glasgow for William Beardmore (later Lord Invernairn), a Clydeside industrialist. By the beginning of 1907 Shackleton, with the help of Beardmore, a uniquely understanding employer, had found the money needed for his Antarctic plans. On February 11th, he announced his expedition. It was to be an attempt on the South Pole from the old *Discovery* base at McMurdo Sound.

I am astonished, [Scott wrote to Scott Keltie when he heard the news]. Shackleton owes everything to me ... I got him into the Expedition - I had him sent home for his health but I spared no pains to explain & publish reasons which should destroy any idea that reflected on his character – First & last I did much for him.

This was self-delusion. It was hardly Scott who got Shackleton on to the *Discovery*, but Llewellyn Longstaff's patronage. Scott was plagued by jealousy, suspicion, perhaps even by bad conscience and, in this telling passage, he revealed the heart of his bitterness:

> I believe, that every explorer looks upon certain regions as his own, Peary certainly does and I believe there are African precedents.

'Every explorer' was hardly justified; Nansen, Sverdrup, Amundsen were three who took a very different view. The invocation of Peary is telling. He laid down that a route once pioneered by an explorer was

> as much a part of his capital as the gold and silver in the vault of a bank ... no one else, without his consent, has any more right to take and use it, than a stranger has to enter the vaults of the bank and take its treasure.

Scott laid claim to *Discovery*'s winter quarters at McMurdo Sound. As he put it to Scott Keltie:

> I hold it would not have been playing the game for anyone to propose an expedition to McMurdo Sound until he had ascertained that I had given up the idea of going again – and I think I am justified in a stronger view when steps of this sort are taken by one of my own people without a word to me.

Behind this tirade lay the fear that Shackleton would leave no Pole to conquer. Scott now bombarded Scott Keltie with emotional demands. He wanted the R.G.S. to stop Shackleton; to proclaim his own rights; to warn the Americans off; to keep the foreigners out.

1907 Shackleton could hardly be accused of poaching, since he had no inkling of Scott's Antarctic plans. Scott had revealed his intentions to a few privileged initiates alone. The Admiralty was still smarting over the *Discovery* affair and secrecy was vital.

Scott Keltie was one of the few in whom Scott confided, and he was a man who liked being at the centre of events. As the Secretary of the R.G.S., he was also one of the first to hear from Shackleton. Scott bitterly reproached him for not stopping Shackleton, knowing his, Scott's, intentions. Scott Keltie gently pointed out that a confidence was a confidence, and Scott was hoist with his own petard.

In fact, Scott Keltie was more deeply implicated than he cared to admit. As usual, he was exploiting his privileged double rôle of R.G.S. Secretary and specialist writer for *The Times*. He was uniquely placed for the inside story, and what journalist can resist that? An explorer's quarrel was too good to miss. Scott Keltie probably wrote the original *Times* report of Shackleton's announcement which gave Scott the news, including the slur on Scott, 'that the southern sledge party of the *Discovery* would have reached a much higher latitude if they had been more adequately equipped'.

Scott was furious, and immediately tried to stop Shackleton, rather as if he were reprimanding a junior officer. Shackleton, controlling his anger, refused to comply. He pointed out that in the Antarctic, Scott had said he would not go south again because of his position in the Navy. Unable to make an impression on Shackleton, Scott asked Wilson to take a hand.

Wilson was in a unique position to enforce his ideas. Shackleton held him in great respect and affection, having indeed unsuccessfully tried to persuade him to join his expedition. Wilson was in no doubt that Shackleton ought to 'throw the whole thing up'. Wilson himself, in such a position would have done so, because of his self-sacrificial tastes. Shackleton would not submit to such advice; not even from Wilson. Then, at any rate, said Wilson, he ought to keep clear of Scott's old base

I think if you go to McMurdo Sound [he wrote] & even reach the Pole – the gilt will be off the gingerbread because of the insinuation which will almost certainly appear in the minds of a good many, that you forestalled Scott who had a prior claim to the use of that base.

Wilson's unbending sense of moral rectitude finally overcame Shackleton. With the knowledge that in a public brawl with a Naval officer, he was bound to come off worst, he reluctantly gave in. Early in March, he visited Wilson at his home near Cheltenham, and Wilson dictated terms compelling Shackleton to keep to the east of the 170th meridian of west longitude, with everything to the west reserved for Scott. Shackleton telegraphed Scott that he was giving up McMurdo Sound. 'By doing so,' he wrote to Scott Keltie, 'I much diminish any chance of success in the way of a long journey.' That was undoubtedly Scott's intention.

At Scott's insistence, Shackleton recorded their agreement in a letter. Since the base at McMurdo Sound, Shackleton wrote, was

discovered by you and ... as my plans cut across yours, you asked me to change my base.
This I agreed to do ... I am leaving the McMurdo Sound base to you, and will land either at the place known as Barrier Inlet or at King Edward

VII Land, whichever is the most suitable, if I land at either of these places I will not work to the westward of the 170 Meridian W., and shall not make any sledge journey going W of that meridian unless prevented when going to the South from keeping to the East of that meridian by the physical features of the country.

This is a harsh and unprecedented document. Scott had scored off Shackleton; Shackleton, for his part, had one more cause for resentment.

On August 7th Shackleton sailed down the Thames in *Nimrod*, a small and underpowered Newfoundland sealer, which was the only ship he could afford. He went like a corsair. The R.G.S. practically disowned him – leaving themselves, however, a loophole to bathe in his reflected glory, should he succeed. He had no official standing. But King Edward VII, who perhaps knew more than he admitted about the preliminaries, commanded *Nimrod* to Cowes at the last moment, so that he could inspect her before she left. So, with Royal sanction, Shackleton departed for the south, and for the moment, sails out of the story.

After Scott came back from the Antarctic, he had twice requested, and twice been granted, leave to give his lectures and write *The Voyage of the 'Discovery'*. He was then unemployed for six months, and in the autumn of 1905, a year after coming home, still had no appointment. The situation was perplexing the Lords of the Admiralty. Scott was still a Naval anomaly.

He had now been away from Naval service for more than five years, yet in between had risen from a rather senior lieutenant to a very junior captain. Influence had got him where he was.

During his twenty-one years in the Navy Scott had never yet been a chief executive officer. This is the post of running a ship, usually considered an indispensable preliminary to command. Amongst other things, it teaches the future captain what it is like to translate orders into action.

In the words of one Naval officer,

There is no greater test of character ... than to be the executive officer of a big ship. Many shun the responsibility ... but few captains can efficiently command a great ship's company unless they themselves have been through the mill, and can realize [his] difficulties day by day and feel the pulse of the sea.

This explains much of the trouble on *Discovery*. The whole pattern of Scott's career, before going to the Antarctic, points to mistrust of his ability to handle ships, and a tendency to keep him away from the pathway leading to command. The Admiralty were reluctant to put a modern battleship, ten or twenty thousand tons of expensive iron-mongery, in his hands. They eventually returned him to Naval service through a brief war course and a shore appointment. At the end of 1905, he was made Assistant to the Director of Naval Intelligence, Rear Admiral Sir Charles Ottley, a post he held until August 1906. Scott worked with about twenty officers in the same department, including Captain Maurice (later Lord) Hankey, a future Cabinet Secretary, but seems to have made little impression. There is nothing from this period to compare with the flattering portrait of Amundsen penned by the French Ambassador to Norway.* Scott did his work competently, how-ever, suggesting that his bent may have been with facts and figures rather than with men and ships.

From the Intelligence department, Scott went to sea on H.M.S. *Victorious* for his first experience as the captain of a warship. His last Naval service afloat had been six years before, as torpedo lieutenant of H.M.S. *Majestic*.

It was now that Scott decided to return to the Antarctic. He had been toying with the idea for some time, but he seems to have made up his mind in the summer of 1906, shortly before taking over *Victorious*. It was as if he could not face the return to Service life; almost as if, at the prospect of Naval command, his first thought was of escape.

Sir Clements Markham, with whom Scott maintained regular contact, was remarkably lukewarm. Sir Clements was no longer President of the R.G.S. In 1905 he had retired, or been forced from office, discredited by his conduct of the *Discovery* expedition and its relief. Nonetheless, even in retirement he remained a formidable figure. At the age of seventy-six he was still vigorous; still an eminent intriguer, and a patriarch in geographical circles; an oracle whom it might be profitable to consult.

Another expedition, Sir Clements wrote to Scott, required 'much con-sideration from several points of view'. Scott, he felt, ought now to concentrate on the Navy and think of his promotion.

Scott held two commands within the year; first H.M.S. *Victorious*, then H.M.S. *Albemarle*, both battleships in the Atlantic Fleet, both under curiously unsatisfying circumstances. In each case, he was brought in towards the end of the commission, the ship already 'worked up'. His predecessor had trained the crew and got the vessel functioning as an organic whole. He found himself with strong executive officers, like Commander (later Admiral Sir) W. W. Fisher, who really ran his ships.

* See p. 193.

In two and a half years, Scott held four commands, all under like conditions.

Rear Admiral George Le Cl. Egerton, the old 'Arctic' officer who, as his captain on H.M.S. *Majestic*, had written his testimonial for command of *Discovery*, asked for Scott as flag captain, i.e. captain of his flagship. In this way, Scott was given command of first *Victorious* and then *Albemarle*. In February, 1907, just after Scott had taken over *Albemarle*, she rammed *Commonwealth*, another battleship in night manoeuvres off the coast of Portugal. No lives were lost, nor did either ship go down. For Scott, however, the implications were disturbing.

There was the suggestion of an unlucky officer. Sixteen years before, Torpedo Boat No. 87, his first command, had run aground where it required exceptional ill fortune to do so. In the service of the sea, luck is a very real personal attribute.

But beyond this was the light thrown by the incident on Scott's character. He was not on the bridge at the time of collision. To the other captains the dangers were apparent at the time. The fleet was in close formation in quarter column (i.e. echelon); a delicate situation in which the slightest error of course or speed could mean disaster. A fleet change of speed was ordered; under any circumstances, a critical manoeuvre; on a dark night with a heavy sea running doubly so. This was the moment that Scott chose to leave the bridge. He did so to fetch a wireless message, which he decoded himself, and then took personally to Egerton in his Admiral's cabin. These are all menial tasks, normally left to subordinates. Scott was running errands and fussing round a superior, when he should have been concerned for the safety of his ship, the overriding concern of any captain at all times.

Meanwhile *King Edward VII*, the flagship at the head of the line, in giving the order to increase speed had not done so herself. To avoid overrunning and possibly colliding, the ship astern swerved to starboard, followed perforce by the next, and so on down the line until *Commonwealth* astern of *Albemarle* missed her cue, turned too late, and collided. The fault was *Albemarle*'s in not signalling with her siren as the others had done. As far as Scott was concerned, the nub of the matter was that he had not remained on the bridge until the fleet had settled down to a change of speed. It was one of those crises of command, when the instinct of every captain ought to be – and indeed of every other captain in this fleet was – to stay at his post. Scott alone deserted it. At the very least, this argues failure of judgment under pressure. It also suggests running away from responsibility, with all that implies for personal inadequacy. It was the thread running through his career. He was unsuited to command. He was faced with a situation that was beyond him; the predicament of talent failing ambition.

Scott's Naval career might have been in serious jeopardy, but for the present he was safe. The formation of the fleet and the signals controlling it were at least partly the cause of the collision. The ultimate responsibility rested with Admiral Sir William May, commanding the fleet, and Sir William – another old 'Arctic' officer – told Scott he proposed to hush the whole thing up. He did, and nobody was blamed – officially. But there were some awkward moments of suspense before the matter was arranged.

The Shackleton affair burst on Scott while he was still under the strain of this unpropitious incident. It was enough to explain his violent emotional reaction.

Since 1905, another old *Discovery* officer, Michael Barne, had been trying to organize an Antarctic expedition. Scott did not take umbrage, since Barne was aiming at the Weddell Sea, and thus not poaching on what he considered his preserves. In any case, Barne found he could not raise the money. The R.G.S., still smarting from *Discovery*, categorically refused all support. Even with family influence and Royal interest, he got nowhere with the Admirality.

When Scott heard this he realized how prematurely advertising his Polar ambitions could jeopardize his career. He had to bide his time and work with discretion. At the end of September 1906 he wrote to Barne asking him to come with him to the Antarctic as his second in command and, in the meanwhile, act as his front man. Barne, resigned to the collapse of his own project, went on half pay to work for Scott. He could afford to do this as he had a private income: the Navy was a hobby and, although a good officer, he was not too seriously obsessed with promotion.

At this point, Scott received a letter from Lieutenant E. R. Evans, who had been on *Morning*.

> I am very disappointed that I shall not be [Barne's] Navigator, but will you take me as yours? ... If you will only let me sail with you I promise that you will have no keener officer ... I am tremendously enthusiastic about Antarctic exploration.

This was the first application to join Scott's next expedition, and as such has an historic interest. But Scott had a long and tortuous path before he could start accepting volunteers.

*

In some ways, Scott's eyes had been opened by the setbacks on *Discovery*. To interest potential backers for a new expedition, he wrote a memorandum bearing the suggestive title: *The Sledging Problem in the Antarctic: Men versus motors.*

> To reach the South Pole from and return to the *Discovery* Winter Quarters ... necessitates a journey of *1466* miles. Is this possible?

The answer was unequivocal: 'A glance at the figures ... for men haulage will show that it cannot be done in that way.' Nor, said Scott, were dogs the answer: 'It is only in considering the possibility of motor traction that the problem becomes practical.' In these words, then, Scott launched his concept for another expedition:

> I am of opinion that a very high Southern Latitude could be achieved and the possibility of the South Pole itself could be reached by the proper employment of vehicles capable of mechanical propulsion over the surface of the Great Southern Barrier.

This is virtually a paraphrase of Skelton's original suggestion on *Discovery* in 1902. It reveals Scott's attitude to the Polar environment, and the inconsistencies within himself.

As a result of his Antarctic experience, Scott has sensibly discarded man-hauling. He has less sensibly persisted with his idea that dogs are useless. He does so in the teeth of more evidence presented since his return. There were Sverdrup's long treks on *Fram*; and Godfred Hansen's great journey to Victoria Land on Amundsen's North-West Passage expedition. And, in the Antarctic itself, there was Nordenskjöld who, on his notably efficient traverse of the Larsen Ice Shelf, a miniature of the Ross Ice Barrier, had pointed the way with dogs in the south.*

Scott, however, ignored the lessons of these successful contemporaries, and put his faith in a technological panacea. In this he was following his training and his times. The Royal Navy was in the hands of the *materielists*: that school of thought which saw in bigger and better gadgetry the guarantee, *by its mere possession*, of superiority and success: putting machines before men, in other words.

Scott may have been wrong-headed in all this, but the technically-minded author of *The Sledging Problem in the Antarctic* is not the romantic idealist of *The Voyage of the 'Discovery'*. The man who says that it is only

---

* After losing his ship *Antarctic* in the ice of the Weddell Sea, Nordenskjöld had to spend a second winter involuntarily at his base on Snow Hill Island. Together with *Antarctic*'s crew, he was eventually rescued in 1904 by an Argentine relief expedition. Nordenskjöld's expedition is one of the unsung sagas of Polar exploration; it was one of the best-run enterprises.

in considering the possibility of 'motor traction' that the problem of reaching the Pole 'becomes practical' is not the same one who could write that 'the conquest is more nobly won' by 'hard physical labour'.* Scott seemed to have learned an important lesson.

To Scott a motor sledge was the new key to the South Pole. But, except for some experimental devices in Canada and Sweden, none existed. A model had to be developed, and Barne's first task was to find a backer, which eventually he found in Lord Howard de Walden, one of the motoring pioneers.

The obstacles were great. Motoring was still in its infancy; the petrol engine yet unreliable. Scott, finding after some time that his technical knowledge was inadequate, needed professional assistance. He turned to Skelton who, as Sir Clements Markham had put it, gave 'the impression of a supremely able man', which the Navy was proceeding to recognize. Scott approached Skelton through Barne, who reported that Skelton seemed 'just the least bit piqued at not having been consulted earlier'. Barne having broken the ice, Scott wrote to Skelton.

It is an interesting document, displaying subtlety and charm. Skelton had not been happy on *Discovery*; nor did he particularly like Scott. But he had an inventive mind, and this was a project calculated to appeal to him. Scott played on that.

After a long resumé of the situation, including the bait that he had 'got in touch with the King – got Wilson to say he would come again' and a disarmingly frank reference to 'the difficulty of ... my position in the service [which] pointed to the advisability of keeping my ideas to myself', Scott came to the point:

Traction is the main thing and of course one turns to the motor; it matters not who first thought of it since it is so natural a thought to come to anyone.

This shows considerable poise. Arctowski, of *Belgica*, and Dr. J. B. Charcot, who had led the French expedition to the coast of Graham Land in 1903–05 were already experimenting with motor sledges. Possibly this turned Scott's attention to the subject. In any case, Skelton, on the evidence of his own diaries, had already made the suggestion on *Discovery* in 1902.

Barne, Scott explained in his letter, was a person who might be

usefully employed in making certain enquiries concerning motor people [but it] was not the sort of business one would expect Michael to excel.

This was hardly fair since it was Barne who introduced Scott to Lord

* See p. 188.

Howard de Walden. But Barne had served his purpose; now it was Skelton's turn:

> I have not told you of my scheme before because it seemed to me the moment had not come ... Now the moment has come   There is only one person in the world that combines a knowledge of southern conditions with engineering skill and that is yourself.
>
> I have cherished the idea that if I went South again you would join what I want now is, not a promise that if all goes well you will come South, but your engineering skill and expert knowledge in designing and pushing forward the design of the ... motors Lord Howard will build ... I will only go South with a pretty good certainty of success and I believe that that can only be obtained by universal patience in getting the machine that is required.

There is, however, no mistaking the urgency of the peroration:

> You see how I am situated and how hopeless it is for me to push things on my own account at present — Therefore I rely the more on you to push them.

Skelton answered this call by telegram. Within a week, he had started on Scott's motor sledge.

Meanwhile, Shackleton — doubtless inspired by Skelton — was also working on Antarctic motor transport. Now preparing to leave on *Nimrod*, he was having a modified motor car, made by the Arroll-Johnstone Co. who were testing fuels and lubricants. 'We must,' said Scott, 'get hold of the results sometime.' Shackleton had started his ambivalent rôle as enemy and pacemaker.

Scott's sledge was based on a caterpillar track. It was the first tracked vehicle to be designed specifically for snow, although not the first tracked vehicle, which was an American invention. The idea of using a caterpillar track was jointly due to Skelton and B. T. Hamilton, one of Lord Howard de Walden's engineers. Skelton worked out the details and originated the device of putting slats on the track to grip the snow.

This vehicle was far ahead of its time. It needed careful experiment and design in every detail. Because a few motor cars had started in cold weather in Canada and Russia, however, Scott told Skelton not to 'waste time in freezing chambers' testing his motors. Again, Scott was showing his characteristic impatience where caution was necessary, not to mention his ignorance of technology and the Polar environment.

With a backer and a trusted helper advancing his project, Scott now devoted himself to his professional duties and his personal affairs.

17

An Edwardian Marriage

EXTRAVAGANT, POSSIBLY VULGARIAN, Edwardian society was eager for celebrities and catholic in its tastes. Explorers were made much of. This was the world into which Scott plunged on his return from the Antarctic. As the Polar explorer, he had attained a social standing that otherwise would have been denied him. For the first time, with doors opened that heretofore had been closed, he did the London season. In Sir Clements Markham's words, Scott was 'very flourishing, and the ideal of a smart captain of a battleship'. He was caricatured (cruelly) as a bit of a dandy and a roué by 'Spy' in *Vanity Fair*. He had arrived.

Scott enjoyed the taste of success. He could now indulge himself, for he had a captain's pay and royalty payments from his book. Moreover, he was at last able to make his mother an allowance without financial strain. She had moved to a new house at 56, Oakley Street, Chelsea, and Scott still lived with her.

Through his sister Ettie Ellison-Macartney, Scott was introduced to a raffish world of artists, writers and actors. When she had been on the stage, Ettie had toured with Mabel Beardsley, the sister of Aubrey Beardsley, the *fin-de-siècle* artist. Now married and settled down, Mabel was a determined lionizer. Through Ettie, she secured the presence of Scott at her 'Thursday afternoon teas' in her home in Pimlico. There, in an ambiance of ageing aestheticism and cultivated decadence, Scott met Max Beerbohm, friends of Oscar Wilde, and other survivors of the Nineties. He conducted a flirtation with Mabel substantial enough to support a correspondence. 'I'm serving my King and Country once more,' he wrote to her with unwonted flippancy when he returned to sea. 'No theatres or tea parties for quite a long time.'

At one of Mabel's luncheon parties in March 1906, Scott met Kathleen Bruce. She was what Max Beerbohm – next to whom, incidentally, she was sitting, with Barrie on the other side – called 'rather a talented sculptress'. Her maternal grandmother was Greek. For the rest, she was pure Scots, the youngest of a country parson's eleven children. Intended for teaching, she took to sculpture instead and trained at the Slade School in London. She lived for a time in Paris, where she met Picasso, Rodin and others. She appears to have been the kind of person often found on the fringes of the famous. She had a passionate infatuation for the dancer Isadora Duncan, and lived a self-consciously Bohemian life with undertones of bisexuality. Gertrude Stein, the American avante-garde writer and a known Lesbian, found her 'a very beautiful, very athletic English girl'. A compulsive flirt, she had an impressive capacity for self-dramatization.

Scott was now consciously or not looking for a wife and at this delicate juncture the Admiralty, in their occult wisdom, gave him the necessary leisure to attend to his own affairs. On August 25th, 1907, he left H.M.S. *Albemarle*, and went on half pay for five months.

Scott was what his family called 'a ladies' man'. Among his recent affairs was one with an actress called Pauline Chase, an early Peter Pan, engineered by Barrie. Despite all this, however, Scott's knowledge of women was extremely superficial. Kathleen Bruce, with her extravagant Bohemianism, her continental travels, and a spell of nursing in one of the Balkan wars, was outside his experience. She was a predatory female; more predatory than usual, that is. For, approaching thirty, she was in danger of being left on the shelf. Scott was child's play for her.

He always admired clever women, and he was (partly) attracted to Kathleen by her art and conversation. For some months, they were almost constantly together. Apart, they wrote a stream of love letters, almost devoid of humour, and curiously lacking in passion. Scott's approach was hardly that of the masterful lover but of self-searching and abasement. In one of his letters, he revealed a flash of insight that goes far to explain his inadequacy as a leader; at least it convincingly suggests why he could not *inspire* people. It has authentic echoes of *Discovery*:

> I've a personality myself – a mean poor thing beside yours, something that can neither inspire or content others, but yet has a tendency to dominate by sheer persistency – you've seen the effect I know in those that have been much with me – I hate it myself and hate the sense of responsibility it brings but I don't seem to have the power to make it different.

By January 1908, marriage was in the air. Scott also had a ship again. Towards the end of the month, at short notice, he was given command of H.M.S. *Essex*. She was a cruiser; a step down from the battleships he had commanded and which, taken with the long time on half pay, might have been interpreted as oblique censure for the collision of *Albemarle*.

Early in March, his motor sledge was ready. Dr. J. B. Charcot, the

Frenchman who had been in the Antarctic while he was there, and who was now also working on a motor sledge, invited Scott to joint snow trials at Lauteret, in the French Alps. Scott decided to go himself, instead of working through an agent, although it meant risking premature disclosure of his plans to the Admiralty. It also meant breaking regulations because, although on leave, he was on twelve hours' notice to join his ship at Portsmouth. He got his mother to telegraph the Admiralty after he had departed, requesting an extension to thirty-six hours, and crossed the Channel. In Paris, he learned from the *Continental Daily Mail* that *Nimrod* had returned to New Zealand and Shackleton, after all, had landed at 'his' quarters at McMurdo Sound. He was overcome by a childish torrent of emotion, instantly vented in a letter to Kathleen:

> Did I show you his agreement with me – it was a perfectly plain distinct statement absolutely binding in an honourable sense – he definitely agreed not to approach our old quarters ... it makes it definitely impossible to do anything till he is heard of again ... you can guess something of my thoughts.

Shackleton, barred from McMurdo Sound by his 'private word of honour given under pressure' as he put it, had in fact first tried to land on the Barrier itself, at Balloon Bight. When that failed, he made for King Edward VII Land but, there too, he was defeated by the ice. Then and only then did he put the helm about and sail to the forbidden base. 'My conscience is clear,' he wrote to his wife, 'but my heart is sore ... I have one comfort that I did my best.' Scott, and certainly Wilson, expected him to keep his word, cost what it might, even if it meant risking the lives of himself and all his men.

Scott continued to brood over the morals of the case. He sent Kathleen the text of the agreement he had forced out of Shackleton giving up McMurdo Sound. 'Don't trouble to return [it] as I have many copies,' he wrote.

After torrents of emotional prolixity, they had decided to marry. Of Scott's fervour, there is no doubt; whether Kathleen was in love with him is another matter. Scott was only too conscious of the shortcomings of a Naval education. He willingly allowed Kathleen to repair the deficiency, for he respected her intelligence. She introduced him to books, plays and ideas which she, in turn, had acquired from her intellectual friends. Scott's education, in a sense, began when he met Kathleen. She was evidently trying to mould him into her image of the ideal man; the complete hero.

To the conventional pursuit of a husband, Kathleen had added an unusual twist of her own. She had decided that one day she would bear a hero as a son, to a father of whom none but a hero would be worthy. It was a Wagnerian idea – she was fond of Wagner – with which she amused her friends, although she herself, eventually, took it seriously enough. She was, after all, merely saying explicitly what every woman feels, and dramatizing it rather more than most. Scott, as a Polar explorer, was the kind of heroic figure of whom she could approve, although he had, to her, manifest imperfections which she felt she ought to remove.

Of Scott it might well be said, as it has been said of Don Quixote, that he was 'a knight-errant with small faith in his own credentials ... his attitude to his own destiny [being] that of secret uncertainty held down ... by a continued effort of will'. It was now that this 'secret uncertainty' got the upper hand.

Marriage loomed ahead to a woman both physically and emotionally demanding. Shackleton was reaching heaven knows where in the Antarctic. In the midst of this turmoil, Scott was faced with the dangerous Naval intrigues which signalled the end of Admiral Fisher's tempestuous reign and could imperil a promising career. It behoved the prudent officer to keep clear of the backwash. Scott had to tread carefully, avoiding unpopular admirals, making his number with rising ones. Each of these burdens was strain enough by itself for an insecure and highly-strung man. But it was the pressures of command that told on Scott. It was obvious towards the end of the *Discovery* expedition, but it became more marked after his first Naval commands. It was then that the doubt and introspection which had always lurked just underneath the surface, took a morbid turn and seized him in their grip.

By training and temperament, Scott was reserved and inhibited. He had found in Kathleen someone to whom he could unburden himself. 'I want someone to anchor to,' as he expressed it in a letter to her. At the same time he told her he was 'a little frightened vaguely. You are so uncommon and I conventionalised. What does it all mean?'

It was a favourite phrase: 'What does it all mean?', as if he could not find a meaning in life; perhaps it was the expression of the black depression that regularly descended on him; a hopelessness that alternated with bouts of violent elation.

At the eleventh hour, Kathleen had doubts about marriage, partly because she saw that Scott was a mother worshipper, and therefore might not be quite the man she wanted. She took a dislike to Mrs. Scott; also to Wilson because he was the other person who dominated Scott. Kathleen especially disliked Wilson, in after years bitterly denouncing him as a prig with no humour. She resented him almost as if he had been another woman threatening her hold on Scott.

Mrs. Scott, for her part, disapproved of the match. Puritanical and infinitely middle class, she was not at ease with artists. She expected her son to marry money, or at least position; besides which, she flinched at the prospect of a masterful daughter-in-law. Scott, however, after one or two tentative forays had learned exactly his standing in the marriage market, and made his mother understand that Kathleen was the best he could get. Kathleen overcame her doubts, and they were married on September 2nd, 1908. It was, Max Beerbohm wrote in his inimitable style to Kathleen (whom he had, briefly, considered marrying himself), 'very congratulable a matter for you, not less than for *him!*'

Scott bungled the announcement, so that privileged associates heard not privately in advance, but with the public via the newspapers; in those days a solecism of the very gravest kind. Kathleen was not pleased, because it gave her the idea that her future husband was 'unlucky', and her attitude to the unlucky was, in the words of a Spanish proverb, that 'they are best avoided'.

The wedding took place at the Chapel Royal, Hampton Court, a privilege not granted to all. Royal permission was necessary. The wedding was one of the extensively reported functions of the year.

After a week's honeymoon at Etretat, near Le Havre (Kathleen's idea), the couple returned to London for a few days together in their new home, at 174 Buckingham Palace Road, a small house conveniently close to the Admiralty. Scott then returned to duty at Devonport, and H.M.S. *Bulwark*, a battleship of which he was now captain.

Marriage began with an inauspicious echo from *Discovery*. The scientific results had begun to appear, inspiring Dr. Chree, President of the Physical Society of London to say that

> When referring to any British national undertaking, such as a war or a scientific expedition, one is expected to apologise for a greater or less amount of preliminary muddle.

He hinted that Scott was 'some one whose knowledge of physical science is very limited', and that 'a scientific court martial' might not have been out of place. The meteorology came in for particularly heavy criticism. The elementary error of confusing true and magnetic compass bearings had been made, and the wind observations were thus largely worthless. *The Times Literary Supplement* rubbed home the point:

> The meteorological observations, instead of being made by people familiar with such work ... were entrusted to officers who had no previous training, and were not even properly instructed ... How much longer shall we have to wait in England for those entrusted with national

affairs to appreciate a little more seriously the requirements of scientific investigation? Probably until the constant leakage and loss which we suffer in ignorance are made plainer by one or more exceptional disasters.

Scott's reaction was a copious, violent and not entirely coherent flood of protest. The criticism or, as he put it in a letter to Sir Archibald Geikie, Secretary of the Royal Society, the attack, was 'so gratuitous, so utterly unprovoked, and, in view of the circulation, so unpatriotic ...' Scott, tellingly, equated all criticism with personal vindictiveness. He demanded a public enquiry to put an end 'to this irresponsible criticism by *responsible* persons'. When Mostyn Field, now Rear Admiral and Hydrographer of the Navy, heard of this, he remarked that

> The hyper-sensitiveness that refuses to accept criticism is very unfortunate ...
> I fear Captain Scott will retain his own opinion in spite of what any one
> may say, but in my judgement by pressing for an enquiry he will do himself ...
> much harm ... and give cause to the Continental nations to draw unfavour-
> able conclusions.

Scott took the hint and retreated. Skelton had gone through the records and uncovered incompetence which, had it been made public, would have given Scott's enemies a field day.

Kathleen, meanwhile, was working hard at Scott's career. She had declined to follow him to Devonport, very sensibly preferring to stay close to the rulers of the Navy in the Admiralty building at the entrance to the Mall. She had a great capacity for championing a person wholeheartedly, making him appear larger than life. She built up Scott; the very fact that she was his wife suggested that perhaps he had hidden qualities. A man, after all, is known by his woman. She cultivated influential Admiralty officers; two in particular: Captain Mark Kerr, and Captain Henry Campbell, an old shipmate of Scott. On them she exerted her forceful and fascinating personality. By the end of the year she had wangled for her husband an Admiralty appointment as Naval assistant to Admiral Sir Francis Bridgeman, Second Sea Lord.

At a country house one weekend Kathleen managed to interest Sir Edgar Speyer, a City banker and philanthropist, in supporting the expedition, when it came about. She was so vehemently keen on an expedition that it sometimes seemed as if she would not have married Scott unless he was fairly certain to go.

Meanwhile, there was the business of a baby which, after all, was Kathleen's main reason for marrying. She summoned Scott to London at the proper time in her menstrual cycle, but otherwise seemed to bear his absence very well, so that his function was made almost comically clear. He could hardly complain. At great length she had revealed how she was devoted to the overthrow of male domination. She belonged to the advance guard of the feminists. 'The war of the sexes', a fashionable slogan just then, was to her a living reality. She wished to turn the tables on the men, and dominate them instead of being dominated. By her own account, she was a virgin when she married Scott, and made much of it.

'Throw up your cap & shout & sing triumphantly,' she wrote to him with a more exuberant scrawl than usual in the New Year when, for the first time, she was a few days overdue, 'meseems we are in a fair way to achieve my end.' The 'my' instead of 'our' was a revealing slip of the pen; for Scott, perhaps a little too revealing. He protested, mildly.

Kathleen had, indeed, conceived and provisionally chosen names: Peter if it turned out to be a boy, Griselda if a girl. Still the black mood clung to Scott.

> I'm obsessed with the view of life as a struggle for existence [he wrote in a typical letter to Kathleen]. I seem to be marking time ... impotent to command circumstances – I seem to hold in reserve something that makes for success and yet see no worthy field for it.

Towards the end of 1908, the second version of Scott's motor sledge was ready for snow trials. Scott wrote to Nansen, asking advice on where and when.

> I am contemplating your country ... I need not try to explain to you ... that the real conditions required cannot be obtained outside the Polar circle.

To which Nansen, like anyone else reasonably familiar with the mountain world, could reply that on 'one of the big glaciers, ... of course you may have almost exactly Inland Ice conditions ...'

Scott settled instead for Lillehammer, a valley town on a lake in Eastern Norway, because it was more easily accessible. He was unable to get leave, so Skelton ran the trials instead, returning with the hopeful report that it would 'require very slight modification for useful work in the Antarctic'.

Then, on March 24th, 1909, the very day that he took up his new Admiralty appointment, Scott heard the news of Shackleton's arrival in New Zealand bearing the tale of his achievement. Shackleton had got within ninety-seven miles of the Pole, 360 miles beyond the old Furthest

South. It was the biggest single advance that had ever been or ever would be made towards either Pole of the earth. But the South Pole, after all, had been left for Scott – and Amundsen.

On June 14th, 1909, Shackleton returned to London and to a tumultuous welcome, painfully unlike Scott's own muted homecoming from *Discovery*. Hugh Robert Mill has described how, calling in at the R.G.S. the same day, he

> met Scott there, gloomily discussing with Keltie whether he ought to go to meet Shackleton or not. He did not wish to go, but Scott was always a slave to duty, and we persuaded him that it was his duty to greet his former subordinate.

Amundsen, who understood what Shackleton had done, wrote a spontaneous tribute to the R.G.S.

> I must ... congratulate you ... upon this wonderful achievement ... The English nation has by the deed of Shackleton won a victory in the Antarctic exploration [sic] which never can be surpassed. What Nansen is in the North Shackleton is in the South.

Shackleton had stopped with the goal within his grasp, one of the bravest acts in the history of Polar exploration. When his wife asked him how he found the strength of will to turn, he answered: 'I thought you would rather have a live donkey than a dead lion.' Turning back and living with the might-have-been requires a special brand of courage.

Shackleton had more to his credit than merely the Furthest South. Some of his men, under Professor Edgeworth David (at the age of fifty-four) had been the first to reach the South Magnetic Pole, and others had climbed Mount Erebus, the first ascent of an Antarctic mountain, all in the course of a single season. It really was attainment of no ordinary kind. Shackleton laid England at his feet. But it was not so much because of the deed as the style. The country was looking for a hero, and Shackleton filled the bill.

While Britain still appeared the greatest power on earth, unease was gnawing just beneath the surface. Imperial Germany, bursting with the crude aggressive energy of a rising and ambitious state, untroubled by the tortured moralizing that was eating away the spirit of the British, had become the overhanging threat. Strikes and social unrest gave forebodings of upheaval to come. Into this atmosphere laden with uncertainty and doubt, burst Shackleton, genial, swaggering, breezy, the precise figure of reassurance for a troubled country.

King Edward VII, a shrewd monarch, understood this when he

knighted Shackleton, while Scott had to make do with a C.V.O. Scott, with his neurotic worries and suspicion, was too much a mirror of the times for comfort; Shackleton was a tonic.

It was not only that he had carried the Union Jack closer to the Pole than any other flag, he had done it in a way far more acceptable than if he had actually reached his goal and done it too easily. He had provided a glorious near miss and enjoyed the right kind of British adventure with all the proper ingredients; heroic battling against the odds, an epic race against disaster, triumph by sheer grit and, by the very finest of margins, a happy ending: a moral tale for the times.

Beyond all this, Shackleton was the stuff of which the necessary kind of hero was made. He radiated a simple unaffected patriotism. 'I am representing 400 million British subjects,' he had written to his wife. He belonged, said a contemporary journalist, 'most closely to the type ... pictured ... in old tales and sea romance ... a living "Midshipman Easy"'. The publicists, so keenly sensitive to the public mood, harped on this point. 'In our age,' said the *Daily Telegraph* in a leader, 'filled with vain babbling about the decadence of the race, he has upheld the old fame of our breed.'

Shackleton brought the South Pole into the British public consciousness; more, he made it the universal and easily understood goal of his day, like the race to the moon our times. Shackleton would have been a godsend for television, for he had presence, charisma, the actor's gift of simplifying and projecting himself. Not since Nansen returned from the drift of the *Fram* had any explorer made such an impact. Scott did not impress journalists; in fact he faintly antagonized them. Consequently, at the time, he was never as popular as Shackleton. It is a little ironic, that Shackleton, who is half forgotten today, was the better able to enjoy contemporary success.

In public, the two men masked their hostility by a façade of mutual esteem. But Shackleton could not trust himself to talk to Scott in private, for he was bitterly hurt by malicious and unfounded rumours that he had faked his latitudes, probably blaming it on Scott himself, although Sir Clements Markham almost certainly was implicated.

Within a few days of hearing the news, Sir Clements was writing to Scott that 'it draws rather a long bill on my credulity'. Sir Clements, however, did not pursue the subject until the middle of April, when Scott came to dinner and, Sir Clements wrote in his diary, said that he 'does not believe in the latitudes'.

Sir Clements' opinions were coloured by his disapproval of what he considered Shackleton's poaching on Scott's preserves at McMurdo

Sound. He could not, however, entirely suppress admiration for Shackleton's achievement, going so far as to observe at one point that 'something should be allowed for his very impulsive character'. Sir Clements' spark of generosity, however, seems to have been snuffed out by Scott who, by his own account, now mistrusted everything about Shackleton.

This did not, however, prevent Scott from presiding at a dinner for Shackleton at the Savage Club in London on June 19th. In his after dinner speech, Scott (to the punctuation of loud cheers) suggested that the South Pole must be discovered by an Englishman, and that he was prepared 'to go forth in search of that object'. 'All I have to do now,' Scott concluded by saying, 'is to thank Mr. Shackleton for so nobly showing the way.' He had indeed. Shackleton had proved beyond reasonable doubt that the Pole lay high up on an ice cap; and he had found the gateway to the heights; a vast glacier over a hundred miles long which he named the Beardmore in honour of his benefactor.

The speech at the Savage Club was virtually Scott's declaration of intent to organize another expedition. Again Sir Clements was lukewarm. The Pole, he wrote to Scott, 'ought to be done, but I do not think you should swerve from your naval career for it'.

Scott, however, ignored Sir Clements' views. He started badgering the R.G.S. to force Shackleton to define his future actions, for Shackleton was suggesting that he too was going South again.

> All I want [Scott wrote to Leonard Darwin] is freedom to make an announcement without incurring suspicion that I am cutting across Shackleton's plans; ... if he leaves his own intentions in the present vague form I cannot act without causing that suspicion.

Scott was a slave to forms and etiquette; but also he seemed like someone putting off decisions. He made few friends by it. The R.G.S. had no desire to become involved in a repetition of the previous squabble, especially since, having sat on the fence, they now very handsomely accepted Shackleton and partook of his reflected glory.

Admiral Sir Lewis Beaumont, the R.G.S. Vice-President, wrote to Major Leonard Darwin, now the R.G.S. President, saying that

> Scott would make a very great mistake ... by trying to compete with Shackleton on a Pole-hunting expedition ... the [R.G.S.] Council's attitude ... ought not only to be neutral but actually opposed to it.
> The more I think of the difference between what Shackleton has done, and the mere act ... of standing at the position of the Pole itself - the less I think of it! ...
> Let him [Scott] lead another Antarctic expedition if he will ... but

let it be a scientific expedition ... He is looking at the thing now from too close, individually ...

All this is to incline you to put Scott off from making ... a mistake – that is, competing with Shackleton in organizing an expedition to go over the old route merely to do that 97 miles ...

Sir Lewis was a new-found admirer of Kathleen Scott, one of Scott's Naval patrons and an old 'Arctic' Admiral. In the light of history, it was perceptive advice.

Scott, having been plainly told that the R.G.S. declined to run his errands for him, finally tried the direct approach to Shackleton:

I propose to organize the Expedition to the Ross Sea ... My plan is to establish a base in King Edward Land ... I should be glad to have your assurance that I am not disconcerting any plan of yours.

A week later, Shackleton, doubtless influenced by Darwin, replied that Scott's expedition would not

interfere with any plans of mine ... I wish you every success in your endeavour to penetrate the ice and to land on King Edward VII Land.

It was thus, in the shadow of an enemy, that Scott started on the road back to the Antarctic.

It was now that Scott took his first definite steps towards another expedition. He tried to get a ship. Unlike Amundsen, he had no *Fram* to turn to. Norway, poor and small, could afford to keep a vessel for Polar exploration but not the British Empire, with the mightiest Navy and mercantile marine afloat. After her return from the Antarctic, *Discovery* had been sold to the Hudson's Bay Company, and Scott had to start again from scratch. As Sir Clements Markham said, in strangely familiar words, 'The great fault in this country is the absence of continuity in all our efforts.'

Scott tried to get back *Discovery*, but Lord Strathcona, chairman of the Hudson's Bay Company, was uncharitable and unwilling. Scott then started negotiating for *Terra Nova*, the second *Discovery* relief ship.

For almost two months, Scott's plans hung fire; and then suddenly, in the middle of September, he announced his new expedition. To the outside world, it was quite unexpected. The R.G.S. was taken by surprise. Offices were rented in Victoria Street at forty-eight hours' notice. The decision bore all the signs of haste. Something evidently had happened to precipitate action. One explanation is obvious: the same Cook and Peary sensation of those first days of September that made Amundsen turn about.

The claims to have reached the North Pole brought home to Scott the dangers in the south. As it was, there were rumours of an American Antarctic expedition. America was still in England looked upon as a rival and half an enemy. The Germans and the Japanese were actually preparing expeditions. With Pole-seeking now extinguished in the north, the pressure would be redoubled in the south. Shackleton had left what Amundsen called 'a little patch' behind. But the respite might be short. Time was running out for Scott. If he was to reach the Pole; if he was to have his revenge on Shackleton – for that was now his goal – if he was to make the one last throw of the dice that would make certain of his Admiral's flag in the now generally expected war, he would have to act swiftly. The Admiralty (thanks to Shackleton's overwhelming success) was no longer implacably opposed to Polar expeditions. Everything pointed in the same direction.

On September 11th, Kathleen entered in her diary 'The office 36 Victoria St. was taken. Went to see it.'

And on the 13th: 'Sent for Dr. & Nurse. Announcement of expedition in *Times* and *Daily Mail*.'

She had gone into labour as the news of the expedition appeared, giving birth the following day to their only child, christened Peter Markham, after Peter Pan and Sir Clements Markham.

The battle was on. The race had begun. In a letter to Admiral Sir Arthur Moore, Scott wrote bluntly, 'I don't hold that anyone but an Englishman should get to the S. Pole.'

The danger with this kind of thought is that *should* imperceptibly glides into *can*. Scott proposed to leave the following year, about the same time as Amundsen. The difference was that Amundsen had been preparing since 1907; Scott, except for developing the motor sledge, had done nothing. The years he might have used for training had been cast away. He was still as incompetent as the day he blundered off the ice cap at the end of 1903.

The difference between the rivals was equally profound at the deeper levels from which motives and behaviour spring. When Scott announced his marriage, he wrote to Dr. Charcot that 'It does not stop my plans for my work in the South, which is as well, for I tire of this life of regularity.'

This is a revealing hint of the essentially negative impulses driving Scott. Fear was at the head; fear of professional failure, but fear of boredom above all. The power of boredom is great; it has spurred men to do much. Unfortunately, it involves the mentality of escape, and thinking by reaction, which means dangerous emotionalism and rashness. Amundsen had the advantage of the positive force of undiluted ambition, perhaps even narcissism; a search for fulfilment instead of avoidance of what might be worse; the goal ahead instead of the goad behind.

Part Two

Part Two

18

Volte-Face

IN SEPTEMBER, 1909, Amundsen returned from Copenhagen to his home at Bundefjord, where Betty, his old nursemaid was reigning as housekeeper. There, as the birch trees began to turn yellow, and the first breath of autumn came down from the hills, he sat in his study looking through the window at the gently rippled waters of the fjord, and worked out his plan of campaign.

He held both the strategic and tactical advantage. Scott had by now disclosed his intentions, while he himself had not shown his hand. Amundsen knew he had a rival. Scott was working in the dark.

Psychologically, too, Amundsen held a trump. The shock of being forestalled (perhaps) by Cook and Peary was quite impersonal. It soon passed off, allowing him to think and act dispassionately. Scott, by contrast, had been goaded by the personally upsetting clash with Shackleton, and feelings still held sway. To Amundsen, Shackleton was the rational and detached embodiment of lessons to be learned; not, as in the case of Scott, a provoker of the dangerous emotions that encircle envy and imperil judgment.

The heart of Scott's plan, as published in *The Times* on September 13th, was the establishment of *two* bases; one at McMurdo Sound, the other on King Edward VII Land, 'the advance to the Pole [being] made from one or other ... according to circumstances'.

Amundsen saw this as a copy of the *Nimrod* expedition. He rightly concluded that Scott, having a conventional mind, would probably stick to known paths, and make for the Pole over Shackleton's route from McMurdo Sound.

Amundsen decided to land on the Ross Ice Barrier itself. This was a stroke of audacity. No one had yet dared to camp on an ice shelf for fear of floating out to sea on an iceberg when it calved. It was a challenge from which even Shackleton had shrunk.

On January 24th, 1908, when in *Nimrod* Shackleton had reached the position of Balloon Bight, first sighted six years before on *Discovery*, the Bight had disappeared. The ice shelf had broken away for miles, floating out to sea and leaving instead a wide bay with hundreds of whales blowing in the water. Shackleton called it the Bay of Whales. Icebergs and pack ice pressing in from the north made their point to Shackleton's imaginative mind.

The thought of what might have been [he wrote], made me decide then and there that under no circumstances would I winter on the Barrier and that wherever we did land we would secure a solid rock foundation for our winter home.

Amundsen nonetheless chose the Bay of Whales for his base. He was not being reckless.

I had given this formation in the Barrier a special study [he wrote] and came to the conclusion that what today is known as the Bay of Whales is nothing else than the selfsame bay observed by Sir James Clark Ross, admittedly with a number of big changes, but nonetheless the same. For 70 years this forma-tion ... remained in the same place. I decided that it could not be fortuitous. What had ... stopped the giant ice stream at precisely this point and formed a permanent bay in the ice front, which otherwise runs smoothly, was not some caprice but ... terra firma.

Amundsen was right, although for the wrong reasons. The Bay of Whales is a permanent feature, although not, as we now know, be-cause it is aground. Like the rest of the Barrier, it is in fact afloat. But it is in the lee of Roosevelt Island, a shoal to the south, which slows the advance of the ice, and also causes a disturbance like eddies in a stream.

In any case, Amundsen had read his history. Sir James Clark Ross, Borchgrevink, Scott in *Discovery*, Shackleton all told the same tale of a constant feature in the ice. A picture from Ross' voyage of the mysterious bay in 1841 showed a distinct dome in the background. This was the prediscovery of Roosevelt Island, first noticed from the air a century later. To Amundsen, ignorant of its existence, the message of the dome was none the less clear. It was the form taken by ice as it flows over an underlying obstruction of solid material.

Amundsen was the first to draw the obvious conclusion because he was the first to study the sources; the first to look with the experienced eye of one with a feeling for ice in all its forms; the first with an historic sense. Amundsen, like Nansen, was that rare creature, an in-tellectual Polar explorer; with the capacity to examine evidence and make logical deductions. And he had flair, talent, perception; possibly the elements of genius.

In the balancing of risks, the odds were heavily in favour of the Bay of Whales. It was a whole degree of latitude – sixty miles – closer to

the Pole than McMurdo Sound: a saving of 120 miles in a journey of
1,364 miles as the crow flies; or almost nine per cent. Where every mile
and minute counted, this was an advantage worth much. It outweighed
the dangers of the Barrier calving precisely where winter quarters would
stand. Having started on a race, as Amundsen remarked, he 'had to
be the first past the post; everything had to give way to that'. For the
same reason, he proposed to follow the shortest path from the Bay of
Whales to the Pole, along a meridian of longitude, and find his own
way up to the Polar Plateau. This meant pioneering a new route across
unknown territory, and doing so quickly. That was in itself an act of
faith.

Amundsen saw various advantages of the Bay of Whales. It lay on
the Barrier itself; the road to the South would start at the front door.
Shackleton had shown that in that respect McMurdo Sound was chancy:
a land base could be cut off from the Barrier when the ice went out.
A ship could always get close to the Barrier front, whereas at McMurdo
Sound – as *Discovery* had so graphically demonstrated – this was not
necessarily so. There were plenty of seals to feed men and dogs.
Amundsen also reasoned that, because the Bay of Whales was further
than McMurdo Sound from the mountains of South Victoria Land, the
weather would be better, and the ice less disturbed. As we now know,
he reasoned from false premises; but he reasoned correctly from the
facts as they were known at the time.

Although Amundsen kept away from McMurdo Sound to avoid
crossing Scott's path, it is conceivable that, even had the field been free,
he would have stuck to the Bay of Whales because the advantages were
so overwhelming. Saving distance was his concern; distance and time,
not only to beat Scott, but because of working his dogs.

But Amundsen did not care for Scott's assumption of prescriptive
rights to McMurdo Sound.

> I do not belong to that class of explorer who believes that the Polar sea has
> been created for myself alone [he once pointedly said]. My view is the
> diametric opposite. The more the merrier; simultaneously at the same place
> if you like. Nothing stimulates like competition. [That is] the sporting spirit
> that ought to reign in these regions. First come, first served is an old saying.

To Amundsen, his route had the moral justification of being Norwegian. It was Borchgrevink – a Norwegian, even if he sailed under
the British flag – who first landed on the Barrier at about the same
spot, and showed that it was the highway to the south. And if there
were claims to privilege in the Ross Sea, then the Norwegians' were

as good as any. For were not the first men ashore on South Victoria Land Norwegians from *Antarctic* in 1895? That was years before Scott had the remotest interest in the Polar regions.

Having decided on his base and his route, Amundsen set about analysing Shackleton's performance, in order to learn from his mistakes. It is much harder to learn from success than from failure, and nothing illustrates Amundsen's calibre better than his refusal to be mesmerized by Shackleton's dazzling performance. He had the perception to see behind to the near disaster which loomed throughout, and which was the real lesson to be learned.

Shackleton had taken risks on a monumental scale. He had cut his rations to the bone. Depots were too small, too few, and too sketchily marked. Reaching them in time, a matter of life and death, was often a close-run thing. To Amundsen it was a vivid demonstration of the vital necessity of generous margins of safety.

From Shackleton's experience, Amundsen deduced that the fight for the Pole would be a ski race writ large. Indeed, Shackleton admitted this himself afterwards in a lecture. 'Had we taken ski on the southern journey and understood how to use them like the Norwegians,' he said, 'we would presumably have reached the Pole.'

So Amundsen, whilst he might admire the dashing buccaneer and the leader that was Shackleton, had no desire to emulate his methods. The heroic struggle that made such good reading, was in reality a warning. In transport, Shackleton was an example of what to avoid. It was not only that, misled by his *Discovery* experience, he had eschewed skis, but man-hauling, by then outmoded and discredited outside England, had once more been the backbone of the deed. Dogs, though taken, were misjudged and wrongly handled. The more Amundsen studied Shackleton's approach, the more he believed that he was on the right track.

Money remained the problem. His fear that Cook and Peary would kill his chances of raising what he needed were soon confirmed. Donors called back contributions. Manufacturers revoked promises of free supplies. Lord Northcliffe, who had offered £5,000 for newspaper rights to the attainment of the Pole, was now unwilling to pay anything at all – still under the impression, of course, that he was dealing with the North Pole. Amundsen was left in the lurch.

He asked the Government for 25,000 kroner* more to pay eight extra men – twenty-two instead of fourteen – for an extra sixteen months. This happened to be the shore party for the Antarctic and the time that

* £1,360 or $6,600; £22,000 or $44,000 in present terms.

the excursion to the South Pole would add to the main expedition. He disguised it as extra scientific work. That, said Herr Alfred Eriksen, a Socialist opponent of Amundsen, in the Storting debate, would bring the State's contribution 'to more than a quarter of the total annual cultural budget' and anyway, in the debate the year before, the Storting had been assured 'in the most binding manner possible that [it] would be the final grant'. This time, Eriksen carried the house, and Amundsen's request was rejected by sixty-six votes to forty-two.

This, to Amundsen, made the Storting a Judas assembly and, in his own mind, further justified deception. Private and public sources had now dried up and, needing 300,000 kroner*, he was inescapably faced with a deficit of 150,000 kroner.†

In all this, the R.G.S. in London played a poignant rôle; giving Amundsen £100 in the belief that he was going North. They could only afford to give Scott £500.

Amundsen had long ceased worrying about the niceties of balanced budgets. His aim was to get his ship out of reach of his creditors. If he won the Pole, all would be forgiven. Failure would be the only crime.

He got credit where he could. He mortgaged his house and put at least 25,000 kroner into the expedition funds. To Leon he turned over the entire business management of the expedition. In return he agreed to pay a fee of 25,000 kroner and '10% of the net proceeds of *Fram*'s Antarctic and Arctic voyages'. He then washed his hands of money matters so that he could devote himself to essentials; notably to the design of his equipment.

He took nothing for granted, and was indefatigable in his attention to detail. For example, he rejected existing snow goggles, having his own made up after a pattern of Dr. Frederick Cook's. He insisted on designing special skis, for in the basic tool of his enterprise he saw the grand necessity of adaptation to a purpose. Like any skier worth his salt he was cheerfully obsessed by equipment. Skis were then, not the laminated confections we know, but laths of solid wood, and the main controversy was on kind, origin, grain, age, seasoning. Nor were the proportions stabilized. Amundsen ordered a model, something between a jumping and cross country ski. It was extremely long – about eight feet – and narrow for its length. This, Amundsen believed, was what the Antarctic required. The length was to bridge the widest possible crevasses. By giving a large bearing surface it avoided breaking snow bridges or thin crust and sinking into loose snow. Such a ski, reproducing

* £16,500 or $79,000; £263,000 or $526,000 in present terms.
† £8,150 or $39,500; £131,500 or $263,000 in present terms.

the characteristics of a cross-country racing model in a more robust form, is easy to run on, because resistance is lowered. Also, it is stable, holds a straight course, and puts less strain on the legs in keeping them steady. Other refinements were a narrow waist and a deep flared tip to ride over drifts and extract the last ounce of advantage in sliding – and hence saving energy and precious food. For material, Amundsen chose hickory. It was heavy but strong, elastic, close grained, kept water out, held wax, and seemed to act best in low temperatures.* He had the wood; bought in Pensacola nine years before so he was sure of its quality.

The one drawback to these skis was their length, which made them fiendishly difficult to turn. But this would only have to be paid for on the descent from the plateau, at the most a hundred miles out of 1,400. The waste of energy on that score would be infinitesimal by comparison with the savings on the rest.

Like any skier, Amundsen was preoccupied with boots and bindings. He chose the tensioned heel bindings then coming on to the market because by giving efficient control, they saved energy. A boot had to be designed that was longitudinally rigid enough to be used with the bindings, and also with crampons on ice slopes, while flexing easily to allow the heel to be raised, and avoiding the constriction and frostbite associated with stiff footwear in low temperatures. An unconventional boot with leather soles and canvas uppers was adopted. It was enormous, to provide space for several socks and inner soles. Bindings, too, were imperfect. Amundsen began a frustrating process of development lasting, with various setbacks, for almost two years, and not finished until the last moment in the snows. In the end, he settled for the Huitfeld binding, an early form of heel strap, with Høyer-Ellefsen snap levers.

Food was another preoccupation. Still haunted by *Belgica*, Amundsen was worried about scurvy. Fresh meat, he decided, was the only preventative; still no toxin theory for him.† He also turned his attention to pemmican. On a quick visit to America at the end of 1909, he found that Armour's, the Chicago meat packers who had promised free pemmican, joined the other firms who withdrew their offers, because, the North Pole having been attained, the Arctic no longer pulled as

* His judgment was vindicated. When laminated skis came on the market twenty years later, hickory was used for the sole and to give strength to the weak parts where the ski thins at heel and tip.

† In 1907, as Amundsen began his preparations, there took place up the fjord in Christiania the epoch-making experiments of Holst and Frølich, which led to the discovery of Vitamin C. They induced scurvy in guinea pigs by deprivation of fresh food, this indicating a deficiency disease.

advertising. It was a blessing in disguise, because it forced Amundsen
to develop a better product.

Pemmican, being concentrated fat and protein, has very little bulk,
and therefore can militate against well being, putting stomachs wildly
out of order. The Norwegian Army had been experimenting with
pemmican as an iron ration, adding peas to give fibre and make it
more digestible. Amundsen heard of this, and, after some trials of his
own, ordered pemmican to which oatmeal and peas had been added.
It was one of the little details which might mean everything. In extreme
conditions, the simplest habit becomes a conscious effort; bladder and
bowels can become an obsession. A leaden stomach means sluggish
work, wasted effort and ill temper. Diarrhoea, where defaecation may
be a whole performance in a blizzard with snow sand-blasting one end,
and frostbite menacing the other, is no joke; constipation, if possible,
even worse. The time to prevent all this, Amundsen believed, was
before he started.

Likewise, in clothing, Amundsen took infinite pains. Through
Daugaard-Jensen, together with the dogs, he had already ordered Greenland Eskimo sealskin clothing, with material for repairs. He now had
the Netsilik pattern of clothing made up in reindeer, wolf skin, Burberry
windproof cloth, a tough kind of Norwegian cotton gaberdine, and even
old, matted military blankets for rough shipboard and base wear.

Amundsen left no detail to chance, took nothing for granted. To
everything he brought an imaginative touch. Even the sledging cases,
for example, he specially designed. Mistrusting plywood, he had them
made of solid ash. To be absolutely sure of the quality, he imported
the wood from an estate in Denmark. Instead of a conventional lid on
hinges, each case had a circular opening, which was closed with a press
lid like a tea canister. This made a stronger case and a snowproof seal.
Most important of all, the lid could be opened and closed *on* the sledge
without having to undo the lashings, thus saving time and energy.

> If one is tired and slack [Amundsen remarks], it may easily happen that one
> puts off for tomorrow what ought to be done today; especially when it is
> bitter and cold. The lighter and simpler one's sledging equipment, the sooner
> one can rest. And that plays a not unimportant rôle on a long journey.

The lids to the packing cases, incidentally, were a little project on
their own. To save weight and avoid corrosion they were made of
aluminium – one of its very early uses – and had to be specially manu-
factured.

With the same critical specialization he devoted to equipment,

Amundsen chose his men. 'Have you asked your parents?' was one of the first things he said to Lieutenant Frederick Gjertsen, the Naval officer who became *Fram*'s second mate. It was one of the first questions he usually asked, varied by: 'Have you asked your wife?', an innocent-sounding question, it told much. Amundsen wanted no misfits, drop-outs, failures, adventurers; the legions of the alienated and discontented who more than ever were beginning to cluster round exploration as an escape from the strains of civilized existence. The traumatic ex-perience of *Belgica* had taught him the dangers of unsuitable personality on a Polar expedition. The wrong companion was infinitely more dangerous than the worst blizzard. He was one of the first explorers fully to grasp the importance of mental as well as physical health. He looked on his men as a means to an end, their main qualification being suitability for their task. In selecting them, he put sentiment aside.

Amundsen knew that he was not a master dog-driver. Admittedly, he was vastly better than his English rivals, but among his own kind, and in his own eyes, he was no more than competent, and competence was not good enough. He wanted the best. Helmer Hanssen, his old companion from the North-West Passage, agreed, after some hesitation, to join him. Hanssen, having his mate's certificate, could navigate as well. With Bjaaland and Hanssen, Amundsen had the nucleus of his Polar party.

He paid Helmer Hanssen, signed on before the mast, twice as much as Gjertsen, the second mate. Neither thought it particularly unfair. Dog-drivers were scarcer than second mates, and in the Polar regions the dog-driver was king. It was a professional attitude, but this, after all, was a professional enterprise; as Scott was running an amateur enterprise. To make certain of having a proper Polar cook, Amundsen secured Adolf Lindstrøm, who had been with him on *Gjøa* and was now fishing off the West Coast of Alaska.

In the summer of 1909, Oscar Wisting, a naval gunner, was working on *Fram* in the dockyard at Horten. Amundsen, on one of his periodical visits, came up 'and said, as he patted me amiably on the shoulder, "You can come North with me." To put it mildly, I was surprised.'

Wisting had not even troubled to apply. But Lieutenant Kristian Prestrud, one of his officers, who was going with Amundsen, had recommended him. And Amundsen, after suitable inspection, had made the proposal. For Wisting had been whaling round Iceland and ended up a gunner; he had his mate's certificate, was a competent small ship handler. Although by Norwegian standards a very moderate skier, and ignorant of dog-driving, he none the less was used to working outside in cold weather. He was adaptable, quick to learn and a good handyman. Amundsen wanted people who willingly and absolutely submitted to his personal authority. 'I affirm on my honour that I will obey the leader of the expedition in everything at any time,' ran a clause in the contract his men were required to sign, 'and promise to work for a successful outcome with indefatigable resolution.'

Despite the expertise at his disposal, Amundsen insisted on taking an ice pilot. This was the specialist who could save weeks getting through the pack ice, when every hour might count in the race for the Pole. Amundsen asked his old friend Zapffe to find one in Tromsø. Zapffe eventually selected an Arctic sealing skipper called Andreas Beck: 'a big, good humoured bear of few words'.

Although Gustav Wiik had died on *Gjøa* through illness, Amundsen still declined to take a doctor. He asked Zapffe to come instead.

> I believe [wrote Amundsen] that with your knowledge of medicine – for after all a pharmacist will learn a lot about that in the course of time – you could take over the position of doctor etc. etc. etc. on board. A doctor may often have the drawback that only reluctantly will he concern himself with anything outside his profession. But I have no place for such a man. A non medical man, in my opinion, will not suffer from that fault.

This concealed a fear of the academically trained as a threat to his authority by making him appear ridiculous before his men.

Since Zapffe could not come, Amundsen sent Gjertsen and Wisting to hospitals on what he called a 'snapshot course' in practical dentistry and surgery. Amundsen was convinced that a layman could cope with most of the medicine required on an expedition; a view, incidentally, that some doctors might well endorse.

There was one dark moment, when Amundsen had to abandon principle and submit to a choice forced on him.

In the autumn of 1908, he received a letter of application from Hjalmar Johansen, who had been with Nansen in the north. Johansen was a good dog-driver with rare experience of Polar travel. A short, squat man, agile, wiry and immensely tough, he was a trained gymnast and competition skier; on the face of it, just the man for the expedition. But he suffered from personal failings that made him a serious risk.

In 1896, when he returned to Norway after his epic journey with Nansen over the Arctic ice, Johansen was one of the heroes of the hour. After the cheering was over, however, came the return to workaday. That is a shock which requires certain qualities to overcome, and it was too much for Johansen, as for many others.

Johansen had come home thinking his fortune was made; he soon discovered that Polar adventure was not necessarily a passport to success. He was rewarded with a permanent captain's commission in the Army, but that merely meant a return to the monotony which, in the first place, had driven him out into the snows.

From the start, Johansen found himself neglected by Nansen, having to live in his shadow, the predestined number two. For Johansen who, quiet, unassuming, modest, yet nursed greater hopes, it was a bitter disappointment. He found it hard to bear and things soon started to go wrong. A few months after landing, he had to ask Nansen for a loan of 500 kroner* 'until better days come' and thenceforth was almost constantly in need, appealing to his old chief again and again for help. Ten years of setback culminated in separation from his wife and children, bankruptcy and resignation from the Army. Drink was Johansen's burden; he had become virtually an alcoholic.

In 1907, he was living in a Tromsø hotel, destitute at the age of forty, unable to pay his board and lodging and, as he wrote to Nansen,

> If you think I have been any use to you during the [Fram] expedition, and for that reason perhaps want to help me out of this desperate situation – then help is wanted in the highest degree.

But the Tromsø police chief, to whom Nansen had written to find out what was happening to his old companion, believed that 'any financial help will only go on drink. He ought to get away from this place.' Johansen himself wanted to

> join some expedition or other. It almost doesn't matter what kind, to get away from this existence which, during the past few years has been anything but attractive – I am grateful for the life on board Fram!

He was not the only man to see in the Polar deserts an escape from the wastelands of everyday existence. But an expedition, as Nansen, who knew the feeling well, put it, 'would be no solution; it will be just as bad when he comes back'. None the less, he had always answered Johansen's calls of distress; and now he helped him to get Polar work.

For the next few seasons, Johansen accompanied foreign expeditions to Spitsbergen. As one of his employers put it, he worked well, 'with none of the disastrous results associated with life in more temperate latitudes'. But, as Nansen had foreseen, he relapsed into his old habits when he returned home.

When Amundsen announced his expedition, with its original prospect

* £27 or $130; £450 or $900 in present terms.

of a five-year Arctic drift, it seemed the opportunity for which
Johansen had been waiting.

Johansen had saved Nansen's life in the Arctic, and Nansen therefore
felt under an obligation. He also had a sentimental idea that he wanted
one of his old men on his old ship. He pressed Amundsen to take
Johansen.

It was the last thing Amundsen wanted to do. He felt sorry for
Johansen but sentiment had no place in selecting followers. A heavy
drinker implied to Amundsen a fault of character that meant danger
under stress. Yet, more seriously, he feared that Johansen, being older,
equally experienced, a better skier and, above all, having lived with
thwarted ambition in Nansen's reflected glory, would prove a threat
to his own authority.

But Amundsen was more or less in Nansen's hands, and, all his
instincts flouted, he found himself compelled to take Johansen on
Fram. By then, Amundsen knew he was going south instead of north,
and could ill afford extra strain and risk.

Like a general preparing a surprise attack, Amundsen had to be ever
on his guard, thinking of his secret in the midst of intricate preparations. Together with Bjørn Helland-Hansen, he had planned a heavy
extra programme of oceanographical work in the Atlantic, which gave
the expedition additional scientific worth and, incidentally, gave him
a convincing pretext for sailing with *Fram*, instead of his advertised
intention of leaving later and joining her at San Francisco. He would
have to be on board to supervise the work. He used the Press to foster
the impression that he was still going north, for he had developed an
impressive rapport with journalists. His plan, he took care to say in
one newspaper interview, was

> a scientific investigation of the North Polar Basin, together with a thorough
> investigation of Atlantic oceanography [for which] we will have plenty of
> time ... during the voyage round Cape Horn to San Francisco.

This contained a good deal of truth – the art of the 'story' fed to
the Press.

In photographs taken at this time, Amundsen seems to be putting
on a poker face; almost as if he were enjoying a private joke. He found
a grim pleasure in keeping his secret, for he believed in Ibsen's words
that 'the strongest man in the world is he who stands most alone'.

Amundsen had to watch his every step and weigh every word, for
one chance hint might give the game away. He left his house and came

back at irregular intervals. He hid, none knew where. He refused to answer the telephone. To all but a few privileged initiates, he was never at home and strangely elusive. Nansen, especially, had to be kept in the dark because if he knew the truth, so Amundsen feared, he would be the first to stop the enterprise.

It was not only against outsiders that Amundsen had to be on his guard; he had to keep the secret from his men as well: for the time being they had to continue in the belief that they were going north. The one exception was Lieutenant Thorvald Nilsen, the second in command.

When Nilsen reported for duty in January 1910, Amundsen, under pledge of secrecy, revealed his true intentions. This was unavoidable. Nilsen was to be the master of the *Fram*; he had to know where he was going well in advance, in order to make his preparations.

For after leaving Madeira there would be no ports of call, except possibly some remote island for water, until the Bay of Whales, a distance of 14,000 miles. Once his true intentions had been revealed, Amundsen wanted to give civilization a wide berth, for fear of distraint by creditors and Government. He wished to avoid cableheads and consuls; writs, journalists and lawyers.

Nilsen, too, had to work deviously. He could not, for example, openly order any Antarctic charts; at least not through local agents; for that would soon have been broadcast. Instead, he got them on some specious excuse through the Norwegian Embassy in London. This did not at the time arouse any suspicion.

One of the worst threats to Amundsen's secret remained the wintering hut, which he had built by a carpenter called Jørgen Stubberud, who had renovated his house. When Stubberud heard about the 'North Polar expedition', he

got a burning desire to join. [Amundsen] was so pleasant and easy as an employer, gave instructions you could understand, and never fussed: 'Do it when it suits', he would say.

Stubberud was accepted and, having signed the contract, was asked to build the hut. Again, it was a matter of specialized accomplishment. Stubberud knew how to build for a harsh climate; for simple transport and assembly using prefabricated sections.

It is one of the most surprising episodes in this story that Stubberud's suspicions were not aroused when he discovered what he was expected to build. To cloak his intentions and avert awkward questions, Amundsen told the Press and all who cared to ask, that it was 'an observation hut' for the Arctic pack ice. It was, however, a large, robust structure, with separate kitchen furnished with a table, eleven bunks and linoleum on the floor, clearly designed for prolonged habitation It was hardly consistent with an expedition whose home was to be a ship. Stubberud, however, completely dominated by Amundsen's personality, accepted his story and carried on in the belief that he was going north

But others were puzzled. The hut was built and given its trial assembly in Amundsen's garden by the side of the fjord, away from main roads and prying eyes. But, in a country where Polar knowledge was so common, it was hard to avert all suspicion. This, luckily, stopped at very local gossip. But Amundsen could never be sure from one day to the next, whether his secret would not be surprised.

One morning, in March 1910, the telephone gave its now unwelcome jangle. The concierge of a Christiania hotel was on the line. Captain Scott, the English Polar explorer wanted to talk to Captain Amundsen. Amundsen had been dreading such a call. Scott had written to say that he was coming to talk about scientific cooperation between himself in the south and Amundsen in the north. Amundsen was incapable of meeting Scott and lying to his face. He sent the usual message that he was not available and began the nerve-racking business of prevarication and avoiding an encounter.

19

On the Terra Nova

SCOTT HAD COME to Norway for the final trials of his motor sledge. The manufacturers had been late with delivery and the trials were a hurried and ill conceived event, to be run at Fefor, a ski resort north of Christiania. Even an English mountain skier questioned the choice. Scott, he wrote, ought to have gone higher above the treeline where the snow was

> usually wind-driven and hard, i.e. more like the snow commonly encountered on Polar expeditions than at Fefor, which is comparatively sheltered.

Finse, on the edge of Hardangervidda, Amundsen's old Polar school, would have been entirely suitable. The sledge could have been taken directly to the foot of a glacier by the newly-opened railway between Christiania and Bergen. Scott, however, had been offered free accommodation at Fefor, which lay in familiar country near Lillehammer, the site of the previous trials.

As usual, everything was rushed and details were scamped, for Scott had left himself a bare nine months to organize the expedition, whereas most Polar explorers considered two years necessary. Scott hoped for great scientific and extensive geographical discoveries and the Pole into the bargain. He had no clear perception of what he wanted most, and his efforts were correspondingly dispersed.

Much of his equipment was bought over the counter, or made to obsolescent patterns from *Discovery* or before. Scott was following in old footsteps, in the words of one Norwegian writer, 'avoiding with diligence the experience of his Arctic predecessors'.

While *Fram* was being modernized from the keel up, *Terra Nova*, the ship that Scott eventually settled for, was given the proverbial lick and a promise. Money was partly, although not entirely the explanation. While, for example, an expensive ice house was installed to carry mutton superfluously all the way to Antarctica, with its inexhaustible supplies of seal, *Terra Nova*'s antiquated hand pump was left unchanged, its deficiencies such as to threaten the safety of the ship and hence the survival of all.

The works of Peary and Astrup, not to mention Sverdrup's *New Land*, and Amundsen's *North-West Passage*, with their striking evidence in favour of dogs, were now open to inspection. There is no evidence that Scott read any of them; or if he did, he ignored what they had to say. He persisted in the wilful mistrust of dogs garnered on *Discovery*; still blaming the beasts, unable to admit even to himself, that the fault could have been his. When, in the middle of 1909, he realized that the motor sledges were unlikely to get him all the way to the Pole, and animal transport was going to be needed, he decided on ponies instead – because Shackleton had used them.

This is one of the more bizarre incidents in Polar exploration. Shackleton, too, had been deceived by the failure of the dogs on *Discovery*, and jumped to the conclusion, in the face of all the other evidence, that they were therefore useless in the snows. He got the idea of horses from Armitage, who had used them on the Jackson–Harmsworth expedition in Franz Josef Land, and who persuasively argued their merits in the Antarctic on *Discovery*.

Scott saw only that Shackleton had nearly reached the Pole; he was unable to discern that a man may succeed for the wrong reasons. Shackleton's experience had clearly shown that ponies could not stand the harsh Antarctic climate. They were wholly unsuited to glacial terrain, since the pressure of their hooves broke through snow bridges, and their weight made them hard to man-handle. His last pony ended his days in a crevasse long before reaching the Polar Plateau.

But the most serious objection to horses was the obvious one that their food did not grow in the Antarctic. The only vegetable life was a little moss or lichen here and there. Every scrap of fodder would have to be taken on the ship. The Antarctic, with its abundant seal and penguin, was for carnivores. Horses could not live off the land, but dogs could.

Scott not only copied Shackleton's methods, he wanted his men as well. He asked Shackleton's agent in Christchurch, N.Z., Joseph (later Sir Joseph) Kinsey, to be his agent. Kinsey, reluctantly, agreed. Scott also attempted to get Douglas Mawson.

Mawson (later Sir Douglas Mawson) was an Australian geologist who had been on the party which, under a compatriot, Professor Edgeworth David, had reached the South Magnetic Pole, and added lustre to Shackleton's achievements. When, in January 1910, Mawson visited London, Scott, helped by Kathleen, tried to cajole him into coming. Mawson, however, declined. Amongst other things, he formed the opinion that Scott was trying to steal his ideas. He decided instead to organize an Antarctic expedition of his own. Scott was surprised and annoyed.

Meeting Frank Wild at a reception in London, Scott then and there tried to persuade him to join his expedition. Wild had stood with Shackleton at the Furthest South, and could have shown the way almost to the Pole. As a seaman on *Discovery*, Wild had experienced Scott the Naval martinet; now exposed to the charm of Scott's social person, he was unimpressed, and categorically rejected the invitation. Scott pleaded so emotionally that fellow-guests overheard. He offered money, Naval promotion. But Wild was adamant. He had promised to follow Shackleton on *his* next expedition. That was a bitter thrust. The rivalry between Scott and Shackleton had crystallized into two opposing factions. Wild was wholeheartedly Shackleton's man.

Scott did, however, get two men who had been on the *Nimrod* expedition: Bernard Day, the motor mechanic, and as the result of a last-minute vacancy Raymond (later Sir Raymond) Priestley, a geologist and future Chancellor of Birmingham University.

The man Scott most wanted was Wilson: Wilson his guide, counsellor, saviour and alter ego; the peacemaker from *Discovery*. And Wilson was coming. Scott had made it clear over the past two years how much he needed his old companion and when the call came (by telegram), Wilson answered it. 'Scott is ... worth working for as a man', Wilson wrote to his father. 'We want the Scientific work to make the bagging of the Pole merely an item in the results'.

Wilson was made chief of the scientific staff. One of his appointments was that of Dr. George Simpson, the meteorologist whom Scott had discarded on *Discovery* from personal dislike. Simpson was now a distinguished member of the Indian meteorological service. He was a product of the Victoria University, Manchester; but the other scientists were preponderantly from Cambridge: Debenham and Griffith Taylor, the geologists; Lillie and Nelson the biologists and Wilson himself. This led a local newspaper to call it the 'Cambridge and Admiralty expedition'.

Although the same air of incompetence and improvisation that characterized *Discovery* also hung over this expedition, the tide of public interest had turned in the intervening years. For this, much credit belonged to Shackleton, who had made Antarctic exploration intellectually respectable. Partly, but not entirely, this was due to the quality of scientist he had taken on *Nimrod*, which was far higher than that on *Discovery*. As a result, the intellectual calibre of those now seeking to join was much higher, and the pressure of volunteers enormous. There were about 8,000 all told; all kinds and conditions of men.

The Admiralty had relented since the *Discovery* expedition, allowing Scott to have all the officers and ratings he wanted. Scott was a Captain now, and his chief at the Admiralty, the Second Sea Lord, i.e. Admiral Sir Francis Bridgeman, was in charge of the Navy's personnel. Perhaps most important of all, Kathleen Scott was energetically at work. But though Scott was given leave to chance his arm, he had to find his own funds. The expense of the *Discovery* relief was still a vivid memory in Whitehall; money was out of the question.

Although so fundamentally different, the British and Norwegian expeditions displayed certain parallels. Scott, having liberated himself from committees, was now, like Amundsen, running a personal venture, which nonetheless had become a national enterprise. As Amundsen had Hjalmar Johansen thrust upon him, so was Scott driven to take someone by force of circumstances.

Lieutenant E. R. Evans who, two years earlier, volunteered to go back to the Antarctic with Scott, had in the meantime tired of waiting and decided to organize an expedition of his own. In May, 1909, he began discussing his plans with Sir Clements Markham.

Towards Scott, Sir Clements' attitude remained that of a jealous impresario and in Evans he saw awkward competition. Evans' plan was to explore King Edward VII Land,* so far only a sighting on *Discovery* in 1902 and *Nimrod* six years later. It was a good plan, promising new discoveries in the yet sketchily known Antarctic continent. It appealed to Sir Clements, who deprecated what he called 'these rushes to the Poles'. It appealed more than Scott's intention to go over old ground merely to beat Shackleton.

Sir Clements discreetly revealed Evans' intentions to Scott and, when Evans came to lunch with Sir Clements on July 8th, in order to present his detailed plan, he discovered that Scott had adopted it as his own. Evans now found himself in the position of intruder, about to play another Shackleton. Sir Clements suggested that he go to Scott 'and be perfectly open and above board'. The next day, as Sir Clements had intended, they decided to join forces, Scott making Evans his second in command. Sir Clements actually had a high regard for Evans, and his motives for manoeuvring him into this position were not only to save Scott uncomfortable rivalry. The undertones in Sir Clements' diaries speak of some tiny hidden doubt over Scott's capabilities, and he saw Evans as a desirable prop.

As soon as fund raising began, Scott found that in 'Teddy' Evans he

---

* Today the King Edward VII Peninsula in Marie Byrd Land.

had acquired an invaluable asset. Evans could play the bluff sailor to landlubbers, and knew how to wheedle an audience into giving money. By the spring of 1910, Scott and Evans had collected the first £10,000. The Government (Liberal), until then non-committal, now made a grant of £20,000. This was five times what the Storting gave Amundsen.

In the selection of their men, Amundsen and Scott followed a fundamentally different approach: Amundsen was organizing a raid; Scott a general offensive. Amundsen depended on nimbleness and mobility; Scott saw safety in numbers. Amundsen retained his faith in the small party, with its cohesion and simplicity. He was in any case by nature a leader of small groups, he had the insight to see this, and he stuck to his metier. His whole landing party would be ten or less; Scott was thinking in terms of twenty to thirty.

Amundsen could afford no passengers. He methodically chose his men for a purpose, like a workman his tools. Besides Polar experience and the specific accomplishments of skiing and dog-driving he wanted them generally inured to isolation and hard outdoor work in a cold climate.

Scott worked on no obvious pattern, beyond a preponderance of Naval men. On the one hand, there was a small nucleus of old *Discovery* people: Wilson, and the seamen Crean, Lashly, Edgar Evans, Williamson; on the other the large heterogeneous majority with no Polar or, indeed, cold weather experience.

There was, for example, Henry Robertson Bowers, a tough, redheaded, wiry little Clydeside Scot who had rounded the Horn in a sailing ship, served the apprenticeship of the sea, and now, at the age of twenty-six, was a lieutenant in the Royal Indian Marine. He had early conceived an interest in the Polar regions. He knew nothing of ice and snow, however, except by hearsay or through books.

Like 'Teddy' Evans, Bowers was a product of *Worcester*, the merchant service training ship in the Thames; indeed there is something of the Old Boy network in the way Bowers was brought into the expedition. He had met Sir Clements Markham, who took a keen interest in *Worcester*, and impressed him with his Polar enthusiasm. When Scott was about to announce the expedition, Sir Clements remembered Bowers and wrote to him in Burma, where he was at the time, asking if he would like to join. Bowers jumped at the chance. Sir Clements, helped by 'Teddy' Evans, persuaded Scott to take him, sight unseen.

Another kind of person came to the expedition because of its financial straits.

As a means of raising funds Scott followed Shackleton in accepting paying volunteers.* Two joined *Terra Nova* at a fee of £1,000 each. One was a recent Oxford graduate, Apsley Cherry-Garrard. He was a cousin of Reginald John Smith, Scott's publisher, and a particular friend of Wilson. Scott would probably have preferred Cherry-Garrard's money without Cherry-Garrard. But Wilson interceded on his behalf, manifestly at Smith's urging.

Smith and Wilson were evidently thinking more of what the expedition could do for Cherry-Garrard, than of the expedition itself. The young man was suffering from a debilitating upbringing, between the bullying of a tyrannical father and the tender domination of a mother and sisters. It had left him something of a child. It was felt that the Antarctic would do him good by toughening him both physically and mentally.

The other subscribing volunteer was a cavalry captain, Lawrence Edward Grace Oates. He was an Old Etonian who came (like Cherry-Garrard) from the landed gentry. He had a private income but always lived mildly beyond it. An officer in the 6th Inniskilling Dragoons, he played polo, went shooting, hunted, rode point to point, kept a yacht and a racehorse or two, in fact indulged in all the usual recreations of his time, class and regimental background. Less conventionally, he rode a motorcycle, one of the first men in England to do so. He was also ahead of his times in advocating a private swimming pool for Gestingthorpe, the Oates country house in Essex. He was quiet and self-contained and though he liked, on occasion, to act the part of the horsey oaf, he was far from being so in fact.

Nor was he the ordinary kind of schoolboy romantic frequently attracted to Polar exploration. In fact, he was no romantic at all. He was innocent of cant. He was a rational eighteenth-century squire born into the surroundings of the twentieth century. From his schooldays he despised snobbery and affectation. He happened to be introduced to the Duke of Connaught, who asked if he knew his son at Eton. 'No,' answered Oates, 'I can't be expected to know *everybody*.'

Oates was a fighting soldier. He had fought in the Boer War and been severely wounded in the thigh. He was in India when he volunteered for the Antarctic expedition, acutely bored with peacetime routine and dispassionately aware of the path to preferment:

... if you happen to know one or two of the nibs at the war office or better

---

* Sir Philip Brocklehurst paid to join the *Nimrod*.

still their wives, soldiering is rather fun but if you don't it's better to stay at home.

It was in this frame of mind he offered to join Scott. The seed of Polar interest may have fallen from his father who, a keen traveller, had once sailed on a yachting cruise to Spitsbergen.

Oates' father had died when he was an adolescent. Mother and son had since been very close. To disarm her worries, Oates wrapped up the announcement of his approach to Scott in a wry, perhaps flippant humour that nevertheless contained a serious, self-revealing core:

> It will help me professionally as in the Army if they want a man to wash labels off bottles they would sooner employ a man who had been to the North Pole than one who had only got as far as the Mile End Road.

Oates wanted hard work and something new. Scott was looking for someone to care for the horses. Oates' offer came providentially and he was accepted, like Bowers, sight unseen. Scott asked the War Office to release Oates, which eventually they did – provided he paid his own fare home and that of his replacement out to India. He complied with pleasure; together with the £1,000 subscription, it was still cheaper than two years' Army living.

Early in May, he presented himself on *Terra Nova*, which was fitting out at the West India Docks in London. His coming had been awaited with considerable speculation. As he himself expressed it 'cavalry officers are not generally taken for these shows'. The appearance of an upper-class captain of Dragoons in a middle-class enterprise was an interesting prospect. Oates was doubtless conscious of this. He dealt with the situation in his own way by appearing in a battered bowler hat, his tall form wrapped in a disreputable raincoat buttoned up to the neck. Crean, one of the seamen on deck when Oates arrived,

> never for a moment thought he was an officer, for they were usually so smart. We made up our minds he was a farmer, he was ... so nice and friendly, just like one of ourselves, but oh! he was a gentleman, quite a gentleman, and always a gentleman!

When, at the beginning of March, Scott went to Norway for the motor trials, he also took the opportunity to buy furs and sledges. In Christiania, on the way to Fefor, he met Nansen, who now had the British strategy revealed to him.

Nansen did not particularly like Scott – although he definitely did like Kathleen who accompanied her husband – but, in the Greek sense, he was a man of charity, who could not stand coldly by and watch a fellow human being apparently bent on self-destruction. Scott's plans – insofar as they existed – were absurd. His irrational mistrust of dogs, his reliance instead on horses, his faith in the yet unproven capacities of petrol engines in cold weather all seemed an invitation to disaster. Nansen felt he had to save Scott from himself; at the same time a Norwegian Polar apprentice needed unobtrusive help.

This was Tryggve Gran who, at the age of twenty, had started organizing an Antarctic expedition of his own. His Polar interest had been started by Captain Victor Baumann, who had been with Otto Sverdrup on the second *Fram* expedition. Gran had met Baumann during a brief spell as a Norwegian Naval cadet. But it was Shackleton who inspired Gran to act. Gran had met him when he came to Norway in October, 1909, and heard him lecture in Christiania on his journey almost to within sight of the Pole.

> For an hour and a half I seemed to be nailed to my seat. In words and pictures I seemed to experience reality's fairy tale. Indeed, the Antarctic was the place where Norwegian skiers could make history.

Amundsen was also present and, in after years, Lady Shackleton once said she would never forget the look on his face while her husband was speaking.

> His keen eyes were fixed on him, and while Ernest quoted R. Service's line 'The trails of the world be countless', a mystic look softened them, the look of a man who saw a vision.

Before Shackleton left Christiania, Gran had an interview with him.

> I asked him straight out if he would advise me to go South on my own initiative, young as I was, and without any other experience than I had acquired at sea and in the mountains as a skier. Shackleton's answer made my heart hammer violently against my ribs. 'Listen here, my young friend,' he said 'I will not advise you to do it, but give my frank opinion. Provided you can get enough experienced men to get your ship down to the Ross Barrier, your youth is anything but a handicap.' And Shackleton continued: 'An English expedition under Captain Scott is in preparation and will presumably start next summer. It is necessary to act quickly. You can count on a cheque from me.'

Shackleton must have been unusually off his guard when he so patently encouraged a total stranger to compete with Scott; he did not often reveal to outsiders the resentment he felt against his rival. Possibly he was carried away by his reception in Christiania, a torchlight procession and an emotional oration by Amundsen. 'Nowhere have hearts beat more warmly for you,' ran a passage that touched Shackleton, 'and perhaps no assembly has been better qualified to judge of your undertaking.'

Gran, an impressionable young man, was fired by the same scenes, and by the encounter with Shackleton. He went away and ordered a ship. He was rich enough to indulge his whims. He began gathering companions. In January, 1910, he visited Nansen to discuss his plans.

Nansen was worried by what he heard. Gran's boat was about as big as a fishing smack – ludicrously small for the Antarctic. And at the age of twenty, Gran was exceptionally young even to be thinking of leading his own expedition.

Yet it was not just his youth and inexperience that worried Nansen. Gran was not untried. He had been intended for the Navy which, in Norway, meant twenty-one months' sea service on merchant ships before becoming a cadet. Between the age of sixteen and eighteen Gran had shipped before the mast on sailing ships; crossed the Atlantic several times, been shipwrecked on the Norwegian coast. In between he had been ski touring in the Norwegian mountains.

Gran had given up the Navy when he seized on the idea of an Antarctic expedition. It was not the happiest background for the enterprise. All this, and much else besides, Nansen understood. The question was: how to dissuade Gran from pursuing his enterprise? To tell him not to would almost certainly have disastrous effects. Setting a devious little scheme in train, Nansen offered to introduce Gran to Scott; Gran was delighted: he was raised at a stroke, as it were, to the company of recognized explorers.

Nansen arranged the meeting at Hagen's, the shop where Scott was going to buy his sledges. Scott's unreasoning aversion to skis - another outcome of the *Discovery* expedition – seemed to Nansen crass stupidity. He hoped that exposure to the seductive ambience of skiing equipment en masse, aided by some judicious propaganda, would overcome it. So all three men went down to Hagen's, and browsed among the sledges and the skis. At a suitable moment, as Tryggve Gran recollected in after years, Nansen turned to Scott and said:

> Now you're going to take ski with you. Shackleton didn't take ski and [he] told me when he had lunch with me if he had known how to use ski he would have reached the pole. He would have done!

This showed considerable percipience; Nansen had divined Scott's Shackleton fixation. Or had Kathleen Scott told him?

> But remember, it's no use having ski unless you know how to use them

properly. You ought to [let] a Norwegian show [you]. Well, if you can point out a man who can show me, says Scott, I would be very thankful to you. So [Nansen] knocked me on the shoulder and said, well, Gran, can't you do it? And I said, with the greatest pleasure.

So, next morning Gran caught the train with Scott to Fefor. Gran was deeply conscious of his rôle as exponent of the noble art of skiing. A horse and sleigh took Scott's party from the railway station at Vinstra up to Fefor. When they reached the snow at the foot of the first rise, Gran jumped off the sleigh, put on his skis and, as he said 'soon grasped that Scott was impressed' at the way he managed to keep up all the way to the top.

Next day, the motor sledge, which had been sent ahead, was put through its paces on the frozen lake outside the hotel. At the controls sat Bernard Day, Shackleton's motor mechanic, the first Antarctic driver. Men from the Wolseley motor company, which had made the engine, were there to watch. So too was Skelton, now engineer commander, busy with the application of the first diesel engines to British submarines but still, at Scott's urgent appeals, finding time to supervise the manufacture and testing of the sledge.

Soon after breakfast the mountain silence was shattered by the splutter and pop of an early petrol engine; across the snow the monster crawled, cheered to the echo by the little crowd of holidaymakers. People clambered on the sledge, hung on, and were pulled along behind on ski. This miracle lasted exactly a quarter of an hour. Without warning there was a sharp crack and the sledge stopped dead, like a horse refusing a fence, throwing Day head foremost into the snow. An axle had broken. That was Gran's opportunity to show what ski could do. Time was short; Scott had to return to London. Repairs could only be done by a workshop in the valley. Carrying the pieces on his back, Gran swished off down on ski in best racing style. 'Scott could scarcely believe his eyes,' when Gran returned after five hours, having skied some ten miles, running down and climbing 1,000 feet, with the repaired axle, a load of twenty-five pounds, on his back.

The axle was replaced, and all afternoon the sledge triumphantly clattered to and fro; pulling three tons at four and a half miles per hour. At that rate it would clear the Barrier in fifty-five running hours from McMurdo Sound. Scott was in splendid humour. Gran recalled how they were skiing across the lake when

Scott suddenly stopped and asked me if I would consider postponing my own Antarctic plans and follow him South instead. I thought I had heard wrongly, and it was only when Scott explained that now, for the first time he realized what ski properly used would mean to him and his expedition, that I grasped that my ears had not been playing me tricks.

It is entirely characteristic that, ten years after Scott began his Antarctic work, he had finally gone to source and seen skiing in its homeland. Widely regarded as a Polar expert, until he went to Fefor he had never seen ski properly used. He had floundered, the first, into the heart of the Antarctic; but Gran was the first accomplished skier he had seen in action.

Gran showed what could be done with two sticks; how they made sliding effortless, and climbing almost a pleasure. This was the revelation that converted Scott. He had never before seen two ski sticks in action but used only the obsolescent single pole. Gran also demonstrated other refinements; chiefly stable boots and bindings giving proper control over the skis.

With the fervour of the convert, Scott now invested with quasi-miraculous attributes the implements which, a few hours before, he had totally rejected. Gran's dramatic performance had been admirably timed. Scott had been plunged into despondency by the breakdown of the sledge; the elation following the repair simply magnified the uncertainties now brought to his attention. Skelton's final report enumerated over sixty mechanical faults, any one of which would be enough to cause a breakdown. There was no time for more snow trials before going into action. Skis now appeared as a providential insurance: the extra kind of transport which, added to motors and animals, must get him to the Pole.

Scott's idea was that Gran should turn his followers, some of whom, like Oates and Bowers, were absolute beginners, into accomplished skiers between landing in the Antarctic and the start for the Pole; doing in a few months what normally took years. Besides instilling technique, Gran was also expected to supply motivation. Scott wanted him by personal example to show what skis could do, and thus overcome the prejudice which had so inhibited him and which, as he so rightly judged, blinkered his subordinates. All this was to be done while the pupils were working in dead earnest; rather like first teaching a soldier to shoot as he goes into battle. Gran, understandably, asked for time to consider his reply.

In fact – and doubtless as Nansen had slyly calculated – for Gran, too, the development was opportune. Gran was rich but, alas, not rich enough. He had plunged into his preparations without counting the cost. Scott offered to take over the skis and sledges he had bought, not so much out of kindness, as out of necessity. Scott had waited until the last moment to give his order to Hagen's; and Hagen's could hardly finish in time. Taking over Gran's stock solved that difficulty. To Gran the arrangement meant that he could honourably renounce his plans and extricate himself from his financial difficulties. It also offered him experience on a platter. Early the following day, he told Scott that he would go. Kathleen Scott, as Gran describes the scene,

> was standing next to her husband, grabbed my hand with both hers. 'How glad I am; and how relieved I shall be,' she burst out, visibly and audibly enthused. 'Ski can work wonders.'

Since recovering from the birth of her baby, Kathleen had been very much in evidence. To Gran – incidentally, tall, well-built, flamboyant, a Nordic Don Juan – she gave the impression of

> a very very clever woman very very pushing ... very ambitious ... I don't think Scott would have gone to the Antarctic if it hadn't been for her.

Almost certainly she had a hand in Scott's conversion to skis and his decision to take Gran. After a day or so, they returned to Christiania where Scott continued his attempt, now helped by Gran, to run Amundsen to earth.

When Gran had started organizing his own expedition he wanted to talk to Amundsen, but also found him elusive. Eventually, it was only by going out to Bundefjord unannounced that he managed to catch him at home. Amundsen, in Gran's words,

> did not seem to be particularly interested, and answered rather oracularly to most questions. His knowledge of the Antarctic regions was confined to the drift ice south of Cape Horn. The Ross Sea he knew only through books ... After about a quarter of an hour ... I left, about as wise as when I came. It was not thus that I had imagined my first meeting with Roald Amundsen.

Gran was chagrined, but not suspicious, since a general reputation for wilfulness surrounded Amundsen after his return from the North-West Passage. It never occurred to Gran that Amundsen had anything to conceal; much less that he had changed his plans, and now was going south himself. At any rate, when Scott continued to find Amundsen elusive, Gran did his best to arrange an interview, and thought he had succeeded. He went with Scott to Bundefjord, where they were met by Amundsen's brother Gustav, who, says Gran, informed us that Roald had been told that Scott wanted to see him that afternoon, and it was quite incomprehensible that he had not yet returned home.... We waited a good hour, but not a sign of life from the conqueror of the North-West Passage.... If Scott was disappointed, I was ashamed.

Gustav, incidentally, was not in the secret; he still thought his brother was going north.

Without a glimmer of suspicion of the true reason for all the evasiveness, Scott returned to London without meeting Amundsen. The two had never spoken face to face and now they never would.

Scott sent Amundsen certain instruments matched with his own for comparative observations; the Norwegians in the north, and the British in the south. Amundsen was terribly embarrassed. But refusal would have raised a hornet's nest. He therefore accepted, in evasive terms but without the lie direct.

At Fefor, Skelton, having seen the success of the motor sledge on which he had worked so long, was told by Scott that he could not, after all, go south again. 'Teddy' Evans had declared that he, Evans, as a mere *lieutenant* could not possibly command *Terra Nova* with *Commander* Skelton in the engine room and therefore a senior officer, albeit an engineer, under him.

Remembering how Scott had written: 'I have cherished the idea that if I went South again you would join'*, Skelton's bitterness was understandable and he could hardly be blamed for feeling he had been used and cast aside. He embarked on an impassioned correspondence which, however, produced little more satisfaction than Evans' cool reply that he had 'really nothing to add' and an elaboration by Scott of his motives:

As far as I am concerned personally, I should be delighted† to have you ... but it would be folly for me to indulge in a personal predilection when this may lead to friction.... Evans would of course assent if I put my foot down but I don't think I ought to do that; the yielding on his part should be voluntary.

Scott had thrown over an old friend for a new one. But, whatever the morality of the affair, in jettisoning Skelton, Scott had jettisoned Antarctic experience and the one man who fully understood the motor sledge; by his own estimation the chief hope for reaching the Pole and

* See p. 224.
† 'Very glad' scored out.

returning safely.

On May 17th, 1910, when Tryggve Gran joined *Terra Nova* in the West India Docks, he observed

> a hurry and scurry that impressed me almost as much as the traffic in the streets of the metropolis. Men tore about like busy ants. Sailors were crawling over rigging and spars.

Terra Nova had been handed over on November 8th, 1909, with sailing day the following August 1st. Halfway through the fitting out, Scott decided this was too late for the southern summer, and made it June 1st instead. The ensuing rush, spiced by the British love of a crisis, produced the unfamiliar scene that greeted Tryggve Gran when he stepped aboard *Terra Nova*.

Below decks, in the wardroom 'where chaos also reigned' he unexpectedly found an old acquaintance, Lieutenant Victor Campbell, whom he had met skiing at a Norwegian mountain hotel.

Campbell was an errant Old Etonian who had gone to sea, starting in the merchant service before transferring to the Royal Navy from which he retired as a lieutenant in 1902.* He then lived part of each year in Norway on a salmon river in Sandsfjord, on the West Coast, where an uncle owned the fishing rights. Campbell had learned to ski in the Norwegian mountains, which gave him the impetus to volunteer for Scott's expedition. He was the only member of the expedition who had been taught to ski properly and one of the very few with any knowledge of snowcraft.

Campbell was to lead the party going to King Edward VII Land. The expedition as the announcement in *The Times* had shown, was an amalgam of Teddy Evans' plan for King Edward VII Land, and Scott's original intention of returning to McMurdo Sound. Campbell, however, had the subsidiary task; for Scott, as Amundsen had guessed, had by now decided on McMurdo Sound as his main base. On the ship, Campbell was first mate,† the chief executive officer. 'He had a very nasty temper', was Gran's abiding memory of him, '& the nickname "the wicked mate" was a right one. But he was a very good sailor'. Campbell had the knack of compelling obedience and driving men to the limit: like 'Teddy' Evans, he was a born leader of a forlorn

* He returned to the Navy in the Great War, reached the rank of Captain, and served at Gallipoli.

† As in the case of *Discovery*, *Terra Nova* was that singular anomaly, a merchant ship run by Naval men. The officers officially were mustered under merchant titles. Evans was the Master; Campbell First Mate, and so on.

hope, and he could take much of the credit for getting *Terra Nova* ready in time. That was not an easy job.

Terra Nova was an old Dundee whaler, 700 tons gross, built in 1884; well worn and scarred by the time Scott bought her, straight off the whaling grounds, still reeking of whale oil and blubber.

> I was much taken aback when I got my first sight of her [said Davies the shipwright], she looked an absolute wreck, fit only for the knacker's yard. [She had been] squeezed in the pack ice, once so badly, I was told, that all her hatches were out of shape.

But eyes unused to wooden Polar ships were easily distressed. *Terra Nova* was no shining yacht but she had plenty of life left in her. In the event, Davies was more troubled by the base huts – at least to begin with.

Davies, as shipwright, i.e. master carpenter, was responsible for checking the quality of the huts. He discovered that the East End firm building them had by a trick of the trade skimped on the planking for the walls, with potential embarrassment on site in the Antarctic, 2,000 miles from the nearest tree. Scott had to use dire threats to force the firm to make up the deficiency.

Halley's comet was in the sky. The day Gran arrived in London, the earth was passing through the comet's tail which, according to sensational predictions, would mean the end of the world.

Ten days before, on May 6th, Edward VII had died; and the collector of historical coincidences will note that the sailing of *Discovery* had also been marked by the death of a sovereign; on that occasion Queen Victoria. Scott's Antarctic preparation was spanned by the short Edwardian era, that time, as one historian put it,

> of growth and strain, of idealism and reaction, of swelling changes and seething unrest. At home, politics had never been so bitter; and abroad, the clouds were massing for Armageddon.

Scott's expedition was being played up as a symbol of national vitality; a living refutation of prophecies of national doom. Peary who, for all his failings, was a brilliant Polar traveller – far superior to Scott – saw the cracks behind the façade of the British expedition. He was in London at the time to receive an R.G.S. medal (partly) for priority at the North Pole, and, like Nansen, felt he ought to try and save Scott from himself. 'I was,' wrote Peary 'with Scott for two weeks before his expedition started ... and I talked dogs and dogs with him, but without results.'

On May 31st, the day before *Terra Nova* left London docks, the R.G.S. gave a farewell lunch. Scott, said Major Leonard Darwin, the R.G.S. President, in one of the speeches, was

> going to prove once again that the manhood of the nation is not dead and that the characteristics of our ancestors, who won this great empire still flourish amongst us.

Scott's reply was oddly in keeping; no blustery Viking self confidence; no Elizabethan cockiness; but an unconscious suspicion that something was awry. The presence of Captain 'Bob' Bartlett, who had been with Peary in the north, suggested one obvious short-coming:

> We have [said Scott] the men necessary for the success of a polar expedition. But yet, complete as this provision seems to be, one cannot fail to realize that there are many other men in this great empire (and remember that I have tried to make this an empire expedition) who might greatly help forward our work ... One knows, for instance, that in Canada there are hard men who wrestle with the difficulties of frontier life, and who would be invaluable on such an expedition. One knows (and we have an example here in Captain Bartlett, who I see is sitting opposite me) the hardy breed of sailors which Newfoundland has produced ... but there are limits beyond which an expedition cannot go. Apart from the limit of number, it is desirable that the people who come together should have the same sentiment, and to some extent the same up-bringing, and, furthermore, there are insuperable difficulties in selecting men who are far removed from us geographically.

Bartlett's reactions are not recorded, but he did give his thoughts the following day, June 1st, when, by special invitation, he saw *Terra Nova* off as she left the London docks.

> Two things especially struck me about what I saw; the attitude of the country and the kind of equipment ... there were gold lace and cocked hats and dignitaries enough to run a Navy. I couldn't help comparing all this formality with the shoddy, almost sneering, attitude of the American public towards Peary's brave efforts ...
> The basis of all Peary's work was application of Eskimo methods ... In contrast to this, the British worked out their own theories. [They] proved on paper that it wasn't worth while to use dogs ...
> I thought of these things as I looked at the fine woollen clothing, the specially designed (in England) ... other gear. None of it looked like the Eskimo stuff that we were used to.

Sir Clements Markham, venerable, white-haired, bewhiskered, a monument to the already distant certainties of the Victorian age, had also come down to see *Terra Nova* off. At four p.m., an hour before she sailed, he watched Lady Bridgeman, wife of the Second Sea Lord, break the White Ensign at the maintop. (The Admiralty had relaxed their hauteur of *Discovery* days, and allowed *Terra Nova*, although no warship, to fly the Naval flag.) At last, after thirty years, Sir Clements saw his ambition fulfilled, and a British Antarctic expedition set sail under the White Ensign.

Lady Markham broke the burgee of the Royal Yacht Squadron, to which exclusive body Scott had been elected a temporary member. Like *Discovery*, *Terra Nova* had been registered as a yacht to avoid merchant shipping regulations.

By a strange coincidence, *Discovery*, still a humble merchantman with the Hudson's Bay Company, was berthed in the same dock, and Scott passed his old ship as *Terra Nova*, all new black paint, gilding and squared yards, swung out into the Thames and began her voyage.

At Greenhithe, down the river, Scott and his wife, who had been on board for the farewell, went ashore to rejoin *Terra Nova* for the next send-off, at Portland. Thither – shades of her relief voyage for *Discovery* – she was ceremonially towed by a cruiser for a Naval review. This is how the scene appeared to the impressionable Gran:

> At that time, the British Home Fleet – the world's mightiest naval force – lay gathered in Portland Harbour. Little *Terra Nova* – decorated with flags from topmast to deck, steamed as it were through a crowded street of battleships and battle cruisers. On the decks of the armoured colossi, the crews were drawn up along the railings, and the cheers from the many thousand of throats fairly made the air quiver on that blazing summer afternoon.

Finally, on June 15th, after calling at Cardiff for coal, *Terra Nova* left the shores of Britain.

> Neither before or since in time of peace have I heard such an uproar as that which made the air tremble as *Terra Nova* glided out through the docks [wrote Gran]. People in their thousands yelled as if they had taken leave of their senses. Railway wagons were rolled over a line covered with dynamite detonators, and vessels in their hundreds completed the noise with whistles and sirens. At the last lock gates we were met by a little squadron of beflagged boats, and with this as escort we steamed out into the open sea.

Scott came off with the pilot boat. Wanting to make a last-minute bid to collect more money, to make newspaper arrangements and generally to tie up loose ends – besides being with his wife and child – he decided to stay behind and travel out by mailboat later, joining the expedition in New Zealand. Until then, Teddy Evans was to captain *Terra Nova*.

As Scott returned to shore, he could hardly fail to appreciate how the country was looking over his shoulder. Here at Cardiff was the authentic roaring of the plebs. There had been voices raised against his enterprise as a waste of money while there was unemployment and social inequality at home. Those same voices were now howling for glory, not for bread. Like a bullfighter, Scott sensed the tyranny of the crowd; he was its hero, and therefore its sacrificial victim. It would be a strong man, stronger than Scott, who could hold his own course. Now, he could never turn back.

Few were wholly unaffected by this atmosphere. Some of the seamen could hardly be blamed for cutting a dash as intrepid explorers off to the frozen wastes.

There was a third departure, this time from Waterloo station in London. On July 16th, Scott left by the eleven thirty-five a.m. boat train for Southampton to sail on R.M.S. *Saxon* for Cape Town. At the last moment, Kathleen had decided to travel out with him as far as New Zealand, leaving her baby behind with a nurse. Wilson's and Teddy Evans' wives were also travelling out to New Zealand to see their husbands off.

20

The Secret Disclosed

THERE WAS A profound difference in the spirit of the two expeditions, as the Press, that mirror of the public soul, suggested in covering the departure. 'I feel it is good to be setting forth ... to uphold the exploring traditions of our race, and proving that the spirit of enterprise is still alive,' the *Sheffield Daily Telegraph* quoted Scott as saying. On which its leader writer commented,

> It may be that ... we are a race of degenerates, living in a flabby age. But at least there can be no degenerates aboard the *Terra Nova* ... These men are the spiritual sons of the great Elizabethans ... where a Shackleton fails gloriously, a Scott is found ready ... to renew the attempt. While England has such men to lead ... we may thank God and take courage ...
> This is a case in which failure – if failure there must be – is only less glorious than success.

Fram set off in an altogether different atmosphere. There were no heroics. Even had Amundsen wanted to play the hero, his public would not have been amused.

The Norwegians were supremely, some would say, grotesquely, self-confident. In Polar exploration where, with its combination of the skier's and the whaler's skills, they could call themselves masters, they tended to take a cool, professional view. The Norwegian Press concentrated on technical details. For instance, *Social Demokraten* explained how

> single cabins have been built for the crew; [to each] a diminutive room in which artificial lighting is always necessary; inside a bunk and cupboard have been fitted, and when the occupant is added, the space is filled.

With measured pace, *Fram* had been made ready, Unnoticed, on April 25th, 1910, her refit done, she hoisted her silken swallow-tailed ensign – the blue cross of St. Olav outlined with white on a red ground – and left the dockyard at Horten to sail up the fjord to Christiania. There she moored under the medieval walls of Akershus Castle. The whole of May was spent in stowing ship, for *Terra Nova* could, and would be restowed at Cape Town, Melbourne and Lyttelton, New Zealand;

but *Fram* had to be stowed once and for all. There would be no second chance before the Bay of Whales.

On June 3rd, *Fram* sailed down to anchor outside Amundsen's home at Bundefjord.

Here, *Fram* loaded the hut which Stubberud and his brother had finished and which now stood on the lawn at the water's edge, a guilty intimation of the truth. The structure was dismantled, the parts carefully numbered for reassembly and stowed on board. There was some mystification among the crew, but the Press – doubtless steered by Amundsen – suspected nothing and spoke of other things. A critical point had been safely passed: Amundsen's secret was still safe; the world still thought he was going north on an Arctic drift.

Late in the evening of June 6th, Amundsen came out of his house, shut the door behind him, leaving things as if returning in an hour or two, walked briskly through the trees, and boarded *Fram*. There was a rattle of chains; the anchor was raised, and slowly she swung out into the fjord.

'Sailed at midnight', ran the opening entry of Amundsen's diary; echoing the words with which he had begun his diary on *Gjøa*. Again, he had chosen the hour from a sense of drama and the desire of a quiet farewell. Deliberately, too, as a patriotic symbol, Amundsen had chosen June 7th, Norway's Independence Day, for his departure. He was vouchsafed clear skies and calm weather; so different from the rain that, seven years before, made *Gjøa*'s sailing dismal.

Across the fjord, in the tower at Polhøgda, Nansen kept a lonely vigil, watching *Fram* steal round the headland and, like a ghost ship, melt into the long northern summer twilight, as she vanished down the channel to the sea. She seemed to take something of himself with her; his old ship, his conception, the vessel of now unattainable desires. Still he hankered after the South Pole. His wife was dead now and *Fram* was a symbol of what might have been. Nansen, in his heart of hearts knew he was too old, his moment past, but as he saw *Fram* sailing, he thought how he had given her to the younger man, and felt the melancholy of those who are left behind. Years after, he told his son that it was 'the bitterest moment in my life'.

Amundsen did not feel truly under way until – as on *Gjøa* – he had reached the open sea. He recorded the moment in his diary:

Quietly and calmly we stand out of the Christiania Fjord. Soon the land will have disappeared from view and *Fram* will have begun her third voyage. God grant it will be to our credit.

Amundsen took pains to call this the *third* voyage of the *Fram*, looking on himself as the heir to Nansen on the first and Sverdrup on the second cruise of the selfsame ship. So began the third voyage of the *Fram*. First, she spent a month on a preliminary North Atlantic cruise, ostensibly to take oceanographical readings for Nansen; in reality to test *Fram* in her new guise; especially the motor and the men. It would never occur to Amundsen to do what the British expedition was happily doing, set off for the other end of the world without putting men and material through their paces.

Bjaaland, the ski champion, was thrown in at the deep end. In a calm spell on the fourth day out, he was told to take the helm. He had never been to sea before, much less steered a ship.

> You can take it from me [he confided to his diary], that she made some beautiful swerves ... for *Fram* is slow to turn, so she always overshoots the mark if you don't stop her in time. But a lovely hour it was, and just imagine being allowed to steer *Fram*, that historic thingamobob which has brought the country so much honour.

Fram was supposed to be slow, so Amundsen was encouraged when she did almost ten knots in a storm under power and sail. As he put it, however, he had 'a heartily unpleasant night ... water had penetrated everywhere [and] I was fairly swimming in my cabin.' *Fram* had developed a leak above the waterline. Other defects were shown up in time to be repaired before sailing South.

On July 10th, *Fram* put in to Bergen at the end of her cruise. The diesel engine had given trouble by fouling up and constantly having to be decarbonized. The fuel was too thick, and the engineer incompetent. Amundsen ordered thinner oil, sent off a telegram to Atlas Diesel in Stockholm, demanding 'qualified help as soon as possible', and departed for Christiania on urgent business. The motor was the least of his troubles; a technical trifle that the manufacturers, with the future of their invention at stake, could be relied upon to deal with. Money was the more intractable problem.

He still was short of 150,000 kroner* with no prospect of raising it in the month that remained before the final departure for the south. When Nansen asked him what he was going to do, he answered that he would collect the rest in San Francisco – no trouble in America – which made Nansen shake his head. Amundsen had to act with the greatest circumspection, because if his creditors got wind of the truth, he would

---

* £8,150 or $39,500; £131,000 or $262,000 in present terms.

find *Fram* under writs of distraint. At all costs, the creditors had to be kept at bay until *Fram* was beyond their reach.

It required a cool head and a reassuring front, both of which Leon, his brother and impresario, luckily possessed. The position was that there would be no money to refit, refuel and reprovision *Fram* after landing the shore party at the Bay of Whales; in other words, the wherewithal of relief was yet lacking, and the possibility of being marooned in the Antarctic not entirely academic. It is at this point that in a well-constructed drama, the *deus ex machina* ought to appear upon the stage. Oddly enough, that is precisely what he did.

Ten days before departure, Amundsen, who was now in Kristiansand, waiting to embark his dogs, received a telegram from the Norwegian Foreign Ministry:

> The Norwegian Minister in Buenos Aires Christophersen writes: Herr landowner Peter Christophersen of this place has expressed to me his willingness to provide the Expedition both with Coal and the necessary supplies at his expense on condition that 'Fram' on her forthcoming voyage touches Montevideo to take on coal. On behalf of the expedition I have accepted Herr Christophersen's kind and altruistic offer of which the Foreign Ministry is asked to apprize Herr Roald Amundsen Unquote stop Put me in a position to convey your answer to minister Christophersen.

Amundsen might well, as he had told Nansen, trust in his 'good fate'. At the eleventh hour a total stranger had appeared, unexpected and unasked, to rescue Amundsen from a financial wilderness, and guarantee that, having reached the Pole he could return to civilization without delay.

'Herr Landowner Peter Christophersen' belonged to a generation of Norwegians who found their own country too small. In 1871 he had emigrated to Argentina and made his fortune. 'Don Pedro' he was called; the mark of a big landowner, a man of substance; as 'Don Pedro' he has gone down in history.

Don Pedro wanted to do something for the old country; helping *Fram* had appeared a suitable way. He had been kept in touch with Amundsen's financial state, probably through a brother who until recently had been Norwegian Foreign Minister and who knew Nansen. (Another brother was the 'Minister Christophersen' of the telegram, Norwegian Minister in Buenos Aires.)

> I have received your magnificent no less than kind offer to supply my Expedition both with [fuel] and provisions when *Fram* touches Montevideo [Amundsen wrote in stilted gratitude the day the telegram arrived],

and I hereby permit myself to convey my recognition and warmest thanks for the generous manner in which it is your intention to support my enterprise.

Don Pedro naturally believed he was helping a northern voyage; Amundsen did nothing to correct that view; because a misplaced word could still mean ruination. However, through the Foreign Ministry, he explained that he needed oil, not coal; and that *Fram* was bound for Buenos Aires if that were convenient. Within forty-eight hours he received the comforting reply that Don Pedro 'offered petroleum and provisions in Montevideo or Buenos Aires'.

Tolerably certain of his finances for the next eighteen months, Amundsen could now devote himself to the essential business of the embarkation of the dogs.

Daugaard-Jensen had gone to infinite pains to secure good animals. Immediately after Amundsen's visit to Copenhagen in September, he had sent out a request for dogs between two and three years old to be collected during the winter at Egedsminde, Godhavn and Jakobshavn, the North Greenland trading stations. He himself would then pick out the dogs himself when he arrived from Denmark in the Spring. Daugaard-Jensen used to conduct his official tours of inspection by dog sledge. He had made himself into a good driver, and knew the Greenland breed. He offered twice the usual price* but for that he would 'buy only good, strong animals ... and reserve the right to select from each team only those [dogs] which meet my requirements'. Amundsen could be sure of the pick of the North Greenland dogs; the cream of the cream.

The Danish authorities showed their esteem for Amundsen by voluntarily shipping all 101 dogs free to Kristiansand in the care of two Eskimos.

Ninety-nine were delivered alive and well to a small island off Kristiansand, which Amundsen had borrowed. There they were looked after by Lindstrøm, who had just returned from Alaska, and a dog-driver called Sverre Hassel.

Hassel, like Lindstrøm, had been with Otto Sverdrup on the second voyage of the *Fram*. Amundsen had been trying hard to get him for the expedition, but Hassel, now having a comfortable berth in the Customs service, at first declined. By the beginning of July, Amundsen had persuaded him, or rather had persuaded the Customs service to

---

* Daugaard-Jensen offered 10 kroner for bitches and 12 kroner for dogs; 10/6 or $2.60 and 14/- or $3.40; £8 or $16 and £10 or $20 in present terms. But a good Eskimo dog now costs £50, or more.

send him, to care for the dogs at Kristiansand, and look after the twenty tons of stockfish that was to be part of their diet.

Amundsen now exerted all his charm and force of character to coax Hassel, after all, to sail with him. In the end, Hassel, worn down by his persistence, agreed, up to a point. Guaranteed against loss of salary (by Amundsen) and seniority (by the Customs), he promised to sail as far as San Francisco to look after the dogs. That was all that Amundsen wanted. Hassel, under the impression that *Fram* was going north, had all unknowing been earmarked for the dash to the South Pole. Together with Helmer Hanssen, Amundsen now had the two dog-drivers that he wanted.

Amundsen next had to make sure of his officers. On the eve of departure, under pledge of secrecy, he now told Lieutenants Gjertsen and Prestrud that they were going south. Both were charmed with the idea. Amundsen could now face the future with equanimity. With his officers behind him, he had every prospect of carrying the crew with him when the time came for them to be told the truth.

Seven people were now party to the secret; Amundsen, his brother Leon, Nilsen, Gjertsen and Prestrud, Herman Gade and Bjørn Helland-Hansen.

Helland-Hansen was the oceanographer under whom Amundsen had worked in Bergen on the elements of oceanography. He knew Nansen well, and Amundsen had let him into the secret so that he could break the news to Nansen when the time came. He had taken Amundsen's bombshell very calmly; at any rate he refrained from moralizing, and promised to do as bidden.

Thus reassured, Amundsen could turn to the final preparations for departure. The engine was now working; the oil had been changed, and a better engineer sent by the factory in Stockholm. He was a Swede called Knut Sundbeck, who had helped to build the motor. Looking back, Sundbeck remembered Amundsen as

a laconic and decided gentleman, and not many words were exchanged at our first meeting.
'I shall do what I can,' I said.
'Excellent,' he answered, 'because no one can do more.'
And our agreement was thereby in order.

On their island, the dogs, in Gjertsen's words, 'had the time of their lives with lovely horsemeat, lying and lazing in the sun, swimming expeditions to the mainland, and fighting to the death'.

After three weeks' rest and recuperation the dogs – or, as Amundsen calls them, his 'new shipmates' – were embarked on August 9th, the last item before departure. In three hours they all – now ninety-seven in number – had been brought off. It was a noisy circus, ferrying them in relays from the island in a lifeboat and hoisting them aboard by the scruffs of their necks.

'A wonderful feeling to cast off at last, and head for the goal,' Amundsen wrote in his diary. 'Clear and calm. Hot as the warmest summer's day.... All well.'

At half past eight in the evening, as soon as the last dog was on board, anchors were weighed. To make sure of a quiet departure, Amundsen had not announced the time. Almost unseen, *Fram* slid through the skerries in the gathering dusk and made for the open sea, in Bjaaland's words, 'headed for the Pole, that Promised Land'.

From the start, there was something wrong with the atmosphere on *Fram*. Amundsen's companions were subdued and ill at ease. They sensed something awry.

There was indeed cause for perplexity. If they really were going north, why the dogs, when they could so much more easily be obtained in Alaska without the bother of hauling them all the way round Cape Horn and twice through the tropics? It had struck Nansen as odd without, however, arousing his suspicions. After all, *Fram* was supposed to be going round the Americas and through the Bering Strait into the Arctic.

Not only the dogs puzzled the crew; much else was causing mystification. 'Their very faces,' as Amundsen put it, 'began to resemble question marks.'

But it was the 'observation' hut that really worried them. It seemed dangerously heavy, and no power on earth, Helmer Hanssen remarked to Nilsen,

would get me to sleep in such a house built in the pack. But at that Nilsen did a vanishing trick, and afterwards wouldn't hear any more talk on the subject.

A few incidents like these, showing evasive officers before puzzled men, especially coming from a community where obedience, although absolute, was not blind, but depended on mutual confidence and explanations of ultimate purpose, was quite enough to generate suspicion and low spirits. Head winds, trying at the best times, caught *Fram* in the Straits of Dover, and dampened feelings yet more.

In his diary, Johansen wrote a little while afterwards:

I am compelled to make comparisons between this voyage and the first one of *Fram*'s. The difference is great. This time there is too much fuss. There is no *esprit de corps*. There is not the comradeship, not to mention anything so elevated as friendship, which is necessary if an expedition as serious as this is to have a fortunate outcome.

Already there were cross-currents between Amundsen and Johansen; the one ill at ease with the subordinate forced on him, the other comparing his new chief with the old, to the detriment of the new. The shadow of Nansen was long.

Round tub as she was, *Fram* wallowed like a crab, close-hauled. She took ten days to clear the Channel, creeping against the gales. On August 22nd, the wind finally veered north, to let her run free once more. At last, she could head into the open waters of the Atlantic, and leave the narrow seas behind.

It was the end of a stage; to Amundsen it meant the breath of escape. The same night, he turned to a labour which he had been dreading; his apologia to Nansen, which would be sent back from Madeira. Shutting himself up in his cabin, he sat down before his typewriter, and carefully started picking out the words. Usually he wrote in longhand, but while *Fram* rolled and lurched as only she knew how, it was hard to control the pen. There was, too, something symbolic about the use of a machine, as if unable quite to face his emotions, he wished to hide behind its mask:

Herr Professor Fridtjof Nansen [he wrote],
    It is not with a light heart that I send you these lines, but there is no way round, and therefore I might as well go straight to the point.
    When the news from Cook and later from Peary about their journeys to the North Pole arrived in the autumn of last year, I understood immediately that that was the death blow to my enterprise. I understood immediately that after this I could not count on the financial support that I needed ...
    To give up my enterprise did not for one moment occur to me. The question for me became what I had to do in order to raise the necessary means. To acquire these without something special was out of the question. Something had to be done to rouse the interest of the public. In that way alone would it be possible to realize my plan. Only one problem remained in the polar regions that could be depended on to awaken the interest of the masses; the attainment of the South Pole. If I could carry that out, I knew that the means would be secured for the expedition I had originally planned.

Yes, it is hard for me, Herr Professor, to tell you, but in September 1909, my decision to take part in the contest for the solution of this question was taken. Many a time I have been on the way to confide the whole matter in you, but always have turned back for fear that you would stop me. I have often wished that Scott could have learned of my decision, so that it would not seem as if I wanted to sneak down there without his knowledge in order to forestall him: but I have not dared to make any kind of announcement, for fear of being stopped. I shall in the meanwhile do everything possible to meet him down there and tell him my decision, and then he can act accordingly.

So, since September last year, my mind has been made up, and I believe I may say we are well prepared. But at the same time I must point out that, had I succeeded in obtaining the funds still needed for the expedition I originally intended – about 150,000 kroner – I would have left out this extra excursion with pleasure; but there was no question of that.

From Madeira we set our course Southwards for South Victoria Land. With 9 men it is my intention to be landed there, and then let *Fram* go out on an oceanographic cruise ... Where we will go ashore down there, I have not yet decided, but it is my intention not to dog the Englishmen's footsteps. They have naturally the first right. We must make do with what they discard.

In February–March 1912, *Fram* will again come down to fetch us. We will then first go to Lyttelton in New Zealand to cable, and from there to San Francisco to continue my interrupted work with, as I hope the equipment necessary for a voyage of this nature.

I have asked Helland [Hansen], who for some time has known this plan, to deliver this letter, in the hope that possibly he will be in a position to put my case in a more favourable light than I myself am able.

And when you pass judgment on me, Herr Professor, do not be too severe. I have taken the only path that seemed open, and now events will just have to take their course.

Simultaneously with this letter, I am informing the King as well, but no one else. A few days after the receipt of this, my brother will arrange the announcement of the addition to the expedition's plan.

Once more, I beg you, do not treat me too harshly. I am no humbug; necissity forced me.

And so I beg your forgiveness for what I have done. May my coming work help to atone for that in which I have offended.

With my most respectful
greetings
Roald Amundsen

Writing this was perhaps the hardest thing Amundsen ever had to do. What it cost him may be faintly judged by this: his spelling, which already was idiosyncratic, now took a step for the worse.

For Amundsen was not a monster of indifference. Underneath the granite shell, behind those shrewd eyes glinting out of that carved, impassive face there was a sometimes unbearable sensitivity, and he who was hurt most by betrayal, who forgave anything but disloyalty, now had to bear the knowledge that he had betrayed another.

The letter to Nansen needed tactful delivery, and Amundsen had chosen to confide in Helland-Hansen believing (justifiably) that he was best suited to that unenviable task. He now wrote to Helland-Hansen, explaining that he had asked Leon to arrange matters

> so that you deliver the letter to Nansen, and one of similar content to the King, simultaneously. In this way, both receive the message *at the same moment*. It means much to me that this is done.
>
> Do what you can to temper feelings, please. They will screech to begin with, I can imagine, but it will blow over with time.

These were the worst letters to write. Thus unburdened, it was with evident relief that Amundsen turned to the remainder, to be delivered after the news had been published and therefore written as comment. To Professor Axel Steen, of the Meteorological Institute in Christiania who had helped him on the North-West Passage he wrote with ironic gusto:

> I won't bother you with asking what you think of my abilities as a juggler. Good God, if it is necessary to be an acrobat, well, one must bite on the bullet and become one. You must expect nothing whatsoever of worth from this excursion. On this occasion I am compelled to put everything aside for coin of the realm.

There were letters to Axel Heiberg, to Don Pedro Christophersen and finally, to Daugaard-Jensen thanking him yet again for getting the dogs, 'stronger and more beautiful animals cannot possibly exist'.

At Madeira, the crew would be told where the ship was really bound. They would then have to be persuaded to volunteer for the south. Amundsen knew the gamble this involved.

He was an acute psychologist, observing his men all the time, searching out their foibles. After two months in the close confinement of a ship, he was beginning to know their strengths and weaknesses; who could be depended on, who not.

Amundsen was fairly certain that he could carry almost everyone on board with him by moral force. But there was one man who could spoil the game for him; the same one who could win the race with Scott; Sverre Hassel, the dog-driver.

Hassel, Amundsen saw, was exactly the kind of person who, if wrongly handled, could take over the psychological leadership at least during the critical moments. He might easily persuade the rest of the crew not to carry on, especially if he felt he had been duped. Amundsen solved this difficulty by taking him into his confidence, under pledge of secrecy, just before arriving at Madeira. Hassel was flattered by the trust put in him. He saw nothing morally wrong in Amundsen's deception at least now that he was party to it. He agreed to go south, as Amundsen asked.

Amundsen had now made all the moves he possibly could. He had got the leaders – real and potential – on his side. There was nothing more he could do. The rest, truly, was in the lap of the gods.

On the morning of September 6th, *Fram* arrived at Madeira, and anchored in Funchal Roads. Shortly afterwards, Leon Amundsen, who had gone on ahead to make arrangements in advance, came off from the shore in a boat. He had ordered fresh fruit, vegetables and water, ready to be taken on board; and also two whole horse carcasses to be fed to the dogs, so that they could eat their fill of fresh meat before the long haul ahead. As Gjertsen put it, 'oof, what a stench on board!'

Unfortunately, *Fram*'s propeller bearings had to be repaired, and her stay was longer than intended. To avoid the discontent of waiting in the torrid heat of a windless anchorage, the crew was sent ashore under the officers' supervision to see the sights at the expense of the Amundsen brothers.

Both Roald and Leon were worried by the risks entailed by the delay. As it was, the local Press, drawing conclusions from the visit of *Terra Nova* late in June, blithely announced that *Fram* too was going south. Had this got abroad the whole plan of campaign, with its finely calculated timetable, would have been dangerously disrupted. Luckily the news stayed on the island, although at the time there was no certainty of this. With so much hanging in the balance, it is doubtful whether Amundsen paid a great deal of attention to the fact that Scott had gained three weeks on him.

Fram's repairs were finally completed on September 9th. At six in the evening, everybody was aboard, preparing for departure. Sandvik, the steward, discharged for incompetence and incompatibility of temperament, was already ashore. Leon was the only outsider on the ship.

Amundsen gave the order to raise anchor.

Suddenly, without warning, the windlass began to grind, and the anchor chain to rattle as it was shortened in.

What was this? Sailing time was three hours hence. Was *Fram* leaving early? There was a ripple of annoyance; the murmur of curses *sotto voce*; for most were in their cabins, bent over last letters home.

The windlass stopped; all hands were called on deck. This was totally outside the normal routine of putting to sea. Annoyance gave way to the tingling of the unfamiliar. Mystified and mildly disturbed, Johansen, Bjaaland, Wisting, Hanssen, and the rest came tumbling up the hatchways. This was the scene that met their uncomprehending eyes:

Nilsen was waiting on deck with a large scroll, which he proceeded to unfurl and hang on the mainmast, revealing a map of the Antarctic. Amundsen placed himself alongside.

There was on board a Russian oceanographer called Alexander Kutchin, a keen student of human nature, and a devoted admirer of Amundsen. 'This always remarkable man,' Kutchin wrote in his diary, 'now was noticeably agitated.'

Amundsen baldly recorded: 'I announced my intention to make for the South Pole.'

Luckily there was someone present with the sense of historic obligation to put down his exact words while fresh in the memory.

There are many things on board which you have regarded with mistrustful or astonished eyes, [Amundsen began by saying, Lieutenant Gjertsen wrote a few hours later], for example the observation house and all the dogs, but I won't say anything about that. What I will say is this; it is my intention to sail Southwards, land a party on the Southern continent and try to reach the South Pole.

There was a church-like hush, broken only by the faint creak of *Fram* pulling on the tautened anchor chain as if straining at the leash.

Prestrud and I [said Gjertsen], already initiated into the affair ... were hugely entertained by the expressions on the various faces. Most stood with mouth agape, staring at the Chief like so many question marks.

But it was no joke; this was a moment of true drama. Amundsen had now collected himself. He stood at the map, physically dominating the assembly, for he was the tallest of them all. There radiated from his extraordinary gnarled, prematurely aged face with its hooded eyes, half Viking, half ascetic, a moral force that could almost be felt.

In short, concise sentences, straight to the point, without attempt at evasion, circumlocution or histrionics, Amundsen spoke on. In his reedy, high-pitched voice, that seemed to possess some electric quality, he calmly explained how he had deceived them and why, using roughly the same argument as he had in the letter to Nansen. He spoke prosaically, underplaying the whole affair. There was no sentimentality; no visible emotion; except perhaps for a lurking hint of double irony, a glint in those pale blue eyes playing over the faces before him, as he suggested that he wasn't proposing anything particularly remarkable. It was no change in any plan; merely an 'extension'. After all, in any case, they had to go round Cape Horn on their voyage north, which was three-quarters of the way to the South Pole, so why not go the whole hog? It was a comparatively little detour, it wouldn't take very long. It would be a pity not to do it while they were there anyway. He contrived to give the impression that he was talking about nothing more extraordinary than a weekend trip to Nordmarka.

Amundsen knew the psyche of his countrymen. Behind the seeming casualness of his talk, there lay an acute capacity to play on feelings, a sense of walking on eggshells, the knowledge that one ill-chosen word, the slightest suspicion of heroics and he was lost.

The news, said Kutchin,

astonished all. Nobody had suspected it ... weariness soon overcame us – a kind of drunkenness - new thoughts, new plans, as far from the old ones as the South Pole from the North.

I remember [Wisting afterwards wrote], that he used 'we' and 'ours' ... It was not his expedition but 'ours' - we were all companions and all had the same common goal.

Now, Amundsen continued, it was a question of racing the English.

'Hurrah,' shouted Bjaaland. 'That means we'll get there first!'

They were the first words spoken; relieving the tension a little. Bjaaland was naturally thinking as a ski champion, used to winning, looking on the South Pole as a cross-country ski race, longer and harder than any other, but still, basically a ski race. And, as everybody knew, the Norwegians were better skiers than the English.

Amundsen now proceeded to explain his strategy for the descent on the Pole. He was considerably more frank than he had been in his letters home. He told his men where they were going to land. This had been revealed to no one else, not even Nansen. On that point, the public was to be left in doubt, and the information deliberately made vague. Only Amundsen, Leon, and the men listening on the deck of *Fram* knew that their destination – if they chose to carry on – was the Bay of Whales.

There was a sound tactical reason for keeping his secret within a secret. The base was rather more than half the battle, and careless talk might still lose it for, if Amundsen disclosed exactly where he was going, Scott might yet forestall him. Amundsen understood sufficient of Scott's mentality to grasp that he was the kind of person who, unoriginal in himself, when presented with an original idea, had a compulsion to adopt it as his own. Dangerous ideas must not be put into his head; he had to be lulled into sticking to his plans and going to McMurdo Sound.

But now, on *Fram*'s deck, illustrating his points on the map, like a teacher at the blackboard, he candidly revealed the whole plan for winning the race to the Pole. He could not, he ended up by saying, compel anyone to accept what he had done. He had broken his side of the agreement, therefore they were released from theirs. Anyone who wanted to could leave now, with passage paid home. Nevertheless, he would ask them to follow him to the South Pole.

In spite of the intense heat down there in the tropics [Helmer Hanssen said in after years], I think a cold shiver ran through most of us when we heard the South Pole mentioned as our journey's aim. We began to think back and forth, to the South Pole – when after all we were supposed to be going to the North Pole –- but there was no time to succumb to meditation ... [for now] came the steel-hard moment when each man was asked, one by one, if he would agree to this new plan   and make a South Pole out of the North Pole. The consequence was that each and every one answered – yes – and the performance was thereby at an end.

It was indeed a masterly performance. Amundsen had established complete domination, and willed them into saying 'yes', playing on the fear of drawing back. He pressed home the advantage; allowing no one time to think. He gave them an hour to write home.

As most of the letters were already prepared [wrote Kutchin], it only remained to add the [latest] news.... 'Before going North', wrote one of the men to his wife, 'We will make a small excursion to the South Pole.' And that was all.

The letters were then collected, and given to Leon, who would post them in Christiania after the news had been published. This would be some time yet. Even now, it was essential that the plans did not leak out too soon.

The mere fact that *Fram* had put in at Madeira was not in itself suspicious. The Panama Canal was not yet open. To reach the Bering Strait necessarily meant going round South America. As far as Madeira, the route to the North Pole or the South therefore was the same.

The timing of the announcement was vital. *Fram* had to be well clear of land, beyond the possibility of recall. Scott, as it was always intended, had to be told before he left civilization. On the other hand the world had to know before *Fram* was due at Montevideo to ship the supplies offered by Don Pedro. The beginning of October was probably the best date under the circumstances.

At nine p.m. Leon was rowed ashore. As he landed, the oarsmen – Gjertsen and Wisting* turned back. Since Amundsen had spoken, no one else had boarded or left the ship.

As soon as Leon went over the side, the windlass resumed its interrupted winding, and the chains rattled into their locker. 'Never,' remarked Kutchin, 'has an anchor been so quickly weighed.'

The boat returned; was hoisted aboard, the motor started and, under power alone, *Fram* started moving out to sea, vibrating to the rhythmic stamp of pistons. As she gathered way, a breath of air stirred to break the still suffocating heat of the anchorage and the dogs, as if at the sign of a conductor's baton, started up their age-old melancholy chorus, a hundred throats in unison voicing a slowly ululating wail, like wolves howling forlornly at the moon. For once nobody on board complained; the animals seemed to be speaking for their masters.

At first, in Helmer Hanssen's words,

when we ... had time to think over what had happened, one heard everywhere: why did you say yes? If only you had answered no. I would have done the same. But we also understood that what is done, cannot be undone.

But after shock and second thoughts wore off, another mood swept over *Fram*. Puzzlement and suspicion had dissolved. The atmosphere had cleared. 'It was,' said Wisting, 'as if we had started on something new.' To quote Johansen's diary,

---

* Officer and man; Amundsen was taking no chances of a last-minute defection.

Since the day we sailed from Madeira, we have done nothing but discuss the wintering and the sledging tour [to the Pole] and who will winter [ashore] and who will sail with *Fram* to Buenos Aires.

They followed Amundsen because he was their leader; he dominated by superior will. Even the foreigners in their midst, Sundbeck, the Swede and Kutchin, the Russian, agreed to carry on.

'For my part,' Sundbeck said, 'I didn't have much time for unnecessary rumination, since *Fram*'s motor gave me enough to think about.' The motor was regularly needed to prevent speed falling below five knots, and it had to be dismantled every fortnight for decarbonizing.

Kutchin's enticement was nicely pitched. ('His wages,' Amundsen had written to Helland-Hansen, 'will be 60 kroner per month and good treatment.') Instead of the old beaten track doubling Cape Horn and up to San Francisco, he was offered something of more interest to an oceanographer. *Fram*'s voyage round the Cape to the Bay of Whales, and thence to Buenos Aires, meant a virtual circumnavigation of the globe at high latitudes. Moreover, while *Fram* was waiting to go down to fetch the shore party, she would make the first oceanographic survey of the waters between South America and the African coast.

This had been arranged by Bjørn Helland-Hansen; the reward, as it were, of his acquiescence in Amundsen's stratagem and his silence. Kutchin was Helland-Hansen's pupil, and it was through Helland-Hansen that he was on board.

On the wall of *Fram*'s charthouse a map of the Antarctic, with the route to the Pole inked in, and a summary of the expedition's plans, was hung, in Amundsen's own words, 'for everybody's use'. Every man on board, from cook to captain, was thus taken into the leader's confidence and early made to understand his rôle. Every man had a precisely defined rôle to play.

Amundsen's plan was worked out in detail. It revolved round two objectives: to beat the British to the Pole, and get back first with the news. Amundsen clearly grasped, what Scott did not, that the Press made its own reality. The winner was not necessarily he who won the race, but he who got the headlines first. That, for Amundsen, had been the moral of the whole Cook and Peary episode. Cook, by getting through first, had brought off a kind of victory. If Peary had only beaten him to the cablehead all the trouble would have been prevented.

So the plan for the Pole not only showed how Amundsen proposed to land, set up his base, lay depots, reach the goal and return to the

Bay of Whales, down to details of when, and approximately where, dogs were to be slaughtered, but how *Fram* was to fetch the shore party and bring back the news to civilization.

Scott, according to his published intentions, would reach the Pole about December 22nd, 1911. Amundsen expected to beat him by a fortnight or three weeks. With luck, although *Fram* was slower than *Terra Nova*, he could hold on to that lead as far as the cablehead. The unknown factor was the motor sledge. On known evidence, however, it was unlikely to get very far. The drawbacks of the ponies and Scott's evident inferiority as a skier would further slow him down. He might very well miss the relief ship, and be stranded in the Antarctic for another winter, leaving the field clear for a twelve-month.

All this rested on the assumption that wireless would not awkwardly obtrude; Scott, so far as Amundsen could make out, was not equipped with it.*

Amundsen had told Nansen that he would return to Lyttelton, New Zealand, in order to cable his news. This was deliberately misleading; what nobody except for Amundsen and his brother Leon yet knew was that *Fram* would go to Hobart, Tasmania. For Amundsen had not forgotten the 'stolen' telegram and the leakage of news, after the North-West Passage. There would be no repetition of *that*. He would take no risk with 'collect' cables this time; certainly not make arrangements in advance and give notice of his intentions He would walk into the cable office, anonymous and a cash customer. After the behaviour of Major Glassford† of the U.S. Signal Corps, he trusted nobody working anywhere for any cable company whatsoever, so had also arranged a cipher to which he and Leon alone had the key.

Much depended on Leon. Roald worked out how to get to the Pole and back again: it was probably Leon who planned how to mislead the world. Leon, in a way, was his brother's chief of staff.

More than five thousand miles ahead, *Terra Nova* had already left the Cape and was making her easting down across the Indian Ocean. It was a largely illusory lead. In *Terra Nova*'s charthouse there was no plan for

---

* In fact, wireless was first used in the Antarctic only a year later by Douglas (later Sir Douglas) Mawson's Australian expedition. His base on the coast of George V Land was about 500 miles closer to New Zealand, and he had a relay station on Macquarie Island. It would have been quite feasible for Scott to arrange a wireless link, imperfect but effective, using relay stations at Cape Adare and Macquarie Island. This was another reason for Amundsen's secrecy. He did not want to frighten Scott into trying wireless, which would have put him at a crippling disadvantage.
† See p. 114.

public inspection, for the very excellent reason that no such plan as yet ex-existed. The difference between the expeditions is enshrined in two diary entries.

On *Fram*, three days out from Madeira, Amundsen wrote:

We have now begun the preparations for our South Polar journey. Rønne [the sailmaker] is sewing floors into our 16 man tents [for the base camp]. Bjaaland has started on the sledges.

On board *Terra Nova*, Cherry-Garrard recorded on August 7th that '[Lieutenant] Evans, Campbell & Wilson have formed a sledging committee and I am nominally the secretary, but there seems very little for me to do.'

This was written almost a year after Scott had announced his expedition; and Amundsen sat in his study at Bundefjord finishing his plan of campaign.

On board *Fram* there were exactly nineteen men; on *Terra Nova*, sixty-five all told. The numbers were out of proportion to the size of the ships. *Fram* was 126 ft. overall, 35 ft. beam, 440 g.r.tons; *Terra Nova* 187 ft. overall, 31 ft. beam, 747 g.r.tons. Both had three masts, but *Terra Nova* was rigged as a barque, against *Fram*'s topsail schooner rig. *Fram* had been built for economy of hands. Her diesel motor ('Old Whooping Cough', as Bjaaland called it) was served by one man.

Terra Nova was technically inferior and prodigal of manpower. Her venerable coal-burning steam engine required two or three stokers to keep the boilers going, besides auxiliary attendants to trim bunkers and an engineer at the controls. Her rig needed many hands and much going aloft.

Terra Nova was not carrying one expedition, but two; Scott's main party for McMurdo Sound, and Campbell's group for King Edward VII Land. She was overburdened, and too small for her task. *Fram* was nicely adjusted to what she had to do.

This was more than a race between explorers: it was a contest of philosophies. On *Terra Nova*, as Wilson said, there were 'many men shoved together at random'; on *Fram* a small band of chosen specialists. Scott with a large, clumsy organization, was marshalling his forces for a ponderous campaign. In *Fram*, 'The Viking Ship of the Twentieth Century', as Borchgrevink called her, Amundsen was sailing on a raid.

Amundsen was obsessed with the necessity of perfecting his equipment. The four months from Madeira to the Bay of Whales seemed not a minute too long; every moment had to be used. Not even the time-honoured ceremony of 'crossing the line' was allowed to interfere with the working routine. Indeed, on October 2nd, a Sunday, they had what Amundsen called their

> Equator dinner, even although we were a few degrees North. We did not have the time to waste a weekday on that kind of nonsense.

Unlike the British expedition which, on the verge of action, was still debating whether motors, ponies, dogs or human power were to win the Pole; whether skis, or the manly use of feet; the Nor-wegians had no doubt on doctrine. The Pole depended on skis, sledges and dogs. All had to be brought safely through the tropics.

If skis and sledges warped, it would be an unmitigated disaster, meaning hard travel and squandered effort. They were sensitive to damp and heat; in need of understanding treatment. The skis were slung from the ceiling of the fore saloon. 'We could not,' as Amundsen put it, 'offer anything better.'

Both Scott and Amundsen had bought their sledges at Hagen's in Christiania. Only Amundsen observed that the workmanship was defective; in particular the lashings. Bjaaland had to get to work with chisel and plane – on that infernally rolling ship – to make the sledges true, and bad workmanship good. By October 24th, he had finished. In six weeks he had rebuilt ten sledges and made for each a pair of loose runners. They had a double purpose: to guard against wear and for coating with a thin layer of ice, as Amundsen and Helmer Hanssen had learned from the Netsilik Eskimos in order to slide properly in deep cold.

One of the sledges was a sophisticated device, with no iron or steel in its construction. This was the non-magnetic steering sledge, on which the main travelling compass would be mounted.

After the sledges, Bjaaland had to true the skis, adjust bindings, besides a plethora of jobs like making sledging boxes for the Primus stoves. Rønne, the sailmaker, sewed new tents, and did all the saddlery and sailmaking for the landing party besides relashing the sledges; between five and six hundred joints in all. These two, Rønne and Bjaaland, worked from six a.m. to six p.m. six days a week, and were excused their watches. That, on a ship with so small a crew, meant a burden on the rest. But, as Amundsen remarked, 'If we are to win, not a trouser button must be missing.'

There was on board a seaman called Ludvig Hansen, who had

been selected for his skill as a tinsmith. A fortnight out of Funchal, he started making paraffin tanks for the sledging journeys.

On the North-West Passage, Amundsen had observed that paraffin has a capacity to 'creep'. Tins left in depots were inexplicably depleted after a few weeks, something to do with the behaviour of petroleum products at low temperatures. Then it had merely been an annoyance, but in the sterile fastnesses of the south, it might be a matter of life and death. Thus warned, Amundsen decided to have tanks specially made up from galvanized iron sheet. To make them absolutely tight, all seams were to be brazed, and the contents eventually sealed in by soldering the spout. Hansen made ten tanks in all, holding fifteen litres each.

Amundsen refused to entrust his work to a commercial enterprise. He could only trust the workmanship, if it was in the hands of someone spurred on by the knowledge that on his skill and conscientiousness depended the lives of his companions. The faith in detail; the knowledge that every little item of equipment can be trusted absolutely, is an essential part of the psychological armour in a hostile environment. Doubt is a dangerous travelling companion.

On the heaving deck, Jacob Nødtvedt, the second engineer and another veteran of the second *Fram* expedition, a skilled blacksmith, set up his forge and, off watch, produced countless gadgets, like patent shackles for the dog harnesses.

There was a reason for this uncharacteristic flurry. For his original Polar drift, Amundsen intended having much of his sledging equipment made on board during the long winters in the ice. He could not alter this without giving himself away. Instead of pleasant immobility in the pack, his craftsmen now had to work on a ship that everlastingly lurched and rolled in the ocean swell. At least it gave a mood of urgency and purpose from the start.

With *Fram* undermanned, basic duties were rotated to spread the strain. Each man, for example, had so many dogs to look after and a regular trick at the wheel, The Chief, as Amundsen was known, not excepted. This was a deliberate act of leadership.

On they sailed through the doldrums and the Trade Winds, the only break in isolation the occasional glimpse of a distant sail, carefully avoided.

A shortage of fresh water was Amundsen's main concern, and the men were rationed in favour of the dogs, for the dogs could not be stinted. He could have put in at Cape Town and got all he wanted. But he had no desire to come in contact with people now. Everybody will want to write home and the newspapers naturally will have a lot to say.

At whatever cost to the men, the dogs were pampered. When, in the colder waters off the Cape of Good Hope, they began to lose condition through want of fat, and the tallow brought for them was running low, they were quite simply given butter, though that, too, was short. Nobody minded. Everything turned on getting the dogs to the Bay of Whales physically and mentally sound. Everybody understood, in Johansen's words that 'The dogs are the most important things for us. The whole outcome of the expedition depends on them.'

Amundsen had had the deck covered by a raised wooden grid, allowing air to circulate under the animals, keeping them comfortable in the tropics. Also it simplified washing down. Twice a day the deck was swilled, besides constant removal of ordure. Twice a week the wooden grille was taken up and scrubbed. But with so many dogs on board, absolute cleanliness was an unattainable ideal:

> Working sails in the dark [Wisting said] [one heard] fairly unambiguous expressions about dogs on a ship, when ropes slid a little too easily through fingers well greased with 'soft soap'.

Nonetheless, the dogs were the great diversion. More than the men, they fill the diaries on board. Sometimes it almost seems as if the Norwegians found most of their companionship among the dogs. At any rate, the animals were a safety valve, stopping many a feud. Great observation of character, together with much tolerance and humour, were lavished on them, as Johansen's diary suggests:

> The names of [some of] my dogs are: 'The Corpse' presumably the oldest of the dogs on board - has undoubtedly once been a whopper of a taskmaster, but now he's come down in the world ... Then I've got 'The Scalp' and 'Pimp'. They are inseparable [and] stalwarts both.

As Amundsen put it in his diary, 'To look after all these our children, we had to go to work systematically.' At first they were chained to their places to discourage their favourite hobby of fighting, and prevent wholesale slaughter.

In the beginning, some of the dogs were so shy and vicious, food had to be thrown to them from a distance. Within a few weeks as Amundsen wrote, all this had changed:

> What a commotion at feeding time. It was like a howl from the depths of Hell. What love these animals conceive for those who look after them.

Of course it is cupboard love - but so it is often the case with our own love; look carefully, and you'll see!

Early in October, when masters and dogs knew each other thoroughly, the dogs were muzzled and let loose. There was a glorious set-to all along the line, but all they could do was make a little fur fly. They were now allowed to get their fighting out of their system.

Before we loosed the dogs, [wrote Amundsen], we noticed that there were a few who ... did not seem as happy as they ought. They were shyer and more agitated than the others ... The day we let them loose, we saw what was the matter ... they had good old friends, who by chance had been placed in another corner of the deck, and separation from their companion was the cause of the bad humour. It was absolutely touching to see the happiness they showed at the reunion. The animals were quite transformed. Naturally, in these cases, it was so arranged ... that ... in the future they were in the same teams.

Amundsen not only considered friendship among the dogs. They were divided among eight watchmen, so that men and animals could learn to know each other in manageable and compatible groups. Some men could not get on with some dogs, so suitable exchanges were made.

On October 31st, when they appeared to have got the fighting out of their systems, they had their muzzles removed. All – mostly – went well. Thenceforth, they had the run of the ship. It is an unusual example of animal management; the first recorded case of letting Greenland dogs run free on board an expedition ship.

By the beginning of November, there were twenty-one pups on board, all born since sailing. Only the males had been kept; within a year they would be at work. It was not only to maintain the stock that the bitches had been taken. The domestic rhythm of pregnancy and parturition brought normalcy to an all-male community. Cuddling puppies, little bundles of bulging fur palpitating with life, gave an outlet for sentiment and feeling to men suffering from sexual deprivation. At least dogs stopped monotony ever getting the upper hand.

After three months, men and dogs had got their sea legs, but neither could ever quite get used to *Fram*'s lurching and rolling.

In a storm [Johansen observed], over 20 dogs can be pressed together ... like a jumble with heads sticking out, and when the ship lurches, the whole mass moves. And then there's a fight ... Intelligent as dogs are in many respects, they cannot understand a lurch as anything but some devilment on the part of their neighbour who, naturally, needs a hiding ... (Well, for that matter, it takes something for human beings to manage as well.)

Fram rolled and bobbed and tossed and yawed and corkscrewed, plunged and pitched as few ships did. This was because of her round bottom and broad beam, constructed for the ice. The received opinion was that *Fram* was built exclusively for the ice, not the water; to drift beset, not to sail. Like so much received opinion, it was fallacious.

Fram was a masterpiece of the shipbuilder's art. In seven years beset in the Arctic ice, she was never once in danger; in the 16,000 miles from Kristiansand to the Bay of Whales, she never shipped a sea. The wind could rake the deck with spume, but the bridge stayed dry and cleared to receive the dogs. In bad weather up to fifty would congregate there at a time. The charthouse was another favoured refuge.

By December, *Fram* was in the Roaring Forties. Here, in the long surging swells where the seas towered up to thirty feet or more, *Fram* showed her mettle. It was, in Amundsen's words during a storm,

> almost unbelievable. The one sea towers up more menacingly than the other, and one might expect it over one every moment. But no – she gives a little twist, and the sea passes under ... Archer can be proud of *Fram*.

On December 1st, Amundsen announced the landing party, which was to consist of himself and Prestrud, Johansen, Hassel, Lindstrøm, Helmer Hanssen, Wisting, Bjaaland and Stubberud; nine in all.

Taking Johansen was a gamble. By little hints and undertones, Johansen made it clear that he felt himself a better Polar traveller than Amundsen. Amundsen was sometimes hard put to keep his temper. Nor did Johansen get on well with others, Hassel in particular. Yet Johansen did have experience; and to keep him on the ship would smack of vindictiveness which would be even worse for morale. The lesser risk was to take him ashore.

> I have increased the wages of those sailing back with *Fram* by 50% [Amundsen noted]. I think it is only right. Many are family breadwinners, with all their wages drawn. They would thus have been absolutely without money on arrival at Buenos Aires.

Partly this was consolation for bitter disappointment. Almost all the ship's party wanted to go ashore; Gjertsen so much so, that he asked Amundsen if he could change places with Prestrud. Amundsen agreed, if Prestrud did. Prestrud did not; Gjertsen stayed on board. Anyway, Amundsen had meted out rough justice by making up the shore party (with one or two exceptions) out of those who had originally signed on for the whole Arctic drift; the ship's party being those who were to have sailed only as far as San Francisco before returning home. The equity of this was, with fairly good grace, accepted.

Now, Amundsen noted on December 8th, 'we are storming to our goal'. They were passing the 100th meridian, approaching the longitude of Australia, seven-eighths of their journey done. They also, although they did not know, had hauled in on Scott, and were only 2,500 miles behind.

High latitudes were now approaching. The first icebergs were expected. The look-out, on that account was now left to what Amundsen called 'the experienced', i.e. those who had sailed most in Polar waters before. The one watch was taken by the Tromsø men, Beck, the ice pilot, and Ludvig Hansen; the otner by Wisting and Helmer Hanssen. Between them they had something like half a century's experience of ice navigation. (*Terra Nova*, by comparison, had no ice pilot, and could muster five years' ice navigation all told.)

Whatever the violence of the seas and the gyrations of *Fram*, preparations for the Polar journey went on. Rønne was making a special lightweight emergency tent for the Pole: another little piece of pioneering. It was the aerodynamic model invented by Dr Cook on *Belgica*, thirteen years before.* Dr Cook had offered it to the Royal Geographical Society, and been snubbed, on the grounds that their own experts had achieved perfection. Rønne cut it on the heaving chartroom table in a storm, a feat that aroused Amundsen's unstinted admiration.

Some of the crew, notably Beck, the ice pilot, had persuaded Nilsen to start a refresher course in English, so that they could consult the main works in *Fram*'s Polar library. That included *The Voyage of the 'Discovery'*, and *The Heart of the Antarctic*, Shackleton's story of the *Nimrod* expedition. Both were read, re-read, and avidly discussed.

Nilsen himself, who was responsible for the navigation, significantly stuck to Sir James Clark Ross' account of his expedition of 1839–43, which, as he remarked, still, after almost seventy years, said everything about sailing in the Southern Ocean.

The critical point of the voyage was approaching. Where was *Fram* to enter the pack? Upon the answer depended the passage, whether short or long; of days or weeks. Much hung upon the choice; whether the timetable for laying depots before the winter could be kept, and hence, ultimately, the outcome of the race to the Pole.

Meanwhile, there was Christmas. Officers and men sat down together in the forward saloon for dinner on Christmas Eve. Amundsen had arranged a little surprise. As they took their places, he wrote, describing the scene in his diary,

* See p. 72.

'Holy Night, Silent Night', burst out, sung by Herold, Heavens, what a ceremony – what an effect. One had to be made of more than steel not to feel the tears coming. The gramophone was completely hidden. No one expected it. The wonderful voice brought Christmas greetings to us like fresh breath from home. It would have been interesting to be a thought reader at that moment.

Fram was, by and large, a happy ship. She was also a lucky one. On January 2nd, she crossed the Antarctic Circle, to find the water free of ice further south than anyone else before. But perhaps this was not luck alone.

It was a commonplace to the Polar experts gathered on *Fram*, that most pack ice has clearly defined contours, shaped by wind and current. Unfortunately, since Ross first went that way there had only been eight voyages; hardly enough to give a pattern. However, carefully analysing the published records – *all* of which were on board – led Amundsen to two conclusions: that there was a clear passage in the ice where the pack was slackest and narrowest, and that at that time of the year, it was probably a few degrees west of the 180th Meridian. He acted on this, but only as a general directive to Beck, the ice pilot, the huge, placid bear of a man from North Norway, who had the feel of the pack, and knew how to exploit its weaknesses. Further than that, he let Beck have his head. The tale is simply told. *Fram* entered the pack on January 3rd, 1911 at 175° 35′ E. longitude, and ran out into the open Ross Sea three days and fourteen hours later, one of the fastest passages yet.

The diesel motor had entirely vindicated itself, another little milestone in technological history, the first motor passage of the pack. Amundsen had instant power exactly where he wanted and, unlike Scott who found *Terra Nova*'s ancient steam engine eating far more coal than he had hoped, was pleasantly surprised by fuel consumption less than he had anticipated. Amundsen was now only 300 miles behind.

In the pack, Amundsen had seen to it that plenty of seals were shot, to give the dogs fresh meat and blubber after four months on dried fish, and feed them up properly before getting into harness. 'Great activity reigns on board,' wrote Amundsen on January 9th. 'The last touches are being put to all the work. Clothing bags must be packed ready to go ashore.'

The atmostphere was now the tensed expectancy at the end of an ocean voyage, when there is still a distance to run, but port is just below the horizon. And there was a longing for solid earth – or ice – after four months without intermission on a rolling deck. Amundsen's thoughts were with his dogs:

They are now, almost without exception, all big, round and fat. I dare say they are at the top of their power and appetite for life ... Now that all danger of disease seems to be over, I must admit that our transport of these dogs a distance of 16,000 miles, in all kinds of weather and almost all temperatures was not only a complete success but also bears witness to a specially good and considerate care. This [will be] a reminder to the many people who opined that the expedition would be cruelty to animals from first to last. If only I had these sensitive persons under my care. Hypocrites all! Bloody hell!

Sailing over the open Ross Sea, under a clear and crystal sky, Bjaaland was moved by his first sight of the midnight sun, north or south to write:

One could wish one's home here in the icy regions where the sun shines day and night. One would think that it was everlasting summer here if it were not for the chill [in the air] that speaks of ice and desolation.

On January 11th he wrote:

At long last, the ice barrier hove into sight today. It is a strange feeling that grips one as the sight now reveals itself. The sea is still as a pool, and before one stands this Great Wall of China and glitters. Far off, it is like a photograph that has just been developed on the plate.

Amundsen saw the sight with different eyes:

There it lay – this infamous 200 ft. high snow wall – wall of ice one cannot call it – and gleamed at us. I had expected it to impress me more than it does, but the excellent reproductions in Shackleton's book meant that I had got used to it and looked on it as an old acquaintance. So here we are.

None of them had been there before. (On *Terra Nova*, there were two who had.) Now they had to find the Bay of Whales. Their only guide was Shackleton's description in *The Heart of the Antarctic*, with a rather approximate position. Nilsen had brought *Fram* to the Barrier at 169° 40′ W. longitude, a little too far to the west. Slowly *Fram* coasted eastwards along the Barrier, overshot the mark, turned, retraced her tracks, and on January 14th, found a wide bay which was evidently what Shackleton had seen. Amundsen then did what even Shackleton never dared: put his ship into the bight.

Past a headland gleaming in the sunlight as if it had been carved out of crystal, *Fram* glided through grey waters, loose pieces of ice grating her sides with the sound of skis rasping on crust, while the steady beat of her engine drummed in the air. Whales hissed and spouted; overhead,

a skua circled and dived. Men and dogs crowded the port bulwarks to peer at the 'Promised Land' as *Fram* followed the glinting
cliff of the Barrier edge.

In the south-east corner of the bay, she was brought up by bay ice.
Amundsen, Nilsen, Prestrud and Stubberud had their skis ready. As
soon as the ice anchors were out and moorings secured, they were over
the side, and off to reconnoitre.

The brown-speckled seals strewn over the ice ignored the intruders.
They had not yet learned to fear man. Penguins streamed inquisitively
from all quarters like spectators at a race.

After months cooped up on *Fram*, Amundsen and his companions
were a little unsteady on their skis. It took some time to limber up.
After about two miles, in Amundsen's words, they found that

> the ice foot led onto the Barrier by a small, even slope; an ideal
> connection in other words. We continued in a south-easterly direction,
> and after about 15 minutes reached one of the [previously observed]
> ridge formations on the barrier. These formations looked like small
> morain ridges with certain irregularities on the top.

Shackleton, too, had noticed this phenomenon and taken it to be more
proof of underlying danger. Amundsen, however, saw it differently:

> The irregularities turned out to consist of huge ice blocks on edge.
> Something must have stopped the barrier in its regular progress and caused
> this. What else can it be but underlying land? ... A sounding on return
> gave 175 fathoms. Bottom-grey and fine sand. Land, land and land again
> forms this bay. Nothing else ... Every formation I see ... confirms me
> in my assumption that disturbances in this inner part only occur very
> rarely, and therefore we have got nothing to fear from it. I selected a
> place – in a little valley, on a fine, flat foundation, about 4 nautical miles
> from the ... sea, as our future residence. Here we will build our home,
> and from here our work will be carried out.

It had been an extraordinary voyage: 16,000 miles from Norway, 14,000
miles non stop from Madeira. When *Fram* lay to on the 14th January, it
was exactly one day earlier than Nilsen had calculated.

With his mixture of poetry and peasant realism, Bjaaland wrote:

> By letting thoughts wander in over the [Barrier] surface, one finds oneself in
> a melancholy mood. One thinks of what is to come, the hardships one is going
> to face, the use one will be, and if we can get there before the Englishmen –
> who are surely burning with the same ambitions.

Scott Sails On

LATE ON THURSDAY, October 12th, *Terra Nova* reached Melbourne from the Cape. Kathleen Scott, who had arrived ten days before, braved a heavy running sea and a dark and filthy night to come off in a launch and claim her husband. Scott went back with her to spend the night ashore and fetch his mail. He still did not know that he had a rival in the field.

Next morning early, Scott returned on board and immediately summoned Gran into his cabin.

> When I entered [Gran wrote in his diary], he handed over to me an opened cablegram, saying, 'What can you make of this?' I read with mounting astonishment: 'Beg leave to inform you *Fram* proceeding Antarctic Amundsen'.

Scott hoped that Gran, being Amundsen's fellow countryman, might be able to help. The fact that he had consulted Gran at all showed the depth of his perplexity. It was not Scott's habit to take juniors into his confidence.

Gran was as astounded and mystified as Scott. He noticed that the cable was dated October 3rd, while *Terra Nova* was still in the middle of the Indian Ocean. It was sent from Christiania but, according to what he had heard in Cape Town, *Fram* had already left Norway with Amundsen on board.

To neither Scott nor Gran was it immediately apparent that they had received a challenge for the Pole. Gran noticed that the cable was signed simply 'Amundsen', which led him to wonder, since Roald was at sea, whether perhaps Leon was the sender. Gran did not quite trust Leon. He kept his doubts, however, to himself, and made what was to him an obvious suggestion: cable Nansen for more information. 'Hope Nansen answers quickly,' Gran noted in his diary, doubtless for his own peace of mind. He had given Scott his complete loyalty; he did not particularly want to suffer for the sins of his countrymen.

Scott was extraordinarily secretive about the cable. Even his officers were kept in the dark. When Gran told Campbell what had happened, he was met with blank amazement. With journalists, Scott avoided the subject. Gran was forced to the conclusion that 'Scott wants as much as possible to suppress this Amundsen affair, which has come like a bolt from the blue.'

Gran now temporarily parted from *Terra Nova* to travel by mailboat to New Zealand and see a little of Australia. In Sydney, he visited the Norwegian Consul, Olav Pauss

To Pauss, the whole affair came as a surprise. He was unaware of the very existence of the cable. He had heard nothing from Norway. As far as he knew, the Australian Press had not mentioned the matter by a single word.

It was indeed Leon Amundsen who had cabled Scott. It was not his fault that the message was unclear. The cable was not intended to inform. It was a courtesy to be taken in the context of the news. Scott was supposed to learn of the Norwegian plans through the Press.

Leon left *Fram* at Madeira on September 9th, and arrived in Christiania late in the evening of the 30th. Next morning he had an audience with King Haakon to tell him about his brother's change of plan. At the same time, Bjørn Helland-Hansen, who had been forewarned, delivered Amundsen's letter to Fridtjof Nansen.

When Nansen had read it through he is reported to have burst out: 'The idiot! Why couldn't he have told me. He could have had all my plans and calculations.'

In his mind's eye, Nansen saw the Norwegian flag already waving at the Pole; he knew, better than most, Amundsen's strength and Scott's weakness. His reaction was that of an explorer, a patriot, a loyal colleague, and one who suspects he has picked a winner. For Amundsen, out in the Atlantic, nearing the Equator, it was a hidden triumph; he had secured his vital ally at a blow.

In the dignified surroundings of the Hotel Continental, that evening, Leon called a Press conference. Next morning, Sunday, October 2nd, the front pages of the Christiania Press told the story:

'FRAM' FORGES TOWARDS THE SOUTH POLE
SENSATIONAL ANNOUNCEMENT BY ROALD
AMUNDSEN
FRIDTJOF NANSEN: 'A WONDERFUL PLAN'
OVER THE SOUTH POLE TO THE NORTH POLE

To their eternal credit, the Norwegian newspapers allowed Amundsen to speak for himself. His letter to the public, written at sea and distributed by Leon at the Press conference, was printed in extenso.

From Madeira, *Fram* sets her course South for the Antarctic Regions to take part in the fight for the South Pole [ran its winged opening words]. At first glance this will appear to many to be change in the original plan for the third voyage of the *Fram*. This is, however, not the case. It is only an extension of the Expedition's plan; not an alteration.

The papers went on to repeat Amundsen's argument in the letter to Nansen. He was plain, uncompromising; he scorned an appeal to patriotism and waved no banner but his own: 'Alone I have taken this decision; alone I bear the responsibility.'

The challenge had been unequivocally issued. Notice had been copiously served on Scott that his march on the Pole had turned into a race. As one Norwegian newspaper put it, 'With a single blow ... Roald Amundsen ... reawakens the attention of the world when the exciting fight for the South Pole is on.' The Amundsens quite reasonably assumed that sensation of this vintage would be picked up by the British Press, and thus conveyed to Scott.

The judgment of news editors, however, is not invariably rational. *The Times*, as a Norwegian newspaper reported with amazement, 'has not mentioned the matter by a single word'. Only *The Daily Telegraph* and *The Morning Post* carried the news, albeit truncated and, in the case of the latter, partially misleading.

Scott Keltie, the R.G.S. Secretary, wrote to Nansen, asking if *The Daily Telegraph*'s report was 'really true? ... Amundsen ... of course ... has a perfect right ... to run a race with Scott ... I simply want to know the truth and the facts.'

This was one of the few sensible reactions in Polar circles. Sir Clements Markham poohed-poohed the whole affair, maintaining that Amundsen could not possibly take enough dogs to get to the Pole, while Shackleton could not see

how Amundsen can hope to reach the South Pole unless he has a large number of ponies on board. He may have dogs, but they are not very reliable.

Then, in the middle of October, Sir Clements' condescending equanimity was disturbed by letters from Norway saying that Amundsen was going to McMurdo Sound. This rumour originated with Dr. Reutsch, the President of the Norwegian Geographical Society, who, in a newspaper interview, hazarded it as a guess.

Sir Clements billowed with righteous indignation.

What rascals these poles are producing ... [he wrote to Scott Keltie]. He has been deliberately forming a plan to steal a march on Scott. He is a blackguard.

This is a caricature, but it mirrors English feelings at the time, in so far as there were feelings on the subject. Very few, even among the geographically interested, had taken notice. The result was that the British Press let the matter drop, and by Australian newspapers it was ignored. When Scott came off at Melbourne, then, he had nothing to guide him beyond that single, enigmatic cable.

It has been suggested that Amundsen's announcement was deliberately timed to inhibit British preparations. An early foreign challenge could have helped Scott to whip up public interest, getting all the money he needed, perhaps even inducing him to get more dogs, and becoming altogether a more formidable proposition. By waiting until Scott left the Cape on September 2nd, Amundsen would reduce his ability to change his plans and thus minimized the risks.

If that were the case, it showed an intelligent understanding of the situation. Indeed Scott was unable to find all the money he wanted before leaving England. Continuing his efforts in South Africa he got a derisory £500 from an unenthusiastic Government as a sop to Imperialist sentiment. The gold and diamond millionaires did not consider him a proposition worth investing in.

But intentionally or otherwise, the greatest effect was in another and, perhaps ultimately, more fateful direction. By temperament and character, Scott was unsuited to emergencies: they exacerbated his fluctuating moods and heightened his already taut nerves. Outside Melbourne on *Terra Nova*, waiting for the tide to turn, he was in a state of considerable tension, torn between complacency and fear; convinced that plans were running to perfection, gloomily afraid that something would go wrong. Amundsen's cable knocked him off balance.

Gran had noticed that Scott wanted to conceal the affair. What he did not see was that Scott had been paralysed by the appearance of the unexpected. There were many things that Scott could have done. As Gran suggested, he might have cabled Nansen; he could have cabled Scott Keltie for information. He could have shown the cable to a Melbourne newspaper which would rapidly have paid dividends in the shape of the whole story, complete in every circumstantial detail, obtained over the wires at urgent rates for the next edition. Scott did none of these things. He remained ominously passive.

Scott left *Terra Nova* at Melbourne to spend the next ten days in Australia making official calls, and by playing on Empire sentiment, trying to raise funds. Amundsen's cable could have been exploited to sound the tocsin of foreign intervention.

The news that a Japanese expedition was on its way to the Ross Sea had been enough to persuade the Australian Government to grant *Terra Nova* £2,500, after first flatly declining to contribute a penny. What could not have been achieved by a judicious waving of the Norwegian cable? Why did Scott refuse to profit by it? Cherry-Garrard afterwards made the significant remark that 'though we did not appreciate it at the time ... we were up against a very big man'.

At any rate, if it was the intention to bring Scott into disarray by playing on uncertainty it succeeded. 'Beg leave to inform you *Fram* proceeding Antarctic', is not explicitly a challenge; but it carries a veiled threat. This much is certain: when Scott embarked at Sydney for the crossing to New Zealand, it still was not clear to him that Amundsen was heading for the Pole. Antarctica was so vast, so unknown, that there was plenty to explore elsewhere.

Landing at Wellington on October 27th, Scott was interviewed by a local newspaper. Reports of Amundsen's challenge for the Pole were now beginning to filter through, the gist of which the interviewer gave Scott, and then asked for his comment. At that, according to Tryggve Gran,

> Scott fell silent. But the interviewer did not give up. Then Scott became angry and brushed the man off by saying, 'If, as [your] rumour says, Amundsen wants to try for the South Pole from some part of the coast of the West Antarctic, I can only wish him good luck.'

This was how Scott learned of Amundsen's challenge. Until that awkward, conscientious, obliging interrogator raised the point, he had refused to face the possibility.

Meanwhile, in London, nobody had seen fit to keep Scott in touch with developments. It was Sir Clements Markham, industriously collecting information from Norway, who finally, on November 4th, got the R.G.S. to cable Scott (erroneously) that Amundsen was going to McMurdo Sound. But Scott, now in Lyttelton, waiting to sail for the south, remained curiously inert. He still seemed to shrink from facing the truth, concerned most to hide it from his men. Only when some of them showed him the newspaper paragraphs about the Norwegian expedition, was he driven to act. On November 14th, a month after receiving Amundsen's cable, Scott finally did what Gran had suggested and cabled Nansen to ask about Amundsen's destination.

The answer arrived the same day; a single word; 'Unknown'.

Nansen had not been entirely frank. Amundsen had told him in his letter from Madeira that he was going to South Victoria Land. But Nansen had rallied unreservedly to Amundsen's support, and considered that all hints of his destination ought to be suppressed – especially when it appeared to impinge on British interests.

My telegram to ask Amundsen's intentions may need some explanation [Scott wrote to Nansen]. As you can imagine it is very difficult to get information in this part of the world and having no information ... I thought it best to communicate with you ... I do not believe the report that he is going to McMurdo Sound – the idea seems to me preposterous in view of his record – but the fact that he departs with so much mystery leaves one with an uncomfortable feeling that he contemplates something which he imagines we should not approve.

Finally Scott cabled Scott Keltie the same day he received Nansen's reply asking for *Fram*'s last port of call and date of departure, getting the misleading reply that 'Fram left Madeira beginning October.' This adds to the picture of confusion and ignorance surrounding Amundsen's intentions. Most of it was due to slovenly staff work – inactivity on the part of Scott's associates – for which Amundsen can scarcely bear the blame.

As a result of Nansen's cable, Scott wrote to Keltie, he concluded that Amundsen

has not thought fit to even inform his supporters in Norway in respect of his intentions. Well, we shall know in due course, I suppose. Meanwhile, rumours must be rife.

Scott now tried to put Amundsen out of his mind. He refused to discuss the subject. He gives the impression of someone who believes that by ignoring an uncomfortable fact, it can be made to go away. A wilful complacency makes its way into the annals of the expedition. In so far as Amundsen was discussed, it was the other-worldly question of his ethics, not the hard realities of the threat he posed. To this there was one solitary exception. It was Oates:

What do you think about Amundsen's expedition [he wrote to his mother]. If he gets to the Pole first we shall come home with our tails between our legs and no mistake. I must say we have made far too much noise about ourselves all that photographing, cheering, steaming through the fleet etc. etc. is rot and if we fail it will only make us look more foolish. They say Amundsen has been underhand in the way he has gone about it but I personally don't see it is underhand to keep your mouth shut - I myself think these Norskies are a very tough lot they have 200 dogs and Yohandsen [*sic*] is with them and he is not exactly a child, also they are very good ski-runners while we can only walk, if Scott does anything silly such as underfeeding his ponies he will be beaten as sure as death.

Scott had been pursuaded by Nansen to take some dogs in addition to ponies and motor sledges. He did not know, as Admundsen did, that the best sledge dogs came from Greenland, and even if he had, it was too difficult and too late to get any. As dog-driver Scott had selected Cecil Meares who, early in 1910 went out to buy animals in Eastern Siberia.

The ponies Scott was going to take were a special cold-weather breed from Manchuria. Since it was in the same general direction as Siberia, he decided at the last moment that Meares might as well buy the ponies as well.

So someone ignorant of horses did the notoriously difficult business of buying them, while the one member of the expedition, Oates, who knew everything about them stayed at home on *Terra Nova* doing work that any ordinary seaman could have done.

Scott assumed that anyone who knew about dogs was qualified to buy horses. It was an oddly casual way to select the beasts on which not only the outcome of the enterprise but his own life would eventually depend.

Oates was surprised, since he had joined the expedition as a horse expert and so presumed he would have a hand in their choice. But he was not the kind to question orders. Scott, he decided, 'had his own way of running things', and left it at that; at least as far as public comment was concerned.

Meares' journey to fetch the animals is a little saga on its own.

In January he went overland by the Trans-Siberian Railway to Khabarovsk. Thence, by horse and sleigh, he travelled down the frozen River Amur to Nikolievsk near the Sea of Okhotsk, a little matter of 660 miles.

Nikolievsk was a bleak Russian settlement in a bleak, sub-Arctic region, then known for dogs and dog-drivers; one of various remote corners of the Far East with which Meares was familiar. To Scott, he appeared a wanderer on the face of the earth. That, no doubt, was the impression he wished to give.

The son of a major in the Royal Scots Fusiliers, Cecil Henry Meares wanted to follow in his father's footsteps, and enter the Regular Army but, for some unknown reason, he failed.

In 1896, at the age of eighteen, he went to the East. There, with an interval spent fighting (despite his earlier rejection for the Army) in the Boer War, he stayed for the next decade. He knew India but spent most of his time in Siberia and Manchuria. Over exactly what he was doing there hangs a veil of mystery. He hovered on the outskirts of military affairs. He spoke Russian, Chinese and Hindustani. He seemed to specialize in Eastern Siberia and the frontier lands of the Russian Empire.

It is not quite the pattern of the usual aimless traveller. He manifestly had excellent connections with Russian officialdom. His later career suggests considerable trust on the part of the British authorities. He was connected with Intelligence.

Somewhere along the line he had learned dog-driving. He had made considerable winter journeys. He crossed Siberia to Cape Chelyuskin, on the Arctic Ocean, the northernmost promontory of the Asiatic mainland, a distance of some 2,000 miles. Someone at the Admiralty recommended him to Scott.

It was, Meares wrote to his father from Nikolievsk, in the spring,

> a very big contract indeed to choose all these animals ... I have been kept very busy ... trying teams and picking out one or two dogs and making up a team and trying it on a run of 100 miles and throwing out the dogs which do not come up to the mark and collecting others.

This was much the same method as that followed by Daugaard-Jensen in Greenland on Amundsen's behalf.

There the similarity ends. Daugaard-Jensen collected one hundred dogs to Meares' thirty-three. Daugaard-Jensen was not expected personally to deliver the animals as well; Meares was, single-handed. This was expecting too much. At Nikolievsk, he persuaded a Russian dog-driver, Dmetri Girev to join the expedition as his assistant.

In late May, the dogs were taken by steamer up the River Amur to Khabarovsk, whence they travelled on by train to Vladivostok. There, on the way through the streets from the station to the kennel, a mad dog rushed into the procession. But the Governor had prudently supplied a military escort, and the creature was shot before it could bite.

There remained the Manchurian ponies. Meares, being no judge of horseflesh, had deputed an unnamed friend to buy them at a fair in Harbin. To help him, the friend took along a Russian jockey from the Vladivostok race course, Anton Omel'chenko. Anton also joined the expedition.

Since, on Shackleton's expedition, the dark ponies died before the white ones, Scott jumped to the conclusion that white ones must in all cases necessarily be superior, and insisted on white ponies for himself. It was a characteristic example of Scott's muddle-headedness, and his Shackleton fixation. It was at any rate an unfortunate complication. White ponies were only a fraction of those on offer at Harbin, and among them, the choice was not large. The deal having been clinched, the vendor departed, as Anton afterwards put it in his broken English 'with a plenty big smile'.

To get his cumbersome menagerie from Siberia to New Zealand, Meares quite reasonably cabled Scott for an extra assistant. Now Wilfred Bruce, Kathleen Scott's brother, a P. & O. merchant officer, who had joined the expedition, was then in the Far East. It was characteristic of the whole expedition that Bruce hurried home by Trans-Siberian Railway – a fortnight's hard travelling - only to find that Scott had tried to stop him by telegram at Irkutsk so that he should turn back and help Meares. Bruce took it imperturbably:

I suggested that if I could have two or three weeks in England, the return journey by rail across the continent would be no great hardship and the plan was settled at once.

He reached Vladivostok in time to help with the embarkation of the livestock. It was, as he recorded in his diary,

Awful ... raining hard, streets *feet* deep in mud. Two ponies broke away twice, Anton recovered them each time. Trying to fix a rope on one, with Anton on his back, [the pony] reared up over my head and came down with one forefoot on each of my shoulders. Hurt less than I should have thought.

After a harrowing Pacific crossing of five weeks and three transhipments, Meares reached Lyttelton, New Zealand, without losing a single animal, but no longer on speaking terms with Bruce. 'Quite "One of the boys",' as he put it, 'but too "kid glovey" for this job.' Bruce heartily reciprocated: Meares 'wasn't a bit my style'. Meares elicited fellow-passengers' complaints for being untidy, unshaven, and appearing on deck in his pyjamas. They now had two months in which to recuperate before *Terra Nova* arrived on October 28th, followed a day later by Scott. Scott was relieved to see Meares; until then he had been uncertain whether Meares had succeeded in his task.

Two days later when Scott went out to Quail Island, where the dogs and ponies were quarantined, he was, as he wrote in his diary, 'greatly pleased with animals ... thinks dogs finest ever got together'.

Oates was not so pleased, 'Narrow chest. Knock knees ... Aged. Windsucker ...' And so on, a monotonous catalogue of equine defects; such was the survey he entered in *his* diary. 'In mentioning the ponies' blemishes I have only mentioned those which appear actively to interfere with their work or for identification.'

What Meares had brought 8,000 miles from the recesses of Manchuria was a troop of ancient crocks. When Oates communicated this to Scott he was met by condescension tinged with annoyance. Scott knew nothing about animals but he liked to think that everything under his command was the best possible. Oates was given to understand that his opinions were uncalled for, besides being the hairsplitting of a perfectionist. This was not Oates's first experience of the obstinate side of Scott's character, but it seems to have been the incident that sealed his opinion.

Oates had gradually been taking a dislike to Scott. They were in any case incompatible. Scott had an uneasy emotional attitude towards animals, his reaction towards animal suffering was mawkishly sentimental; he was moreover short-tempered and humourless; Oates, rational, equable with a sardonic sense of humour, felt animals should be treated well but was realistic about the problems they posed. Scott stood on his dignity, very much aware of little social distinctions; Oates was at home with kings and beggars. Before him, Scott had the nervous uncertainty of the ambitious middle class faced with a natural aristocrat, especially when he found fixed upon himself a faraway, enigmatic gaze, which regimental friends recognized as Oates in the process of summing people up. Oates had been aware of Scott's social inferiority; he now realized that he was not a born leader of men.

For a month *Terra Nova* remained at Lyttelton, where she was restowed and the threads of the expedition were drawn together. Scott, like the others, enjoyed the open-handed New Zealand hospitality. He was caught up in the official round and Kathleen was much in evidence. It was, in parts, a pleasant time; but there were disagreeable undertones.

Scott quarrelled with Oates about fodder. Scott, still his old self, wanted to cut things fine. Oates did not. In the end, Oates got his way, at the expense, however, of extra coal, thus shortening the ship's steaming range. As sailing day approached, nerves grew taut, especially among the wives:

> Mrs. Scott and Mrs. Evans have had a magnificent battle [Oates wrote to his mother in his graphic, schoolboy unpunctuated style]; they tell me it was a draw after 15 rounds. Mrs. Wilson flung herself into the fight after the 10th round and then there was more blood and hair flying about the hotel than you would see in a Chicago slaughter house in a month the husbands got a bit of the backwash and there is a certain amount of coolness which I hope they won't bring into the hut with them.

In fact, cross-currents between Scott and 'Teddy' Evans had been growing for some time.

When *Terra Nova* sailed from Cardiff, leaving Scott to follow on with Kathleen, it was the first time that Evans had captained a ship. He naturally wanted to prove himself. Short, stocky and genial, the picture of a young sea dog, he had a talent for getting the best out of people.

He won considerable respect for the way he licked his heterogeneous crowd into shape and got them working as a team. He exuded high spirits, albeit of a schoolboyish kind; but then, his companions were rather like overgrown schoolboys on a jaunt; a shipload of Peter Pans. There was much ragging in the mess, led by Evans himself. One day he was making up verses to the tune of *Cock Robin*, and brought the house down with:

Who doesn't like women?
I, said Captain Oates,
I prefer goats.

It was a shrewd hit: Oates did indeed regard women as a monstrous regiment, best avoided. He took no offence, however, for Evans was a good messmate. 'But I should be sorry,' as Oates put it, 'for the person who hesitated to do what Evans told him.' Evans could be friendly and yet authoritative; he could keep discipline and also run a happy ship. He reached the Cape with the satisfaction of a job well done.

It was a great blow, therefore, when Scott, having first arranged to join *Terra Nova* in New Zealand, now suddenly decided, having caught up, to send Kathleen on by mailboat and take over command himself for the voyage from Cape Town to Melbourne. Malicious tongues suggested a desire to get away from Kathleen, who by now had assumed the air of leader of the expedition, or at least its inspector-general. Perhaps Scott was jealous of Evans' popularity. Whatever the real explanation, he caused the unease associated with unexpected and impenetrable changes. Worst of all, his decision was tactless. Evans took it as a slur on his professional ability. He hid his feelings, acquiring considerable respect thereby, but the foundation of an unfortunate antagonism with Scott had been laid. In New Zealand P.O. Evans now exacerbated the situation.

Over the years, P.O. Evans had turned into a beery womanizer, exposed to the risk of venereal disease, and running a bit to fat. 'Teddy' Evans wanted him discharged, believing that on a Polar expedition there was no room for men of his type, since the weakness of one could be the death of all.

P.O. Evans, however, was a favourite of Scott. A huge, bull-necked beefy figure, he was the image of jolly Jack Tar, and Scott went by appearances.

Evans responded by toadying to Scott. But underneath it all there lay a streak of genuine devotion.

On November 26th, when *Terra Nova* sailed for Port Chalmers where she was to take on coal and bid farewell to New Zealand, P.O. Evans was left behind. He had got drunk and had fallen into the water while going aboard. That was too much even for Scott. He told Evans to pack his gear and leave the ship.

Next morning, Evans waylaid Scott, who had stayed behind in Lyttelton to finish off some business, and pleaded for another chance. He was rebuffed several times, but persistently returned to ask again. Scott finally relented and they travelled down together on the same train to rejoin *Terra Nova*, at Port Chalmers, Evans acting, Scott took pains to record, 'as though nothing had happened!'

The other Evans was furious. This was softness, rank favouritism, once more demonstrating the captain's lack of judgment.

In his diary, Scott conceded that Evans' grievance was 'reasonable ... smoothed him down'.

Terra Nova was supposed to sail on the 28th; at the last moment Scott postponed departure until the 29th. Oates found it

> annoying as it means 24 hours more in the ship for the ponies and the only reason for staying is that the crowd may have the fun of cheering us.

Scott very much felt that *Terra Nova* had a duty to show the flag. A local holiday was declared for her departure. At two-thirty she cast off to a repetition of the rousing and emotional farewells at London, Portland, Cardiff, Cape Town, Lyttelton.

Amundsen haunted Scott's leave-taking:

> Perhaps you will say something about the rival expedition? [a journalist asked at the quayside] The one from Norway and its prospects of success   that is, if there are any prospects? Captain Scott replied, with an expression that was without form and void, 'No I don't think I would care to say anything on that subject.'

There was an odd echo of *Discovery* nine years before. Then, before sailing from New Zealand for the Antarctic, Scott had written to Nansen with otherwise unexpressed forebodings; now he did the same:

> We may have made a mistake in having such an extensive organization but I am most anxious to get really good scientific results and for that one ought to have a number of experts   as to the travelling we might have improved matters by having more dogs and fewer ponies   it is difficult to say   the animals we have are splendid and all in good condition.

Two days out from New Zealand, *Terra Nova* nearly foundered in a storm. Scott saw it as undeserved bad luck. There were, however, rational explanations for what happened.

If, as Tryggve Gran put it, *Terra Nova* 'was deep laden on leaving England, she was ready to sink after departing from Port Chalmers'. The deck was smothered in cargo, the centre-piece being the cumbrous packing cases containing three motor sledges which, after last-minute alterations, had been sent out by cargo ship from England to New Zealand. Nineteen ponies and thirty-three dogs had been crammed on board. The dogs were chained wherever there was space to stand, exposed to every cloud of spray. In the fo'c'sle, occupying part of the crew's quarters stood the ponies.

Men were crammed in to bursting point. In New Zealand, seven more had joined: Raymond Priestley from Cheltenham, and the Australian geologists Griffith Taylor and Frank Debenham; Meares, Bruce, Bernard Day, and Herbert Ponting, a well-known photographer. On the mess deck, the seamen had to share hammocks; the one watch tumbling out as the other turned in. With twenty-four now having to find space at mealtimes, the wardroom was noticeably congested. Thus, overcrowded, overburdened, *Terra Nova* shaped for the South.

The main feature of the waters for which she was headed, to quote that treasury of wisdom, *The Admiralty Pilot*,

is the circumpolar trough of low pressure ... Frequent depressions move E. or SE at about 20 to 30 knots in the vicinity ... gales are common ... Brief periods of fair weather occur at intervals, as a ridge of high pressure intervenes.

Scott was hoping to slip through between the storms. In those days of imperfect meteorological forecasting, it was rather like stepping blindly off the kerb into the path of heavy traffic and trusting to luck not to be run over.

On December 1st, a little before noon, *Terra Nova* ran into the predictable storm. The battering of the seas on an overloaded hull wrenched her in a way she was not designed to stand. With every twist her deck planking opened at the seams, letting in water which cascaded down into the bilges. During the night the main bilge pump choked.

At Melbourne, *Terra Nova*'s chief engineer, Lieutenant (E) Edgar W. Riley, R.N., had been discharged, by Scott's own admission, on a mere whim, because of personal dislike. Riley was not replaced and the ship sailed south without a commissioned officer in the engine room, leaving warrant officers in charge. This meant a break in the chain of command; an invitation to disaster, in the rigidly hierarchical Navy of the time.

When the pump clogged, the engineer failed to report it immediately to the bridge, as an officer would normally have done. He was, perhaps, afraid of a reprimand, and tried to clear the pump himself. By morning, the stokehold plates were awash.

The hand pump suctions had also clogged. Time and time again on the way from Cardiff to Lyttelton, the pump choked and was put out of action. In heavy weather it was impossible to repair, because the well hatch could not be opened and the working parts were therefore inaccessible. There was ample and graphic warning of what was in store.

Thousands of pounds had been spent on motor sledges and elaborate scientific instruments. In all the weeks at Lyttelton, nothing had been done to correct the faults of the one cheap but indispensable item whose failure could send it all to the bottom. *Terra Nova* entered the stormiest waters in the world with the same defective pump that repeatedly had failed.

The water rose unchecked, put the fires out, and the engines stopped. There *Terra Nova* lay in the hollow of the storm, no longer a ship, but a waterlogged hulk, raked from stem to stern by green walls of solid water, rolling rail under with the sickly, sluggish sagging movement that means a ship in peril. Oates and Atkinson, one of the Naval surgeons, stayed forward, labouring all night through to care for the horses, who were being hurled against their stalls by the plunging of the ship and were in a miserable state.

The seamen, in Davies' words,

> were getting a very rough time; they lived in very cramped quarters on the lower mess deck ... under the ponies ... Every bit of their clothing ... was stained with urine from the ponies that soaked through the leaky decks as the ship groaned and strained.

Scott was silent, noticeably unhappy and passive. It was Teddy Evans who, at this crisis, had taken command.

Evans got the engineers cutting through a bulkhead to reach the pump suctions. It took ten hours working in bilge water slopping up to their necks. In the meantime, he organized a bucket chain from the engine room in order to bale out the ship. Possibly it was more to keep up morale among the landlubbers than for the good it did.

In cold figures, as the log of *Terra Nova* records, the wind was blowing Force 10 on the Beaufort Scale, between forty-eight and fifty-five knots, with waves up to thirty-five feet high. It so happens that on November 11th, *Fram* logged a replica of that storm, south-westerly direction and all. Amundsen's record reads:

> Ran before the wind under only foresail and inner jib ... how beautifully she takes [the waves]. If one takes care to swing the stern towards [them], on board one doesn't know that one is on the sea at all. If they come on the beam, then one notices it of course, she lurches beautifully, but ships no water whatsoever.

But *Fram* was not overloaded. Her voyage had been planned on the assumption that she would meet the worst conceivable weather. Her pumps were modern and functioned well.

Scott's luck held. In the small hours of December 3rd, after thirty-six hours of a screaming inferno, the wind providentially began to drop. Scott was through at the cost of no more than a bad fright, and the loss of two ponies, two dogs, ten tons of coal, sixty-five gallons of petrol, and about ten feet of the port bulwarks.

The men thought Evans had saved the ship, and cheered him when he came on deck. Scott did not like that.

On December 9th, *Terra Nova* ran into the pack ice, and there Scott's luck ran out; he fell a victim to his obsessions. Because Shackleton had got through easily to the east with *Nimrod* in 1908, Scott blindly followed, although reason told him that it was outside the pattern of experience, including his own in *Discovery*. He was rewarded, as he put it with unconscious irony in a letter home, 'by encountering worse conditions than any ship has had before'. He was held up in the pack for three weeks.

'No other ship ... would have come through so well,' wrote Scott when at last on December 30th *Terra Nova* ran out of the pack into the open Ross Sea. 'Certainly the *Nimrod* would never have reached the South Water had she been caught in such a pack.'

For Scott, the weeks beset, with coal burning away, had been a miserable trial. He kept to himself and hardly spoke to anyone but Wilson. But for everyone else the great white field of ice, with its teeming seal and birds, was an exotic interlude. Gran in lyrical mood wrote in his diary about 'the leads, where the night frost spun its fine, delicate web ... It was as if we sailed over a lake where thousands of white lilies lay and swayed in the evening breeze.'

On a convenient floe, Gran opened his ski school, optimistically expected by Scott to turn the little cohort of tyros into expert skiers in a week or two. Officers and scientists were (mostly) willing pupils. But the seamen, on the whole, declined to learn. Gran never forgave P.O. Evans for calling skis 'planks'.

On January 2nd, Scott once again saw Mount Erebus, with its wispy plume of vapour. Ice blocked the way to the old *Discovery* quarters in McMurdo Sound, and after some hesitation Scott decided to land on a small promontory of rock and moraine about six miles south of Cape Royds, called, from *Discovery* days, 'The Skuary'. This he now renamed Cape Evans, 'in honour of our excellent second in command'.

All four forms of transport were mobilized to haul the cargo over the ice from *Terra Nova* to dry land: dogs, horses, motor sledges and man-hauling. Disembarkation, however, had not been properly planned, and the scene was one of confusion and disarray. Raymond Priestley, the old Shackleton man, made blunt comparisons

> between the way the work was carried out and the way when we were landing stores at Cape Royds ... there [are] too many officers superintending and the men never knew when and where to go for orders ... an Expedition to make a complete success should be entirely away from any Navy ideas ... in this one particular give me Shackleton's expedition over and over again.

One morning Ponting, enthusiastically working at the first professional Antarctic photo reportage, noticed killer whales cruising near the ice edge and ran up close to get a picture. In Campbell's words,

> they thought he was a seal and getting right under the floe bumped so hard they split off one piece with him on and it was only by the greatest agility he escaped .. what irony of fate to be eaten by a whale thinking one was a seal and then spat out because one was only a photographer.

This was the first warning of the state of the ice. The next was early on January 8th, the day that the third motor sledge was to be brought ashore, when a seaman went through up to his neck. Scott dismissed the incident. It had been thawing heavily for two days, and a strong current was running. The motor sledge was hoisted over the side on to a floe adjoining the ship. Scott then went ashore, leaving Campbell in charge of the proceedings. Shortly afterwards the ice next to the ship began breaking up. About the same time a message arrived from Scott to say he had found the ice rotten and the sooner the sledge was taken ashore the better. The order was unthinkingly obeyed, although common sense indicated hoisting inboard as the only reasonable proceeding. There was no time to start the motor. A tow rope was attached and all hands began hauling the sledge ashore. Simpson, the meteorologist, was sent ahead to sound the ice. But his sounding rod was too thick and he too inexperienced to gauge the danger. Before a hundred yards, the ice gave way. The sledge broke through and sank into the depths, nearly taking some of the men with it. Salvage was impossible. At the bottom of McMurdo Sound, a hundred fathoms deep, the motor sledge rested; a silent omen.

Cherry-Garrard asked 'Uncle Bill' (Wilson) what would happen if Scott did not reach the Pole, recording the answer in his diary:

> We shall probably stop here and have a 2nd go at it —'with fewer ponies and dogs, but more experience', as Bill said. Two good failures and we could be forgiven for not succeeding.

22

The Base at Framheim

AT THE BAY OF WHALES, the Norwegians started disembarking on January 15th, ten days after the British at McMurdo Sound.

'There lies the barrier, probably as it lay thousands of years ago, bathed in the rays of the midnight sun,' wrote Amundsen on the day the work began. 'It seems as if the princess is still sleeping in her shining castle. May we be able to awaken her!'

Tellingly, to express his feelings, he had turned to a childhood tale; to the Sleeping Beauty myth, with its moral of victory going to the strong, the resolute, the man who takes his destiny in his hands.

Amundsen's landing had been carefully worked out in detail. Each man knew the plan to which Amundsen was working; and therefore could see himself in relation to the whole. The Norwegians knew they had to have their base ready before the end of April, with all seal meat laid in for the winter, and that they were to run three depot journeys to advance supplies to the 83rd parallel of latitude for the Polar dash in the spring. At McMurdo Sound, nobody yet knew what they were going to do because, even after landing, Scott was not sure himself. He had not chosen to take his officers into his confidence. All that remained was rigid unquestioning literal obedience to orders, without regard for circumstances, to which the sunken motor sledge was an outstanding monument.

Fram was moored to the edge of bay ice filling a protected inlet at the south-east corner of the Bay of Whales. The western point of this inlet was formed by a high promontory of the Barrier, fancifully dubbed Kap Manhue, 'Cape Man's Head'. The eastern side was bounded by a tongue of ice on which the hut was to be built.

Once the site had been selected, a track from the ship was reconnoitred and marked out along the whole length of 2.2 nautical miles with blue pennants on low sticks every fifteen skiing paces. These details had been anticipated and discussed; the pennants made up well in advance. It was the kind of forethought alien to Scott. Despite his Antarctic experience, the necessity of staking out a track on the ice at Cape Evans took him by surprise, and he had hastily to improvise markers out of paraffin tins.

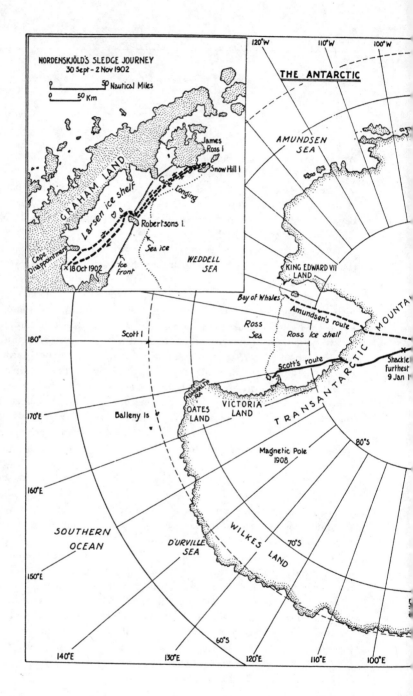

NORDENSKJÖLD'S SLEDGE JOURNEY
30 Sept - 2 Nov 1902

0   50 Nautical Miles
0   50 Km

James Ross I.
Snow Hill I.
GRAHAM LAND
Larsen ice shelf
Longing
Robertsons I.
Cape Disappointment
Sea ice
× 18 Oct 1902
Ice front
WEDDELL SEA

THE ANTARCTIC

120°W   110°W   100°W

AMUNDSEN SEA

KING EDWARD VII LAND

Bay of Whales
Ross Sea
Ross ice shelf
Amundsen's route
TRANSANTARCTIC MOUNTAINS

180°
Scott I

Scott's route
Shackleton furthest 9 Jan 1

170°E

ADMIRALTY SEA
OATES LAND
VICTORIA LAND
Balleny Is

160°E

80°S

Magnetic Pole 1908

SOUTHERN OCEAN

D'URVILLE SEA

WILKES LAND

70°S

150°E

140°E   130°E   120°E   110°E   100°E

60°S

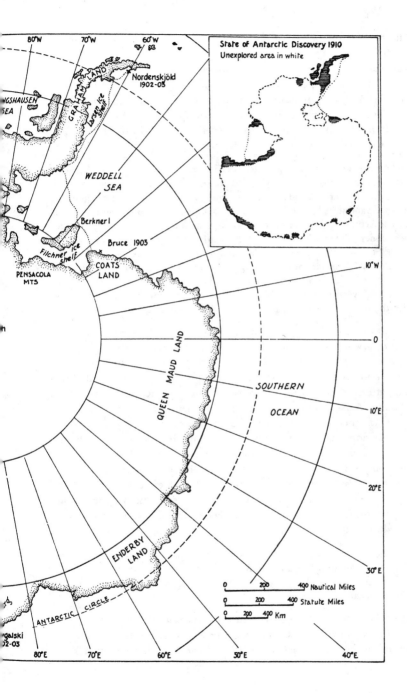

State of Antarctic Discovery 1910
Unexplored area in white

80°W 70°W 60°W
63

NGSHAUSEN
SEA

GRAHAM LAND

Nordenskjöld
1902-03

Larsen Ice Shelf

WEDDELL
SEA

Berkner I

Filchner Ice Shelf

Bruce 1903

COATS
LAND

PENSACOLA
MTS

10°W

0

QUEEN MAUD LAND

SOUTHERN

OCEAN

10°E

20°E

ENDERBY
LAND

30°E

0   200   400 Nautical Miles

0   200   400 Statute Miles

0   200   400 Km

ANTARCTIC CIRCLE

rgalski
)2-03

80°E   70°E   60°E   50°E   40°E

The first transport was ready to leave *Fram* for the future base at 11 a.m. on January 15th. It was the opening of the land campaign, the start on the road to the Pole, and made a little occasion. A sledge was hoisted over the side on to the ice and loaded with 300 kilos (660 pounds) of advance supplies. Eight dogs were hitched before. As leader of the expedition, not to mention conqueror of the North-West Passage, Amundsen by tacit agreement was given the honour of driving.

It was, as Amundsen afterwards reported,

a defeat; no two ways about it. The dogs had now done nothing for half a year except eat and drink, so they apparently believed they did not have anything else to do ... After they had moved forwards a few yards, they sat down as if at a command and stared at each other. The most unfeigned surprise was to be read in their faces. We finally managed with the help of a sound thrashing to make them understand that we really expected work out of them; but it did not help much. For, instead of obeying orders, they turned on each other in a glorious battle – God help me, how we struggled with those 8 hounds that day! ... During the hullabaloo, I stole a glance on board. But what I saw caused me quickly to avert my eyes. They simply hooted with laughter, and loud cries with the most infamous suggestions rained down over us.

Somehow, that first dog sledge was got two miles to the base. Something in the confusion went beyond ordinary canine devilry. This was made plain as more dog teams were brought into harness, and the transport got under way. Amundsen was soon convinced that the trouble lay in the pattern of harnessing. Because of his experience on *Gjøa* he had adopted the Alaskan style, with the dogs attached pair by pair to a central trace. It was theoretically efficient, because all the traction was parallel. But these dogs had been trained to pull in the Greenland fashion, spreading fanwise from a central point of attachment. It was - again theoretically – not so efficient, but it was what the animals were used to. In this instance, they were entitled to their preference. Amundsen decided to change over to the Greenland system immediately. On January 17th, together with Johansen, Hassel and Wisting, he returned to the ship to alter the traces.

With the help of the ship's party, we were able to make 46 traces in the course of an afternoon, or full equipment for the 4 teams we can use at the moment [Amundsen recorded in his diary]. That was the splendid result, and a good proof of what co-operation can do.

After the change, the dogs started running properly; the drivers got control. Like railway trains, five sledges now shuttled regularly between *Fram* and the base site. Each sledge moved five or six loads a day, about two tons in all. Forty-six dogs and five drivers were shifting ten tons and more a day. Upwards on to the Barrier, with full loads, the drivers ran on ski; back to the ship they rode on the empty sledges.

Bjaaland and Stubberud, the carpenters, were living in a tent and putting up the hut. Nobody before had put up a building on a southern ice shelf. As Amundsen guessed, however, it resembled Norway, where housebuilding usually means hacking foundations into bedrock. Translated to the environment of the Ross Ice Barrier, it meant digging down through the snow to the underlying ice. 'There was,' Stubberud recalled, 'constant snow drift, so that the site drifted up again quicker than we could shovel away.'

That too, was familiar from home. With spare planks he and Bjaaland contrived a plough-shaped windbreak that kept the snow out.

In that way, we managed to dig out the site and get down to solid ground, i.e., blue ice, hard as rock. Because of the sloping terrain, we had to hack down about 3 metres for a length of 8 metres along the upper part to get the site horizontal. It was naturally a hard job; severe cold . . . delayed the work. But in the end we did it.

On January 27th, ten days after the first spade was turned, the hut was finished, complete with all interior fittings, including a patent table that could be hung from the ceiling out of the way while the floor was scrubbed.

Meanwhile, with the aid of the rest of the party, seals and penguins were being slaughtered and flensed. 'We live in a veritable Never-Never land,' wrote Amundsen. 'Seals come up to the ship and penguins to the tent, and allow themselves to be shot.'

This had been too much for the hunting instincts of the old Arctic hands. One day some of them went out and shot a few seals for fun, leaving them on the ice. When Amundsen heard what had happened, he flew into a rage. 'The members of the expedition are absolutely forbidden to kill any animals we cannot use,' he announced, and ordered the carcasses to be brought back.

A few days later, Amundsen, together with Helmer Hanssen and Wisting went out to slaughter about thirty seals but the ice broke away before the carcasses could be fetched.

That evening [says Wisting], Amundsen was simply miserable, because we had killed all those animals for nothing. I have rarely, if ever, in my life met a man with such a love for animals as he. It was a characteristic which also helped us to appreciate him more. Even those of us who had allowed nature to over-power upbringing, were naturally compelled to agree after a little reflection that he was right and never more were animals killed unnecessarily.

Supplies had to be laid in for 110 dogs and ten men for a year, with generous margins of safety, a matter of 200 seals, and as many penguins. The men worked twelve hours a day, dogs in shifts of five hours so as not to overstrain them.

After three weeks shuttling between ship and hut, each team covering over 500 miles, the dogs had settled down, the experienced drivers got into form again, and the novices, like Wisting and Prestrud, were over their teething troubles. It was all undramatic and workaday.

On Saturday, January 28th the landing party moved into the hut.

Here on the same barrier where Shackleton praised his God that he had not landed [Amundsen wrote in his diary] – here we have put up our house – here we will have our home. That [Sir James Clark] Ross did not want to come too close to this ice giant in his sailing ships – that I understand. But that S. did not come here and take the great chance offered by an extra degree of Southern latitude; that I don't understand. Not *one* of us has given a thought to any danger in doing so. The future will show if we were right.

At a little past midnight on February 4th, *Fram*'s watchman was in the galley, fortifying himself with a cup of coffee, when he heard strange noises off. He jumped up and dashed topsides, seeing in his imagination the Barrier calving and about to send them all to perdition. He was considerably relieved on coming out on deck to find that it was only *Terra Nova* which had arrived while he was below and was putting out ice anchors. In Gjertsen's words.

We had long expected her to come into the bay when she went Eastwards with the party [for] King Edward's Land. Our watchman ... saw two men go ashore, put on skis, and, with reasonably good speed for foreigners, rush off up towards the barrier, following the dogs' tracks. 'Well,' thought the watchman, 'if they have any nefarious intentions, (one of our constant subjects of discussion was how the Englishmen would take our challenge) the dogs will manage that job, and get them to turn round all right. It'll be worse if they sneak up to *Fram*, where I'm alone on watch. Best to be ready for all eventualities.' ... He dashed into the charthouse, carefully loaded 9 bullets into our old Farman gun ... dug out an old English grammar, and looked up 'How are you this morning' and similar expressions. Thus armed to the teeth, both physically and mentally, he crept out on watch again. He might have been waiting $\frac{1}{2}$ an hour ... when suddenly a shock went through him. The Englishmen were coming down again, with a course straight for *Fram* ... He looked carefully: No, they had no weapons; if so, it must be a revolver in a pocket ... He put down the gun and the grammar just under his coat, so that both could be retrieved in a hurry, raised himself and calmly awaited the Englishmen's movements.

*

Terra Nova had left McMurdo Sound on January 28th to take Campbell and the eastern party to King Edward VII Land. Scott and Evans having left the ship, Campbell was in command on board with Lieutenant H. Pennell second in command and captain for the voyage back to New Zealand.

On February 2nd Campbell's intended landing place, Cape Colbeck, was in the offing. He had unwittingly chosen the point with the worst ice conditions in the Ross Sea. Like Scott in 1902 and Shackleton in 1908, he was stopped by grinding floes and swirling currents from going ashore. King Edward VII Land stayed tantalizingly just out of reach. Campbell was forced to turn, and *Terra Nova* coasted back along the face of the Ice Barrier looking for a place to land.

At ten p.m. on the 3rd they entered the Bay of Whales. For Raymond Priestley, who had been with Shackleton and now was the geologist on Campbell's party, it was a moment of vindication. Scott and his faction had always cast doubt on the existence of the Bay of Whales, as they had cast doubt on Shackleton's Furthest South. Priestley, very much a Shackleton man, had taken this to heart; he was vastly cheered when *Terra Nova*'s observations 'wonderfully upheld' Shackleton's. 'There is no doubt now,' Priestley wrote in his diary, 'that Balloon Inlet and the neighbouring Bay marked on to the *Discovery* Chart had been merged into one.'

It was perhaps just as well for Amundsen's peace of mind that he never learned of Priestley's next remark that

since that period the resulting Bight has broken back considerably more, indeed it seems to have altered a great deal on its Western Border since our visit to it in 1908.

It was, Priestley continued,

satisfactory to find ... everybody backing up the Shackleton expedition and I turned in ... feeling quite cheerful and believing that there would be a good chance of ... finding a home on the Barrier here – our last hope of surveying King Edward's Land. However, Man proposes but God disposes and I was waked at one o'clock by Lillie [one of the biologists] with the astounding news that we had sighted a ship at anchor to the sea ice in the Bay. All was confusion on board for a few minutes, everybody rushing up on deck with cameras and clothes. It was no false alarm, there she was within a few hundred yards of us and what is more, those of us who had read Nansen's books recognized the *Fram*.

'Curses loud and deep,' Lieutenant Wilfred Bruce wrote to his sister, 'were heard everywhere.' *Fram*'s watchman had not been entirely fanciful in ascribing aggressive thoughts to *Terra Nova*'s company. They knew that Amundsen was in the Antarctic. They did not know where. It was not a subject on which Scott encouraged speculation. The received opinion was Graham Land or the Weddell Sea; certainly nowhere near the British preserves. The last thing they expected to see as they turned the headland into the Bay of Whales was, therefore, the stubby shape of *Fram*. 'An eruption of Erebus,' as Wilfred Bruce put it in his diary,' would fall flat after that.'

It was Campbell who had approached *Fram*, and so alarmed the watchman. Speaking Norwegian, he had gone to open negotiations, and friendly or at least diplomatic relations were established between the two ships. He learned that Amundsen was up at the hut, expected at the ship early in the morning. At six o'clock Amundsen and his companions, in Gjertsen's words,

> came galloping down. Never before had it gone so swimmingly, and once down on the flat ice, they formed a line and there was a veritable race to reach the ship. The Englishmen [were] absolutely flabbergasted. No, they had never dreamt that dogs could run in that way before a sledge, and already they felt contempt for their dear ponies. Suddenly they were gripped by wild excitement, cheered, and waved their caps. Our drivers returned their greetings and cracked their whips.

This was showing off. Amundsen had seen *Terra Nova* as he came to the edge of the Barrier. It was not his normal way of driving to the ship.

Campbell, Pennell and Levick, the eastern party's surgeon, were invited to the hut for breakfast; Amundsen's base was inaugurated, as it were, by his rivals.

The Norwegians enjoyed impressing their visitors. In the course of the morning, *Terra Nova*'s officers and men, in Gjertsen's words,

> came ... to see 'The famous ship' and everyone broke out in eulogies over how nice and comfortably we lived. ... When they saw that every man had his own cabin, and everyone had a large common saloon, their eyes grew wide with astonishment.

The British seamen regaled the Norwegian with spicy (and wholly authentic) details of their life. Their mess table lay exactly underneath the ponies, who provided dripping yellow 'mustard' at mealtimes. Sanitary arrangements involved a balancing act over the side on a chute suspended above the rolling deep.

The only recorded Norwegian comment after being shown over *Terra Nova* was Nilsen's: 'I must confess it did not look very inviting.'

Both sides found themselves getting on with the other. Johansen recorded that the visitors were 'good humoured, and were particularly pleasant to us.' To Wilfred Bruce, the Norwegians 'individually ... all seemed charming men, even the perfidious Amundsen.'

But Campbell had at a blow been cut off from the exploration of King Edward VII Land. He was deeply disappointed. As Priestley put it, 'we cannot according to etiquette trench on their country for winter quarters.'

The scruples were all on one side. Amundsen told Campbell to land and make his base where he wanted; the Antarctic was free to all. Campbell wanted to accept but, said Bruce, 'we dissuaded him, as the feeling between the two expeditions must be strained'.

Amundsen, Nilsen and Prestrud were invited to lunch on *Terra Nova*. As Amundsen came aboard, he stopped, glanced up at the rigging and, seeing no aerial, casually asked about wireless. He tried to hide his relief when Pennell told him there was none. One awful uncertainty had been eliminated; he did not, after all, labour under an insuperable handicap in getting the news through first.

It was, in Tryggve Gran's words, 'a known fact that Englishmen, as long as there is any possibility, drag many of the luxuries of civilization with them into the wilderness. And the Scott expedition was no exception.' To *Terra Nova*'s Norwegian guests who, since leaving Madeira, had been living very simply, the lunch seemed like a banquet.

Under the bonhomie, however, it was a strained meal. The conversation was like a fencing match, each side trying to find out the other's intentions without being too obvious, and determined to give nothing away in return. Amundsen refused to be drawn about his plans. But, worried more than he cared to admit about Scott's motor sledges, he asked bluntly, towards the end of the meal, whether they were working.

Campbell was in a mood of bitter dejection at the collapse of all his hopes. Nobody had yet set foot on King Edward VII Land; he had (rightly) regarded the landing there as the one piece of true exploration on the expedition. He now had little to look forward to but a winter in some landlocked corner of South Victoria Land. He took Amundsen's question about the motor sledges as an opportunity to vent his feelings.

'One of them,' he said enigmatically, 'is already on *terra firma*.'

Campbell was thinking of the sledge reposing at the bottom of McMurdo Sound. But Amundsen, as indeed was the intention, understood it to mean that the sledge had already crossed the Barrier and possibly reached the Beardmore Glacier. The Norwegians were silent for a moment, neither requesting nor receiving elucidation. Shortly afterwards, they rose to leave, with perfect politeness but a touch of frost. Half an hour later, *Terra Nova* sailed. Amundsen and Nilsen stood on *Fram*'s deck, watching her as she steamed across the calm waters of the Bay of Whales and disappeared out of sight. They did not say much to each other, but their thoughts were full. A terrible fear had exploded in Amundsen. Might the motor sledges not at the last moment rob him of the victory?

The day after *Terra Nova* left, the Norwegian base was given its name: Framheim, 'The home of *Fram*'. This was an allusion to the names of Norwegian mountain ranges like Jotunheimen, 'The home of the giants', with their Norse mythological overtones. The idea, Amundsen remembered to record, was Prestrud's.

As a housewarming gift, Sundbeck, *Fram*'s chief engineer, had made what Amundsen called 'the most magnificent weathercock ... I have not seen a finer from any firm in civilization'.

Framheim resembled a whole little village rising out of the snow. Fourteen sixteen-man military bell tents had been pitched round the hut for stores and kennels. Despite the Greenland dogs' proven toughness, Amundsen believed they would best be kept in condition if protected from the elements when not working.

By February 7th, a Wednesday, Amundsen decided that, with Framheim established and *Fram*'s unloading practically complete, he could go south on his first depot-laying journey: exactly what Scott then was doing four hundred miles to the west. But Scott was going over old ground. When Framheim was lost to sight, Amundsen would be launched into the unknown.

On February 9th, Amundsen reconnoitred the start of the road to the south. It ran down from the spur of the Barrier on which Framheim stood, across the south-eastern arm of the Bay of Whales, then up on to the Barrier again. The run down to the sea was easy; on the other side, the Barrier, about sixty feet high at this point, was approached by a snow drift forming a short, sharp slope. From the top, this Barrier was flat as far as the eye could see. 'The skiing conditions,' Amundsen noted, 'were of the finest kind.'

Since *Fram* possibly would have left by the time he returned, Amundsen finished off his mail, and said his farewells to the ship's party. His instructions for Lieutenant Nilsen, who now had taken over command on board, had been written and handed over at the beginning of January, before reaching the Bay of Whales.

After a brief summary of *Fram*'s intended movements, to go direct to

Buenos Aires, carry out her oceanographical cruise and return to relieve Framheim, the document ends on this characteristic note:

> The earlier you can force your way to the Barrier in 1912 the better. I give no time, as everything depends on circumstances, and I leave it to you to act according to your judgment.
>
> For the rest, I give you complete freedom of action in everything concerning the interests of the expedition.
>
> If on returning to the Barrier you should find that I am prevented by sickness or death from taking over the leadership of the expedition, I give it into your hands, and I beg you most earnestly to try and carry out the expedition's original plan – exploration of the North Polar Basin.

On February 10th, a Friday, at nine-thirty in the morning, Amundsen started on what Johansen accurately called a 'combined reconnaissance and depot-laying journey'. With him were Prestrud, Johansen, Helmer Hanssen, three sledges, eighteen dogs, and half a ton of supplies, mostly dog pemmican for the depot. The 80th parallel was their goal. Down from Framheim, across the sea ice, pattered the dogs, Amundsen and his men swinging by their side on skis. Bjaaland, Hassel, Wisting, Stubberud, four of the landing party who were staying behind, followed them as far as the Barrier to help them up the slope with their loads. 'It was,' Amundsen laconically recorded in his diary, 'a hard push.' At the top, the helpers returned after a quick handshake and a brief farewell. There was no cheering. 'None of us,' says Amundsen, 'was sentimentally inclined.' In his diary he wrote: 'There, far away, lay *Fram* with flag at the mainmast, – a last farewell.'

Amundsen's vision of Antarctic travel had been coloured by *The Voyage of the 'Discovery'* and *The Heart of the Antarctic*. Although he discerned the incompetence that lay behind most of the adventure, he made inadequate allowance for the distortions of men ill adapted to their environment, for the effect of a public putting its money on heroic struggle, and, in the case of Scott, for the subtleties of the romantic delusion.

The reality was anti-climax. 'The so-called Barrier,' wrote Johansen, 'runs like any other glacier.' 'The skiing on the barrier,' said Amundsen, 'is splendid', continuing in mild astonishment, 'We covered 15 geographical miles, a good result the first day.' From the first mile of that first depot trip, their first steps to the Pole, the Norwegians found that, after all, they were at home.

> 11th February: The dogs pull magnificently, and the going on the barrier is ideal. Cannot understand what the English mean when they say that dogs cannot be used here.

13th February: Today we have had a lot of loose snow ... For us on skis it was the most magnificent going. How men [on foot] & horses are going to get through in these conditions I cannot understand, not to mention an automobile. The Thermos flask is a splendid invention. We fill it every morning with boiling chocolate and drink it piping hot at noon. Not bad for the middle of the Barrier.

15th February: A fine performance of our dogs this: 40 geographical miles yesterday – of which 10 miles with heavy load and then 51½ miles today – I think they will hold their own with the ponies on the Barrier.

Helmer Hanssen summed it up by saying that this first attempt showed that 'it was much easier to travel down here than up North during the *Gjøa* expedition'. Even allowing for the fact that the Antarctic was on its best behaviour – no blizzards; temperatures between – 7° and 17° (C.), like a bracing winter's day at home – this was the main point. As far as the technique of snow travel went, the Barrier had rapidly lost its mystery and the terrors. It was in any case preferable to Hardangervidda as Amundsen had known it.*

The skis were right, the dogs were right, and very soon Amundsen discovered that he had got the order of running right as well. First came Prestrud, alone, as forerunner to give the dogs something to follow, a lesson from the North-West Passage.† Next came Helmer Hanssen with the leading dog team and steering compass, followed by Johansen, also with a compass. Last came Amundsen, with spare compass and sledge-meter. The latter was the device for measuring distance run, consisting of a bicycle wheel with a revolution counter, running in the snow, and attached to the back of the sledge.

In the snows Amundsen grasped that it was usually best to lead from behind. He could see his men and survey the situation, the foundation of command. And the last man has the responsibility of retrieving what falls off the sledges. However careful the stowing, somehow something vital usually drops by the wayside.

In his diary for February 11th, Johansen notes that Amundsen

had trouble with his dog team ... in the end he had to take off his reindeer trousers and ski in shirt and underpants. The temperature was 12 degrees below zero. One can do this sort of thing here, where colds do not exist.

'Shirt and underpants' were in fact Netsilik reindeer skin under-garments. They were travelling in Netsilik reindeer fur clothing and found the full set too warm. Thus did another lesson from the North-

* See pp. 49–50 and 57.
† See pp. 106 *et. seq.*

West Passage* bear fruit. Amundsen had learned how to dress against the cold – except for one crucial item.

In Johansen's words,

> the boots ... ordered in Christiania, of which so much was expected, turned out to be unusable in the cold. Both Prestrud and I got blisters from them. And at supper today I had to put on *kamikks* [Eskimo boots of seal-skin] instead.

This was disaster indeed. Boots – ever the weak link in skiing and Polar travel – had once more turned out to be a plague. They would have to be rebuilt; there was much work ahead.

By the side of this depressing discovery the other defects of the journey paled. It took, for example, four hours to strike camp and get off in the morning. 'Dawdling', was Amundsen's bald comment. The theodolite was found to be damaged, so he was deprived of astronomical observation and had to depend on dead reckoning.

On February 14th the Norwegians reached their goal of 80° S., as near as they could judge. Building their depot, they immediately turned and, with lightened sledges, raced for home. Their chief worry now was the marking of the track. Reading Scott's and Shackleton's accounts, Amundsen had perceived that their signposting was sketchy; he proposed at all costs, to avoid a repetition of their error. On the outward journey, he had put out bamboo stakes with numbered black flags every eight miles. But this proved to be too far apart. To fill the gaps, Amundsen used the ingenious expedient of sticking stockfish (part of the dog food) in the snow, alternating with pieces of a broken up packing case, every quarter of a mile.

The return journey was an uneventful ski tour of two days, fifty miles being covered on the second.

Amundsen had hurried to bid farewell to *Fram* if he could. He missed her by twelve hours. It was strange, he wrote, not to see her 'any longer. It made a melancholy, forlorn impression on us all. But the time will come, I hope, when we meet again with work well done.'

Amundsen's disappointment masked a considerable achievement. His depot journey was a mere 160 miles, it lasted but a week, and was recorded in decidedly unheroic diary jottings. Nonetheless it was one of the milestones of Polar history. It proved that the Norwegian school of Polar travel, using the creative interplay of skis and dogs, was suited to the south. It was the journey that brought the technique of pre-

* See pp. 102 *et. seq.*

mechanical Antarctic exploration to fruition. In terms of the race to the Pole, the results were eloquent.

Although Amundsen could not know it at the time, he had wiped out his rival's lead. He had reached 80°, while Scott on his depot journey never got beyond 79½°. Having started 6,000 miles behind, Amundsen was now thirty miles ahead. His technical superiority is illuminated by two simple figures. The average speed on his depot journey was twenty miles a day, twice that made by Scott.

While Amundsen was absent, Framheim had been completed under Wisting's command. 'Very fine work,' Amundsen noted in one of the rare personal comments in his diary. Amongst other things, one of *Fram*'s whalers had been hauled inland several miles as a lifeboat in case, after all, the Barrier calved, and Framheim started drifting out to sea.

Stubberud and Bjaaland had dug a passage round the hut and roofed it in by an extension to the eaves. This impressed Amundsen.

Besides its protective function [he expatiated in his diary], it will also have great use as a store for all kinds of things. For example, here L[indstrøm] can cut out shelves and have his fresh meat. The snow he cuts out he can use for fresh water.... Two things are achieved thereby. I. Always having reliably clean snow for water available   and that is particularly difficult here, with so many puppies loose and mucking up the place. II. Not be compelled to go under open skies to fetch snow. If we have a lot of bad weather, this will be of considerable importance.

At this point, Scott, 400 miles to the west, was retreating from the Barrier for the season. Amundsen was now hurrying to return. Before winter set in, he was determined to advance a depot to 83° S.; at the very least 82°. Nothing less satisfied his concepts of safety. He gave his men a week to get ready. All were going out this time; except Lindstrøm, the cook, who would stay behind alone to look after Framheim and the remaining dogs. Lindstrøm looked forward to getting everybody out of the way, so that he could put the house in order, he said. Equipment was being examined and overhauled.

The place is just one big workshop [Amundsen recorded]. In particular, the shoemaker's trade seems to thrive. We must alter our enormous ski boots from Andersen's [in Christiania]. They turned out to be too stiff in the cold. All possible – and impossible – patents now appear.

Except for Wisting, nobody had any experience of shoemaking. This was no obstacle. The boots were unstitched and successfully rebuilt. Several layers of sole leather were removed, and huge wedges sewn into the toes to give extra space.

On the evening of February 21st, the work was finished and the following day they set off, a caravan of seven sledges with six dogs each and eight men. Prestrud again was forerunner. Each sledge carried about 300 kilos (660 pounds). They started in a spirit of the grossest self-confidence.

In the week since the previous journey, the snow had changed. Abrasive drift snow had swept over the landscape and the thermometer had dropped nine degrees, so that ski and sledges slid a little worse than before, but not so much as to inhibit speed. Three days after starting, they ran into their first blizzard, a nice, south-east gale whipping the Barrier into a violent whirl of drift.

'These Norskies are a very tough lot,' as Oates had written. This was the kind of blizzard that kept Scott in his tent. Amundsen set off as usual with the trite remark that 'nobody knows the day before the sun goes down'. Eventually it ceased to drift, and that day they did thirty-nine miles.

One of Scott's misconceptions was that Eskimo dogs could not run into the wind because the drift hurt their eyes. Nothing apparently could shake this obstinate and wholly erroneous conviction. Scott's ignorance of the dog was such that he did not know about the nictitating membrane, the inner eyelid that can be drawn over the eyeball for protection. Amundsen's dogs were suffering now, but not from the wind. He had not realized that the long ocean voyage had made them soft. They needed far longer than the five weeks they had been ashore to acclimatize. Their paws had lost the hard resistant skin developed by constant work. They broke through the thin wind crust which, when in form, would hardly have troubled them. Now they cut their pads, so that their paws were a mass of blood at the end of each day. They were untrained, underfed, tired easily, and soon began to lose weight.

Among the men, there was discontent, Johansen, who had already quarrelled with Hassel, now fell out with Prestrud. In a diary entry, which graphically conveys the irritations of dog-driving and living cramped up in a small tent, Johansen described how

> Prestrud, who goes loose and unhindered in front on ski was impatient and bad tempered because he could not get into the tent and begin cooking. 'They began cooking in the other tent long ago,' he said. I had to inform him that not all dogs are equally good, and some have to be behind. There is nothing to be done about it. It is the heaviest job to come behind with the less good dogs. And when I finally arrive – he creeps into the tent and begins cooking, but I've got to finish feeding my dogs, *and* arranging sledges, harnesses etc., and take in [sleeping] bags and clothes. When everything is in order, Amundsen

and Hassel come in, and we creep together and eat our pemmican – It is silent in the tent. We have not exchanged a word since our quarrel.

Keeping to their old tracks was easy. They followed the dried fish in the snow which, in Amundsen's words, 'proved to be excellent markers'. The forerunner had to pick up each piece as he passed, and throw it to one side, because, had the dogs come upon it, there would have been a battle royal for possession. The first sledge driver then picked it up, collecting the pieces on his sledge, and in the evening divided it among all the dogs as extra food.

After five days, they reached the depot at 80° without incident. This time they had brought plenty of instruments for an astronomic fix. Two sextants and a theodolite gave a mean of 79° 59'; vindication of their sledgemeter and dead reckoning navigation.

Amundsen had viewed the way Scott and Shackleton marked their depots as verging on criminal negligence. That, too, he proposed to avoid. The problem was an awkward and vital one in a featureless desert. The method he adopted was a line of black pennants on short sticks running east–west across the course. Twenty were laid out half a mile apart; ten on each side of the depot, making a transverse marking of ten miles in all. This was well within any conceivable instrumental error, so that even in thick weather, the chances of missing a pennant were small. Each pennant was numbered, giving the distance and bearing of the depot.

Onwards from the 80th parallel the temperature dropped to 30–40 degrees (C.) of frost. The difficulty, as in most skiing, was not freezing, but sweating. Running with the dogs, they were kept all too warm. In deep cold, sweat condenses in its passage through the clothing, forming a deposit of rime, which then melts with horrible discomfort. Amundsen had to sit up late, drying his Netsilik reindeer fur *kamikks* over the Primus stove. But there are no complaints of feeling cold, which suggests that food (especially the supply of Vitamin C) was in order.

On March 3rd, they reached the 81st parallel, or to be precise, 81° 1'. There they put up the next depot, containing half a ton of dog pemmican. Hassel, Bjaaland and Stubberud then turned home. Amundsen, Prestrud, Helmer Hanssen, Wisting and Johansen continued south to try to get to 83°.

Until 81°, the going had been reasonable. The animals were tired and hungry, but willing. The only casualty was Odin, one of Amundsen's dogs, chafed by an ill-fitting harness. He was put on a sledge and sent home with the returning party.

Beyond 81°, it was a different tale. Johansen's diary for March 6th sums it up:

16½ miles covered today – the last part of the way terribly slowly. The poor dogs had to be whipped on.

The following day they

did 13 miles with greater difficulty than hitherto, and it goes very sluggishly; it nearly didn't go at all the last part of the way. The Chief's dogs are the worst, they don't take any notice of thrashing any more, just lie down in their tracks, and it is a terrible performance to get them going again.

Amundsen drew the necessary conclusion: 'I have decided only to take the depot to 82 deg. S. It will not pay to push on further.'

It was only fifteen miles on, and the day after, they arrived. It was a whole degree short of what Amundsen wanted. But in his words, it was

the uttermost that my 5 dogs could manage ... they were completely worn out, poor creatures. It is my only dark memory from down there – that my lovely animals were destroyed. I demanded more of them than they could manage. My consolation is that I did not spare myself either.

This was not empty posturing. The day after leaving Framheim, Amundsen suffered a recurrence of a painful rectal complaint, probably a severe form of haemorrhoids, to which Polar travellers are particularly prone. Every yard of the 160 miles since then had been agony, but he had driven himself, concealing what was happening as best he could. He *had* to reach a certain point or the whole enterprise would be jeopardized.

They celebrated their arrival at 82° South by a post mortem on the journey. Johansen had pronounced views on the deficiencies revealed. 'I have slept in many kinds of tent,' he wrote, 'and without tent, but this is the worst, and ditto the cooking arrangements.' The five of them were crowded into two small tents, the cooking done in one, food carried over to the other. The general mood was one of fiasco. It was not evident that something remarkable has just been achieved. Over half a ton of supplies including 880 pounds (400 kilos) of dog pemmican had been brought to within 480 miles of the Pole. It was 150 miles further than Scott had managed to get his furthest depot.

The second night at 82° S., they continued their discussion. All five, as Johansen put it in his diary,

gathered in the cooking tent in various squeezed up postures in order to profit a little from the warmth of the Primus. And then we discussed how best we were to reach our goal in the spring, by using our dogs in the best possible way. Now we have seen that they have been strained because the load has been too heavy and time too short. A. gave it as his opinion that the motto from 82 degrees must be as few people and as many dogs as possible.

This depot was more carefully marked than the preceding ones: sixty pennants being laid out instead of twenty; six to the mile instead of two. Amundsen deposited his own sledge, dividing his dogs between Helmer Hanssen and Wisting for the homeward journey. He knew he was the worst dog-driver in the company, and the others would get more out of the animals.

To go by the diaries of the homeward run, it was no more demanding, for the men, than a winter's ski tour at home. The weather was stormy and cold, with thirty to forty degrees (C.) of frost, the same conditions that in Scott's record set the scene for struggle. Differences of style apart, the fact is that Amundsen and his men were inured to the climate, both physically and mentally.

The monotony of the Great Ice Barrier that is a feature of Scott's and Wilson's diaries is totally absent from the Norwegians'. Their dogs saw to that. It was like having dozens of demanding and entertaining children to look after. There was no time for monotony or brooding.

On the morning of March 23rd, the dark water sky of the open Ross Sea appeared over the northern horizon; the homecoming landmark in that rolling Sahara of snow. In the late afternoon, the caravan breasted a rise and the Bay of Whales sprang into sight below. Amundsen was relieved to see that 'No change had taken place in the Barrier's appearance since we left, to the smallest detail, it lies as we saw it last.'

Prestrud, still forerunner, set off down the slope to the sea ice, but was overtaken by the first sledge, careering down unbraked, and barely saved himself at the last moment by flinging himself on board. The others followed similarly out of control. A concertina crash ensued, and dogs, sledges, men and skis ended up in a glorious heap at the bottom, to a cacophony of laughter, curses, barks and snarls. Thus ended the great Norwegian depot journey, like the beginners' class in a ski school.

They had been out a month, working in severe cold; the last fortnight at an average temperature of about −40° (C.). At that point mercury freezes and each breath burns like fire. Even on men used to outdoor work in a harsh climate, the strain was beginning to tell. Fingertips were frostbitten, faces beginning to crack from exposure. But they had accomplished much. They had taken more than a ton and a half of supplies to between 80° and 82° South. This included pemmican for twenty-five dogs for three months, and at the depot at 82°, 110 litres of paraffin, enough for four or five men travelling for 200 days, or twice the estimated duration of the Polar journey. It was the first time in the short history of Antarctic land exploration that a sane foundation had been built for an assault on the Pole. It had cost the lives of eight dogs in all, but still left eighty-five adult and twenty-two pups, who would be ready for work in the spring. As far as the men were concerned, it had been accomplished without undue suffering.

Mentally, the outcome was vital. Despite the physical hardships, relief was the dominant emotion. The Ross Ice Barrier was just another snow-field, made for ski and sledges. This removed the strain and unease of an alien environment. The Norwegians were at home, able to identify themselves with this new world, instead of fighting it. Antarctica was only Hardangervidda writ large.

The abiding lesson Amundsen had learned from Scott's and Shackleton's heroic risk-taking, was the absolute necessity of generous margins of safety. So far, he was working with a figure between 100 and 200 per cent. It was far more than Scott ever contemplated, but for Amundsen it was not enough. Before winter set in, he wanted a ton of seal meat taken to 80°, so that the dogs could gorge on fresh food before starting for the south. It meant having fresh dogs more than a degree nearer the Pole and therefore, in effect, advancing the Norwegian base a hundred miles beyond Scott at Cape Evans.

To be back before the sun disappeared for the winter, they had to start within ten days and, in the meanwhile, the failings revealed by the last journey had to be corrected.

The most serious defect lay in the tents. Amundsen acknowledged his mistake in having small, two-man models under the impression that they would be warm. Hassel and Wisting made the suggestion, and proceeded to execute the work, of sewing two together to make four- or five-man tents. The outcome was a kind of dome shape, rather like an elongated igloo, with no surface to catch the wind. Two were ready within a week.

Hassel and Wisting were the kind of all-round men whom Amundsen set great store by. Both could navigate (Hassel had a mate's certificate) besides doing sailmaking and saddlery with professional competence. As they were going to live in the tents themselves, their workmanship could be trusted – absolutely.

The forthcoming journey was also to mark the road to 80° S. properly. Amundsen wanted this done beyond a peradventure, because he considered 80° the real start of the Polar journey, and wanted it to be seen as such. Route finding in the wilderness is always a strain, and any strain saved was, in Amundsen's view, effort well spent. Anxiety can be as bad as hunger; coming on top of each other, it can be a disastrous combination, especially if it impedes judgment. It is in the awareness of these subtleties that Amundsen was superior to Scott.

Amundsen wanted a flag every mile. Unfortunately, there were not enough bamboo sticks which, because of lightness, were being reserved for route marking beyond 82 degrees. So Bjaaland and Stubberud cut up one-inch planks and spliced the lengths to make up eight-foot posts. This particular size was chosen because it was visible for half a mile and therefore in clear weather at least one would always be in sight. Eighty were ready in five days.

Six extra large, fat, blubbery seals were shot just before the start, heads and flippers removed to save useless weight, and loaded on the sledges. Since the journey was a short one of about 170 miles, the men would not waste pemmican but live on seal.

Amundsen was still in pain from his rectal complaint and decided not to go. On the eve of the start, he told Johansen that he would be in command. Johansen recorded in his diary that Amundsen said this 'in the others' hearing, so that they could act accordingly'.

It is not the remark of a contented man. Johansen was the everlasting number two, and his temporary promotion made him more conscious of this than ever.

At ten the next morning, the depot party set off. Helmer Hanssen was ill with some abdominal complaint, but insisted on going. As the best dog-driver, he felt his responsibility.

Amundsen was left behind along with Lindstrøm, whom he now proceeded to help, like any menial, to clean out the hut. The return from a journey had been dubbed 'the dirty days'. With sleeping bags and fur clothing slung from every square inch of ceiling space to dry, equipment from end to end and nine human beings neatly slotted into a space none too big, the result was a regular deposition of reindeer hair, discarded socks and the detritus of mountain huts. Everything had to be cleaned and scoured, ready for the next 'dirty days'.

Rubicund, solid, imperturbable, Lindstrøm holds a special place in Polar history as the prince of major-domos. Chef, baker, pastry-cook, he provided surrogate domesticity. He was also instrument maker, taxidermist, housepainter as circumstances required – and clown.

He had an alarm-clock, set to wake him at six-thirty a.m., which frequently rang in the evening as well. It sounded like a telephone. Amundsen got the idea of telling him to answer it. Lindstrøm would then rush out into the galley, mimic a telephone conversation and, with a perfectly straight face, return to report what had happened.

And then [Amundsen says in his diary], we both laughed and enjoyed ourselves like children. The odd thing is that this has happened three evenings in a row, always with the same result – amusement.

Lindstrøm now showed that besides his other accomplishments he was also a cabinet maker, quickly and professionally turning out a meteorological screen to replace one left behind on *Fram*. This caused Amundsen to say that, after three years together on *Gjøa*, Lindstrøm still surprised him.

I thought I knew him quite well, but he continually shows new sides of himself. A better man has never set foot inside the polar regions. I hope from the bottom of my heart to be in the position one day to do something for him. He has done Norwegian polar explorations greater and more valuable services than anyone else. May the Norwegian peasants – Good God, that one must be beholden to such a crew – understand this some day.

This hints at the bitterness beginning to well up as he brooded over the niggardly support at home: a patriot beginning to despise his fellow countrymen.

The depot party was expected back on Saturday, April 8th; a week was considered ample for 160 miles by now. It was not until the following Tuesday that Amundsen and Lindstrøm, regularly scanning the Barrier with more concern than they were prepared to admit, saw the looked-for caravan break the southern horizon and, like a line of dark insects scurrying over a counterpane of white, start their descent to the bay. The men were riding, the dogs evidently pulling well. Even from afar, it suggested the air of success.

So it turned out to be. The delay had been caused by straying, in thick fog, into a maze of hidden crevasses where, as Hassel drily put it, 'The abyss yawned darkly under my sledge.' It took two days to escape from this labyrinth, snow bridges collapsing to right and left. The only casualties were Johansen's two leading dogs, who fell through, broke their traces and were lost. This incidentally demonstrated graphically the advantages of the fan system of harnessing. When a dog fell, he fell alone. With the parallel system attached to a single trace, he would drag his companions as well.

At least it was a danger now charted. For this was *terra incognita*. In the crevassed uncertainty of ice, they could only be sure of the line they had trodden before.

For the rest, it was an uneventful dog sledge and skiing trip over now familiar terrain, the daily distances as usual between fifteen and twenty miles.

There were two surprises. The temperature was between ten and fifteen degrees higher. There was fog most of the way, putting the depot marking to the test. The result was this. With visibility down to less than a mile, running by compass and sledgemeter alone, they missed the depot by a mile and a half, but ran into marker flag No. 8, to the west, with no difficulty, as a result, in finding their goal. It was an unlooked-for tonic; proof that, come what might, they need never miss a depot.

Lindstrøm had sent a small tuck box to be opened at the depot. It contained, as Bjaaland recorded,

> a cake, and [tinned] pears and pineapples, and finally a glass each of vermouth; that was something to savour at 80 degrees S. latitude.

In rebuilding the depot, Johansen arranged the six seals standing up on end, round the monolith of cases and snow blocks. This was to prevent their being drifted up and save the trouble of having to be dug out on the Polar journey. This shows the true forethought of the professional.

As far as Amundsen was concerned, the journey had been an unqualified success. The dogs were as round and fat as when they started. To the 80° depot they had added, besides a ton of seal meat, 165 litres of paraffin and various other useful supplies. There were now almost two tons all told at 80 degrees, making three tons out on the Barrier. There was a depot every whole degree of latitude up to 82 degrees South. The road was marked every mile all the way to 80 degrees.

The one doubt was those motor sledges of Scott's. Amundsen never spoke about them, nor did he encourage discussion, but they were beginning to prey on his mind. The success of Johansen's journey, however, was a comfort.

> Tomorrow [wrote Amundsen on the evening the party returned], we celebrate the end of the autumn's work, and truly we can celebrate it with a good conscience. *Thereafter* comes Easter, so we can celebrate a whole week on end.

23

Sledging with 'the Owner'

WHEN *TERRA NOVA* left the Bay of Whales after the encounter with *Fram* there were, in the words of Wilfred Bruce,

> heavy arguments in wardroom about the rights and wrongs of Amundsen's party and the chances of our being able to beat them. Their experience and number of dogs seem to leave us very little.

Campbell was in particularly low spirits. Events at the Bay of Whales had been depressing in more ways than one. Comparisons beyond the number of dogs obtruded themselves. Framheim, with its evident meticulous planning and smooth organization, was far from the muddles at Cape Evans. Even more dispiriting, perhaps, was the contrast between the aura of quiet, yet aggressive self-confidence surrounding Amundsen and the sour undertones of Scott's profoundly defensive mentality. Campbell did not put it exactly in those terms but he sensed the superiority of the Norwegian's leadership. To cap it all, he had been deprived of his chosen field of work, and thus suffered more than Scott by Amundsen's incursion.

He now had to find another base for the winter, and there was not much time before the season closed in. But first he gave the order to head for McMurdo Sound in order to report the meeting with the Norwegians.

> Our thoughts are full, too full of them [Priestley wrote in his diary]. The impression they have left with us is that of a set of men with distinctive personalities, hard and evidently inured to hardship, good goers and pleasant good humoured men: All these qualities combine to render them very dangerous rivals ... We have news which will make [Scott] as uneasy as ourselves.

After a stormy passage, *Terra Nova* arrived on February 8th off Cape Evans where Campbell landed the two ponies he had been given for King Edward VII Land. In the mountainous country of South Victoria Land, whither he now was bound, there would be no use for ponies, while Scott, with Amundsen in the field, would need all those he could get. The poor beasts had to be swum ashore through the icy waters, Anton, the Russian groom, humanely resuscitating them on arrival with half a bottle of brandy apiece.

Scott was away on his depot journey. To make sure he learned of Amundsen's doings as soon as possible, *Terra Nova* steamed up McMurdo Sound and delivered Campbell's report at the old *Discovery* hut. Now running short of coal, she hurried away to find Campbell and his men a landing place. Eventually, after various setbacks due to heavy ice, they were as a last resort put ashore at Borchgrevink's old haunts at Cape Adare. There, the eastern party became the northern party and, in Priestley's words, 'spent a pleasant winter, but it [was not] exploring'. And, there, for the moment, they pass out of the story.

In the lifeless Antarctic hinterland, the depot journeys were more than a matter of tactics; they were the very instruments of survival. The manner in which they were launched and carried out embodied, indeed caricatured, the essential difference between the Norwegian and British expeditions. Amundsen set out with the matter-of-fact calm of workaday routine; Scott, as Cherry-Garrard put it, left 'in a state of hurry bordering upon panic'. Amundsen was issuing the executive order for an operation prepared months in advance. Scott gave the signal for a stupendous act of improvisation.

Scott had been ashore for a fortnight, while the ship was unloaded and the hut built, before on January 19th suddenly ordering P.O. Evans and Bowers to have everything ready for the depot journey to start on the 25th. They had to start from scratch. Scott himself had to 'work out sledge details' as he put it, 'but my head doesn't seem half as clear on the subject as it ought to be'. He was optimistically hoping to rush through in less than a week the work for which Amundsen considered a year hardly enough. Amongst other things, Bowers was expected, single-handed, to unpack provisions and make sledging rations for thirteen or fourteen men for two months.

Scott's treatment of Bowers is an apt illustration of his vacillating judgment. Bowers was a red-headed, ungainly person, short, squat and heavy, with legs too short and nose too long. He had the profile of a parrot and was immortalized under the name of 'Birdie'. When first presented with this strangely featured character, Scott said to 'Teddy' Evans: 'Well, we're in for it now, and must make the best of a bad job.' Scott was usually deceived by appearances.

In fact, on the voyage to Australia, Bowers proved himself a thoroughly competent ship's officer, making Scott revise his judgment.

Scott then went to the other extreme. Having originally intended Bowers for the ship, he now put him in the main landing party and proceeded to load him with more and more responsibility. Bowers, earnest, good-humoured, anxious to do his duty, responded with a gluttonous appetite for work, to become Scott's willing prop. In the end, he took over all the lading, stores, navigation and arrangement of sledging rations. His one failing was that he did not know much about snow and ice. But then, in spite of his previous experience, neither did Scott.

The drawback of a coastal base on Ross Island was that overland, because of the glaciers and ice falls cascading down the ramparts of Mount Erebus, the road to the south was impassable, at least to any but practised mountaineers, of whom there were none on that expedition. The sea ice was the only practicable route. It usually went out during the summer, however, cutting off the base from the Barrier. Both *Discovery* and *Nimrod* expeditions told the tale. Gran was astounded that Scott had not thought to bring along a motor boat to maintain communications.

As it was, the road from Cape Evans depended on a remnant of the winter's ice still clinging to the coast, but steadily melting away and, to the practised eye, distinctly unreliable. Scott, however, assumed it would hold long enough for him to get away or, in his own words, 'it would be poor luck if it failed'. On January 23rd, he woke to find that the start of the road to the south had stolen away in the night. The open sea was now lapping at the foot of Cape Evans. Winter quarters were almost cut off. A hurried reconnaissance showed one last chance of escape over a fringe of ice remaining in a bay to the south of Cape Evans. The ponies could – with luck – be got across. There was no question of taking any loads. Dogs, sledges, all the remaining impedimenta, would have to be taken by the ship to where firm bay ice began. Scott, now thoroughly alive to the foibles of late summer ice, ordered a start for the following day, twenty-four hours earlier than originally intended. 'Everything,' he noted, 'has been rushed – and a wonderful day's work has resulted. . . . One breathes a prayer that the road holds for the few remaining hours . . . We are doing it on a very narrow margin.'

Food, sledges, equipment and dogs, were bundled back on to the ship whence they had with such toil been disembarked three weeks before. Letters were scribbled, clothes hurriedly sorted and roughly altered. With Bowers' help, Scott completed such arrangements for a second season as could be suggested on the spur of the moment. Men stayed up all night perforce to complete what, with a little care, could have been done at leisure. When, at nine o'clock next morning, the ponies set off, Bowers, according to Cherry-Garrard, had not slept for seventy-two hours. It was a good old British muddle.

'Things are not as rosy as they might be,' Oates now wrote to his mother.

We shall I am sure be handicapped by the lack of experience which the party possesses. Scott having spent too much of his life in an office, he would fifty times sooner stay in the hut seeing how a pair of ... puttees suited him than come out and look at a ponies [*sic*] legs or a dogs feet.

Terra Nova joined the ponies at Glacier Tongue, the snout of a glacier jutting out into McMurdo Sound about five miles south of Cape Evans, where the edge of the sea ice lay. There, she disembarked the rest of the depot party. They were without the motor sledges, which had already developed serious faults due to slovenly manufacture and defective metallurgy.

It took two days to discharge the depot party's supplies – about ten tons – and transport it to what looked like safety about a mile from the edge of the ice. *Terra Nova* then sailed for the western shore of McMurdo Sound to land a geological party under Griffith Taylor, before setting off on the voyage that eventually took her to the encounter with Amundsen at the Bay of Whales.

The depot party – thirteen men, eight ponies and twenty-six dogs – now spent four days ferrying their supplies about eighteen miles on to the Barrier, to a point called Safety Camp, a few miles back from the edge, which Scott considered safe from calving. It was a cumbrous and ragged performance bearing out Oates' forebodings.

Scott was soon initiated into the drawbacks of ponies in the Antarctic, when they broke through the sea ice or wallowed up to their bellies in snowdrifts. The dogs showed their insulting superiority by such diverse exploits as charging enthusiastically with a full load over polished sea ice in pursuit of a whale that had surfaced in a lead, and efficiently scampering over powdery drift and grainy crust for mile after mile. Wilson, for the first time seeing trained animals and a competent driver, rapidly dropped his old prejudice. 'Dog-driving like this,' he wrote, 'is a very different thing to the beastly dog-driving we perpetrated in the *Discovery* days.'

Scott's reaction was different.

I withhold my opinion of the dogs [he wrote], in much doubt as to whether they are going to be a real success – but the ponies are going to be real good ... They work with such extraordinary steadiness, stepping out briskly and cheerfully.

From Camp 2, on the sea ice, the whole party, except for Scott, visited the old *Discovery* hut to see about digging it out. On an earlier visit, Scott had found a broken window pane, which had let in the blizzards to fill the place with hard, compacted snow. He blamed Shackleton, who had used the place on the *Nimrod* expedition. Scott waxed indignant. 'The report is unfavourable, as I expected,' he wrote on the return of the party. 'It would take weeks of work to clear it ... in no case can we inhabit our old Hut.' This was hyperbolic, and not quite what he was told. In the event, Atkinson and one seaman cleared the place in a few days, and made it habitable.

At Safety Camp Scott, as he put it,

held a council of war ... I unfolded my plan, which is to go forward with five weeks' food for men and animals; to depot a fortnight's supply after twelve or thirteen days and return here.

This was the first intimation of what was going to happen. Scott had divulged his plans to no one, possibly because, until the last moment, there were no plans to divulge. The result was a frenzy of chaotic activity. Even Wilson had been kept in the dark, and now found himself scurrying round for orders like a private on parade.

Such was the introduction of most of the party to Scott as explorer in the field. Sitting up in his sleeping bag after camp had been made and supper eaten, his confusion and irritability disappeared, and he became genial and relaxed. Inside the tent Scott's confusion was replaced by fussiness, everything having to be at right angles, like a Naval rating's kit laid out for inspection. This went beyond the tidiness required for comfort in a confined space. It told on some who shared his tent – even Naval men. 'Sledging with the Owner',* as it came to be known, was generally considered something of a strain.

Chery-Garrard, another Polar apprentice, found that Scott had 'little sense of humour'. Charles Wright, the Canadian, remembered Scott as 'always the naval gentleman', whose tent mates stood so much in awe of him that, in a blizzard or dangerous cold, they would go outside and brave excruciating discomfort to perform their natural functions – even modest urination – or not to do them at all, rather than use a corner of the tent which, during intolerable weather, was common practice on the expedition.

A martinet in petty detail, Scott often became slipshod and abstracted when confronted with essentials. Oates found him the 'most absent-minded person' he had ever known, implying that, while in a private

* 'The Owner' is Naval slang for the captain of a warship.

citizen this might be an endearing trait, it was less so in a leader, responsible for the lives of his subordinates.

Gran was distinctly puzzled. He had come to demonstrate the potentialities of skis, and now found that Scott's enthusiasm at Fefor seemed to have evaporated. There was considerable debate for and against skis. Gran tried to show what skis could do by running errands in the confusion of marching and counter-marching that followed in the wake of Scott's incompetent improvisations. But all too soon he was reduced at Scott's orders, to the farcical procedure of wading through the snow while his skis were dragged uselessly on the sledge. This was because it seemed impossible to lead a pony on skis.

Running Scott's first depot journey caravan was a ponderous and complex business. Each morning, the ponies would first march off, leaving the dogs, who travelled faster, to wait behind, and leave later so as to arrive together at the next camp. There was daily confusion and misunderstanding.

> I see the difficulty with complicated transport [Gran remarked in his diary]. And one thing I am certain of. We will need luck if we are to reach the Pole next year.

They moved at between a half and a third of Amundsen's speed. Periodically they were tent-bound by blizzards. On at least two occasions it was the kind of weather in which Amundsen covered twenty miles. The temperature was the same, about $-20°$ (C.). The animals were the main trouble.

'The poor horses have a hard time now,' Gran remarked, 'so frozen they can hardly eat.' Scott did not apparently connect this with the weakness and thinning he noticed after the first blizzard. He observes in his diary however, that the dogs 'ought to be quite happy. They are curled snugly under the snow and at meal times issue from steaming warm holes.' And again: 'The dogs are in fine form – the blizzard has only been a pleasant rest *for them.*'

Oates had started off with a suspicion of dogs, but soon saw that they were better adapted than ponies to Polar conditions. When he saw the ponies failing from cold, hunger and exposure, he pressed Scott to march on, killing the weakest ponies, depoting them as dog (and if necessary human) food for the following season. Scott refused because, in spite of his philosophizing, he could not bear the thought of killing animals.

Oates was quietly appalled at such mawkishness. Having seen men killed in battle, he knew that nothing was as important as human life; certainly not horseflesh. Thus reasoned that unsentimental cavalryman.

Finding he could not get the point across to Scott, Oates retreated into a pessimistic taciturnity.

Scott carried on, hoping to reach 80° South. The ponies found the going hard. On the 17th, he decided they could no longer face the incessant southerly drift. He gave the order to turn. The actual latitude was 79° 28½'; his furthest South that season. It had taken twenty-four days of struggle to reach this point – called One Ton Depot – from Cape Evans. Amundsen on his first depot journey reached the 80th parallel, and returned to Framheim, in five days.

Scott's depot and route marking were as poor as his travel. He repeated the mistakes of the *Discovery* expedition. A single flag was all that marked One Ton Depot; the road was not marked at all, tracks and old camp sites in the shifting snow being deemed sufficient.

Gran's pony, Weary Willie, was at the end of his tether. Oates now proposed putting him down and marching on with the remaining four ponies to move the depot further south. Scott refused. He had, as he put it, made himself sick watching the poor ponies suffer. Whether this reaction was sorrow for the animals or pity for himself at having to see their misery is not clear.

Oates was a soldier, his god was duty, but he was also the kind of officer who was prepared to argue with a superior when the occasion demanded. He proceeded to argue with Scott. It would, he said, be a great mistake not to continue.

'I have had more than enough of this cruelty to animals,' was Scott's reply, 'and I'm not going to defy my feelings for the sake of a few days' march.'

'I'm afraid you'll regret it, Sir,' said Oates in the end, exasperated by Scott's squeamishness.

After building One Ton Depot (so called after the amount it contained) Scott characteristically was seized with impatience to get back to Hut Point. He joined the dog teams and hurried on ahead, leaving the pony party to fend for themselves. There was a point, called Corner Camp, where the road to the Pole turned south, after first running east, to avoid the crevasses caused by the pressure of the Barrier flowing past a nunatak called White Island. Scott, hurrying on, broke the elementary rules of glacier travel, and cut the corner. He duly paid for his recklessness and lost two dogs in a crevasse, all for the sake of saving a few hours.

On the 22nd, Scott arrived at Safety Camp, where he was reunited with Teddy Evans, who had returned early with three of the weaker ponies. Two had died on the way. But that, and all Scott's other worries, paled during the evening when a party arrived at the camp from the *Discovery* hut, bearing Campbell's letter with the news about Amundsen at the Bay of Whales.

First Shackleton; now this. It was ironic and maybe inevitable, that Scott in whom the sense of prerogative was elevated to a ruling passion, had been singled out to suffer the pangs of jealousy and invasion. Campbell's letter came as an almost physical blow.

> For many hours [wrote Cherry-Garrard, who was in the same tent at the time], Scott could think of nothing else nor talk of anything else. Evidently a great shock for him – he thinks it very unsporting since our plans for landing a party there* were known.

Scott had chosen to believe, and told his companions, that Amundsen was going to try for the Pole from the Weddell Sea, because this minimized the threat, and therefore was the most convenient opinion. He was now so denuded of restraint as to blurt out the contents of Scott Keltie's cable that Amundsen was making for McMurdo Sound, the very existence of which he had been concealing since November. It was altogether an emotional scene. Eventually, Scott calmed down sufficiently to get into his sleeping bag and, as usual, to write up his diary before turning in. Amundsen's 'proceedings have been very deliberate, and success alone can justify them,' was his comment.

> One thing only fixes itself definitely in my mind. The proper, as well as the wiser, course for us is to proceed exactly as though this had not happened. To go forward and do our best for the honour of the country without fear or panic.
> There is no doubt that Amundsen's plan is a very serious menace to ours. He has a shorter distance to the Pole by 60 miles – I never thought he could have got so many dogs safely to the ice. His plan for running them seems excellent. But above and beyond all he can start his journey early in the season – an impossible condition with ponies.

Scott now passed into what Cherry-Garrard called 'a state of high nervous excitement bordering on collapse'. He launched into a succession of aimless little marches and counter-marches, the only discernible purpose of which was activity for its own sake; the sign of a man not quite in control of himself.

Meanwhile, Oates, Bowers and Gran were trailing behind with the ponies on the Barrier. Alone, released from the curiously dampening influence of Scott's presence, they relaxed and, sharing a tent together

* i.e., King Edward VII Land.

for the first time, learned to know each other. Gran, who had felt since leaving England that he did not 'find favour' in Oates' eyes, now discovered why.

Oates said straight out that it was not my person he had anything against, but that I was a foreigner. He hated all foreigners from the bottom of his heart, because all foreigners hated England. The entire rest of the world, with Germany at the head, in Oates' view, were only waiting for a pretext to throw themselves on his country and destroy it if they only could. I would have answered Oates immediately, but Bowers forestalled me. 'There may be something in what you say, Titus [Oates' nickname], but still I'll bet you anything you like that Trigger [Bowers' name for Gran] will be with us if England is forced innocently into a war.' 'Would you?' asked Oates. 'Naturally,'* I answered, and the next instant, his hand had clasped mine. With that, the closed book was opened, and from that moment, Oates and I were the best of friends.

On the night of February 25th, three days after Scott, they ambled into Safety Camp. There, Gran heard the news of Amundsen from the incongruous figure of Meares emerging in his underpants on a nocturnal errand as they arrived. The following day he wrote:

I felt as if the Barrier had opened under me, and a thousand thoughts poured through my head at once. Was I to compete with my own countrymen, with my own flag? No, not a pleasant thought to contemplate . . .

Bowers recorded that when they

heard the news of Amundsen's little game . . . Trigger was so genuinely upset at the behaviour of his countryman that one could not help feeling sorry for him & the awkward position it put him.

It was left to Oates, as usual, to dispense with moralistic rhodomontade:

If it comes to a race, Amundsen will have a great chance of getting there as he is a man who has been at this kind of game all his life and he has a hard crowd behind him while we are very young.

For three days, Bowers, Oates, Gran, Wilson, Meares, Cherry-Garrard, Surgeon Atkinson and Petty Officer Crean hung about at Safety Camp passively waiting for orders, Scott was somewhere else, and over his intentions there rested absolute obscurity. On February 28th, still unbalanced by the shock of Amundsen, he arrived in a flurry and ordered an immediate withdrawal back to Hut Point, the old *Discovery* winter

* Gran joined the R.F.C. early in the First World War, and fought on the Western Front chiefly in 'Camels', being severely wounded. He finished as a major, and had trouble at home for serving a foreign power.

quarters, straight over the sea ice. Wilson pointed out that the ice was dangerous. Scott lost his temper and informed him that orders were orders. Wilson and Meares were to take the dogs and do what they were told. Wilson managed to extract permission to deviate from the prescribed course if circumstances dictated, and then he and Meares got off as soon as they could. Wilson was now exasperated with Scott and glad to leave him to his own devices for a spell.

Scott took command of the ponies. Finding Weary Willie in a 'pitiable condition', he stayed behind with Oates and Gran to nurse the invalid, leaving Bowers, Cherry-Garrard and Crean to carry on and face the crossing of the sea-ice alone. It is strangely reminiscent of the moment, four years before, when Scott deserted the bridge of H.M.S. *Albemarle* on an unnecessary errand just before she collided with H.M.S. *Commonwealth*.

Scott stayed up all night with the poor creature, apparently oblivious to the men and dogs and ponies scattered over the terrain, dependent on his orders. Weary Willie died in the morning. It was, wrote a lachrymose Scott,

> hard to have got him back so far only for this. It is clear that these blizzards are terrible for the poor animals ... and we cannot afford to lose condition at the beginning of a journey. It makes a late start *necessary for next year*.
>
> Well, we have done our best and bought our experience at a heavy cost.

Meanwhile, out in McMurdo Sound, an inglorious débâcle was unfolding.

On the sea ice, Wilson was soon confronted with working cracks and diverse other signs of an imminent break-up. He swung violently at right angles and beat a very fast retreat to *terra firma* with all the dogs. A mile or so behind came Bowers in charge of the ponies. Scott of course was somewhere out of sight tending Weary Willie.

Bowers' orders were to follow the dog tracks. But he also knew that Scott had insisted on the route round Cape Armitage. When he saw Wilson change course he was in a quandary, because he was not sure whether he was supposed to follow Wilson as a pilot or to hold Scott's preordained course. He chose the latter alternative, because it stemmed from higher authority, and he assumed that Wilson had deviated from the original orders, which of course was what he very sensibly had done.

Bowers was frighteningly inexperienced on ice, but he was used to obeying orders. He pressed on blindly. Inevitably he was caught by the break-up of the ice. The men and most of the equipment were luckily saved, but all except one of the ponies were lost. It was an object lesson

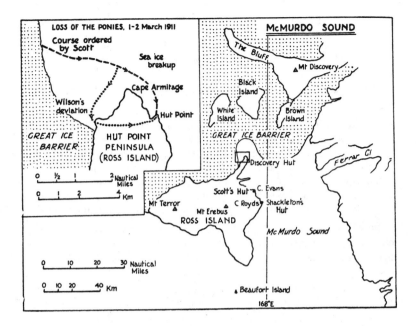

LOSS OF THE PONIES, 1-2 March 1911

Course ordered by Scott

Sea ice breakup

Cape Armitage

Wilson's deviation

Hut Point

GREAT ICE BARRIER

HUT POINT PENINSULA (ROSS ISLAND)

0 ½ 1 2 Nautical Miles

0 1 2 4 Km

McMURDO SOUND

The Bluff

Mt Discovery

Black Island

White Island

Brown Island

GREAT ICE BARRIER

Ferrar Gl

Discovery Hut

Scott's Hut   C. Evans

Mt Terror   C Royds   Shackleton's Hut

Mt Erebus

ROSS ISLAND

Mc Murdo Sound

0 10 20 30 Nautical Miles

0 10 20 40 Km

Beaufort Island

168°E

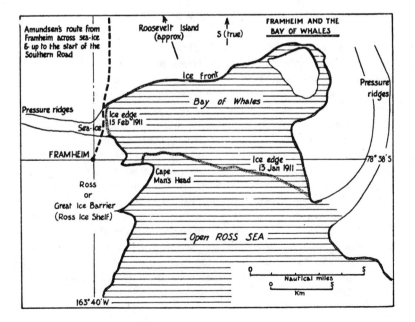

Amundsen's route from Framheim across sea-ice & up to the start of the Southern Road

Roosevelt Island (approx)

S (true)

FRAMHEIM AND THE BAY OF WHALES

Ice front

Pressure ridges

Bay of Whales

Pressure ridges

Ice edge 15 Feb 1911

Sea-ice

FRAMHEIM

Ice edge 13 Jan 1911

78° 38′ S

Ross or Great Ice Barrier (Ross Ice Shelf)

Cape Man's Head

Open ROSS SEA

0 Nautical miles 5

0 Km 5

163° 40′ W

in the consequences of unclear orders, insistence on blind obedience to the letter of command, and a professional training that crushed initiative in subordinate officers.

Bowers accepted the blame for the disaster, yet comforted himself by a piece of fatalistic reasoning.

> It just had to be. Six hours earlier we could have walked to the Hut on sound sea ice. A few hours later we should have seen open water on arrival at the Barrier's edge. The blizzard that knocked out the beasts, the death of Weary Willie · the misunderstanding of the dogs, everything fitted into place ... Let those who believe in co-incidence carry on believing. Nobody will ever convince me that it was not something more. Perhaps in the light of next year we shall see what was meant by such an apparent blow to our hopes.

So ended the great depot journey. Figures tell the tale. Seven out of eight ponies had been lost. Thirteen men had struggled for a month to bring a ton of supplies not quite to 80° South. At the Bay of Whales, eight Norwegians and fifty dogs, working for two months, far later in the season, had moved three tons another two degrees of latitude closer to the Pole. Even without this comparison, it had patently been a shambles. As Gran put it in his diary: 'Our party is divided, and we are like an army that is defeated, disappointed and inconsolable.'

Scott now had to wait at the *Discovery* hut for the sea to freeze so that he could return to Cape Evans. He became so moody, nervous and tense at having to play a waiting game that he made it a trying time for everyone else. Matters worsened with the arrival on March 14th of Griffith Taylor's western geological party. Sixteen men were now littering the hut's incommodious quarters. Taylor was good enough to explain that the mapping on the *Discovery* expedition was a 'disgrace', and that he had done more in six weeks than the *Discovery* expedition in two years. On March 17th, torn by the cumulative strain of Amundsen, Griffith Taylor's home truths, and general inactivity, Scott once more lost control of himself and gave Gran a public dressing down, the burden of which was that he was a lazy malingerer. Scott felt deeply enough to fill two whole pages of his diary on the subject. 'All that remains,' he ended, 'is to rid oneself as far as possible of the nuisance of his presence.'

In Gran's words, Scott 'was not a fatherly man', so that although he suspected what lay behind the outburst, he was afraid to have it out. Like most people on the expedition, Gran turned in his perplexity to 'Uncle Bill', as Wilson was called. On March 22nd, sitting side by side on a boulder in the wind some distance from the hut, they had a long and serious talk.

I had the sort of feeling when I opened my mouth Scott would think of Amundsen [Gran said to Wilson]. I had a sort of feeling that I was a kind of shadow in Scott's life. . . .

You mustn't think like that [Wilson said]. Scott is in a terrible state. But it is natural, because I think he thinks that if Amundsen does not have bad luck, he will get to the Pole first and then you know that the expedition will be ruined, and nothing to what it could have been if Amundsen hadn't existed.

Wilson knew what he was talking about. He was nursing Scott through a debilitating bout of melancholic depression. No one knows what Scott (and the expedition) owed Wilson.

I am impatient of our wait here [wrote Scott]. But I shall be impatient also in the main hut. It is ill to sit still and contemplate the ruin which has assailed our transport. . . . The Pole is a long way off, alas!

Bit by bit I am losing all faith in the dogs and much in Meares — I'm afraid neither he nor they will ever go the pace we look for.

For three weeks the sixteen at Hut Point waited in limbo. Some desultory man-hauling of supplies to Corner Camp came perforce to an end on March 23rd when temperatures of −40° (C.) made work outside unpleasant.

After three weeks, Scott was at the end of his tether, and, deaf to all counsel, insisted on crossing to Cape Evans over the young autumn ice. It was a risk which appalled his companions, because they saw it was unnecessary and irrational. In parts the ice was less than four inches thick. It was not yet settled. A storm could have sent it out to sea. Again Scott's ungovernable emotions had clouded his judgment. Scott got through. But it was a near thing.

24

The Pole-Seeker Prepares

SCOTT HAD ORDERED Pennell to explore the unknown waters west of Cape Adare on his way back to New Zealand in *Terra Nova*. After putting Campbell ashore, this is what Pennell proceeded to do.

On February 22nd, Wilfred Bruce, who had the watch, sighted the snow-capped peaks of new land. Later it was named Oates Land after Captain Oates.

That discovery nearly cost the expedition dear. Navigating pack ice, especially off an uncharted coast, is a specialized occupation. There was no ice pilot on board; nobody in fact with more experience than the passage of the pack on the voyage down.

Terra Nova was very nearly beset. In Bruce's words after 'dodging about like a rat in a trap' she escaped from the ice, having cut it very, very fine. As she finally cleared, the sea began to freeze behind her.

Before *Terra Nova* arrived in New Zealand, she had another close shave. She ran into stormy weather, and the clogging of her decrepit pumps was nearly her bane, as it had been on the outward voyage. Luckily Davies, the shipwright, was on board. Scott had wanted to keep him in the south, but Pennell refused point blank to sail without him, for he was the only man who understood those pumps. Davies saved the ship again. At one point she was kept afloat with a filter improvised by perforating an enamel jug and held *by hand* to the bilge pump intakes. On March 31st, she arrived at Lyttelton, and Pennell's troubles were over. He had all the care and bounty of New Zealand to carry him through the winter.

Fram also started her homeward voyage by looking for new land. Nilsen, now in command, took her east to Cape Colbeck, to see if he could discover more of King Edward VII Land. But there the similarity stops. Finding pack ice, he sheered off before getting entangled. His only task was to get through safely. This meant no experiments, no risks. So *Fram* put her head about and made for charted waters as quickly as she could.

Before leaving the Bay of Whales, Nilsen had taken a swing into the innermost channel, in order to go beyond *Terra Nova* and keep *Fram*'s record of 'Furthest North and Furthest South'.

Nilsen had twice as far to sail as Pennell on *Terra Nova*. *Fram* was going round the Horn, all the way up the coast of South America to Buenos Aires. She ran into a hurricane, but shrugged it off and once again, in Nilsen's words, 'showed herself in all her glory as the world's best sea-boat'.

On April 17th, Nilson dropped anchor in Buenos Aires roads with the satisfaction of an extraordinary voyage in a splendid ship – and insolvent. Small change had been confiscated at the Bay of Whales for silver soldering and sealing paraffin tanks. He did not have the money to pay for a tender to take him ashore.

Having been led to believe that funds would be waiting for him at Buenos Aires, he found that there were none, and was reduced to the beggary of a seaman in distress. The Norwegian Embassy cabled home for him, and Nilsen learned that no money had been sent, because there was none in the kitty. Amundsen had been more or less deserted by his fellow countrymen. Private subscriptions had been virtually impossible to raise, and such was the undercurrent of feeling against Amundsen's behaviour that the Norwegian Government was afraid to ask the Storting for a grant.

Nilsen was left to his own devices. His only hope now was Don Pedro Christophersen, Amundsen's last-minute benefactor. Don Pedro's original offer had been for fuelling and provisioning the ship; he was now expected to pay all the expenses of the relief.

The Norwegian Minister still happened to be Don Pedro's brother, and he arranged an interview as soon as Nilsen landed. Don Pedro quite understood Amundsen's predicament and undertook to pay the bills. He did so in the most gracious manner, remarking only that 'it would have gone badly if I had not taken care of you'.

But, as Nilsen wrote to Alexander Nansen, the expedition's business manager,

> It was not fair to draw too big a draft on one man ... at home they can naturally say that the expedition went South in all secrecy, and therefore it can manage as best it can. But what is one to do? Norway spends money now and then on vessels to represent the country. Is *Fram* not the best vessel that can be sent out? I won't pretend to say [he continued with a touch of bitter irony], that there is anybody on board particularly qualified to represent the country; but who doesn't know *Fram*? Norway can scarcely be better known than by its flag flying in the world's greatest harbours from the gaff of the world's most famous ship ...

Every man from chief to cook has done, and will do everything for the expedition to reach its goal. It is therefore not exactly encouraging to hear in the first port of call that the country has washed its hands of us.

So Don Pedro looked after *Fram*, paying for the refit she so sorely needed after 20,000 miles at sea.

Nilsen's immediate troubles were over. He could engage the extra seamen he so badly needed for his undermanned craft. On June 8th, he was able to leave as planned on his oceanographic cruise between South America and Southern Africa. It was, in its way, quite original. That part of the ocean, as Fridtjof Nansen wrote to Nilsen was,

so to say, all an unknown world, where previous expeditions have ... done little or nothing of significance. It would be splendid if Norwegians could also show themselves superior in this field. In addition, it will show clearly that the *Fram* expedition is not only a sporting stunt, as some say, but also a scientific enterprise worthy of respect.

Nansen had reasons beyond the purely scientific for his urging.

Terra Nova had beaten *Fram* to the cablehead, bringing the first news of the encounter at the Bay of Whales. As a result, Benjamin Vogt, the Norwegian Ambassador in London, had written to Nansen that there was

quite bitter criticism of Amundsen's unexpected decision to go towards the South Pole.... It has been, I believe, a fairly widespread view, that Amundsen's behaviour has not been fair, not gentlemanly.... I write to ask you whether you could do something to rehabilitate Amundsen and thus his fatherland; you know best yourself, what an incomparable effect your word would have. As [public] opinion seems to be now, I do not look forward with unmixed pleasure to the announcement that A. has arrived first at the South Pole.

Amundsen had undoubtedly damaged the Norwegian cause, although not as much perhaps as Vogt suggested. The attacks were personal, and, on the whole, tried to distinguish between the man and his country.

This was true even of Sir Clements Markham, bombarding Scott Keltie with letters about Amundsen's 'dirty trick', calling him variously a 'blackguard', 'rascal' and 'interloper'. In public Amundsen was accused by Shackleton, with unconscious irony, of 'wintering in Captain Scott's sphere of influence'; by a leader in the *Daily Mail* of attempting to ' "jump" Captain Scott's "claim" '.

Major Leonard Darwin, on the other hand, reiterated his view at an

R.G.S. meeting that 'no explorer obtains any vested right merely by exploration'. But his was a lone voice crying against the crowd. Feeling ran so high, at least in print, that Nansen answered Vogt's call and defended Amundsen in a letter to *The Times*, published on April 26th.

I have had much to do with Amundsen, and on all occasions ... he always acted as a man, and my firm conviction is that an unfair act of any kind would be entirely alien to his nature ... Fearing that [his supporters] might advise him not to go to the Antarctic, he decided not to tell any of us ... And in this he was perhaps right ... he thought he had no right to make us co-responsible and so has taken the whole responsibility upon himself. I cannot help thinking that this is a manly way of proceeding ... As regards the question whether Amundsen had a right to enter [another explorer's territory] ... It must ... be remembered that the bases of operations of Scott and Amundsen lie far apart, there being about the same distance between them as between Spitsbergen and Franz Josef Land. I am certain that not even the keenest monopolist would venture to suggest that it would be unfair to go to Franz Josef Land on an expedition in quest of the North Pole, because another expedition with the same object in view was already on its way to Spitsbergen.

Such was Nansen's authority, and such his goodwill in England, that this letter actually mitigated public opinion, or at least newspaper comment which may pass (more or less) for the same thing. *The Times* itself (in the days when it was a power in the land) declared that there was 'no need to defend the Norwegian explorer from any charge of unfair intrusion'.

But in Norway, Amundsen was suffering an undercurrent of disapproval. Partly it was due to the same fears of British reaction that were preoccupying Vogt. Amundsen's financial insouciance, too, may have played a part. When a bill of exchange he had signed in payment for *Fram*'s diesel motor was dishonoured there was, as the manufacturers' lawyer put it,

absolutely nothing in the till with which to pay and Captain Amundsen has left no assets in Norway that can be attached ... The circumstances can, however, change if he is lucky with his expedition.

Leon Amundsen wrote apologetically to Don Pedro:

When my brother received your charitable offer before his departure from Norway, he had no idea he would be compelled to take advantage of it to the extent that now has been necessary; he felt convinced that his supporters and the Norwegian people would sympathize with the decision he had made to go South, when his reasons were so strong and good ... and he believed definitely he could count on the necessary support to carry out his journey. In that belief he remains today.

He does not know, what I know, that his actions have been condemned in nearly all quarters ... It is a fact which in the highest degree will hurt his sense of honour and sow bitterness in his mind when he learns about it.

On April 21st, the sun set at Framheim, not to reappear for another four months. The question was whether the winter would be long enough for all the preparations for the Polar journey, and from April 18th, Amundsen decreed a working routine.

The days now moved into a settled rhythm from seven-thirty a.m. when Lindstrøm woke everybody and laid the table for breakfast, a calculated device. As Amundsen put it in his diary:

Nothing wakes one up so well as the noise of knives, plates and forks; not to mention when he flings the teaspoons into the enamel mugs.

Work began at nine a.m. and stopped at eleven fifty-five to be ready for lunch at midday precisely, when 'we usually have a lot to talk about – if not, well, silence is not depressing. We find it best and most convenient to shut up.'

Then work again from two until five-fifteen p.m., six days a week. Working hours were for collective equipment: sledges, provisions, dogs and so on. Individual items, like boots, clothing, underwear had to be worked on (and there was much to be done) in spare time, which meant chiefly after dinner. Evening after evening, the table in the hut turned into a medley of a cobbler's, a tailor's, and a furrier's workbench – the reindeer fur clothes needed meticulous renovation and overhaul.

Bjaaland recorded in his inimitable half-mocking, half-serious manner,

Each man has got his special work. Wisting is foreman of the fur tent;* there he has absolute authority. Hanssen is igloo sheriff, on account of his long experience and life in the home of the Eskimo. Prestrud is stargazing.

Kristian Prestrud, alone of *Fram*'s Naval lieutenants to go ashore, in fact was preparing the navigation for the Polar journey. He gave a refresher course in the evenings, attendance at which was compulsory – even for Amundsen.

Inspired perhaps by the story of Scott taking only one set of navigational tables on the Western Journey in 1903, and losing it, Prestrud copied out six in the navigation books. He also wrote out standard forms for latitude sights to simplify work in the field and making checking easier. At the time this was unusual.

* All fur clothes were stored in a tent, as they had to be kept dry and cold.

By a ludicrous mistake, the Nautical Almanac for 1912 had been forgotten, the 1911 edition only being landed, and a single copy to boot. One night it was set on fire by an oil lamp. The flames spontaneously extinguished themselves as they reached the page before the vital tables. Amundsen took this as an omen. In any case, he was now obliged by the Almanac to reach the Pole before the end of the year.

Virtually the only scientific work was the routine meteorological observations. They were taken, Amundsen was careful to note, *outside* working hours at eight a.m., two p.m. and eight p.m. and none during the night, even although that limited their worth. In Amundsen's words,

> Our plan is one, one and again one alone - to reach the pole. For that goal, I have decided to throw everything else aside. We shall do what we can without colliding with this plan. If we were to have a night watch, we would have a light burning the whole time. In one room, as we have, this would be worrying for most of us, and make us weak. What concerns me is that we all live properly in all respects during the winter. Sleep and eat well, so that we have full strength and are in good spirits when spring arrives to fight towards the goal which we must attain at any cost.

The great Polar campaign began with a hitch and a piece of ingenious improvisation. Snow shovels had somehow been forgotten. Bjaaland the carpenter, ski-maker, builder, violin-maker, musician, ski champion, made some out of an iron plate, 'Considerably better,' said Amundsen, 'than one can buy.' By then it was the middle of April, and there loomed the Sisyphean task of digging out the hut from three months' accumulation of snow. It then occurred to someone that it would be easier to tunnel into the drift and make the working space so sorely needed, for the hut was really rather cramped.

The proposal was adopted by acclamation. There grew up a warren of snow caves, most linked by tunnel to the hut. Once more, Amundsen had the right professional skill at his disposal. Stubberud, the house-builder, knew how to construct vaults. Large grottoes therefore could be dug without the risk of the roof collapsing.

Framheim was the forerunner of today's elaborate Antarctic bases underneath the snow. There were not only workshops. There was a laundry. There was a W.C., in Amundsen's words,

> quite American as far as hygiene is concerned. Admittedly we don't have water, but instead we have the dogs [who] in a quick and efficient manner remove the night soil.

When Scott was confronted with a dog's habit of eating excrement, he found it 'horrid' and 'the worst side of dog driving'. On *Discovery* he had had puppies slaughtered for the crime. Amundsen, by contrast, took an entirely practical view of the phenomenon. The dog, especially the Eskimo dog, is a scavenger, with the capacity to recycle excrement.* Why not exploit it? Framheim's W.C. was therefore so arranged that the cesspit could be reached by an external tunnel to which the animals had free access. Since there were over a hundred, they had no difficulty in keeping it clean, thus saving the *men* both time and disagreeable work.

The paraffin drums, dumped outside, had naturally drifted up. Hassel who, as Amundsen put it, was 'managing director of Framheim's Coal, Oil and Coke Co. Ltd.', excavated a cave round them *in situ*, thus obtaining

> the finest paraffin store ... under cover. In this way we have once more used the helping hand that Nature has extended. Wouldn't most people have cleared and shovelled the snow the whole winter under similar circumstances? I think so.

This is a veiled comparison between himself and Scott. Amundsen had decided that their books had shown that the main British weakness in the Antarctic was being overcivilized and fighting Nature. *His* strength was that he tried to work with her. Such comparisons intermittently surfaced. Under the outward calm gnawed the awareness of the rival at McMurdo Sound, and the strain of trying to anticipate his every move.

One thing at least was simple; the necessity of building up technical superiority. Before he sailed, Amundsen knew he was a better and faster Polar traveller than Scott; but he wanted a crushing and unassailable lead. The winter had to be devoted to a meticulous overhaul of all equipment.

The sledges had been, comparatively, a failure. They were far too heavy, because Amundsen had been misled by Shackleton's and Scott's highly charged accounts into supposing that the Barrier was something evil, demanding, treacherous. But, in his words, after the depot journeys,

> The mysterious Barrier of the Englishmen has once and for all disappeared, and must give place to a completely natural phenomenon – a glacier.

There was no mystery about that. The sledges had to be lightened.

More disturbing than sheer weight, the sledges on the depot journeys had run badly. They were from Hagen's in Christiania, the ones Bjaaland had modified on *Fram*. They were the same models unquestioningly accepted by Scott. The trouble was that they were production models,

---

* It can extract fat, proteins, vitamins and certain enzymes.

where individual craftsmanship was needed. Amundsen discarded them and, in their stead, Bjaaland reworked four sledges from Sverdrup's second *Fram* expedition, built by a more inspired maker, who unfortunately had gone out of business.

By planing down the runners and thinning the other components, Bjaaland reduced their weight from fifty to thirty-five kilos, without weakening them structurally. He also made three new sledges, light and flexible.

There, in a snow cave, with a few boards laid on a snow shelf for a workbench, Bjaaland turned out his little masterpieces of the ski and sledge-maker's art. The wood he used was hickory; tough, pliable, well seasoned; the same hickory that Amundsen had so prudently bought in Pensacola a decade before.* With primus stoves and tin plate from old paraffin tins, Bjaaland made the steaming chamber to bend the runners. In another workshop, Wisting and Helmer Hanssen assembled the sledges with rawhide lashings. This is a little craft in itself; upon it depends the elasticity of the sledge, and hence the ease of running. Helmer Hanssen, who had driven sledges for thousands of miles, had the particular touch for this work; he *knew* how a sledge ought to behave.

The old *Fram* sledges were adapted to difficult ice, Bjaaland's for speed on level snow. The former were intended for the glaciers leading to the Polar plateau. Once that climb was over and mobility was at a premium, they would be depoted, and Bjaaland's light-weight models would continue. These weighed twenty-four kilos to the renovated *Fram* models' thirty-five, and Hagen's seventy-five. Bjaaland also prepared two pairs of skis for each man, one for running, and one in reserve, to be stowed on the sledges. The work was finished by July 20th.

In deep cold, Amundsen wrote with his wry humour, 'if one is not properly shod, one can soon be without feet, and then, you see, it's too late to shoe yourself properly'.

For the third time the ski boots, having still proved too small, were eviscerated and enlarged with a wedge in the toecap – each man his own cobbler – emerging big enough for two Eskimo reindeer fur socks, plenty of sennegrass, a thick woollen sock with space to move the feet inside, essential to avoid freezing. The original stiff canvas uppers were now replaced with thinner material. After almost two years, the original concept appeared finally to have been realized, and a boot emerged that was rigid enough to control the skis and be used with crampons, but

* See p. 77.

flexible enough not to impede the raising of the heel or (it was hoped) to constrict the circulation.

Much else was modified and rebuilt. Since the dogs ate the narwhal hide heel straps of the ski bindings, Bjaaland fitted them with hooks so that they could be detached from the skis at night and taken into the tents. Stubberud planed down fifty sledging cases to save three kilos each. They were then permanently lashed to the sledges, because, to save time and energy on the march, there would be no stowing and restowing. Food would be taken, as necessary, through the openings in the cases.

Cooking equipment was brought down from thirty to five kilos. On a treadle sewing machine in one of the snow caves, Wisting sewed new tents out of light windcloth to bring the weight down from ten kilos to six. A new pattern with a sewn-in floor (unusual at that time) erected from inside by a single light bamboo pole, they were designed to be easily pitched in a gale.

The trouble was, however, that the cloth was white. On three counts, Amundsen preferred a dark tent: visibility against the snow, rest for the eyes after the day's work in the dazzling sunshine of high latitudes, and superior absorption of solar radiation to heat the inside more effectively. 'Well, well,' as he put it in his diary, 'we rarely allow ourselves to be beaten'; and a dye was concocted out of ink powder and black shoe polish.

And so on and on: snow goggles, anoraks, underwear, ('Of our inner garments,' wrote Amundsen, 'we are fondest of the woollen vests Betty knitted for us'), dog harnesses; all the impedimenta of Polar travel were overhauled and (usually) altered in the restless search for safety and perfection.

Amundsen had the personal magnetism that is the hallmark of great leaders. It was recognized by men of such widely differing characters and backgrounds as Shackleton, Bjørn Helland-Hansen and Lincoln Ellsworth and Admiral Byrd, the American air pioneer. At Framheim, even Johansen recognized it.

Amundsen grasped the psychology of small groups; he had an almost feminine sensitivity for the undertones and cross-currents on which a leader has to play. He worked hard, and with considerable subtlety, to eliminate the strains that beset a Polar expedition.

In a small isolated community, where imaginary mole hills turn into hallucinatory mountains, morning peevishness is a considerable emotional hazard. Scott, for example, was decidedly peevish in the mornings, visited his tetchiness on whoever happened to cross his path, and left it at that. Amundsen, having greater insight, controlled himself, and evolved a scheme to eliminate the same moodiness in his companions.

He organized a competition to guess the temperature, with substantial prizes every month and a telescope at the end of the season for the winner overall. Ostensibly, this was to develop the ability to judge temperature in case all thermometers were to break on the Polar journey.

Because of the prizes [he wrote in his diary] everybody insists on going out to look at the weather. And that's why the prizes have been put up. But nobody knew it. I find this little morning visit out in the open so beneficial. Even if it is but for a minute or two, it is unbelievable how that short time helps to wake a sleepy man and bring feelings into equilibrium before [the day's first] cup of nice, warm coffee.

Even the best-humoured person in the world has a touch of morning peevishness, and that has to be removed as unnoticeably as possible. If a morning peevish person notices that you are putting yourself out to remove his burden, he becomes double peevish.

Amundsen had to tread a narrow path between regularity and monotony.

Because of all the work, recreation was necessarily limited. Prestrud gave an optional English course to a few of the men, teaching in the kitchen to avoid disturbing the others. Bjaaland started making a violin, but found that he did not have enough free time to finish it in the course of the winter. In the end, he took it back to Norway, where it was finished by a professional craftsman, and turned out to be a very good instrument.

For the rest, there was a little reading – mostly Polar literature, of which a small but comprehensive library had been brought – some desultory card playing and, craze of the early winter, darts. This game was new to most of them; a present from Målfred, Gustav Amundsen's wife. Amundsen organized a competition, presenting a pocket chronometer as prize.

To prevent ennui, Amundsen broke the weekly routing with little occasions to look forward to. On weekdays, there was no drinking with meals, but every Saturday there was hot brandy toddy; every Sunday, holiday and birthday, aquavit for dinner. The idea was partly to nip quarrels in the bud: among Scandinavians there is a ritual significance in drinking spirits. The *skål* is a pledge of friendship.

Saturday was sauna night. That, too, was a kind of ritual; a ceremonial cleansing of body and spirit. A small sauna had been rigged up in an igloo, heat and steam provided by two Primus stoves under a metal tray.

A naked sprint through an icy communication tunnel in the Barrier to the hut did duty for the obligatory rolling in the snow.

In many ways, circumstances favoured Amundsen in his concern for morale. Although most of his men lived in towns, they were still Northern country-dwellers under the imperfectly urbanized surface; men of simple tastes, adapted to isolated habitation and, indeed, without being recluses seeking isolation as relaxation and uplift. In their separate workshops under the snow, they were alone for much of the day, so that by evening they were positively glad to see the old, familiar faces. And the dogs were always there as a diversion, as they banished monotony on the march.

Each man had fourteen or fifteen dogs to tend and feed – seal meat (and blubber) and stockfish on alternate days. By midwinter they were fed up with stockfish.

We have [wrote Amundsen, with his eye for a telling anecdote] a rather funny example of a dog's intelligence in this field. Jørgen [Stubberud] has a pup – Funcho – born at Madeira ... He had the habit of not turning up on fish evenings ... But Jørgen [Stubberud] tried the trick of taking the meat box one evening ... and pretending he was ... serving meat. When Funcho saw him coming with the meatbox on his shoulder, he ... followed him ... and was served with a stockfish for supper.

Funcho hadn't yet become acquainted with mankind's many tricks and dodges. But he learned soon enough, and now Jørgen can't fool him any more.

On another occasion, The Shark, a delinquent dog, stole his neighbour's supper. Amundsen tried to force The Shark to make restitution, but he objected. The battle became heated, and in the end they were rolling over and over in the snow, locked in a grip, like wrestlers in the ring. Amundsen did not give up until he had prised the food out of The Shark's jaws and returned it to its rightful owner. Amundsen was unharmed; he would not let a dog get the better of him.

The dogs were tethered in their tents at night,* ten or twelve to a tent, dug down in pits four feet deep, so that the effect was of shallow snow caves roofed with canvas. This was to make them snug and warm – for snow is a good insulator – and save the tents from their teeth and claws.

During the day the dogs were allowed to roam free. They fought little, but several disappeared on illicit excursions, returning hungry and

---

* Although, so close to the Pole, it is dark most of the 24 hours (and light round the clock in summer) by convention the hours of light or darkness at lower latitudes are called 'day' and 'night' if only to preserve something of the normal time sense.

sheepish after a few days. The weather favoured the truants who, with a dog's instinct, doubtless knew exactly what they were about.

The Framheim climate, as Amundsen put it, was 'ideal'. Wind was uncommon; to the benefit of temper and morale. There is nothing so wearing to the spirit as the incessant shriek and battering of storms in the wilderness.

At Cape Evans, Scott had every opportunity to observe this. He had gale force winds (twenty-four m.p.h. and over) more than thirty per cent of the time, to Amundsen's four point two per cent; *seven times as much*.

Framheim was, however, much colder, with an average winter temperature of $-38°$ (C.) against $-27°$ (C.) at Cape Evans. Fifty degrees of frost was common; sometimes the thermometer fell to almost 60 degrees. The dogs were glad to get back to their tents.

> Poor devils [Johansen wrote in a gloomy moment], [they] enjoy life as much as they can in the cold and the dark, they have food enough, eat, sleep, have their amorous adventures when the bitches are on heat; but the pups who have lately come into the world soon succumbed to a relentlessly grim Nature, and happy they are, I think, who escape the little enviable life of a sledge dog — for no animal can have a worse life than the sledge dog.

They were making new whips, with shafts that would hold when they had to lash the dogs on.

> It may seem strange and uncultivated and brutal, that one lashes the dogs so that the [whip] shafts break, but for those who have driven with dogs, tired dogs, hungry dogs, and dogs suffering in the cold with heavy loads and bad going; for him it is different. One does not have to be more brutal than other people; one can suffer because one has to do so, but if one does not use the means he has to get the dogs forward, when it is difficult, he may just as well give up completely. It is at any rate [one's own] life that is at stake.

'The fate of nations,' says Brillat Savarin, 'depends on the way they eat.' How then, are we to judge Lindstrøm, the cook at Framheim?

Norwegians are not gourmets, but sixty years later, Stubberud could still remember with pleasure Lindstrøm's 'hot cakes'.

One of the set pieces of life at Framheim was the appearance at the breakfast table of the solid, beaming form of Lindstrøm surmounting with surrogate domesticity a platter with a pile of 'hot cakes', which he had learned to make in America. They were wolfed liberally covered in preserved whortleberries and cloudberries, traditional Norwegian anti-scorbutics.

Amundsen, haunted still by his experience on *Belgica*, was concerned, indeed, obsessed with the absolute, vital necessity of preventing scurvy; Scott, by comparison, after *his* experience on *Discovery*, did not take the matter seriously enough. Amundsen insisted on a diet of fresh, or at least deep-frozen seal, which was served daily both for lunch and supper; at the latter, covered in whortleberry preserve.

Lindstrøm was a 'Polar' cook, able to prepare seal meat both appetizingly, and nutritiously. Reduced to essentials, this meant underdone dishes which, as we now know, preserved most of the Vitamin C.

All through the winter, then, Amundsen's men were building up their stock of Vitamin C, for the human body, although unable to synthesize it, can store it for a time. Their defences against scurvy were as high as they could make them. Also they ate wholemeal bread fortified by wheat germ, leavened by fresh yeast which Lindstrøm contrived to brew.

This provided the Vitamin B Complex, the importance of which in Polar history has been overshadowed by the more spectacular Vitamin C deficiency. Vitamin B, however, affects the human metabolism; the effects of a deficiency are insidious and can lead to mental and nervous symptoms.

Seal meat, brown bread, 'hot cakes' and berries, were the main food of the Norwegians; a simple, natural and nutritious diet.

At Cape Evans, in Tryggve Gran's words, the British expedition 'lived in a princely fashion [with] things which would be considered delicacies even in civilization'. There was white bread, not brown; much tinned food was used, poor in Vitamin C. Seal meat was not served daily, and then overdone. This was a refined and etiolated diet.

Such, then, was the way each expedition was building up its bodily reserves for the coming trial. Fate was sitting at the dinner table.

Amundsen cultivated simplicity in sledging rations, reducing his ingredients to four: pemmican, chocolate, biscuits and powdered milk. All sugar was in the chocolate. Tea and coffee were abandoned as dangerous stimulants and useless weight.

Pemmican was boiled up into a thick stew (or 'hoosh' as it was known in Scott's camp). The chocolate and powdered milk were combined into a hot, nourishing drink. For quenching thirst, there was the old Eskimo remedy: melted snow in unlimited quantities.

Questions of health apart, Amundsen wanted simplicity because it meant easier housekeeping on the march. He wanted flexibility. He had worked out contingency plans for various circumstances, and all food was arranged and specially packed so that daily rations for any number from two to eight men could be easily extracted.

The dogs' travelling diet was arranged with equal care. Amundsen had devised a special dog pemmican for eating cold. It differed from the ordinary kind in containing fish meal and a higher proportion of fat. The ration was one pound per dog per day and, frozen solid, it was something to gnaw on. It was also fit for human consumption, and could be used as reserve rations. Amundsen had worked out how to cook it so that it was palatable – rather like a full-bodied fish stew – just in case.

Johansen was asked to pack the provisions, a task requiring patience and conscientiousness. These were, as Amundsen had discerned, Johansen's virtues. Amundsen tried hard to suit the work to the man.

Week after week, Johansen patiently crouched over his tins and boxes in the 'Crystal Palace', as he whimsically called his workshop under the snow. Nothing illustrates the concept of the expedition so well as Johansen's instructions and the way he carried them out. 'Not a millimetre must be wasted,' Amundsen had said, not out of pedantry, but to save packing cases, and hence, weight, which in a crisis might perhaps be the little detail that avoided disaster.

Since the pemmican was cylindrical, there were empty spaces in between. Into these, Johansen packed the dried milk in thin bags (sewn by Wisting) like sausages. There still remained some space in the interstices, and into this he managed to fit the chocolate, carefully broken up into individual squares. The biscuits had to be taken out of the maker's boxes, counted, repacked in the sledging cases, and the number, layer by layer, entered in the provision books. Johansen finished this tedious work at the end of July, by which time, he noted in his diary, he had counted 42,000 biscuits, opened 1,321 tins of pemmican, and stowed the contents, likewise 100.8 kilos of chocolate and 203 'sausages' of dried milk holding 300 grammes each. As an extra precaution he had made a light portable scale to take along to the Pole.

Amundsen, who believed in making everyone feel that his work was essential, showered praise on Johansen.

It was, incidentally, one of Amundsen's principles to keep out of the workshops as much as possible, until asked to come and look. He delegated thoroughly, and felt that intrusion, however innocent, might appear as snooping, which definitely was not good for morale.

Amundsen had to tread warily with Johansen, for within them lay the seeds of conflict. And in those circumstances, that meant lives in danger. The mountaineer on the rope; the explorer with his sledge; the astronaut in his capsule; to anyone in an extreme environment, where the external act of treading the frontiers of survival is somehow matched internally by an approach to the borderlands of sanity, the strain of personal conflict is a mortal hazard.

Amundsen had under him four men of roughly equivalent Polar experience. Hassel, Helmer Hanssen, Linstrøm and Johansen. Only Johansen posed a threat to his authority, trying (consciously or not) to assume the psychological leadership. It was like Scott and Shackleton on *Discovery*.

Johansen was physically the stronger; also the better skier and dog-driver, of which he was ever conscious. He considered too, that he knew more than Amundsen about Polar travel. At intervals, he made all this plain, by correcting and contradicting Amundsen, and volunteering advice.

Now behind Amundsen's authority lay a raw sensitivity that often saw in plainly phrased statements a deliberate personal affront. His men quickly learned that things had to be put in the form of a question, given which, he was quite prepared to discuss anything rationally, even his cherished prejudices. Johansen did not bow to this quirk. Amundsen contained his irritation, which, until the crisis came to a head, can only be detected in veiled undertones in his diary. Unlike Scott, who in his diaries could be copiously vindictive about his companions, Amundsen avoided the record of explicit criticism, as if the very act of committing it to paper somehow constituted an act of treachery, poisonous to the atmosphere.

Johansen was suffering from a full measure of frustration, resentment and remorse. He was the everlasting number two, burdened with a sense of failure. On top of it all, he was an alcoholic in a state of abstinence, which added to the strain. It was not an easy situation for Amundsen. He coped by disarming the rivalry and making an ally of Johansen. There was no formal hierarchy under Amundsen, but by implication he allowed Johansen to stand as second in command.

It is a measure of Amundsen's achievement that for most of the winter the note of querulousness virtually disappears from Johansen's diary. Johansen still had bouts of melancholia, but this probably nobody but a guardian angel could help. After his miserable years of drifting, he was touchingly eager to feel useful and accepted. This need Amundsen humanely contrived to meet.

It was only a truce; under the surface the sources of conflict remained. But at least Amundsen had kept tensions under control, his party un-divided, morale high. The work was going well.

Underneath the self-confidence ran the worry about Scott; or rather Scott's motor sledges. As winter waned and the sense of time passing welled up, Amundsen began to fret over the dangers of being beaten to the post. Usually this was expressed in the form of boastful (but nonetheless penetrating) comparisons with the British. He told Johansen, for example, that the morale of Norwegian Polar expeditions was better than the British in the Antarctic.

On July 11th, Amundsen entered in his diary an extensive criticism of Shackleton.

> Either the Englishmen must have had bad dogs [he said about Shackleton's disparagement of those animals] or – they didn't know how to use them.
> Then comes S's reference to fur clothes. [In *The Heart of the Antarctic*.] Furs are not necessary, he opines [because they were not used], on *Discovery* or *Nimrod*. That is enough to prove that furs are unnecessary. Very possibly so. But [why then] does S. complain so often about the cold on his long Southern journey? ... One thing, I think I can ... say, if Shackleton had been equipped in a practical manner; dogs, fur clothes and, above all, skis, ... and, naturally understood their use ... well then, the South Pole would have been a closed chapter. I admire in the highest degree what he and his companions achieved with the equipment they had. Bravery, determination, strength they did not lack. A little more experience – preferably a journey in the far worse conditions in the Arctic ice – would have crowned their work with success.

This is a shrewd judgment and Amundsen returned to the subject:

> The English have loudly and openly told the world that skis and dogs are unusable in these regions and that fur clothes are rubbish. We will see – we will see. I don't want to boast – it's not exactly in my line, but when people decide to attack the methods which have brought the Norwegians into the *leader class* as polar explorers – skis and dogs, well, then, one must be allowed to be irritated and try to show the world that it is not only luck that brought us through with the help of such means, but calculation and understanding of how to use them.

This kind of outburst was rare for the first part of the winter. The darkness, the work, the knowledge that Scott, even with his motor sledges, could not be travelling, allowed him a measure of calm. But as the midday strip of dawn grew daily on the northern horizon and spring was seen to approach, the tensions and misgivings, which he had been keeping under control, began to stir. Amundsen was approaching a crisis.

He could almost hear the English motor sledges stuttering far ahead over the Barrier already on the way to the Pole. But there was something beyond the mere rivalry with Scott. He had obscure forebodings about aspects of his own plan. He intended to take seven companions, leaving Lindstrøm to look after Framheim alone. But, by all known standards, eight was too many for a Polar journey. There would be two tents, with dangers to cohesiveness. And were his margins of safety enough to take everybody on to the Pole? Nor did he like the idea of support parties turning back, because of the emotional strain of separation. He was also worried about Johansen. In a crisis his latent challenge to his leader's authority could surface and cause division and disaster. Mutiny, in the deepest sense, was a possibility.

This was indeed more than a personal crisis; it was a crisis of command. It could not necessarily be resolved by wholly rational and conscious means – even by so pre-eminently a rational leader as Amundsen.

He was now tormented by doubt and vacillation and started changing plans. On July 4th, he presented what he called his 'improved' plan, which involved starting in the middle of September instead of November 1st as originally intended. They would all, eight men with eighty-four dogs, go as far as the 83°-depot. There, they would build igloos and wait for the arrival of the midnight sun, about the middle of October, before finally setting off for the Pole. At the end of July, having preached concentration on a single goal, he suddenly suggested a preliminary thrust into Kind Edward VII Land, as he said, to test equipment. Twice he put it to the vote – something that Scott would never have done – and twice was defeated unanimously. He accepted the result, then returned to his original concept of sticking to the Pole, and now decided to leave on August 24th, the day the sun returned. This was ridiculously early. Johansen warned him against it. He remembered his experience with Nansen in the Arctic when they set off too early only to be driven back by the cold. But Amundsen brushed aside Johansen's protests – and his own misgivings? – and imposed his authority. But there was worry and doubt in the air. Amundsen's unease had communicated itself to his companions. In Hassel's words, 'The thought of the English gave him no peace. For if we were not first at the Pole, we might just as well stay at home.'

25

Wintering at Cape Evans

AT CAPE EVANS, the foreign challenge was met by pretending that it did not exist. For the first few weeks after the return from the depot journey, there was a tacit agreement to ignore Polar matters in general and the expedition's plight in particular. 'It was,' says Gran, 'as if a notice had been put up: "Shop talk not permitted."'

Thoughts however could not be stopped and Frank Debenham probably spoke for the majority when he said in his diary that

> Amundsen's chances ... are rather better than ours. To begin with they are
> 60 miles further South than we are and can make due south at once, whereas
> we have to dodge round islands.... if [Scott] will consult the senior men I
> think it can be done but if he keeps them in the dark as they were on this
> depot trip things are likely to go wrong.

Finally on May 8th, Scott presented his plans for the Polar journey. At the head of the long table in the hut, under the steely glow of the acetylene lamp, using a large map sketched in blue pencil to illustrate his points, he discoursed in his flat, prosaic, oddly uninspiring public manner. It was an astonishing performance. It was obvious that he had arrived in the Antarctic without any plan worthy of the name and, a year and three quarters after the start of the expedition, was offering belated improvisations. It was equally obvious that his audience found nothing strange in such casual behaviour.

The timetable for the Polar dash with which Scott began his exposition was based not on an estimate of his own capabilities, but on Shackleton's figures in 1908. Since Scott and Shackleton were hardly on speaking terms, the figures came not from Shackleton himself, but from *The Heart of the Antarctic*. It is typical of the expedition, that this indispensable work had been omitted from the library, and if Griffith Taylor had not happened to bring his own copy, it would not have been there for Scott to consult. Scott proposed leaving on November 3rd. Taking 144 days for the 1,530 miles to the Pole and back, this meant returning to Hut Point on March 27th.

'Therefore,' said Scott, 'the Pole party will almost certainly be too late for the ship.'

March 27th was dangerously late. It was flying in the face of all experience, his own included. It would probably be cold on the Barrier, especially for tired men. Amundsen, although infinitely better prepared, with wolfskin and bearskin for the very worst conditions, declined under any circumstances to consider a return to Framheim later than the end of January. The beginning of February had been almost too much for Shackleton. But *that* lesson, Scott chose to ignore. Was Shackleton almost overcome by so much cold and so many setbacks? Scott would show that he could endure twice as much.

It was when he turned to transport that Scott revealed to the full his muddle-headedness. Having first put all his trust in the motor sledges, he had now lost faith in them altogether.

The dogs had been a disappointment. This was an arbitrary, not to say irrational statement, made in the face of very considerable evidence to the contrary. On the return from the depot journey, the dogs had run twenty or thirty miles a day, bringing Scott home far ahead of the pony party. Nonetheless, he decided the dogs were unlikely to reach the Beardmore Glacier. He was 'inclined to chuck them for the last part of the journey'.

Ponies, he announced, were the only reliable form of transport, but they could only be taken to the foot of the Glacier. Thence, for the 1,000 miles or so, and 10,000 feet of climbing to the Pole and back, it would be man-hauling all the way.

I for one am delighted at the decision [wrote Bowers]. After all, it will be a fine thing to do that plateau with man-haulage in these days of the supposed decadence of the British race.

Bowers was echoing Scott's heroic yearnings, enshrined in *The Voyage of the 'Discovery'*. George Simpson, the meteorologist, observed in his diary that Scott's plans assumed the best possible conditions, making no allowances for delays. 'It appears that with all our resources,' he wrote, 'there is little margin, and a few accidents or a spell of bad weather would not only bring failure but very likely disaster.'

Scott did consider the question of endurance. They would have to spend seventy-five days at high altitude on the Plateau and its approaches. 'I don't know whether it is possible for men to last out that time,' were his final words. 'I almost doubt it.'

It is illuminating that Bowers, in Cherry-Garrard's words, 'transparently simple, straightforward and unselfish', perhaps the most naive of them all, was practically alone in his unqualified enthusiasm. Like

Simpson, others felt the stirrings of disquiet. 'Things generally turn out for the best,' Wilson enigmatically wrote in his diary, 'and generally in a different way to what one expects.'

Gran was nonplussed by Scott's attitude to dogs.

That dogs are so unusable as assumed, I doubt. I wonder if there is not in this question of dogs a certain consolation before Amundsen with his hundred hounds?

Scott did, indeed, have a sneaking suspicion that dogs might be a trump – for those who knew how to use them. He had fleetingly considered using the ponies to pull the dogs across the Barrier for the final push. He mistakenly believed that dogs could sprint but were not stayers. In any case, he shrank from driving the dogs on, killing them to feed to each other. But, underlying his squeamishness, there seemed to be a tragi-comic resentment against the breed for interfering with his romantic delusions: a working dog has an inimitable capacity to prick the bubble of human self-importance. 'No journey ever made with dogs,' as Scott had written in the *Voyage of the 'Discovery'*, 'can approach the height of that fine conception which is realized when a party with their unaided efforts, go forth to face hardships.'*

Years afterwards, Meares bitterly condemned Scott as a 'sentimental-ist'. At the time, he told Oates that 'Scott ought to buy a shilling book about transport'. Scott overheard this and was not pleased; un-fortunately, it was the only criticism brought to his attention. Most of his people were afraid of him and hesitated to speak out.

Preparations for the Polar journey did not start until after the middle of June, two months later than Amundsen. The ratings alone overhauled equipment, working half days only.

Indeed, Scott's preparations were even more behindhand than they appeared. Almost two years after deciding to go for the Pole, he had not yet considered the subject of Polar diet. After the disastrous outbreak of scurvy on *Discovery*, this argues for a certain insouciance. Now, less than six months before starting for the Pole, he turned his attention to the matter, and got Bowers to read up sledging rations from such books as were available. It is wholly characteristic that Scott turned to an un-qualified tyro. Likewise, Cherry-Garrard, another beginner, was told to prepare a report on igloo-building, Scott's first recorded interest in the matter twelve years after entering Polar exploration.

*

In most things, the British and Norwegian camps made a contrast. At Framheim, everybody lived together in an atmosphere between that of a mountain hut and a sealing ship. Cape Evans, on the other hand, was a hybrid of warship and academic common room. The hut was divided across the middle by a partition of packing cases. On the one side, the officers, scientists, and (broadly speaking) gentlemen; on the other, the Naval ratings (with Anton and Dmetri, the Russian groom and dog boys) lived their separate lives.

This might have been only a matter of style. In social structure, the Royal Navy had changed little since *Discovery* days. Officers and men were still rigidly segregated and, since this expedition was being run in Naval style, it remained logical and sensible, as on *Discovery*, to maintain Naval distinctions in the snow. The contrast with the Norwegians lay deeper, in the quality of leadership.

The all-pervading sense of urgency at Framheim was little in evidence at Cape Evans. Winter passed in leisurely, amateur, almost dilettante fashion, reminiscent of *Discovery* days. Volunteers were depended on for chores, so the willing horses were overworked. Travelling technique was neglected, and Gran, instead of teaching skiing, found himself playing moonlight football. There was, however, a journal – *The South Polar Times*, editor, Cherry-Garrard – sequel to the *Discovery* effort. There were lectures; three a week; too many in the opinion of most. Scott grasped he had a good faculty among the scientists, and got them to lecture by the use of 'compulsory volunteers'. All kinds of abstruse subjects were ventilated; but remarkably few had any bearing on Polar travel. A navigation course was absent, although in 'Teddy' Evans Scott had a navigation specialist.

A different man appears when Scott turns from Polar matters to presiding, at the end of the long table, after dinner, over what was called 'Universitas Antarctica'. Scott now seemed in his element; more an academic than a Naval officer. Simpson was impressed by Scott's 'versatile mind. There is no specialist here who is not pleased to discuss his problems with him.' Scott would have been happy as a technical specialist. With his literary gifts, his true metier may well have been that of scientific popularizer.

He undoubtedly saw in science an agent of prestige. He fretted at the slightest sign of inactivity among his scientists (although it might only have been a pause for thought) fearing the effect on the results and hence his standing as expedition leader.

Scott was now going through a personal crisis. The twin challenge of Shackleton and Amundsen seemed to have unmanned him. The moodiness and irritability of *Discovery* days had turned with the years into long bouts of severe depression interleaved with spasms of euphoria. He had lost any adaptability he might have had, and become frighteningly inflexible. He withdrew into himself, an island among his men, at a distance from reality.

It is easy to see this as an outcome of the isolation with which the Royal Naval captain was surrounded swathed in a mystique, like God Almighty on his ship. It would be more correct to say that Scott was the wrong kind of captain. He was a 'big ship' man, used to the anonymity of large and complex crews, where what was really wanted was a 'small ship man', the captain of a destroyer, a light cruiser, or even a submarine; used to close contact with his men. The Navy recognized the difference; it was concerned with personality, and the one could not be made into the other.

But even within each kind there were, naturally, good and bad. There were plenty of big ship captains who knew how to make contact with their subordinates, and understood exactly what was happening in the furthest corner of their ships. But the strain was great and it required a strong man to bear the isolation. Scott was not strong enough, and he had been marked by a situation beyond his powers.

He now laboured under a sense of being deserted by the Navy. At Cape Town and Lyttelton he had got no help from the Naval dockyards, a humiliating gesture when compared to the aid given him on *Discovery*. The implications were clear; his promotion depended on what happened at ninety degrees South. If all went well, he could expect to be Rear Admiral in 1913. It was the Pole or nothing.

It was enough to try the strength of anyone and Scott needed all the support he could get. He leaned on Wilson as his spiritual prop; on Bowers as his right-hand man in practical affairs. Wilson was a guide and confidant; the intermediary between Scott and his subordinates. Bowers ran the base. Between the two, they exercised certain functions of leadership, and ousted Teddy Evans from his formal standing as second in command.

The animosity that surfaced when Scott took over command of *Terra Nova* from Evans at the Cape had now come to a head. A conflict had arisen between the two that paralleled the one germinating at their end of the Barrier between Amundsen and Johansen.

Evans had not forgiven Scott for his favouritism towards P.O. Evans, but Amundsen was indirectly the cause of their conflict coming to a head. Campbell, after his glimpse of Framheim, had grasped that if Scott was to have a chance of beating Amundsen, he would have to change his plans. However, a lieutenant did not lightly volunteer advice to a

Naval captain, especially one of Scott's irascibility, so Campbell passed the buck to Evans, who thereupon suggested, amongst other things, sending a proposed Western party south instead to concentrate forces on the Pole. It was not a bad idea, but Scott treated it as verging on mutiny, because a junior officer had offered unsolicited advice. Evans merely succeeded in goading Scott too far. He collapsed before Scott's eruption of hostility, and was reduced to a cipher. The psychological leadership – without his seeking it – passed to Oates. It is significant that the Naval ratings turned instinctively for help not to their own officers, of whom there were four (Scott, Evans, Atkinson, Bowers), but to Oates, the Army man – 'Soldier', as he was nicknamed or, inevitably 'Titus', after Titus Oates, the seventeenth-century intriguer. 'Captain Oates good to horses,' as Anton put it, 'good to Anton.'

In that company, there was something poignantly symbolic about Oates. He was the odd man out. He was the representative of the old order; one of the landed gentry, an eighteenth-century squire, among a lot of Edwardian bourgeoisie and, on the other side of the partition, the working class. He stood for a doomed world among the inheritors of a new. Most of his companions appreciated his aristocratic virtues; his detachment, tolerance and disdain for petty social conventions.

Oates had to endure some chaff for his little private cult of Napoleon, whom he admired as a soldier, and a picture of whom was the only decoration in his cubicle. About the only books he was observed to read were the five volumes of Napier's *Peninsular War*. This, too, caused some teasing. On June 18th, the anniversary of Waterloo, Oates was woken by a chorus of 'Now then, get up and salute Napoleon. Who won the battle?' Oates took part in the schoolboy ragging that was a feature of the expedition, and had found much use for his quiet imperturbable humour. Debenham saw the truth. Behind the amiable cavalry officer was 'quite a scholar in war history, and we want him to give a lecture on it'. Oates declined; but he did talk about horses and, as Scott put it in his diary, indulged 'a pleasant conceit in finishing . . . with a merry tale'. Oates was almost alone among the lecturers in making his listeners laugh.

He would spend hours in the stables before a blubber stove. Scott supposed it was because he loved his horses. This was true. It was also true that he preferred their company to that of Scott. When Oates disliked his companions or commanders, he usually went into the stables.

Outward, driving will, as distinct from inward, personal ambition is the hallmark of leadership. Amundsen possessed both; Scott only the ambition. This was the failure of personality that put its stamp on the British expedition. Scott was perhaps too self-centred to be a good leader under any circumstances. He antagonized too many of his men. It was impossible to overcome all the consequences of weak leadership. Underneath the surface amity, the party lacked cohesion and its morale was poor. An eloquent sign was the fragmentation into cliques. None perhaps is so significant as that of Oates, Meares and Atkinson. They were set apart by experience that made them conscious of Scott's immaturity, and drawn together by serious disapproval of his failings as a leader. The cross-currents of conflict boded ill for the future.

June 27th saw the start of a venture that was a classic example of heroism for heroism's sake. It was the winter journey to Cape Crozier undertaken by Wilson, Bowers and Cherry-Garrard. This produced one of the great works of literature to issue from Polar exploration: Cherry-Garrard's *The Worst Journey in the World*.

But that is another story. In the context of the expedition it was an irrelevance. The journey was engineered by Wilson to fetch the egg of an Emperor penguin at a particular stage of incubation. It was also supposed to test rations and equipment - something that could have been done years before with far less risk and suffering. When the party staggered back to Cape Evans, after five weeks in thirty and forty and fifty degrees of frost, miserably cold, their clothing manifestly defective, unsuitable, frozen into icy armour plate, Wilson's verdict was, 'The gear is excellent, excellent.' But, said Scott in his diary:

One continues to wonder as to the possibilities of fur clothing as made by the Esquimaux, with a sneaking feeling that it may outclass our more civilized garb. For us this can only be a matter of speculation, as it would have been quite impossible to have obtained such articles. With the exception of this radically different alternative, I feel sure we are as near perfection as experience can direct.

Amundsen, of course, had no difficulty acquiring Eskimo fur clothing. At the eleventh hour, this was Scott's first recorded hint of ever having considered the idea.

In most respects the Winter Journey had been a bizarre exercise. It had been man-hauling. Skis had been left behind because none of the three was practised enough to use them. Sometimes the trio only did a mile or two a day. On that one experience, the rations for the Polar journey were calculated. The Winter Journey made no contribution to Polar technique, because no one applied the knowledge so laboriously garnered: no one altered clothing, no one reconsidered the dangerous absurdity of man-hauling. What the journey did do was to sap the stamina of the two who eventually went to the Pole, and it showed once again that Scott and Wilson were inept at learning from experience.

And so the winter drew to an end. The sledging season began on September 9th, when Teddy Evans, Gran and Forde, one of the seamen, left for Corner Camp to dig out the depots. It was as well they did, because the depots had been amateurishly built and were hard to find. The journey was all man-hauling and, coming báck, Evans ordered a forced march, covering thirty-five miles in twenty-four hours, all in one stretch. There was no need to do so, and it was an exhausting performance, but Evans felt the need of proving himself before Scott.

On September 15th, Scott, Bowers, Simpson and P.O. Evans went, also man-hauling, to the Western Mountains. 'It is not quite clear,' Debenham commented, 'why they are going or what they are going to do.'

Scott himself called it a 'jaunt'. He wanted to look at a glacier and try out his cameras, but in reality it was, once more, activity for its own sake. Scott went 150 miles in a senseless direction; he would have done better to go on to the Barrier and move fresh seal meat along the road to the south.

On September 13th, meanwhile, Scott had explained his final plans for the Polar journey.

> Everyone was enthusiastic [he wrote in his diary]. Although people have given a good deal of thought to various branches of the subject, there was not a suggestion offered for improvement.

This was, however, not because there were no criticisms to make, but because the critics had been silenced. It is a comment on the atmosphere that Scott had demonstratively got Teddy Evans, his formal second in command, out of the way before revealing what was in his mind.

Scott was going to use four kinds of transport: ponies, dogs, man-hauling and motors, with support parties weaving back and forth, depots being laid until the last moment. There was considerable scope for error and confusion. Late in the season, when accidents were likely to occur, it would be difficult to send out relief. 'A decidedly intricate apparatus', was Gran's very private comment in his diary, repeating his forebodings from the depot journey. The imperfections were also obvious to Simpson, for example, to Debenham, Meares, Wright and Oates. Scott, however, having consistently proved to be stubborn and resentful before criticism, still did not invite frankness, and so they all preferred to keep their opinions to themselves. Once more taking appearance for reality, Scott was content to write: 'The scheme seems to have earned full confidence: it remains to play the game out.'

26

False Start

'IF ONLY WE could wait to start until November 1st,' Hassel wrote in his diary at Framheim on August 20th, 'but if one wants to be first at the Pole, there is hardly any choice.'

It was four days to the start of the Polar journey. For the past week the temperature had stayed below fifty degrees (C.) of frost. One afternoon the thermometer fell to $-57°$ when Amundsen recorded

an odd experience. My nose clogged – as usual in severe cold. Generally ice forms in the nostril hairs ... but yesterday the nostril itself froze up.

Under these conditions, as Johansen put it,

a sledging journey will be fateful. We cannot leave as long as the temperature keeps so low. I agree we must be prepared for proper low temperatures on our forthcoming journey, but I believe it will be terrible for the dogs. They go about now, lifting their legs gingerly, and curl themselves up in a ball with snouts between their paws to keep warm.

On August 23rd, the eve of departure, the sledges were hoisted by block and tackle on to the snow through a hole in the roof of the 'Commisariat'. Weighing almost half a ton each, they were too heavy to be manoeuvred along the corridors through the usual exit. For a month they had been waiting underground, ready packed: cases with the press lids like overgrown tea canisters neatly lined, six to the sledge, lashed down with rawhide thongs.

Twelve dogs, wild with frustrated energy after the winter's luxurious indolence, were harnessed to each sledge. They needed no forerunner now. Fanning out, they hared off in a mad gallop. With the drivers in their Netsilik fur outfits, the cavalcade of seven long sledges looked like an Eskimo migration as it straggled over the sea ice up on to the edge of the Barrier on the other side of the Bay of Whales where the line of flags began, marking the road to the south. There the sledges were left, ready for the start and men and dogs turned for home. 'Our journey has begun,' wrote Amundsen in his diary, 'may it be crowned with good fortune – for that, the Almighty will help us.'

It was light now with the long crepuscule of the Polar spring. On the 24th the sun reappeared, although hidden by an overcast sky. But they were still in the grip of a cold wave, and there was no question of starting yet.

The thought of Scott was plaguing them all. Perhaps – who knew – it was too cold for his ponies and he too was stuck or perhaps, after all – perish the thought! – it was warmer under the mountains at McMurdo Sound and he was already on his way.

Ready to start, the Norwegians could do nothing now but wait for the cold to abate. Dogs pant through their mouths direct into their lungs which cannot stand very cold air for long so it was necessary to wait. All the party were restless and on edge. Johansen remained gloomy and apprehensive. All his instincts, all the vivid recollections of his Arctic Odyssey with Nansen, cried out against starting too soon.

Amundsen knew no peace; a day or two at a time, he postponed the start, but when that day dawned, the thermometer remained in the minus fifties and they had to wait again. On August 31st, the temperature rose to $-26°$ (C.) with a strong breeze of twenty-three knots and a blinding drift. The next day Amundsen, now on tenterhooks, got all the team out with their dogs to take their personal gear over to the sledges waiting at the starting point.

Each man was allowed twenty pounds in addition to his sleeping bag. The prescribed items were: spare underwear and mittens, socks, felt overboots, reindeer skin Eskimo *kamikks* (boots) to wear when not on the march, sennegrass, snow goggles, felt hat for bright sun, face masks for low temperatures, a pocket mirror to check for frostbite on the face (Scott's men were required to check each other), and – a man-hauling harness.

This last was an insurance against emergencies and an incentive to succeed with the dogs. Amundsen used the harness to symbolize the penalty of failure. He reasoned that the daily sight of what to the Norwegians was an instrument of torture rather than a badge of manliness would concentrate the mind wonderfully.

The temperature was now $-42°$ (C.). Everything was ready. Spring, perhaps, was on the way; it was time to go.

Once before, on the North-West Passage Amundsen, when faced with a critical decision, had refused to make up his mind, letting fate, in the form of a compass needle, give the answer instead. Now, again, that archetypal man of action renounced the exercise of free will as if, somehow, afraid of crossing his destiny.

It was a Friday; should they leave on the morrow or the following

Monday? Amundsen ('oddly enough', said Hassel) put it to the vote
by secret ballot. The result was: four for Saturday, four for Monday.
Amundsen let the spin of a coin decide. Monday was the outcome.
Monday came, with a blizzard, visibility down to nil and a temperature
of − 46° (C.). They did not start. How lucky, wrote Johansen,

> that we are now indoors and not lying some miles in over the barrier,
> unable to move, and perhaps lost here at the beginning in the [crevassed]
> terrain to 80 degrees, which must be considered the worst to begin with.

Until the last minute, equipment was being altered. The short sprint
across the bay to the start had exposed shortcomings in the dogs'
harnesses, which had to be corrected. Johansen pointedly recorded that

> Even the Chief, who claimed to have been ready to start the whole of last
> month, and who is extremely worried that the Englishmen will reach the Pole
> before us, and therefore insisted on the earliest possible departure, has been
> altering his under anorak and fur clothes both Sunday and today.

The first stage to 80° South had to be done in good visibility; not only
because of the crevasses, but to avoid the slightest chance of missing
the depot there. Each morning Amundsen turned out at four o'clock
to look at the weather; Tuesday, Wednesday, Thursday, wind, cold and
drift sent him back into his bunk. Various bitches came on heat to
tantalize the dogs and tautening the nerves of these men, so sympathetic
to their animals, like violin strings. For three days, the thermometer
kept well away from the frontier of tolerance at fifty degrees. On
Wednesday and Thursday it was in the minus twenties. 'Without doubt,'
wrote Amundsen, 'it is spring arriving.' On Thursday, they all had a final
rehearsal of igloo building – the art that he had learned from that likeable
rascal, Talurnakto, at Gjøahavn during those carefree days, on the North-
West Passage, which seemed so many, many years ago.

The day after dawned calm, and clear, the thermometer still humanely
at − 37° (C.). Amundsen decided to set off for the Pole. At ten minutes
past noon on September 8th, 1911, the cavalcade of sledges, men and
dogs streamed over the snow, leaving Lindstrøm behind to look after
Framheim alone. The last great terrestial journey left to man had begun.

Fate with its usual sense of the appropriate had arranged poor auspices
and low comedy for the occasion. It happened to be a Friday, the day
of bad luck for starting on a journey.

The dogs bolted, squabbled and tangled at the start, making fools of
the drivers. The second day out, Kaisa, one of the bitches, in Bjaaland's

words, 'was shot for loose living'. She had selected this historic occasion to come into season and produce indiscipline in the ranks.

Saturday and Sunday read in the diaries like any old record of a Norwegian mountain tour. They followed the flags and did about fifteen miles each day. 'The going,' as Amundsen put it, 'was glorious. Rarely have I known the going so good.' The dogs, bursting with spirit and energy after a winter of pampering, rioted to get off. One or two had to be removed from the stronger teams and bound on to the sledges as ballast to keep down the speed. Of a forerunner there was no need; there was a track to follow and everyone was pulled along behind their sledges.

Then the cold counter-attacked.

On Monday, the thermometer sank overnight almost thirty degrees to − 56° (C.). Still they did their fifteen miles.

As the caravan pressed forwards [Johansen wrote], a thick white mist rose from the 86 dogs and 8 men; breath freezes immediately in the cold air. It was not possible to see the team ahead. It was like driving in the thickest fog.

They were wearing their wolfskin outer garments, with reindeer underneath. On the march it was warm enough. But that night it was a different tale. In Bjaaland's words,

It was cold as the devil in the sleeping bag. Everything damp with rime that forms everywhere. God knows where it will end.

The next day the liquid in the compasses froze solid. They stopped after four miles and built two igloos; nobody cared to repeat the experience of the night before in a tent. The igloos were warm and physically they were comfortable. But, wrote Bjaaland,

The Chief's mood is at freezing point and he took the decision to turn for home, and just as well, otherwise we would have frozen to death.

Amundsen in his diary put it this way:

To risk men and animals out of sheer obstinacy and continue, just because we have started on our way − that would never occur to me. If we are to win this game, the pieces must be moved carefully − one false move, and everything can be lost.

There had been an argument about turning or going on, as Johansen hinted in his diary:

Let that be a lesson to start so early on such a long and important journey. One cannot think exclusively about the one thing; to get to the Pole before the English.

Amundsen was not, like Scott, heir to a tradition of blindly following the commander into the cannon's mouth. He could only be sure of his men if they saw reason in his actions. In the untranslatable Norwegian word, they were not *opplagt*; nothing was right, it was not their day, they did not feel like going on; it would be folly, or worse, to persist. In any case, the Pole was not worth danger to life and limb. Amundsen was forced to turn by the moral pressure of his men.

He insisted first on carrying on the twenty miles to the 80 degree depot to dump the loads and be able to travel light that far when finally they started for the Pole. But once he had taken the decision to retreat, his mood lightened, and the atmosphere improved. They reached the depot on the 14th and, without waiting, turned for home, riding now on the almost empty sledges. 'It was,' Bjaaland noted, 'a bloody cold job to drive in 55–56 degrees of frost.' When Amundsen tried to dissipate the gloom that night with a tot of geneva, it was found to be frozen through, the bottle cracked. But another bottle of schnapps, also frozen, was salvaged, and they had their drink. It helped.

But, in Bjaaland's words, the next day

was sour as vinegar, − 47.5 deg. with N.W. wind right in the phizz; delightful.
    The dogs are suffering horribly in the cold; they are miserable, in agony with frostbitten paws. Adam and Lazarus froze to death when they lay down.

There was no need for the whip; the dogs sensed they were racing for their lives. The stronger trotted and galloped tirelessly; the weaker were carried on the sledges.

The day after, the temperature rose to − 44° (C.). The barrier of sluggish snow had been crossed, and the going was good once more; for how long, no one knew. With only forty miles to Framheim, Amundsen seized the chance to get indoors before the cold returned and ordered the distance done at a stretch. They set off at seven in the morning; from the start it was a wild race for home.

Amundsen, having begun the journey as forerunner, had no sledge of his own. He flung himself on Wisting's and, together with Helmer Hanssen, set off at full speed so that, as Bjaaland put it, they were soon 'just a white dot far away'. They reached Framheim at four in the afternoon, in calm and brilliant weather, having put up the respectable performance of forty miles in nine hours.*

Our reception [said Hanssen] was so-so. The first Linstrøm said to us was: 'I told you so!' and we each had a wigging [about starting on a Friday].

──────────
*In similar conditions, on the Winter Journey on Scott's expedition, Wilson, Bowers and Cherry-Garrard took a *week* for the same distance.

But out on the Barrier, the others were still hurrying home. As dogs faltered and weakened from the cold, they were loosed from the traces and left behind to make their way alone. It was every man for himself, a flight, pell-mell, from the cold.

When Amundsen, Wisting and Helmer Hanssen disappeared from sight, Stubberud, who was next, found his dogs slowing down. In pain with frostbitten feet, he had to sit on the sledge. He was

> quite alone. And if there had been a blizzard ... the situation would have been precarious. I had no fuel Primus or tent and little food, only a few biscuits. There was nothing to be done but wait for those behind me, and that took a fairly long time.

Eventually Bjaaland came up, went on ahead and now, with a forerunner, Stubberud's dogs picked up. They reached Framheim two hours after Amundsen. When he heard that they had seen nothing of the other three, he hoped that 'since the weather was turning thick Johansen, as an old, experienced, Polar traveller, would make camp and wait until the next day'. But Hassel, when he arrived, a little later, announced that Johansen and Prestrud, the last two still out on the Barrier, had neither food nor fuel.

They were miles behind. Prestrud's dogs failed; it was as much as they could do to pull the empty sledge. Johansen's team was faltering, but he raced on ahead to make contact with the rest. After six hours of hard driving, he managed to overtake Hassel, who found him

> extremely bitter over the inconsideration shown by Amundsen thus racing away from [him]. He wanted me to wait, but I prefered to continue, as we were still 16 miles from Framheim and had neither Primus, paraffin nor cooking utensils, and the need would be just as great whether we were two or three to share it.

He handed over his tent — neither Johansen nor Prestrud had one — and raced on alone.

Meanwhile, Johansen waited for Prestrud, and probably saved his life. Prestrud arrived after two hours in a miserable state, feet badly frostbitten, staggering along on skis. Johansen realized he had to be got into the warmth as soon as possible and resisted the temptation to stop. They were both on the point of exhaustion after twelve hours of struggle against the cold. They pressed on into the gathering gloom and eventually reached Framheim at half past midnight, after a dangerous descent from the Barrier. The path was narrow and easy to miss. They blundered around in the dark and the fog that had now come down, guided to Framheim only by the barking of the dogs. Lindstrøm was waiting up for them with coffee. The temperature was now − 51° (C.). They had eaten nothing since five that morning.

Barring frostbitten feet, there was nothing physically wrong with the party. But, in Johansen's words, there was 'a woeful aftermath. A profound gloom and misfortune has arisen among us, and no more are we happy and content.'

At breakfast the following morning, Amundsen asked Johansen why he and Prestrud had been so late. At that, Johansen flared up and bitterly rebuked Amundsen for his behaviour the day before. A leader ought not to become separated from his followers. 'I don't call it an expedition. It's panic.' And he launched into a tirade against Amundsen's whole leadership.

Most of the men agreed with Johansen, at least as far as the events of the previous day were concerned. But they recoiled at open rebellion. There was a horrified silence after Johansen had finished. His words, as Bjaaland put it, were 'best left unsaid'.

Johansen had been understandably provoked by Amundsen's conduct the day before. But his outburst had deeper causes. The clash of personalities would have been too much for them in the long run. Amundsen's question at the breakfast table had been the little push that unleashes the avalanche.

For Amundsen it was perhaps the worst crisis in his whole career. It was mutiny. His authority had been blatantly challenged. Personal feelings aside, this was calamitous in an isolated community, where cohesion was life itself.

The gross and unforgivable part of [Johansen's] statements is that they were made in everybody's hearing. The bull must be taken by the horns; I must make an example immediately.

The quarrel was not deliberate on Johansen's part. He was sorry almost as soon as the words were uttered. But he was not fully in control of himself. Ten years of humiliation and failure could not be wiped away without trace. He bore a burden of resentment, brooding on various real or imagined wrongs; one of them, that he had been unfairly saddled with the weakest dogs. On top of it all, his drinking had left him with a dangerous streak of instability.

He was a victim perhaps of the Polar mania. But Amundsen, even had he felt inclined, could afford neither sympathy nor sentiment. For the good of the expedition, he had to re-establish mastery as quickly as he could.

His problem was to isolate Johansen. He began by affecting to leave his outburst unanswered, addressing himself instead to his companions with an explanation of his actions. Two of the fastest dog-drivers, Helmer Hanssen and Stubberud, he said, had frostbitten heels, and needed to be got indoors as soon as possible. This did not really hold water because Prestrud, who was also badly frostbitten, had been left to his own devices. The truth as they broadly grasped, was that Amundsen had lost his head, disgusted no doubt with the check to his plans. He had got on the nearest sledge, and let the driver race as he saw fit, instead of giving orders to hold down the speed and keep contact with the whole party. As Stubberud put it in after years, it was 'quite simply, a mistake'. But in any case, his attempted explanation had mollified most of his companions. Prestrud, however, felt grievously let down and supported Johansen. Amundsen, who had maintained an icy calm throughout, then closed the conversation. They got up from breakfast with the matter hanging in the air.

Amundsen returned to the matter over coffee after the midday meal. In his most matter-of-fact manner he said that after the morning's events, there was no question of taking Johansen or Prestrud to the Pole. Johansen, as the old and experienced Polar explorer, was a particular danger because, as Bjaaland recorded in his diary, he 'could intrigue with the others during the journey and everything would grind to a halt'.

They all saw the point. In any case, Johansen had been at odds with one or two people, notably Hassel. Prestrud now took back his criticisms, and Amundsen seized the opportunity to make peace with him.

Amundsen then announced that Johansen, instead of going south, would travel eastwards on a subsidiary expedition under Prestrud towards King Edward VII Land.

Johansen refused to obey, demanding a written order. At supper, Amundsen delivered one. 'I find it most correct,' he wrote, 'with the good of the expedition in view – to dismiss you from the journey to the South Pole.'

During the evening, Amundsen called his men one by one into the kitchen where, under pledge of secrecy, he asked for, and got, a declaration of loyalty.

Johansen was ostentatiously excluded from the proceedings. He maintained his refusal to go to King Edward VII Land; at least with Prestrud over him. It was, he said in a formal written reply to Amundsen's order, a great disappointment.

When the leader of the expedition decides to put me under the command of a younger man, who is out on this kind of work for the first time, it is obvious that it must be humiliating for me, who has given a part of my life to the ice.

But the expedition under Prestrud was not solely a punishment for Johansen, it was an insurance against failure. Nobody had yet reached King Edward VII Land; if the Norwegians were the first to do so, at least they could return to civilization with something to show in case the Polar journey came to nought. The abortive start had raised the spectre of defeat.

Amundsen came to me and asked if I would be willing to go with Prestrud [Stubberud recalled]. 'If I am to choose,' I said, 'naturally I want to take part in the journey to the South Pole, but I have no alternative but to comply with the Captain's orders.' ...
Then he shook me by the hand, and thanked me.

Without much regret, Prestrud had renounced the Pole; he realized he was not up to it. In the end, Johansen bowed to authority and agreed to follow him. But it was too late. Amundsen never forgave what he considered disloyalty. He refused to speak to Johansen, except to pass the salt.

He regards me as completely outside the expedition [Johansen wrote]. He is mortally affronted because his qualities as a chief have been shipwrecked: he who so often in the course of the winter has spoken so much of how he could not understand how the English expeditions which have been down here have managed, since there has constantly been poor morale amongst them. But he himself is not the man I took him for to lead an expedition such as this.

In his diary, Amundsen defended his actions.

Many have criticized our early departure [he wrote]. Well, it is easy to do so afterwards [but] to sit still without doing anything, would never occur to me, criticize me who will. With the exception of [a few] frozen heels, and some dogs, our little journey has not caused us any loss. It was a good trial run. Besides we got everything up to 80 deg.

It would be too much to say that Amundsen had deliberately engineered a trial, but luck and some obscure unconscious drive accomplished the same end. The inevitable breach with Johansen had been provoked before it was too late. It was one of Amundsen's greatest strokes of fortune to have this happen at Framheim instead of on the road to the Pole. If the whole thing had been contrived, it could not have been better accomplished.

The setback also exposed material weaknesses. The worst were the boots. They were still too stiff, the cause of the frostbitten feet. For the fourth time they were altered.

Perhaps the most important outcome of the whole affair was the

Scott in 1909, before the last expedition.

The newly married Kathleen Scott, *née* Bruce.

Fram, a fine sight under full sail.

Captain L. E. G. Oates tending the horses on *Terra Nova*.

Midwinter 1910, the Norwegian party: (*l-r*) Bjaaland, Hassel, Wisting, Helmer Hanssen, Amundsen, Johansen and Prestrud.

Scott, at the head of the table in the hut at Cape Evans, with his fellow officers, celebrating what was to be his last birthday on June 6th, 1911.

Amundsen's party negotiating the Devil's Glacier.

Amundsen's diary records simply: "So we arrived and were able to plant our flag at the geographical South Pole. God be thanked!"

Two ski sticks lashed together mark the South Pole – the Norwegians, Wisting and Bjaaland on the left, together with one of the dogs, share in the moment of triumph.

Scott's entry in his diary on arrival at the Pole: "The Pole yes, but – under very different circumstances from those expected. We have had a horrible day."

(*l-r*) Scott, Bowers, Wilson and P. O. Evans stand disconsolate at Polheim. "Great God! This is an awful place and terrible enough for us to have laboured to it without the reward of priority."

New York, 1913 – a meeting between Amundsen, Shackleton and Peary.

Shortly after this photograph was taken Amundsen set off to trace the missing airship *Italia* and its pilot Umberto Nobile, but he never returned.

reduction of the Polar party to five, with depots calculated for eight, almost doubling the margin of safety. It had been, on balance, a profitable experience. But the price, as Amundsen put it, was 'the sad end to our splendid unity'.

Amundsen's faithful followers were Wisting and Helmer Hanssen, quiet, simple, loyal people, who did not trust Johansen. Outside, in another circle of allegiance, came Hassel, Bjaaland, Stubberud; no uncritical admirers of Amundsen, but yet accepting his authority, while (except for Hassel) sympathizing to some extent with Johansen. Prestrud had been shaken by the whole experience and, outside them all, stood Johansen, no longer defiant, but sad, remorseful, melancholy; the defeated rebel, who had yet done so much work for the expedition; a truly tragic figure.

> It is unhappy and desolate at Framheim now [he wrote]. Desolation hovers in the air, and nevertheless we are forced to live cheek by jowl, day and night. We cannot move to or from our places without stumbling over each other.

In the midst of this sullen division, Linstrøm tried to be the peacemaker; but not with much success.

> The Chief is in a miserable humour [Bjaaland wrote on October 6th]. But is isn't my fault. He can thank his wanderlust for that. Anyway, I think of the Pole just as much as he. God knows if I will ever get there.

Scott – or rather his motor sledges – continued to torment them with visions of defeat. The thought gave Amundsen no peace; they all talked about it now and then.

Amundsen had no intention of starting until all the frostbitten heels had been cured. Stubberud, Hassel, Helmer Hanssen and Prestrud were bedridden for ten days. They found it hard to keep still at night; Amundsen, usually the most good-natured of hutmates, told them sharply not to toss and turn as they did.

Amundsen who, despite (or because of) his failure at university, liked acting the rôle of doctor, was treating the patients. One day, Helmer Hanssen, consulting a medical book, drew his attention to the fact that the treatment described therein was different from his cure. Amundsen's reply was that he ought not to concern himself with that book but play cards or read novels instead.

So time passed. Outside, the dogs nursed their frostbitten, bloodcaked paws; inside the hut, the patients were on the mend.

The midnight sun returned; gradually the thermometer crept up towards − 20° (C.). Early in October, a petrel appeared; spring now definitely seemed to be on the way. Amundsen decided to start on October 15th. By then, rather to his surprise, men and dogs had recovered and, in Bjaaland's words,

> Now we are ready again. I hope it won't be a fiasco like the last time ... If I emerge unscathed from this journey, I must see that I get out of polar exploration. It's hardly worth the trouble ... and if I should be caught out there, well, my tenderest wishes to friends and acquaintances, my countrymen and fatherland.

They were kept on tenterhooks to the last, gales and fog delaying them for the best part of a week. On October 20th, they finally got off.

The weather was still not auspicious. It was dull, misty, with a nasty shifting breeze.

Lindstrøm prophesied another premature return. They were starting on a Friday again.

Wistful and disappointed, Johansen stood out in the snow, to one side, watching Amundsen, Bjaaland, Wisting, Hassel and Helmer Hanssen marshal their dogs and sledges, while Prestrud prepared to film the departure. Amundsen had hardly spoken to Johansen since the memorable breakfast on September 17th, but now went up to him and bade farewell; and Johansen in return wished him good luck.

> I have told him the truth [Johansen wrote, surveying the scene], and that is not always the best to hear, and that is why I have fallen into disfavour [but] I think I have been of some use to him ... and so departure has come. Sledge after sledge set off ... onto the sea ice, over the bay [and] up onto the Barrier ... Around midday, they had all reached it, and so they disappeared in the old, familiar direction.

The party swinging southwards into the drift, slowly rising and falling as they followed the undulations of the Barrier, like a squadron of warships speeding over the swell, represented the culmination of an era. The men were clad in Eskimo garments, the dogs tearing away with them over the snow were harnessed in Eskimo fashion; but the sledges, the skis, the food waiting at 80° South, the sextants and Primus stoves, tents and all the impedimenta, were the products of Western ingenuity. It was the marriage of civilization and a primitive culture. The technique was already on the point of obsolescence. Aircraft and tractors were waiting in the wings. This was the last classic journey in the old style; and it was to end the era of terrestrial exploration that began with the explosion of the human spirit during the Renaissance.

Everything turned on the personal quality of the men riding placidly on their sledges towards the south. They were the best of their kind;

embodying a formidable combination of physical and mental qualities. They were tough, resourceful, inured to cold. But, beyond that, they had been through their trial; weaknesses had been ruthlessly eliminated. They now unreservedly accepted Amundsen's leadership, since he had shown himself in command. Once their dogs had been hitched to the sledges and fanned out in full cry, the dismal atmosphere of Framheim was swept away by a gale of action and self-confidence. They were soon required to put this confidence to the test.

Their first goal was the depot at 80° South. The journey there took place in notably displeasing weather, with gale and head wind and fog. They lost their way several times, already the first day straying from the flagged route into one of the crevassed areas they were doing their best to avoid.

> I came last ... with Roald Amundsen riding on my sledge [Wisting recalled]. We sat back to back ... Suddenly I felt a tremendous jerk in the sledge, which seemed to whip down by the stern, and wanted to glide backwards with nose in the air. I turned round quick as lightning, and saw that we had driven over an enormous crevasse. Partly over, the snow bridge had broken under us but, on account of our high and even speed, the sledge luckily slid on to firm ice. We did not stop but continued on our way. Then I felt Amundsen tap me on the shoulder ... 'Did you see that?' he said. 'That would have liked both us, the sledge and the dogs.' More was not said.

They had several more brushes with crevasses, with equal good luck. In any case, luckiest of all, they were travelling light, riding on their sledges, dogs wildly racing; so wildly that, as on the abortive start, some had to be bound on the sledges as ballast to keep the speed down. Four animals were discharged for obesity or malicious indolence; turned loose with the chance of finding their way home (one or two did). This left forty-eight dogs; twelve to a sledge.

On the fourth day out, they ran into a fog so thick, said Amundsen, that they 'could not see their hands in front of their faces'. It was the occasion not for complaint but for quiet glee. Navigating blind, with the help of the flags, they struck the depot with no trouble at half past one in the afternoon. 'A brilliant test,' said Amundsen, 'of both sledgemeter and compass.' Crevasses and all, they had done their twenty miles a day.

But to Amundsen, this was no more than a preliminary canter. As far as he was concerned, it was here at 80° South that the Polar journey really began. Here he was to rest and feed and rest again before picking up his loads and setting off in earnest. This really is the measure of his start. He had advanced his base more than a degree of latitude. He was 150 miles ahead of Scott before the race began. The learning and experience of a decade and a half was bearing fruit.

On October 24th, the day after reaching the depot, Amundsen, his four men and forty-eight dogs were sumptuously lolling about. A blizzard was blowing. Nobody cared, least of all the dogs. They were gorging themselves to their hearts' content on the seal meat brought out by Johansen on the last depot journey in the autumn. They were, as Amundsen recorded, 'enjoying life'.

27

Scott's Caravan

ONE HUNDRED AND fifty miles behind, the first part of Scott's intricate apparatus was starting from Cape Evans. At ten o'clock in the morning of October 24th, the two motor sledges, after a preliminary breakdown, stuttered and strained over the sea ice, pulling a ton and a half apiece Bernard Day, the mechanic, and Lashly, the stoker, were driving. Hooper, the steward, helped. Teddy Evans was in charge, on the face of it, a position of trust.

In fact, it was to get him out of the way, as Scott now revealed in a letter to Joseph Kinsey, his New Zealand agent. Evans, he wrote, was

> not at all fitted to be 'Second-in-Command', as I was foolish enough to name him. I am going to take some steps concerning this, as it would not do to leave him in charge here in case I am late returning.

Scott was deliberately taking an antagonist with him, blandly accepting as a lesser evil the injection of conflict into the Polar party.

After the motors had gone, the main Polar party had a week to wait before starting. Scott devoted the time to a stream of farewell letters.

They betray the contradictions, the confusion, the divorce from reality, the self-delusion, which were his drawbacks as a leader. In his feelings towards Amundsen, he gives himself away: 'Of course I never realized that there was any object in haste this season or I should have brought more dogs as Amundsen has done,' he wrote to Sir Edgar Speyer, the expedition treasurer, continuing, however, in the same breath: 'I'm not a great believer in dog transport beyond a certain point.'

The same skein of muddled thinking ran through Scott's other letters. Amundsen would probably beat him to the Pole because, as he wrote to Kathleen, 'he is bound to travel fast with dogs and pretty certain to start early'.

But this was followed by:

> On this account, I decided at a very early date to act exactly as I should have done had he not existed. Any attempt to race must have wrecked my plan, beside which it doesn't appear the sort of thing one is out for.

All of which reveals an absence of the will to win so desirable in a leader. It was, however, not the entire truth, as Scott indicated when he wrote to Admiral Egerton that 'Everything depends on the coming journey, of course.'

So, in fact, there *was* a race for the Pole, although Scott, when it suited him, maintained the gentlemanly pretence that there was not.

In an effort, perhaps, to reassure himself through confession, Scott now, in a letter to Kathleen, described the cloud hanging over him:

> I am quite on my feet now. I feel both mentally and physically fit for the work, and I realize that the others know it and have full confidence in me. But it is a certain fact that it was not so in London or indeed until after we reached this spot. The root of the trouble was that I had lost confidence in myself ... it is significant of my recovery that I do not allow anxieties to press on me where I deem my actions to have been justified.

Whether Scott deceived his wife in writing that his companions now had full confidence in him, he was deceiving himself. Oates was perhaps the most forthright in the criticism on record.

In one of his letters written before the winter he had felt obliged to reassure his mother: 'Don't think from what I say that Scott is likely to endanger anyone, it can be quite the reverse, and I may be maligning the man.' But he could not forgive Scott for the loss of the animals on the depot journey, believing that anyone who squandered horses was capable of squandering men as well. At the end of the winter he was still unnaturally moody.

> The winter here was wretched [Oates wrote to his mother while waiting to start for the south], although we got on very well together ... I dislike Scott intensely and would chuck the thing if it was not that we are the British expedition and must beat the Norwegians. Scott has always been very civil to me and I have the reputation of getting on well with him. But the fact of the matter is that he is not straight, it is himself first, the rest nowhere, and when he has got what he can out of you, it is shift for yourself.

This is the same judgment made by Armitage, Skelton, and others who knew Scott well.

Oates was much occupied by comparisons with the Norwegians:

> I expect they have started for the Pole by this, and have a jolly good chance of getting there if their dogs are good and they use them properly. From what I see I think it would not be difficult to get to the Pole provided you have proper transport but with the rubbish we have it will be jolly difficult and mean a lot of hard work.

He had by now learned that he was to be in Scott's tent for the start of the Polar journey.

> Whether this means I am going to be in the final party or not I don't know but I think I have a fairish chance that is if Scott & I don't fall out it will be pretty tough having four months of him, he fusses dreadfully ... Scott wanted me to stay down here another year but I shall clear out of it if I get back in time for the ship which I hope to goodness will be the case ... Scott pretends at present he is going to stay but I have bet myself a fiver he clears out, that is if he gets to the Pole ... If Scott was a decent chap I would ask him bang out what he means to do.

Oates was, in fact, feeling so low that he had not the least desire to write home. He did so only because Frank Debenham practically forced him to sit down and take pen in hand. And so, while Scott in his cubicle was composing farewells, which included the remark to his wife that he felt himself 'a competent leader over the team', Oates on the other side of the partition was writing to his mother that 'I expect there will be a bit of a circus getting off.'

Oates was not far off the mark. A telephone line had been laid to Hut Point – the first Antarctic telephone link – and on the 26th, someone rang up to report trouble with the motor sledges. Scott, who in any case was now manifestly jumpy, immediately broke off preparations in order to take Wilson and six others out on a man-hauling rescue dash – to find that rescue was unwanted. The only result of this ill-judged foray was to give Scott a strained Achilles tendon and to waste two days, which, as Wilson put it, happening

> just when we wanted them most of all for letter writing and final arrangements has been rather a trial. A host of things have had to be left to the last moment and now it becomes a rush to get them done in time.

It is a bizarre contrast to the Norwegians waiting at Framheim for the start, everything long packed and ready; Amundsen poring over his equipment, until the last moment searching for improvement. Scott, having long ago decided that *his* equipment was incapable of being improved, spends the last few days grappling instead with final orders and farewell letters. Amundsen, so far as we know, wrote no letters at all. Scott seems to be looking over his shoulder at an unseen audience, concerned more with his reputation than his actions. Amundsen believed that his deeds would speak for themselves. In the wonderful stoic words of the *Hávamál*, the piece of ancient Norse poetry that was part of his cultural heritage,

> Cattle die,
> Friends die
> Thou thyself shalt die,
> I know a thing
> That never dies,
> Judgment over the dead.

At last, on Wednesday, November 1st, at about eleven a.m., Charles Wright and P.O. Keohane with Jehu and Jimmy Pigg, the slowest ponies, having gone ahead to wait at Hut Point, the main southern party set off from Cape Evans. Scott, in Gran's words, 'a little – indeed, a good deal nervous,' harnessed his pony to the wrong sledge and had to transfer in some confusion before marching off rapidly to the south. One by one the eight ponies, each with attendant man and sledge, straggled out into the greyness.

A few hours later the telephone rang at Cape Evans. It was Scott on the line, explaining that, in the last-minute confusion, he had left behind the Union Jack for the Pole given him by Queen Alexandra, the Queen Mother. He wanted it sent on. As the best skier and the fastest traveller, Gran was told to do so. A blizzard however, stopped him until the following day.

He set off early in the afternoon, the silken ensign wrapped around himself to avoid creasing. Racing as best he knew, he did the fifteen miles to Hut Point in three hours, against a head wind, by any standards not a bad performance,* and caught the party just before it left.

'The irony of fate,' Scott said with a smile as Gran handed over the flag. A Norwegian had carried the British colours the first few miles towards the Pole.

Just before he led off his cavalcade over the sea and on to the waiting Barrier, Scott went up to Gran who was not going south, for by common consent he was absolved from competing with his countrymen, and said: 'You're young, you've got your life before you. Take care of yourself. Good luck, my boy.'

Those were his parting words. To the impressionable Norwegian they sounded like the valediction of a doomed man.

Amundsen was now 200 miles ahead.

*

---

* By comparison, a modern cross-country ski racer will do a thirty-kilometre race (Gran's 'course' was twenty-seven kilometres) in one and a half hours, or twenty kilometres an hour. Gran's speed was nine kilometres an hour, with heavy clothes, and ski weighing fifteen pounds to the modern nordic racer's five pounds or so.

Five days later, just past Corner Camp, the two motor sledges were found abandoned and broken down. 'The dream of great help from the machines,' wrote Scott, 'is at an end!' An original idea had foundered on haphazard production.

After spending thousands of pounds on the devices, neither tools nor sufficient spares had been brought, and the mechanics had to improvise with makeshift equipment. What would have happened if Skelton, the part-inventor, had been present? Perhaps there was a price to pay for betraying an old shipmate. One sledge had already pulled a ton and a half fifty miles; proper expertise could have coaxed another fifty or hundred miles. In terms of the expedition's outcome, this is not insignificant.

The derelict sledges, forlornly drifting up, stood as monuments to Scott's great foray into modern technology (Amundsen's was the diesel engine on *Fram*). The trouble was that even after the *Discovery* expedition, Scott had never come to terms with the Polar environment.

The ponies alone, totally unsuited to the conditions, fighting their way into the drift, their nearest food growing 2,000 miles away, bear witness to Scott's inability to grasp the implications of the cold, storms and unpredictable surfaces of the Antarctic world. Perhaps he lacked the competence, the application, even possibly the intelligence to carry technical aids through to success.

For at least four years he had known he would return to the Antarctic. He could have visited Norway or the Alps; learnt to ski and drive dogs himself; aquired a grounding in the internal combustion engine, (he was, after all, a torpedo expert), or even tried some mountaineering. He had done none of these things.

Incompetent design penetrated into most details of equipment. Scott had learned nothing and forgotten nothing. He still used neither furs nor anoraks, but wore the same inefficient garments with separate hoods that had disfigured the *Discovery* expedition. His tents, without sewn-in groundsheets, slipped over a cumbrous framework of poles, like a tepee, were difficult to erect in a gale. And where transport was concerned, Scott trusted neither ponies, nor skis, dogs or sledge; in truth all he really believed in was human effort.

There now occurred one of those incidents that seem to illuminate whole histories. On November 7th, Scott was tent-bound, because of a southerly blizzard against which he considered travel impossible. In the middle of the morning Meares unconcernedly drove up with the dogs cheerfully trotting into the supposedly impenetrable blast.

Meares had been left behind at base on desultory errands, with orders to catch up afterwards, for dogs were naturally the fastest transport in the organization. He had been told to join Scott together with the motor party at 80° 30′ South, just beyond One Ton Camp and he had been so presumptuous as to overtake Scott. Scott was annoyed but his annoyance went beyond that of orders disobeyed. In an illogical diary entry, he wrote that Meares had 'played too much for safety in catching us so soon, but it is satisfactory to find the dogs ... can be driven to face such a wind as we have had'.

Meares had travelled without apparent trouble in conditions which had stopped Scott. He had assuredly done much worse than merely disobey orders. He had cast a shadow on his commander's judgment and ability. He had proved the fact of the superiority of dogs. Scott disliked uncomfortable facts and in general ignored them. Understandably, he was irritated at Meares' unexpected arrival.

Oates at any rate was pleased; Meares was about the only man he could talk to seriously.

We both damned the motors. 3 motors at £1,000 each, 19 ponies at £5 each. 32 dogs at 30/- each. If Scott fails to get to the Pole he jolly well deserves it.

Scott was showing considerable nervousness. On November 18th, in Oates' words, 'he had a breeze up with Bowers ... about the loads', accusing Bowers of deliberately overloading his, Scott's, pony in order to save his own. It was not a wholly rational proceeding. Bowers was responsible for distributing the weights and checking stores. Oates too 'had words with Scott' that day: 'He's a very difficult man to get on with.' Scott was fretting about the slow progress; and had long refused to believe that the animals were such poor material as he had been told. At last, Oates recorded with sardonic glee, 'Scott realizes now what awful cripples our ponies are and carries a face like a tired seaboot in consequence.'

In the tent one night, Scott started speaking of the Southern Journey on *Discovery*. He said, as Cherry-Garrard wrote in his diary, that 'he thought they did everything wrong with their dogs'.

This is Scott's first recorded admission of a mistake; that the fault might have been his and not the animals'. It was manifestly too late, and doubtless associated with the fact that now, also too late, he could no longer ignore the significance of seeing dogs run properly. Scott, as Cherry-Garrard recorded in his diary, had begun 'to feel very doubtful whether the ponies will do their job & evidently thinks Amundsen with his dogs may be doing much better'. The sight of a commander not only rueing his actions, but lacking the self-control to hide it, was hardly uplifting.

Scott's uncomfortable suspicion was driven home with irritating lucidity. Day after day, when he halted to camp, worn out, dispirited, complaining of poor snow and bad weather, after seven, eight or nine hours of slogging, Meares and Dmetri would romp up, having done the distance in a third of the time, and breezily report good going. A crop of minor injuries suggested that the party was not in perfect health. A defective and over-civilized diet during the winter was already beginning to tell. Scott had fed his men as if they had been at home, in the face of considerable published evidence that diet had to be adapted to climate, not only out in the field, but beforehand at the base. What might happen at the Pole and after would have been decided months before. It was a lesson which both Scott and Wilson could have learned from Shackleton, had they wished. The change from base to sledging rations was too abrupt; this and dietary deficiencies suggest that Scott's irritability on the march might partly have been due to physical causes.

On November 21st, the main caravan overtook Teddy Evans and the erstwhile motor party, now man-hauling. When Scott heard that they had been waiting almost a week, he patronizingly said: 'My dear Teddy, always the same.' Evans, determined to show Scott that he was twice the man he thought he was, had raced ahead, tiring his party out in the process. They killed the intervening time by building a monster cairn, fifteen feet high, dubbed 'Mount Hooper'.

The conjunction of Scott and Evans added the strain of conflict and suspicion to an already divided party. Meares and Oates had found no reason to revise their contempt for Scott, at least as far as transport went.

The caravan had now attained its full complexity, with sixteen men and three kinds of transport; man-hauling, ponies and dogs. Travelling routine became even more intricate than before. Each day began with five separate starts, spread over several hours to allow for different speeds and ensure that everyone arrived, more or less, together. First came the man-haulers, who were the slowest, then three pony teams, in descending order of decrepitude, and finally Meares, Dmetri and the dogs, the fastest of all, bringing up the rear. It was a clumsy performance, reminding Scott himself of 'a somewhat disorganized fleet'. With gallows humour, the slowest pony party was soon dubbed 'The Baltic Fleet', after the ramshackle Russian squadron that, under the ill-fated Admiral Rozhdestvensky during the Russo-Japanese War, struggled halfway round the world from Europe to the Far East, only to be annihilated at the Battle of Tushima.

Camp work was as trying as the day's march. Only the dogs could look after themselves. A dog is well adapted to cold because, amongst other things, he sweats only through his tongue, and his fur remains dry. A horse, on the other hand, sweats through his hide and in cold weather the sweat turns to ice. Standing still, unable, like dogs, to dig themselves down into the comforting, protective snow, Scott's ponies froze; their flanks sometimes encased in armour plate of solid ice. They were not built for these conditions, and they suffered. They had to be rubbed down at the end of every stage and covered with blankets while snow walls were built to protect them from the wind.

Scott's transport system involved parties successively turning back as they laid depots, or consumption reduced loads, dispensing with the need for their traction. The first of these return parties, Day and Hooper, left on November 24th, at 81° 15′, 525 miles from the Pole. With them went a letter from Scott to Simpson, now in command at Cape Evans, changing the orders for Meares and the dogs.

Although Scott nursed an irrational, indeed a paranoiac dislike and mistrust of dogs, he had nonetheless staked his life on them. He had not left enough in his depots for the return of the Polar party, expecting the dogs to come out later and make up the deficiency. His plan required them to bring out food and fuel to One Ton Camp and beyond before March 1st. *Scott depended on those supplies to get through safely.*

At the same time, Meares was expected to take his teams south a certain distance, carrying fodder for the ponies, before dashing back to Cape Evans in time for his vital mission and, incidentally, also help unload the ship when she arrived. It was, in any case, a complex and ill-conceived procedure, earning Meares' undying contempt.

The sight of what Meares had actually accomplished with his animals, and the nagging thought of what Amundsen might do, made Scott now suddenly decide to take the dogs on further than he had originally intended. They might, he wrote to Simpson,

> be late returning; unfit for further work or non existent. So don't forget that the [supplies] must be [got out] somehow.

This was irresponsible tampering with already thin lines of retreat, for margins of error there were none. It also thrust unfair responsibility on Simpson. The new orders, as he impenetrably wrote on receiving them a month later, 'left me with the problem of laying out the depot at "One Ton Camp".'

With Day and Hooper, and the letter to Simpson, also went two useless dogs, including 'Stareek' ('Old Man' in Russian), Meares' leader dog, who, for no apparent reason, had gone on strike. In a curious comment which says worlds about thoughts beneath the surface, Bowers wrote that

> 'Stareek' ... is a splendid leader and the most intelligent of the dogs, and that I think is his undoing. The fact seems to be that he has come to the conclusion that he does not know where he is and that we are still heading away from home, so he had chucked his hand in.

There is a kind of heroism for which there are no medals because it is unmentionable. It is that of the subordinate stoically following a leader whom he *knows* is taking him to disaster. A dog is not that kind of hero.

The familiar landmarks sank one by one below the horizon; last of all Mount Erebus with its plume, and the long trek across the Barrier went on. It was a dismal saga. Men and ponies sank in the snow to their knees; the former, because they were on foot, their skis perversely carried on the sledges; the latter because Nature never intended them for the conditions, and their hooves ploughed through the crust.

But the greater burden lay in morale, not technique. It was a tensed party crawling over the endless frozen desert, the mirror of Scott's moodiness. The tension was also that of men who had failed to come to terms with their surroundings. Even Wilson, imbued with a romantic Franciscan nature worship, sketching the scenery on every possible occasion, seems somehow cold and estranged from the country. And there was something else.

The Norwegians were fired by the willpower of a leader who understood that the human personality is an instrument to be played with a living touch. Scott saw his men as puppets on a string. He was rewarded with a party depressingly passive, waiting, like regimented automata, for orders from above. When the going got bad Scott, in the words of Raymond Priestley, 'drove and cajoled his men along. They made up much leeway, but it left them stale.' 'It was our simple job to follow,' wrote Cherry-Garrard, 'to get up when we were roused, to pull our hardest.'

It was part of Scott's plan to kill his ponies as they finished their work. On November 24th, Oates shot Jehu, the first pony. 'Scott,' Cherry-Garrard observed in his diary, 'feels this kind of thing a lot.'

When Jehu was shot, Wilson noted in his diary, it was 'a good few miles further South than the lat. where Shackleton shot his first pony'. Wilson, playing Sancho Panza, to Scott's Don Quixote, had joined his master in his illusory battle with an imaginary foe. Shackleton had stalked with them across the Barrier as the ghostly rival in their tracks; the shadow, to Scott's and now to Wilson's eyes, of more substance than Amundsen. When reality is harsh, the flight into illusion is comforting.

Shackleton was their pilot. Scott had with him a copy of Frank Wild's diary of Shackleton's Southern Journey obtained through Priestley. Also he had extracts from Shackleton's book *The Heart of the Antarctic* typed by Cherry-Garrard. Scott mentions them to sneer at Shackleton or bolster his own self-confidence. It was left to Oates to show generosity. On December 4th, when they raised the approaches to the plateau, and the Barrier stage of the journey was all but over, Oates said in his diary:

> Saw several enormous glaciers coming down between the mountains, and some of the chasms which stopped Shackleton. And now one is here one can realise what a wonderful journey his was and the daring which prompted him to strike up the glacier instead of following the coastline.

28

The Devil's Ballroom

Drove off 9 a.m. Dogs as if possessed, careered off like madmen. Going good and terrain flat and fine. Distance 15.6 miles from 9.a.m. to 1.30 p.m.

THIS QUOTATION FROM Bjaaland's diary on October 26th, the day the Norwegians left the depot at 80° S., 600 miles from the Pole, catches the spirit of their race across the Barrier.

This is not to say that the Norwegians had uniformly plain sailing. They had their fair share of blizzard and drift; and a generous helping of fog. That the weather was Scott's particular enemy, while Amundsen was blessed with exceptional and by implication wholly undeserved luck, is part of the Scott legend. Amundsen has only himself to blame. He made things seem too easy, which was all very well for the intellectual aficionado of the elegant solution, but not for the world at large. He had forgotten Corneille's dictum, '*A vaincre sans péril on triomphe sans gloire.*'

The diaries tell another tale – as far as the facts go. But there is a strong subjective element in judging weather, and against Scott's self-pity must be set Amundsen's cold understatement. This is not style alone, but expresses a fundamental difference of approach. Amundsen had a proper humility before Nature, accepting a rough justice in her dictates. He knew that if it snows today it will be hard crust tomorrow; that after the storm skiing is good; that a blizzard is a time to rest.

Scott, by contrast, expected the elements to be ordered for his benefit, and was resentful each time he found that they were not. This was a manifestation of the spiritual pride that was Scott's fatal flaw.

The difference between the two rivals is expressed in the way each called on the Deity. Scott did so only to complain when things went wrong; Amundsen, to give thanks for good fortune. In any case, Scott was an agnostic and believed in science; Amundsen was a Nature-worshipper. For that reason alone, Amundsen found it easier to accept the caprice of blizzard and storm. He and his companions were in tune with their surroundings; they were spared the *angst* that tormented Scott and, through him, pervaded the British expedition.

After five days' travel, including one day stormbound, Amundsen reached the depot at 81° S. He had now travelled 140 miles, and been pulled on skis all the way. Each sledge carried 400 kilos (880 lbs); twice Scott's loads. Amundsen's average speed was three and a half miles per hour; Scott's half to two miles per hour. But this conceals a greater supremacy. Scott's men and ponies trudged eight hours and more to cover ten to thirteen miles a day; Amundsen's daily stage of fifteen to twenty miles was done in five or six hours with plenty in reserve, and nothing to do but eat and sleep – especially sleep – for the rest of the day. Bjaaland 'suggested we do 25 miles a day, but got the reply that this could not be risked for the sake of the dogs'. His men and dogs knew that they would do a certain regular amount of work each day, to set off fresh on the morrow.

Scott was not quite so self-controlled. He had a Dionysian urge to show off his undoubted physical strength and drive his companions to exhaustion. He did not believe that a day's work had been done unless there was visible distress. Cherry-Garrard has left an account of what it was like. After nine or ten hours on the march, Scott would say,

'Oh, well, I think we'll go on a little bit more' ... It might be an hour or more before we halted and made our camp: sometimes a blizzard had its silver lining. Scott could not wait ... any delay was intolerable.

On November 1st, after a day's rest at the 81 degree depot, Amundsen put his head out of the tent door to be greeted by thick and clinging fog. Two hundred miles behind, Scott was gathering his forces for the main start from Cape Evans.

Of this, Amundsen was naturally ignorant. What he did know, however, was that, running his own race – the only sensible proceeding – he had to maintain a certain speed; which happened to be a degree of latitude in four days.

Amundsen measured, indeed chose, his distances in degrees, not miles, so that effort was visualized instinctively on the surface of the globe, and thus a progress towards the goal, one of many little devices to keep up the spirits of the party.*

Amundsen's timetable speed was, then, one quarter of a degree per day. He proposed to maintain it. Fog or no fog, he decided to travel. Visibility was four sledge lengths.

Amundsen had been that way once before on the third depot journey

---

* An intelligent use of the power of numbers and the significance of units. The geographical, or nautical mile is one minute of latitude, or one sixtieth of a degree. Nonetheless, the relation only makes an impact when simple fractions are involved.

in the autumn, and the route was marked – after a fashion. But it was uncharted country.

What Amundsen did not know, however, was that directly in his path lay particularly nasty terrain. It is what today is called the Steers Head crevasses, a part of the Barrier distorted by the glacial outflow from Marie Byrd Land to the east. Almost predictably, the Norwegians ran off course in the fog and right into the trap. Crevasse after crevasse, stretched as far as the fog allowed the eye to see. They were not very broad, however – about a metre – and they seemed to run athwart their course, which reduced the risk of falling in. Amundsen decided to go on. All went well for twelve and a half miles. Then Helmer Hanssen, who now habitually led, had the kind of accident that inevitably happens when skiing with dogs. His ski tips got caught in the traces and he fell. He fell in the middle of a crevasse. He remained where he was, having the presence of mind to realize that, although the snow bridge held under his outstretched body, it might break under the strain of getting to his feet again. He had to lie where he was until he was rescued. The party was not roped because it was against the Norwegian nature: better to take the risk of being unsecured, than the greater risk of inhibiting the skiing rhythm.

Hanssen's dogs had crossed over safely and instantly profited by the temporary neutralization of their lord and master to have a joyous, snarling riot on the edge of the abyss. The sledge had slewed round, almost edgewise along the crevasse, the snow bridge broken, ready to disappear into the depths and drag the dogs with it.

Amundsen cleared the crevasse and somehow stopped the battle. Wisting rescued Hanssen, who seemed wholly unperturbed; he loved the sight of chasms and the more sensational the better. The three then got the sledge to safety. Hassel also fell in the middle of a crevasse and was nearly swallowed into the depths.

These crevasses are impressive when one lies at the edge and stares down in them [Amundsen remarked in his diary]. A bottomless chasm goes from light blue into the thickest darkness.

The ugliest formations we have found here, are huge holes that could take *Fram*, and a lot more besides. These holes are covered by a thin wind crust, and the little hole that is visible doesn't seem so difficult. But if one gets on to such a delightful spot, one is irrevocably lost. We passed one of these holes in the 'pea souper' today.

Luckily H[elmer] H[anssen] saw it in time. There is not much that escapes his sharp eye.

We are all clear. What risk we run in our march over such unpleasant stretches. We go with our lives in our hands each day. But it is pleasant to hear nobody wants to turn back.

There is in the Norwegian character a streak of flamboyant fatalism to which risk appeals. It is the kind of audacity, at any rate, that sometimes seems to impress Dame Fortune. The Norwegians scurried out from the crevasses into safety unharmed, still having done their 'regulation' fifteen miles – one quarter of a degree of latitude – for the day.

It was a skier's and dogs' terrain; old ice for foundation, with no temperamental soil below, and snow strewn on top; somewhat preferable to Hardangervidda, as Amundsen remembered it.

Driven in a 'pea souper' the whole day [wrote Amundsen on November 4th]. The going has been brilliant – could not be better. Great change from one day to the other. Yesterday the going was sticky as fish glue.

The philosophic mood, with its soupçon of humour, is unmistakable – and virtually indistinguishable from that of a winter ski tour in the Norwegian mountains.

Scott, a few hundred miles behind in substantially the same conditions, inhabits another world:

I expected these marches to be a little difficult, but not near so bad as today ... Another horrid march in a terrible light, surface very bad ... A tired animal makes a tired man, I find, and none of us are very bright now after the day's march.

After sixteen miles on November 4th, Amundsen's compasses and sledgemeters indicated the vicinity of his depot at 82° S., 480 miles from the Pole. But the fog was thick, and it seemed senseless to grope in the murk at the end of the march; much more sensible to pitch camp and wait for another day.

At 4 a.m. the sun came out for a moment [wrote Amundsen] and we were not slow in getting out of our sleeping bags. There the depot loomed up about 2 miles E.S.E. The small flags were just as they had been left, standing out beautifully against the white background. We took the depot's bearings, and got back into bed again. After breakfast we packed up and set off. It had then closed in again, but we had our bearing, and after 2½ miles' march we stood by our southernmost depot. Everything was in the finest order.

Here was the frontier. This was the last opportunity to rest the dogs, and for the next two days they rested, stretched out in the snow, basking in sunshine of a warmth that made Amundsen's thoughts 'stray now and then to the tropics'.

Fur clothes were shaken out and dried; men and animals were relaxed. And in that receptive mood, plans were altered, or rather Amundsen got his men to accept a plan which he had long had in mind. The original intention had been to go on with fully loaded sledges to the Pole and back. But, finding this last depot, as Amundsen put it, had been

a victory for *us. We* have shown that it is possible to lay out depots on these endless expanses and mark them so that with careful navigation we can find them again.

And now he suggested that instead of taking everything on, they should lay depots every degree of latitude. After a short discussion, the proposal was accepted.

The new scheme, Helmer Hanssen wrote afterwards,

lightened the sledges for the poor dogs [who], would have to be driven and lashed forward, if the journey was to end well. The theosophists teach something about us after death coming back in one or another form, and I for my part devoutly hope that I do not come again as a draft dog on polar expeditions.

After replenishing the sledges with pemmican and paraffin from the depot, Amundsen was now fully loaded, as he had been at Framheim. In effect he had pushed his base forward 200 miles to 82 degrees. All, he now wrote in his diary,

that is to say, men, animals and equipment, is in the finest condition. The hounds are now in a far better state than when we left. All the sore feet have healed, and a little of the superfluous obesity has gone.

The morale of the party was rising as it went; contrast to Scott's where it was gradually being sapped. One explanation is to be found in their underlying assumptions.

On his departure from 82° S., Amundsen carried supplies for a hundred days, taking him to February 6th, 1912. According to his time-table, *and on his performance so far,* he would return to Framheim by January 31st. This meant that even in the unlikely event of missing all depots laid so far, he could still reach the Pole, return to Framheim, turn around, and do another hundred miles to the south before his food gave out. He had three or four times as much paraffin as he needed. He allowed one day in four for rest and bad weather. He assumed that he would be forced to man-haul from 86° S. on the return journey. The margin of safety was great and was seen to be great.

Scott, by comparison, had allowed no margin of safety in food, fuel or weather. Simple figures make the point. When Amundsen started, he had three tons of supplies in his depots; Scott had one ton. There were five in Amundsen's party, making 1,300 pounds per man; Scott started with seventeen men which meant 124 pounds per head. Amundsen had ten times more food and fuel per man than Scott. For Scott to miss a single depot would be fatal.

This is enough to explain the feeling of forlorn hope hanging over the British expedition, and the quiet self-confidence of the Norwegian.

On the morning of November 7th, the Norwegians prepared to leave the last familiar landmark at 82° S. But first the dogs disgraced themselves. Bjørn, one of Hassel's animals, got under his sledge and tipped it over. In the ensuing riot, as Bjaaland put it in his diary,

'The Sheep' took the opportunity to serve 'Lussi', who in consequence got a lead bullet in the forehead and was put on the depot.

It was an inexorable rule that for a bitch to come on heat in the field was a capital crime; it caused confusion, poor running and therefore danger. Likewise, Jålå, everybody's favourite bitch had been put down at the depot because she was found to be pregnant, and could not pull properly. Uranus was shot for laziness, '*pour encourager les autres*'. They would all help to feed their surviving comrades on the way back.

At last the whips cracked in the silent air, the dogs heaved, the sledges came away, and the Norwegians glided away into the unknown. 'Now,' wrote Amundsen, 'the journey has begun in earnest.' At two p.m. he remembered to note, 'Passed *Discovery* expeditions' southernmost latitude 82° 17″, and camped – as intended – at 82° 20′ for the night.

Amundsen had now passed the limits of human knowledge. For 500 miles he would be pioneering every inch of the way. He was a discoverer with every step and racing at the same time. He had accepted the double challenge of the unknown and a human rival. He not only had to find a way to the Pole, but also to do it quickly. Every day, every hour, perhaps counted. He bore the twin burdens of the discoverer and the long distance runner. In the history of exploration, the challenge is unique.

Amundsen had long ago decided to take the shortest route and follow a meridian of longitude, forcing whatever obstacles that happened to appear in his path. Neither he nor his companions were overawed by the prospect.

The Norwegians saw what they were doing as not so much discovery as sport. The atmosphere of racing on their own, against the clock, rivals out of sight, was not so very different from that of a cross-country ski race, with its staggered starts and lonely slog and a world that shrinks to the track ahead and the snow around your skis. Bjaaland, at any rate, regarded the whole thing as a race, somewhat longer than any he yet knew but still, basically, a ski race. His companions had the decided uplift of knowing that in his person they had one of the finest skiers in the world.

For his start into the unknown, Amundsen was vouchsafed ideal weather and splendid going.

There were four sledges. First came Helmer Hanssen, because he was the best of the dog-drivers. He had no need of the whip yet – nor did he have to shout. He had the capacity to get his dogs on with a word and a gesture; the quiet talent of the born dog-handler. He was also the best of the navigators, and he had the special non-magnetic steering sledge* with its large compass mounted on gimbals, in protective casing, as if on board ship.

Behind Hanssen came Hassel, then Wisting and last of all Bjaaland, the best of the skiers but the worst of the dog-drivers who, indeed, regarded his team with humorous exasperation. Amundsen had no sledge of his own, roaming up and down the column as command required; sometimes going ahead as forerunner. Still they were all being pulled along on skis by the dogs.

They were marking the route as they went along with a cairn at every third mile, made of nine large snow blocks according to a settled pattern, about the height of a man, visible the one from the other. In each was inserted a record with the position, the distance from the last depot and the bearing of the previous cairn.

Forty-five dogs were now left, pulling just under eighty pounds each. They scampered off, the sledges coming away easily; and hour after hour they moved in their tireless trot, tails in an upward curve, and accompanied by the nostalgic sounds of panting breath, paws pattering, the quiet creak of the sledge and the silk-like rustle of skis on powder snow.

Amundsen deliberately selected the intervals between the cairns to rest his animals every hour. Dogs need frequent rests to preserve stamina; they work best in a succession of sprints. So do their drivers, at least if they happen to have the Norwegian temperament. Amundsen had got his animals and his men working in tune.

They followed a routine devised for economy of effort. When they stopped for the day, the tent was first unloaded. Amundsen would then crawl inside, erect it with the single pole and while his companions drove in the pegs and arranged the guys outside, he got the Primus going and started supper. Getting the food was a matter of opening the small lid of

* See p. 290.

a provision case like a tea canister; the sledges were left permanently lashed and loaded.* The dogs were unhitched, fed with their pound of pemmican and allowed to roam free until harnessed the next day – the best for their comfort. Bjaaland then detached the ski bindings, bringing them into the tent for the night to avoid their disappearing into the dogs' stomachs: the Eskimo dog will devour anything. A low snow wall was thrown up to stop the dogs urinating on the fabric of the tent. In an hour, camp was made, men and animals fed.

Under Amundsen, each sledge-driver was responsible for the supplies he was carrying, keeping a precise tally in a combined provision and navigation book as each meal was served. This meticulous accounting was absent from the British expedition, with fateful results.

In their tent at night, the Norwegians were silent, not from surliness, but because it was their nature. The evening meal was eaten quietly, broken only by an occasional remark.

'We are going like greyhounds over the endless flat, snow plain,' Amundsen wrote on November 8th. Clearly the longer that terrain continued, the better. The same day a bank of cloud appeared over the south-west horizon. Next morning, it still hung there, motionless and unchanged, and through the telescope turned out to be land. Amundsen identified it with the mountains observed distantly to the south-east by Shackleton in 1908. He was much more excited with the fact that 'Right in our course – South – we can see not a trace of land, and that promises well.' Amundsen was hoping against hope that the Pole lay not on the Plateau but on the Barrier; nothing was certain.

They had now reached the 83rd parallel, and stopped to build the next depot. The depot was a now standard structure: a cube of two metres, built of hard snow blocks cut from the solid, wind-packed crust, with a dark pennant on top.

The next day, November 10th, they rested, but a storm during the night sent Amundsen – ever in search of perfection – back to the previous cairn to investigate the effect. The cairn was standing, but bent to leeward. 'We shall,' he noted, 'give the cairns a new form hereafter.'

Unfortunately Karenius, The Sheep and Schwartz followed Amundsen, and vanished northwards. 'They were Lussi's lovers,' he wrote. 'I am afraid they have taken the road back to where we shot her.' They were Bjaaland's best dogs, and they had gone for good.

This left forty-two dogs, but since Amundsen had allowed for wastage,

---

* Scott's packing cases, of conventional design with large lids, could not be opened without undoing the lashings. The sledges were loaded and unloaded at every camp, adding perhaps half an hour to the work.

and the animals therefore were not working at full stretch, the loss had no corporate effect, although Bjaaland with a weakened team now found it harder to keep up. It did not affect his spirits. 'Sun and summer,' he wrote in his diary about this time, speaking for them all, 'splendid going.'

To 82°, Amundsen had taken four days for a degree of latitude; this he then reduced to three days. The daily stage of twenty miles, in his own words,

we polish off ... in 5 hours. With cairn building, 6½ hours in all. The night is thus long. It doesn't seem to strain the dogs. They are a little thinner, but in better condition than ever.

On November 11th, there appeared over the horizon ahead, a row of glistening pyramids; the summits of a high mountain range miraged up to the south. This was Amundsen's first undoubted discovery. He later called it the Queen Maud Range, after the Queen of Norway; the Queen Maud Mountains as it is known today. At the time he was anything but elated. The peaks, as he sketched them in his notebook, were bleakly labelled A, B, C, D, E ..., symbols, not of romantic accomplishment, but merely of an obstacle in his path. 'A climb,' he drily observed, 'will apparently be unavoidable.'

It was at this point that Bjaaland heard 'unpleasant thundering in the ice in the distance ... it began at 4 o'clock but by 8, nothing was heard. Can it be the tide?'

It was to be more than sixty years before scientists proved that the Barrier was afloat, and affected by the tides.* Bjaaland made the first recorded suggestion.

The sensation of discovery came to Amundsen by delayed action. When it came, it was overwhelming.

Glittering white, shining blue, raven black ... the land looks like a fairytale [he wrote on the 13th]. Pinnacle after pinnacle, peak after peak – crevassed, wild as any land on our globe, it lies, unseen and untrodden. It is a wonderful feeling to travel along it.

What he had seen was not only the continuation of Shackleton's mountains to the south-west, but a completely unknown chain to the east, fixing the south-eastern limit of the Ross Ice Barrier. This was all very well, but where was the way up?

Amundsen had to find a pass through that high, gleaming wall of untrodden ice looming up ahead. It had to be found quickly. Amundsen

---

* The work was finally done in the Antarctic summer of 1977-78, when the U.S. Antarctic Research Programme drilled a borehole through to the underlying seawater.

chose to continue due south along his meridian and overcome what obstacles happened to obtrude. He had no time to spare; not only because of Scott, but because of his own timetable.

He could feed all his dogs for another ten days. Before that he had to reach the Polar plateau or risk his transport on the return. The spectre of man-hauling was sufficient spur to succeed.

On November 13th, Amundsen made the 'marvellous discovery' of a huge bay running due south, right in his course, where he assumed his climb must go. He thought perhaps he might not meet land before 87°; he certainly could not do so before 85°. By accepting the challenge of an unknown route, he had found land at least a degree of latitude further south than Scott and therefore would have 120 miles less on the plateau. That meant a fortnight less in the rarefied atmosphere of high altitude, a strain for which Amundsen happened to be the better prepared.

After a day navigating blind through the fog, the Norwegians found the mountains startlingly nearer. But there was no obvious way up. Amundsen carried on due south.

The Barrier began to roll in high, frozen waves. The transition to land was approaching. Influenced by Shackleton and Scott, Amundsen expected an infernal honeycomb of ridges, chasms, seracs, topped off by a monstrous bergschrund. Reality was an anti-climax; no fuss, no drama, in keeping with the rest. On the morning of November 17th, the Norwegians switchbacked over a few icy undulations, like waves running on to a shore, and negotiated some minor crevasses. With a hop, skip and jump, they left the Barrier and found themselves at the foot of the mountains.

The view from the foot of a mountain is misleading. Perspective is distorted and size often masked. The scale of these mountains, however, was gigantic; they dwarfed anything Amundsen had ever seen and, even from where he was, he had few illusions over the magnitude of the task ahead.

He was faced with the Transantarctic Mountains. In a long, unbroken curve they wind their way for over two thousand miles across the continent from Cape Adare in the east to the Pensacola Mountains in the west. From sea level, they rise in one sweep twelve or fifteen thousand feet – a sight seen nowhere else. But size alone is not what sets them apart. The great ranges of other continents – the Alps, the Andes, the Caucasus, the Himalayas – are divides across the land. This is a buttress holding back the Ice Cap. It is like a huge dam wall, with the threat of pent-up power behind.

The task before Amundsen was of a different order from that awaiting

Scott. Scott was following the route pioneered by Shackleton, and it was to be his second crossing of the Transantarctic Mountains. The previous one, on the Western Journey in 1903, had also been in another's footsteps, since Armitage had shown the way. But there was no one to guide Amundsen. A gulf separates the man who goes first from everyone who comes after. The pathfinder is denied the comfort of knowing that what he is attempting has already been proved possible. There is a world of difference between knowing and believing. From Amundsen, an act of faith was required.

Armitage and Shackleton had pioneered the only two crossings yet known. But that was hundreds of miles away, and Amundsen could not be certain of a path through the colossus of a mountain range straddling his path. Somewhere in the array of glaciers spilling over from the heights probably lay the key. But Amundsen had no time to scout, no time for second thoughts. Time, not terrain, was his enemy; time because of Scott, and the limitations of his own transport.

Amundsen had about a week left in which to find a crossing, where Armitage had taken three weeks and Shackleton a fortnight. Amundsen had long ago weighed up the problem, and decided that his only course was to drive on to the south, looking neither to right nor left. He was the prisoner of his determination, and he was now forced into the uncharacteristic position of fighting an obstacle instead of turning it.

He had landed under the spur of a massif he had seen ahead for days.* From the new perspective, the bay towards which he had been steering lost its attraction. An easier route seemed to present itself in the direction of a peak he called 'The Beehive'.† Since this involved but a minor deviation from his course, Amundsen turned aside without more ado.

The plan had been to use all the dogs for the climb, then slaughter twenty-four, whose traction would then be superfluous, take eighteen on to the Pole, and put down another six to enable twelve to return to the Barrier.

Amundsen now decided to lay an extra depot where they were, at the foot of the mountains, although their latitude was only 85° 5'. The previous depot was five miles behind at 85°, and the next one ought to be at 86°. As usual, he discussed the change with his men and got their approval.

The distance to the Pole and back, as the crow flies, was 600 miles. Taking fifteen miles a day as the speed on the Plateau, this gave forty days' travel. Amundsen decided to take sixty days' food, depoting the

* Now known as the Herbert Range.
† Subsequently Mount Ruth Gade, after the wife of Amundsen's friend, F. Herman Gade.

remainder, about thirty days', together with the sealskin clothing. Only the reindeer fur and Burberry cloth outfits were kept.

After supper, leaving Hassel to look after the dogs, Amundsen, Wisting, Bjaaland and Helmer Hanssen reconnoitred the start of the climb, going eight miles south and 2,000 feet up.

We were [says Amundsen], extraordinarily lucky. All crevasses filled. The going in the heights was splendid. Just enough loose snow for the dogs' paws, and a gradient not steeper than they can manage – the first day, at any rate.

They had a quick ski run down to the camp, out of sheer pleasure. The last slope before the Barrier was so steep that they got all the speed they wanted, the snow kicking up in little spurts. Bjaaland and Amundsen decided to make a detour to a rocky knoll in order to set foot on solid ground after fourteen months' wandering on sea and ice.

They climbed the knoll, which Amundsen immediately dubbed Betty's Knoll, after his old nursemaid and housekepper, waiting at Bundefjord for his return.

The excursion was rather tiring; the dogs had pulled the men almost all the whole way from Framheim and they were a little out of training.

In the tent that evening, someone quoted a well-known Norwegian poem:

> Fain would I know, what I once may see,
> Over the mountains high.

Then somebody, records Amundsen, recited the next line, which ran: 'Only snow shall meet the eye.'

'It came out drily,' he continues, 'and caused roars of mirth.'

The next day, the 18th, Bjaaland succinctly recorded that 'the horrible climb has begun at last' – though, he concedes, 'the snowfield where we went, was fine and smooth.' It was also steep. Up the worst pitches, the sledges had to be relayed with double teams, but, said Amundsen with quiet admiration, 'the dogs have done work today that has surpassed my greatest expectations'. They had moved their load of a ton and a half ten miles and climbed 1,500 feet. The weather, as Amundsen put it, remained 'pure summer', and that evening, looking over the Barrier gleaming like a burnished shield in the midnight sun, surrounded by an amphitheatre of ice-clad mountains, they had what he called 'the loveliest camp site in the world'.

Unfortunately, their mountain amphitheatre blocked the further road from view. While Amundsen and Hassel fed the dogs and prepared the supper, the others skied up to reconnoitre. They returned – Bjaaland speeding down unconcernedly as if he were on the outrun of a familiar ski jump – to report a navigable pass and a clear, unobstructed way on to the summit.

> On condition [Bjaaland sagely remarked], that behind those mountains [we can see] there is no awkward obstacle of parallel mountains! ... [Helmer] Hanssen says he thinks we can reach the Plateau in 2 days. If we manage it, well—

The next day began well, the dogs climbing the pass without relaying. On the other side was a descent of about 800 feet, so harsh that the sledge had to be braked by winding ropes round the runners to keep them under control. Then came the traverse of a minor glacier, elaborately crevassed, but securely bridged with snow, then up another climb, this time so steep that, in Amundsen's words, he had to relay and 'harness all [42] dogs before two sledges at a time – and still they found it hard'.

Bellies flattened on the snow, they panted and clawed their way up. They needed no whip, only shoves of the sledge and yells of encouragement for in front went Bjaaland as forerunner, leaning on his sticks, clambering up the slope with the deceptive effortlessness one expects of a champion cross-country skier.

At the top was another pass, the run down from which, as Bjaaland put it, being 'more violent than the first, so dogs and sledges ran into each other. Broke the bow of my sledge and the stern of Hassel's.'

The worst now seemed to be over, the visible contours smooth and reasonable. They now turned slightly westwards to head for a vast mountain, at least 12,000 feet high, which Amundsen at first called Haakonshallen, after its resemblance to a Norwegian castle of that name, but later changed to Mount Don Pedro Christophersen, in honour of his benefactor.

In that direction, it seemed, the way was clear to the top.

They ran out from the pass on to a small hanging glacier and, as they did so, the perspective abruptly changed. To Amundsen's stupefaction, the ground opened at his feet, revealing 'a huge, mighty glacier, absolutely fjord-like, running East–West,' across his course and interposed, like a frozen moat, between himself and Mount Don Pedro Christophersen. Contours, distance, the foreshortening of mountain perspective had played a well-known trick. The easy way up had been an illusion.

Glaciers are proverbially the highways of the mountains, but this one was more like a rampart. It was a treacherous cataract of ice, miles from shore to shore, tumbling from the edge of the Polar Plateau down to the

Barrier. It fell nearly 8,000 feet in only twenty miles and of that, twelve miles were virtually flat.

After his momentary consternation, Amundsen's attitude to the glittering white monster at his feet was wholly matter of fact. From the new vantage point, it seemed the only way to the Plateau. Even at a distance it looked appalling. It was dangerous to try. But for the distant goal it was even more dangerous not to. He was now in a cold fury. Speed was the cry; speed to use the dogs while they were there, speed to avoid man-hauling, speed to win the race with Scott. The only way seemed to be to keep on his course and overcome the hurdle Nature had thrust in his path. He decided to carry the rampart by storm.

First he had to find a way down to the new glacier, which on the spur of the moment he dubbed 'Folgefonni', after a glacier on the West Coast of Norway, but later changed to Axel Heiberg after his patron on *Gjøa* and *Fram*; the name it bears today.

It is part of the English legend of the South Pole to say that Amundsen found an easy way up and, therefore, by implication acquired an unfair advantage over Scott. Today, aircraft fly regularly over the long, steady gradient of the Beardmore Glacier on the English route pioneered by Shackleton, but very few willingly try the Axel Heiberg, since they have to use their *maximum rate of climb* to overcome it. Someone, seeing the ice falls for the first time from the air, called them 'a frothy extravaganza of crevasses'.

There was a comparatively simple, albeit steep route, up the Northern edge of the glacier, but ice blocks and sinister piles of snow told their tale of avalanches constantly tumbling from the mountains on the flank. *That* way up was a death trap. The ice falls were the only reasonable alternative. Amundsen first had to ski down to the glacier, a drop of almost 2,000 feet in a few miles. It was all deep, glistening powder snow, stable because of the cold; even now, in the summer time, the air temperature was − 20° (C.). Nonetheless, even by modern Alpine standards, it was a notable performance. The slope was equivalent to a stiffish downhill racing piste; and on this the Norwegians were running, not on modern engineered confections, but on long, narrow, solid wooden skis, hard to control, lacking steel edges, and handicapped by loose bindings that allowed the heels to lift. In addition, they had to steer their sledges, each weighing almost half a ton, and command a cohort of now exuberant Eskimo dogs in wild career.

Then came a long, enervating plod across the glacier. At any rate, they had covered nine miles that day, recouped their forced descent, and were camped 4,000 feet above sea level; 1,600 feet higher than the night before.

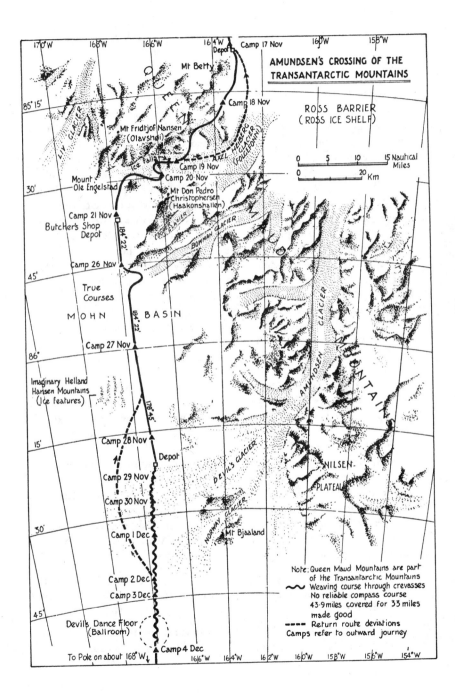

AMUNDSEN'S CROSSING OF THE
TRANSANTARCTIC MOUNTAINS

ROSS BARRIER
(ROSS ICE SHELF)

Camp 17 Nov
Depot

Mt Betty

Camp 18 Nov

Mt Fridtjof Nansen
(Olavshøi)

Ice Falls

Camp 19 Nov
Camp 20 Nov

Mount
Ole Engelstad

Mt Don Pedro
Christophersen
(Haakonshallen)

Camp 21 Nov
Butcher's Shop
Depot

184° 22'

Camp 26 Nov

True
Courses

M O H N   B A S I N

184° 22'

Camp 27 Nov

Imaginary Helland
Hansen Mountains
(Ice features)

176° 45'

Camp 28 Nov

Depot

Camp 29 Nov

Camp 30 Nov

DEVIL'S GLACIER

NORWAY GLACIER

Camp I Dec

Mt Bjaaland

Camp 2 Dec

Camp 3 Dec

Devil's Dance Floor
(Ballroom)

Camp 4 Dec

To Pole on about 168° W

AMUNDSEN GLACIER

MOUNTAINS

NILSEN-
PLATEAU

LIV GLACIER

AXEL HEIBERG GLACIER (FOLGEFONN)

BOWMAN GLACIER

0   5   10   15 Nautical
                      Miles
0   20 Km

Note: Queen Maud Mountains are part
of the Transantarctic Mountains
~ Weaving course through crevasses
   No reliable compass course
   43.9 miles covered for 33 miles
   made good
---- Return route deviations
Camps refer to outward journey

They were just under the lower ice falls, through whose maze of crevasses, pits, chasms and seracs Amundsen intended to go, because that was the direct way.

There was difficulty finding a camping place that evening among the crevasses. When they found a patch big enough, the snow was so loose that they had to tramp it down before the tent could be pitched. But the setting was magnificent, under 'Haakonshallen' with, as Bjaaland expressed it 'mighty ridges that stretched their 15,000 feet up to God'.

There are few places on earth where the might of Nature is felt with such naked force. The sheer scale is awesome; an alien immensity assaults the sense, almost as if it were a landscape from another planet. Antarctica is a land of violent extremes and yet, paradoxically, it is one of the few places where man comes closest to controlling his own fate.

The dangers are impersonal. Away from the coast, there is no life, and therefore no bacteria; no disease, no pests, no beasts of prey, no mobs, no human interference. It is a clinical environment, where a man survives by his own intelligence and foresight alone; he has to create the conditions to support his life. It can only be compared with life under the ocean or in space.

In some ways the Antarctic may seem friendly, or at least benign. Snow, after all, is a great ally. It offers shelter, insulation, drink, building material and a highway. But the friendliness is a dangerous illusion. The Antarctic is a hostile environment. It is like a passive giant now and then bestirring himself to deal a blow. One must always be on one's guard and take nothing for granted. Survival is a matter of physical and mental balance, like walking a tightrope or traversing a knife edge in the mountains, where disaster is never more than a step away, on either side.

Perched above the glacier, Amundsen now had the folly of his actions presented to his eyes. He could see how 'Folgefonni' ran down evenly to the Ice Barrier, in the bay towards which they had for days been steering before turning off at the end. The dogs, incidentally, had shown a decided wish to follow in the old direction, constantly having to be forced into what with hindsight turned out to be a disastrously mistaken course; another enigma, perhaps, of animal perception. At any rate, as Amundsen ruefully acknowledged, had he only listened to his dogs he could have

followed this glacier right up to the tent site we have this evening. Ah, well, we couldn't have done it that way under two days either. [But] this is the glacier that will be our way back when we come down from the plateau.

All the effort of the day before had been for nought. But Amundsen's mistake was scarcely resented by his companions. They had, after all, been party to the decision which led to it; an advantage of his particular style of leadership.

Amundsen now proposed quite simply to carry the ice falls by frontal assault. A trained mountaineer, sparsely loaded, would have thought carefully about finding a way through that unplumbed labyrinth of chasms and seracs. Amundsen was going to take forty-two dogs and a load of a ton and a half. From where he was, he could only have a general idea of the way to go; he could not possibly be certain that there was a route. All he knew was that the ice fall was in his way and, frightful as it looked, he simply decided to try it out. W. W. Herbert. the New Zealand explorer, who followed in Amundsen's footsteps fifty years later to see how he did it, has written that

> This is to me the most impressive example of Amundsen's determination in the face of an obstacle that would have turned away any lesser man.

Wisting once said of Amundsen that

> I never heard him say, Here we turn back. But nor did he take unnecessary chances, where it was obviously impossible to do anything.

This then was the hold Amundsen had on his men; there was no pathological isolation in that party. There might well have been. Wisting, Helmer Hanssen and Bjaaland, got on well together. But Hassel, somehow, seemed outside; he was the one inwardly most critical of Amundsen. Amundsen sensed this and took great care to share the worst camp chores with him to discourage him from feeling resentment. It was here, on the glacier, that, with bad leadership, a party could crack, as Scott's all but did on the Southern Journey in 1902.

After making camp, Amundsen sent Bjaaland and Helmer Hanssen to scout the falls for a way up as far as they could go. There was a breath of doubt in the air. Amundsen deliberately stayed behind to exploit the prestige of a ski champion and avert the dangerous, albeit silent reproach of a fool rushing in where angels feared to tread.

The next day, November 20th, the climb began. The clear weather held. Up on the heights, plumes of drift were blowing off the plateau like white chiffon streaming against a cloudless sky; down on the glacier it was 'calm, absolutely calm ... and boiling hot' in the sun, like a summer's day on an Alpine glacier. But instead of coarse, wet snow, there was powder, about a foot over wind crust. It gave grip and steerage without impeding; good, dry winter going under a summer sky, one of the hidden pleasures of high latitudes.

> Helmer Hanssen and Bjaaland [said Amundsen, in his usual, deceptively under-

played style], had found an excellent route up the glacier. There were many crevasses and chasms, but we found good [snow] bridges everywhere. The glacier ... was fairly steep at a number of places, and relaying with double teams had to be resorted to. We got a good photo of one of these 'claw drives'.

Bjaaland again led the way; for here the ski champion came into his own. The art in skiing is not only in running down, but in climbing up. Because waxing was still rudimentary, Bjaaland depended on sheer technique. He was an artist on skis, a master of balance, strength and suppleness. With the elegance of the great cross-country skier, he slid up-hill, fast enough to keep ahead of the dogs. With that moving target they followed with a touch of inspiration.

Not only were the dogs inspired. To have a ski champion in front of them, to know that their rivals had no one to touch him; this was belly-comfort to the men.

The end of the climb brought the party on to the fairly flat, middle terrace of the glacier between the upper and lower ice falls. They had come straight through the lower fall, but the upper one looked atrocious, and since this was the limit of Bjaaland's and Helmer Hanssen's pioneering, Amundsen decided to turn the obstacle, instead of forcing it.

Amundsen had been climbing straight up the middle of the glacier; he now turned aside towards Mount Don Pedro Christophersen on his left. This brought him to a pitch yet steeper than the first. Again, it was double teams and relay; the shouting, pushing, straining, clawing; the sheer *willing* upwards of the dogs, a process both mentally and physically exhausting. They were hovering in uncertainty. No one knew whether there was a way ahead.

Away on the other side of the glacier, like a twin sentinel to Don Pedro, lay the highest mountain within sight. This, Amundsen symbolically named Fridtjof Nansen. From the flanks of that ice-bound peak, there came, with impeccable timing, a cannonade of avalanches, as an obbligato to the efforts of the dogs and men. Bjaaland, at least, was vaguely disturbed, as if in the roars across the valley he heard the ominous mutterings of distant thunder.

At two in the afternoon, having climbed fifteen hundred feet or so, they reached a shelf of a distinctly uninviting aspect. It was, however, the furthest point attainable without more reconnoitring, since the upper ice falls still remained in their path. So they pitched camp, and Amundsen immediately set out to find a way through what he called

the terribly chaotic crevasses which surround us. Enormous blocks of ice, mighty abysses and wide crevasses blocked the way everywhere.

He had with him Bjaaland and Helmer Hanssen. First they attempted the direct route upwards, and were balked. They returned to the tent, and tried another route, closer to Don Pedro, towards the edge of the glacier. Again there were crevasses, but this time, with a practicable way through and over. They reached the upper terrace of the glacier, above the falls, and there, somewhat to their surprise, they saw, in Amundsen's words,

a reasonably acceptable pass at the head of the glacier ... about 8,000 ft high.... Conditions seemed quite decent. Not a crevasse or unevenness to be seen.

Bjaaland observed laconically that 'we were 8 miles up, and a hard march it was'. But they had found a route to the Plateau. The only doubt was a passage obscured by a mountain named Ole Engelstad, after the officer who was to have been the second in command.* Barring that, the crisis was over; next day almost certainly would see them on the Plateau. With some pleasure, they turned to ski back with the news to Hassel and Wisting at the camp. In their old tracks, the descent was easy; in parts, downright enjoyable; a splendid soft snow run.

As skiers will, they paused to survey the landscape.

It was [wrote Amundsen], a beautiful and impressive view we had [of] our tent ... far below, surrounded on all sides by huge crevasses and open chasms ... The wildness of the landscape from above is indescribable. Pit after pit, crevasse after crevasse, and huge ice blocks scattered helter skelter. It was easy to see that here, Nature was at her mightiest ... It was not without satisfaction that we regarded the scene. The tiny dark patch down there – our tent – in the midst of this chaos, gave us a feeling of strength and power.

The effort had taken its toll. Men and dogs were now ravenous. The dogs prowled about the camp like wolves, gnawing at anything they could get their teeth into. The sun shone, the air remained calm; it was boiling hot in the tent. Everybody, man and beast, was resting for the final effort.

This is Bjaaland's account of the following day, November 21st, 1911:

Got out of the thousands of metres deep crevasses where we had our camp. The excitement was great as we approached the side of [Mount Ole Engelstad], not knowing if it was snow covered and passable, and it was a pleasant surprise. We got up with single teams, it was heavy, but we managed. It was the hardest day we have had.

* See p. 205.

After having managed the worst slope, [the terrain] went in wave after wave with disgusting sastrugi hard as flint, and [after 12 hours] we reached the top ... and pitched tent ... and then you can bet that pemmican and chocolate went down and then into the sleeping bag; heigh ho, polar life is a grind.

From such a record it is hard to discern that Amundsen and his men had just performed one of the most extraordinary feats in the history of Polar exploration.

In four days they had found a way from the Barrier to the Polar Plateau. They had travelled forty-four miles and climbed 10,000 feet* with a ton of supplies. In charted terrain it would have been a respectable performance, even by modern standards with mechanical aids. But they had been faced by unknown mountains. It was as if they had pioneered the first crossing of the Rockies or one of the Tibetan passes. Amundsen had brought off a *tour de force*.

Perhaps, after all, he had been lucky. He had struck the Trans-antarctic Mountains at their narrowest. Not many miles to either side, and the passage would have been considerably longer.

As we know now, Amundsen had made one serious mistake. He had chosen the most difficult route in the region. To the east, he would have found an easier way up the glacier which now bears his name. But the sheer scale of things discouraged scouting. Even with dogs, it would have taken days to move from the mouth of one glacier to another. The contours were so broken that, from where Amundsen stood, all directions seemed equally impassable. He could afford to look neither to right nor left. He had no guarantee that another route existed. The only realistic alternative was forwards.

The Norwegian character is not adapted to defence or holding ground; it must attack or give way. Amundsen took a risk going up the Axel Heiberg Glacier. He would have taken a bigger risk not to, because he might have demoralized his men. And, in the event, the Axel Heiberg, with its short, concentrated strain, matched the Norwegian temperament. Amundsen had surmounted his chief obstacle in the style that became him best.

He was in no doubt to whom the credit was due. 'It was a sheer marvel ... that the dogs accomplished today,' he wrote in his diary on the evening of November 21st, at the edge of the Plateau, '17 miles, with 5,000 ft. climb. Come and say that dogs cannot be used here.'

As soon as they arrived, the dogs were put down. Each man shot

---

* During the same four days, Scott travelled fifty-two miles on the flat.

his own – that had been agreed. Amundsen, having no team of his own, was excused. As usual, being cook, he was first into the tent. But

what went faster that evening than usual was to get the Primus going and pump it to high pressure. I hoped in that way to make the most noise possible and avoid hearing the many shots that soon would sound ...
 It was hard, but it had to be. We had agreed to stop at nothing to reach our goal ... There went the first shot. I am not nervous, but I admit, that I started. Shot now followed shot – it sounded gruesome over the wastes. A faithful servant lost his life for each shot ... The festive mood which should have reigned in the tent that evening – the first on the plateau – did not come. There was something oppressive, miserable in the air; we had grown so fond of our dogs. The place was called 'The Butcher's Shop'.

At least Amundsen made no attempt at self-delusion, nor did he resort to sentimental cant. He faced the fact that, for his own ambitions, certain creatures had to pay the price. He could also truthfully say that, from the moment they arrived at Kristiansand from Greenland, eighteen months ago, his 'faithful servants' had lived a good life. They had eaten, slept, made love and drunk to their hearts' content. On this journey at least, they had not been asked to work more than they could comfortably manage, and then, at the end, they had swiftly been put down with a bullet.

It was now a month since leaving Framheim. In that time, Amundsen had got himself, his men and his dogs 430 miles across the Barrier and up to the heights in reasonable condition, although Wisting probably strained his heart on the climb. It was the first time in Antarctic history that animals had been got up to the Polar Plateau. That, too, was an outstanding exploit.

Like stage scenery changing at a cue, the weather which, as Bjaaland said, had been 'sun and summer' for the ascent, broke when the top was reached. Amundsen had, in any case, decided to halt at the Butcher's Shop, resting and feeding up his company for the last lap to the Pole.

After the effort of the climb, the eighteen surviving dogs were yet hungrier than before and noticeably thinner. As he originally planned, Amundsen proceeded to feed them up on the slaughtered animals. He was convinced that fresh meat and a change of diet were essential to restore condition, the daily pound of pemmican was not enough.

Once the carcasses were skinned, the dogs needed little persuasion to wolf their fallen friends, who thus performed their last service to the expedition.

Amundsen also believed – correctly – that the fresh dog meat would help to prevent scurvy, and persuaded the men to eat their old companions. Hunger in any case overcome revulsion at the thought. 'Wonderful dinners have we enjoyed from our good Greenlanders,' said Bjaaland, 'and I'll say they tasted good.' The monotony of an unvarying diet can be awful especially when it is concentrated and devoid of anything fresh.

At the Butcher's Shop, 274 miles from the Pole, Hassel abandoned his sledge. The eighteen surviving dogs were reorganized into three teams; Bjaaland, Helmer Hanssen and Wisting driving.

The Butcher's Shop was not a pleasant place. It lay on an exposed spur of Don Pedro, the snow ominously wind-packed hard as flint, with tell-tale sastrugi carved by constant gales. Amundsen intended staying for two days; he was storm-bound for four. It was, as he soon discerned, a blessing in disguise for the animals at least. They needed the rest. Filled with fresh meat, snoozing contentedly in the snow, uncaring of the blast, the two extra days let them recover from the climb. For better or worse, a dog quickly changes condition – the beginning of wisdom in his management. For the men, delay meant a heaven-sent opportunity to acclimatize to the altitude, although this was not clearly understood. 'Bugger this lying still,' wrote Bjaaland with feeling after four days pinned down in his sleeping bag, trying to rest eighteen hours out of the twenty-four; tossing, turning, breathless and restive from the thin air of 10,000 feet above sea level, while the tent walls drummed with the wind and hissed with the driven snow. On the fifth day – November 26th – the blizzard was still raging. But now, in sheer exasperation and, perhaps, goaded by the thought of Scott, they all willingly followed Amundsen when he decided to travel, blow high, blow low.

It was a miserable day, with a north-easterly gale. The dogs were distinctly reluctant to move because, as Amundsen said, 'They had overeaten on their comrades.'

Amundsen was now in a region where the Ice Cap starts streaming into the glaciers that drain it. It is a mass of disturbed ice; sinister country, shot with snares in the form of fissured fields riddled with hidden crevasses. Mapped and in good weather, it needs caution. When Amundsen plunged into it, it was unfathomed, unknown and veiled in blizzard and drift.

It was, as he recorded in his diary, not an ideal day to start into the unknown:

To begin with it went badly. We had to surmount enormous sastrugi, [but they] gradually decreased, until finally we had the smoothest, finest terrain. The going, however, was rotten   sticky as glue. Heavy for the dogs. The drift was so thick   mixed with falling snow - that we could hardly see the dogs in front of the sledges.

It was a 'whiteout', and Amundsen had difficulty in gauging whether the terrain rose or fell. In fact, for the first few hours, he was crossing the basin between the two spurs of Mount Don Pedro Christophersen, and almost certainly was climbing gently. But about one p.m., the snow unmistakably began to fall away. Amundsen did not know whether he was joining the Plateau or was on his way back to the Barrier; whether he was running across a dip or heading for a precipice. Meanwhile, the slope increased, and the dogs began galloping wildly down, almost out of control. 'To continue this chase completely in the dark', as Amundsen expressed it in his diary, 'would be the work of a madman', and he ordered an immediate halt. He had to bellow against the storm to make himself heard. Helmer Hanssen, up in front, had to fling his sledge sideways to obey, and the others tumbled to a standstill against him. They camped, where they were, in the middle of an awkward slope, having, in spite of all, done ten miles for the day, and went to bed hoping for a break in the weather.

It came at three the next morning. It did not last long, but they were sleeping with one eye open, and were up and out of their sleeping bags in time to get their bearings, shivering in their underclothes before the icy blast. In the direction they had been travelling, the slope was un-invitingly steep but, by turning east, they would have a gentle run down to a smooth, safe-looking snow field, apparently leading to the Plateau.

At eight a.m., they were off again, in the teeth of an easterly blizzard. The snow, in the words of Amundsen's diary, was 'sticky as fish glue' and to make the dogs pull he had to ski ahead. But soon they reached the safety of level ground a few hundred feet below, turned south, and did fifteen miles for the day, reaching 86° S.

The road to the Pole was not yet clear. For the next ten days the weather, with occasional respites, was appalling: the price, as it were, for perfect conditions on the climb.

Fog, fog and fog again, [ran a typical record in Amundsen's diary] and in addition fine snow crystals that make the going impossible. Poor beasts, they have struggled hard to get the sledges forward.

For the men, it was like skiing on sand. Blizzard and fog shrouded the landscape. Vague shapes like trolls looming out of the mist were all that

Amundsen could see of what he called 'mighty mountains' to the east. A fleeting glimpse on November 28th of a dark mass to the E.S.E. was his discovery of what today is called the Nilsen Plateau.

Even though warmed by a sense of relief at having found his way up to the Plateau, and thus overcome the main obstacle to the Pole, Amundsen was still awed by what he could see. It is spectacular landscape. The mountains are buried under more than a mile of ice, with only the tops sticking through, and still they rise five or six thousand feet, like the peaks above an Alpine valley. The very shapes hint at immensity truncated; the sprawling mass of rock and ice, the sheer scale of things is overwhelming.

The same day that he discovered the Nilsen Plateau, Amundsen saw to the west what he later called, in a letter to Bjørn Helland-Hansen, 'a gloriously beautiful mountain, in fact two, in the distant, wonderfully lovely land around the Pole which I have given you'. In that quarter, however, there is only ice, although so distorted that in the play of light it may easily suggest whole mountain ranges. Amundsen had been the victim of a common illusion. All land, as we now know, lay to the east, in the opposite direction. But the Helland-Hansen mountains went down in the maps, and were only removed after the first complete survey, forty years later.

Amundsen displayed a supreme disregard for the details of topography. He had neither the time nor the desire for surveys. He was the precursor; his task was to get to the Pole. Those who came after could fill in the gaps. His record of the uncharted country through which he was now passing consisted of a few rough drawings, a photograph or two, and sketchy compass bearings taken hastily through rifts in the fog and snow. Later travellers found difficulty in identifying several features that Amundsen named, for the diagrammatic map that he eventually published was very little help, and to this day some uncertainty remains.

Where it mattered, however, Amundsen turned out to be sufficiently precise. There is no doubt whatsoever of the identity of the main landmarks, such as the Axel Heiberg Glacier, Mount Fridtjof Nansen, Mount Don Pedro Christophersen, the Butcher's Shop, the Nilsen Plateau. When the region was finally mapped, his dead reckoning position at the Butcher's Shop proved to have been within a mile of the true one, fixed by his own latitude observation and a bearing on Mount Fridtjof Nansen. (See map, p. 413.) Since he had depended for longitude exclusively on compass and sledgemeter after leaving Framheim, now 400 miles behind, this was by any standards an astonishing degree of accuracy. Without maps or the footsteps of others to guide him, however, Amundsen had no way of knowing this at the time.

At this point, Amundsen displayed an awesome faith in himself, driving on south by the compass, trusting blindly to his instruments, while the unknown maze around him was swathed in veils of mist. As it was, something now affected the compass needle so that he drifted over to the east.

On November 29th, through a break in the fog and snow, Amundsen was surprised, first by the discovery of the isolated cluster of peaks round the Norway Glacier (see map) and then, further off, by the sudden appearance of what he called 'a colossal mountain'. This was, in fact, the Nilsen Plateau again, but unrecognizable from a different angle. But 'the biggest and most unpleasant surprise,' to quote his diary, 'was a mighty glacier ... right across our course.' Glacier was a misnomer. What he had come to was a region of strain and disturbance in the Ice Cap, like the rapids on a river. Here, at 86° 21′ S. latitude, just over 200 miles from the Pole, he laid another depot, to lighten each sledge by twenty-five kilos. He took bearings on the mountains to fix his position, and then continued on his way. He elected to follow the compass, and go straight across the disturbance straddling his path. He soon regretted his choice.

Ice is not an immobile solid. It creeps like an immensely viscous liquid whose flow is sensed, not seen, and this gives to Antarctica its feeling of movement and lurking power. The Ice Cap is in a constant state of flux, and Amundsen was at a point where its flow starts to be channelled over the edge onto the Barrier below. It also happens to be one of the most powerful ice streams in the whole of the Transantarctic Mountains. He could not know this, but he soon understood that he had run into something special in the way of glaciated nastiness. He was enmeshed in a cobweb of crevasses and fogbound into the bargain. With difficulty he found an unbroken patch of ice big enough for tent and dogs, ordered camp to be made and, with Helmer Hanssen, went on to try to find the way ahead.

It was a dangerous and trying setback. Amundsen, however, did not descend into self-pity. His diary is free of whining, suggesting instead sober recognition that he had no one to blame but himself, and anger at having been such an ass. At moments such as these, it is an exhilarating document to read.

Roped together, Amundsen and Helmer Hanssen fumbled blindly among the fissures and seracs. The fog lifted to reveal a sinister confusion of mauled and fractured ice tumbling in chaos, suggesting to Amundsen the remains of a bygone cataclysm. 'I was glad,' as he whimsically put it, 'not to have been there when it happened.'

They tried another direction; the fog descended, and they stumbled on a giant pressure ridge, where the ice seemed to have been crumpled in two, and found a gap which they dubbed 'The Gates of Hell'. On the other side, they caught a glimpse of marginally better going and a way, perhaps, to the south. They then turned and painfully picked their way among the crevasses back to the tent. As they crawled in through the entrance, with the swirling fog behind them, Amundsen, with a glint in his eye, proclaimed that 'Hereafter this shall be known as the Devil's Glacier.' This was greeted by raucous applause. 'Devil', in Norwegian, 'Fanden', has the force of a four-letter word. As the 'Devil's Glacier' it remains to this day on the maps. For four days, the Norwegians were caught there and in Amundsen's words, it

> proved to be worthy of its name. One has to move 2 miles to advance 1. Chasm after chasm ... has to be circumvented ... The dogs struggle and the drivers not less. It is tiring for us 2 who go ahead.

Bjaaland, for one, declined to be wholly depressed or rail against the gods:

> It was a lovely sight [his diary ran at one point], when the fog lifted again, and mountains and glacier came through in the most wonderful tints, no artist could achieve anything so magical; the blue green reflection in the fog.

When Bjaaland wrote this, his life was in his hands at every step. Chasms and crevasses gaped to right and left, forward and behind. No one knew, from one moment to another, when the snow would open underneath their feet and swallow them, men, dogs, sledges and all. Often, only skilful skiing and distributing weight carefully stopped them from breaking through. Once a snow bridge collapsed under Wisting but he saved himself by presence of mind. 'Some people,' Amundsen remarked, 'would call it luck.'

The third day in this frosted inferno, they came to a stretch of hard, polished ice, picked clean of snow. Unfortunately, on the assumption that the worst was over, all the crampons had been left behind at the Butcher's Shop.

> Without them [wrote Amundsen] climbing on sheer ice is supposed to be practically an impossibility. A thousand thoughts raced through my brain. The pole lost, perhaps, because of such an idiotic blunder?

Somehow, slipping and slithering, they got the sledges up inch by inch. Why, with nothing to grip, they did not fall to perdition, none of them quite understood. That evening they could not find a patch of snow for the tent, which had to be pitched on the inconvenient surface of hard ice. At least it offered a good material for melting into water, a matter of some moment. Snow and ice have an infinite variety of forms, and it is essential to avoid the kinds with too much air, because they shrink during melting into a derisory fraction of their bulk, besides wasting fuel. Finding the right kind usually involved a little walk. But on this occasion Hassel, whose job it usually was, did not have to go far.

Right outside the tent door [in Amundsen's words] 2 feet away, lay a fine little haycock that seemed entirely suitable. Hassel lifted his axe and gave a really good blow. Without resistance, the axe slipped in to the handle. The haycock was hollow. As the axe was withdrawn, the surrounding section loosened, and one could hear how the ice fragments tumbled down the gloomy shaft – 2 feet outside the door we thus had the most convenient entrance to the basement. Hassel seemed to enjoy the situation ... The raw material offered by the haycock was one of the best kind and lent itself excellently to melting into water.

The next day, December 2nd, Amundsen described how

the plateau over which we are now travelling resembles a frozen sea – a domed cupola of ice ... excellent going for a skater, but unfortunately unsuitable for our dogs and ourselves. I drag myself with my sticks ahead on skis. It is not easy. The dog drivers are without skis, at the side of their sledges, ready to help the animals.

Bjaaland solemnly headed his diary that day, 'The Devil's Nameday'. Besides the assortment of other miseries, they were travelling in the teeth of a Force 7 gale, with thick snow and drift so that

we couldn't see in front of our nose tips, and our faces were white and hard as wax candles ... Wisting's jaw looks like the snout of a Jersey cow. Helmer [Hanssen] has thick scabs [from frostbite] and skin as rough as a file. It was a damned hard day, the hounds slid on the ice, and stopped when the sledges hit a sastrugi, but we forced our way 13 miles against the ... wind which burned like a flame, oh, oh what a life.

Looking back, Amundsen chose 'The Devil's Nameday' to portray a typical picture of tent life:

It was a Saturday evening ... Outside the Sou'Easter howled [but inside] it looks cosy enough. The innermost half is occupied by 3 sleeping bags. The respective owners have found it most convenient ... to go to bed ... nearest the entrance ... Wisting and Hanssen are still up. Hanssen is cook ... Wisting is his sworn friend and helper ... Hanssen appears to be a careful cook. He doesn't like to scorch the food. The spoon goes round uninterruptedly in the contents of the saucepan ... cups are filled with [piping hot] pemmican [which] disappears with amazing speed [and then] everyone clamours for ice cold water [which] disappears in vast quantities ... the Primus roars gently during the whole meal, and the temperature in the tent is quite pleasant.

Aftjer the meal ... the polar travellers are observed to tidy themselves for the coming Sunday. Beards are cut short with clippers every Saturday evening ... Lumps of ice easily form on a beard. For me, a beard on such a journey seems quite as impractical and uncomfortable as, for example, to walk with top hats on your legs.

Blizzard followed blizzard, of a violence that kept Scott tentbound more than once. But the thought of his English rival gave Amundsen no rest, and he drove on through the storm. The winds were Gale Force 7 and 8 – thirty knots and more. Under these conditions, the landscape seems to be boiling with snow. It is an effort to move on skis; at high altitude every step is a strain. It is practically impossible to carry skis over the shoulder, as the wind tears them from one's grasp. It is very hard to follow even well-marked tracks in more civilized surroundings. For most people – even well-trained skiers – it is a heavy mental and physical strain.

The fact that Amundsen could travel at all was due to the Eskimo cut of his clothes, and the furs around his face. But although the few square inches of exposed cheek and chin were tormented by the blast, at least by Antarctic standards it was not cold. The temperature hovered around − 20° (C.). Since the start of the climb to the plateau, only the Burberry cloth outfits had been worn. The reindeer fur garments were too warm and lay on the sledges, unused. To save weight, they were abandoned on the Devil's Glacier, the hoods however cut off and saved for extra protection round the face on the windproof cloth outfits.

Ignoring a succession of narrow escapes, Amundsen plunged blindly on into the unknown. His temerity aroused the private worries of his men, but they followed compliantly, sensing that fortune was with them.

The Devil's Glacier [wrote Bjaaland], we could have avoided by driving round to the West, but no-one could believe that it looked like that; that we came through without loss of people or animals, is a miracle.

The infernal regions were then much on their minds. On December 4th, they passed what Amundsen called 'The Devil's Dance-Floor',* a freakish, treacherous surface of thin ice overlying crevasses. Here,

* Later changed to, and perpetuated as, the 'Devil's Ballroom'.

Wisting, who seemed to be a scapegoat of Fortune, nearly came to grief again, twice in quick succession. The first time, his sledge was caught with one runner hanging over a bottomless pit, while his dogs clawed for dear life, and Bjaaland, with considerable sang-froid, took a quick snapshot before jumping to help with the rescue. The second time, Wisting's dogs all went down to the length of their traces, but were rapidly hauled up.

This was the last of the disturbed terrain. 'It was at 87 deg. South,' Amundsen wrote in his diary with quiet feeling, 'that at long last we reached the plateau.' A few miles further on, he had his last view of the mountains, as they swung away to the south-east and were swallowed by the fog. They were the most southerly mountains yet seen by man – the Nilsen Plateau again – and ahead lay nothing but the unbroken surface of the Antarctic Ice Cap, at last.

It was now a clear run to the Pole, except for a minor jungle of sastrugi, some perhaps three feet high. In the whiteout which now enveloped them the forerunners – Amundsen and Hassel by turns – were helpless, because the sastrugi were invisible until they fell over them.

Soon the sastrugi, too, had ceased; it was a smooth sea of snow, a skier's eldorado. But the weather remained appalling. Thick fog and snow fall obstinately persisted for three days in a row, dismissed by Amundsen with the remark, 'Travelled completely blind ... nonetheless we have done our [daily] 20 miles.' A little later, however, he cut his speed to fifteen miles a day in order to nurse the dogs.

The climax came on December 7th, with an easterly blizzard, when Bjaaland, on the point of exasperation, irreverently decided that the great Polar Plateau was to be called *'Grisevidda'*, the Swinish Plateau. That day, in the storm, the 88th parallel was passed. Amundsen, however, did not lay the usual depot, but wanted to break Shackleton's record first, and get within a hundred miles of the Pole.

The following day, December 8th, Amundsen's diary begins with the words, 'One of our big days.' The fog lifted, the wind dropped: the weather gods had shown an uncanny sense of occasion. Early in the afternoon, Amundsen, who was leading,

suddenly heard a stout, hearty cheer behind. I turned round. In the light breeze from the South, the brave, well-known colours [of the Norwegian flag] waved from the first sledge, we have passed and put behind us [Shackleton's] record. It was a splendid sight. The sun had just broken through in all its glory and illuminated in a lovely manner the beautiful little flag ... My goggles clouded over again, but this time it was not the South wind's fault.

There was no jealousy; no gloating over a fallen rival. Amundsen's admiration for Shackleton was boundless.

As my dogs were horribly worn [wrote Bjaaland], I was 1 mile behind, and when I came up, 88° 23′ it *was* and I seemed to walk on springs. I congratulated the Captain, he was in a shining humour, you can be sure. Extra chocolate in honour of the occasion. Tomorrow rest day. The sun is shining.

29

Man-Hauling Begins

IN SCOTT'S CAMP, two hundred and fifty miles behind, Wilson was reading Tennyson's *In Memoriam*,

and have been realizing [he wrote in his diary] what a perfect piece of faith and hope and religion it is, makes me feel that if the end comes to me here or hereabout ... All will be as it is meant to be.

These are revealing words. *In Memoriam* is the quintessence of Victorian morbidity. It includes the lines, 'This year I slept and woke with pain,/I almost wished no more to wake.' It is an odd poem for the frontiers of survival.

Since December 5th, Scott had been stopped by a blizzard near the foot of the Beardmore Glacier. 'One cannot see the next tent,' he wrote, 'let alone the land ... I doubt if any party could travel in such weather, certainly no one could travel against it.'

As it happened, the weather was much the same as that facing Amundsen on 'The Devil's Nameday', although he was handicapped threefold by the rarefied atmosphere of an altitude of 10,000 feet greater, a temperature fifteen degrees lower, and completely unknown country with no predecessor's footsteps to guide him. *His* diary read: 'It has been an unpleasant day – storm, drift and frostbite, but we have advanced 13 miles closer to our goal.'

When Oates had said that Amundsen would 'have a great chance ... as ... he has a hard crowd behind him',* he had discerned the weakness within his own party. In plain figures Scott had, in all, six days of gale-force winds, and travelled on none of them; Amundsen had fifteen, and travelled on eight.

Like the Norwegians at the Butcher's Shop a fortnight before, the British were now four days blizzard-bound. Scott's self-pity:

It is more than our share of ill-fortune ... How great may be the element of luck! No foresight – no procedure – could have prepared us for this state of affairs. Had we been ten times as experienced or certain of our aim we should not have expected such rebuffs ... It's real hard luck.

* See p. 345.

contrasts with Amundsen's stoicism: 'We just had to make a virtue of a necessity and turn in again. We all benefit from the rest even if it is monotonous.'

But Scott, unlike Amundsen, had cut things fine. In his own words, 'we can't afford' the delay. In a journey of four months, he had not allowed for four days' bad weather. At the most, said Bowers in his diary, 'the delay will mean nothing worse than a little short commons on our return journey, a trifling matter'.

Bowers knew all about the stores.

They had already started on their summit ration, which they were not supposed to do before reaching the Glacier. They had already started overrunning their supplies.

This was beginning to look ominously like the Southern Journey on the *Discovery* all over again. Wilson who, alone of Scott's companions, had been on that near-disaster as well, could make comparisons. He could see how Scott appeared to have learned nothing and was repeating old mistakes. It is enough to explain his sense of foreboding.

There was another danger.

Even now, on the march, Scott shut his eyes to the foreign threat, followed for the most part by his men. Reality was sometimes too strong to be ignored as, for example, when the Transantarctic Mountains were seen trailing off to the south-east, forcing Scott ruefully to remark that 'If Amundsen journeying that way has a stroke of luck, he may well find his summit journey reduced to 100 miles.' Bowers in his diary was more blunt: 'Amundsen has probably reached the Pole by now. I hope he has not, as I regard him as a sneaking, back-handed ruffian.'

But aside from such outbursts, Amundsen did not seem to exist; certainly not for Scott. He was living in a fantasy world, looking over his shoulder at the shadow of Shackleton; squat, energetic, with burning eyes, striding masterfully over the snows. There, to Scott, was the real antagonist. 'Our luck in weather is preposterous,' he complained, to continue in a revealing outburst, 'It makes me feel a little bitter to contrast such weather with that experienced by our predecessors.'

When he wrote this, Scott had been comparing his fortunes with Shackleton's. He had built all his plans on an exact repetition of Shackleton's weather, and now he grudged his ghostly rival his luck.

In fact Scott could read in his own diary the record of nineteen good days out of thirty-four on the march so far. At the comparable stage, on November 22nd, Amundsen could say precisely the same. Scott could not know this, but he could read in his extract from *The Heart of the Antarctic* that Shackleton, on December 4th, 1908, only had seventeen good days out of the first thirty-four. Scott's luck was, therefore, in reality no worse than that of his rivals; marginally better perhaps than Shackleton's. He hardly had grounds for complaint.

On the fourth day of the blizzard, still tent-bound and idle, Bowers was 'prognosticating good signs out of everything to cheer up Captain Scott, who naturally feels a bit down on his luck'. In another telling passage, Bowers remarked he was glad Scott had 'Dr. Bill [Wilson] in his tent; there is something always so reassuring about Bill, he comes out best in adversity'.

There were sound technical reasons for Scott's delay. His clothing was unsuited to bad weather. His men could not ski well enough to cope with the soft snow now facing them. The ponies were helpless because their hooves drove straight through the snow and they only had one set of snowshoes among them. The depot journey had shown how useful such devices were, and since proved models (of which many existed in cold-weather countries) had not been brought in sufficient number, P.O. Evans had been told to improvise. The improvisations had soon broken down.

Another technical deficiency made lying still unpleasant. The tents lacked sewn-in groundsheets, so that, to quote P.O. Keohane, 'We bails the water off the floor cloth, but that is small comfort.'

It was a freakish warm blizzard, and that was what had caused Scott's lamentation. He need not have been surprised. During the *Discovery* Southern Journey, on January 6th, 1903, he had had precisely the same experience. Now, exactly as on that occasion, the snow was melting as it fell. The going was heavy.

Yet, in Scott's own words, 'With the help of the dogs, we could get on, no doubt.' But he shrank from driving the ponies into the gale for fear of seeing them suffer, as he shrank from driving dogs to the limit.

Amundsen had the insight to grasp that he had to overcome his emotions to make sure of survival; that what he had set out to do, demanded a price. Scott lacked that insight. He lacked the resolution and consistency in the daily round demanded by his consuming desire for the distant goal.

In any case, Scott's proceedings were now irrational. The ponies were at the end of their tether, their fodder finished. Starving and shivering as they stood in the gale, they suffered as much as on the march.

On December 8th, as the blizzard started to drop, an astonishing spectacle was enacted in the English camp. As Bowers once said when discussing Anton and Dmetri, the two Russian boys on the expedition, 'Foreigners generally think Britons are a trifle mad.' They might well have thought so now. Four men sat on a sledge, while three others were harnessed before them to prove, on the last 400 miles to the Pole, that loads could be pulled on skis; a proceeding that recalled Captain Mostyn Field's opposition to putting Scott in command of *Discovery*.

> If an officer inexperienced in these matters be appointed, the price will be paid in time and material, neither of which can be afforded on an Antarctic Expedition.*

Time was now Scott's most precious commodity, and time was running out. He was at the end of the Barrier stage, about to start the climb. He had been on the way for thirty-eight days, covering 379 miles, a speed of nine point eight miles a day. Amundsen, at the corresponding point, had covered 385 miles and taken only twenty-nine days, a speed of thirteen point three miles a day, including rests. Scott was falling behind at the rate of three and a half miles a day.

The ponies' last march was on December 9th. Starved, tired and frozen, they were lashed on, sinking up to their bellies in the soft snow. They took twelve and a half hours for six miles. Two miles from the entrance to the Glacier called by Shackleton the Gateway, the procession stopped and Oates shot the ponies. 'Thank God the horses are now all done with,' wrote Wilson in his diary, 'and we begin the heavier work ourselves.'

Scott too was glad that the man-hauling was about to begin; it was now he came into his own. He was relieved that all distasteful beasts were out of sight, obviously enjoying the sense of struggle.

Scott now tackled the self-imposed task of man-hauling all his loads up to the heights; a prospect regarded by Amundsen with unmitigated horror, and one which it had been his fundamental aim to avert. Even Scott had a trace of doubt. The dogs were supposed to turn back at the foot of the Glacier: with a sudden change of mind he ordered them on for two days more. That was another error of judgment. It helped him a little way up the Glacier but it lessened the chances of having them bring him supplies on the very last lap of all and so of getting home safely. Also, to eke out Meares' food on his return, everybody else gave up one biscuit daily, which meant 200 calories, or almost five per cent of what in the circumstances was already a starvation diet. These were two more risks to add to the others in the chain. On December 11th, when Meares and Dmetri finally turned home with the dog teams, 360 miles from the Pole, Cherry-Garrard remarked that 'They have done splendidly. It looks as if Amundsen may have hit off the right thing.'

* See p. 135.

Scott blandly said that 'the dogs should get back quite easily; there is food all along the line.' This was all the thanks that Meares got for his effort. Scott was like an officer on some hair-raising mission, taking self-sacrifice in his subordinates for granted. He had done little to help Meares on his way.

Between the Glacier and 80° S. Scott had put down exactly two depots; Amundsen on the corresponding stretch, *seven*, regularly spaced sixty miles from each other. It was 120 miles between the Mid-Barrier and One Ton Depots. Scott's depots were too few and too far apart even for his dogs to run in comfort. What would happen when tired men had to walk the distance on their way back from the Pole?

As it was, Meares had a hard run back. By going on longer than originally intended, he had stretched his rations to the limit. He had to go short. This angered him because he felt his life had been unnecessarily risked, and he bore a lasting grudge. Scott, he said in after years, was an incompetent organizer and 'should not have been put in charge of such an expedition'.

With Meares and Dmetri gone, Scott had eleven men left: Oates, Bowers, Teddy Evans, Charles Wright, Cherry-Garrard, Petty Officers Edgar Evans, Crean and Keohane, Lashly, and the two doctors, Wilson and Atkinson. They were expected to pull 200 pounds a man, uphill, for 120 miles along the immense Beardmore Glacier up to the Plateau at 10,000 feet. They started off in deep, loose snow. Skis, wrote Scott, 'are the thing, and here are my tiresome fellow-countrymen too prejudiced to have prepared themselves for the event'.

This was shifting the responsibility. Scott had failed to organize systematic training. Having brought Tryggve Gran halfway round the world to give ski instruction, he had then refused to make use of him. Partly, this was another example of Scott's inconsistency, partly his illogical reaction to Amundsen's challenge, which took the form of shutting his eyes to things Norwegian. As a result, the party on the Glacier was ill-prepared, squandering energy with poor technique. Hauling the sledges, said Bowers, was

> the most back-breaking work I have ever come up against ... The starting was worse than pulling as it required from ten to fifteen desperate jerks on the harness to move the sledge at all ... I have never pulled so hard, or so nearly crushed my inside into my backbone by the everlasting jerking with all my strength on the canvas band round my unfortunate tummy.

Straining as if each mile was his last, Scott provided the heroic self-punishment so dear to the heart of the British public of whom he was ever aware. Underneath the lamentations he accepted the agony. So too did Wilson, sitting out on a packing case at each camp to sketch the landscape with his well-mannered, oddly impersonal realism. Oates was the odd man out. No genteel stoic, he knew that a horse or a dog was built to pull, but not a human being. To him, the whole proceeding appeared mildly insane, but he kept his counsel. Sapping their vital energy, the British endured struggles far more heroic than Amundsen on his climb up to the Plateau.

The Norwegian and British routes are totally different in style and atmosphere. The Axel Heiberg Glacier, short, steep, broken, in a narrow defile hemmed in by high mountains, makes a dramatic impact, like an Alpine valley. The Beardmore Glacier is altogether vaster; the mountains are almost as high, but the view is from the middle distance, and the impression is of wide vistas and sheer scale instead of form and almost claustrophobic height; the Himalayas rather than the Alps.

The ice falls of the Beardmore Glacier are neither as high nor as steep as those of the Axel Heiberg, but longer; the dangers less intense but more protracted. The British, however, had the advantage over the Norwegians in a gentler climb, giving acclimatization to altitude. Miles from shore to shore, winding interminably onwards like a white, frozen Amazon, the Beardmore was the better stage for Scott's dogged trudge.

While Amundsen was pioneering every inch of the way, Scott was following in Shackleton's footsteps; relieved at not having to blaze a trail, yet resenting the obligation. Each night in the tent, studying Frank Wild's diary and the extracts from *The Heart of the Antarctic*, Scott was jealously measuring himself against Shackleton. 'We are now 6 days behind Shackleton,' he wrote dejectedly on December 16th, 'all due to that wretched storm'. It was Shackleton, Shackleton all the way. Scott does not share Amundsen's (or Oates') admiration for what Shackleton did; where he comments, it is in sour disparagement. 'We see that there is great and increasing error in the charting.' 'His latitudes are out by 7 miles or so.' 'We gain on him,' Scott writes triumphantly on December 17th, as he passed Mount Hope and entered the upper reaches of the Glacier under the Wild, Marshall and Adams ranges, called after Shackleton's three companions on his southern journey. The very place-names were a reproach and a reminder of the rival who had been before.

As the top of the Glacier approached, so too did the time for another support party to turn. 'I dreaded this necessity of choosing,' Scott lamented in his diary, 'nothing could be more heartrending.'

Those now selected to return were Atkinson, Wright, Cherry-Garrard and P.O. Keohane. They left on December 21st.

The evening before, Wilson took Atkinson aside and, as one doctor to another, put the following question: Of the seamen, Edgar Evans, Lashly and Crean, whom did he consider, on mental and physical grounds, the fittest to go on to the Pole?

Atkinson's reply was: Lashly.

Wilson agreed.

Atkinson then said that, next to Lashly, on physical grounds he would take Crean. Wilson did not altogether agree. But about Lashly he had no reservations.

This conversation had its origins in a desire of Scott, as a Naval officer, to have the Lower Deck represented at the moment, as he thought, of victory. For that honour he had selected P.O. Evans. Wilson was unhappy over this. Having known Evans since *Discovery* days, he noticed his deterioration and saw in him physical and mental flaws, hinting at danger under stress. Evans' drinking alone had been enough to raise doubts. Wilson argued that if a seaman was to go on, it ought to be Lashly or Crean instead.

Lashly was quiet and articulate. A teetotaller and non-smoker, he attracted the clichés 'hard as nails' and a 'tough old sportsman', indicating that his companions regarded him as physically and mentally sound beyond a peradventure.

Crean, an Irishman to Lashly's West Country, was, in Tryggve Gran's words, 'a man who wouldn't have cared if he'd got to the Pole and God Almighty was standing there, or the Devil. He called himself "The Wild Man from Borneo".... And he was!'

Both were intelligent and resourceful. Either would have been preferable to Evans. Wilson sought Atkinson's professional opinion to reinforce his arguments with Scott. But Scott was not open to argument. Evans was big and beefy, and Scott, who went by appearances, persisted in equating size with stamina. His crippling incapacity to judge character made him blind to defects which were obvious to others. He stuck to his old favourite, for once ignoring Wilson's advice. Scott insisted on taking Evans to the Pole out of sentiment.

On the Western Journey in 1903, during the *Discovery* expedition, Evans had fallen into a crevasse with Scott, while it was Lashly who, by a combination of luck, strength and presence of mind had kept his footing and hauled them up. Scott preferred the man who had fallen into the depths with him to the one who had stayed on top and saved his life.

Scott possessed great physical courage and phenomenal stamina. One of his weaknesses as a leader was to expect the same powers in everyone and ignore the differences in men.

Beyond this, he was a man who always raced; against a rival, a friend, and, in the last resort against himself. It was as if he wanted to reassure himself of his physical strength. He revealed a glimpse of the neurotic doubts underlying this behaviour when writing to his wife that he could 'go with the best of them, so that I am not ashamed to belong to you'.

On the march, Scott had an irrational, almost sadistic love of driving his companions to exhaustion. On the border of survival, such men are dangerous.

Amundsen's companions knew that when they had done their fifteen or twenty miles, they stopped, outspanned and camped. There was rhythm, regularity, discipline, certainty, finite compass to their days. Whatever his *angst* over being forestalled, Amundsen had the intelligence and self-control to filter his emotions and avoid driving his men to the limit. Scott, with manic urge, drove his followers on, whatever the consequences. Bowers conveys the atmosphere in his diary for Christmas Day.

> Scott [he wrote] got fairly wound up and went on and on ... my breath kept fogging, my glasses and our windproofs got oppressively warm and altogether things were pretty rotten. At last he stopped and we found we had done 14¾ miles.*
>
> He said, 'What about fifteen miles for Christmas day?', so we gladly went on - anything definite is better than indefinite trudging.

The doctors had remonstrated at this hysteric race, but without result.

Wafted on the winds of his emotion, Scott was more than usually fretful when, on December 27th, Bowers reported breaking the thermometer belonging to the hypsometer (an instrument for determining altitudes by the boiling point of water).† He

> got an unusual outburst of wrath in consequence, in fact my name is mud just at present. It is rather sad to get into the dirt tub with one's leader at this juncture, but accidents will happen.

It was hardly Bowers' fault. A thermometer is a fragile instrument. However, only one had been brought, and Scott now had no accurate method of measuring altitude. (Amundsen had taken four thermometers for his hypsometer in case of accidents.)

There was a rational foundation for these emotional outbursts. Self-

---

* Man-hauling, and plodding and skiing badly. To expend the same energy, the Norwegians, dog-driving and skiing properly would have to travel about thirty miles.
† Based on the fact that the boiling point drops as the altitude rises.

delusion has its limits. As Scott climbed up the Glacier, and the forlorn sense of isolation squeezed him in its grasp, he found it harder to escape the uncomfortable consciousness that he had left his lines of retreat in disarray. Could the dogs, after all, come out and meet him? Would there be food and fuel enough at the final depots to get him back safely? Meares would not be there to make certain. They had quarrelled during the winter, mainly because Scott had tried to tell him how to run the dogs. Meares had thereupon informed Scott that he was going to clear out and go home with the ship. There was now no love lost between them, and Meares plainly had no intention of changing his mind. Scott would, therefore, be deprived of his dog expert precisely when he needed him most. Dmetri would then be the only qualified dog-driver remaining, but he could not work without supervision, something of which Scott had long been aware. It was near the top of the Beardmore, four hundred miles from base, when the cold light of reality began to dawn, that he first considered the matter. Just before Atkinson turned back, Scott unexpectedly told him, in terms suggesting hasty improvisation, that he was to bring the dog teams south on the last lap instead of Meares. 'Come as far as you can,' he said, in a tone which left Atkinson uncertain whether it was an order or a suggestion. In any case, the instructions were verbal, when all prudence suggested writing. This was the third time that the orders for the dogs had been changed.

Among Scott's troubles was a spate of snowblindness, which Amundsen escaped because he had better goggles. The explanation went back to the early preparations. Scott had ordered conventional goggles, of the small, round type that misted up easily and gave inadequate protection. Amundsen, on the other hand, discovered that Dr. Frederick Cook had constructed a radically new kind while in the Arctic. It was based on an Eskimo model, which was a wide visor with ventilation slits on the top, rather like modern ski goggles, and therefore much in advance of its time. Instead of the narrow slits used by Eskimos to mask the light, however, Dr. Cook had substituted photographic filters. Apart from giving proper protection, and not misting up easily, this design gave a wide angle of vision, essential in route-finding. Amundsen had these goggles copied for his party, and secured another advantage over Scott.

Various technical defects plagued Scott on his climb up the Glacier and tried his temper. He continued to worry over his poor luck compared with Shackleton. He was particularly upset by having loose snow which Shackleton did not.

In fact, on the climb, Scott had little to complain of. As he moved along the glistening white road, he had plenty of sunshine, not once being weatherbound. The deep snow, of which he complained because it made his own hauling harder, also more securely bridged crevasses, and therefore gave him a considerable advantage on that score. Again, figures tell the tale. Shackleton was in danger from crevasses for twenty-five days, Amundsen for eighteen, Scott for *only three*. Scott, however, failed to grasp the point, and it was not in his nature to give thanks for favours received. He was self-absorbed to the point where he expected the gods to order things for his benefit, as of right.

All this was ominous enough. More serious yet, the party was riven by conflict. The hostility between Scott and Teddy Evans had grown under the strain of the climb until now it was poisoning the atmosphere.

All the way up the Glacier, sometimes on skis, sometimes not, Scott was racing Evans, and Evans, aggressively competitive himself, responded by straining every muscle and nerve to show that he was, after all, his captain's equal. After Atkinson had turned, 300 miles from the Pole, the dénouement came.

Two sledges were now left on the road to the Pole. One was hauled by Scott, Wilson, P.O. Evans and Oates; the other, by Teddy Evans, Bowers, Lashly and Crean. Rivalry was simple and obvious.

Scott forced the pace. He covered thirteen miles a day, not far short of Amundsen's fifteen. But the effort was prodigious. Scott was on the march for nine or ten hours, hauling heavy weights. Evans kept up gamely but on December 27th, he began to falter. Scott was annoyed; after some trial he discovered that the other sledge was running badly and blamed Evans for strapping the loads too tightly, thus distorting the framework and the runners. Evans' team, he unfairly decided, were 'not done, ['Fagged out'] and I have told them plainly that they must wrestle with the trouble and get it right for themselves'.

What Scott did not understand – or perhaps he did – was that Evans was tiring. Evans had been man-hauling 400 miles further, almost the whole length of the Barrier since the motors broke down. He was already in the early stages of scurvy. He now consistently dropped behind. When they reached the Plateau on New Year's Day, 1912, his party, as Scott put it, were 'not in very high spirits, they have not managed matters well for themselves'. Scott had worn Evans down, but he had also worn his own men out, although this was not yet obvious. Dragging 200 pounds per man up to 10,000 feet was inhuman enough, without the strain of quarrels and forced marches.

Wilson was worried about the tension between Scott and Evans. He was very unhappy after a visit to Evans' tent on December 30th. Evans desperately wanted to go on to the Pole and the final party had not yet been announced.

That announcement could not be long delayed. On New Year's Eve, Scott ordered Evans' team to abandon their skis and continue on foot. This is quite staggering, and Scott nowhere gives his motives. He did, however, make his own party keep their skis, and gives a hint of what was in his mind when he wrote that it was 'a plod for the foot people and pretty easy going for us'. He had patently decided by then to take his own team on to the Pole, and wanted to break Evans so as to ease the task of sending him back.

After a short march, Scott camped, so that P.O. Evans and Crean could dismantle the sledges and shorten them from twelve feet to ten feet. The purpose was to lighten them and improve their running. It took eight hours, rather longer than Scott expected. It was hardly work that men would choose to do on the march, when sledging in bitter cold, with fingers freezing. Scott, however, had deliberately intended it all along. Evans cut his hand badly in the process; he was prone to this kind of accident. During the *Discovery* expedition, Skelton had observed that he was 'clumsy'.

Scott promised a lie-in until nine-thirty on New Year's Day; then routed everybody out as usual at seven-thirty. The march to the south was resumed with a distinct feeling that 1912 had not begun auspiciously.

By the following day, the Beardmore Glacier had ebbed out, and the Plateau seemed to have been reached, obstacles put behind. All that remained was a straight run to the Pole, a bare 150 miles away. Their work done, the supporting party could now turn back. The next morning, just before starting, Scott visited Teddy Evans' tent to break the news. It was a moment he had been dreading, and put off as long as he could, because from the start he had led Evans to believe that he would go to the Pole.

As Scott entered, the tent was full of tobacco smoke, and Crean happened to be coughing.

'You've got a bad cold, Crean,' said Scott.

But Crean saw through him.

'I understand a half sung song, sir.'

Scott smiled and, as casually as he could, announced that he was taking his own team to the Pole. He then ordered everyone out of the tent except Evans and, when they were alone, asked him if he could spare Bowers from his team, making the return journey one man short. Evans rashly consented; his pride allowed no other course. Scott wanted Bowers for the Polar party.

This was quite astonishing. Scott had based his plans on taking four men to the Pole. Now, at the last moment, he unexpectedly added a fifth and considerably increased his risks. His food would only last for four weeks instead of five but, as he casually remarked, 'it ought to see us through'. One of his waves of euphoria had welled up on discovering that now, after superhuman efforts, he was actually *ahead* of Shackleton's dates. That is to say he had arrived at 87° 30′ S., in a few days less than Shackleton three years before, over a journey of 600 miles, lasting two months. To Scott this appeared as victory and a comforting margin of safety.

It was not only the Polar party that Scott had put at risk. He had thrown his whole intricate organization dangerously out of joint. Everything was arranged for four-man units: tents, gear, cookers, fuel and the depots along the route. The tent would be crowded. Evans on his way back would have to break into the ready-packed portions, take three-quarters, and leave a quarter. He had with him neither scales to weigh food, nor a measure for paraffin. Scott himself offered no explanations. His companions had by now grown so accustomed to his caprice and irresolution that they accepted this latest change of mind as a matter of course, without recorded comment. Probably the prospect of parting brought Scott for the first time face to face with the chill reality of man-hauling another nine hundred miles. The undertones in his diary speak of failing faith in his own calculations. In a moment of panic he might have decided that he needed more power, and five men would be safer than four.

When, on New Year's Eve, he had clearly decided to send back Evans and his party, Scott did not consider that it would leave him without a navigator. One week before leaving Cape Evans, Wilson had spent a few hours learning latitude sights. 'It will be wiser,' as he put it in his diary, 'to know a little navigation on this southern sledge journey.' It was not enough. Using a theodolite, which Scott had chosen in preference to a sextant, needs considerable practice; so, too, does working out the sights. To all intents and purposes, Wilson could not navigate; neither could Oates or P.O. Evans, and Scott himself was out of practice. Competent astronomical navigation was vital in travelling over the featureless interior of the Polar Plateau, not to mention finding the goal of the journey. No navigator, no Pole, about sums it up. (Amundsen had *four* qualified navigators on his Polar party.)

A long talk with Bowers on New Year's Day brought Scott back to his senses. Until then, his mind had been blocked by his obsessive concern for getting rid of Evans. He now grasped that he had to take a navigator to the Pole, and Bowers filled the bill. Unfortunately, by now Evans' party had abandoned their skis, and Bowers perforce was plodding along on foot.

Bowers was more than just a navigator. In Scott's words, it was 'an immense relief to have the indefatigable little Bowers to see to all detail arrangements.' Bowers was Scott's physical prop, as Wilson was his mental one. It speaks eloquently of Scott's confused state of mind that he had condemned so indispensable an assistant to the handicap of trudging through the snow, while his companions skied in comparative comfort. Bowers, for his part, was willing to face the slog; he wanted to go to the Pole at almost any price.

As Cherry-Garrard had said of his own parting, 'a very mournful air' pervaded the camp, affecting 'those going on and those turning back'. A strange undertone haunts Oates' last letter home:

The Plateau, 3 January 1912.
I have been selected to go on to the Pole with Scott as you will have seen by the papers. I am of course delighted but I am sorry I shall not be home for another year as we shall miss the ship – we shall get to the Pole alright. We are now within 50 miles of Shackleton's Furthest South.
It is pretty cold up here ... and the work has been very heavy but ... I am very fit indeed and have lost condition less than anyone else almost. I hope the alterations at Gestingthorpe have been carried out. I mean the archway between Violet's room and my room. It would be nice in the room opposite the bathroom as 1 can have a fire in there at night better than in my old one. Can you please ... send me ½ doz. books so that I can start working for my Major's exam. on my way home ... What a lot we shall have to talk about when I get back – God bless you & keep you well until I come home.

Atkinson, who was Oates' particular friend, told Cherry-Garrard that after their last conversation, he

did not think Titus wanted to go on, though he (T.) did not actually say so. He thinks Titus knew he was done – his face showed him to be so and the way he went along.

Oates was worse off than Atkinson suspected.

My feet [Oates wrote in his diary], are giving me a bit of trouble. They've been continually wet since leaving Hut Point. And now walking along this hard ice [on the Glacier] has made rather hay of them.

Oates, indeed, did not want to go on. His Boer War wound was worrying him. The bullet that shattered his thigh had left one leg about an inch shorter than the other. He had been passed fit for ordinary Army work, which meant mostly riding. There is no evidence that he was ever found fit to march for 1,500 miles. He was now perceptibly limping. He had got his ponies across the Barrier and done his job. He had reached the top of the Glacier and satisfied ambition. Now he wanted to go home. This, Scott, so isolated from his companions, was incapable of sensing. Oates was brought up with a code of behaviour which made it honourable to conceal his infirmities. He had enormous self-control. Atkinson saw through this; so did Wilson. But Scott took the outer shell for the reality, and ignored Wilson when he tried to warn him, as he had ignored him over P.O. Evans.

Scott was now screwed to a pitch where he was no longer accessible to reason. He could quite well have sent Oates back in place of Bowers and kept his numbers down to four. Atkinson and Wilson agreed that Oates was unfit to continue but Wilson, according to what Atkinson later told Cherry-Garrard, explained that 'Scott was keen on his going on, he wanted the Army represented.'

Oates had, indeed, started off with similar ideas. Just before leaving Cape Evans, he had written to his mother:

> I have half a mind to see Scott and tell him I must go home in the ship but it would be a pity to spoil my chances of being in the final party especially as the regiment and perhaps the whole army would be pleased if I was at the Pole.

By now, however, Oates had ceased such sentimentalizing. He knew he ought not to go on, but his contempt for Scott made it doubly humiliating to admit weakness. His rigid sense of discipline made him regard his commanding officer's wish as an order to be obeyed, whatever the cost. He went forward, driven only by a sense of duty, half-hearted and uninspired.

On January 4th came the parting. They were now less than 150 miles from the Pole. It was another emotional occasion. Wilson was 'very sorry for Teddy Evans as he has spent 2½ years in working for a place on this polar journey'. In Scott's words, 'Poor old Crean wept and even Lashly was affected.'

Evans, Crean and Lashly followed the Polar party a mile or two to see them on their way. Then they stopped, gave three cheers that whispered wanly in the bitter breeze, and turned for home, looking back constantly until Scott and his companions were a speck on the horizon and disappeared from human ken.

Oates' farewell was characteristic:

> I'm afraid, Teddy, you won't have much of a 'slope' going back, but old

Christopher [Oates' pony] is waiting to be eaten on the Barrier when you get there.

Evans carried letters from Scott. One was to Kathleen, saying that he had

led this business – not nominally but actually – and lifted the other people out of difficulty – so that no man will or can say I wasn't fit to lead through the last lap.

Another was a message in a different vein to the Press: 'I am remaining in the Antarctic for another winter in order to continue and complete my work.' This was his public posture in case he missed the ship.

Evans also carried a message from Scott changing the orders for the dogs yet again – for the fourth time. Meares now was to come out and meet Scott between 82° and 83° S., some time towards the middle of February. The ostensible purpose was to hurry him back in time to catch the ship. Like Amundsen, Scott, too, wanted to be first with the news. But it also hinted at anxieties. This was the furthest Scott had yet wanted the dogs brought out. It was in any case a vital alteration to his plans. It was verbal. It bore the stamp, once more, of last-minute improvisation. Scott assumed that Evans would deliver it in time.

It was an optimistic assumption. Scott had done nothing to ease the homeward path. There were too few cairns on the Plateau; none to mark the path through the ice falls on the Glacier. Until he reached the Barrier, Evans would have to depend on his outgoing tracks in the shifting snows. He had no sledgemeter, so that navigation would be largely guesswork. And, as he very soon discovered, he had made too great a sacrifice by giving up one of his party. Three was too few to drag a loaded sledge for hundreds of miles. He also found that Scott had put the depots too far apart for man-hauling. It was going to be a struggle to get through at all.

The consequences of his actions were soon brought home to Scott.

Cooking for five [he recorded the day after parting from Teddy Evans] takes a seriously longer time than cooking for four; perhaps half an hour on the whole day. It is an item I had not considered when re-organizing.

Another item he had not considered was the difficulty of Bowers hauling on foot together with men on ski. Their rhythms were so different, it was hard to synchronize the pull. Bowers was hitched to the central trace in the middle of the team. There he plodded along, sinking sometimes to his knees with every step, handicapped by his short legs;

determinedly keeping up with his companions floating on the surface on their skis.

He faced more than 300 miles of this to the Pole and back before finding his skis again.

There was ominously little joy in the party. 'The marching,' wrote Scott in a typical diary entry, 'is growing dreadfully monotonous.' Hour after hour, day after day, they plodded along, each mile like the last, each man wrapped up in himself, his harness tugging at every step, the creak of the sledge the only sound in the silence of the dead white plain rolling interminably to the horizon.

Scott was still haunted by Shackleton. 'It is amusing to stand thus,' he wrote on a fine evening, able to remain comfortably outside the tent, 'and remember the constant horrors of our situation as they were painted by S.' He was soon punished for his presumption. 'Dreadfully trying', he was already writing in his diary the following day, when the snow turned sticky.

They were doing about ten miles a day now; just about keeping up with their timetable, and found the going uniformly bad. On January 6th, running into heavy sastrugi, where skiing was difficult, Scott, in one of his irrational outbursts, decided to dump their skis. The next day they set off walking, but argued over the skis. In the end, Scott was persuaded to return to fetch them. They lost one and a half hours by this piece of confusion and did only nine miles for the day.

Marching again [said Scott], I found to my horror we could scarcely move the sledge on ski; the first hour was awful owing to the wretched coating of loose sandy snow. However, we persisted, and towards the latter end of our tiring march we began to make better progress, but the work is still awfully heavy. I must stick to the ski after this.

Scott had not considered the question of steering. Down on the Barrier, with the long caravan of animal transport; up the Glacier with topography defining the road, steering had been relatively simple. Now, alone on a plain without landmarks, it had become a problem. Their wrist compasses were unreliable. They steered by the sun when they could. But, tightly bunched together on the trace, without forerunners to give a mark, distracted by the constant tug of the sledge, they found it hard to keep a straight course, even in clear weather. In poor visibility, steering was excessively difficult.

That was why they were weatherbound on January 8th. They were stopped by a Force 4–6 wind from the south (about twenty-five knots), slightly better conditions than those under which the Norwegians had gone out and done thirteen miles in the teeth of a southerly blizzard. With his insignificant margin of safety, Scott could ill afford this delay. Yet he was unworried at the setback, anticipating the taste of triumph. It came the following day, January 9th. The weather lifted, he was able to march again, and began his diary with '*RECORD*' in large capital letters. He had passed what he sneeringly called 'the record of Shackleton's walk'. This referred to the dash from their southernmost camp by Shackleton, Marshall Wild and Adams to reach their Furthest South; a very courageous act. Shackleton's diary read: 'We have shot our bolt and the tale is latitude 88 deg. 23' South, longitude 162 deg. East... Whatever regrets may be, we have done our best.'

The date had been January 9th, 1909. It was three years to the day. Scott had beaten his rival – at last.

30

The Race Won

Among the Norwegians, beyond Shackleton's Furthest South, exactly one month before, the spirit was very different. 'We stayed in bed late today,' Amundsen had written on December 9th, 'to prepare for the final onslaught.'

Here, ninety-five miles from the Pole, the last depot was laid. Wisting's and Bjaaland's sledges were lightened by about a hundred pounds each; Helmer Hanssen, dog-driver with a touch of genius, was to carry on with the same load.

The depot was marked with extra care. On either side the usual transverse line was laid out with thirty planks taken from empty sledging cases, painted black at Framheim, months beforehand, in preparation for this purpose. The planks were set out a hundred skiing paces from each other, covering about three miles, so that across the route was a grid of six miles.

Every other plank, Amundsen precisely noted in his diary,

carries a black pennant. Those planks to the E. all have a notch under the pennant to indicate the direction they lie in relation to the depot ... In addition we will put up a few snow blocks every other mile, [for the first few miles] on the way South.

On December 10th, Amundsen gave the order to strike camp and set off on the 'final onslaught', past Shackleton's Furthest South.

Helmer Hanssen, Wisting and I [he drily wrote], look quite awe-inspiring since our faces were frostbitten in the ... storm a few days ago. Sores, pain and scabs the whole of our left sides. Bjaaland and Hassel, who went last, got off scot free. The dogs have begun to be quite dangerous [from hunger] and must be considered as ... enemies when one leaves the sledges.

The Major, one of Wisting's dogs, disappeared. 'Presumably,' in Amundsen's words, 'he had gone away to die.' This left seventeen dogs, who as he put it, were 'tired, and quickly we do not go, but we go evenly, and we have covered the planned 16 miles [for the day].'

Wisting still had The Colonel, his leader dog. He had been on all the journeys so far, and eventually went to live with his master at Horten on the Christiania Fjord. There, in Wisting's words,

he enjoyed his retirement, with gusto. He wasn't a bad fellow at all ... there's an old saying that when [the Devil] is old, he goes into a monastery; so too with 'The Colonel'. He went to the Salvation Army! He sat outside their premises every evening in all kinds of weather and listened reverently to the speeches, songs and music.

At last his days were numbered. It was as if I had lost one of my own, so much did I miss him.

With characters like The Colonel, monotony was banished. Tired and hungry as they were, the dogs yet trotted gamely on, as if driven by the fever of their masters.

On and on went their masters, with the deceptively lazy lope of the nordic skier that hides power and economy of effort. Skis gently soughed on the fine, crystal snow. Ski sticks gave the tell-tale creak of deep frost. The same conditions which drove Scott to lament over inhuman struggle against snow that would not slide, Amundsen described in these terms:

— 28 deg. [C.]. Breeze from the Southward. ... A little cool to go against with our sore faces, but nothing to make a song about. Terrain and going the same old kind – first class. Quite even and flat, the *Vidda* lies before us. Sledges and ski glide easily and pleasantly.

Like Bjaaland, Amundsen had chosen the homely word *vidda* to describe the Antarctic Ice Cap. The word means, literally, a plateau, but its associations to a Norwegian are familiar. It is part of his own mountain world, the heath at the end of the valley, the playground on his doorstep. By calling the great South Polar Plateau the *vidda*, Amundsen had somehow demythologized it. Dangerous it might be, and vast, but not alien.

The Pole was now in the offing and the question was how to find it. Travelling over the featureless expanses of the Polar Ice Cap is like navigating a ship at sea. Navigation at high latitudes, however, has certain peculiarities, the most important being the convergence of the meridians. It is a specialized field.

In November 1909, A. R. Hinks, Lecturer in Surveying and Cartography at Cambridge University, held a seminar at the Royal Geographical Society in London on determining position near the Poles. It was occasioned both by the Cook–Peary controversy over which, if either, reached the North Pole, and by Scott's forthcoming attempt on the South Pole. It was attended by some highly qualified navigators and explorers. Scott was present, but he politely ignored what the specialists had to say. He eventually arrived on the Polar Plateau using conventional Naval routine, which Bowers, a conventional Naval officer, obediently followed.

What it meant was this. Every day, around noon, Bowers took an ex-meridian sight for latitude, and in the evening another for longitude. The calculation of both is tedious, taking (in those days without pocket calculators) perhaps an hour of laborious arithmetic and Bowers, as Scott described it, used to be 'coiled in his [sleeping] bag . . . working out sights long after the others are asleep'. Scott clearly approved of this as praiseworthy devotion to duty. He did not consider that with the exhaustion of man-hauling at high altitude, rest was more important. It was, in any case, an unintelligent waste of effort. Bowers was racking his brains for a few hundred yards of meaningless accuracy.

At high latitudes, the convergence of the meridians makes the degree of longitude small. At the head of the Axel Heiberg Glacier, 86° S., for example, it is a bare four miles, instead of sixty miles at the equator.

The Hinks seminar indicated that longitude fixes were therefore mostly unnecessary. What was required was to steer accurately due south towards the Pole, for which the simpler observations for latitude and compass error would do.

Amundsen saw the report of the Hinks seminar in the *Geographical Journal*, and took the advice that Scott ignored. He used the meridian sight for latitude, which is simple to calculate and takes a few minutes. He believed that saving mental as well as physical energy was a vital rule of safety.

Amundsen reasoned that in any case an elaborate procedure would be needed to fix the Pole, so he might as well save himself trouble on the march. He therefore navigated with a sextant, instead of a theodolite like Scott because, although less accurate, it was simpler to use.

Its one drawback was the necessity of an artificial horizon. This is because a smooth, absolutely level natural one, on which a sextant depends, is only found at sea. The artificial horizon was a tray of mercury to reflect the image of the sun. In case the mercury froze, Amundsen also took an artificial horizon made of silvered glass, levelled with a spirit bubble. For speed and simplicity, he depended on accurate steering and dead reckoning.

One of the more worrying of the Norwegian setbacks the previous season had been the sledgemeters. They were periodically clogged with snow, and had to be nursed constantly.

The sledgemeter was vital for navigation and had to function without fail. Amundsen's pattern was more robust and legible than Scott's, because the revolution counter was larger and the wheel more securely

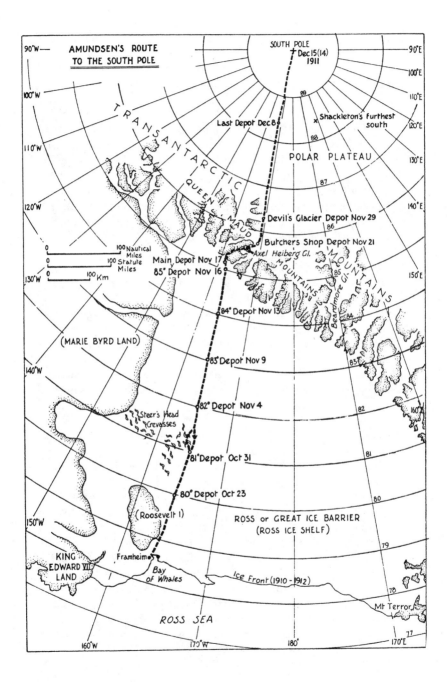

mounted. The weak link lay in the transmission from the wheel. This allowed fine drift snow, which has an unbelievable capacity to penetrate where it is unwanted, to enter the counter mechanism and jam it, as if it had been so much sand. All winter, Lindstrøm had worked away, until he had got every sledgemeter absolutely snowproof and utterly reliable in any kind of weather.

Scott's sledgemeters had developed the same faults as Amundsen's. In his case, however, nothing was done about it. He set off for the Pole with the same unreliable and inaccurate instruments constantly clogged by snow, and regularly breaking down, that he had used on the depot journey; rather like the pump on *Terra Nova*. Despite generous warning, therefore, he had no dependable method of logging his day's run. His steering too, because of inferior sledging compasses and the inherent drawbacks of man-hauling, was doubtful.

The result of all this was that Amundsen, but not Scott, was prepared for navigation in bad weather; nor was Amundsen so dependent on astronomical fixes. He could, and did, skip an observation or two without ill effect. But Bowers absolutely had to take every available one or risk seriously being off course. Even so, the British course was jagged, with perceptible zig-zags, costing perhaps ten or twenty miles over the journey. The significance of that would be grim. The praise afterwards lavished on Bowers for taking more observations than Amundsen on the march was really glorying in, or perhaps covering up, a singular inefficiency. Amundsen's and Scott's navigation reflected exactly their respective margins of safety in transport and supplies. Amundsen could afford more mistakes.

More important, Amundsen understood how to get the best out of his equipment. All his experience, from his first, halting attempts at crossing Hardangervidda onwards, went into devising the order of running, with which he was now bearing down on the Pole.

First came Helmer Hanssen with his non-magnetic sledge and the standard compass to steer the course. That was no sinecure. He had to drive his dogs, with all that meant in constant vigilance to see that no rascal slackened. Since he was leading, he also had to break the trail, which required extra care and energy. He had to watch the terrain all the time to make certain no irregularity overturned the sledge; and in between all this, he had to watch the compass, his cracked and frostbitten face constantly lashed by the incessant wind from the south. Ahead of him, to encourage his dogs and to keep a straight course, went the forerunner, on the last lap to the Pole, alternately Amundsen and Hassel, who had no sledges of their own.

The position of forerunner, in Amundsen's words, was not

enviable. Admittedly he escapes all the trouble with the dogs, but it is damnably unpleasant to go there alone and stare at nothing. His only entertainment is the calls from the leading sledge; 'A little to the right - a little to the left' ... It is no easy matter to go straight in terrain where one has no distinguishing marks ... An Eskimo can manage, but none of us. We swing from right to left and back again, and give the leading driver constant trouble [and] in the long run he is irritated, working himself up to believe that the unsuspecting, innocent forerunner makes these swings just to annoy him.

On December 8th, round about Shackleton's Furthest South, Amundsen had had his navigation put to the test. For five days the weather had stopped all observations, so that he had to steer blind by compass and sledgemeter alone. Now, 'His Grace', as he called the sun, emerged and he found the observed latitude, 88° 16' agreed with the dead reckoning to within a mile, 'a brilliant victory,' as he put it, 'after 1½ deg. [90 miles] in thick fog and snow drift ... so now we are ready to take the pole in any kind of weather on offer.'

But the weather now turned perversely glorious. It was as if the gods had decided that it was no use trying to fight these persistent men and their loyal dogs any longer, and the men knew it.

'Four long days more,' wrote Bjaaland in his diary on December 11th, 'and there's the Pole.' The same day, Amundsen recorded that the altitude was telling on him; it was hard to work, and breathing was an effort. But, he tersely commented, 'We'll get our breath back, if only we win.'

There was no depression on this party. Their morale was high. They needed no coaxing or cajoling, or even conscious leadership now. They seemed to be moving along under their own momentum, Amundsen almost a spectator, watching his plans unfold; leading, without appearing to do so.

It was uncanny how the weather arranged itself for Amundsen, as if he were the centre of some play. It had smiled on him for the critical ascent of the Plateau; and now it was smiling for the climax. December 12th was so uneventful, with sunshine, clear skies, and seventeen miles done instead of the stipulated fifteen, that all Amundsen could find to say was 'same fine terrain and going'.

But this concealed rising tension and tautening nerves. It was now forty-five miles to go. Amundsen could tell almost to the hour when he would arrive, and the race would be won or lost. The thought of Scott, the prospect of being beaten by him at the post had been haunting him like a vivid nightmare. So much stood or fell by the result. To be second would not only be failure but disgrace. It would have been easy to succumb to panic and race his men and dogs to exhaustion. But he had the willpower to control his feelings and keep his pace down to fifteen miles a day, apparently idling. He suppressed the tension within him, but the strain came through, and communicated itself to the others.

This was not a struggle; it was a race. Bjaaland, at any rate, declined to be impressed by anything, least of all the great Antarctic Ice Cap. As far as he was concerned, there was no difference between beating Scott and overtaking some slowcoach on the track at Holmenkollen or Chamonix.

It was all a ski race to him. What annoyed him most of all was that patently worse skiers than himself, Helmer Hanssen, for example, kept ahead of him. The dogs were the trouble. Bjaaland was convinced he had been saddled with the worst animals. This was hardly fair; he was not a very good driver. Anyway, it was a useful thing about which to get angry and where there is anger, there is no room for brooding.

From about 86° onwards, Scott haunted the conversation. Wisting and Hassel, the most phlegmatic of Amundsen's team, showed signs of agitation. All scanned the horizon with unspoken dread. Even the dogs seemed to understand that something was in the air, showing an uncanny interest in the southern horizon, craning forward to peer and catch a scent.

'Do you see that black thing over there?' Hassel called out urgently as they were making camp on the 13th.

Everybody saw it.

'Can it be Scott?' someone called.

Bjaaland ran forward to investigate. He did not have to run far. 'Mirage,' he reported laconically, 'dog turds.'

The latitude was 89° 30'. They had done their fifteen miles without particular effort.

The going was of the best; hard, snow crust over which sledges and skis skimmed with a familiar, sensuous musical rasp. 'Our finest day up here,' wrote Amundsen, 'calm most of the day, with burning sunshine.'

Now the strain within Amundsen was overlaid by a haunting touch of anti-climax. As he came to the end of that long race which started 16,000 miles behind on the fjord outside his home, he seemed to sense that the game was in his grasp, and it was not an entirely pleasurable sensation. Win or lose, the end of any race is bittersweet.

The next day, the eve of attainment, the dogs had to be whipped forward for practically the first time (except when Bjaaland was trying to overtake Hanssen) since the Devil's Glacier. It was not the terrain. On December 12th, at a latitude of 89° 15', after reaching an altitude of 10,500 feet, they had started to go gently downhill, and were still sinking gently from the summit. Perhaps it was because, in Bjaaland's words

The dogs are so hungry they're eating their own crap, and if they can get to it, they eat the bindings on the sledges, and bite deep into the wood.

Perhaps the weather had something to do with it. The sky clouded over and frost crystals fell during the afternoon. Perhaps, too, the dogs noticed that their masters were unnaturally tense.

That night their camp was at 89° 45': exactly fifteen miles from the Pole. Amundsen could barely write up his diary, reduced to an unnaturally laconic four lines, which had nothing to do with the Pole. Bjaaland was not afraid to express his thoughts:

We can now lie and look towards the Pole [he wrote in his diary] and I hear the axle creaking, but tomorrow it will be oiled. The excitement is great. Shall we see the English flag - God have mercy on us, I don't believe it.

December 15th, a Friday, dawned – if one can speak of dawn when the sun circles overhead – bright and clear. They finished breakfast and packed up a little quicker than usual, and set off on the last few miles. The going was mixed; sometimes good, sometimes heavy in patches of loose snow. They strained their eyes, staring, staring to see what lay ahead, pretending to each other, but not to themselves, they were not nervous or worried – what if, after all, a Union Jack was there to greet them? But hard as they stared, they could see nothing but the endless, unbroken snow ahead.

Helmer Hanssen, as usual, was leading; the best dog-driver and the best navigator. With about eight miles to go, he called back to Amundsen to go up into the lead.

'Why?' asked Amundsen.

'Because,' Hanssen slowly replied, 'I can't get the dogs to run if nobody runs in front.' This was a lie of sorts. The dogs were spurting so the snow flew up; they needed no forerunner now. But Hanssen had no wish to be first at the Pole. That honour belonged to Amundsen. So Amundsen went ahead. He was still there, when the dog-drivers, who had been carefully watching their sledgemeters the last few miles, cried out, in chorus: 'Halt!' The time was three o'clock in the afternoon.

It was journey's end; they had reached the Pole.

*

So now [wrote Bjaaland in his diary], we have attained the goal of our desires, and the great thing is that we are here as the first men, no English flag waves, but a 3 coloured Norwegian. We have now eaten and drunk our fill of what we can manage; Seal steak, and biscuits and pemmican and chocolate.

Yes, if only you knew *mother*, and you Susanna and T. and Svein and Helga and Hans, that now I'm sitting here at the South Pole and writing, you'd celebrate for me. Here it's as flat as the lake at Morgedal and the skiing is good.

Helmer Hanssen, on the other hand, had no feeling of triumph at that moment.

I was relieved to know that I no longer should have to stare down at the compass in the biting wind which constantly blew against us while we drove Southwards, but which we now would have behind us.

And Amundsen? 'So we arrived and were able to plant our flag at the geographical South Pole,' he wrote. 'God be thanked!'

That was all.

Scott was 360 miles behind, still fighting his way up the Beardmore Glacier.

During the night, Tryggve Gran, asleep with Debenham and Taylor in the Western Mountains, woke with a start. 'I dreamt I received a telegram,' he wrote in his diary, 'Amundsen reached the Pole 15th–20th December!'*

I cannot say – even although I know it would have a much greater effect – that I stood at my life's goal [Amundsen afterwards wrote]. That would be telling stories much too openly. I had better be honest and say right out that I believe no human being has stood so diametrically opposed to the goal of his wishes as I did on that occasion. The regions round the North Pole – oh the Devil take it – the North Pole had attracted me since the days of my childhood, and so I found myself at the South Pole. Can anything more perverse be conceived?

Amundsen had learned what the Duke of Wellington had meant when in the moment of victory he wrote that 'Nothing except a battle lost can be half so melancholy as a battle won.' Such, then, was the attainment of the South Pole; a muted feast; a thing of paradox, of classic detachment; of disappointment almost. It was the antithesis, conceivably deliberate, to Peary at the other end of the earth, two and a half years before: 'The Pole at last. The prize of three centuries. My dream and goal for twenty years. Mine at last!'

When the navigators cried 'Halt!', and the Norwegians had arrived as

---

* Tryggve Gran, Diary, December 15th, 1911. Attested by Taylor. The first cable from Amundsen, when it came, took almost exactly this form.

close to the so desirable point as they were provisionally able to decide, this is what happened:

Without a word, they shook hands with each other. Then Amundsen got out the Norwegian flag, which had been bent to a pair of ski sticks lashed together the night before in readiness. But, as he put it,

I had decided that we would all take part in the historic event; the act itself of planting the flag. It was not the privilege of *one* man, it was the privilege of *all* those who had risked their lives in the fight and stood together through thick and thin. It was the only way I could show my companions my gratitude here at this desolate and forlorn place.... Five roughened, frostbitten fists it was that gripped the post, lifted the fluttering flag on high and planted it together as the very first at the Geographic South Pole.

As the improvised flagstaff entered the snow, Amundsen pronounced these words: 'So we plant you, dear flag, on the South Pole, and give the plain on which it lies the name King Haakon VII's Plateau.'

Amundsen then photographed the scene.

Bjaaland, who had brought along a snapshot camera as part of his personal gear, also took some pictures. It was as well that he did. Afterwards, it turned out that Amundsen's camera was damaged and Bjaaland's photographs were all that remained. Thus it was that attainment was recorded by snapshots at the Pole.

The Eskimo-like figures of four Norwegians stand in their Netsilik pattern of anorak under the Norwegian flag streaming in the breeze, next to a pair of skis, and a dog; not forgetting the dog. It is artless, but it neatly sums up all the whys and wherefores. The Stone-Age lore of the Eskimo had brought the Norwegians safely and comfortably to their goal.

Bjaaland and Amundsen shut their cameras and put them away. As Amundsen afterwards remarked in the curious, flat style he reserved for notable occasions, that moment, short as it was, would

certainly be remembered by all who were there. One soon gets out of the habit of protracted ceremonies in those regions – the shorter the better.

Workaday resumed immediately.

First, Helmer Hanssen had the bitter duty of killing his best dog, Helge. Poor Helge, he had pulled loyally and uncomplainingly, and Hanssen loved him. But he had worn himself out. A week before he had collapsed, and simply dragged himself in the harness, no longer any use; a brave and faithful friend. Hanssen had insisted on getting him to the Pole.

After the ceremony of the flag, Helge was put down, divided and immediately devoured by his unsentimental companions, ravenous on their daily portion of half a kilogram of pemmican each. Sixteen dogs remained, and were now reorganized into two teams, Bjaaland giving up his animals, and abandoning his sledge, Wisting and Hanssen remaining as the last two drivers. 'Thank God, I am quit the fuss and bother of my dogs', was Bjaaland's heartfelt comment. Henceforth, with vast relief, he could stick to skiing.

'Naturally we are not exactly at the point called 90 deg.,' as Amundsen put it, 'but after all our excellent observations and dead reckoning we must be very close.'

He now set about making certain of the Pole. He did so with a thoroughness that surprised his companions. 'But,' says Helmer Hanssen, 'the Chief wanted it that way, and that was the way he had it.' Amundsen considered that with the instruments at his disposal he could hardly fix the Pole closer than a mile. He was preparing for carping on return. He had to prove beyond a doubt that he had reached his goal.

The day after arrival was, as he put it, 'extremely agitated'. The Poles are Looking-Glass world; a graphic illustration of how the ideal, necessarily, means a reduction to absurdity. Familiar concepts break down. There is only one direction; at the North Pole, South; at the South Pole, North. The meridians converge to vanishing point, so that longitude is meaningless, and only latitude remains. Fixing the position of this strange spot is an alien and arduous exercise.

In the immediate vicinity of the Pole, the path of the sun as it circles overhead is so flat that its zenith is hard to determine and the noons around the horizon coalesce. The well-tried midday observation of lower latitudes therefore will not do. A tight series of altitudes of the sun is required, preferably over a complete revolution of the earth; right round the horizon.

After a few hours' sleep, Amundsen roused the camp at midnight to take the first observation.

They woke, as Bjaaland put it, 'to the most beautiful sunny weather, and the observers were charging all over the place with their instruments to decide where the place is'. It is uncanny how, once more, the weather arranged itself for Amundsen's benefit. The breeze died, the air cleared, and the sun proceeded to shine uninterruptedly as long as necessary to make certain of the goal. Amundsen could scarcely have asked for more, and his tale makes a singular contrast to all the heroic Polar sagas of hardship and misery. 'The dogs lie stretched out in the heat of the sun,' he wrote at one point, 'enjoying life despite their insufficient food.'

The first observation showed the camp to be about four miles from the Pole itself. Until more readings were taken, the direction was unknown.

When the position was fixed, Amundsen was going to send out three of his companions to 'box' the Pole and make sure that the party had covered the area in which it lay. Bjaaland, who was one, preferred to start immediately, so as not to presume on the weather. Amundsen agreed. At two thirty a.m., after an extra breakfast of hot chocolate and biscuits, Bjaaland, Wisting and Hassel set out each to ski ten miles; Bjaaland on a continuation of their course from Framheim, Wisting and Hassel at right angles to left and right respectively. Each was alone, without compass, because their sledging compasses were too heavy to be carried. Their only food was thirty biscuits – not quite a day's allowance.

That march [Amundsen afterwards wrote], was not entirely without danger. . . . On that endless plain our tent, without marks of any kind, can well be compared with the proverbial needle in a haystack. . . . They had the sun to steer by when they started. . . . If it was obscured, their own tracks would help. But to depend on tracks in that region is dangerous. One, two, three and the whole plateau is a whirling drift of snow, and all tracks are wiped out as quickly as they have been made. With the sudden changes we had experienced, this was not impossible. That those 3 risked their lives that morning . . . there is no doubt whatsoever. And they knew it so very well.

They were not, however, being asked to risk their lives for an academic exercise, but to save their work from futility. After Cook and Peary and the whispers against Shackleton, Polar explorers could no longer count on being taken at their word. Amundsen knew that his deception in going south laid him particularly open to doubt and suspicion. In the testimony of his rival, lay a heaven-sent opportunity of conclusive proof. Bjaaland, Wisting and Hassel were going out to forestall the slander of their critics by putting up marks that Scott could hardly fail to see.

The mark was a spare sledge runner, a solid strip of wood twelve feet long, to one end of which was attached a black flag and a small bag containing a note for Scott with the bearing and distance of the camp. Each man carried one of these awkward objects slung across his shoulders and, having skied his ten miles – by elapsed time – stuck it securely in the snow.

The weather – naturally – held, and the three skiers re-appeared on Amundsen's horizon almost simultaneously, after about six hours as expected, arriving at the tent about ten a.m. 'No English flag to be seen anywhere', Bjaaland noted, and tumbled with gratitude into his sleeping bag, having covered thirty-five miles in twenty-four hours, with very little sleep, quite a trial at an altitude of over 10,000 feet.

In the meanwhile, Amundsen and Helmer Hanssen had been taking frequent altitudes of the sun. For the sake of accuracy, Amundsen had intended bringing a theodolite for the Polar observations alone. But both his instruments had been damaged, so he had to make do with a sextant instead. It was a tedious business, focusing on the artificial horizon at an awkward downward angle, and getting the direct image of the sun and its reflection to touch exactly.

It is quite interesting, to see the sun wander round the heavens at so to speak the same altitude day and night [Amundsen remarked]. I think somehow we are the first to see this curious sight.

This is a bland reflection on Cook's and Peary's claims to have reached the North Pole. It is the one recorded hint that in his heart of hearts he disbelieved them both. The poignancy of this remark is that he had gone to such trouble to attain the 'wrong' Pole, while the *other* one was really still unconquered.

Not until late in the afternoon of the 16th, did Amundsen find his position. To his astonishment, he found he was on the 123rd meridian of East longitude instead of the 168th West, that he had been following on the plateau, a shift of 69° to the west. However, at that latitude, a degree of longitude is a mere 200 yards, instead of sixty miles as at the Equator, so that they had only come about seven miles out of their way. The final calculations put them five and a half miles from the Pole, well within the 'box' traced by Bjaaland, Hassel and Wisting.

Meanwhile, for the second time in a few days, Amundsen had been checking his supplies. He found he could feed his men for another eighteen days; his dogs for ten days. Allowing for head winds and bad weather, it was, *on his performance so far*, six days' travel to the first homeward depot at 88° 35'. Of fuel he had a glut; it was not yet Midsummer and the weather promised fair. He decided he was justified in staying to take a second set of observations at the newly-found Pole and make sure of his mark.

On December 17th, he broke camp early in the morning. The dogs were harnessed, the sledges lined up along the meridian.

To lead the procession to the Pole was regarded by them all as an honour. Amundsen gave it to Bjaaland. He did so out of respect to a great skier, and as a compliment to the men of Telemark, who had pioneered skiing. It was they, Amundsen felt, who had enabled him to win; without skis he would have got nowhere. Bjaaland, as the one Telemarking among them, was entitled to be first at the Pole. The others' acclamation left no doubt that they agreed.

'Thank you,' said Bjaaland quietly when Amundsen ordered him to go ahead, 'The blokes in Morgedal will be grateful. It'll be fun, the finish to this race.'

He had to run dead straight, because reaching the Pole depended on precisely following the calculated course. Amundsen put himself last to check the line of march. It was, he said, 'pure pleasure to see Bj. hold the course. He moved as if he had a flagged route to follow.'

At eleven a.m. Bjaaland, as it were, passed the finishing post, followed by Hassel, and Helmer Hanssen's leader dog, in that order.

So the first man at the Pole was not, strictly speaking an explorer, but a ski champion and a pioneer of modern skiing. To Amundsen it expressed the fitness of things. The conquest of the Pole as he himself had said was 'a sporting stunt', and it was wholly appropriate that the final honour should fall to a sportsman. It was equally appropriate that the third living creature to tread the South Geographic Pole was a sledge dog: an Eskimo dog from Greenland.

Amundsen pitched camp and prepared for the final observations. Two solid snow pedestals were constructed: one to hold the artificial horizon, the other to rest the sextant when not in use. From the middle of the morning, hourly observations were taken for twenty-four hours. All four navigators, Amundsen, Wisting, Helmer Hanssen and Hassel, shared the readings, taking them in pairs, watch and watch, six hours on and six hours off. All countersigned each other's navigation books. This too was by implication a rebuke to Cook and Peary, who had only their own word to prove they had been at the Pole.

As souvenirs of the Pole, watches, knives and various small things were engraved or, more correctly, scratched, in between observations, with the date and place.

That evening in the tent after the usual pemmican and biscuits, Bjaaland called for silence and made a little speech in honour of the day, delivered in the formal manner of the after-dinner oration that lingered as a custom of Norwegian society.

When he had finished speaking, Bjaaland produced a cigar case and handed it round, for all the world as if it had been some homely function. Then he presented the case and its remaining cigars with a ceremonial gesture to Amundsen, bowing slightly in a way he managed to invest with dignity, although squatting on the ·floor, and saying in his rich dialect, 'And this I give you in memory of the Pole.'

Amundsen was deeply touched. Bjaaland did not himself smoke, and he had brought the cigars (a Christmas present) all the way from Framheim in order to please his companions. He had turned the everlasting pemmican into a banquet.

During the day it had become apparent that they were still about one and a half miles from the Pole. Bjaaland and Helmer Hanssen were sent out about four miles in the indicated direction to mark the place with pennants.

It has been so clear today [wrote Amundsen some time about midnight on the 17th], that we have been able to see for miles around. We have all used our telescopes industriously to see if there is any sign of life in any direction   but in vain. We are the first here all right.

To make even more certain of the Pole, Amundsen 'boxed' the 'remaining few minutes of arc' as he put it, by putting pennants a few miles in each direction. He had now covered the Pole three times. 'We have done what we can,' as he put it. 'I think our observations will be of great interest for the experts.'

When the observations were eventually checked, the polar camp, Polheim, as Amundsen called it, 'The Home of the Pole', proved to have lain within 2,500 yards of the mathematical point, its position fixed with an accuracy of 200 yards. It was a tribute to the skill of the men handling the sextant, not an instrument designed for extreme precision.

The work was finished at midday on the 18th and they prepared to start that evening 'for our home on the Barrier', as Bjaaland put it. 'Thank God for that.'

To mark Polheim, Amundsen raised his now superfluous reserve tent, the light, aerodynamic model devised by Dr. Cook on *Belgica** and made by Rønne on *Fram* as she pitched and tossed over the South Atlantic.

The first congratulations now arrived, on two yellow leather labels found sewn on to the tent. The one said 'Bon Voyage', the other, 'Welcome to 90 degrees'; each signed by Rønne and Beck, the ice pilot on *Fram*.

The tent was securely stayed, and to the top was lashed a long bamboo on which was fixed the Norwegian flag, together with a *Fram* pennant, a device of red and white sent by Helland-Hansen for the Pole; for *of course* the ship was entitled to her share of the credit.

Inside the tent, Amundsen put some discarded equipment, and a letter to King Haakon.

Your Majesty [he wrote]. We have determined the Southernmost extremity of

* See p. 72 above.

the great 'Ross Ice Barrier', together with the junction of Victoria Land and King Edward VII Land at the same place. We have discovered a mighty mountain range with peaks up to 22,000 ft. a.s.l., which I have taken the liberty of calling with permission, I hope - 'Queen Maud's Range'. We found that the great inland plateau ... began to slope gently downwards from 89° ... We have called this gently sloping plain on which we have succeeded in establishing the position of the Geographic South Pole - with I hope Your Majesty's permission - 'King Haakon VII's Plateau'.

This succinctly recorded the Norwegian discoveries. It was put in an envelope, together with a covering letter, addressed to Scott who, as Amundsen remarked, 'I must assume will be the first to visit the place after us', asking him to forward it.

'The way home was so long,' as Amundsen put it, 'and so much could happen that could deprive us of the possibility of reporting on our journey ourselves.'

At half past seven in the evening, three days and five hours after arriving, Amundsen and his men got on their skis, turned their faces to the north, and began their journey home. Their last action before leaving was to shut the tent and salute the Norwegian flag flying from the top.

'And so, farewell, dear Pole,' Amundsen wrote in his diary, 'I don't think we'll meet again.'

We got away in the most wonderful weather conditions one could possibly desire [said Bjaaland]. − 19 deg. [C.] must be said to be fine at the South Pole. The dogs, poor devils, have not been over fed at the Pole, yet they are quick and lively.

While their masters pottered about with farewell ceremonies, the dogs were hopping up and down in a frenzy of impatience, and when at last they were told to go, they broke away like runners at the crack of the starter's pistol. They knew they were homeward bound, and there was food over the horizon.

Amundsen, too, was now straining at the leash. Scott, he remarked to Helmer Hanssen, 'will arrive during the next day or two. If I know the British, they won't give up once they've started.'

The fight was yet far from won. Amundsen still had to get back first with the news, for if he was beaten to the cablehead achievement would be blurred. Priority of attainment was thrown away without priority of print. The scoop was half the prize; indeed, in a way, it *was* the prize.

Amundsen could not know that Scott was over 300 miles and more than a month behind. It never occurred to him that anyone in full possession of his faculties would deliberately choose to man-haul. The return to Framheim was going to be a long, hard race.

Now heading north, Amundsen changed to night travel in order to have the sun behind him and avoid dazzle from the snow; another detail that evaded Scott. Bjaaland, the fastest skier of them all, was made forerunner for the journey home. '700 miles will be quite tough,' he remarked, considering the course before him, 'but I'll manage.'

He started by returning to the original Pole camp to pick up the outward track, and then led off down the fifteen miles to the first homeward camp. Here, as an extra precaution, Amundsen put another black flag to warn Scott. It was on about the 180th meridian, and thus approximately on the British route from the Beardmore. Scott would be more likely to see it while he might well miss the other flags if the weather was bad.

For Amundsen, the start of the homeward run was auspicious. The incessant southerly wind was now behind him. While he had been at the Pole, wind and sun had worked the surface of the snow into a fast, crystalline crust, just soft enough for the dogs to get a grip. The skiing, as the diaries consistently record, was 'splendid' and

In Bjaaland [to quote Amundsen], we have found a forerunner of class. He sees like nobody else, and he goes like nobody else. Thus he has kept our old spoors Northwards ... although they are very indistinct.

When Amundsen's and Scott's first reports reached civilization, a Norwegian newspaper remarked that

Amundsen ... leaves the impression that it was all basically a comparatively simple affair   [while] Scott brings out and underlines the 'inhuman exertion' ... 'the tremendous dangers' ... 'the exceptional ill fortune' and the 'unsatisfactory weather' both when it froze and when it thawed.

This was fair comment. Scott wanted to be a hero; Amundsen merely wanted to get to the Pole. Scott, with his instinct for self-dramatization, was playing to the gallery; Amundsen thought of the job in hand, not of an audience.

Even had the Norwegians hankered after conventional heroics, they would not easily have found a convincing pretext. The journey had settled down to rhythm and unexciting regularity. They ate, slept, and did their fifteen miles a day. Their chief diversion was Bjaaland's race to keep ahead of Helmer Hanssen's dogs. Bjaaland did not like being beaten by a dog. He was chagrined at the four and a half miles an hour which was all he could average now, when four years before he was doing seven miles an hour as runner up in the fifty-kilometre race at Holmenkollen. It was at any rate twice what Scott could manage and, at 10,000 feet, quite an impressive performance. As Bjaaland secretly admitted, 'I wish to God we were down on the Barrier, here it is hard to breathe, and the nights are as long as the Devil.'

They were spending up to sixteen hours a day in their sleeping bags, by Amundsen's design. He would not allow the daily fifteen miles to be exceeded, and insisted on plenty of rest. He felt the altitude called for it; at almost any cost, he wanted to avoid playing men and dogs out. He needed to conserve all his physical and mental resources for the descent from the plateau. Once down on the Barrier he could start to sprint.

Anybody watching the party would hardly credit that they had been out in the harshest climate in the world for two months on end. Bjaaland speeding ahead, seemed to be finishing off a ski race, utterly at home on the track, instead of an explorer at the end of a great journey. On the polished crust, he moved with the effortless-looking double-stick heave, throwing himself forward, leaning on the sticks, and pulling himself on with the sinuous power of a spring uncoiling, mile after mile.

The drama came from the dogs. Sixteen were left, of the fifty-two which had started, and they had to be got back to 86° S., for Amundsen's plans to work out. Two days after leaving the Pole, the first dog died; Amundsen's own favourite, Lasse. He collapsed, worn out with work. The day after it was Per, one of Wisting's best animals, then Black Patch.

All three were immediately divided among their companions, who devoured them, hair and hide. Thenceforth the thirteen remaining animals picked up condition and showed every sign of lasting the course. Their normal diet of pemmican alone, did not seem adequate. They needed fresh meat periodically to keep up their strength.*

On December 21st, now sure he was running to time, Amundsen raised the daily allowance of pemmican from 350 grammes to 400 grammes per man. 'God reward him for that,' Bjaaland feelingly wrote, expressing the thoughts of them all. 'Now I'm so full and satisfied, I can't express it in words.'

The first homeward depot at 88° 25' was reached, as planned, on Christmas Day, to general relief. Owing to exuberance at the Pole, they had overspent their chocolate allowance and had had to go short since then. Since it was their only source of sugar, they suffered in varying degrees; the lack of sweet stuff in the snow can be a trial.

It was eight days to the next depot at 86° 25', 130 miles away, the

---

* The reason is obscure, but is probably connected with a need for the Vitamin B complex, which the pemmican could not supply.

longest gap along the whole route, and Amundsen now had twelve days' full rations for men and dogs, besides a reserve of pemmican.

So we are [as he said], well provided for. I am [therefore] putting aside a sample of each item of food that has been at the Pole. The suppliers will presumably appreciate it.

They had brought no extra food for Christmas. Wisting collected biscuit crumbs which, with some powdered milk, were made into a concoction reminiscent of the traditional Norwegian rice porridge. That, together with the roar of the Primus, allowed for once to burn for warmth, and the aroma of Bjaaland's cigars, created in the tent a festive and nostalgic atmosphere.

Now you're lighting the candles at home [Amundsen wrote in his diary]. We are there also [in spirit], even although the distance is great. But wait a little – it won't be long before you will have us again, and then it will be with victory in our hands.

They had now come 100 miles, with 600 left to Framheim. 'A long hard jump,' in Bjaaland's words. 'Oh, my old pals at home, you don't need to envy me yet.'

The crossing of the coastal mountains was now looming up ahead. The weather, at least, continued fair. 'Boiling sun on our backs,' wrote Amundsen on the day land hove into sight. 'Brilliant going that puts the dogs in top form, [and they] really seem to be putting on weight.'

On December 29th, they reached the summit of the Plateau, and started descending gently to the coast. The going continued fast; a polished, icy surface, shot with sharp sastrugi on which, in Amundsen's words, 'We went with the speed of lightning.' The sastrugi made for a bit of a slalom, but Bjaaland, who had flown faster in worse terrain, kept ahead as usual. In Amundsen's words, he and Hassel, neither in Bjaaland's class as skiers, 'had a hard job to keep up with the sledges. The drivers support themselves on their sledges, are pulled along on skis, and have halcyon days.'

For his part, Bjaaland found the skiing

as easy as it could possibly be [but] had my work cut out to keep ahead of Helmer [Hanssen's] dogs. Just as I thought they were well behind, I found them sticking their noses in front, just next to me.

Helmer Hanssen was chasing for fun. Wisting rigged a sail on his sledge, and his dogs galloped after Hanssen, howling and yapping with pleasure.

On December 29th, Amundsen again raised the pemmican allowance, to 450 grammes. This meant that the Norwegians were now getting approximately the amount of food they needed. At last they were all satisfied; even Bjaaland who, the previous day, had ingenuously asked for more – and got it. As forerunner, he considered himself entitled to a little extra.

'Dear Diary,' wrote Bjaaland on New Year's Day, 1912, with the comfort of a full belly, 'wasn't the first day of the New Year fine and easy; the loveliest day of all.' That was the moment when the two expeditions came closest to each other, barely a hundred miles apart. Scott was just emerging from the Beardmore Glacier, still outward bound. Amundsen was approaching the crisis of the homeward journey; the descent from the Plateau on to the Barrier below.

Amundsen was retracing his steps to the Axel Heiberg Glacier, and the one route he knew. This meant finding his way through the tangled ice flow and ridge of the coastal mountains with the aid only of his own observations. But, because of blizzard and fog on the way up, he was now seeing the view from the south for the first time.

Recognizing mountains from an unfamiliar angle and in changing light is notoriously difficult, especially the weathered, indistinctive shapes of this region. When Amundsen raised land on December 27th, he thought he had discovered something new, when in fact he was looking at mountains seen on the outward journey.* He took days to discover his mistake. The sun and crystal-clear air shimmering with mirage played havoc with distance and perspective, and Amundsen's short sight (which he still carefully concealed) intensified the distortion.

His confusion was aggravated by a combination of circumstances. To find his way back, he had relied on a single landmark, one of the mountains round the Norway Glacier, known as Mount Bjaaland today. It was capped by a distinctive ice dome, with what looked like a crown of jagged crystals at the top. It seemed unmistakable, at least from the north, on the outward journey. But now, from the south, on the return, it was masked by the contours of the terrain. Moreover, Amundsen had ceased astronomical observations since leaving the Pole, and he had lost his line of cairns after 88° S. To cap it all, in his hurry on the way up, he had muddled vital bearings, so that his points of reference were confused.

This does not emerge clearly from the published account. It was Amundsen's style to play down difficulties, and draw a veil over circumstances that suggested plans going awry. His diary, however, is free of

---

* Today called the Nilsen Plateau and the Rawson Mountains, the one a continuation of the other.

dissimulation. 'We are in truth running through an enigma,' he wrote. 'To recognize where we are is an impossibility.'

At this moment of unease, Wisting provided a diversion with an unbearable toothache. Unfortunately he was the one with dental training and, since, in his words,

> it was a little far to the nearest dentist, I asked ... Amundsen ... if he would take care of the beast. He instantly declared himself willing, and our forceps were got out. On account of the cold, it first had to be warmed over the Primus. Then I knelt in my sleeping bag, and he sat over me in his, and pulled as hard as he could. After a tremendous fuss the operation – eventually – succeeded, and with that all my troubles were over.

Amundsen was, in fact, not quite as lost as his diary suggests. He had a general compass course.

By New Year's Eve, he had in fact picked up the mountains round the Butcher's Shop in the distance, so he knew where he was heading but not, exactly, where he was.

To identify the vital landmarks on which the fixing of his position depended, Amundsen had only fleeting glimpses through the fog on his way up a month before. Even when, as he thought, he now recognized some of the peaks, he remained in uncertainty. On the outward journey, he had confused the Nilsen Plateau with the mountains round the Norway Glacier, some ten miles to the west. (See map p. 413.) This meant that the compass bearings he had taken then were misleading, and he could not tell where he was in an east–west direction. Unfortunately, this was at the approaches to the Devil's Glacier, where it would be desirable to know where one was.

On January 2nd, Amundsen reached the Devil's Glacier. 'We were,' he wrote, 'bloody lucky.... In a few hours the whole glacier was conquered' – the same glacier that had caused three days of misery, struggle and danger on the way southwards. Amundsen had hit on a smooth, narrow path between the chasms and he escaped the Devil's Ballroom completely. Partly this was because the weather was now clear, where it had been thick on the way out. It was also due to the fact that he had arrived back at a different point. Dame Fortune had shown the way.

Exactly where he was, however, Amundsen still could not say. This was a serious state of affairs, because his next depot lay at the edge of the Devil's Glacier, and finding it depended on precise recognition of the surroundings.

> The Captain thinks we are East of the depot [wrote Bjaaland], so do the others.

I, on the other hand, believe just as firmly that we are a little to the West. Tomorrow we shall see.

They did. Starting off as usual at seven p.m., they were soon forced by fog to camp. However, in Amundsen's words

just as we had got our pemmican down, the sun broke through, and shortly after it was the finest weather. In a quarter of an hour, we had packed up and were under way ... directly West in the hope of finding the depot ... but no depot was there to see.

The terrain was broken by deep wave formations that cut off their view of the surroundings. They were soon quite lost and, rather than waste time floundering about for a depot they might not find, agreed that the safest course was to head straight for the Butcher's Shop, and reach the Barrier as quickly as they could.

Amundsen had enough pemmican in reserve to get his men down to the Barrier; but only three days' dog food. There was a chance of missing the depot of dog carcasses at the Butcher's Shop. The spectre of man-hauling rose up. The mood of the Norwegians as they started was distinctly under par.

They had not gone far when somebody recognized a ridge in the tumbled confusion of the ice. But whereas on the outward journey, they had seen it to the west, now it lay to the east. They had strayed, after all, too far to the west. They turned eastwards and, at the top of a rise, had a view over the surroundings for the first time. They got their bearings and could clearly see the point at the foot of the Devil's Glacier where the depot lay, not far behind.

'Under these circumstances,' as Amundsen put it, 'we all thought it would be wrong to leave the depot without trying to find it.' They were all willing to make the attempt, but there was no point in the whole caravan turning back. Amundsen selected Helmer Hanssen and Bjaaland. Without waiting to rest or eat they set off, Hanssen, as Bjaaland said, 'with empty sledge and his good Greenlanders, and I on my light ski as forerunner'.

But the terrain was harder than expected; wave after icy wave like a frozen sea. They soon regretted not having taken sleeping bags in case they were caught by the weather. In Bjaaland's words,

the Captain said he thought it was 8 miles, but rubbish I said. We went 11 miles, partly in fog and drift, without seeing anything. Luckily it cleared a little ahead, and soon we saw the [depot flags] across our course [about two] miles away, and our pleasure was vast, you can be sure.

Reaching the depot, they loaded the contents on to the sledge, after first giving their dogs a double ration of pemmican, and eating a little chocolate themselves. Without delay, they then began the return journey which, as Bjaaland said, 'went like a bomb.... After 10 hours on the march we were back at the camp [and] now we are rich in provisions.'

Amundsen stayed up the whole time waiting for them, restlessly prowling up and down in the snow, watching the weather anxiously, searching the distance with his telescope, unable to rest. When, at last, he saw them reappear on the crest of a frozen wave he rushed into the tent to wake Hassel and Wisting, who had prudently turned in. 'They must have found the depot,' he said, unusually excited, 'for neither is sitting on the sledge. They've got something else to carry on it.' He immediately started the Primus in order to melt snow, so that there was plenty of water ready to slake their thirst, and then to boil up the pemmican, for they would surely be ravenous. He was beaming when they arrived, and insisted on taking care of their dogs.

Bjaaland and Helmer Hanssen, he recorded, had done forty-two miles with no rest and very little food 'at an average speed of 3 miles an hour! Come and say that dogs are useless in this terrain.'

Now it was about five days to the next depot, and Amundsen had ten days' food for men and dogs, besides emergency reserves. He was, as he put it, 'on the right footing' again.

He now discovered why he had been lost. Through some error of navigation, he had been one and a half points (17 degrees) off course. But that had been a blessing in disguise, since it had steered him away from land, and led him to the easy crossing of the Devil's Glacier. With a rational explanation, Amundsen was calm again.

He now had to make for the Butcher's Shop, and find the start of his route down the Axel Heiberg Glacier. He had an urgent desire to see around him when he did so. Since the weather *now* was fine, he logically made a dash while the going was good.

Abandoning his time table, he drove twenty miles on January 4th, rested five hours, and continued on his way. The dogs seemed to sense what was in the wind and, of their own accord, pulled as hard as they knew. After the first ten miles, Amundsen picked up his line of cairns again. Early in the morning of January 5th, he reached the Butcher's Shop and found his depot of dog carcasses. It was, as he said, Helmer Hanssen

who, with sharp eyes discovered [the depot]. Had that not been the case, I don't quite know what would have happened. The place was completely unrecognizable – just as if we had never seen it before.

Again it was the treachery of changing light. On the first occasion, Amundsen had seen through curtains of obscurity; now it was sunny and clear. It took time before it dawned on him that a mysterious peak looming overhead was in fact Mount Fridtjof Nansen. He had seen it for days without recognizing what it was. Also for the first time, from the vantage point of the Butcher's Shop, he was able to see what he had forced his way through in fog and drift six weeks before. 'No, to travel blind in these surroundings,' he drily remarked, 'is fairly dangerous.'

Also, he realized that he had 'overestimated the heights of the mountains a lot in the misty atmosphere on the southwards journey'. They were, he now decided, correctly, as it subsequently turned out, only 12–13,000 feet, instead of 18–20,000 feet as he had written to King Haakon, and which Bjaaland 'had found so damned difficult to believe'.

At least Amundsen had now got his bearings. Round the corner, as it were, lay the Axel Heiberg Glacier, and the way down. There was no incentive to linger. Even now at Midsummer, the Butcher's Shop was scarcely hospitable. The temperature was − 25° (C.), a good five degrees lower than the Norwegians had grown accustomed to. There was also an unpleasant breeze, and for the first time on the whole journey, they felt the cold in their bones; it was time they were off the Plateau.

Stopping just long enough to give their animals an extra feed of dog meat at the depot, they slung a carcass on each sledge and, as Bjaaland put it, 'we shot off, pell mell, down the slopes, the one worse than the other'. These were the slopes under Mount Ole Engelstad at the head of the glacier, where the dogs had desperately clawed their way up inch by inch going south. It was a place to impress even a modern Alpine skier and Bjaaland, leading down the course, 'had his work cut out', as Amundsen observed.

Luckily, the snow was loose, so they could all – more or less – run under control. The sledges were braked with ropes wound round the runners. In about an hour and a half they had dropped 3,000 feet from the Butcher's Shop, done twenty-three miles for the day, and reached the upper terrace of the glacier. The first part of the descent was safely over. They camped at about 7,500 feet in the lee of Mount Ole Engelstad.

Day and night had now lost their meaning; even the date was a matter of confusion. 'Just as well we can remember the year,' as Amundsen put it. After a suitable rest, they were up again at one a.m. for the descent of the ice falls.

Amundsen was quite calm. What he had once climbed, he could presumably descend. In any case, he was not afraid of physical danger, and he happily lacked the tortured imagination that suffers in advance.

The little caravan set off. Bjaaland, still forerunner, was the first to reach the edge of the upper ice falls. Between his skis he was abruptly presented with the vertiginous sight of empty space and an apparently disconnected runout far below. It is the sight that betokens something special in the way of slopes, and brings butterflies to the stomach. Once more the sledges were braked by ropes round the runners, and they all, men and dogs, launched themselves over the top.

> It was [in Amundsen's words], a good day for us skiers. Loose snow, so that the ski sank about 2 inches: iced and grainy so that the ski glided as if on an oiled surface. . . . The loose snow gave control. The one slope steeper than the next. . . . We whizzed down. A wonderful sport.

To Bjaaland, 'The skiing was wonderful. I had many good runs and raced with the Captain.' Amundsen, Bjaaland and probably Hassel were enjoying themselves; there was every reason why they should. They had perfect spring snow. The descent from the Plateau had become sheer pleasure. Their light-heartedness makes a contrast with Scott's Puritanical earnestness. Did Scott enjoy himself at all?

But Amundsen was a master of understatement. His casual phrases mask an extraordinary performance. This was a downhill run of Alpine proportions and these men were unused to Alpine conditions. Their background was Nordic; they lacked specialized Alpine technique and equipment. Without fixed downhill bindings, they were handicapped by long skis, difficult to turn. Nonetheless they overcame the obstacles, swinging down in wide Telemark and Christiania turns, stick-riding when the slope was too steep. They ran a tremendous slalom between crevasses, round the pits, seracs and abysses of the Axel Heiberg's monstrous cataracts of ice, albeit down the course marked on their way up.

The dog-drivers, Helmer Hanssen and Wisting, did not find it quite such fun. A slalom with a loaded sledge that tends to yaw across a slope is doubtful entertainment with grinning chasms waiting for the slightest slip beneath. And the dogs, sinking to their knees in the loose snow, found the going hard. But they all managed without mishap and, in a short while, drivers, dogs, sledges and unencumbered skiers had run through the ice falls. After eleven and a half miles and a drop of 4,500 feet, they stopped to camp at the same spot at the foot of the lower fall where, in Bjaaland's words, they

> lay 47 days ago and had so much toil and so many hard days ahead. . . . Thank God we are back in the lowlands . . . and can breathe in a decent way . . . after 6 weeks' hard existence in the [thin] dry cold air.

The terrible descent was over.

Instead of the unnecessary mountain crossing of the way up, they followed the Axel Heiberg Glacier down to the Barrier, swung north, and just before midnight on January 7th, reached their depot at $85° 5'$ S., under Betty's Knoll. Now there was thirty-five days' food for men and dogs on the sledges, more than enough to get them all back to Framheim – and still there were depots strewn over the Barrier at every degree of latitude. In Amundsen's words, they were now

> really living among the fleshpots of Egypt. It's just a matter now of eating as much as possible to lighten our sledges as quickly as possible.

Amundsen sent Helmer Hanssen and Wisting up to Betty's Knoll, to build a stone cairn to show that people had been there. In the cairn was put a message saying what the expedition had done,* and a seventeen-litre tin of paraffin, together with twenty boxes of matches. 'Possibly,' said Amundsen, 'they will be useful in the future.' One more dog, Fridtjof, collapsed and was shot there. They set off with twelve dogs for Framheim, as originally calculated.

Except for some crevasses at the junction of Barrier and land, the objective dangers were over and Amundsen now was conscious of the race again. For all he knew, the British were drawing level down the Beardmore Glacier, which ended a full degree north of the Axel Heiberg. He became, in Bjaaland's words, 'impatient; tolerates no opposition. Sharp dispute over my goggles. Is he annoyed that I'm not using the Roaldish snow goggles?'

This is quite revealing. Bjaaland had made his own model based on an Eskimo pattern with slits, and abandoned Amundsen's pattern.

Now Amundsen decided to sprint; there was no longer any need to hold in men and dogs. The Barrier became a racecourse. They ran fifteen or twenty miles, camped for eight hours, went on again, rested, and so on without heed of day or night. In this way, they raised their speed by a half, cut down the time to Framheim by almost a fortnight, and therefore, with luck, would return that much earlier to civilization.

On January 11th, they saw the last of the mountains, 'a wonderful sight', as Bjaaland put it, 'like a home of the trolls, glittering with silver and crystal'.

On the same day, exactly halfway between Framheim and the Pole, two

---

*Found by Admiral Byrd's expedition in 1929.

skuas appeared. These were the first living creatures they had seen in the wilderness for over two months, the first sign of the outside world. The birds were greeted by cheering and waving. Bjaaland got out his revolver (for putting down the dogs) and fired a volley into the air.

Snowstorms, gales, drift, fog and generally unpleasant weather now swept down. The sealskin anoraks and trousers retrieved from the depot under Betty's Knoll were donned and everybody was warm, too warm perhaps, because the temperature hovered around $-10°$ (C.), mild by Antarctic standards.

His men now grasped the value of Amundsen's planning and foresight. Whatever the wind, weather or visiblity, they could do their distances, moving from cairn to cairn. Depots always found, they were reduced to navigational checks. Originally laid out at four days' travel from each other, this had now shrunk to two or three days, the time it now took for a degree of latitude. Their contents were now superfluous, and at least half a ton of food was left strewn across the Barrier. The dogs were put on double rations of pemmican, seal meat, biscuits, and in the end, chocolate as well, anything to lighten the loads.

Amundsen conveyed his sense of urgency to his companions. They were on form; they felt perhaps they were winning. They were working as a team, men and dogs, racing together in step. So they went on, at three miles an hour, twenty and thirty miles a day; day in, day out, men and dogs putting on weight. It was a triumph of skill, forethought and organization.

On January 17th, they reached their depot at 82° S. This had a particular significance. It was the southernmost of the depots laid the previous autumn. In Amundsen's words,

> We had a special meal to celebrate our arrival at civilization's furthermost outpost in the South. Wisting has to be cook on such occasions. He plied us with a mixture of pemmican and seal steak. For dessert: chocolate pudding.

They were now on their line of flags, and as good as home. The last two hundred miles was like following a marked ski track, but the weather continued poor. Just before the 81 degree depot, the clouds lifted, they had their first clear day for a long time and, having had poor visibility on each of the three occasions they had been that way before, were now for the first time able to see their surroundings. An impressive array of shattered ice towers and serried crevasses met their eyes. In Bjaaland's words, they also 'saw several rock and snowclad mountains which seemed to run in a N.E. direction ... 30 miles off'.

Amundsen declined to deviate an inch from his course to investigate this apparent discovery of new land. It was as if, having got to the Pole, he was afraid of tempting the gods by asking too much. Besides, *his* job was now to get home first with the news, and nothing else counted. The next expedition, whosoever commanded it, could investigate the sighting. Amundsen knew that it might well turn out to be a chimera; and so, in the end, it did. We know now that what he probably saw were the distant disturbances of the Steers Head crevasse system. The blue shadows and shining highlights often produce the illusion of snow-covered land.

Once past the depot, the skiing became tricky, with fast going on breakable crust, awkward for the dogs as well. Then the snow turned soft. The skiing worsened, with little glide, the going heavy for men and dogs. 'Ha ha,' recorded Bjaaland with friendly malice. 'Those fellows who thought they would be pulled ... will just have to traipse to Framheim.' Still they did their thirty miles a day, and they seemed impervious to depression. In the mood in which they found themselves, there was an astringent exhilaration in the whirling of the snow.

On January 25th, during the morning they arrived within eighteen miles of Framheim. The going had suddenly turned better again. 'The dogs,' as Amundsen put it, 'flew as never before.' But, as he made camp, 'the Sou'Wester broke out with drift and other abomination'. At ten in the evening when he set off again, the weather was still 'of unpleasant kind. Calm, with thick snowfall and fog, so one couldn't see one's own ski tips'.

They now lost the marked track and when, after an hour or so, they broke out into clearer weather, there was not a flag to be seen. Amundsen ordered a compass course and

After 8 miles march a large, dark object hove into sight – 2 points off our course – to the West. We struck out for it. It turned out to be one of our sledges, which we had left at the start on October 20th, 1911. Before we knew it, we had reached our point of departure. *Fram* we saw nothing of, but that was hardly to be wondered at, because the whole inner part of the bay was covered with ice. Framheim on the other hand lay, as we had left it, bathed in the morning sun.

It was Friday, January 26th, 1912.

Bursting with health, men and dogs careered down from the Barrier and across the ice of the Bay of Whales. By the way they moved, it would be hard to tell that they were just finishing off a journey of 1,400 miles.

It is entirely appropriate to the whole spirit of the enterprise that Bjaaland, to sum up his experience, chose the language not of heroic endeavour, but of ski racing: 'It was,' he wrote 'a damned hard job being forerunner.'

The Race Lost

AT THE POLE the black flags were waiting. Scott, slowly approaching over the last hundred miles beyond Shackleton's Furthest South, found it 'wearisome work this tugging and straining to advance a light sledge.' Also, 'one gets horribly sick of the monotony and can easily imagine oneself getting played out'. He and his companions were dispirited before they had reached their goal, and with more than half their journey ahead.

Scott had worn his men out on the climb, without thinking of the return. In any case, by his basic decision to man-haul, he had graphically proved Nansen's point that 'taking the dogs is cruel, but it is also cruel to overburden human beings with work'. That Scott faced temperatures between five and ten degrees lower than Amundsen was his own fault. By taking ponies and consequently delaying his start, he had made certain of being on the Plateau three weeks after the summer solstice and the turn of the season. Low temperature was a strain he could ill afford. Excepting mittens and boots, Scott had no furs, the absence of which around the face was enough to explain some of the party's persistent frostbite. Poor skiing technique, unintelligent navigation, a badly-loaded, ill-maintained and ill-running sledge, inefficient camping routine, the disruptions caused by the last-minute addition of a fifth man; the list of defects was comprehensive. Scott had been so consistently inept as to almost suggest the workings of a death wish.

He had certainly made things difficult for himself. Beyond everything else, he had condemned himself and his companions to the dangers of thirst.

Working hard at high altitude and in great cold, the human body loses an enormous quantity of liquid through perspiration. The loss must be made up, and plenty to drink is a necessity. Scott, in spite of his own experience and the information readily available, had not considered the subject. He barely had enough fuel to cook his food, let alone melt snow to produce all the water that was physiologically necessary. So he and his companions suffered the pangs of dehydration, with its physical weakness and mental distress. They were also slowly starving.

Amundsen found he had put on weight on his Polar journey; food had played its part in his victory, as it was to decide what happened to Scott. Amundsen's sledging ration of pemmican, biscuits, dried milk and chocolate, contrasts with Scott's pemmican, biscuits, butter, cocoa, sugar and tea. Scott's rations produced about 4,500 Calories per man, exactly what Amundsen was getting until he increased his allowances on the way home. It was probably enough for Amundsen, skiing unencumbered; for the grotesque hard labour of Scott, man-hauling, it was between 1,000 and 1,500 Calories too low. The Winter Journey had shown unmistakably that acting their own sledge dogs on that amount, men did in fact starve. Scott and Wilson missed the point, Atkinson did not. But, as a Naval surgeon, he knew that Naval captains in general, and Scott in particular, regarded criticism, however. reasoned, as bordering on mutiny, so he held his tongue.

Amundsen's diet not only provided enough energy but, according to modern ideas, it was better balanced than Scott's, containing more carbohydrate in relation to fat and protein. It was also richer in certain important vitamins.

By the time Scott and his companions reached the Plateau, they were suffering from vitamin deficiencies. Compared to the Norwegians, they were getting too little thiamin (Vitamin B_1), riboflavin (Vitamin B_2) and nicotinic acid. These belong to the Vitamin B complex, and a deficiency can have mental and nervous effects.

This difference in diet was partly the result of Amundsen's taking more chocolate and dried milk, both sources of Vitamin B, but mostly it was due to the biscuits used by each expedition on the march. Both were specially produced for concentrated nourishment. But Scott's biscuits, baked by Huntley and Palmer's, contained white flour, with sodium bicarbonate as leavening. Amundsen's, on the other hand, made by Saetre, a Norwegian firm, were based on wholemeal flour and crude rolled oats, with yeast as the main leavening. Yeast and whole grain are potent sources of Vitamin B.*

The biscuits symbolize two different worlds. Vitamins, admittedly, had not yet been discovered, but the Norwegians ate more naturally, and instinctively sensed the source of their essentials.

In their biological requirements, men are individuals. Accepted standards are average figures. So much of a particular vitamin will be enough for one man, but too little for another. On the whole, however, civilization seems to demand a greater supply, and those leading a more

* See Note on Diet, p. 545.

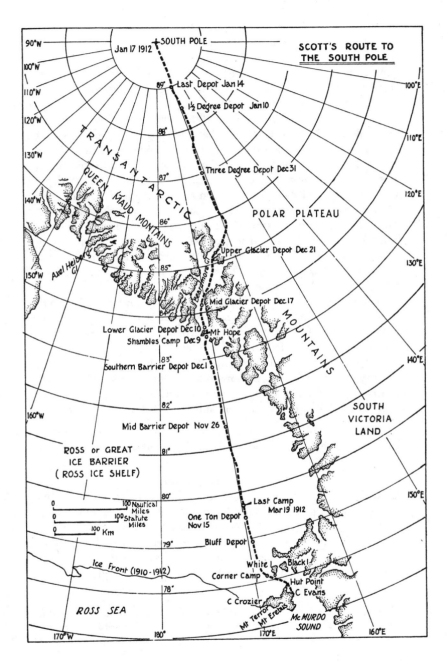

natural, outdoor life can keep healthy on a smaller quantity of vitamins than urbanized men with a more artificial existence.* For this reason, Amundsen's advantage in the Vitamin B complex was almost certainly even greater than the figures suggest. For the same reason, Scott faced scurvy sooner, although the basic sledging rations of both expeditions were practically devoid of Vitamin C.

Scott, moreover, did not understand the importance of what he ate at base; a point which, incidentally, Shackleton had grasped. This gave Amundsen yet another advantage. Because he understood that his survival on the march might well depend on what he had eaten before the start, he had insisted on a more natural and balanced diet throughout the winter, and therefore set off in better condition than his rival.

But mobility was the crux. Three months is about the longest the human body can store Vitamin C. Amundsen who, reducing his philosophy to its simplest terms, had seen safety in speed, was back to his sources of Vitamin C at the seal meat depots in two and a half months. Scott had now been on the road for almost exactly the same time, and he had not done half his journey yet.

Vitamin deficiencies and general malnutrition go far to explain Scott's afflictions from about 88° South: his susceptibility to cold, his manifest weakness. Lack of Vitamin C would account for the festering cut on P.O. Evans' hand and its obstinate refusal to heal.

A vitamin deficiency also explains some of the depression clouding the party. But here the plot is complicated by low morale and the effect of Scott's melancholic nature. What is certain is that, as they approached the Pole, the British were ailing in body and mind.

> We noticed the cold [said Scott]. It is a critical time, but we ought to pull through ... Oh! for a few fine days! So close it seems and only the weather to baulk us.

Since his injury, Evans had become unnaturally silent and downcast. Oates, not normally prone to self-pity, had fallen into an uncharacteristically gloomy state of mind. On January 15th, about thirty miles from the Pole, he wrote: 'My pemmican must have disagreed with me at breakfast, for coming along I felt very depressed and homesick.'

The next day, on the threshold of attainment they set off in slightly better spirits, buoyed up by the belief that victory was as good as theirs.

---

* Differing needs have, for example, been demonstrated by a study of Norwegian trappers in Greenland. They seemed in good health on levels of Vitamin B and C that in urban dwellers produce symptoms of deficiency. (See Kåre Rodahl, *Vitamin Sources in Arctic Regions*.)

Failing to find traces of Amundsen on the Beardmore Glacier, they assumed he had met with an accident, since they took it for granted that he would follow the same route and not try another. Despite his premonitions at the foot of the glacier, Scott encouraged that opinion, because his style of leadership involved concealing uncomfortable thoughts from his subordinates. He tried to conceal them from himself, even if past experience suggested that any disillusion would thereby be doubly hard to bear. How far he succeeded in this particular self-deception, however, must remain open to doubt. At the last moment, when he – rashly – wrote in his diary that 'It ought to be a certain thing now,' he remembered nonetheless to add the rider, 'the only appalling possibility, the sight of the Norwegian flag forestalling ours.'

It was not the cross of St. Olaf that told Scott he had lost the game but, as Amundsen had intended, the black flag planted in his path.

Somehow it was in keeping that neither Scott on skis in front nor Wilson by his side first sighted the dark speck breaking the whiteness ahead, but Bowers stumping along on foot in the middle of the trace, wearily lifting his legs out of the snow like a soldier marking time in slow motion. The time was five o'clock in the afternoon.

Slowly the speck turned into something that moved, and then they were standing under the black flag of disillusion. Dog stools and paw marks in the snow told their simple tale. The pitiless wind in their faces seemed colder than an hour before.

'We're not a very happy party tonight,' said Oates.

They did not sleep much after the shock of their discovery.

Scott [said Oates] is taking his defeat much better than I expected ... Amundsen – I must say that man must have his head screwed on right ... The Norskies ... seem to have had a comfortable trip with their dog teams, very different to our wretched man-hauling.

Thus gaunt, hungry, frostbitten, Oates with aristocratic detachment, stands at the end of the earth, weighing up the commander who has led him to inevitable defeat, and the opponent, who has just as inevitably triumphed. He takes a rational pleasure in seeing that the best man won; standing apart with quiet scorn for an incompetent leader. Bowers wrote:

It is sad that we have been forestalled by the Norwegians, but I am glad that we have done it by good British man-haulage. That is the traditional British sledging method and this is the greatest journey done by man since we left our transport at the foot of the Glacier.

Bowers did not have much in common with Oates. In that company, Oates was the odd man out.

Even Wilson lacked Oates' bald courage in facing defeat. Amundsen, said Wilson, 'has beaten us in so far as he made a race of it. We have done what we came for all the same and as our programme was made out.' It was the argument he used to comfort Scott; and of comfort Scott was in sore need.

To Scott, the black flag had been not defeat but failure. The fact that it was wholly expected; that he had only himself to blame, did not make it any the easier to bear; on the contrary. His decision to carry on as if Amundsen had not existed, 'to go forward', as he had put it, 'and do our best for the honour of the country without fear or panic', was in the spirit of Balaclava. He knew very well that only an accident to Amundsen could save him. Yet he blindly led his men on to what he knew was almost inevitable defeat.

He had tempted the gods. Rashly he had written to his wife before starting for the Pole:

There are a number of circumstances which make me doubt [Amundsen's] ability to achieve his object, on the other hand he would find it difficult to acknowledge defeat, and I cannot imagine him reporting it.

And now the black flag fluttering in the Polar wind: 'Certainly also the Norwegians found an easy way up.' Besides being unworthy, this was dangerous self-delusion.

The next morning, they struck camp and left the black flag to drag their sledge the last few miles to the Pole, a hollow little anti-climax in Amundsen's wake. They reached what they considered to be the point at six thirty p.m. It was Wednesday January 17th, 1912, thirty-four days after the Norwegians had cantered up with their dogs.

Scott wrote gloomily in his diary:

The Pole. Yes, but under very different circumstances from those expected. We have had a horrible day – add to our disappointment a head wind 4 to 5, with a temperature − 22°, and companions labouring on with cold feet and hands ... Great God! this is an awful place and terrible enough for us to have laboured to it without the reward of priority.

The one original piece of work left to Scott was finding the height of the Pole. But that was impossible because the hypsometer was broken; the whole expedition in a nutshell. What remained was to check Amundsen's positions, an essentially futile proceeding since, in Wilson's words, they 'all agreed that he can claim prior right to the Pole itself'.

It was a very different scene from that of a month before. Instead of the Norwegian quartet taking twenty-four leisurely observations round the clock, Bowers and Scott had to make do with five during the night; there was no time for more. Bowers set up the theodolite and took the readings; Scott booked them.

The temperature was − 30° C., a full eight degrees lower than for Amundsen. There was no calm air and clear sky, with dogs stretched out in the heat of the sun, but a bitter wind, drifting clouds, and two men shivering, as Scott wrote, with

> that curious damp, cold feeling in the air which chills one to the bone in no time ... there is very little that is different from the monotomy of past days ... Well, it is something to have got here, and the wind may be our friend tomorrow ... Now for the run home and a desperate struggle to get the news through first. I wonder if we can do it.

For publication, this was altered to read 'a desperate struggle. I wonder if we can do it', a rather different thing. In fact, Scott did not yet quite grasp that the return was going to be a fight for survival, although he did understand that there was no time to be lost.

At five in the morning they were off again. Having completed their observations, and worked up the results, Bowers and Scott decided they were about three miles from the Pole. Looking in the calculated direction, Bowers saw Amundsen's tent about two miles off. Dragging their sledge, they went up to it and found the Norwegian flag and *Fram* pennant still flying from the top. But nothing could equal the shock of the first scrap of black bunting.

Scott admired the neat design of the tent.

Inside, he found Amundsen's letter to King Haakon and the covering letter to himself:

Dear Captain Scott,

> As you probably are the first to reach this area after us, I will ask you kindly to forward this letter to King Haakon VII. If you can use any of the articles left in the tent please do not hesitate to do so. With kind regards I wish you a safe return.

> Yours truly,
> Roald Amundsen

'I am puzzled at the object,' Scott wrote in another remark edited out for publication. This speaks worlds for his state of mind. He did not understand that Amundsen was simply taking precautions in case of accident; he probably suspected some veiled attempt at humiliation.

In any case, the effect was depressing. At one blow, in Raymond Priestley's words, Scott 'was degraded from explorer to postman'.

Amundsen's discarded equipment came in handy; Bowers was glad of a pair of reindeer mitts to replace his dogskin ones lost a few days before. 'It looks as though the Norwegian party expected colder weather ... than they got,' Scott remarked in his diary, surveying the fur garments neatly piled on the tent floor. 'It could scarcely be otherwise from Shackleton's overdrawn account.' Scott was pursuing the vendetta with his ghostly rival to the last.

Leaving a note to say they had been there, the British party shut the tent, and marched off towards what they decided was the Pole. There, in Scott's words, they 'built a cairn, put up our poor slighted Union Jack, and photographed ourselves – mighty cold work, all of it'.

This hides a pathetic little irony. After a night of broken sleep, cold, tired, still shocked by defeat, Scott and Bowers had made an error in their calculations. They decided they were beyond the Pole, when in fact they were not. Thinking they were going towards it, they were actually moving away. By their own observations, *they never quite got to the Pole at all.**

Their belief that they had reached the mathematical point was reinforced by finding another of Amundsen's black flags about half a mile from the British cairn. Amundsen's note attached to it, said:

> The Norwegian Polheim is situated in 89 deg. 58' SE by E. (comp.) 8 Miles. 15 Decbr, 1911. Roald Amundsen.

It was written in English. Scott mistook it for the Norwegian Pole mark, which clearly it was not. It was the left-hand flag used by Amundsen to box the Pole.

After another round of observations, Scott carried the 'poor slighted Union Jack', as he thought a little nearer the Pole but, in fact, taking it further away, and then set off on the homeward march. In his words, 'We have turned our back now on the goal of our ambition with sore feelings and must face our 800 miles of solid dragging – and good-bye to most of the day dreams!'

Compared to Amundsen, Scott's way back was straightforward; no Devil's Glacier, no broken terrain, no uncharted mountains, but a smooth mapped and pioneered route to the wide entrance of the Beardmore Glacier. With the incessant Polar wind behind him, a sail rigged on the sledge, fast wind crust and the slope down from the summit of

---

* Hinks, A. R., 'The Observations of Amundsen and Scott at the South Pole', *Geographical Journal*, Volume CIII, p. 160.

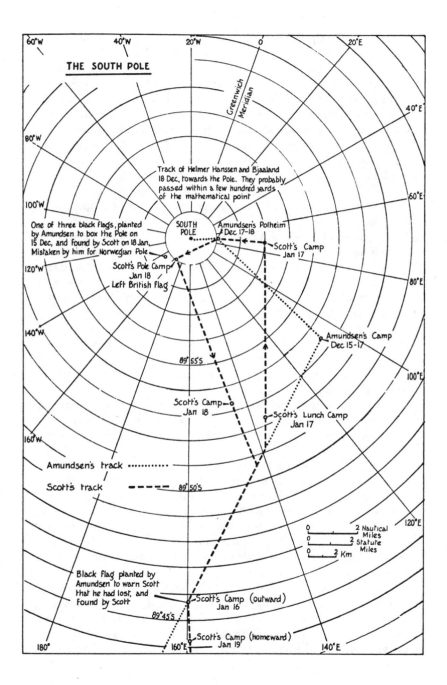

THE SOUTH POLE

Track of Helmer Hanssen and Bjaaland 18 Dec, towards the Pole. They probably passed within a few hundred yards of the mathematical point

One of three black flags, planted by Amundsen to box the Pole on 15 Dec, and found by Scott on 18 Jan. Mistaken by him for Norwegian Pole

SOUTH POLE

Amundsen's Polheim Dec 17–18

Scott's Camp Jan 17

Scott's Pole Camp Jan 18
Left British flag

Amundsen's Camp Dec 15–17

89° 55'S

Scott's Camp Jan 18

Scott's Lunch Camp Jan 17

Amundsen's track ⋯⋯⋯⋯⋯

Scott's track ━ ━ ━ ━ ━   89° 50'S

0 ⊢———————⊣ 2 Nautical Miles
0 ⊢———————⊣ 2 Statute Miles
0 ⊢———⊣ 2 Km

Black flag planted by Amundsen to warn Scott that he had lost, and found by Scott

Scott's Camp (outward) Jan 16

89° 45'S

Scott's Camp (homeward) Jan 19

60°W   40°W   20°W   0   20°E
80°W
100°W
120°W
140°W
160°W
180°

Greenwich Meridian

40°E
60°E
80°E
100°E
120°E
140°E

160°E

the plateau to help him, he began well. Over the first three weeks, he averaged fourteen miles a day, not far behind Amundsen's fifteen miles. Nonetheless the British journey was a dismal contrast to that of the Norwegians. Amundsen was victoriously racing home with the news; Scott's return was like the rout of the vanquished. At first he buoyed himself up with hopes of salvaging something from the wreck by beating Amundsen to the cablehead and telling the story to the world. He had begun to compose his message. 'It is satisfactory,' runs a surviving fragment, 'that the above facts prove that both parties have been at the Pole.' But the delusion soon faded away. Something within Scott had been broken by defeat at the Pole, and his companions sensed it.

There was no fire and little laughter among them, no Bjaaland to race ahead, no running, but a dogged, interminable plod. Scott, now that it was too late, realized that he had cut his food too fine and left himself no leeway. He had condemned his men to march or die. Their reasonable mileage concealed a cruel exhaustion. They had to drive themselves so many miles a day to reach the next depot before supplies gave out. Their already minimal rations were reduced to spin them out, and by now they were probably down to little more than half the food they needed. To do their distances they had to drag their sledge for anything up to twelve hours out of the twenty-four at an altitude of 10,000 feet; a strain on healthy men. One can safely do without either food or rest in emergencies, but to deprive oneself of both is to ask too much of Nature.

Scott and his men had no animals to provide companionship and diversion. They had only their thoughts for company, and a crushing monotony oppressed them on the march. They were suddenly feeling the cold more.

Finding each depot now became a crisis, because there were none of Amundsen's ingenious transverse markings, but merely a single, inadequate flag. Cairns were too low, badly made, and too few for navigation. Scott depended on his outward tracks to find his way back. So too, for convenience, did Amundsen. But he was driving dogs, and he had Bjaaland ranging ahead, scouting for spoors in the snow. With man-hauling that was impossible where the tracks were poor. They had to unharness and scratch about so that route-finding was tedious, for fair-weather only. Twice in the first week the British were unnecessarily stopped by *following* blizzards because they found steering impossible. In any case, their old tracks, drifted up and obscured, were often hard to detect with the sun ahead, throwing up a glare in their faces. For the same reason, Wilson in particular suffered from snowblindness. It did not occur to Scott, as it occurred to Amundsen, to change to night travel as soon as he turned north, and have the sun behind him. Camping unnecessarily squandered effort because of the tent's crass error of design. 'We had the dickens of a time getting up the tent,' wrote Scott of a typical experience in a wind, 'cold fingers all round.'

It was, Bowers remarked, 'soft plodding for me on foot. I shall be jolly glad to pick up my dear old ski.' He did so on January 31st, having trudged through the snow without them for 360 miles. Two days earlier, he wrote his last diary entry in his normal chatty style. From February 4th, he ceased keeping a diary altogether.

Bowers was an extrovert and an optimist, and such men do not usually dilate on unpleasantness. It was about this time that he began to grasp Scott's incompetence. The first alarm came on January 25th, when searching for the depot at 88° 30': 'We have only three days' food with us and shall be in queer street if we miss the depot.' Bowers had been in charge of stores; he knew that Scott had cut things fine, but how fine he only now was beginning to realize.

At breakfast on February 7th, there was what Scott called a 'panic' and Wilson, a 'discussion' when it was discovered that one day's biscuit was missing. Scott vented his wrath on Bowers who, as stores officer, was responsible. Bowers, in Scott's words, was 'dreadfully disturbed'. Wilson, as usual, tried to calm Scott and keep the peace. Scott had forgotten the presence of P.O. Evans, the one rating in their midst, who was thus treated to the unedifying sight of his officers in total confusion. It was no time to show feet of clay, especially in this case, where a subordinate depended utterly on his leader. Evans, unfortunately for himself, had shared a tent with Scott on the Western Journey on the *Discovery* expedition, and therefore knew from personal experience how Scott could run things close. It was knowledge that, perhaps, required the moral strength of a Wilson to bear.

That day, they started the descent of the Beardmore Glacier, reaching the upper glacier depot the same evening. They now had exactly five days' food, with five days to the next depot, the mid glacier depot – according to the outward journey. On a glacier, with ice falls, crevasses and all kinds of potential delay, Scott had left himself no safety margin. The following day he found lee under Mount Buckley, with sunshine and calm after weeks of cold winds on the plateau. It was a moment to seize, and cover distance while the going was good. Scott, with grotesque misjudgment, stopped for the afternoon to collect geological samples, and thenceforth dragged thirty pounds of stones on the sledge. Geology cost him six or seven miles, and time when time was against him.

Next day, Scott discovered that food was running out.

We are in rather a nasty hole tonight [Oates remarked on February 12th]. Got among bad crevasses and pressure, all blue ice. We struggled in this chaos until about 9 p.m., when we were absolutely done.

Scott had lost his way. He had not marked the route through the labyrinth of crevasses on the way up; nor, as he now belatedly regretted, had he kept any bearings to help him find safety. The upshot was that on the wide expanses of the glacier, where perspective could play tricks, and the ice falls were mostly invisible from above, he blundered into some of the worst.

Scott had not only lost his way, he did not know exactly where his depot was; Amundsen's predicament on January 2nd, at the Devil's Glacier.* But Amundsen had food in reserve, Scott had none. He had exactly one thin meal left. Missing the depot was a disaster that would not bear thinking about. 'We *must* get there tomorrow,' he wrote. 'Meanwhile we are cheerful with an effort. It's a tight place.'

They camped among the crevasses and Scott, justifiably worried, found it hard to sleep. By morning, fog had rolled down. With the hollow feeling in the pit of the stomach that comes either from despair or a poor breakfast, they drove on blindly because there was no alternative. When, in a clear interval, Wilson caught sight of the depot flag, a little bit of pemmican and some tea was all the food they had left. They had got through by the skin of their teeth. It was, to quote Scott,

the worst experience of the trip and gave a horrid feeling of insecurity ... In future food must be worked so that we do not run so short if the weather fails us. We mustn't get into a hole like this again.

It was rather late in the day to think of this.

Apart from lacking any margin of safety, Scott had no proper system of accounting. He could not be sure of how his food would last. It is another contrast to Amundsen, meticulously keeping records. The mismanagement was obvious even to Scott's companions.

But they had other burdens now. In Oates' words,

It's an extraordinary thing about Evans, he's lost his guts and behaves like an old woman or worse. He's quite worn out with the work, and how he's going to do the 400 odd miles we've still got to do, I don't know.

It was not the least of Amundsen's achievements to take his men fourteen hundred miles to the Pole and back without sickness or

* See p. 466.

accident. One case of toothache and heavy breathing while trying to *race* at 10,000 feet, are the complaints of healthy men. The British, on the other hand, were ailing when they left the Pole. Oates' toes were turning black from frostbite. Scott fell and hurt his shoulder. Snow-blindness was rife. On January 29th, after a march of almost twenty miles – practically the longest of the whole journey – Wilson found his leg overstrained and for several days could only hobble along by the sledge without pulling. '400 miles about to go before meeting the dogs with ship's news', he wrote. This wistful thought of outside help begins a series of diary comments shot through with pessimistic undertones. He knew Scott well from the Southern Journey of 1902, and how near disaster that had been. It was beginning to look more and more like a repetition. This was a party under stress. From about 88°, it started to disintegrate, and Evans was the first to crack.

Scott had been blind to the flaws concealed by Evans' bull-like figure; flaws obvious to others. It did not help the spirit of the party that Oates, Wilson and Bowers disliked Evans, so that now, when loyalty and cohesion were vital, there were cross-currents of hostility and, in the case of Wilson, a hint of reproach.

Evans was suffering badly from frostbite, to which, as Wilson could remember from *Discovery*, he had always been prone. On January 30th, Scott observed that Evans had 'dislodged two fingernails ... his hands are really bad, and to my surprise he shows signs of losing heart over it – which makes me much disappointed in him'.

Scott lacked sympathy for invalids and, moreover, he expected his men to be silent in adversity. He did not understand that Evans was mentally as well as physically failing.

In a way, the Pole meant more to Evans than the others. He had made up his mind – encouraged by Scott – that it would mean financial security; promotion, money, honourable retirement to keep a nice little pub for the rest of his days. Conversely, defeat would mean ruin. Scott had made the point by asking the officers and scientists to forego their salaries for the second season, because the expedition funds were low. When Evans saw Amundsen's flag fluttering over the snow, his world collapsed. His leader had failed, his hopes were overthrown. He grew unnaturally silent and withdrawn; no longer his usual extrovert self, the compulsive raconteur. Then he gave vent to his anguish in babbling speech. They would be a laughing stock when they got home, second; they were finished, there was no point in carrying on. It was as if Scott were faced with a caricature of himself.

Someone – probably Oates – managed to calm Evans and persuade him to carry on pulling. Physical complications intervened.

Biggest and heaviest of the party, Evans nonetheless had to make do with the same rations as the others. He was, therefore, starving more, deficiencies were accelerated, and his condition grew proportionately worse. Everyone was thinning, but Evans most of all. The injury to his hand, received while shortening the sledges, refused to heal and by the end of January he was unable to help with the camp work. Alone in being so incapacitated, he was on that account oppressed by a sense of failure. This probably helped to break him. Scott had always expected too much of him and had driven him too hard.

Early in February, Evans began to deteriorate rapidly. With lucid intervals, he grew dull, slow and apathetic. He progressively weakened with, eventually, intermittent paralysis. Beyond a vague remark of Scott's that Wilson thought he must have 'injured his brain by a fall', no diagnosis was recorded, and exactly what ailed Evans has always been something of a mystery. One conceivable explanation is hypothermia – lowering of the bodily temperature. But, so far, the most convincingly argued possibility is scurvy. The reasoning turns on the fact that a fall appears to have precipitated Evans' deterioration.

On February 4th, starting to descend the glacier, Scott and Evans fell into a crevasse up to their waists – Evans twice. As mountain accidents go, these were trivial, but the same evening Scott recorded that Evans was 'becoming rather stupid and incapable' and the next day he was 'very stupid about himself'.

The wound that refused to heal, also suppurating cuts and continual nose bleeds, all suggest that after leaving the Pole Evans was suffering from advanced Vitamin C deficiency, and may have been in the early stages of scurvy. One of the effects of the disease is to make blood vessels fragile. In that condition the normally insignificant shock of falling waist-deep into a crevasse, as Evans did, could be enough to injure a blood vessel within the skull and cause a slow brain haemorrhage. That would explain what was happening to him.*

The five men were crammed into a tent made for four. It was an eerie experience to live cheek by jowl with one of the number losing his reason. They could not know if Evans would turn violent, but most of the time he seemed sunk in a stupor, scarcely conscious of what

---

* Concussion was given as the cause in *Scott's Last Expedition*, the first published edition of Scott's diaries. This, however, was a device to conceal, or at least explain away, mental breakdown. Concussion requires a blow to the head, of which there is no record in Evans' case. All the medical evidence is against it.

was happening around him. In any case, they were all tired, hungry, weak and sluggish with cold and malnutrition. Nobody – least of all Wilson, the doctor – had any desire to face mental derangement at close quarters, when they could not bear to look too deeply into their own minds.

They were running out of food again. With enough for three and a half days, they left the mid-glacier depot on February 13th, but in Scott's words, 'We don't know our distance from the next depot ... We are pulling for food ... We have reduced food, also sleep; feeling rather done.'

The uncertainty, and the brutal evidence of Scott's recklessly incompetent preparations were enough to try men in full possession of their faculties. Perhaps it was just as well that they were in varying degress apathetic. For Evans, the crisis came on February 16th. In the afternoon he collapsed, sick and giddy. Oates as usual faced the situation squarely:

> Evans ... first had to get out of his harness and hold on to the sledge and later said he could not get on. If he does not get by tomorrow God knows how we're going to get him home. We cannot possibly take him on the sledge.

Evans was by now an emaciated wreck of a man, but he had been pulling to the bitter end. The next day he seemed better, started in harness, but then, for the first time, was unable to pull. His companions were now quite desperate. Again, they *had* to reach the next depot quickly, for food had nearly run out and they could afford no delay. Evans was having trouble with his boots. He was unhitched and left behind to fix himself up, and told to come on as quickly as he could.

> After lunch [Oates wrote], as Evans was not up, we went back on ski for him, Scott and I leading. We found him on his hands and knees in the snow in a most pitiful condition. He was unable to walk, and the other two went for the empty sledge and we brought him into the tent.

Does this mask a more or less unconscious attempt to abandon Evans? A subsequent remark by Scott in his diary points in that direction:

> I take this opportunity of saying that we have stuck to our sick companions ... In case of Edgar Evans ... the safety of the remainder seemed to demand his abandonment, but Providence mercifully removed him at the critical moment.

Evans was comatose when he was brought into the tent, and he died that night without recovering consciousness.

Almost immediately Scott struck camp, made his way down through some pressure ridges, and found his lower glacier depot. There he and his remaining companions had their first proper meal for a week and, as he put it, 'we gave ourselves 5 hours' sleep ... after the horrible night', before continuing through the Gateway to Shambles Camp, where the ponies had been shot.

They dug up a carcass, and with pony meat that night, they were comforted by the sensation of a full belly for once. The momentary optimism did not last. When they set off from Shambles Camp it was the same tale of struggle in conditions under which the Norwegians were skating along. Little strains began to tell. Scott chid Bowers for not having 'quite the trick' in skiing. Bowers was justifiably hurt; it was late for this kind of criticism. They were all indifferent skiers, which meant moil and toil and a drain on their dwindling strength. When every inch counted, they were losing perhaps a hundred yards a mile from poor technique alone; thirty miles in the journey from the Pole to the yet far off One Ton Depot at 79° 28½'. In the end, that would mean a great deal.

They were struggling for pitiful marches of six and seven miles. 'Heavy toiling all day,' wrote Scott on the 21st, 'inspiring gloomiest thoughts at times ... We never won a march of 8½ miles with greater difficulty, but we can't go on like this.' On the 24th, they reached the Southern Barrier Depot. They found a shortage of fuel.

'Wish we had more fuel,' 'The fuel shortage is still an anxiety,' 'Fuel is woefully short.' Thus the litany of remorse. And then on February 27th: 'Pray God we have no further set-backs. We are naturally always discussing possibility of meeting dogs, where and when, etc.' So, the dogs were to be their salvation after all.

'It is a critical position. We may find ourselves in safety at next depot, but there is a horrid element of doubt.'

Now Scott grasped it was going to be a race for life.

On that day, Wilson ceased keeping his diary, as if he could no longer bear to face his thoughts. They were more than 300 miles from home.

32

Back to the Fram

AT FOUR IN the morning of January 26th, the Norwegians drove up to Framheim. Speaking in undertones, they unhitched the dogs as quietly as they could and, like conspirators, stealthily entered the hut. The occupants – Lindstrøm, Stubberud, Prestrud and Johansen – were fast asleep. It was a gratifying sight. Amundsen had arranged the last lap expressly to catch Framheim abed. He felt that the Polar journey could appropriately end with a prank.

'Good morning, my dear Lindstrøm', said Amundsen as he stepped inside. 'Have you any coffee for us?'

In Wisting's words, 'It would be very difficult for me to describe the various phizzes that emerged from their respective bunks and stared at us – they had to be seen.'

All Lindstrøm could say at first was, 'Good God, is it you?' The Polar party had not been expected for another ten days.

'Get up boys,' he called when he had gathered his wits together, 'it's the first cuckoo of spring.' Stubberud recalled that 'Roald came up to me, and shook my hand; I didn't ask about anything.' Somebody, as Wisting remembered the scene, finally put the question,

'Have you been there?' 'Yes, we've been there,' answered Roald Amundsen, and then there was a hullabaloo. Soon after, we were all seated round the table and savoured Lindstrøm's hot cakes and heavenly coffee. How good a cup of coffee can really taste one only realises when, like us, one has had to go without so long.

That came from the heart; for ninety-nine days, the Polar party had drunk nothing but chocolate.

Amundsen made a short speech. There had been no quarrels on the Polar journey, he said, but good team work. And he was glad that everyone had got back safely.

'That gathering round the breakfast table at Framheim after the end of the trip,' wrote Helmer Hanssen, 'belongs to the moments in one's life one never forgets.' Amundsen was happiest at these festive moments with a small chosen group around him. He knew how to create a sense of occasion. To finish off, in Bjaaland's words, they 'quaffed a welcoming cup ... a really good schnapps'.

By audacity and something not far short of genius Amundsen had snatched the prize, and brought all his men safely back again. It was one of the greatest of Polar journeys; perhaps the greatest, as Amundsen, because he had the gift of good fortune to add to his other talents, was among the greatest of Polar explorers.

'We haven't got much to tell in the way of privation or great struggle,' he said at the breakfast table that memorable Friday morning. 'The whole thing went like a dream.'

And indeed all things considered, Amundsen did have rather more to hear than to tell. In his absence, a Japanese expedition in the *Kainan Maru* ('Opener up of the South') had arrived. 'What they intend to do,' he wrote, 'I haven't the slightest idea. They hardly know themselves.'* Prestrud, Johansen, and Stubberud had reached King Edward VII Land, becoming the first 'men to set foot on it.† But best of all, *Fram* had arrived on January 9th. She had since been driven out to sea by wind and ice, but came in again the day after Amundsen's arrival.

On board, Nilsen had seen the large swallow-tailed Norwegian Naval ensign flying from Cape Man's Head, the prearranged signal of the Southern Party's safe return. He hooted triumphantly on the siren as he came in and everybody at Framheim, excepting Lindstrøm, hurried down to the ship.

> Great, jubilant reunion [in Nilsen's words]. First aboard was the chief; I was so certain that he had reached the goal, that I didn't even ask about it. First, after an hour, when so much else had been discussed, I asked: 'Well, you've naturally been to the South Pole???'

Now Amundsen had his first news of the outside world since meeting *Terra Nova* a year before, and heard how his coup had been received. It gave him a taste of gall:

> A number of people seem to be indignant over our activities down

---

*R. Amundsen. Diary. January 26th, 1912. A little unfair. The Japanese wanted to achieve their own Furthest South, and even then, the 'Dash Patrol', under Lt. Shirase, the expedition commander, was on its way, setting the record two days later, the latitude being 80° 5′ S. There, Lt. Shirase 'raised ... the national Sun-Flag and raised a threefold *Banzai* for His Majesty the Emperor.' (*Geographical Journal*, Vol. LXXXII, 1933 p. 420). It was the first Japanese Antarctic expedition.

† But only just. They arrived on November 29th. The *Kainan Maru* landed a party over the pack ice on January 23rd doing, incidentally, what neither *Discovery*, *Nimrod*, nor *Terra Nova* had managed. It was the first landing from the sea.

here – a breach of 'etiquette'? Are these people mad? Is the question of the pole exclusively confided to Scott for solution? I don't give a hang for these idiots. Nansen, as usual, with his cool, clear understanding, has cooled emotions. Oh well, people are idiotic.

He also now discovered what he owed Don Pedro Christophersen. As he put it in his diary,

It is to the intervention of this man that the 3rd *Fram* Expedition owes its continued existence. At home, everything was closed – with the exception of the King and Fridtjof Nansen. May the confidence that they have shown me not be disappointed! I admire the King for his manly behaviour. [He] was not afraid to give a contribution to the South Polar expedition, even if parliament or the majority wanted *Fram* to be ordered home. But it didn't go the way those gentlemen wanted. Just wait a bit, we'll soon have a talk. Perhaps you will be pleasanter the next time you hear from *Fram* ... I owe the King, Nansen, and Christophersen more than I can express. When *everyone* turned their backs – they stretched out their hand. God bless them!

Amundsen did not dwell long on such thoughts, for the moment. The race was not yet won. He still had to get through first with the news and he imagined that Scott was still in the running. 'Time is precious,' he wrote, 'and we've got to reach civilisation before anyone else.'

On Sunday after returning from the Pole, Amundsen nonetheless made time for a farewell dinner at Framheim. With the air of a magician pulling rabbits out of a hat, Lindstrøm produced champagne. He had brought it with him from home, and slept with the bottles in his bed all winter to stop them getting too cold at night.

Amundsen made a little after-dinner speech, thanking everybody for work well done. The expedition had accomplished everything it set out to do: the conquest of the South Pole; first to reach King Edward VII Land, and the first oceanographic survey of the South Atlantic between America and Africa; but above all, the Pole.

Now there was a hurry to embark. Only the dogs and more valuable equipment were taken. Everything else was left behind. Because of the ice, *Fram* was moored further out than the year before, and it took two days' hard shuttling with dog teams to load her. Indispensable to the end, it was the dogs who gave the speed.

On January 30th in the evening, Amundsen shut the door of the hut carefully behind him and for the last time, followed the track down to the ice edge where *Fram* was waiting, dressed overall and ready for sea. It was, in his words, a heavy moment to leave Framheim. A more splendid or cosy winter quarters no one has had. When we departed, Lindstrøm had scoured it from top to bottom and it was shining like a new pin. We won't be accused of untidiness or dirt if anyone should happen to go there and look.

All that remained was to heave the dogs on board. Thirty-nine had survived. They were being taken back to civilization, some to be given to Douglas Mawson's Australian Antarctic expedition, and some to found the stock for *Fram*'s Northern Drift. It was, said Amundsen,

> Strange to see how many of the old veterans immediately recognised *Fram*'s deck. Wisting's sturdy dog, old 'Colonel', with his two adjutants 'The Whopper' and 'Arne' immediately took the place where they had stood many a fine day during the long voyage South ... 'Mylius' and 'Ring' - Helmer Hanssen's special favourites - began playing there in the corner of the fo'csle to port, as if nothing had happened. Nobody could see by the two jolly rascals that they had trotted at the head of the whole caravan both to the Pole and back. There was one, stalking alone and reserved, always unsettled and unapproachable. Nothing could replace his fallen friend 'Fridtjof' who had long found his grave in his comrade's bellies hundreds of miles away in the Barrier.

As soon as the dogs were on board, *Fram* cast off, and, as Bjaaland put it in his diary, left 'These regions and Framheim with all their splendour to anyone who wants them.'

With her unerring sense of drama, Nature dropped the curtain with a fog. There was no last lingering view to sour the moment with anticlimax. The Barrier, Cape Man's Head, and all the well-remembered landmarks were cleanly cut off from sight.

A shadow in the fog, *Fram*, like a Viking ship coming away from a raid, stood out of the Bay of Whales and headed for the open sea. About Amundsen himself there was, indeed, a touch of the Viking. It was not only the heroic vision that led him to switch from one Pole of the earth to another. It was also the other and equally authentic side of the Viking spirit: the man following his destiny; the shrewd realist born, as one historian has expressed it, of 'folk wisdom, peasant cunning, mercantile caution, and the soldier's prejudice against being caught with his pants down'.

Amundsen had kept to his original choice of Hobart, Tasmania, for his landfall. Lyttelton, New Zealand was closer, but that was Scott's citadel, and he had no wish to tempt Fate by intruding on the enemy in his stronghold.

Fram crossed the Antarctic circle on February 9th, and sighted the last iceberg two days later. But in Bjaaland's words, she 'crept forwards miserably slowly, headwinds and fog and rain and high seas on the beam'. *Fram* had plenty of scope for her famous rolling and yawing. Now lightly laden, she tossed about like a cork. On one occasion by the violence of her lurching, she broke a gaff; on another, she threw a young dog overboard.

> After long and hard work [wrote Amundsen], we managed to get a lifeline round him, and up he came. He was then rather exhausted. Lt. Gjertsen and Wisting were outboard during [the rescue] and got some really good duckings.

It was a long and trying voyage.

To begin with, at any rate, Amundsen had plenty to do. For hours every day, he sat working in his cabin, under the eyes of Nansen looking down from the portrait that hung like an ikon, above his desk. It was the same portrait that had hung in *Gjøa* through the North-West Passage.

In that formidable presence, Amundsen ploughed through a complete year's file of *Tidens Tegn*, a Christiania newspaper sent out for him to catch up with the world. He prepared his telegrams. He wrote his story for the Press. He wrote and rehearsed the lecture which he was going to repeat so inhumanly often in the months ahead. Nilsen, a superior linguist, did the English translations.

Amundsen was doing what has been given to few Polar explorers; recording an enterprise carried through as he had intended. Not even Nansen could boast of that.

Unshakable in loyalty and gratitude, Amundsen was implacable in hostility. The Pole had not changed that. Even in victory, he could not and would not forgive Johansen his luckless quarrel on the first start for the south.

Johansen was profoundly miserable. His exclusion from the Polar party seemed the final humiliation to cap the disappointment that had been his lot since the return of *Fram* from her first voyage, sixteen years before. To his wife, he now wrote a melancholy apologia:

> When one is so far away and left to one's self in the great loneliness, one broods about one thing or the other ... For my part, I can still be glad that I have not suffered any injury, but still possess my indomitable strength ... I did not get to the Pole. I naturally would have liked to ... The main thing is that ... we did good work [on King Edward VII Land]. But you know the great public asks who has been to the Pole. Well, I don't care. I dare to say that nevertheless I have also helped the Southern party to reach the Pole,

even if I couldn't be on the final assault, and I know that I was appreciated by those with whom I worked ... Ah well, as things are, it has all turned out for the best.

Fighting the weather is a wearing business, and everlastingly beating up into the wind worst of all, especially on a ship like *Fram* that makes leeway like a crab. After the middle of February, spirits on board began to droop.

To Amundsen, the conquest of the Pole was now past, attainment being its own reward. In any case, the attacks on his behaviour, and what he saw as the desertion of his countrymen, had seared the raw nerves under a very thin skin.

He was already thinking of his Arctic drift. Because of the 'deviation' to the South Pole, his men had been released from their original contracts and, as *Fram* plunged and tossed her way through the spume towards Hobart, he asked them to continue on the original Arctic drift. Most did. Wisting and Helmer Hanssen by now would have followed him anywhere. Bjaaland, in the face of urgent persuasion, declined. 'It will be a long and hard trip,' he confided darkly to his diary, 'if I know the old blighter properly.'

By the end of February, Amundsen was on tenterhooks once more. He had been a month under way; still the winds were perverse, as if trying to keep him away from land. He was plagued by visions of Scott beating him to the cablehead and taking half the game; yet, on the other hand, oddly content to put off the end of the voyage. There is comfort in the suspended animation of a ship at sea, even if she lurches about like *Fram*, in the teeth of a gale. There may only be disillusion ashore. Like Columbus, that archetype of the discoverer, Amundsen was really only happy on the move, going from here to there.

On March 4th, the Tasmanian coast was finally raised. But, in Bjaaland's words,

It was a stinking job to get in to Hobart. Storm and calm followed each other, and when we finally were at the approaches to our goal, so God help me we were blown past, the result being we had to lay to in a storm with torn sail and splintered gaff.

At last, on Thursday, March 7th, *Fram* reached Hobart and anchored out in the fairway. A little knot of spectators had gathered on the waterfront. Amundsen alone went ashore and booked in at Hadley's Orient Hotel. 'Treated as a tramp,' he noted in his diary, 'my peaked cap and blue sweater – given a miserable little room.'

Thus ended the last classic journey of terrestrial discovery.

33

The Ultimate Defeat

FAR BEHIND ON the Barrier, at about 82 degrees S. latitude, Scott was struggling on. The shortage of fuel at the Southern Barrier Depot was repeated at the next depot on March 1st. Instead of the gallon expected, he found hardly a quarter.

That paraffin 'creeps' in extreme cold was familiar to Polar explorers. Amundsen, having met the phenomenon on the North-West Passage, took great pains to overcome it for the South Pole. Scott had observed it on *Discovery*, but neglected to find a proper answer. He used tins with screwed bungs seated on leather washers. Polar literature offered sufficient evidence that this was ineffective. Again, Amundsen makes the point. Fifty years later, one of his hermetically sealed tins of paraffin was found on Betty's Knoll, at 85° S., the contents still intact.* Three months after laying his depots, Scott's life-giving fuel had escaped.

In any case, he had cut things fine. Amundsen, travelling twice as fast between Barrier depots consistently closer, allowed three times as much fuel. Scott was paying for his ineptitude: unfortunately his followers would have to pay as well.

Starving and ill-clothed, they were feeling the cold horribly. They were starving because the depots were too small, too few and too far apart. Scott had spaced them for animal transport, knowing full well that he would be man-hauling on the return. His benumbed state of mind comes through when he writes about being 'two poney [*sic*] marches and 4 miles from our depot' when he only had the use of his own two feet. Too late he realized that 'we cannot do distances without the ponies'.

Oates' feet had now turned gangrenous from frostbite. From mistaken gallantry, he had hidden the fact until, on March 2nd, he could stand the pain no longer, and revealed what was the matter. Scott was shocked at the sight of the swollen and discoloured members.

Three days later, Scott recorded:

poor Soldier nearly done. It is pathetic enough because we can do nothing for him ... We none of us expected these terribly low temperatures.

* By Dr. Charles Swithinbank, then of the U.S. Antarctic Program

Yet all his experience told him what to expect. The *Discovery* told him so. Shackleton told him so. His own men told him so; or could have, if he had been prepared to listen. The year before, at the same time, Teddy Evans had found low temperatures and hard going on the Barrier. Scott nonetheless planned to be out three or four weeks later. Naval officers have been court-martialled for less.

In fact, the temperatures, between $-30°$ and $-40°$C., were not exceptionally low for the season of the year. But all their defences against the cold were down. By now they were all probably suffering from scurvy in varying degrees.

At this point one is thrown back on deduction. No medical records have survived, since by now Wilson had stopped keeping his diary. It was in any case intended for his family, and therefore suppressed unpleasantness. He was always sparing of clinical details. His sole explanation of Evans' collapse, for example, was that it had 'much to do with the fact that he has never been sick in his life and is now helpless with his hands frost-bitten', into which worlds can be read. But Wilson was not a practising doctor. His clinical experience was limited, and he showed no evidence of being able to diagnose the complicated progress of scurvy, except in its final stages. And since he was now sick and miserable himself, his desire and capacity to diagnose sickness in others would have been blunted.

What remains are the two records still being kept: Scott's diary, and Bowers' meteorological log. From the former comes a tale of dismal pulling and bad surfaces; from the latter, evidence that conditions were not unrelievedly bad, but often the same as those which to Amundsen meant good going. Scott and his companions, however, were so weak that it was clearly an effort to move even their featherweight sledge. They were struggling nine hours or more for their six or seven miles a day.

By now Scott was almost certainly in the early stages of scurvy. He had been out for more than four months without any significant intake of Vitamin C, and his position was complicated by another threat. Stress is a drain on Vitamin C, and of stress Scott and his men had too much. They were beset by fear and anxiety, much of it due to Scott's negligence. He had, for example, not built enough cairns and now, when every minute counted, had to waste time looking for tracks. The sense of being lost is wearing because it strikes at the fundamental human craving for security; nothing can cause panic so easily. Such worries and uncertainty, on top of strains within the party, were enough to waste the life-giving vitamin. Amundsen and his men were spared that drain on their resources.

Oates, Bowers and Wilson were labouring under a terrible burden. Scott alone was still keeping a diary, and his words give a glimpse of what his companions were going through. 'I don't know what I should do,' he wrote on March 4th, 'if Wilson and Bowers weren't so determinedly cheerful over things.' As a leader Scott had collapsed, and Wilson had taken over.

For Oates, it was a *via dolorosa*. He was now unable to pull, just limping along in pain by the side of the sledge, resting when he could. It took him more than an hour to get his swollen feet into his frozen *finnesko* each morning.

One of the effects of scurvy is to make old wounds reopen, because Vitamin C is needed to keep scars together. There are records of injuries opening up again after more than twenty years, as if they had never been healed. Before this stage is reached, there is degeneration in the tissues, which may cause great pain. The lack of Vitamin C from which Oates was now suffering, almost certainly affected his old war injury, which was about ten years old. The bullet which smashed his thigh bone had left a massive scar, which by now would have begun to dissolve under incipient scurvy. What he suffered can only be imagined; on top of his frostbitten feet, it merely added to his agony. He was miserable, unnaturally miserable; his old humour dead. He was silent in the tent. As Scott put it in his diary, he had 'become a terrible hindrance' going on to say that he

must know that he can never get through. He asked Wilson if he had a chance this morning, and of course Bill had to say he didn't know. In point of fact he has none. Apart from him, if he went under now, I doubt whether we could get through. The weather conditions are awful, and our gear gets steadily more icy and difficult to manage. At the same time of course poor Titus is the greatest handicap ... Poor chap! poor chap. It is too pathetic to watch him.

Poor Oates, indeed. He sat there in the tent, Scott staring at him, with the unspoken expectation of the supreme sacrifice.

At Cape Evans, Oates had emphatically said that on the Polar journey no man should be a burden to his companions. He thought that a pistol should be carried, and 'if anyone breaks down he should have the privilege of using it'.

Perhaps Oates remembered another conversation, a year before, when he told Scott he would regret not taking the ponies on to move One Ton Depot further south, and Scott had replied that he had 'had more than enough of this cruelty to animals, and for the sake of a few marches, I'm not going to defy my feelings'. Scott had saved his feelings, but he had not yet paid the cost.

Alone among them, Oates had been to war and faced death in the field. He had no immature fantasies of martyrdom. He was playing to no audience; he clutched at no heroic delusions. He was a brave man. Coming second – especially to someone like Amundsen – was a disgrace with which he, at least, could live. He wanted to go home and take his major's exam. After Amundsen he could see how he had been betrayed by bad leadership. He had never wanted to go to the Pole; he had been ordered there against his wishes. There was no reason why he should give up to oblige Scott – yet.

On March 9th, they reached what was to be the depot of their salvation; Mount Hooper. In Scott's words, it was

Cold comfort. Shortage on our allowance all round. I don't know that anyone is to blame – but generosity and thoughtfulness has not been abundant.

Again, Scott had brought it on himself. By taking five men at the last moment, and bringing Meares on much further than originally planned, he had disturbed the whole organization of the depots. The return parties had been forced to broach stores and redistribute quantities instead of taking prepared rations. They had neither measures nor scales; it was an unfair burden, especially on men sick and exhausted with judgment impaired.

The shortage at the depot had serious implications. As Scott put it: 'The dogs which would have been our salvation have evidently failed. Meares had a bad trip home I suppose – It's a miserable jumble.' Scott had not only left himself with barely enough supplies to get him from one depot to the next, but he had left the depots without reserves in case of accidents. By his own efforts, the chances of getting through were thin. Salvation, after all, depended on the dogs. But the dogs were not coming.

Behind him at Cape Evans, Scott had left voluminous and intricate orders. They contrived to destroy initiative, bind his subordinates and throw responsibility on to others. They were, in the vital parts, imprecisely phrased, and open to misinterpretation.

The dogs, upon whom so much depended, were the subject of particularly diffuse, ill-conceived and contradictory instructions. On the one hand, they were to hurry Scott home; on the other, they were not to be risked but saved for the next season. In any case, Scott had gone off without leaving final instructions. His meeting with the dogs was to be fixed by orders sent back with the return parties. If there was any hitch, the commander at Cape Evans would not know what to do, because Scott, still declining to take his officers into his confidence, had not explained his intentions. Moreover, the responsibility for executing the orders would shift as Simpson, left in charge at Cape Evans, handed over to the first Naval officer returning from the south.

In all the marching and counter-marching, Scott had somehow failed to put enough supplies along his route to get him safely home. It was the dogs who, from the start, were expected to close the gap at the last moment. This was the vital operation that Scott had left in uncertainty and muddle.

Simpson expected Meares and the dogs back by December 15th. He remained in uncertainty until the 26th, when Day and Hooper arrived with the wholly unforeseen news that Scott was taking the dogs on further than originally intended. They might, as Scott put it in his new orders to Simpson, 'be late returning unfit for work or non-existent. So don't forget that [the supplies] must be got to 'One Ton Camp' ... somehow'.* Simpson immediately sent Day and Hooper back to do the job – none too eagerly – man hauling.

On January 5th, Meares finally arrived with the dogs. He had nothing to do except wait for orders from the south.

Three weeks later, Atkinson returned, but without the orders that Meares had been led to expect. The only hint of Scott's intentions was his vague remark to Atkinson at the top of the Beardmore Glacier to 'come as far as you can'.† Against this were instructions not to start too early because dogs, in Scott's opinion, were unable to wait; because they suffered from lying in the snow. This of course was nonsense, but it was an order.

On February 19th, Petty Officer Crean arrived alone at Hut Point to say that Teddy Evans, nursed by Lashly, was out near Corner Camp, seriously ill with scurvy. In that crisis, Scott's vital message that the dogs were to meet him between 82° and 83°, casually mentioned just before parting with Evans, was forgotten.

Atkinson, as a doctor, now concentrated on rescuing Evans. Together with Dmetri, he went out with the dogs, brought Evans back, and saved his life – just.

It occurred to nobody that if Evans had scurvy, then Scott or some of his men might also be suffering from it by now. Slight symptoms

* See p. 396.
† See p. 437.

among Atkinson's own return party ought already to have suggested the possibility, in which case the Polar party might be in trouble, and an immediate attempt to relieve them ought to be made. But even had the thought arisen, no one would have dared to act, for Scott had given categorical orders that he was *not* to be relieved on any account. It might well have been bravado, but it was an order.

The interpretation of orders, especially in extreme conditions and, above all, in the Polar regions, requires judgment. It is dangerous to bind with rigid instructions. Obedience *au pied de la lettre*, may spell disaster. It is best to be able to adapt to circumstances and carry out ultimate intentions. That is why Amundsen had said to Thorvald Nilsen on *Fram*, 'I give you complete freedom of action.'

But the base at Cape Evans was run in Naval fashion. Atkinson, the man now in command, although a doctor, was a Naval officer. In a situation calling for judgment and initiative, Naval discipline failed. The training and tradition of the Royal Navy was still absolute, unquestioning, literal obedience to orders. Scott, the martinet, rigidly enforced this. His subordinates were, as a result, mentally fettered.

Nor could Scott count on affection to disregard orders and brave hardships to save him. 'If the Pole is won I believe you'll have a pleasant winter,' as Griffith Taylor, who was going home on the ship, pointedly expressed it to Frank Debenham, 'If not, *Gott Ihnen hilft*!' ['God help you!']

On February 5th, *Terra Nova* arrived. She brought news that decided Simpson to change his plans and go home. He handed over to Wright in a hurry as best he could, and prepared to embark. Meares, intent on catching the ship, dropped all work. He was by now quite disgusted with the expedition, and wanted to wash his hands of the whole affair.

Atkinson was now supposed to go out with the dogs and hurry Scott back to catch the ship. But he felt he ought to stay and look after Evans instead. Dmetri was the only dog-driver left. Cherry-Garrard or Wright would have to go with him. Wright was tough, level-headed, and a navigator. But he was a scientist, and, with Simpson out of the picture, his place was considered to be at Cape Evans with the instruments. So he stayed, and Cherry-Garrard went.

On every count, Cherry-Garrard was unsuited to the task. He had never driven dogs before. He was short-sighted. He could not navigate. Scott had laughed at him when he tried to learn the subject. 'Of course there is not one chance in a hundred that he will ever have to consider navigation', Scott had written home just before the start; and now the hundredth chance had arrived.

Together with Dmetri, Cherry-Garrard started with the dog teams for the South on February 25th. As far as he knew, it was just a welcoming excursion. He got to One Ton Camp on March 4th, having done twenty miles a day without trouble under Dmetri's tutelage, mildly bemused by the discovery at the eleventh hour of what dogs could do.

There was no sign of the Polar party. A blizzard now broke out and blew for four days, pinning Cherry down. An experienced dog-driver could have gone on, but Cherry was not an experienced dog-driver and Dmetri had no desire to drive on into the storm.

In any case, a supply of dog food mentioned by Scott did not exist. It was to have been brought out by Meares, but had somehow been forgotten in the general confusion caused by Scott's shifting plans and unclear orders. The dogs, therefore, could not go on as far as he expected, although there was food enough on the sledges for them to continue for a day or two before turning home. They could have been taken further on, some being killed to feed the others.

But Scott's orders emphatically stated that the dogs were not to be risked, and Atkinson had explained that he was not in any way dependent on them for his return. What Atkinson did not grasp, however, because Scott had not made it clear, was that the danger point had moved significantly south. The original plans assumed that the Polar party would be able to get through to One Ton Camp before needing the supplies brought out from base. Because of all the changes, notably the fact that Meares had been taken on much further than originally intended, this no longer held.

All of this, of course, was hidden from Cherry-Garrard. Moreover, since he could not navigate, he dared not go any further for fear of missing Scott. Besides, Scott was not yet due at One Ton Camp, and Scott himself had led Cherry-Garrard to believe that time tables were inviolate. The situation seemed hardly urgent. Cherry felt justified in staying where he was, and waited for six days. On March 10th, he turned back, still suspecting no danger to the Polar party.

When Cherry-Garrard turned, Oates was almost at the end of his tether. Scott compelled Wilson to hand over his stock of opium tablets for each one to do away with himself, if he wanted.

It was only the hope of meeting the dogs that now kept Oates going. By March 14th or 15th – they were losing track of dates now

– when the dogs still had not appeared, he could no longer carry on. The pain of his gangrenous frostbitten feet, the burden of hunger and cold, was too much. Oates had reached a stage of apathy that comes with privation in great cold. He asked to be left behind in the snow in his sleeping bag, but was persuaded to struggle on for a few more miles, in the faint hope that the dogs were, after all, just over the horizon. After the inevitable disappointment, he finally gave up.

In the tent that night, Oates turned to Wilson as those in trouble usually did. He had no wish to confide in Scott, for whom by now he had lost any lingering vestige of respect. Oates had to face the hideous realization that he had been betrayed by incompetent leadership. If only he had not been so mistakenly silent, he could have avoided this futile disaster. It was a heavy burden of regret to bear.

He had left writing until too late, and handed over his fragmentary diary to Wilson, asking him to give it to his mother. She was, he told Wilson, the only woman he had ever loved, and his greatest regret was that he had not written to her how, before the end.

According to Scott's dairy, Oates 'slept through the night' – implying that this was no longer usually the case – 'hoping not to wake.' What does this mean? If he could, he would have taken the opium tablets and put himself out of his misery, but that was a moral barrier he could not cross. Probably he appealed to Wilson, and Wilson gave him a morphine injection. It would not have been a fatal dose. For that we have Wilson's word: 'Our record,' as he put it in a letter to his parents, 'is clear.' But he may have given Oates enough to quell his pain, with perhaps the half-admitted thought that in his condition it might be his quietus.

But there was no easy way out for Oates. In the morning he woke. It was, if the dates were right, March 17th, and his thirty-second birthday. The tent walls cracked with the noise of canvas whipped by the wind. He struggled out of the worn, damp furs of his sleeping bag, crawled over his companions' legs across the tent and, taking hold of the entrance, hanging down like an empty sack, he started to undo it. It was the ordinary and familiar act of many a camp. Three pairs of eyes stared; someone made a half-hearted attempt to stop him.

The knot loosened; the sack opened and became a tunnel. Like an animal creeping away to die, Oates limped out into the whirling drift and was seen no more.

Wilson wrote to Mrs Oates that he had never seen or heard of

506 / scott and amundsen

such courage as her son had shown. He died, said Wilson, like a man and a soldier, without a word of complaint.

In Scott's version, as it appeared in his diary, Oates, as he left the tent said: 'I am just going outside and may be some time.' Oates, said Scott,

> took pride in thinking that his regiment would be pleased with the bold way in which he met his death ... We knew that poor Oates was walking to his death, but ... we knew it was the act of a brave man and an English gentleman.

Wilson implies that Oates was suffering so much that, when there was no longer any hope, he took the only way out. Scott ascribes heroic thoughts, leaving the unanswered question of how he knew. Scott, however, was by now writing for publication, some day. Wilson was writing a very personal letter and, if Oates had expressed heroic intent, he would have told Mrs. Oates so, including presumably his last words. Where independent testimony exists, Wilson is always reliable.

Scott, however, was preparing his alibi. A subordinate driven to the extremity of suffering would be damaging in the extreme, so Oates simply *had* to have a story-book ending. In any case, Scott, who always went by appearances, may well have interpreted Oates' action as the correct gesture.

The weather lifted and, for a few days more, Scott, Wilson and Bowers struggled on. On March 21st, they came within eleven miles of One Ton Depot, food and fuel almost gone. They pitched their tent and a blizzard came down from the south-west. Scott's right foot had been frostbitten, and he was almost unable to walk. Now he was the drag on the party, and in the predicament of Oates. Wilson and Bowers, in marginally better shape, prepared to set off for the depot and fetch food and fuel. Something stopped them; it is not clear what. Bowers was not the man to give up while there was the ghost of a chance.

Even in top form they had been stopped by the same kind of following gale because of the inability to steer in bad weather. Because of slovenly marking, they needed good weather to find the depot. But the storm is unlikely to have been as fierce or unrelenting as Scott suggested, for even in health he dramatized events. Now he was cold, starving, ill, things might easily seem worse than they were. Scott himself probably held Bowers and Wilson back.

Even if they reached the depot, they were probably finished, with

130 miles still to safety and the season closing in. Scott's frostbitten foot threatened gangrene. 'Amputation is the least I can hope for
now,' he wrote, 'but will the trouble spread?' If, by some miracle,
they got through, they would probably be crippled for life. All this
Wilson, and certainly Bowers, were prepared to accept; but Scott had
to face the terrible words MENE MENE TEKEL UPHARSIN ...
Thou art weighed in the balances and art found wanting.

'I stand or fall by the expedition', Scott had written home before
starting. He had nothing to look forward to. He had been beaten to
the Pole. He had bungled the whole enterprise. He had departed in
triumph, and now he would have to return home and face his public
in defeat. At best, what awaited him was the humiliating sympathy
reserved for the also-ran. His enemies would laugh at him. Indeed,
on March 20th, Armitage, embittered by the *Discovery* expedition, was
writing to Nansen with 'heartiest congratulations' on Amundsen's
success:

> It proves once more, the value of practical experience & logical reasoning ...
> I fear that Scott, with his dislike for Ski, to say nothing else, will find
> great difficulty in reaching his goal ... I see that Amundsen intends making
> the Bering Sea passage across the North Pole, and I sincerely hope that
> he will be as fully successful as in the South.

Scott would have to answer for the men he had lost.

Shackleton would have the last laugh.

That was something Scott could not face. It would be better to
seek immolation in the tent. That way he could snatch a kind of victory
out of defeat. Wilson and Bowers were persuaded to lie down with
him and wait for the end, where the instinct of other men in like
predicament was to keep going and fall in their tracks. For at least
nine days they lay in their sleeping bags, while their last food and
fuel gave out, and their life ebbed away.

They wrote their last letters, believing they would be found some day.
That indeed was the argument that Scott probably used to persuade
Wilson and Bowers to lie down and wait in the tent. If they had
fallen in their tracks, they and their records would have been lost.
In the tent, they would have a chance of being found, and their tale
saved from oblivion.

Wilson and Bowers penned a few hasty, poignant, private notes. Scott,
however, had been preparing his farewells for some time. The earliest
was dated March 16th, to Sir Edgar Speyer, the expedition's treasurer:
'I fear we must go.' Scott had already given up.

Letter after letter poured out; Scott was addressing his audience. In the approach of extinction, he showed an exultation he had never otherwise displayed; the true spirit of the martyr. The paradox was that Wilson, who for so long had nursed morbid death-wishes, now had regrets.

He had promised Oates that he would go to see his mother. The only way he could now keep that trust was by writing to Mrs. Oates to convey her son's last message and describe how he met his end. Wilson was on the verge of breaking down as he wrote, for now, as he expressed it, he was in the same can. He could no longer hope to see either her or his wife or his own mother and father again. He was a born loser, that he understood. But his life had been thrown away – for nothing. They were now ten miles *north* of the point to which Scott had been urged to take the depot so tragically just out of reach.

> I leave you in the lurch [Scott wrote to William Ellison-Macartney, his brother-in-law, who managed the family finances], but without intention as you know ... I left my money, about £2,000 to Mother. Other money ought to come in. See Speyer and talk over Kathleen's rights. You have been a brick.

Then Scott prepared his exit from the stage.

> I was *not* too old for this job [he wrote to Admiral Sir Francis Bridgeman, his last Naval chief]. It was the younger men that went under first ... We are setting a good example to our countrymen, if not by getting into a tight place, by facing it like men when we get there.

This was his constant theme. He wrote to Sir James Barrie, putting it in these words:

> We are showing that Englishmen can still die with a bold spirit, fighting it out to the end ... I think this makes an example for Englishmen of the future.

For Sir Clements Markham, however, the man to whom Scott owed his chance in life, there was no letter. 'I haven't time to write to Sir Clements,' Scott wrote to Kathleen. 'Tell him I thought much of him, and never regretted his putting me in command of the *Discovery*.'

Scott did, on the other hand, write a message to the public:

> The causes of the disaster are not due to faulty organisation but to misfortune in all risks which had to be undertaken ... The loss of the pony transport ... The weather ... The soft snow in lower reaches of

glacier ... Every detail of our food supplies, clothing and depots ... worked out to perfection ... I do not think human beings ever came through such a month as we have come through ... We should have got through ... but for the sickening of ... Captain Oates, and a shortage of fuel in our depots for which I cannot account.

This is special pleading. Scott had brought disaster on himself by his own incompetence, and thrown away the lives of his companions. He had suffered retribution for his sins. But he was justifying himself; finding excuses, throwing the blame on his subordinates. It is the testament of a failure, but because of its literary style, heroic failure.

Bowers, who was probably the last to die, wrote to his mother; a sad little note:

> my trust is still in Him and in the abounding Grace of my Lord and Saviour whom you brought me to trust in ... I should so like to come through for your dear sake. It is splendid to pass however with such companions as I have ... There will be no shame however and you will know that I have struggled to the end ... Oh, how I do feel for you when you hear all, you will know that for me the end was peaceful as it is only sleep in the cold.

Outside, the wind roared, died, sprang up, dropped and blew again. The snow rasped the canvas; little by little the green tent was buried in a drift. A hundred miles away, the first attempts at rescue were being made, too feeble and too late.

34

Birth of a Legend

WHEN THE PILOT boarded *Fram* outside Hobart on March 7th, the first thing Amundsen asked was about *Terra Nova*. He was cheered when told she had not been heard of. But the race was not won until the news was through. *Terra Nova* might even then be steaming up towards Lyttelton Heads. The theft of the cable from Eagle City six years before remained as a vivid reminder of what could yet occur.

As soon as he landed, Amundsen sent a cable in a private code to Leon in Christiania. But until the story reached the rightful columns, *Fram* stayed out in the fairway, incommunicado, to prevent any chance of a leak. Local reporters, as Amundsen put it in his diary, 'were intrusive, but they ran up against a brick wall'. One of them called him a 'dour Norse sea king', primly adding that 'Silence is golden puts a very sordid aspect upon the heroism of exploration.'

Amundsen also cabled in confidence to King Haakon, Nansen and Don Pedro to tell them before the general public. It was taking a risk, but gratitude required it.

> Oh, is it not strange how things happen in this world [Nansen wrote in a letter]. As I am just writing these lines, I am called down to the telephone to get the news.

The addressee happened to be Kathleen Scott.

> There is a whirlpool of feelings inside me ... I think of you and what you may wish, more than of him, and am in a strange mood, unhappy and uneasy. Oh, why are there so many difficulties in the world and why is life so complicated? [Amundsen] has evidently sailed very fast, and my old ship has done well – but still I wish that Scott had come first. Yes, life is very complicated indeed!

This is a little more than the courtesies due from one explorer to the wife of another. By a melodramatic improbability, Nansen and Kathleen Scott had been having a love affair while Scott was on the Southern Road. It was consummated in a Berlin hotel while Scott was facing defeat at the Pole and, just before the telephone rang, Nansen was asking Kathleen, 'What kind of place are you going to arrange for us in Paris?'

Amundsen came between them. Kathleen had taken a venomous dislike to him, and told Nansen so. Nansen was soon defending him before her:

> People in England do not understand Amundsen; he is in every respect a fine and noble fellow, and is really a man; ... Anyhow I am sure that it is after all a comfort to you to know that the man is really a fine specimen of the race who deserves his success and not a common brute who has chanced into it.

For, by now, Amundsen's historic, and characteristically terse little cable to Leon, 'Pole attained fourteenth–seventeenth December 1911. All well,'* had burst on to the front pages everywhere. 'The whole world,' as the *New York Times* put it, 'has now been discovered.' Amundsen was a man of whom every Norwegian could now be proud.

Amundsen's success, or rather her husband's failure, overwhelmed Kathleen with pity, remorse and regret. There was no assignation in Paris. The affair with Nansen died.

The London *Daily Chronicle* had secured Amundsen's publication rights outside Scandinavia and, after receiving a coded message from Leon, he cabled his story. Nothing leaked. The story was exclusive. It was without competition from Scott. *Fram* had beaten *Terra Nova* to the cablehead handsomely. Amundsen had won the long race that began in those heated September days in 1909, when Cook and Peary robbed him of the North Pole. It was a scoop of the very finest vintage. It earned him £2,000,† a respectable sum for those days, and a good start in his quest for funds.

For three weeks, while *Terra Nova* belatedly ploughed her way to New Zealand, Amundsen held the stage alone. In England, he had to compete for public attention with a coal strike, which was paralysing industry and increasing the cost of food. But the headlines erupted everywhere, most violently of course in Norway: NORWAY'S FLAG AT THE SOUTH POLE was splashed across the page when the news first came through. 'Today, town and country put out all flags,' ran one newspaper announcement. 'We are all Roald Amundsen's fellow countrymen.' Among Norwegians, the national flag is brought out on auspicious occasions. So too now on March 8th, to mark that 'the South

---

* Amundsen had omitted to put back his calendar when crossing the International Date Line, so that the expedition was one day out in its reckoning. On returning to civilization, the dates were (pedantically) revised.

† £31,000 or $62,000 in present terms.

Pole has become ours', as Amundsen expressed it in a letter to Don
Pedro.

> On days like this [wrote a Christiania newspaper columnist], everything is
> changed ... It is more warmth and pride that we feel that we are all
> children of the same, happy country. Smiles are more frequent – in bold mens'
> deeds we are richer and more united and happier.
>   Ay yes – at one blow, we are far forwards!

In a Christiania variety theatre, this ditty was sung:

> Roald Amundsen ran,
> Faster than Scott can.
> Miles ahead of Scott,
> Roald to the Pole has got!

Yet, Bjørn Helland-Hansen, Amundsen's friend, wrote to Nansen that
he could not 'understand why people don't show more pleasure than
they do'. Even among Amundsen's countrymen there was a chill
underneath the cheers.

A Norwegian newspaper hinted at one explanation:

> We are glad that Roald Amundsen chose a new route to the South
> Pole, so that he avoided going directly in Scott's path. The English had
> the exclusive right to the route from McMurdo Sound. That was their
> opinion at any rate.

Many Norwegians uneasily felt that Amundsen's great journey was
not so much a national accomplishment as a political *bêtise*, antagonizing
a great Power. British huffiness, expressed by the *Times* in a fairly typical
comment, that the Norwegian expedition was 'a mere dash for the
Pole, designed to forestall the British expedition in the most spectacular,
though not the most valuable part of the work', confirmed that
opinion. Nansen who, in any case, admired what Amundsen had done,
threw the whole force of his reputation behind his countryman.
Amundsen, he wrote in the *Daily Chronicle*,

> had set his course, as he had determined, and without looking back ... what
> does it not convey of a sage, well-laid plan, and splendid execution of
> determined courage, endurance and manly power!

This, unfortunately, defeated its own purpose. To the British public,
a man who avoided the hard way was 'too clever by half'; he was not
a hero but a cheat. Sir Clements Markham, denouncing Amundsen as an
'interloper' and 'that gadfly', was more in tune with conventional
opinion. With the same innuendo he had used to discredit Shackleton,
Sir Clements also gave tongue to a general hope when he told

Scott Keltie that Amundsen 'was pretty sure to hurry back to have the first say. We must wait for the truth until the return of the *Terra Nova*.' But *Terra Nova* brought no consolation. She arrived at Akaroa Harbour, New Zealand, on April 1st, without Scott, but with evidence that he must have lost the race. The last news came back with Teddy Evans, 150 miles from the Pole, on January 4th, three weeks after Amundsen had reached it.

Terra Nova brought back other hints of failure and mismanagement. Teddy Evans was on board, sent home to recuperate from scurvy. Thick ice had stopped the relief of Campbell and the northern party. They had been picked up at Cape Adare on the way down and landed on the coast of South Victoria Land for the summer. They had broken the law of the Polar regions by not guarding against the absence of relief. They were left to face the winter unprepared.

With the arrival of *Terra Nova*, killing hopes of victory after all, British feelings of chagrin were let loose. It was akin to the American sense of shock when the Russians beat them with the first satellite and the first man in space. Benjamin Vogt, the Norwegian Ambassador in London, was worried about the effect on British goodwill. He wrote to Nansen:

How the bitter feeling against Amundsen ... emerges despite all formal recognition .., Scott Keltie in a private conversation ... used the expression 'a dirty trick altogether', and regretted that the South Pole had first been attained by 'a professional'.

The implication was, of course, that Scott and his companions were amateurs. It was only too true, although not quite in the sense that Keltie meant. Feeling ran high; so high, as almost to persuade Nansen that, for the sake of Anglo-Norwegian relations, Amundsen ought to cancel his projected lecture tour in England. 'I have no intention of meeting Roald Amundsen,' declared Lord Curzon, a former Viceroy of India, now R.G.S. President. 'I do not care a farthing whether Amundsen comes or not.' Wisely, perhaps, Nansen decided the damage would be worse if Amundsen did not come.

It was characteristic of Britain at the time that very few asked *why* Amundsen had succeeded. The most astonishing manipulations of facts were performed in order to prove that the British had not been worsted and, but for a little bad luck, all would have been well. Scott's histrionic message sent back with Evans, that 'I am remaining in the Antarctic for another winter in order to continue and complete my work', was exactly what the public, or at least the leaders of public opinion wanted. It was the text taken up by the Press, of which J. L. Garvin's leader in the *Pall Mall Gazette* is a fair sample:

> It suffices to tell the country that ... there has been no ... 'race' to the Pole ... Captain Scott ... was not lent by the Admiralty to take part in a Marathon race. There are questions of the utmost scientific importance to which he is seeking the answer ... The message is one of which Captain Scott's countrymen may be prouder than if he had been able to announce that he had arrived at the South Pole slightly in advance of Amundsen.

Shackleton was almost alone to give Amundsen ungrudging public recognition or rather, as Kathleen Scott put it, he 'was delighted at the turn things have taken. I would willingly assist at that man's annihilation.' It was not Amundsen's triumph so much as Scott's defeat that gave Shackleton pleasure. He had got his final crushing revenge.

Outside England, Amundsen obtained full recognition. When Scott's story, sent back with *Terra Nova*, was published a Christiania newspaper made a point widely noticed. Scott gave

> the impression that terrain and weather were much worse [than] Amundsen's. This can hardly be the case. From Amundsen's account, one can see, for example, that he was forced to lie still for four days in a snow storm. But he considers it as something that belongs to such a journey – it's 'all in the day's work', and he doesn't make a fuss about it.

Even in England, Amundsen had recognition of a kind. 'His was a very fine feat wasn't it,' Kathleen Scott wrote to Skelton, with whom she had kept in contact, '& in spite of one's irritation one has to admire it.' Eventually, when Amundsen arrived to give his lectures, he had full houses and, generally, made a good impression by his modesty and serious approach. When Ponting, Scott's photographer, came to show the films he had made in the Antarctic, he discovered that Amundsen, as he put it, had

> completely knocked the bottom out of them & about 60% of the possible profits, by robbing the Expedition of the glamour of its main achievement.

As long as Scott appeared to be alive Amundsen's victory was complete.

In Hobart Amundsen, for the moment, was at ease. The Tasmanians offered unstinted recognition. The Governor received him. Churches held services of thanksgiving for his safe return. On March 8th, the day after his arrival, the cables of congratulation, in his own words, 'began to rain down'. He eventually had them bound in a red morocco leather book, labelled in gilt on the cover 'South Pole'.

The cables ranged from President Theodore Roosevelt, whom Amundsen had met in America after the North-West Passage, to a Norwegian tinned fish packer who wanted Amundsen's picture on his tins – reply paid, four words. Peary, who later wrote to a friend that Amundsen had 'deliberately stolen the prize from Scott', nonetheless now cabled: 'Congratulations your great journey. Dogs are only motor for polar work.' Scott's rejection of his advice still rankled.

In the first fruits of victory, Amundsen felt a touch of bitterness. He craved recognition and he was hurt by the few and, as he considered, grudging messages from England. He seemed to value English recognition most of all. The R.G.S. did send a cable, but the President, Major Leonard Darwin, wrote to Kathleen Scott explaining that it was only because they had felt bound to. 'Of course,' she replied. 'Let us at any rate if we don't win be good losers.' She wanted to cable Amundsen herself, but was stopped by Scott's publisher, Reginald Smith.

King George V sent a cable with a real or imagined edge: 'I have received with the greatest of pleasure the news that it is on British soil that you have first landed after your successful expedition . . .'

The day after arrival, Amundsen wrote his first letter of thanks. It was to Don Pedro Christophersen:

I look forward . . . to thank you personally for all you have done for me . . . I hope now that with hard work I shall manage . . . My splendid shipmate and *Fram*'s captain, Lt. Thv. Nilsen – brought me your . . . welcome assistance. Without that I would have been absolutely broke on arrival here.

Amundsen's feelings towards Nansen were more complicated, and it was some time before he was able to write:

Again and again I have tried to find expression for the thanks I so much want to send you, but in vain. Words cannot express it. With your name, you have gone surety for my actions. With your authority you have shamed all the gossiping people into silence. In my heart of hearts I have felt that you wanted to help me, and often, often, it has helped me forwards, when things became difficult.

Unfortunately my letter does not only bring good news – I have been compelled to send Johansen ashore. From the start his behaviour on board has been anything but pleasant. During the winter, he refused to obey orders on one occasion, and on that account I was compelled to exclude him from participation in the Southern party. That naturally made things worse. On our arrival here, he got drunk and began to pick quarrels with his shipmates, and obstruct them in their work. To have peace on board, I have therefore been compelled to send him ashore.

This was all true, but the account of the abortive start for the Pole was misleading. Amundsen feared Nansen's disapproval, and wished to present his version first.

Johansen in any case wanted to go home. Amundsen gave him his passage money and he left Hobart on a cargo boat, reaching Norway in the middle of June, once more a melancholy and disappointed man.

Amundsen cabled the President of the Norwegian Geographical Society that Johansen was being sent home because he had committed mutiny. He was to be excluded from the official celebrations, and his arrival was to be kept quiet. The whole affair was to be hushed up. Amundsen could not forgive, and Johansen's offence had been grave.

On March 21st, Amundsen left Hobart for the Australian mainland to start on the dreary lecture trail. The day before, *Fram* sailed for Buenos Aires where, with Don Pedro's financial assistance, she was to refit and reprovision for what Amundsen called 'the real journey', the Arctic drift, which was to begin in 1913.

After his lecture tour in Australia and New Zealand, Amundsen sailed for Buenos Aires to rejoin *Fram*. At Montevideo, a reception committee from the Norwegian colony met the ship. In the words of one of them,

> We rushed on board and asked, 'Where is Captain Amundsen?' The ship's captain smiled and said, 'No one by that name on board this ship, sir.' But then, from a man with long beard and dark glasses nearby came: 'Perhaps it is me you want?' Quite right; there was the polar explorer before us.

Having attained the last geographic goal and become a household name, Amundsen had felt the need to travel, not only incognito but in disguise. He was down on the passenger list as Engebreth Gravning. He wore a false beard. Only the ship's captain knew who he was.

Now, for the first time, Amundsen met Don Pedro, who up to then had been but a distant benefactor. It was an emotional encounter. Amundsen, usually undemonstrative and self-controlled, embraced the old man who, like an indulgent father, had saved the expedition. Don Pedro took Amundsen under his wing.

It was at Buenos Aires that Amundsen first received the acclaim of his countrymen, the Norwegian colony giving a banquet for himself and *Fram*'s crew. He prepared a large photograph of the mountain he had named after Don Pedro on the way to the Pole. He arranged for the photograph to be brought in while he was speaking after dinner, and as he was thanking Don Pedro for everything he had done, it was presented to him. Don Pedro was quite overcome, and tears poured down his cheeks.

In his speech Amundsen, as Hassel put it, admitted

> he was an unpleasant man to work with ... in which he is right. In the meanwhile it is extraordinary how a frank admission of a fault helps to mitigate the distaste it causes.

Amundsen now had to finish the book about the South Pole which poor, optimistic devil – he hoped would be a best-seller and put him on an even keel. William Heinemann, the publisher, was not too hopeful, on the grounds that the story in *The Daily Chronicle* was dull.

> I am ... disappointed with the want of imagination he displays ... in even so thrilling a thing as his achievement ... I cannot help feeling that however great Amundsen's feat is, he is not likely to write a good book.

To finish his book, Amundsen went to one of Don Pedro's estancias. In the meanwhile *Fram*'s departure for her Arctic drift was postponed. Most of the crew sailed home by liner. Amundsen could not afford to provide much pocket money. 'Broke and miserable,' as Bjaaland put it, crossing the Equator. 'God knows when I shall have money as becomes a man.'

Bjaaland and his companions arrived at Bergen on July 2nd. Asked by a newspaper about Scott,

> They had little wish to make any comments, but they were all agreed that Scott had reached the Pole. On the other hand, they could not avoid the fear that he had not reached his main depot on the way back. In their view, winter had stopped him ... Scurvy, in their view, could also be a dangerous enemy. They would be extremely sorry if anything were to happen to him.

In July, Amundsen left Buenos Aires for Norway, again incognito.

> Without any adventure of any sort, unrecognised and unnoticed, I reached my office in Christiania [he wrote to Don Pedro]. Thus was this journey also crowned with victory

At Cape Evans, the British expedition was waiting for another spring.

On March 16th, Cherry-Garrard and Dmetri had arrived back at Hut Point after their journey to One Ton Camp, without Scott, but with a tale of blizzard and cold and woe. This gave Atkinson, who had been waiting at Hut Point alone with Keohane, his first intimations of disaster. But the weather was entirely predictable from the year before.

Atkinson felt that for the sake of conscience another rescue attempt had to be made. But Cherry-Garrard had collapsed mentally and physically; Dmetri, too, was *hors de combat*. Until the freezing of the sea, they were cut off by open water from their companions at Cape Evans. After ten days Atkinson went out on a forlorn hope with Keohane.

It is characteristic of the whole ill-fated expedition, that they went out *man-hauling*, while the dogs were left to laze at Hut Point. Neither Atkinson nor Keohane had driven dogs before and Atkinson felt it would be cruel to take the dogs out again so soon after their last journey with Cherry-Garrard and Dmetri. On March 30th, just past Corner Camp, plodding into the teeth of gales and drift, he decided to turn, morally certain that the Polar party had perished.

In fact the last entry in Scott's diary was dated March 29th.

The survivors now had to get through a second winter.

It was a sobered little company which reunited at Cape Evans at the beginning of May. The hut was half empty, with thirteen occupants instead of the previous twenty-seven. And there were the five empty bunks of the Polar party to remind them every moment of the day.

Yet they were kept happy; in some ways happier perhaps than the year before. This was due to Atkinson, who now was in command. Of him, Gran wrote that

> everyone had got respect and admiration for him ... His wonderful qualities of leadership soon appeared in the winter hibernation at Cape Evans. He never gave orders – only expressed wishes – and more was not needed.

All winter, Atkinson had hanging over him a heavy decision. South, for certain, lay the dead Polar party; in the north, were Campbell and his companions, alive perhaps. What was more important: to find the dead or search for the living? In the end, he decided that sentiment and public opinion at home both demanded the saving of the Polar party's records from oblivion, so his first duty was the finding of the dead.

On October 29th, the search party started for the south. There were twelve men with dogs and seven Indian Army Himalayan mules landed for the second season at Oates' suggestion. They were prepared for a long journey up to the Polar Plateau.

They kept to the old route as closely as possible. On November 12th, in Tryggve Gran's words, 'It has happened! We have found what we sought! Great Heavens how fate can strike hard.'

At six in the morning, about ten miles south of One Ton Depot, just as they were going to camp, they saw what they thought was a cairn to the right of their course. Charles Wright, who was navigating, went over to investigate, stopped, and motioned the others to follow. It was a tent drifted up. The entrance was closed from the inside.

I must own I shed a few tears [wrote Petty Officer Thomas Williamson] and I know the others did the same, it came as a great shock to us all, although we knew full well for months past that we should meet with this sort of thing everyone seemed dumfounded [sic] we did not touch anything but just stood gazing and wondering what awful secrets the tent held for us.

Atkinson ordered camp to be made a little way off while the tent was dug out. He then entered, and, before anything was removed, insisted on everybody going in one by one to look, so that there could be no dispute over what had been found.

I did not go over for quite a good time [said Williamson] for fear I could not look on this most pityable [sic] scene, but when at last I made up my mind I saw a most ghastly sight, those sleeping bags with frozen bodies in them the one in the middle I recognized as Capt. Scott ... the other two bodies I did not see, nor did I care to see them poor fellows.

When it was all over, Atkinson took out the watches and documents. The tent was collapsed over the bodies of Scott, Wilson and Bowers, and they were buried where they lay, as they had been found, in their sleeping bags. Over them was built a high cairn, on top of which was placed a cross made of a pair of skis, and under the cairn and the cross, Atkinson read the burial service.

It was [in Gran's words] a solemn act. It was moving to see 11 weatherbeaten men stand with bared heads and sing. To the South the sun flamed through threatening storm clouds, and the great plain lay in fairytale colours. The drift snow swept down, and when the hymn was finished, a soft white 'blanket' rested over the dead.

Scott had left instructions for the finder to read his diary, after which it was to be sent home. Atkinson retired to his tent and read, it seemed, for hour upon hour, until he learned what had happened. Then he gathered the little company around him, and told them the story.

As the tale sank in, the shock of the discovery was overlaid by a sense of unease. Scott, Wilson and Bowers had perished so close to succour and, as Gran expressed it in his diary,

I cannot rid myself of the thought that we ought to have been able to save Scott. Perhaps we might have succeeded if Cherry could have navigated. My companions are too phlegmatic. It is sometimes a good thing to raise Hell. Perhaps Scott himself is most to blame. He did not want to risk others' lives to save his own. But I wonder if he didn't also think that if Shackleton managed to come back without help, so could he   and so he could, if it had been Our Lord's intention ... Atkinson was too much the calm, conservative doctor. He is capable, but too unimaginative. Ah yes, it is sad indeed.

For Cherry-Garrard, feelings were more personal. He had led the last realistic rescue attempt. Wilson and Bowers had been his great friends and now he knew that eight months before, when he turned with Dmetri and the dogs at One Ton Camp, they had been fighting for their lives only sixty miles away.

If only we had travelled for a day and a half [he wrote], we might have left some food and oil on one of the cairns, hoping that they would see it ... It will always to the end of my life be a great sorrow to me that we did not do this.

And again:

The question of what we might have done for them with the dog teams is terribly on my mind - but we obeyed instructions.

For the rest of his days Cherry-Garrard was haunted by self-reproach. If only he had been a navigator; if only he had been a practised dog-driver instead of a beginner; if only he had been able to impose his will on a mulish Russian peasant, he might have saved his friends. In the end, his reason was to be clouded by the thought.

Now, however, his concern was for the criticism, and worse, he feared he would have to face on returning home. He need not have worried. Clamour was quelled by Scott's literary powers. The masterly self-justification which threw the blame on his companions and left among them a legacy of guilt, by the same token covered up for them all.

They had a foretaste out in the snows, in the forlorn setting of Scott's last camp. Atkinson finished telling the tale of the last march by reading Scott's message to the public. The effect was immediate.

Of their sufferings, hardship and devotion to one another [wrote Williamson], the world will soon know, the deeds that were done were equally as great as any committed on Battlefield and won the respect and honour of every true Britisher.

Thus did the legend take root so swiftly and naturally. Scott had known how to speak to his countrymen.

The sledge was dug out, with its load of geological specimens. Cherry-Garrard found it 'magnificent that men ... should go on pulling everything they had died to gain'.

'I think,' said Gran, from another point of view, 'they might have saved themselves the weight.'

They had dragged those thirty pounds of rock to show themselves martyrs to Science; a pathetic little gesture to salvage something from defeat at the Pole and the wreck of their hopes. Half the weight in seal meat would have saved them. A pint of paraffin or a tin of pemmican would have been worth more to them than the most valuable stone in the world. And, in the end, the specimens meant almost nothing. Shackleton had already done most of the work and, by the time Scott's results were finally published, they had been overtaken by events.

Besides the geological collection it was, as Gran put it in his diary, 'absolutely incredible how much they had on the sledge ... a mass of empty provision bags, and worn out articles of clothing'.

The party continued south to look for Oates, but only found his empty sleeping bag a few miles away. There, they built another cairn and a cross, to which was attached a note: 'Hereabouts died a very gallant gentleman, Capt. L. E. G. Oates, of the Inniskilling Dragoons.'

Immediately they turned back to what Williamson called 'Sorrowful Camp'. There, while going through the material to be discarded, Gran and Williamson discovered by chance a bag containing Amundsen's letter to King Haakon. It lay among the debris on Scott's sledge; buried all winter under the snow.

At the cairn of the Polar party, Gran put on Scott's skis for the journey back; in his own words, 'they shall and will complete their 2,000 kilometres wandering'.

The party now hurried north to save Campbell and his men.

They reached Hut Point on November 27th, to find that Campbell had saved himself. He and his party had spent the winter in a snow cave at Evans Coves, on the coast of South Victoria Land, living off seal and penguin. It was a splendid tale of survival. But Abbott, one of the seamen, went mad after arriving at Hut Point.

Now there was nothing to do but wait for the ship. She was

late. On January 17th, with heavy hearts, they started preparing for
the third winter. The next day, Gran wrote in his diary:

Terra Nova in sight. Hurrah! Hurrah! Great joy - Hurrah!

Teddy Evans, having recovered from scurvy, was now in command.
After thirty-six hours' working round the clock, *Terra Nova* was loaded
and she sailed up the Sound to Hut Point, to put up a memorial cross
to the Polar party on Observation Hill. The inscription, chosen by
Cherry-Garrard, was the same line from Tennyson's *Ulysses*, 'To strive,
to seek, to find, and not to yield', that Nansen chose when praising
Amundsen's attainment of the North-West Passage in London six years
before.

Terra Nova then sailed away. On February 10th, at three a.m., she
reached Oamaru, New Zealand, where Pennell and Atkinson went ashore
to send off the Press telegram, while *Terra Nova* cruised up and down
along the coast to prevent any leakage of news. She entered Lyttelton
on February 12th. Flags were at half mast. The headlines streamed
across the page. The death of Scott had gripped the world. 'The
adventure is finished,' Gran wrote in his diary, 'and our journey lies in
the past.'

In London, Lieutenant Barry Domville, R.N.,* when he heard the
news, commented: 'I have never been keen on these Expeditions for
naval officers and though of course I am sorry about Scott, I cannot
unduly enthuse over it.'

More typical was the diary of a Bristol schoolgirl:

Tuesday Feb. 11th 1913 a dreadful day never to be forgotten and a
sadder day for some women who learnt that by the valiant efforts of
Captain Scott and his 4 other brave companions to reach the S. Pole
(and so give Britain a proud day) 5 human souls had to be sacrificed to all
the toll of the Antarctic - those men had wives and children at home
and Captain Scott's last wish was that the people at home should be
cared for. This will be done.

Kathleen Scott, who had travelled out to New Zealand to meet her
husband, soon got to the heart of the matter: 'They would have
got through if they hadn't stood by their sick,' she wrote to Admiral
Egerton, Scott's Naval patron, '& so I am very glad that they did
not get through.'

Indeed, if Scott had got through, second and nowhere, with all the

*Later Admiral Sir Barry Domville.

evidence of mismanagement, he would probably have been discredited and died half forgotten. Hugh Robert Mill's response to a request for an article for the *Geographical Journal* in April 1912, after *Terra Nova* had brought confirmation of Scott's defeat, but not news of his end, makes the point:

> I would gladly write ... on Scott's results, but ... there are none ... He kept so close to Shackleton's track that he could discover nothing unless Shackleton had never been there ...
>
> Even if Scott reaches the Pole he ... can accomplish nothing except to bring his party back alive.

As it was, things could not have turned out better. To adapt Shackleton's saying, Kathleen and the country preferred a dead lion to a live donkey. In the words of Hannen Swaffer, a contemporary journalist, 'With the sole exception of the death of Nelson in the hour of victory, there has been nothing so dramatic.' The Admiralty announced that Scott and his companions were considered 'killed in action'. In an unprecedented gesture, Kathleen was granted the title of Lady Scott, as if her husband had lived to be knighted. The Lord Mayor of London opened a fund for the dependants of the dead, and the British public responded with its usual generosity at a time of disaster; there was a memorial service at St. Paul's Cathedral; all for one of the most inefficient of Polar expeditions, and one of the worst of Polar explorers.

The country was roused by Scott's message to the public:

> Our wreck is certainly due to this sudden advent of bad weather ... I do not think human beings ever came through such a month as we have come through ... I do not regret this journey, which has shown that Englishmen can endure hardships, help one another and meet death with as great a fortitude as ever in the past.

Amundsen had made the conquest of the Pole into something between an art and a sport. Scott had turned Polar exploration into an affair of heroism for heroism's sake. Mrs. Oates, miserable over her son's suicide – to give it its proper name – was perhaps going too far when she called Scott his 'murderer', but that Scott was responsible for his companions' deaths, was evident.

For public consumption, a story was contrived that Oates had sacrificed himself to save his companions, although between the lines of Scott's diary the real tragedy could be glimpsed:

> Titus Oates [Scott had written on March 11th], is very near the end ... We discussed the matter ... he is a brave fine fellow and understands the

situation but he practically asked for advice. Nothing could be said but to urge him to march as long as he could.

But all evidence that poor Oates had done away with himself when his pain became too great to·bear, especially Wilson's letter to Mrs. Oates, was concealed. Tragedy had to be gilded with heroic gesture, or Scott would have been held responsible, which would not have redounded to his credit.

Nowhere in the records of the Polar party is Oates explicitly said to have given up his life out of heroic self-sacrifice. The tale depends on the hint in Scott's account.

The Oates family were oddly restrained. Mrs. Oates had evidently discerned the truth and never forgave Scott. She acted like the mother not of a hero, but of a victim. Nonetheless, she acquiesced in bending her son's behaviour to an acceptable pattern. 'One cannot state facts plainly,' as Teddy Evans wrote to her in all too familiar words, 'when they reflect on the organisation.'

In a typical sermon, preached at the Naval dockyard chapel, Devonport, Oates and his companions were praised for 'the reminder they bring us of ... the glory of self-sacrifice, the blessing of failure'. A great deal of verbiage was expended on the theme of 'snatching victory from the jaws of death'. Oates was not that kind of person at all; he was far too plain and rational. There was something poignantly symbolic about his action, the aristocrat seeking his end because there was no longer any place for him; it was the only way out.

It was Scott who suited the sermons. His actions and, above all, his literary style, appealed to the spirit of his countrymen. He personified the glorious failure which by now had become a British ideal. He was a suitable hero for a nation in decline.

Few attempts were made to analyse the reasons for disaster. It was less disturbing to make a virtue of calamity and dress up incompetence as heroism. In the face of overwhelming evidence to the contrary, the *Daily Chronicle* wrote that 'Captain Scott's expedition was undoubtedly the best equipped of all those which have explored the Antarctic Continent.' *The Times* offered a typical sophistry. 'Let us put out of our minds all the gossip which ... has been circulated about a "race",' it urged – adding that the real value of this Antarctic expedition was

> spiritual, and therefore in the truest sense national. It is proof that in an age of depressing materialism men can still be found to face known hardship, heavy risk and even death, in pursuit of an idea ... That is the temper of men who build empires, and while it lives among us we shall be capable of maintaining an Empire that our fathers builded.

35

The Last Adventure

AMUNDSEN WAS IN Madison, Wisconsin, when he heard the news. 'I would gladly forgo any honour or money,' he said to a journalist, 'if thereby I could have saved Scott his terrible death.'

The next day in Chicago, another waiting journalist described how he

looked the picture of grief, and strove unsuccessfully to conceal his emotion ... 'Horrible, horrible!' exclaimed Amundsen, as he walked back and forth ... 'I cannot read that last message of Scott's without emotion ... And to think,' [he added] in a hushed tone, 'that while these brave men were dying out there in the waste of ice, I was lecturing in warmth and comfort in Australia.'

Amundsen was now touring America to lecture on how he had attained the South Pole. For almost a year he had held the stage alone. All seemed to have been forgiven. In Norway, there was a move to make him a titular professor. 'A regular annual salary,' he wrote to Nansen, 'would be good to have but,' he continued with the perverse irony he had made his own, 'professor – I'm not qualified for that. I must reject the flattering proposal, with thanks.' All other honours – and they were many - he impartially accepted wherever they appeared, so that Bjaaland was moved to write, 'Congratulations on your triumphal progress round the world.' Then came *Terra Nova* bearing a tale of what one of the headlines called a 'death march in Antarctica', and Amundseon the victor was eclipsed for a season by Scott the martyr.

Before the news arrived, the British had consoled themselves by saying that Amundsen only won because he was 'lucky'. This annoyed Nansen to the point where he wrote in the introduction to Amundsen's book about his expedition: 'Let no one come and prate about luck. Amundsen's triumph is that of the strong and the far-seeing.'

Now, in England, Amundsen was made a convenient scapegoat. Scott, so the story ran, died because his heart was broken by defeat at the Pole; ergo, the fault was not his own, but that of the man who had the impertinence to get there first. It was a romantic device that dispensed with the awkward necessity of asking *why* Scott was second. It was not calculated to appeal to Amundsen's rational mind. From the start, he openly argued that Scott had brought disaster on himself as, indeed, Nansen suggested in a bitter exchange of letters with Sir Clements Markham:

> I was very sorry that he would not listen to my advice to take plenty of good well broken dogs and to trust to them and not to ponies ... had he done what I would have him to, we should still have had him amongst us. [His] equipment ... was not adequate to the task.

Reason, however, was not all. Amundsen was haunted by a doubt. Of course, Scott had been weak, incompetent and stupid. Of course, he had brought it all upon himself. But Amundsen was no monster of unconcern. Who could say that not one iota of responsibility was his?

The death of Scott, or rather the effect upon himself, was the one eventuality Amundsen had not foreseen. On the sledge that Scott had dragged was the evidence that this Norwegian had been to the Pole, even down to a photograph of the tent he had left behind. In the last resort, Scott had died to prove that Amundsen had won. The irony was cruel, and Amundsen could not bring himself to write a letter of condolence, getting Leon instead to do so on his behalf. 'Scott,' Leon wrote to Scott Keltie, 'has shown us how to die.' It was all that could be said.

The world largely saw the tale through Scott's eyes. His diaries were rapidly published and, quite simply, he was a better writer than Amundsen. Amundsen lacked the power of advocacy. He was too much the man of action; like so many of his kind, he squandered his talent on his deeds. Living the moment so intensely, he was denied the surplus energy to convey it to others. 'The last of the Vikings' expected his deeds to speak for themselves; they were in any case his art. Scott, by contrast, seemed to have sought experience as a means to other ends; as the path to promotion, the raw material for writing. He appealed to everyman, where Amundsen did not try to hide his contempt for the crowd. There was nothing to counterbalance Scott's masterly self-justification. His literary talent was his trump. It was as if he had reached out from his buried tent to take revenge.

He not only set an example, but left a legacy of heroic failure. In 1914, Shackleton set out to make the first crossing of Antarctica. Before he could land, his ship, *Endurance*, was crushed by the ice in the Weddell Sea and sank. He sailed almost a thousand miles in an open boat to South Georgia to fetch help, and got every one of his men back alive. It is one of the sagas of the sea. Shackleton died of heart disease on January 5th, 1922, at the start of his next Antarctic expedition, and was buried in South Georgia. His last words, to a doctor remonstrating with him over his way of life, were: 'What do you want me to give up now?'

The Norwegian postscript to the classic age of Antarctic exploration was different. In 1929, an expedition under Captain Hjalmar Riiser-Larsen discovered Queen Maud Land and filled in the last major gap in the continental coastline.* It was done efficiently, without setback or fuss. Thus, among their countrymen, Scott and Amundsen each had his characteristic successor.

Scott was a heroic bungler. He added nothing to the technique of Polar travel, unless it was to emphasize the grotesque futility of man-hauling. As Helmer Hanssen put it: 'What shall one say of Scott and his companions who were their own sledge dogs? ... I don't think anyone will ever copy him.' Scott was a monument to sheer ambition and bull-headed persistence; he was, after all, the second man at the South Pole. His achievement was to perpetuate the romantic myth of the explorer as martyr and, in a wider sense, to glorify suffering and self-sacrifice as ends in themselves.

Scott instantly became a legend. From the start, there was tacit agreement to tamper with the record in order to protect his name and conceal uncomfortable facts. 'The tragedy ... was not due to any lack of forethought,' said *The Times*, leading the way. 'Captain Scott had no share of the English failing of muddling through a task.' For publication, his diaries were purged of all passages detracting from a perfect image; particularly those revealing bitterness over Amundsen, criticism of his companions and, above all, signs of incompetence. Lord Curzon, the R.G.S. President, wanted an enquiry into the disaster, especially the fuel shortage and question of relief, in order to exonerate Scott and forestall the massive public criticism which – mistakenly as it turned out – he feared would soon arise. He was dissuaded, however, by Admiral Sir Lewis Beaumont, who pointed out that no one could 'say beforehand where an Enquiry might lead to'. Atkinson, who had examined the bodies, refused to divulge anything he knew about the medical details of the Polar party's end, a burden that probably helped to send him to an early grave. There are stray hints that

---

* Called the *Norvegia* expedition, after the expedition ship. Lars Christensen, a Norwegian whaling ship owner, paid for the whole enterprise out of his own pocket, including two aircraft.

he might have been concealing evidence of scurvy, which could not be revealed because it would have reflected on the whole conduct of the expedition.

There was a morbid preoccupation with glorifying Scott to the bitter end. It began with Kathleen Scott who, at her husband's request, was dealing with his papers. 'He was the last to go,' she wrote to Admiral Egerton, sending Scott's farewell letter to him – which happened to indicate otherwise. It was one of the letters found loose in the tent. On the back was a note in Bowers' hand, suggesting that Bowers may have been the last survivor, or at least casting doubt on Scott's claims – if in the circumstances that had any meaning.* In any case, it was inconvenient evidence. It was suppressed and, instead, there was issued an official reconstruction of the closing scene in the tent, contrived at the request of Kathleen Scott by Sir J. M. Barrie.

> Wilson and Bowers died first [wrote that practised playwright] and Captain Scott ... thereafter ... unbared his shirt and ... with his head flung back awaited death. We know this because it was thus that the three were found ... Some of the wording may not be quite right, but the brevity is.

Scott had become a myth figure. He was a necessary one. A year later the Great War broke out and, as one writer put it after a notable bout of disaster, he had given his

> countrymen an example of endurance ... We have so many heroes among us now, so many Scotts ... holding sacrifice above gain [and] we begin to understand what a splendour arises from the bloody fields ... of Flanders ... and Gallipoli.

It was a tradition that lingered on. A Norwegian official on Spitsbergen, who had seen expeditions of diverse nationalities come and go, once remarked that the British university students stood out, because they 'seemed to want to be heroes'. Scott remains the inspiration of the romantic idealist. His power transcends national boundaries. He has been accepted as an orthodox martyr figure even among Marxists in the grotesquely alien surroundings of the Soviet Union where, in the words of one author, he has been sent as the personification of 'A fight to the death with the forces of fate [like] the tractor man driving his machine into a wheatfield which is on fire.'

Amundsen is *not* a Soviet hero. He was too much an individualist, too rational and detached to be harnessed to a barbaric ideology; indeed,

---

* The note was to the finder and read: 'Dr. Wilson's Note to Mrs. Wilson is in the satchel in the Instrument Box with his diary and two sketch books.' (SPRI)

ideology of any kind. It was not what he wanted. It was Scott who had set out to be an heroic example. Amundsen merely wanted to be first at the Pole.

Both had their prayers answered.

Scott early paid the price.

And Amundsen?

In America, just before he learned the fate of Scott, he was reached by the news of Hjalmar Johansen's suicide.

After returning to Norway from Hobart in June, 1912, Johansen relapsed into his old life and stayed in the low quarters of Christiania, drinking and drifting. He avoided family and friends. He was like a man gone into hiding. From a mixture of loyalty and shame, he kept silent about the quarrel with Amundsen. He became withdrawn and apathetic, 'sitting in a corner in the twilight', in the words of someone who met him, 'silent and heavy-hearted. When anyone addressed him, he started, and his answer showed that he had been far away.'

When, after months had passed, Johansen's friends learned of his plight, they tried to help but he was by now past helping. He had ceased brooding over failure. He was resigned to the sense of a fate gone awry. He had come to the end of the road. One day he moved to an hotel in the centre of Christiania, the best he could afford; and there, in the small hours of January 4th, 1913, he shot himself. 'It was, maybe, the best thing for him, poor devil,' as Thorvald Nilsen put it. When Johansen arrived at his last abode, his luggage consisted of a cigar box with his shaving tackle.

Johansen's friends accused Amundsen of hounding him to his death. Nansen, at least, knew that things were not so simple. Humiliation in the Antarctic was probably the last straw, but it was not all that drove his old companion to do away with himself. Not by a word did Nansen betray his feelings for he was bound by loyalty both to Johansen and Amundsen, but he offered to pay Johansen's funeral expenses, which was interpreted as oblique reproof of Amundsen. It was also an admission that some of the blame was his own for neglecting Johansen after the first voyage of the *Fram*, and then forcing him on Amundsen. Johansen had paid the loser's penalty.

The suicide of Johansen, the self-destruction of Scott, cast their shadows over Amundsen. It was as if upon the South Pole there had lain a curse.

Amundsen had sailed for the Antarctic expecting Sigrid Castberg to divorce her husband and be ready to marry him when he came home.

He returned to find that she had not done so. 'For that reason,' as he put it, 'I consider I am absolved from my responsibilities in that direction', and broke off the affair, calling in Herman Gade, their mutual friend, as intermediary.

> Please tell [Sigrid] in the best and most considerate way [Amundsen wrote to Gade]. I do not want to write to her now that once and for all I have broken off. Please fix this up as well as you can ... as I have told you, I am now bound hand and foot – and for ever 'a good boy' in that sphere.

Exactly what Amundsen meant by this it is hard to glean. Wherever women are concerned he is impenetrably ambivalent. He undoubtedly felt a sense of betrayal, remarking years afterwards, in a rare moment of frankness: 'That a human being could trample so ruthlessly on my heart in that way I can never forget.' But this is reconstruction after brooding, and is unlikely to be the whole truth. In the background lurks some hindrance locking him out from full satisfaction of a woman. Perhaps Sigrid sensed this and for that reason drew back on the brink. Equally, Amundsen may have been showing an element of renunciation for the sake of conscience and career.

Since landing at Hobart a year before, Amundsen had been working to resume his original plan of an Arctic drift. And then, in Ottawa, still on his North American lecture tour, he suddenly wrote to Nansen that he was suspending preparations. The Norwegian Government, said Amundsen, had dishonoured an undertaking to reward those who had helped him and

> You, Herr Professor, will be the first to understand my action. To go into the polar basin for a drift of years, one must have all one's papers in order. There is no point in starting *that* journey with broken promises.

To which Nansen replied that:

> all those lectures over there in that nerv-racking land have drained your strength, and ... knocked you off balance ... This is the only way I can explain ... your letter, which otherwise would be incomprehensible to me, unless you have tired of the whole expedition with *Fram*, and would prefer to give it up; but then you would presumably say it straight out ... If it is your intention to threaten not to continue with *Fram* unless all promises are fulfilled ... it will put you in a most unfavourable light, as one who would break his great promise, in comparison with which, all the other things that you mention, are insignificant. When you told us that you were going to the South Pole before you started on the drift in the ice, you said it was to get the means for that expedition. With this as the point of departure,

the Government and we others have defended you and broken lances for you, and, dare I say it, for your honour ...

You can perhaps reproach me for not doing enough to get these promises that you mention, carried out. But in the first place I have not known about them before your letter ... I do not feel that you have anything to reproach me with. I have really done my best for you and your expedition; I can say what you perhaps have not understood, that I have made a greater sacrifice for you than for any other living person, in that I gave up my expedition to the South Pole, the crown of my work as a polar explorer and renounced *Fram* so that you could carry out your drift over the Polar Sea. You might think that was not much; but you might consider that it was a plan that I had already considered before sailing on *Fram*, and which I had planned in all its detail in the hut on Franz Josef Land ...

So you went, and I saw *Fram* for the last time, and I got your announcement that you had gone to carry out the expedition I had given up for your sake. It was so strange – but I was glad. It would in any case be a Norwegian, and precisely in the way I had thought. What I most regretted was however, that you did not say anything to me beforehand; for I could at any rate have given you valuable advice ... I had thought it all out ... but all's well that ends well ... I repeat all this here, so that you can see that I for my part at any rate have sacrificed something for you and your expedition, and that your bitterness against Norway because you consider that promises are so cheap here at home, is not entirely justified ... it seems to me that higher values are involved here than Lt. Nilsen gets a decoration and is promoted to commander ... or if Consul Gade gets an order etc.

It was, however, not merely a matter of baubles and gold braid. Amundsen had lent Bjaaland 20,000 kroner* to start a ski factory, although he could ill afford it, because he felt bound by his obligations. He wanted to keep faith with those who had helped him. His reply to Nansen contained this bitter little shaft of irony: 'I am grateful that you made me see that in ... dark moments one can forget the big things for bagatelles.'

Then, in a rare reference, albeit oblique, to Scott:

But, Herr Professor, do you not also believe that details must be thoroughly looked after and not neglected? It seems to me that many great enterprises have failed, because bagatelles have been neglected.

Nansen had discerned that Amundsen had been seeking a pretext to abandon his Arctic plans, and Amundsen admitted

It is possible I needed the correction you gave me. I would have resisted anyone else from whom I had received such blows. But I owe you so

* £1,080 or $5,300; £16,500 or $33,000 in present terms.

much – I see now more than I ever knew – that I calmly bow my head and accept it.

The prospect of an Arctic drift had become appallingly hollow. It could only be a repetition of what Nansen had already done.

Amundsen had no more worlds to conquer. He was not an explorer; he was a discoverer, which is very different. He had attained the last great terrestrial goal. The only way he could recapture the sensation would be by being the first man on the Moon. Everything else was doomed to be an anti-climax. At least he could try something new, and not follow in the footsteps of others.

If Scott had come back vanquished but alive, Amundsen could have abandoned his Arctic drift with impunity. But since Scott had died, that was now unthinkable. As Nansen had so lucidly expressed it, there was no way out with honour; Amundsen had to sail on, like the Flying Dutchman, until he found peace.

The winning of the South Pole had been a work of art, a masterpiece. Amundsen could not hope to repeat it. No longer did he know the power of overriding will. He suffered the conflict of duty and desire. Others could sense something gone awry. 'He seemed distinguished,' in the words of someone who met him at this time, 'but somehow a little decayed.' Fortune, his sometime faithful shipmate, had turned aside. He was pursued by setbacks, while *Fram* gathered barnacles in South American harbours. Eventually, after various changes of plan including an abortive possibility of being the first ship through the Panama Canal, then nearing completion, she returned to Norway in July, 1914. A few weeks later, the Great War broke out, and all plans were brought to a halt.

Fram was now worm-eaten and unseaworthy. For two decades she languished in Norwegian backwaters, quietly rotting away, while committees wrung their hands. In the end she was rescued by a public-spirited ship owner and given a final resting place under cover in Oslo, as Christiania in the meanwhile had become. And there she remains by the banks of the fjord, a national monument and Polar shrine.

Meanwhile, Amundsen had to find another vessel. Money, as usual, was his stumbling block, and there the war came to his aid. Norway was neutral, her merchant ships in demand among the Allies. Amundsen, like many of his countrymen, invested in shipping, quickly made a million kroner* and ordered a new vessel. She was built on

* £60,000 or $301,200; £640,000 or $1,280,000 in present terms.

the lines of Fram and called *Maud*, after the Norwegian Queen.

In July, 1918, *Maud* left Norway to follow the Siberian coast and start her drift across the Arctic at the Bering Strait. Seven years later, she finished her voyage in Seattle, having got no further north than the New Siberian Islands.

In the sense of achieving its stated goal, the expedition was a failure. *Maud* was, however, the second ship to pass through the North-East Passage, and Amundsen had been seen to attempt his Arctic drift. That the South Pole had not been the goldmine he expected, that wind, ice and currents had been against him in the north, was hardly his fault.

Amundsen had now devoted a quarter of a century to the Polar ice and snow. The first Antarctic night, the North-West Passage, the South Pole, the North-East Passage; his career read like a saga. He had spent ten years trying to keep his word, and his conscience on that account was clear. It would have been enough for most men, but Amundsen was still restless and knew no peace.

A decade of setback had obliterated the triumphs of the past, and Amundsen now knew the fate of the fallen hero, which in Norway happens to be particularly hard. He could not retire in disgrace: he first had to retrieve his reputation. It was the South Pole all over again.

The technique of dog-sledging that Amundsen had worked so hard to perfect was already obsolescent. He had closed an era. He at least had no nostalgic regrets. 'I stood with fresh memories of the long sledge journeys in Antarctica,' he said after first seeing an aeroplane fly (in Germany in 1913) and 'watched the machine in the air cover distances in one hour that would have taken days and cost fearful effort in the Polar regions.' He saw where the future lay, and immediately started learning to fly. In 1914, he took the first civilian pilot's licence in Norway. Now, at the age of fifty, as the *Maud* expedition petered out, he became possessed of the idea of being the first man to fly across the Arctic.

In 1923, leaving *Maud* to finish her voyage under Wisting, who had faithfully followed his old chief, Amundsen attempted to fly from Wainwright, in Alaska, to Spitsbergen. His aircraft, however, crashed before the start. He returned to Norway to try again.

'When Amundsen came back in triumph,' as a Norwegian journalist put it, 'we vied with each other to honour him. But when things went badly ... we were immediately ready with our sickly criticism.' The Norwegian press openly taunted Amundsen, amongst other things, with having engineered the crash at Wainwright because of being afraid of the flight. He was accused of a hoax in order to get publicity. Gossip suggested (impossibly, as the calendar would show) that two Eskimo girls he had adopted on *Maud* and brought to Norway for their education were his illegitimate daughters. Even if they had been, it would have reflected creditably on his sense of responsibility. But he took it all very much to heart.

So soon had victory begun to turn sour. It was as if the South Pole had become the albatross around his neck. A few snubs, some possibly unintentional went deep. Flying had introduced him to an unfamiliar world of business and finance in which he was ill at ease. He fell into the clutches of what he called 'a criminal optimist', and had difficulty in extricating himself. His trusting naiveté gave way to a low opinion of human nature and suspicion of his fellow men. He isolated himself behind a glacial crust of dignity built upon his natural reserve. 'I have so terribly few friends,' he wrote to Herman Gade, in a rare admission of the loneliness and unhappiness within. He was like a child who has been hurt, and trusts no one any more. It was given to few to breach the shell and glimpse the suppressed affection underneath.

Amundsen had come home in financial distress, as he expressed it, 'a permanent state of affairs' since sailing on *Gjøa*, twenty years before. He had begged ten thousand dollars for his abortive flight from Don Pedro Christophersen, who had remained his faithful and open-handed patron.

Money had no value for Amundsen; it was merely the means to realize ambition. Despite a Norwegian Government grant of 500,000 kroner* to help clear *Maud*'s deficit, his affairs had fallen into calamitous disarray. He quarrelled over money with his brother Leon, his business manager for more than a decade, and then made himself bankrupt. It was unnecessary, and against all advice: Amundsen's behaviour now seemed so strange that his sanity was questioned: the penalty, sometimes, of obsession with a single goal.

In the way an artist may be obsessed with his art, Amundsen was obsessed with exploration to the exclusion of all else. He neglected other sides of himself, so that to those who did not share his obsession, he appeared unbalanced. Calmly dismissing insolvency and the hounding of his creditors, he had ordered some German Dornier-Wal all-metal flying boats, the latest of their kind. All he needed was the money to

* £18,100 or $82,800; £157,000 or $314,000 in present terms.

pay for them – a mere detail. Don Pedro Christophersen and Herman Gade, his faithful friends, tried to save him from himself: they had bought his home to save it from the bankruptcy proceedings, let him have the use of it, and categorically forbade him to raise money on it, as he had done to finance his previous expeditions. Since, as he put it, 'all purses were closed' in Norway, Amundsen went to America to raise money by lecturing and writing.

In America, however, his star had also waned. The first results, in his words, were 'not encouraging. I worked out that if nothing unforeseen occurred, I could be ready to start when I was 110 years old!'

The unforeseen happened. 'Not the first time,' as Amundsen had put it on the South Pole journey, 'I have observed help at the right moment.' In New York, an American called Lincoln Ellsworth appeared, offering to finance a flight to the North Pole.

Ellsworth was a millionaire's son, heir to a fortune. Eleven years later, he was to make the first crossing of Antarctica. At the time, he was trying to make a reluctant father finance an Arctic expedition of his own. An obscure newspaper paragraph, announcing Amundsen's presence in New York, by chance gave him the key. Ellsworth Senior, unwilling to trust his son in the frozen wastes was, after some persuasion, prepared to trust the conqueror of the South Pole. For Amundsen, the funds were forthcoming.

Ellsworth regarded Amundsen as a 'virtuoso of exploration', and provided not only the money, but the unqualified respect which Amundsen craved, and of which he had lately been starved at home. Amundsen, on the other hand, gave Ellsworth the heroic example and the means of realizing ambition that he needed. All that Ellsworth wanted for his money was the privilege of serving under Amundsen as leader, and in deference to Amundsen, he let the expedition take place under the Norwegian flag. They were godsends to each other; it was an ideal partnership.

Ellsworth *père* put up $85,000, Amundsen was able to take delivery of his Dornier-Wals, and in May the following year, 1925, he and Lincoln-Ellsworth, with three Norwegians and a German mechanic, flew from Spitsbergen towards the North Pole in two machines. In some ways, it was a hasty and ill-conceived venture. Just short of the 88th parallel, they were forced down on to the pack ice, and one of the aircraft was damaged. After three weeks of epic struggle, they got the remaining one back into the air and returned to civilization, having been given up for lost.

At the age of fifty-three, Amundsen had spectacularly returned to the

the centre of the stage. He had reached 87° 44', the Furthest North yet in the air, and shown the way to the Pole. His escape from the jaws of the Arctic was in itself a triumph. All failure forgiven, his countrymen gave him a rapturous reception.

The following year Ellsworth, now come into his inheritance, gave $100,000 towards a trans-Polar flight by airship under Amundsen's command. The airship was built in Italy; her pilot was Umberto Nobile, who had designed her, and her crew was partly Italian. But she flew the Norwegian flag, and was called *Norge* (*Norway*).

While the *Norge* was waiting at Kings Bay on Spitsbergen for the start, the then Commander (later Admiral) Richard E. Byrd arrived with an aeroplane to be the first man to fly to the North Pole. In England, there was a certain pleasure in seeing the biter bit, as it were. In fact, Amundsen deliberately allowed Byrd to get his flight in first. Amundsen wanted to be first across the Arctic; to ask for priority at the Pole as well was hubris. Besides, with doubt still clinging to Cook's and Peary's claims, Amundsen felt it best for the record to stay in America, so as not to reopen old wounds. Byrd having returned with the claim to have reached the Pole, Amundsen started on his flight.

Norge left Kings Bay on May 11th, and landed at Teller, Alaska, two days later, passing over the Pole on the way. Amundsen had satisfied ambition. He was welcomed home with admiration yet more frenzied than the previous year. He was popular as never before; more so than after the South Pole. He would go down in history as the man who had made the first flight across the Arctic; he was the first to reach both Poles of the earth. He had closed the old era of dog and sledge, and opened the new one of the machine. He had risen from the depths to climb to the top again. It was the moment to leave the stage. Amundsen announced his farewell to exploration, and retired to his home at Bundefjord, Nansen's valedictory oration ringing in his ears:

> Your work is a man's work, sprung out of a man's will ... and if anyone can achieve what is called happiness, you must have done so. For the greatest happiness is to be capable of the complete fulfilment of one's uniqueness ... Such fulfilment you, Roald Amundsen, have achieved.

But happiness, as Nansen well knew, was not for Amundsen: he recognized a fellow tortured soul.

The aftermath of the *Norge* flight was miserable. For the first time, Amundsen had not been in command of people who accepted his authority without question; he no longer combined within himself leadership and technical expertise. His talents required a small group of hand-picked men. He was uneasy in the face of a heterogeneous crew. There was friction from the start and, soon after the flight, Amundsen fell out with Nobile whom, with some justice, he accused of claiming too much credit. Amundsen pursued a vendetta with Nobile in public, for he was the most relentless of enemies, as he was the staunchest of friends.

Dr. Frederick Cook had fallen on evil times. He was now in prison at Fort Leavenworth, near Kansas City, serving a long sentence for alleged share frauds. Amundsen took it as the most natural thing in the world, when on an American lecture tour before the *Norge* flight, to visit his old companion from the *Belgica*. This required the courage to defy public opinion, for by now Cook was cast as a villain and, more tragically, a clown. Amundsen was accused of taking sides with Cook against Peary, who now was the official American hero, while Cook's claims to have reached the North Pole were officially discredited. In displeasure, the National Geographic Society in Washington cancelled a lecture by Amundsen, causing him severe financial loss. (In 1913 they had given him $20,000.) Amundsen was unrepentant; in his code, loyalty to friends stood above all.

It was a moot point, however, who stood most in need of comfort, for according to Cook, Amundsen poured out his bitterness, saying amongst other things that 'There is a relation between the tongue and the harpoon. Both can inflict painful wounds. The cut of the lance heals, the cut of the tongue rots.'

Loneliness and disillusion lurked behind the now legendary figure, 'The White Eagle of Norway' as he was sometimes called. He had prematurely aged. He never married although there are tales of a mysterious American woman who stayed with him at his home at Bundefjord.

He was still in debt, pursued by creditors in two continents. It was not easy to shrug off. Amundsen became increasingly embittered. He appeared proud, distant, quarrelsome. He seemed to be fighting some demon. Ellsworth once described how Amundsen and he were walking down a street when suddenly Amundsen

> without looking round ... said tensely: 'Ellsworth, we are being followed!' ... sure enough some little boys were trailing us ... quite unaware that they were also rasping their hero's pet phobia.

In 1927, Amundsen published his memoirs, *My Life as an Explorer*. It was a bitter and, in parts, an unbalanced work that pained his friends and dimmed his reputation. It was totally different from his earlier books, almost as if his personality had changed. Instead of his old modesty and quiet humour, he was boastful, deadly serious and engrossed in attacking his enemies; towards Nobile he was ruthless and cutting. He revealed next to nothing about his private and inner life, but he gave a glimpse of what was preying on his mind.

Despite unstinted recognition elsewhere, Amundsen was galled by neglect in England. He called the English 'bad losers'. It rankled that English schoolchildren were taught that Scott discovered the South Pole, and his own expedition was overlooked. He described how, at a dinner given by the Royal Geographical Society in 1912, Lord Curzon, the President, made a speech which ended

> with the following words: 'I propose three cheers for the dogs', while he clearly emphasized his satirical and derogatory intention by turning towards me with a deprecatory gesture ... and earnestly bade me not to answer this transparent insult.

The R.G.S. denied the accusation, and requested an apology. Amundsen took this as a slur on his honour, refused to comply and resigned his honorary fellowship, which the Society declined to accept. That there had been some kind of insult is more than likely; Curzon could be very rude indeed. At the time, Amundsen had hastily left the Royal Societies' Club, where he was lodged by the R.G.S., and moved to a hotel where he paid for himself, but never gave an explanation. He had brooded on the incident for fifteen years, only now letting it come out.

Amundsen also now wrote that

> Scott and his companions died on the way back from the Pole, not because they were broken by our earlier arrival, but on account of hunger, because they were not in a position to obtain sufficient food.

There was the shadow of an accusing finger. It was the closest Amundsen came to admitting publicly that the death of Scott was preying on his mind. Years before, he once revealed that just before leaving the Pole he debated with himself whether or not to leave a tin of paraffin in order to save weight, and help Scott in case of need. In the end, however, he decided that Scott would be so well supplied, it would be superfluous, and he might just as well take it back as extra insurance.

That tin of paraffin might, in retrospect, have saved Scott and some of his companions. It was a doubtful might-have-been, but enough to foster a gnawing sense of guilt. Amundesen had never really forgiven himself. That was the burden he had borne; the price he had paid. He had to live with the knowledge which could never be quite suppressed and, down the years, might have driven him to the edge of sanity. Victory at the South Pole had been bitter indeed.

At the end of May, 1928, Amundsen was called out of retirement. Nobile had returned to the Arctic, this time under Italian colours, and disappeared on a flight to the North Pole in an airship called *Italia*. The Italian ambassador in Oslo asked the Norwegian Government for help, and Amundsen was one of the Polar experts hastily summoned for consultations about a rescue expedition. Amundsen assumed he would be put in command.

The Italian dictator, Benito Mussolini, however, told the Norwegians that their help was *not* wanted, at least not under Amundsen. Mussolini disapproved of Amundsen for his quarrel with Nobile, which he took as an insult to the Italian nation.

Despite Mussolini's snub, the Norwegian Government persevered with their rescue plans, since Nobile might have crashed near Spitsbergen, and therefore within their jurisdiction. In order not to offend the Italian dictator, however, Amundsen was quietly dropped. Besides, the rescue was to be an air operation, run by Naval flyers and Amundsen, not being an officer, could not be put in command. In any case, since the publication of his memoirs, he was thought too difficult to deal with. He was sent back to Bundefjord, with thanks.

Amundsen was furious; he felt cheated and betrayed, especially since Hjalmar Riiser-Larsen, his old companion from the *Norge* and the flight to 88° North, had accepted command. His feelings, however, ran deeper than pique.

The call to action came as if upon a cue. For the two years since retiring, Amundsen had been working to clear his debts. He had sold his medals (they were bought by a generous fellow countryman and presented to the nation) and the first royalties from his memoirs would complete the payment of his creditors in full. 'Make me an honest man!' he had told his lawyer. The task was almost done.

Scott had shown that when human destinies were intertwined, they could not be unravelled. Amundsen had Hjalmar Johansen on his conscience and he knew that he was partly responsible for driving Nobile back to the ice. After their quarrel, Nobile wanted vindication, for he was a man of heroic aspirations. Amundsen feared that he would be weighed in the balance and found wanting. He did not want another life on his conscience. In public he said he wanted to go to Nobile's rescue as a gesture of reconciliation; to a friend he confessed that he could not face a repetition of the jeer of cowardice raised after his first attempt at an Arctic flight. It was a play acted out on the open stage. Amundsen had been at a public dinner when the original appeal to help Nobile arrived. 'Right away!' he had said; words reported in the Press. That left him no retreat. He *had* to do something; he could not stand idly by and watch and wait.

If nobody wanted Amundsen to look for Nobile, he would do so on his own. He frantically set about organizing a private rescue expedition. Money, alas, blocked him yet again. Amundsen would cheerfully have spent his last penny on the enterprise, but he was just solvent, and no more.

Once again he knew the humiliation of begging and importuning. He sat in his house, looking out at the fjord where *Fram* had moored, and waited helplessly while the telegrams flew to and fro and the wireless in the corner announced the rescue expeditions setting off, one after the other.

An Italian journalist who visited Amundsen at this time described him as restless and abstracted. In the course of conversation he reviewed his life in the Polar ice and said:

> Ah, if only you knew how splendid it is up there, that's where I want to die. And I wish only that death will ... overtake me in the fulfilment of a high mission, quickly, without suffering.

A few days later Sverre Hassel, Amundsen's old companion, one of the four who had stood at the South Pole with him, came on a visit, and fell down dead, while they were talking.

Amundsen craved action and there were those who felt that his inactivity was a national disgrace. Through the intercession of a Norwegian businessman in Paris, the French Government overnight provided a flying boat, complete with pilot and crew. Such was still the magic of Amundsen's name. It was a superfluous gesture, for by now there were at least twenty aricraft and a fleet of ships on the way. The search for Nobile, however, had become an international scramble for prestige, an end in itself, and the French, like the other Governments involved, hoped for some of the pickings.

Within two days, the French machine – a Latham, with the serial No. 47 – was on its way to Bergen, on the Norwegian west coast. On June 16th, Amundsen left Oslo by the night train to meet her there. A crowd had gathered on the platform to see him off and as the train drew away, Amundsen stood at the window waving slowly until he could see faces no more. It was twenty-five years ago, to the day, that he had left for the North-West Passage.

Early in the morning of Monday, June 18th, Amundsen landed in Tromsø to find a Swedish, a Finnish and an Italian flying boat, all bound for Spitsbergen on the same mission. The Swedish pilot suggested all waiting a day to make the crossing of the dangerous Barents Sea together. Amundsen, for one, refused. Radio contact had by now been made with Nobile. He had crashed and, with a few survivors, was on an ice floe north of Spitsbergen. It was now a race to reach Nobile first and take him off.

By now Amundsen knew that his machine was unsuited to her task; so did Leif Dietrichsen, his Norwegian companion, and Captain René Guilbaud, Latham 47's commander. The aircraft was overloaded and too weak for the Arctic. They all knew that to go on was foolhardy, but they had gone too far to turn back.

At four o'clock the same afternoon, Latham 47 taxied out into the fairway. In the crystal-clear light of a perfect northern summer's day, she skimmed heavily over the water. With the spluttering of engines and the whirl of spray she took the air. A little while later, a fisherman off the coast saw her fly low over the water to the northwest until, in his own words,

> a bank of fog rose up over the horizon and then the machine began to climb presumably to fly over it but then it seemed to me she began to move unevenly but then ... she ran into the fog [and] disappeared before our eyes.

Soon after, radio contact ceased. It was the last seen or heard of Roald Amundsen. He had vanished into the Polar sea which had been his only true home on earth.

Months later, one of Latham 47's floats and a petrol tank were recovered from the sea, screwed off and clearly used as improvised life rafts. Amundsen and his companions must have fought to the last. Perhaps they might have been saved if a search had been made as soon as they were overdue at Kings Bay. But Amundsen's countrymen remembered, vividly, how he had changed course in midstream when he went to the Antarctic; they believed he could do it again. It was imagined that he had decided after take-off to head straight for Nobile on his ice floe, and surprise the world as he had done before, and take the game. By the time the alarm was raised, it was too late and all searches were in vain.

Nobile was rescued by someone else; Amundsen had thrown away his life. But he would only have been unhappy if he had gone on. His end was worthy of the old Norse sea kings who sought immolation when they knew their time had come. It was the exit he would have chosen for himself.

On December 14th, the anniversary of Amundsen's arrival at the South Pole, Norway observed a two minutes' silence in his memory. But for long his countrymen refused to believe he was dead. He had landed on some remote, ice-bound coast, ran a popular belief, and would reappear one day. In the north of the country, on the Arctic coast, a tale arose of two men sitting and staring out to sea in the direction in which Latham 47 had last been sighted; paid and fed by their neighbours to watch for Amundsen's return. He would have liked to have lived on as that kind of legend.

Thus perished one of the greatest of Polar explorers. By his countrymen he was remembered as a hero; someone from another age; remote, yet dominating, a Napoleonic figure. At the same time, they seemed half ashamed of him, the result of British disapproval over the years.

There was very little to be ashamed of. Amundsen had brought prestige and self-confidence to Norway at the time when she was finding her feet as an independent nation. He was to his countrymen what a general or a statesman meant elsewhere: the personification of the national genius. He had paid dearly both for his sins and for having his prayers answered. With the passage of time, his secret change from the North Pole to the South appears a necessary deception. Stripped of moralizing cant, it bears a striking resemblance to the Drake touch; the Nelsonian stratagem. The main thing was, he *won*.

His virtue was loyalty, both in giving and inspiring in others. Wisting followed him for sixteen years and mourned him long. In the winter of 1936, a year after *Fram* had safely been brought up on dry land, Wisting asked permission to sleep aboard, and was found dead one morning in his old cabin, like a figure from the sagas, faithful to his lord.

The other two who had stood at the Pole with Amundsen, Bjaaland and Helmer Hanssen, lived to a ripe old age, Bjaaland long enough to meet Sir Vivian Fuchs, who had led the British trans-Antarctic expedition of 1957–1958. Sir Vivian had reached the Pole by tractor, and told Bjaaland all about it. Bjaaland was unimpressed. 'Nothing much been changed there, as far as I know', was his comment. He hadn't changed much, either.

He remembered Amundsen as a 'straightforward and honourable fellow', a judgment that explains much. It was Amundsen's straightforwardness, his lack of self-dramatization, his gift for making things seem easier than they were, that deprived him of unbounded popular hero-worship. He had all the instincts of an artist; he was the explorer's explorer.

Amundsen was the supreme exponent of Polar technique. He towered above his rivals; he brought an intellectual approach to exploration and stood, as he still stands, the antipole to the heroic delusion. 'The victory of human kind over Nature,' he wrote in the closing lines of his autobiography, 'is not that of brute force alone, but also that of the spirit.' It remains his testament.

An unsentimental realist, Amundsen was the great master for all those who came after. The new generation of Polar travellers learned from him their dog-driving, planning, avoidance of risks, attention to detail. Wherever else they got their morality, the new school of English explorers, especially those on the Greenland ice cap between the wars, were careful to take their technique from Amundsen.

Although Amundsen considered the North-West Passage the best of his expeditions, the journey to the South Pole remains his masterpiece, the culmination of the classical age of Polar exploration and, perhaps, the greatest snow journey ever made. It has the touch of genius, and the great general's gift of luck. It remains the grand example of how a venture should be run.

The year Amundsen died, Admiral Richard Byrd took an American expedition to the Bay of Whales. It was the first human visit since *Fram* had sailed away, and the first large, modern Antarctic expedition. Polar exploration was moving into the domain of the coming superpowers, for they had the resources and vitality for the complex scientific enterprises whose day had dawned. Byrd was the new kind of explorer, but he did not attempt to hide what he owed to Amundsen, the pathfinder.

Byrd had sat at Amundsen's feet, adopted his principles, and even had some of his men. He built his base, which he called Little America, near the site of Framheim. He tried to find Amundsen's hut, but in vain. By now it had probably been carried out to sea, for the Barrier had flowed on remorselessly.

Byrd had aircraft and flew to the Pole. He had radio and all contemporary aids. When he saw what Amundsen had overcome with dogs and willpower alone, his admiration was boundless. In an act of pilgrimage Laurence Gould, one of Byrd's men, while exploring the Queen Maud Range, searched for Amundsen's cairn on Betty's Knoll. Eventually he found it.

What a thrill we did all get ... to stand where Amundsen had once stood, and to find, perfectly intact, the cairn he had erected eighteen years before. We couldn't help standing to attention, with hats off, in admiring respect for the memory of this remarkable man.

Note on diet

SCOTT'S SLEDGING RATION from the Beardmore Glacier onwards, per man and day, was 20 gm. (0.7 oz.) tea, 454 gm. (1 lb) biscuits, 24 gm. (0.86 oz.) cocoa, 340 gm. (12 oz.) pemmican, 56.75 gm. (2 oz.) butter, and 85.13 gm. (3 oz.) sugar, a total of 980 gm. (2lb. 3 oz.).

Amundsen's basic sledging ration per man and day was 400 gm. biscuits, 75 gm. dried milk, 125 gm. chocolate and 375 gm. pemmican, a total of 975 gm.

Scott's ration gave 4,430 Calories per man and day, Amundsen's 4,560 Calories. A healthy male doing manual work under normal conditions needs about 3,600 Calories per day. On the return, Scott's ration decreased because of failing supplies, so that he was probably averaging under 4,000 Calories. From the 29th December, when Amundsen increased his pemmican allowance to 450 gm., he was getting 5,000 Calories. Scott probably needed about 5,500 Calories for the work he was doing, Amundsen, 4,500.

Scott's daily intake of thiamin was 1.26 mg., riboflavin, 1.65 mg., and nicotinic acid, 18.18 mg. The corresponding figures for Amundsen on his basic ration were 2.09 mg. thiamin, 2.87 mg. riboflavin and 25.85 mg. nicotinic acid, rising to 2.24 mg., 3.04 mg., and 29.3 mg. respectively, after the increase in pemmican. The accepted requirements for work at 4,500 Calories per day are 1.8 mg. thiamin, 2.4 mg. riboflavin and 29.7 mg. nicotinic acid. Lack of thiamin is associated with beri-beri; of nicotinic acid, with pellagra, both fatal if left untreated.

Bibliography

For the full list of sources see the hardback edition. Wherever possible, I went back to original diaries and papers.

Here is a short personal selection of books I found particularly useful or enjoyable.

First of all, the books written by Roald Amundsen:

My Life as a Polar Explorer, London, William Heinemann, 1927.
The North-West Passage, London, A. Constable & Co., 1908.
The South Pole, London, John Murray, 1912; reissue (facsimile), London, C. Hurst & Co., 1976.
Roald Amundsen and Lincoln Ellsworth, *The First Flight across the Polar Sea*, London, Hutchinson & Co., 1927.

A book by one of Amundsen's followers:

Helmer Hanssen, *Voyages of a Modern Viking*, London, G. Routledge & Sons, 1936.

Next, something about Norway and the Norwegians:

T. K. Derry, *A Short History of Norway*, London, George Allen & Unwin, 1957.
Frede Castberg, *The Norwegian Way of Life*, London, William Heinemann, 1954.

For insight into the Norwegian character:

Two plays by Henrik Ibsen: *The Master Builder*, translated by Una Ellis-Fermor, London, Penguin Books, 1981; *Per Gynt*, London, Penguin Books, 1970.
Knut Hamsun, *Hunger*, London, Picador, 1976 (a *roman à clef* that might have been written by Amundsen himself).

Three marvellous books which tell much of the Norwegians in the polar regions:

Fridtjof Nansen, *The First Crossing of Greenland*, London, Longmans & Co., 1890; *Farthest North* (The Voyage of the Fram, 1893-1896), London, A. Constable & Co., 1897.

Otto Sverdrup, *New Land*, London, Longmans & Co., 1904.

A biography of Nansen:

Liv Nansen Høyer, *Nansen, A Family Portrait*, London, Longmans Green & Co., 1957.

Polar history:

L. P. Kirwan, *A History of Polar Exploration*, London, Penguin Books, 1962.

About dogs, Eskimos and polar travel:

Eivind Astrup, *With Peary Near the Pole*, London, C. Arthur Pearson, 1898.
Sir Martin Conway, *With Ski and Sledge over Arctic Glaciers*, London, J. M. Dent & Co., 1898.
Robert E. Peary, *Secrets of Polar Travel*, New York, Century Co., 1917.

The *Belgica* expedition:

Frederick A. Cook, *Through the First Antarctic Night*, London, William Heinemann, 1900; reissue (facsimile), London, C. Hurst & Co., 1976.

On the British historical background, two essential books by Correlli Barnett:

The Collapse of British Power, London, Eyre Methuen, 1972.
The Swordbearers, London, Eyre & Spottiswoode, 1963.

On the *Discovery* expedition:

R. F. Scott, *The Voyage of the 'Discovery'*, London, Macmillan & Co., 1905.

And, as a complement:

Albert Armitage, *From Cadet to Commodore*, London, Cassell & Co., 1925.

On Scott's last expedition:

R. F. Scott, *Scott's Last Expedition, being the journals of Captain R. F. Scott, R.N., C.V.O.*, arranged by Leonard Huxley, London, Smith, Elder & Co., 1913.

To check the arranging:

R. F. Scott, *The Diaries of Captain Robert Scott*, facsimile edition, Tylers Green, Buckinghamshire, University Microfilms, 1968.

Apsley Cherry-Garrard, *The Worst Journey in the World*, London, Chatto & Windus, 1965.

Admiral Lord Mountevans, *South with Scott*, London, Collins (n.d.).

Finally, two indispensable books on British Antarctic exploration:

Sir Ernest Shackleton, *The Heart of the Antarctic*, London, William Heinemann, 1909.

Sir James Clark Ross, *A Voyage of Discovery and Research in the Southern and Antarctic Regions*, London, John Murray, 1847; reissue (facsimile), Newton Abbott, David & Charles Reprints, 1969.

Index

Active, H.M.S. 130, 131

Adams, Lieutenant Jameson Boyd 445

Adams Range 434

Adare, Cape 63, 69, 150, 288n; first landing at 60; Borchgrevink's winter at 129; Campbell's winter at 338, 513

Addison, Joseph 93

Adventure (Captain Cook's ship) 21

Aftenposten 199–200

Aigle (Bouvet's ship) 20

Akaroa Harbour (New Zealand), *Terra Nova*'s arrival at 513

Albermarle, H.M.S.: Scott in command of 219–20, 226; ramming of *Commonwealth*, 220, 226, 346

Amphion, H.M.S., Scott's tour of duty on, as lieutenant 121, 122–3

Amundsen, Gustav Sahlquist (brother) 26–7, 33, 46, 54, 265–6; Amundsen's letters to, 50–53, 77, 81–2, 89; and Amundsen's finances 82, 86

Amundsen, Hanna Henrikke Gustava Sahlquist (mother) 26, 29–30, 33, 39, 41, 43

Amundsen, Jens Engebreth (father): early success as shipowner 26; marriage 26; move to Christiania 27; as disciplinarian 27–9; concern for son's education 30; death 32–3

Amundsen, Jens Ole Antonio (Tonni) (brother) 14, 41; plan for ski expedition with Amundsen to Graham Land 53–4

Amundsen, Karen Anna (cousin) 32, 41

Amundsen, Leon Henry Benham (brother) 26–7, 77; attempt to ski over Hardangervidda with Amundsen 56–9; help for Amundsen's North-West Passage expedition 90, 112–13; as secretary to Amundsen's Polar expedition 205, 275–6, 281–3, 290, 354; in secret of Amundsen's real aim 276–7, 285–6, 290; revelation of this 299–301; told of Amundsen's success 510, 511, 511; on Scott's death 526; Amundsen's quarrel with 534

Amundsen, Målfred (wife of Gustav) 359

Amundsen, Ole (grandfather) 25

Amundsen, Roald Engebreth Gravning:

ancestry 25–6; birth 26–7; boyhood 27–30; and father's death 32–3; decision to become Polar explorer 33, 36–7, 43–4; ambition to achieve North-West Passage 36–7; first long ski tour 38; education 38–40, 43; creative pause 40, 41; fails university examinations 43, 45; attempts to join Polar expeditions 43–5; acquires art of mountain skiing 45–9; takes up profession of ship's officer 50–54; season on sealer 50–53; first definite plans for exploration 53–4; obtains mate's certificate 54; military service 54–5, 77; attempt to ski over Hardangervidda 56–9; first published work 57–8; serves sea time 59, 61–2, 63; second mate on *Belgica* Antarctic expedition 61, 63–74; on first Antarctic sledging journey 67–8; initiation into ice work 68; resigns over succession of command 72–3; secures Nansen's goodwill 75–6; finishes mariner's training 77; studies Polar literature 77–8, 243; ambition to navigate North-West Passage 77–9; achieves this on pretext of visiting North Magnetic Pole 78–113; training in taking magnetic observations 80, 86, 88–9, 91; obtains Nansen's approval 80–82; preparations 81–92; buys *Gjøa* 82; training cruise 83–5; takes master's certificate 86; financial difficulties 88–92, 114–15; gathering of crew 90–91; departure, and beginning of first command 92–3; succession of near calamities 99–100, 112; frozen in at Gjøahavn 99–109; contact with Eskimos 100–104, 105–7; reaches Pole at third attempt 104–9; graduation as Polar traveller 109–10; financial loss through breaking of exclusive news 114–15; public acclaim 117–18, 191–2; his writing 192–4; lecture tours to repay debts 193–4, 198–9; promised *Fram* 195–7, 531; first recorded sexual adventures 197–8; purchase of house 198; oceanographic course 198–9; plans for North Polar expedition 199–203; preparation for 204–5, 208; falls in love 205; changes destination to South

Amundsen, Roald Engebreth Gravning – *continued*

Pole 208–9, 279–82; first intimation of Scott as rival 211, 240; success over changed plans 210–12, 245–6, 250–52, 265, 273, 276–7; plan of campaign 242–4; difficulty in raising funds 245, 275–6; preparations 245–51; and equipment 245–6, 250–51; choice of men 247–50, 260–61, 276; tribute to Shackleton 263–4; departure 273–4, 278; finds financial backer 275–6; reveals real destination to officers 276–7; apologia to Nansen 279–80, 290, 301–2; tells truth to crew 281–7; summary of plans and aims 288, 289, 315; perfecting of equipment 296, 356–8; announces landing party 297–8; landing at Bay of Whales 298–9, 315; publication of real aim and challenge to Scott 301–2, 303; drives first dog sledge to future base 319; and meeting with *Terra Nova* 322–4, 340–41, 344; concern over Scott's motor sledges 324, 336, 365–6, 384–5; depot-laying journeys 321–34, 337; ahead of Scott 327; rectal complaint 331, 334–5; generous margins of safety 333, 404, 407, 498; criticism of his plan to go South 352–4; morale-building at Framheim 358–60; insistence on preventing scurvy 362; forebodings and crisis of command 366; false start on Polar journey 378–82, 384; his leadership questioned by Johansen 382–4; fresh start 385–7; rate of travel 400, 407, 432–3, 439–40; narrow escapes in crevassed terrain 401; changed plan to lay depots 403–4; beginning of journey in earnest 404–5; routine for economy of effort 405–6, 437–8; crossing of Transantarctic Mountains to Plateau 408–21; and last lap to Pole 422–9; setbacks and narrow escapes in disturbed terrain 424–8; passes Shackleton's Furthest South 427–8, 446; 'final onslaught' 446–54; order of running 450–51; reaches Pole 455; plants Norwegian flag 456; observation and fixing of Pole 458–60; journey back to Framheim base 461–74, 490–92; raises pemmican allowance 462, 463–4; disorientation 465–70; his victory discovered by Scott 479–80, 482, 484; return to *Fram* 492–54; voyage to Tasmania 495–6, 510–11; public acclaim 510–12, 515, 526; Norwegian ambivalence towards 511–12; British bitterness towards 514; lecture tours 516, 525–6, 530, 535; completion of both 487–9; made scapegoat for Scott's death 526; disappointment over love affair 530; tries to drop

plan of Arctic drift 530–31; abortive attempt in *Maud* 532; as fallen hero 534–5; takes first civilian pilot's licence in Norway 533; attempted Arctic flight 533, 539; misfortunes and financial distress 536, 538; Polar flight with Ellsworth 535–7; loneliness and disillusion 537–40; publishes memoirs 538; sense of guilt over Scott's death 538–9; lost at sea in search for Nobile 540–41; as supreme exponent of Polar technique 542

characteristics: animals, love of 298, 321, 330–31, 431; destiny, sense of 85–6, 379; intellect 291; leadership, capacity for 92–4, 157–9, 197–8, 286, 293–5, 358, 386, 414–15, 450–51; loyalty 198–9, 529–30, 541–2; magnetism 358; modesty 193; physical fitness 55; rectitude, sense of 38; religion 33, 85–6, 398; sensitivity 193, 280, 356–7; sexual reticence 40–41, 110, 205, 530; short sight 43, 55, 100, 465–6; singlemindedness 55–6, 80, 81–2; stoicism 430; vanity 193

diet 86, 246, 361–2, 476, 478

equipment and clothing 90, 103–4, 106, 245–6, 252, 290–92, 325–6, 334, 355–7, 375, 450

transport: dogs 87–8, 105–6, 109, 114, 208–14, 275–7, 296–8, 306, 319, 323, 360–62, 376–82, 403, 410–12, 446, 464, 493–4, 501–2; skis 246, 294, 326, 400, 410–11, 416, 472, 474; sledges 110, 115, 290, 319–20, 356, 376–8, 386, 402–3, 410–11, 424–5

Angell, Captain H. A. 48

Antarctic (Norwegian whaler) 60; (Swedish ship) 182, 222n, 244

Antarctic Circle: *Discovery* crosses 183; *Morning* crosses 189; *Fram* crosses 298

Antarctic Ice Cap: Armitage's discovery of 177, 180, 189; in state of flux 422, 424

Archer, Colin: builder of *Fram* 43; Scott unimpressed by 140

Arctowski, Henryk 63, 67, 73; experiments with motor sledges 223

Armitage, Albert, second in command on Scott's *Discovery* expedition 142–3, 146, 148, 178; and use of ponies 151–2, 255; on Scott's lack of magnetism 158; treatment of scurvy 165; first to reach Antarctic Ice Cap 177, 179–80, 189, 408–9; Scott's jealousy of 179, 189; congratulates Amundsen on success 507

Armitage, Cape 346

Armour, Jonathan Ogden 201

Arroll-Johnstone Co. 224

Askeladden, myth of 34, 118

Astrup, Eivind 163, 255; lecture on Peary's pioneering work 41–2, 210; death in

Rondane Mountains 56, 210; Amundsen's debt to 210

Astrup, Cape 212

Athenaeum, The 188

Atkinson, E. L. (surgeon on Scott's Polar expedition) 313, 341-2, 345, 476; forms clique with Meares and Oates 375, 442; and man-hauling 435; advice on fittest seamen to go on to Pole 436; return from Glacier with support party 436-7, 438; told to bring dog teams south on last lap 438, 502, 504-5; considers Oates unfit to continue 442-3; rescues Evans from scurvy 503; in command at Camp Evans 503, 517-18; forlorn rescue attempt 517; later search party and discovery 518, 520-21; refusal to divulge medical details 527

Austin, Captain Horatio 126

Axel Heiberg Glacier 423-4, 436, 449, 465; Amundsen's crossing of 414-16; Amundsen's return down 468, 471

Baffin Bay 96

Balfour, A. J. (later Earl) 130

Balloon Bight 152, 241; disappearance of 241-2, 322

Barbados 130

Barents Sea 84, 144, 540

Barne, Lieutenant Michael: on Scott's *Discovery* expedition 144, 158; sledge journey to Cape Crozier 154, 156; in advance supply party for Scott's journey south 167-8; abortive attempt to organize Antarctic expedition 222; as Scott's front man 222-3

Barrie, J. M.: friendship with Scott 225-6; Scott's last letter to 508-9; reconstruction of closing scene 528

Barrier Inlet 217

Bartlett, Captain 'Bob' 269

Baumann, Captain Victor 261

Beardmore, William (later Lord Invernairn) 215

Beardmore Glacier 234, 414; pony transport to foot of 368, 432-3; blizzard near foot of 429, 431; Scott's man-hauling along 434-40, 442, 454, 465, 478-9, 502-3; Scott's descent of, a return from Pole 485-7

Beardsley, Mabel, Scott's flirtation with 225

Beaumont, Admiral Sir Lewis 202-3, 527; disapproves of Scott competing with Shackleton 234-5

Beck, Andreas, ice pilot on Amundsen's Polar expedition 248, 296

Beechey Island 96, 97

'Beehive, The' (later Mount Ruth Gade) 409

Beerbohm, Max 225, 229

Belgian Geographical Society 73

Belgica: De Gerlache's Antarctic expedition on 61, 63-74, 80, 141; Amundsen as second mate on 63, 65, 67-9, 94, 192-3, 210; beset by ice pack 69-73; scurvy on 70-71, 100, 210, 246, 361-2

Bellingshausen, Captain Baron Thaddeus, and claim to be discoverer of Antarctica 21

Bellingshausen Sea 73; Charcot's charting of land in 185

Bergen 274, 518, 540; Amundsen's oceanographical course in 199

Bering Strait 117, 195

Berlin 137, 141

Bernacchi, Louis 129, 163, 177; as physicist on Scott's *Discovery* expedition 144, 151; his advice rejected 160

Betty (Amundsen's nurse, later housekeeper) *see* Gustavson, Betty

Betty's Knoll 410, 471, 498; Amundsen's cairn on 472, 543

Bjaaland, Olav 525, 531; career and skiing progress 206; on Amundsen's Polar expedition 206, 248, 274, 277, 291-2, 354, 404; and Amundsen's revelation of real aim 284-5; work on sledges and skis 290, 295, 356, 358; in landing party 295-6, 320, 325; on first sight of midnight sun and ice barrier 297; erects hut at base 320, 327; depot-laying 330-31, 336; improvises snow shovels 355; recreation 354; and false start 381-4; fresh start, 386, 400, and rate of travel 400; as dog-driver 405-6, 452, 456-7; and idea that Barrier was afloat 407-8; climb to Plateau 410, 411, 415; eating of dog meat 421; four days storm-bound 422; and last lap to Pole 425, 426; and 'final onslaught' 446, 450-51; arrival at Pole 454-5, 459; gives up dogs 456; 'boxing' of Pole 458; as forerunner on journey back 460, 467-9, 472-3, 484; voyage to Tasmania 495-6; declines to continue on original Arctic drift 496; sails home 518; later life 531, 542

Bjaaland, Mount 465

Bjørnson, Bjørnstjerne 36, 62

Boothia Felix 99, 107; North Magnetic Pole on 108

boots and bindings 246, 326, 328, 358, 384

Borchgrevink, Carsten 28, 63, 144, 146, 151, 291; first to set foot on South Victoria Land 60, 244; ambition to be first to winter in Antarctic 60, 128; fulfils ambition 128-9, 140, 157, 160; record for Furthest South 140, 152; quarrel with Nansen 140

Bouvet de Lozier, Captain Jean-François Charles 20
Bouvet Island 20
Bowers, Henry Robertson 348, 370, 376, 396, 433, 486; joins Scott's Polar expedition 260; depot-laying journey 338, 340–41, 344–5; Scott's vacillating treatment of, 339; loss of ponies in break-up of the ice 346; enthusiasm for Scott's plans 369; as Scott's practical right-hand man 373, 441, 500; winter journey to Cape Crozier 375, 380n; 'breeze up' about loads 393–4; on delay and Scott's depression 431; and man-hauling 435, 438–9, 443; and Scott's rages 438; added to final party 441; as navigator 441, 450; and discovery of Amundsen's prior arrival 479; takes observations 482; finds Amundsen's tent 482; journey back 484, 500; begins to grasp Scott's incompetence 484–5; criticized for indifferent skiing 489; takes over leadership 500; last days 507, 510, 528; letter to mother 509; discovery and burial 518–19
Brabant Island, first Antarctic camp on 67
Brand (Ibsen) 40, 56
Bransfield, Edward, as discoverer of Antarctica 21
Brett (cook on Scott's Discovery expedition) 152–3, 165
Bridgeman, Admiral Sir Francis 230, 257; Scott's last letter to 508
Bridgeman, Lady 270
Britannia training ship, Dartmouth 120
Brocklehurst, Sir Philip 259n
Bruce, Kathleen see Scott, Kathleen
Bruce, Wilfred: with Scott's Polar expedition 307, 311, 350; and meeting with Fram 322–3, 336–7
Bruce, William Spiers: expedition to Weddell Sea 144; discovery of Coats Land 185
Bryde, Johan 61
Buchan, John 146
Buckingham Palace Road (No. 174), Scott's married home 229
Buckley, Mount 485
Buenos Aires: Fram's voyage to 325, 350–51, 516; Amundsen's acclaim in 516
Bulwark, H.M.S., Scott in command of 229
Bundefjord: Amundsen's house at 198, 242, 265, 290, 537, 539; Amundsen boards Fram at 273–4
'Butcher's Shop, The' 421, 422, 429, 466, 468–9
Byrd, Admiral Richard E. 358; expedition to Bay of Whales 471n, 543; first to fly to North Pole 536

Camoens, Luis de 70
Campbell, Captain Henry 230
Campbell, Lieutenant Victor 300, 372; as first mate of Terra Nova 267, 314; as leader of group in King Edward VII Land 267, 291, 322; on sledging committee 290; and meeting with Fram in Bay of Whales 324–5, 337, 342–3; disappointed at King Edward VII Land exploration 323, 337; expedition to South Victoria Land 338, 521; makes winter base at Cape Adare 338, 350
Cardiff, Terra Nova departure from 271
Caroline, H.M.S. 121
'Carrey' (procuress) 198
Castberg, Sigrid, Amundsen's affair with 205, 529
Cato (Addison) 93
Challenger, H.M.S. 127
Chamonix 206
Charcot, Dr. Jean 236; expedition to west coast of Graham Land 145, 185; experiments with motor sledges 223, 226–7
Charles Hansson (whaler) 112
Chase, Horace Blanchard 122
Chase, Minnie, Scott's affair with 122
Chase, Pauline 226
Chelsea: Scott home at Royal Hospital Road 124; Scott home at 56 Oakley Street 224
Cherry-Garrard, Apsley: paying volunteer on Scott's Polar expedition 261, 290, 302, 314, 338, 342, 370, 394, 442; depot-laying journey 340, 345; winter journey to Cape Crozier 375, 380n; and Scott's exhausting day marches 400; and man-hauling 435; return with supporting party 436, 441; sets out with dog teams to speed Scott's return 505; turns back at One Ton Camp 505, 518, 520; breakdown 518–19; self-reproach 520
Chicago 192, 198, 525
Chree, Dr. C. 229
Chree Indians 86
Christensen, Christen 54
Christensen, Lars 527n
Christian Frederick, Cape (Boothia Felix) 107, 109
Christiania 27, 29, 61, 86, 199, 205, 263, 265; Amundsen's boyhood life at Little Uranienborg 28–9, 39; Amundsen's flat in 39, 41; Scott visits Nansen in 139–40; Amundsen's triumphant return to (1906) 192; Press reaction to revelation of Amundsen's South Pole aim 301
Christiania University, Amundsen at 39, 41, 43
Christophersen, Peter ('Don Pedro') 281; provides Amundsen with food and supplies 275–6, 286, 493; pays other expenses

351, 354, 516; told in confidence of Amundsen's success 510; Amundsen's thanks to 515; first meeting 516; further help 535

clothing 104, 106, 246, 269–70, 326, 357, 365, 375, 379, 384, 393

Coats Land, discovery of 185

Colbeck, William 129, 176; discovery of two islands 189

Colbeck, Cape 322, 350

Collinson, Richard, neglected explorer of North-West Passage 92, 111, 114

Commonwealth (battleship), rammed by *Albemarle* 221, 345

Conway, Sir Martin 136, 142

Cook, Dr. Frederick A. 141, 209, 245; doctor with De Gerlache's expedition 64, 67, 68–73; tent design 72, 296–7, 460; sledging journeys 67, 72; treatment of scurvy 70, 99; Amundsen's judgment of 72, 210; claim to have reached North Pole 207, 210–11, 244, 289, 457, 459, 537; suggestion that Amundsen should try for South Pole 207–8, 210; controversy with Peary 210, 446, 537; goggle design 245, 438; later misfortunes 537

Cook, Captain James 125; first to sail over Antarctic Circle 18, 20; and prevention of scurvy 164

Copenhagen 141, 208–9

Corner Camp 343, 349, 375, 393, 502, 517–18

Crean, Petty Officer: on Scott's Polar expedition 260, 263, 345, 436; and man-hauling 435, 440; return with support party 440, 442–3, 502

Crichton-Somerville, D. M., considers skis 'overrated' as transport 138

Crozier, Cape: Royds' sledge journey to 153–4, 167, 180; winter journey to 375, 380n

Curzon, Lord 514, 527; insult to Amundsen 538

Daily Chronicle 524; Amundsen's story in 511, 517

Daily Mail 352–3

Daily Telegraph 233, 301

Dalrymple Rock 95

Danco (member of De Gerlache's expedition) 67, 71

Danish Greenland Literary Expedition 96

Dartmouth, Britannia Royal Naval College 120, 121

Darwin Major Leonard 182, 234, 235, 267–8; on explorer's freedom to go anywhere 235, 353; and Amundsen's success 515

Daugaard-Jensen, Jens 210, 247; helps to obtain Polar dogs 209–12, 276, 281–2, 306

David, Professor Edgeworth 232, 255

Davies, F. E. C., *Terra Nova* shipwright on Scott's Polar expedition 267, 313, 350

Day, Bernard: mechanic on Scott's last expedition 256, 263, 311, 502; start from Cape Evans 388; return 396

De Gerlache, Lieutenant Adrien 76, 157; plans Antarctic expedition 60–61; aim to winter in Antarctic 63, 68–9; departure 64; discovery of De Gerlache Strait 67; and first Antarctic sledging journey 68; first Antarctic camp 68; finds pack ice 68–9; tricks crew into wintering in Antarctic 68–72; rift with Amundsen over command 72–3; end of expedition 74; his achievement 74–5

De Gerlache Strait 65, 67

De La Roquette Islands 97

Debenham, Frank, geologist on Scott's Polar expedition 256, 311, 372, 374, 391, 454

Dell, A. B., as dog-driver 166

Devil's Dance-Floor (later Devil's Ballroom) 426–7, 466

Devil's Glacier 424, 426, 453, 466, 467

Devonport: Scott family home at 'Outlands' 119, 124; Scott on duty at 229, 230

Dewar, Vice Admiral K. G. B. 121

Diesels Motorer Co., Stockholm 205

diet 36, 83–6, 164–5, 171, 246, 362–3 476, 478, 545

Dietrichsen, Leif 541

Discovery: design of 137–8, 159; launching of 146; Scott's expedition on 147, 148–90, 222, 228, 242–3, 259, 338–9, 341, 430, 437, 440; inefficient engines 148–9; leak 149; winter quarters 152–4, 156–65, 176–83, 216, 337, 346, 348–9; discipline on 157–9, 217–18, 255; technical defects 158–60; magazine 159; scurvy among sledging parties 163–5, 190, 361, 369–70; relief of ships sent to 176–8, 182; return 184; criticism of scientific results 229, 349; sold to Hudson's Bay Company 235, 270; in same berth as *Terra Nova* 270; expedition's Furthest South passed by Amundsen 404

Ditlev-Simonsen, Olav 92

Dobrowolski, Antoine 64, 74–5

dogs and dog-driving 87, 95, 104, 114, 137ff, 162ff, 180ff, 208ff, 247–8, 276, 296ff, 305ff, 325–6, 330, 355ff, 369, 376ff, 400ff, 420ff, 440ff, 455–6, 463–4, 493–4, 501–2

Domville, Lieutenant (later Admiral Sir) Barry 522

Don Pedro Christophersen 416, 417; Mount 420, 421, 422

Douglas, Admiral 135

Drygalski, Erich von, and German Antarctic expedition 141, 157, 185

Duncan, Isadora 226

Eagle City (Alaska) 113, 114, 115, 116

Eckroll, Martin, rejects Amundsen's application to join Spitsbergen expedition 43-4

Edward VII 146, 147, 232-3; as Prince of Wales 129; patronage of Scott 184; Amundsen's audience with 203; sanctions Shackleton's Polar expedition 218; death 268

Egerton, Captain (later Rear Admiral) George Le Clerc 132, 136, 220, 522, 528

Ellsworth, Lincoln 357-8, 535-6; abortive flight to North Pole 535; finances trans-Polar airship flight 536

Empress of India, H.M.S., Scott as torpedo lieutenant on 131

Endeavour (Captain Cook's ship) 20

Endurance, crushed by ice in Weddell Sea 526-7

Engelstad, Ole 205, 417

Enterprise, H.M.S. 92

Erebus, Mount 153, 312-13, 339, 397; discovery of 23; ascent of 232

Erebus (Ross's ship) 23

Erichsen, Mylius 96

Eriksen, Alfred 245

Eskimos: on King William Land 100-104, 106-8; culture of 102-4; igloo-building 103; fur clothing 104-6, 326-7; dogs 104-5; spring migration 105-6; Amundsen's relationship with 110-11, 295; sledge preparation 110-11, 295

Esquimalt (Canadian Naval base) 121-3

Essex, H.M.S., Scott in command of 226

Etretat 229

Evans, Sub-Lieutenant E. R. G. R. (later Admiral Lord Mountevans) 178, 261, 267, 339-40, 342-3, 371, 499, 524; applies to join Scott's expedition (1906) 222, 258; discards own Antarctic plans to join Scott as second in command 258; and jettisoning of Skelton 266; to captain Terra Nova to New Zealand 271, 308; on sledging committee 290; antagonism with Scott 309, 372-3, 389, 345-6, 439; hurt by Scott's taking command from Cape Town 308-9, 372-3; takes command during storm 313; forced march after digging out depots 376; in charge of motor-sledge party 388-9, 395; and man-hauling 435, 438; increasing tension with Scott 438-9; Scott's plan to break him

and get rid of him 438-40; return with support party 439, 443-4, 502; near-death from scurvy 502-3; return to England 513; in command of Terra Nova 522

Evans, Mrs. E. R. G. R. 308

Evans, Petty Officer Edgar 180-81; on Scott's Polar expedition 260, 376, 485-6; Scott's favouritism towards 309-10, 373, 438; depot-laying journey 338; improvises snow-shoes 431; and man-hauling 435, 440; chosen for final party 437; cuts hand 439-40, 478, 487; aware of leader's confusion 487; mental and physical failing 487-9; collapse and death 489-90. 499

Evans, Hugh Blackwell 129

Evans, Cape (Scott's base): Terra Nova's landing at 313-14; establishment of base 338; depot journey from 338-46; Scott's risky crossing to, from Hut Point 349; climate 360; diet 361-2; wintering at 367-76, 390; contrast with Framheim 370; motor sledges leave 389, 391; telephone link with Hut Point 391; main party's departure from 400, 440; Scott's confusing orders left at 501-3; last winter at 517-18

Farthest North (Nansen) 162

Feather, Thomas 180, 181

Fefor, motor sledge trials at 254, 262, 264-6

Ferrar, Hartley: as geologist on Scott's Discovery expedition 143, 152, 165, 171; Scott's dislike of 158

Ferrar Glacier 180

Field, Captain (later Admiral) Mostyn, on Scott's deficiencies 135, 230, 432

Filchner, Wilhelm, understanding with Scott over Antarctic expeditions 213

First Crossing of Greenland, The (Nansen) 153, 167

Fisher, Admiral Sir John: as First Sea Lord 184, 228; little interest in Antarctic exploration 184

Fisher, Commander (late Admiral Sir) William Wordsworth 219

Ford (officers' steward on Scott's 1901 expedition) 153

Fort Egbert (Alaska) 114

Fram: building of 43, 295-6; Nansen's voyage in, drifting in ice floe across Polar basin 43, 56, 62, 68, 115, 195, 292, 358-9; Sverdrup's expedition on 87-8, 185-6, 193, 223-4, 277, 357; insulation and ventilation 159-60; promised to Amundsen by Nansen 195, 196, 531; Amundsen's plan for Polar expedition on 199-204; financing and supplying of 200-204; made over to Amundsen 204-5; preparation of 205, 208, 253-4, 273, 278; conversion to diesel propulsion 205, 211, 393; destination changed to South Pole 208-9, 279-80, 301; personnel 247-50, 252, 291; departure 274, 278; preliminary North Atlantic cruise 269-70; embarkation of dogs 278; uneasy atmosphere 278-9; delay for repairs at Madeira 283; crew told of real destination 283-8; sledges 290, 292, 356-7; preparations for South Polar journey 290, 292, 296-7; comparison with *Terra Nova* 292, 296-7, 337; transport of dogs 295-8; mastery of bad weather 296-7, 312-13, 495; crosses Antarctic Circle 297; passage through pack ice 297; enters Bay of Whales 298, 315; sledge shuttle service, to establish base 319; meeting with *Terra Nova* 322-4, 340; Amundsen's farewell to 325-6; homeward voyage 325, 350-51, 516; oceanographic cruise 325, 352-3; return to Framheim base 492-3; return to Tasmania 493-6, 510; sails to Buenos Aires and Norway 516-17; final resting place in Oslo 532

Framheim (Amundsen's base): building of 225-7, 322; naming of 324; completion of 327-8; depot journeys from 325-36, 346; working routine 354-5; morale-building 357; climate 360; diet 362; contrast with Cape Evans 370; false start from 378-82; final departure from 386, 391; return to, from Pole 461-74, 491; farewell dinner and departure from 493; disappearance of 543

Franklin, Captain Sir John 93, 157; discovery of North-West Passage 23-4; 77, 94, 96-7, 111; as Amundsen's inspiration 33, 55; expeditions in search of 93, 127, 137

Franklin Strait 89

Franz Josef Land, Jackson-Harmsworth expedition to 44, 61, 77, 128, 255

French Antarctic Expedition 144

Fridtjof Nansen, Mount 416, 422, 469

Fuchs, Sir Vivian 151, 542

Furthest North: Nansen's 62, 140; Nares's 128, 131; Savoy's 140; Vikings' 18

Furthest South: Borchgrevink's 140, 152, 156; Cook's 20-21; Japanese 'Dash Patrol's' 492n; Scott's 152, 157, 172, 177, 182, 185, 445-6; Shackleton's 233, 256, 428, 442, 445, 451

Furthest West, Scott's 180-82

Gade, F. Herman 197, 529, 535; Amundsen's letters to 199, 201, 208, 530, 535; told of Amundsen's plan to seek South Pole 276-7

Gade, Ruth 409n

Garvin, J. L. 514

'Gates of Hell' 424

Geikie, Sir Archibald 230

Geographical Journal 448, 523

George V 515; as Duke of York 129

George V Land 288n

German Antarctic Expedition 141, 157

Girev, Dmetri, dog-driver on Scott's Polar expedition 306, 370, 395-6, 433, 438, 502, 505, 517-18

Gjertsen, Lieutenant Frederick: *Fram* second mate 248, 278, 282-3, 295, 495; takes brief course in surgery 248; and Amundsen's revelation of South Pole as real aim 277, 283, 298; and *Terra Nova's* arrival in Bay of Whales 322-3

Gjøa 88; Amundsen's achievement of North-West Passage on 82-112, 194, 495; training cruise 83-4; as early motor-driven ship 84; preparation of 88, 89-91; crew 89-90, 93-4; 'spontaneous discipline' 94, 156-7; frozen in for two years 99-111; scurvy prevention 100, 163; final lap of North-West Passage 112; third winter frozen in 112; reaches San Francisco 117; clearing of debts on 198-9

Gjøahavn (King William Land), Amundsen's two years frozen in on 99-111

Glacier Tongue 340

Glassford, Major W. A., and disclosure of Amundsen's exclusive telegram 114-15, 290

Godhavn 95

Goschen, George (later Viscount) 134-5

Gould, Laurence 543

Graham Land 21-2, 54, 63, 68; Nordenskiöld expedition to 141; Charcot expedition to 145, 223

Gran, Gerhard 40

Gran, Tryggve 267, 311, 322, 339, 367, 370; inspired by Shackleton to organize Antarctic expedition 263-4; Nansen's anxiety over 263; meets Scott 263; converts him to use of skis 264; accepts his offer to join expedition 265, 266; and *Terra Nova's* departure 270; and news of Amundsen's rival expedition 299-300, 302-3; opens ski school on ice floe 313; and Scott's attitude to skis 342; depot-laying journey 343, 344, 345; Scott's public dressing-down of 348; Wilson's advice to 348-9; and Scott's attitude to dogs 369; misgivings over Scott's plans 376; skiing performance 392; Scott's farewell to 392; impression of Lashly 437; dreams of receiving news of Amundsen's success 454; and discovery of dead 518-21

Great Ice Barrier *see* Ross Ice Barrier

Greely, Brigadier General Adolphus 115

Greenland: first crossing by Nansen 35–7, 42n, 62, 87, 138, 195; Peary's crossing of 41–2, 137, 210; Polar dogs from 208, 211–12, 276

Greenwich, Royal Naval College 121, 125, 131

Gregory, Professor J. W. 141–2

Grieg, Edvard 40, 141

Guatemala City 121

Guilbaud, Captain René 541

Gustavson, Betty 29, 39, 41, 197–8, 241, 358

Haakon VII of Norway 115, 200, 300; Amundsen's letter to, on reaching Pole 460, 469, 482, 521; contribution to expedition 493; told in confidence of success 510

Haakonshallen 411

Hagen's (sporting goods manufacturer) 263, 293–4, 356

Halley's comet 268

Hamburg, Deutsche Seewarte in 80, 86–7

Hamilton, Admiral Sir Vesey 194

Hampton Court, Scott's wedding at Chapel Royal 229

Hamsun, Knut 40

Handsley, A. B. (of *Discovery*) 180–81

Hankey, Captain Maurice (later Lord) 219

Hans Egede (Danish ship) 207

Hansen, Godfred, as Amundsen's second-in-command on North-West Passage expedition 91, 100, 103, 106–12; journey to Victoria Land 111, 189, 222

Hansen, Ludvig, tinsmith on *Fram* 295, 395

Hanssen, Helmer 90–91, 94, 296, 353; as navigator on North-West Passage expedition 91, 94, 103, 294, 363; as dog-driver 105, 106–7, 116, 248, 334; hunting trips into Mackenzie Delta 116; dog-driver on Amundsen's Polar expedition 248, 277, 403, 405, 409, 421, 446; worried by 'observation' hut 278; and revelation of South Pole as real aim 285, 286; in landing party 295; slaughters seals 321; on depot-laying journeys 325–6, 330, 332–3; as 'igloo sheriff' 354; work on sledges 358; and false start 381, 383–4; frostbitten 383, 385; fresh start 386; fall into crevasse 401; and Amundsen's new scheme to lay depots 403; and climb to Plateau 411, 415–16; and last lap to Pole 422, 424–6; and 'final onslaught' 446; first in running order 450, 453–5; arrival at Pole 454, 456, 458–9; and journey back to *Fram* 464, 466–7, 471, 491; on Scott's man-hauling 527–8

Hardangervidda (Norway) 254; Amundsen's attempted crossings 48–50, 53, 56–9, 326, 450

Harmsworth, Alfred (later Lord Northcliffe) 44, 128, 143

Harwich Yacht Club 146

Hassel, Sverre: dog-driver on Amundsen's Polar expedition 277, 363, 366, 378, 384, 405, 409; agrees to go South 281; in landing party 295, 320, 325, 329; depot-laying 330; creation of four- or five-man tents 334; creation of under-cover paraffin store 356; and false start 382–3, 384: frostbitten 385; fresh start 385–6; fall into crevasse 401; critical of Amundsen 415; abandons sledge 421; finds natural entrance to 'basement' 425: as forerunner 451; and 'final onslaught' 452; 'boxing' of Pole 457; at Pole 458: and journey back 464, 468, 470; death while visiting Amundsen 540

Hávamál (Norse poem) 391–2

Heart of the Antarctic, The (Shackleton) 297, 325, 365, 367, 398, 430, 434

Heiberg, Axel 281; appeals for financial help for Amundsen 193, 201–2

Heinemann, William 517

Helland-Hansen, Professor Bjørn 199, 250, 423, 460, 512; told of Amundsen's real plan to go south 277, 280, 289; breaks news to Nansen 281, 300

Helland-Hansen Mountains 422

Herbert, W. W. 415

Herbert Range 409n

Herschel Island 112–13, 114

Hillary, Sir Edmund 151

Hinks, A. R., seminar on determining position near Pole 447

Hobart (Tasmania) 290, 516; *Fram*'s voyage from Bay of Whales to 495–6, 510–11

Hodgson, Thomas Vere, as marine biologist on Scott's *Discovery* expedition 143, 149, 177, 182–3

Holst, Axel 246n

Holst, Vilhelm 49

Hooper (steward on Scott's Polar expedition) 389, 396, 502

Hooper, Mount 395, 501

Hope, Mount 434

Horten 446–7; *Fram* refitting at 198, 205, 248, 272–3

Howard de Walden, Thomas Scott-Ellis, Lord 223, 224

Hudson's Bay Company 235

Huggins, Sir William 145

Huntley and Palmer's 476

Hut Point (old *Discovery* winter quarters) 338, 341, 345, 349, 367, 392, 502; telephone link with Cape Evans 391; Cherry-

Garrard's return to 498; memorial cross on Observation Hill 522
Hvaler (Norway) 24–5, 27
Hvidsten (Norway): Amundsen's birthplace 26; holidays at 29–30

Ibsen, Henrik 36, 40, 56, 195, 251
In Memoriam (Tennyson) 429
International Geographical Congress: Sixth (1895) 60; Seventh (1899) 137
Investigator, H.M.S., in search for Franklin 93, 127
Italia (airship), Nobile's Polar flight and crash in 539–42

Jackson, Frederick, expedition to Franz Josef Land 44, 62, 77, 128
James Ross Strait 105
Jason (sealer) 54, 59, 61
Johannesen, Hans Christian 83
Johansen, Hjalmar: with Nansen on journey over Arctic ice 61-2, 81, 250, 291-2, 366; applies to join Amundsen's Polar expedition 248: drink problem 249-50, 382-3, 529; reluctantly accepted by Amundsen 250, 278; compares atmosphere with that on Nansen's voyage 278, 358-9; and revelation of South as real aim 288; antagonism to Amundsen 296, 364, 382-3; and attitude to dogs 296, 360-61; in landing party 296, 320; on depotlaying journeys 325-7, 330, 334-7, 338; quarrel with Prestrud 329; recognizes Amundsen's personal magnetism 357-8; packs provisions 362-3; Amundsen's wary treatment of 364; warns against tooearly start 366, 377-9; and false start 380, 381-4; outburst against Amundsen 382-3; dismissal from journey to South Pole 384-5, 496, 516; on expedition to King Edward VII Land 384, 492-3, 496; bids Amundsen farewell on second departure 386; and Amundsen's return 491; sent home after mutiny 516-17; suicide 528-9, 539

Kainan Maru, Japanese expedition in 492
Kaiogolo (Eskimo) 102
Kaiser Wilhelm II Land, discovery of 156
Keltie, Scott 88, 177; and Amundsen's scheme for Polar expedition 202-4; and Shackleton's South Pole expedition 217, 232; and news of Amundsen's real aim for South Pole 301, 303, 343, 353; and Amundsen's success 513
Keohane, Petty Officer: with Scott's Polar expedition 392-3, 431; and man-hauling up Beardmore Glacier 435; return with supporting party 436; forlorn rescue attempt 518

Kerr, Captain (later Admiral) Mark 230
Kerr, Lord Walter 135, 184
King Edward VII Land (now King Edward VII Peninsula) 218, 228, 235-6, 350, 366; Scott's discovery of 150; as base for Scott's Polar expedition 234, 241; Evans's plan to explore 259, 267; Campbell's intended exploration of 267, 291, 323, 344n; collapse of exploration idea 323-4, 337; Prestrud's expedition to 383-4, 493
King Haakon VII's Plateau 455, 461
King Point (Yukon), *Gjøa* frozen in at 113, 116, 117
King William Land, Amundsen's two years on 99-111
Kings Bay (Spitsbergen) 541; Amundsen's flight to Alaska from 536
Kinsey, Joseph (later Sir Joseph), as Scott's agent 255, 389
Kipling, Rudyard 188
Koettlitz, Dr. Reginald: on Scott's *Discovery* expedition 142, 143, 157, 159, 177; considered 'good-natured duffer' by Scott 148; sledge journey to Cape Crozier 154-6, 167; insistence on fresh meat 164, 190
Kristensen, Captain Leonard 60
Kristiansand 275-6
Krogskogen (Norway), Amundsen's ski tour across 38
Kutchin, Alexander, and Amundsen's revelation of South Pole as real aim 284, 286-7

Ladyless South, The (*Belgica* magazine) 72
Lapataïa 64
Lapps, materials and equipment 85-6
Larsen, Captain C. A. 54
Larsen Ice Shelf, Nordenskjöld's traverse of 166, 168, 223
Larvik 43, 88, 139
Lashly, Leading Stoker William 181; on Scott's Polar expedition 260, 436, 437; start from Cape Evans 389; and manhauling 435, 439; return with support party 442-3, 502
Latham 47 (French aircraft); Amundsen's fatal crash in 541
Lawrence, T. E. 185, 189
Lecointe, Georges, in De Gerlache's expedition 65, 69, 71-4, 76
Leopold II of the Belgians 61
Levick (surgeon) 322
Lillehammer, motor sledge trials at 232, 254
Lillie, Dennis, biologist on Scott's Polar expedition 256, 321

Lind, James 163–4
Lindstrøm, Adolf Henrik: as cook on Amundsen's North-West Passage expedition 88, 90; on Amundsen's Polar expedition 248, 354, 363, 366, 377–8, 385; in landing party 295, 328; as prince of major-domos 334–5, 336; diet provided by 361–2; protests at too-early start 386; work on sledgemeters 450; and Amundsen's return from Pole 491; farewell dinner at Framheim 493
Little America (Byrd's Antarctic base) 543
London: Amundsen's lecture in 194; other visits to 202, 206
Longhurst, Cyril, secretary to Scott's *Discovery* expedition 144
Longstaff, Llewellyn 129, 143, 216
Loti, Pierre 64
Lübeck 206
Lund, Anton, as navigator on Amundsen's North-West Passage expedition 90, 97, 100
Lund, Henry 113
Lysaker, Nansen's home (Polhøgda) in 273
Lyttelton (New Zealand) 149, 183, 280, 290, 307, 350, 522

Macartney, Sir William Ellison- 124, 135, 183: Scott's last letter to 508
Macartney, Ettie Ellison- (*née* Scott) (Scott's sister) 123, 134, 225
McClintock, Admiral Sir Leopold 88–9, 106, 134, 137–8
McClure, Captain Robert Le Mesurier 127; first to complete North-West Passage 92
McKenna, Captain James 112
Mackenzie Delta 116
McMurdo Sound: Scott's winter quarters in (1902–4) 153–4, 156–83, 216, 313, 338, 341; Scott-Shackleton controversy over, as base for South Pole attempts 215–18, 227, 242–3; Shackleton forced to land at 226–7, 233; Scott's plan for main base at 242, 243, 263, 285, 291; rumoured to be Amundsen's destination 301, 303; *Terra Nova*'s arrival in 313–14; geological party at 340, 348
Macquarie Island 288n
Madeira 147, 149, 280–81; *Fram*'s delayed departure from 282–6
Madison (Wisconsin) 525
Magdalena (sealer), Amundsen's season on 50–53
Magellan, Ferdinand 18
Majestic, H.M.S. 132; Scott as torpedo lieutenant on 124, 219
man-hauling 104–5, 187–8, 376, 395, 434, 435–40, 442, 454, 465, 479, 518–19, 527
Man's Head, Cape 315, 492, 494

Manchuria, ponies from 305–7
Mandeville, Sir John 162
Marie (Bouvet's ship) 20
Markham, Captain (later Vice-Admiral Sir) Albert 131, 134, 135; disapproves of Amundsen's Polar expedition 202
Markham, Sir Clements 88–9, 139, 141, 147, 165, 211, 223–4, 235, 526; rule of 'no ski. No dogs' 45, 138–9, 188; Amundsen introduced to 88; character and early Naval career 125, 128, 129–30; passion for Polar exploration 125, 126, 128, 132; President of Royal Geographical Society 128; seeks money for Antarctic expedition 128, 129, 137; search for commander 129, 130, 133–6; first encounter with Scott as midshipman 130; later meetings 131; and Scott's appointment 134–6, 142–3; outmoded methods 137–9; at loggerheads with Royal Society 142–3, 145–6; and appointment of officers 144, 145; names Scott's *Discovery* 146; his ideas 'ditched' by Scott 152, 153, 160; sends relief ship 176; secret instructions to Scott to remain 177; and rumpus over second relief expedition 183; continued support of Scott 184–5; endorses Amundsen's Polar expedition 202–3; lukewarm over Scott's plan for Antarctic expedition 219, 234–5; impression of Skelton 222–3; impugns Shackleton's veracity 233; manoeuvres Evans into position of Scott's second in command 258–9; persuades Scott to take on Bowers 260; sees *Terra Nova* depart 270; and news of Amundsen's rival expedition 301, 302, 353; no final message from Scott 508; denunciation of Amundsen 513
Markham, Lady 146, 270
Markham (later Scott) Islands, discovery of 189
Markham, Mount, discovery of 186
Marshall, Dr. Eric 445
Marshall Range 434
Matheson Point (King William Land) 107
Matty Island 105, 108, 112
Maud, Queen, of Norway 200
Maud: Amundsen's Arctic drift attempt in 533; North-East Passage in 533
Mawson, Douglas (later Sir Douglas): declines Scott's invitation 255; his own expedition 288n, 494; use of wireless 288n
May, Admiral of the Fleet Sir William 184, 221
Meares, Cecil Henry 305, 344; as dog-driver on Scott's Polar expedition 305, 311, 345, 396, 434, 442–3; purchase of dogs and ponies 305–6; criticism of Scott's 'sentimentality' 368–9; clique with Atkinson

and Oates 375; travels in conditions considered impossible by Scott 393-4; contempt for Scott 395, 396, 435; hard run back from Glacier 433-5, 501; quarrel with Scott 438-9; determined to go home with ship 438-9, 503-4

Melbourne 299, 302

Melville Bay 95

Mid-Barrier Depot 433

Mill, Hugh Robert 152, 232; impression of Amundsen 193; on Scott's lack of results 523

Millais, Sir John 198

Mizner, Addison 121-2

Mizner, Lansing Bond 121-2

Mogg, Captain William, and sledging journey from Herschel Island to Eagle City 113-14

Montevideo 516

Moore, Admiral Sir Arthur 236

Morgenen (sealer, later *Morning*, q.v.) 51-2

Morning (former sealer *Morgenen*) 51-2, 189; as *Discovery* relief 176-7, 180, 182-3, 221

Morning Post 301

motor transport 152, 223-5, 254, 264, 314, 324, 389, 392

Mulock, Lieutenant George 178

Munch, Edvard 40

Murray, George 148

Mussolini, Benito 539

My Life as an Explorer (Amundsen) 537

Nansen, Alexander 115, 197, 351

Nansen, Eva, 43, 195, 197, 214

Nansen, Fridtjof 40, 52, 87, 112, 118, 145-7, 197-8, 232, 275-6; and first crossing of Greenland 35-7, 41-2, 167, 195; use of skis 36, 154; expedition on *Fram* by drifting across Polar basin 43, 56, 61, 68, 195, 292-3, 358-9; reaches furthest north 61-2, 140; retreat over drifting pack ice 62, 248; as national ideal 62-3, 90, 139; his goodwill secured by Amundsen 75-6, 88-9; approves of Amundsen's expedition to North Magnetic Pole 79-80, 85, 87-8; and campaign for Norwegian independence 89-90, 195; support for Amundsen 89, 92, 114, 117; notified of Amundsen's NWP navigation 114; use of dogs 138, 139, 185-6, 526; Scott's introduction to 139-40, 141; quarrel with Borchgrevink 140; farewell letter to Scott (1901) 147; Scott's farewell letter to 149; use of Amundsen for political propaganda 192, 194; dream of conquering South Pole 195-6, 273-4, 293; agrees to let Amundsen have *Fram* 196-8; deceived over Amundsen's plans 212, 251;

and Johansen's appeals for help 249-50; perturbed at Scott's plans 262-3; contrives Gran's joining expedition 262, 263-4; sadness at *Fram*'s departure 274; told of Amundsen's real aim for South Pole 279-81, 300; refuses to divulge Amundsen's destination to Scott 303-4; and Scott's forebodings 310; enthusiasm for *Fram*'s oceanographic cruise 352; defends Amundsen against attacks 353, 492-3, 511, 530; on Amundsen's success 509-10; affair with Kathleen Scott 510-11; concern at British antagonism to Amundsen 513-14; Amundsen's thanks to 516; on Scott's refusal to take advice 526; and Johansen's suicide 528-9; and Amundsen's abandonment of Arctic drift 530-31; valedictory oration to Amundsen 536

Nansen, Liv 196-7

Nares, Captain (later Admiral) Sir George 127, 138, 163

National Geographic Society 537

Nelson (biologist on Scott's Polar expedition) 256

Netsiliks *see* Eskimos

Neumayer, Professor Georg 80, 109

New Land (Sverdrup) 184, 255

New York 197

New York Times, The 207-8, 211, 511

Newnes, Sir George 128-9

Nikolievsk (Siberia) 305, 306

Nilsen, Lieutenant Thorvald: as second in command of *Fram* 205, 251, 287-8, 297-9, 323-4; and Amundsen's revelation of South Pole as real aim 277, 283-4; starts refresher course in English 296; comment on *Terra Nova* 322-3; takes command of *Fram* on homeward voyage 325-6, 350-51, 516; oceanographic cruise 325, 352; financial distress 351-2; and Amundsen's return to *Fram* 492; translates Amundsen's lecture into English 495; on Johansen's suicide 528-9

Nilsen Plateau 422, 423, 465n, 466

Nimrod 313; Shackleton's expedition in 218, 223, 227, 232-5, 242, 256

Nobile, Umberto: *Norge* trans-Polar flight 536-7; Amundsen's vendetta against 537-9; disappearance on flight to North Pole 539-41; rescue 541

Nødtvedt, Jacob (*Fram* second engineer) 291

Nordenskiöld, Baron Adolf Erik, first to navigate North-East Passage 35, 60

Nordenskjöld, Otto: and Swedish Antarctic expedition 141, 166, 183, 186; traverse of Larsen Ice Shelf 166, 168, 222; use of dogs 222

Nordmarka (Norway), Amundsen's ski tours across 38, 46

Norge (airship), trans-Polar flight in 536

North-East Passage: first navigation of 18, 35, 61; Amundsen's navigation of, 533

North-West Passage, 18; Franklin's discovery of, 23, 36 Amundsen's ambition to navigate 77, 81; his achievement of 82–112, 187–8, 191–5, 203–4, 495, 540, 542–3; McClure's completion of 93; Amundsen's lectures on 193–4, 197–8; lessons from 326

North-West Passage, The (Amundsen) 188–90, 198, 255

North-West Passage, The (Millais) 198

Northcliffe, Lord (formerly Alfred Harmsworth, q.v.) 244

Norvegia expedition 527n

Norway Glacier 423, 465, 466

Norwegian Geographical Society 80, 82; Amundsen unveils North Polar expedition plan to 199

O'Reilly, Kathleen, Scott's flirtation with, 123

O'Reilly, Judge Peter 123

Oamaru (New Zealand) 522

Oates, Mrs. Caroline: Wilson's letter to 506, 523; bitterness towards Scott 523–4

Oates, Lawrence Edward Grace 310, 327–8, 429; character 261, 307, 373; volunteers for Scott's Polar expedition 261–2; arrival on *Terra Nova* 262–3; reaction to Amundsen's rival expedition 304; as horse expert 305, 311, 340; not consulted on choice of horses 307; criticizes Meares' purchase 307–8; dislike of Scott 307–8, 390–91; depot-laying journeys 340, 342–3, 345; appalled at Scott's muddle and mawkishness 342–4, 375–6; hatred of foreigners 344; psychological leadership passes to 373–4; cult of Napoleon 374–5; clique with Atkinson and Meares 375; depression over Scott's inadequacies 390–91; disagreements with Scott 393–4; shoots ponies 397, 433; tribute to Shackleton 398; and man-hauling 435; 439; selected for final party 442; reluctance and unfitness to go on 443, 501; contempt for Scott 443; gloom on approaching Pole 479–80; and discovery of Amundsen's prior arrival 480; journey back 485, 498–501, 504–5; frostbite 486, 498, 500, 504–5; and Evans's breakdown 486–9; becomes 'a terrible hinderance' 500, 506; death 506, 521; legend of self-sacrifice 506, 524

Oates Land, discovery of 350

Olav Yrygvason, medieval Norse hero 62

Ole Engelstad, Mount 417, 469

Omel'chenko, Anton, groom on Scott's Polar expedition 306, 307, 370

One Ton Depot 343, 433–4; plan for dogs to bring supplies to 395–6, 502; relief party turns back from 504–5, 517, 520; Scott's last camp near 507–9, 519–21

Oscar II of Sweden–Norway 115; patronage of 89, 91

Oscar, Amundsen completes sea-time on 77

Oscar II Land, discovery of 54

Ottawa 530

Ottley, Rear Admiral Sir Charles 219

Paget, Francis, Dean 127

Pall Mall Gazette 514

Pandora (yacht) 89

paraffin tanks 'creeping' of 291, 312

Parry, Captain, William Edward 157, 171; as original Pole seeker 22; use of dogs 138

Pauss, Olav 300

Peary, Robert Edwin 34, 41, 64, 194, 269; use of dogs 137, 162, 185, 515; claim to have reached North Pole 207, 209–10, 243–4, 288, 455, 457, 459, 537; denunciation of Cook 210, 446; assumption of prescriptive right to certain areas 210, 216; attempt to save Scott from errors of Antarctic plan 268, 515; congratulates Amundsen 515

Pêcheur d'Islande (Loti) 64

pemmican 86, 246, 331, 363, 464, 468

Pennell, Lieutenant, on *Terra Nova* 322, 323, 350, 522

Pensacola 77

Phoenix (J. E. Amundsen's ship) 26

Polheim (Amundsen's Polar camp) 460, 482

ponies 255, 261–2, 305–6, 340–43, 345, 348, 367–8, 392, 396, 431

Ponting, Herbert, photographer on Scott's Polar expedition 311, 314

Port Chalmers 310

Portsmouth, torpedo training school at 123

Potsdam 86–7, 89

Prestrud, Lieutenant Kristian: on Amundsen's Polar expedition 247, 277, 321; in landing party 298, 322–3; suggests Framheim as name of base 324; on depot-laying journeys 325–6, 330, 331–2; quarrel with Johansen 328–9; prepares navigation for Polar journey 354; gives English course 360; and false start 382–4; frostbitten 382–3, 385; delay in return 382–3; dismissed from journey to South Pole 384; leads expedition to King Edward VII Land 384, 492–3; and Amundsen's return 491

Priestley, Sir Raymond 338, 482; in Scott's Polar expedition 256, 311, 312–13, 323,

396–7; and meeting with *Fram* in Bay of Whales 322–3, 336–7
Pytheas, as first recorded Polar explorer 18

Queen Maud Land, discovery of 527
Queen Maud Mountains 407, 461, 543

Racovitza, Emile-G. 63
Rae, Dr. John 83, 137
Rasmussen, Knud 96, 139
Rawson, Vice Admiral Sir Harry 148
Rawson, Wyatt 135
Rawson Mountains 465n
Recessional (Kipling) 118
Resolution (Captain Cook's ship) 21
Reutsch, Dr. 301
Reutsch, Mrs. 140
Richmond, Admiral Sir Herbert 161
Riiser-Larsen, Captain Hjalmar 527, 539
Riley, Lieutenant (E) Edgar W. 311
Ristvedt, Peder 83–4; engineer on Amundsen's North-West Passage expedition 86, 90, 103–4; on final journey to Pole 106–10; journey to Victoria Land 110–11; Amundsen's sense of obligation to 197
Rønne (*Fram* sailmaker) 289, 290; makes lightweight emergency tent 295, 460
Roosevelt, Theodore 515
Roosevelt Island 242
Ross, Sir James Clark 54, 157; reaches North Magnetic Pole 22, 80, 108; discovery of Antarctic ice shelf 23, 242, 295, 320
Ross Ice Barrier: discovery of 23, 140; first landing on 140, 242; Scott's eastward course along edge (1902) 150–52; Scott's sledge attempt on 156–7, 171; his Southern Journey with Wilson and Shackleton over 165, 166–75, 185–6, 215, 392–3; Royds' journey south-east over 189; Amundsen's decision to land on 242–4; Amundsen reaches 297–9, 315; base established on 319, 322, 333–4; splendid skiing conditions 232–3, 326, 333–4; crevasses 400–401; afloat 407–8
Ross Sea: discovery of 22; first voyage to 60; Scott reaches (1902) 150; Amundsen's and Scott's intention to attack Pole from 211, 235; *Fram*'s passage through pack ice to 298; Japanese expedition to 302, 491–2; *Terra Nova*'s passage to 313
Rover, H.M.S., Scott a midshipman on 130
Royal Geographical Society 88, 126, 216, 232, 235; Amundsen's lecture on North-West Passage to 117, 194; and Scott's *Discovery* expedition 128, 134–6, 182–3, 220–21; self-perpetuating clique of mediocrities 128; library 161; endorse-

ment of Amundsen's Polar expedition 202–4; discourages Scott's competition with Shackleton 235; contribution to Scott's and Amundsen's Polar expeditions 245; farewell lunch to Scott 269; rejects Cook's aerodynamic tent 295–6; Hinks' seminar at 447; grudging recognition of Amundsen's achievement 515; apparent insult to Amundsen 537–8
Royal Navy: expedition to observe transit of Venus (1769) 18, 20; backwardness and inefficiency 120, 232; expansion 124; Polar exploration as activity for 127–8, 183–4; and scurvy 163; and relief of *Discovery* 182–3; Fisher's sweeping reforms 185; Scott's sense of desertion by 373–4
Royal Society 18, 20, 128; and Scott's *Discovery* expedition 128, 134–6, 182; at loggerheads with Markham 142–3, 145–6
Royal Sovereign, H.M.S. 131
Royal Yacht Squadron 270
Royds, Lieutenant Charles Rawson 136, 157; assistant to Scott on *Discovery* expedition 135, 143, 144, 149, 150, 153, 160, 183; Scott's jealousy of 148, 190; sledge journey to Cape Crozier 154–6, 167, 179–80; on unhappy atmosphere 158; responsible for high morale 158–9; expedition south-east over Barrier 189
Royds, Cape 313
Ruth Gade, Mount 409n

Saetre (biscuit manufacturers) 476
Safety Camp 340, 342, 344
St. Kitts 130
San Francisco 122, 274, 280
Sandefjord 61, 63, 90
Savage Club 234
Savoy, Duke of 139, 140
Saxon, R.M.S. 271
Schmelck, Ludvig 37
Sclater, Dr. Philip 143
Scott, Archibald (brother) 120, 124
Scott, Hannah (mother) 119, 147, 184, 223–4; dominating character 119; Kathleen Scott's dislike of 229; Scott's money left to 507–8
Scott (later Macartney, q.v.), Ettie (sister) 124, 125
Scott, Grace (Monsie) (sister) 123, 124
Scott, John Edward (father) 119, 120; financial trouble 124; death 124
Scott (*née* Bruce), Kathleen (wife) 235, 255, 263, 507–8; first meeting with Scott 225–6; character and background 226, 264–5, 308–9, 510; courtship 226–9; determination to bear hero as son 227, 230; choice of Scott as father of hero-son

Scott, Kathleen – *continued*
228; marriage 229–30; furthers Scott's career 230–31, 258–9; pregnancy 230–31; birth of son Peter 236; and Scott's conversion to skis 265; travels as far as New Zealand 271, 298–9, 307, 309; affair with Nansen 510–11; dislike of Amundsen 511; recognition of his success 514; and the heroic legend 522, 527; granted title of Lady Scott 522–3; Scott's letters to 226–8, 231, 389, 442, 479, 507–8

Scott, Kitty (sister) 124

Scott, Sir Peter Markham (son) birth 236

Scott, Robert (grandfather) 119

Scott, Robert Falcon: ancestry and childhood 119; Naval education 120–21; promotion to lieutenant 120–21; early flirtations 122; torpedo training 122; runs aground 123, 220; family upheaval after father's death 124; as torpedo lieutenant 124, 131; seeks promotion 125, 132–3, 134; encounters with Markham 130–1, 132, 133; seeks command of Antarctic expedition 131, 132–5; appointed to command it 136; promoted commander 136; visits Nansen in Christiania 139–41; unimpressed by other Polar explorers 140–1; choice of officers and crew 143–5; burdened by committees and intrigues 145–6; departure in *Discovery* 147; first sight of Antarctica 150; endangers ship through ignorance of ice 150; winter in Antarctica 152–83; failure of first attempts at sledge travel 156–7; idea of Southern Journey 160–2; belated study of Polar literature 162, 184; experiments with dog-driving 163; his Southern Journey by sledge 165–75, 177, 394, 430; inadequate preparation 166; ignorance of snowcraft 168; conflict with Shackleton 170, 174, 175, 178, 215, 216–17, 255–6; risks comrades' lives in determination to achieve southern record 172, 174; his Furthest South 172, 177, 182, 185, 445; his western sledge journey 180–82, 353–4; return to England 183–4; anxiety over promotion 183; promoted captain 184; his achievement compared with Sverdrup's 185; exculpation and elaboration in his account 185–90, 215; comparisons with Amundsen 190, 219, 235ff, 260, 272ff, 291, 334ff, 356ff, 400, 429–31, 450, 476, 486, 513–14; announces new Antarctic expedition 211–17, 222–4, 235; controversy with Shackleton over use of *Discovery* base for South Pole attempt 215–17, 226; Admiralty mistrust of his ability 218; shore appointment 219; service afloat

219–20; battleship collision 220; learns from *Discovery* setbacks 221–3; belief in motor sledging 221–3; belief in motor sledging 221–3, 263–5; social life 226; courtship of Kathleen Bruce 226–9; marriage 229; his scientific knowledge criticized 230; Admiralty appointment 231–2; envy of Shackleton's success 232, 233, 235, 242; definite steps towards expedition 236, 242; Polar 'race' against Amundsen 242, 289, 299–303, 343, 350, 365–7, 380ff, 400, 452, 461ff, 480–82, 495–6; attempt to meet Amundsen for talk on scientific cooperation 252–3, 265; organization of expedition 253–75; continued mistrust of dogs 255, 262–3, 368, 395; use of ponies 255, 262, 305–6, 340–41; choice of men 255–62, 264; acceptance of paying volunteers 260; conversion to use of skis 263–5; Shackleton fixation 263, 305, 312, 367, 371, 397, 430, 436, 437–8, 439, 444–5, 508; departure 270; reactions to news of Amundsen's real destination 300, 302, 342; quarrels and tension with companions 309, 372–3, 395, 441, 483–4; arrival in McMurdo Sound 314; sinking of motor sledge 314–15; depot journeys 337–46, 348; plans for Polar journey 366–7, 376; lost faith in motor sledges 367–8; decision on man-hauling 367–8 little margin of safety 368, 396, 430, 439, 443–4, 450, 483, 497–8; question of endurance 368, 400, 435–7, 474; his 'Universitas Antarctica', 370; personal crisis 369; farewell letters 389, 391; departure from Cape Evans, 391; forced to admit dogs' superiority to ponies 395, 396; rate of travel 400, 432, 434, 443; four days blizzard-bound 428–32; shooting of ponies 434; manhauling along Beardmore Glacier 434–40, 453–4, 465, 480, 501–2; snowblindness 437–8; risk in adding fifth man to Polar party 440, 443, 475, 501; faulty sledgemeters 450; thirst and starvation on last hundred miles 476, 478–9; discovery of defeat 480–82; return journey 482–90; loses way 485; final stages 496–508; collapse as leader 500; last camp and immolation in tent 506–9; farewell letters 507; self-justifying message to public 508, 520, 522; discovery by search party 518–21; creation of legend 520, 524, 525–7; as heroic bungler 526–7 Amundsen's sense of guilt over 538

characteristics: absentmindedness 342; agnosticism 160; command, unsuitability for 220, 228, 307–8, 312–13; criticism, refused to accept 230, 368, 377; depression, bouts of 227–8, 348, 370–71; emotionalism 158, 164, 342, 437; impatience 148; improvisation, belief in 149, 153, 161, 170, 367, 441; inadequacy, sense of 132, 149; insecurity 158, 160; insight, lack of 159, 169; irrationality 158, 160, 432, 436, 441, 444; isolation 158,160, 179, 369; jealousy 148, 179, 216, 235, 242; judgment, defective 161, 166, 170, 220, 434; leadership, failure in 158, 226, 375, 389–90; literary gifts 185, 188, 371, 525–6; panic, readiness to 151, 158, 183; recklessness 170, 172; responsibility, instinct to evade 156, 180, 220, 435, 501; sentimentality 160, 306, 343, 370; vacillation 166, 338, 370–71

diet 22, 163–5, 170, 476, 478, 544

equipment and clothing 168, 218, 268–9, 392, 431, 449

transport: dogs 139, 146, 163ff, 178ff, 305ff, 340–42, 369, 394ff, 434, 438, 443; motor sledges 224, 255ff, 314, 324ff, 388, 392; ponies 255ff, 305, 340ff, 345, 368, 392ff, 431; skis 139ff, 155, 168, 265, 341–2; sledges 263ff, 340–46, 440

Scott, Rose (sister) 124

Scott (former Markham) Islands, discovery of 189

Scott's Last Expedition (arr. Huxley) 488n

Scottish National Expedition to Weddell Sea 144

scurvy 70–71, 99, 163–4, 171–3, 245–6, 360–61, 487–8, 499, 502

sealing 513

Seven Pillars of Wisdom (Lawrence) 185, 189

Seymour Island 54

Shackleton, Sir Ernest 180, 312, 358, 407, 409; junior officer on Scott's Discovery expedition 143, 147, 150; as psychological leader 158, 161; as Wilson's particular friend 161, 217; journey south with Scott and Wilson 161, 165, 166–75, 186; in charge of dogs 162, 168, 172; conflict with Scott 170, 174, 175, 177, 215–16; scurvy 171, 173; not invited to reach Furthest South 172; collapse 174, 175, 178, 186, 215; invalided home 178, 215–16; traduced in Voyage of the 'Discovery' 186, 215; plan for attempt on South Pole from McMurdo Sound 215–17; agreement to leave McMurdo Sound to Scott 216–17, 226, 227; departure 217; and motor transport 223; growing rivalry with Scott 227, 232–4, 256; forced landing at McMurdo Sound 227, 242–3; gets to within 97 miles of 232, 244, 367, 440, 445; a national hero 232; knighthood 232–3; veracity impugned by Markham 233; and Bay of Whales 243,

298–9, 322–3; determination not to winter on Ross Ice Barrier 243, 299, 321; his risks and mistakes studied by Amundsen 243–4; use of ponies 255; encourages Gran to organize expedition 263; accuses Amundsen of invading Scott's 'sphere of influence' 352–3; Amundsen's extensive criticism of 365; as Scott's 'ghostly rival' 367, 397, 431, 432, 439–40, 445, 507–8; his Furthest South record broken by Amundsen 428, 446; and by Scott 445; pleasure at Amundsen's triumph 513–14; attempted first crossing of Antarctica 526; death 526–7

Shackleton, Lady 261

Shambles Camp, 490

Sheffield Daily Telegraph 272

Shirase, Lieutenant, leader of first Japanese Antartic expedition, 429n

Shireff, Captain (of Williams) 21

Simpson, Dr. (later Sir) George 143; as meteorologist on Scott's Polar expedition 256, 313–14, 371, 376; on Scott's plans 368–9; in command at Camp Evans 396, 502; hands over to Wright 503–4

Simpson Strait 99, 112

Skelton, Engineer Lieutenant Reginald 230, 390, 514; on Discovery expedition 144, 151, 157, 439–40, 472; suggests motor transport 151–2, 221, 222; sledge journey to Cape Crozier 154–5, 167; on Scott's panic rages 158; and unhappy atmosphere 158; westward journey with Scott 178, 181; and development of motor sledge 223–4, 232, 265; discarded in favour of Evans 265–6

skis and skiing 36, 38, 41, 49, 68, 87, 110, 138–9, 154–6, 168, 206, 246, 263, 265, 294, 326, 342, 400, 410, 416, 471, 473-4

sledgemeters 450

sledges and sledging 36, 72, 110–11, 223–4, 254, 262, 264, 266, 290ff, 314ff, 340–46, 356, 376–82, 386, 402–5, 410–12, 425, 439–40

Sledging Problem in the Antarctic, The (Scott) 222

Smith, Reginald John 259, 515

Smith, W. E., designer of Discovery 137

Smith Sound 127

Smith's Island 64

Smyth, Midshipman Thomas C. 131, 133

Snow Island 64, 222n

snow shovels 355

Snowy Hill Island 156

Social Demokraten 272

South Polar Times (Discovery magazine) 159; (Cape Evans magazine) 370

South Shetland Islands 64; discovery of 21

South Victoria Land 68; discovery of 22;

South Victoria Land – *continued*
first landing in (1895) 60, 244; Scott's winter quarters on (1902-4) 152-83; sledge journeys 156-7, 165, 166-75 185-6; Amundsen's plan to land on 280, 303; Campbell expedition to 337-8, 513, 521

Southern Barrier Depot 490, 498

Southern Cross, Borchgrevink's Antarctic expedition in 128, 129, 176

Speyer, Sir Edgar 230; as Scott's expedition treasurer 388-9; Scott's last letter to 508

Spitsbergen 22, 250; first crossing of 137; Amundsen's abortive attempt to fly to, from Alaska 532-3; Amundsen's success in other direction 536

'Spy' 225

Steen, Dr. Axel 80, 281

Steer's Head crevasse system 401, 473

Stefansson, Vilhjalmur 177

Stein, Gertrude 226

Stephenson, Vice Admiral Sir Henry 132

Strathcona, Lord 235

Stubberud, Jørgen: carpenter on Amundsen's Polar expedition 251-2; builds socalled wintering hut 251-2, 273; in landing party 295, 298, 320, 325-6; erects hut at base 320, 327; depot-laying 330, 334; constructs vaults 355; work on sledges 357-8; trick played on dog 360; and false start 381-4; frostbitten 382-3, 385; agrees to go with expedition to King Edward VII Land 383, 492-3; and Amundsen's return from Pole 491

Sundbeck, Knut: *Fram* engineer 277; agrees to go South 287; makes weathercock for base 324

Sverdrup, Otto 184, 255, 261; and use of dogs and skis 87-8, 222; his expedition compared with Scott's *Discovery* 184

Swaffer, Hannen 523

Swedish Antarctic Expedition 140, 156, 184, 222

Swithinbank, Dr. Charles 498n

Talurnakto (Eskimo) 110-11, 378; and icing of sledge runners 110

Taylor, Griffith, geologist on *Terra Nova* 256, 340, 348, 368, 453-4, 503

Tennyson, Alfred, Lord 117, 429, 522

tents 68, 72, 290, 296, 333, 358, 431

Teraiu (Eskimo) 102, 106; instructs Amundsen in igloo-building 102

Terra Nova: as *Discovery* relief 182; chosen by Scott for Polar expedition 235, 254; preparation of 254, 266; personnel 255-62, 264-6, 272, 291; paying volunteers 261; departure 269-70; comparison with *Fram* 291, 296, 297, 322, 337;

reaches Melbourne 299, 302; Australian grant to 302; restowing at Lyttelton 306, 307; departure from New Zealand 310; overcrowded 311; near-foundering in storms 311-12, 350; three weeks in pack ice 313; landing at 'Skuary' (renamed Cape Evans) 313-14; meeting with *Fram* at Bay of Whales 323-4, 340; puts caster party ashore at Cape Adare 337-8; return to New Zealand 350; arrival at Cape Evans 502; returns to New Zealand without Scott 510, 513; return with news of Scott's death 522, 525

Terror (Ross's ship) 22, 23

Terror, Mount 154; discovery of 23

Thousand Days in the Arctic, A (Jackson) 77

Through the First Antarctic Night (Cook) 141

Tidens Tegn 495

Times, The 44, 115, 188, 216, 217, 301; and comparison between Sverdrup and Scott 185; announcement of Scott's Polar expedition 211, 235, 241-2, 266; Nansen's defence of Amundsen in 353; huffy comment on Amundsen's achievement 512; sophistry on Scott disaster 523-4, 527-8

Times Literary Supplement, The, on meteorology of *Discovery* expedition 229-30

Tizard, Captain Thomas 145

Tollefsen (member of De Gerlache's expedition) 74

Torpedo Boat No. 87, Scott's first command 220

Torup, Professor Sophus 86

Transantarctic Mountains 424, 430; Amundsen's crossing of 408-20

Tromsø 81-2, 84, 85, 541

Two Hummocks Island 67

Ugpik ('The Owl') (Eskimo) 110

Ui-te-Rangiora (earliest known Antarctic voyager) 18

Ulysses (Tennyson) 522

United States Antarctic Research Program (1977-8) 407n, 498n

Urdahl, Laurentius 57; attempt to cross Hardangerfjord on skis 46, 48-50

Valborg (ship) 53

Vanity Fair 225

Vardø 61

Venus, transit of (1769) 20

Vernon, H.M.S. (torpedo training school) 123-4, 136

Victoria, Queen 130, 146, 268

Victoria (B.C.) 121, 123

Victoria Land, Hansen's charting of 111, 189, 222

Victorious, H.M.S., Scott in command of 219

Vikings, Polar travels of 18
Vince (*Discovery* seaman) 156
Vitamin B complex 362, 476, 478
Vitamin C deficiency 362; as cause for scurvy 70, 165, 171, 246n, 476, 478, 488, 499, 500
Vogt, Benjamin 352, 353, 513
Voyage of the 'Discovery', The (Scott) 185–90, 195, 211, 217, 296, 325, 368–9; Shackleton traduced in 187, 215; compared with Amundsen's *North-West Passage* 189–90

Wainwright (Alaska), Amundsen's abortive flight from 533
Weddell Sea 21, 65, 68, 156, 213; Scottish National expedition to 144; Shackleton's *Endurance* crushed in 526–7
Wellington 303
Western Mountains (Norway) 374; Amundsen's skiing trip in 46, 48–50
Whales, Bay of: chosen as Amundsen's base 243, 250–51, 275–6, 285, 288–9; *Fram* enters 298–9, 315; meeting with *Terra Nova* in 322–9, 337, 340, 351, 352; *Fram* leaves 493–4; Byrd's expedition to 543
Wharton, Admiral Sir William 136
White Island 343
Whitfield, A. B. (*Discovery* stoker) 182
Whymper, Edward 34
Wiik, Gustav Juel, as engineer on Amundsen's North-West Passage expedition 91, 95, 104
Wild, Frank: with Shackleton's South Pole expedition 148, 256, 398, 434, 445; declines Scott's invitation (1910) 256
Wild Range 434
Williams (ship) 21
Williamson, Petty Officer Thomas: with Scott's *Discovery* expedition 150, 151, 181; on atmosphere of discontent 157–8; on Scott's Polar expedition 260; and discovery of dead 518–21
Wilson, Major General Charles 143
Wilson, Dr. Edward: on Scott's *Discovery* expedition 143–4, 151, 160, 179, 430; and unhappy atmosphere 158, 159; as complement to Scott 160; told of Scott's plan to journey south 161; moral leadership 161, 170, 174, 175, 349, 485, 506; failure to understand dogs 162, 168; journey south with Scott and Shackleton 165, 166–75; scurvy 172–3, 177–8; compromise over decision to return 172; mediates in Shackleton's plan to attempt South Pole from Scott's old base 217,

227–8; Kathleen Scott's dislike of 229; as chief of scientific staff on Scott's Polar expedition 256, 261, 314, 391; sledging committee 290; and use of dogs 340; crossing of sea ice on return depot journey 345, 348; as Scott's spiritual prop 348–9, 373, 397, 430–31, 441, 500; winter journey to Cape Crozier 375, 380n; and Scott's rivalry with Shackleton 396–7; morbidity 430; and man-hauling 435, 438–9; and choice of seamen to go on to Pole 436–7; learns latitude sights 441; considers Oates unfit to continue 443–4; and Evans' departure 443–4; and discovery of Amundsen's prior arrival at Pole 480–81; pessimistic diary comments 485–6; ceases keeping diary 490, 498–9; limited clinical experience 498–9; takes over leadership 500; and Oates' death 505, 506–7; his own last days 507, 527–8; regrets 507–8; discovery and burial 518–19
Wilson Mrs. 308
Wilton, D. W. 145
Wisting, Oscar: on Amundsen's Polar expedition 247–8, 296–7, 408–9, 415, 416; and revelation of South as real aim 287; in landing party 295–6, 320, 325; slaughters seals 321; completes Framheim base 327; depot-laying 330, 332; work on tents 333, 357–8; 'foreman of fur tent' 354; work on sledges 356–7; and false start 381, 383–4; fresh start 388; brush with crevasse 386–7; as dog-driver 405, 421, 446, 455–6; mishaps on 'Devil's Ballroom' 426–7; and 'final onslaught' 445–6, 452–3; arrival at Pole 456, 458; 'boxing' of Pole 457; and journey back to *Fram* 464, 467–8, 471, 491; loyalty to Amundsen 532–3, 541–2; death 541–2
With Peary near the Pole (Astrup) 163
Wolseley motor company 263
Worcester (training ship) 258
Worst Journey in the World, The (Cherry-Garrard) 373, 400
Wright, Charles 341; with Scott's Polar expedition 341–2, 375–6, 391–2; and man-hauling 435; return with support party 435–6, 502; and discovery of dead 517–18

Young, Sir Allen 89

Zapffe, Fritz 95, 249; friendship with Amundsen 85–6; help in fitting out North-West Passage expedition 85–6, 91; interest in equipment 86, 204

ROLAND HUNTFORD is the author of *The New Totalitarians,* a study of Swedish socialism, and *Sea of Darkness,* a novel about Columbus. During his years as the *London Observer*'s Scandinavian correspondent, based in Helsinki and Stockholm, he also doubled as winter sports correspondent in Scandinavia and the Alps. Since 1974 he has divided his time between Oslo and his home near Cambridge, England, researching and writing *Scott and Amundsen,* as well as his latest book on Shackleton. He is married and has two children.